St Stephen's Chapel and the Palace of Westminster

St Stephen's Chapel
and the
Palace of Westminster

EDITED BY

Tim Ayers, J. P. D. Cooper,
Elizabeth Hallam Smith, and Caroline Shenton

THE BOYDELL PRESS

The publishers acknowledge the generous financial support of
the Marc Fitch Fund in the production of this volume.

© Contributors 2024

All Rights Reserved. Except as permitted under current legislation
no part of this work may be photocopied, stored in a retrieval system,
published, performed in public, adapted, broadcast,
transmitted, recorded or reproduced in any form or by any means,
without the prior permission of the copyright owner

First published 2024
The Boydell Press, Woodbridge

ISBN 978 1 83765 163 4

The Boydell Press is an imprint of Boydell & Brewer Ltd
PO Box 9, Woodbridge, Suffolk IP12 3DF, UK
and of Boydell & Brewer Inc.
668 Mt Hope Avenue, Rochester, NY 14620–2731, USA
website: www.boydellandbrewer.com

A CIP catalogue record for this book is available
from the British Library

The publisher has no responsibility for the continued existence or accuracy of URLs for
external or third-party internet websites referred to in this book, and does not guarantee
that any content on such websites is, or will remain, accurate or appropriate

In memory of Prof. W. Mark Ormrod
(1957–2020)

Contents

List of Illustrations — ix

List of Contributors — xix

Acknowledgements — xxi

List of Abbreviations — xxiii

Introduction: St Stephen's Chapel Westminster and its Legacies, 1292 to the Present — 1
Tim Ayers, J. P. D. Cooper, Elizabeth Hallam Smith, and Caroline Shenton

Part I St Stephen's Chapel and College in the Middle Ages

St Stephen's Chapel, Westminster: Presence and Absence — 13
Tim Ayers

The Plantagenet Purpose: St Stephen's Chapel and English Kingship, 1272–1377 — 41
W. Mark Ormrod

St Stephen's Chapel, Westminster: From a King's to a Collegiate Chapel — 55
John Harper

War, Politics, and Architecture: Iterative Design at St Stephen's Chapel, 1292–1348 — 75
James Hillson

St Stephen's College, 1348 to 1548 — 109
Elizabeth Biggs

The Imagery of St Stephen's Chapel: An Overview — 125
Paul Binski

The Iconography of the St Stephen's Chapel Painting Fragments — 137
Jane Spooner

Performing Spaces: The Art of Polyphony Within and Beyond St Stephen's — 171
Magnus Williamson

Part II St Stephen's and the House of Commons

St Stephen's under the Tudors: From Royal Chapel to Commons Chamber — 189
J. P. D. Cooper

The Wren Commons Chamber *Murray Tremellen*	211
Architecture and Revolution at St Stephen's and Beyond *Paul Seaward*	219
Antiquaries, Architects, and St Stephen's Chapel, Westminster, 1790–1837 *Rosemary Hill*	243
St Stephen's, Temporary Accommodation, and the New House of Commons *Rebekah Moore*	263
'Going to St Stephen's': The Gothic Legacy of the Chapel in the Nineteenth and Twentieth Centuries *Mark Collins*	279
St Mary Undercroft, 1548–1870: 'a dull sort of ecclesiastical lumber-room'? *Elizabeth Hallam Smith*	301
From Valhalla to New Dawn: Commemoration and Gender in the Afterlife of St Stephen's *Caroline Shenton and Melanie Unwin*	333
Index	355

List of Illustrations

Introduction

1. Wenceslaus Hollar, *Civitatis Westmonasteriensis Pars*, 1647. © UK Parliament (WOA 845). — 2

2. Virtual St Stephen's project, visualization of the interior of the upper chapel. © The Centre for the Study of Christianity & Culture, University of York. — 7

Part I St Stephen's Chapel and College in the Middle Ages

Ayers, 'St Stephen's Chapel: Presence and Absence'

Plan of the medieval Palace. © Historic England Archive, Swindon. — 12

1. *Westminster Palace and Westminster Abbey*, probably *c*.1515–32. © Victoria & Albert Museum, London (acc. no. E.128-1924). — 14

2. King's College Chapel, Cambridge. Photograph by R. Boed, Flickr, <https://www.flickr.com/photos/romanboed/51639616443/in/faves-66943724@N06/> [accessed 10 Nov. 2023]. Licence: CC BY 2.0. — 15

3. George Moore, *St Stephen's Chapel Ruins, after the Fire in 1834*. © UK Parliament (WOA 5195). — 18

4. John Carter, *Ground Plan of the present remains of St Stephen's Chapel*, *c*.1791–2. © SAL (236/E, SSC.2). — 19

5. John Dixon, *Eastern bay on the south side of St Stephen's Chapel*, drawing for a plate published 1811. © SAL (236/E, SSC.15). — 20

6. Lady Chapel, Ely Cathedral. Photograph by D. Iliff, Wikimedia Commons, <https://commons.wikimedia.org/wiki/File:Ely_Cathedral_Lady_Chapel,_Cambridgeshire,_UK_-_Diliff.jpg> [accessed 21 Aug. 2023]. Licence: CC BY-SA 3.0. — 21

7. John Carter, *Elevation of the remains of the South side of St. Stephen's Chapel*, *c*.1791–2. © SAL (236/E, SSC.5). — 23

8. Robert William Billings, *Stairs and Passage from St. Stephen's Chapel to Cloister* and *Vestibule to St. Stephen's Chapel, Westminster*, published Brayley & Britton, pls XVI, XXIX. — 23

9. Gatehouse, St Augustine's Abbey, Canterbury. © James Hillson. 25

10. Choir enclosure, Canterbury Cathedral. © Tim Ayers. Reproduced by permission of the Chapter of Canterbury. 25

11. Wenceslaus Hollar, [*Old*] *St Paul's, Chapter House*, published 1658. University of Toronto Libraries: Wenceslaus Hollar Digital Collection, Hollar_k_0977. © Thomas Fisher Rare Book Library, University of Toronto. 26

12. South transept, Gloucester Cathedral. M. Garlick, Geograph, <https://www.geograph.org.uk/photo/4302545> [accessed 24 Aug. 2023]. Licence: CC BY-SA 2.0. 27

13. The Octagon, Ely Cathedral. M. Garlick, Geograph, <https://www.geograph.org.uk/photo/4515960> [accessed 24 Aug. 2023]. Licence: CC BY-SA 2.0. 28

14. Visualization of the interior of St Stephen's Chapel, looking towards the high altar. © The Centre for the Study of Christianity & Culture, University of York. 32

15. John Carter, *Front of the Architrave mouldings [...] in the proper colours*, c.1791–2. © SAL (236/E, SSC.10). 34

16. John Wykeham Archer, *Fragments, St Stephen's Chapel, Westminster*, c.1834. © The Trustees of the British Museum, London (mus. no. 1874,0314.187). 35

17. Richard Smirke, *Queen Philippa of Hainault*, c.1800. © SAL (236/E, SSC.17.3). 37

Harper, 'From a King's to a Collegiate Chapel'

1. Reconstruction drawing of Windsor Castle, by Bob Marshall. Royal Collection Trust, © His Majesty King Charles III, 2023. 57

2. St Stephen's Chapel, visualization showing the western stalls and pulpitum. © The Centre for the Study of Christianity & Culture, University of York. 67

Hillson, 'Iterative Design at St Stephen's'

1. St Stephen's, longitudinal section. Drawing by James Hillson. © James Hillson. 76

2. Frederick Mackenzie, *One of the Windows of the Chapel of St Mary in the Vaults*, c.1844. © TNA (WORK 29/765). 81

3. John Dixon, *Eastern bay on the south side of St Stephen's Chapel*, detail, drawing for a plate published 1811. © SAL (236E, SSC.15). 82

4. John Carter, *Blockings in the frieze of the entablatures over the windows*, c.1791–2. © SAL (236E, SSC.12–13). 83

Illustrations xi

5. St Stephen's, plan of lower chapel. Drawing by James Hillson. © James Hillson. 89
6. John Carter, *Elevation of the remains of the South side of St Stephen's Chapel*, detail, c.1791–2. © SAL (236E, SSC.5). 90
7. John Thomas Smith, *Part of the South side of the same Chapel*, detail, from Smith, *Antiquities*, facing p. 153. © UK Parliament (WOA 3129). 91
8. John Dixon, *Eastern bay on the south side of St Stephen's Chapel*, drawing for a plate published 1811. © SAL (236E, SSC.15). 91
9. Exeter Cathedral, pulpitum, c.1317–25. © James Hillson. 92
10. Exeter Cathedral, doorway to Grandisson Chapel, c.1328–30. © James Hillson. 92
11. Bristol Cathedral, tomb of Thomas II Berkeley, c.1307–9/1320s. © James Hillson. 93
12. Wells Cathedral, Lady Chapel, sedilia, c.1323–6. © James Hillson. 93
13. Frederick Mackenzie, *St Stephen's Chapel*, detail of upper chapel dado arcading, c.1844. © TNA (WORK 29/766). 94
14. John Carter, *Elevation and plan of the lower part of the columns*, c.1791–2. © SAL (236E, SSC.8). 94
15. St Augustine's Abbey, Canterbury, gatehouse, c.1300–8. © James Hillson. 95
16. John Thomas Smith, *Sculpture and Painted Glass from St Stephen's Chapel*, published 1800. © UK Parliament (WOA 1492b). 96
17. John Carter, *Section of the Remains of the East End of St Stephen's Chapel*, c.1791–2. © SAL (236E, SSC.6.2). 99
18. R. W., *Frontispiece*, c.1682–3, published in John Nalson, *An Impartial Collection of the Great Affairs of State* (London, 1682–3). University of Hull Library (sq DA 395 N1, vol. 2). 100
19. John Thomas Smith, *A geometrical view of the East end of St Stephen's Chapel*, published 1807. © UK Parliament (WOA 1903). 101
20. John Carter, *Elevation of the remains of the West Front of St Stephen's Chapel*, c.1791–2. © SAL (236E, SSC.4). 105
21. Frederick Mackenzie, *Vestibule of St Stephen's Chapel*, details, c.1844. © TNA (WORK 29/767). 106

Biggs, 'St Stephen's College'

1. Anthony Salvin, *Topographical view of the Cloisters looking south west*, 1834. © PA (GB-061, SAL/1). 118

xii *Illustrations*

2. Arms of Thomas Wolsey, as Cardinal Archbishop of York, St Stephen's cloisters. RCHME survey of the Palace, c.1925. © Historic England Archive, Swindon.   120

3. Badge of Katherine of Aragon, St Stephen's cloister. RCHME survey of the Palace, c.1925. © Historic England Archive, Swindon.   120

Binski, 'Imagery of St Stephen's Chapel'

1. Sainte-Chapelle, Paris, north wall arcade, c.1248. © Paul Binski.   126

2. Chapel of the Bishops of Ely, Holborn, c.1286. © James Hillson.   127

3. John Carter, *Six Bosses on the Vaulting of the Undercroft and Cloisters of St Stephen's Chapel*, c.1786, published in John Carter, *Specimens of the Ancient Sculpture and Painting, now remaining in this Kingdom* (London, 1780, 1787), facing p. 26. Yale Center for British Art, Paul Mellon Collection.   127

4. Richard Smirke, *Figures of Angels*, c.1800. © SAL (236/E, SSC.18.2).   129

5a. Richard Smirke, *Edward III and his Sons*, c.1800. © SAL (236/E, SSC.29).   130

5b. Richard Smirke, *Philippa of Hainault and her Daughters*, c.1800. © SAL (236/E, SSC.17.7).   130

6. Emperor Henry VII and his consort, from the *Codex Balduineus*, 1340. Koblenz, Landeshauptarchiv (I C, no. 1, fol. 5r). © Alamy.   132

7. Tomb of Edward III, c.1386, Westminster Abbey. © Paul Binski. Reproduced by courtesy of the Dean and Chapter of Westminster.   133

8. John Thomas Smith, *St. Mercure, St. Eustace*, from Smith, *Antiquities*, facing p. 244. © UK Parliament (WOA 1490c).   135

Spooner, 'Iconography of the Painting Fragments'

1. Wall painting fragments, scenes of the Book of Job, from St Stephen's Chapel. © Trustees of the British Museum, London (mus. no. MME 1814, 0312.2).   138

2. Wall painting fragments, scenes of the Book of Tobit, from St Stephen's Chapel. © Trustees of the British Museum, London (mus. no. MME 1814, 0312.2).   139

3. John Carter, *Plan of the present remains of St Stephen's Chapel*, detail, c.1791–2. © SAL (236/E, SSC.3).   140

4. John Thomas Smith, *Part of the South side of the same Chapel*, detail, from Smith, *Antiquities*, facing p. 153.   142

5.	*Muting/Blinding of the Swallows* (left) and *Tobit Dejected* (right), St Stephen's Chapel. © Trustees of the British Museum, London (mus. no. MME 1814, 0312.2).	143
6.	Inscriptions beneath *Muting of the Swallows*. © Trustees of the British Museum, London (mus. no. MME 1814, 0312.2).	144
7.	*Nuptial Feast of Tobias and Sara*. © Trustees of the British Museum, London (mus. no. MME 1814, 0312.2).	144
8.	*Azarias/Raphael at the Door of Tobit's House* (left) and *Raphael Ascending* (right), St Stephen's Chapel. © Trustees of the British Museum, London (mus. no. MME 1814, 0312.2).	145
9.	*Job Instructing his Sons*. © Trustees of the British Museum, London (mus. no. MME 1814, 0312.2).	146
10.	*Daughters Asking Permission to Attend a Feast*. © Trustees of the British Museum, London (mus. no. MME 1814, 0312.2).	147
11.	*Destruction of Job's Children*. ©Trustees of the British Museum, London (mus. no. MME 1814, 0312.2).	148
12.	*Messenger of Misfortune*. © Trustees of the British Museum, London (mus. no. MME 1814, 0312.2).	149
13.	*Sophar the Naamathite*. © Trustees of the British Museum, London (mus. no. MME 1814, 0312.2).	150
14.	*Elihu and Job*. © Trustees of the British Museum, London (mus. no. MME 1814, 0312.2).	151
15.	*Legend of Pope Sylvester*, c.1332–49, wall paintings on the inner side of the choir enclosure, Cologne Cathedral. © Hohe Domkirche Köln, Dombauhütte. Photo: Matz und Schenk.	152
16.	*Destruction of Job's Children*, wall painting by Bartolo di Fredi, Collegiata, San Gimignano. © Bridgeman Images.	158
17.	*Job Instructing his Children*, in a *Bible Moralisée*, c.1233. Oxford, Bodleian Library, Bodley 270b, fol. 204r. © Bodleian Libraries, University of Oxford (CC BY-NC 4.0).	163
18.	*Destruction of Job's Children*, in a *Bible Moralisée*, c.1349–55. BNF, Fr.167, fol. 103v.	164
19.	*Messenger of Misfortune*, in a *Bible Moralisée*, c.1349–55. BNF, Fr.167, fol. 104r.	165
20.	*Job's Comforters*, in a *Bible Moralisée*, c.1349–55. BNF, Fr.167, fol. 108r.	166
21.	*Muting of the Swallows*, in a *Bible Moralisée*, c.1349–55. BNF, Fr.167, fol. 95r.	167

xiv *Illustrations*

22. Infrared reflectogram of the *Muting of the Swallows* and *Tobit Dejected*. © Trustees of the British Museum, London. Photo: H. Howard and D. Saunders.   168

Williamson, 'Art of Polyphony Within and Beyond St Stephen's'

1. View of the Palace of Westminster. © The Centre for the Study of Christianity & Culture, University of York.   173

2. John Bedyngham's rondeau, *Mon seul plaisir*, published c.1470–80. BNF, Rothschild 2973 ('Chansonnier Cordiforme'), fols 44v–45r.   176

3. Nicholas Ludford, Mass *Lapidaverunt Stephanum*, late 1520s. © Gonville & Caius College, Cambridge, MS 667/760, fols 80v–81r. By permission of the Master and Fellows of Gonville and Caius College, Cambridge.   179

Part II St Stephen's and the House of Commons

Cooper, 'From Royal Chapel to Commons Chamber'

1. Anthonis van den Wyngaerde, *Panorama of London as seen from Southwark: Westminster*, 1543–4. © Ashmolean Museum, Oxford (WA.1950.206.1).   190

2. Peter Tillemans, *The House of Commons in Session*, 1709–14. © UK Parliament (WOA 2737).   203

Tremellen, 'The Wren Commons Chamber'

1. Nicholas Hawksmoor, design for remodelling the House of Commons, 1692. Oxford, All Souls College (344 – AS IV.91). © The Warden and Fellows of All Souls College, Oxford. <https://library.asc.ox.ac.uk/wren/>.   212

2. John Thomas Smith, *North East view of the House of Commons*, from Smith, *Antiquities*, facing p. 145. © UK Parliament (WOA 7518).   215

3. James Scott, James Stephanoff, and Augustus Charles Pugin, *View of the Interior of the House of Commons during the Session 1821–3*, 1836. © UK Parliament (WOA 3102).   217

4. Robert William Billings, *Exterior of St Stephen's Chapel*, 1834. © UK Parliament (WOA 1663).   217

Seaward, 'Architecture and Revolution at St Stephen's and Beyond'

1. After François Schillemans, *The Opening of the Synod of Dort*, 1619. Amsterdam, Rijksmuseum (RP-P-OB-77.278).   222

2. Robert Le Mangnier, *Le vray pourtraict de L'assemblée des Estats*, 1577. New York, Metropolitan Museum of Art (acc. no. 1998.4681). 222

3. Bartolomeus van Bassen/Antonie Palamedesz., *The Great Assembly of 1651*, c.1651. Amsterdam, Rijksmuseum (SK-C-1350). 223

4. Claudio Duchetti, *The General Assembly of the Council of Trent*, 1565. New York, Metropolitan Museum of Art (41.72 (3.70)). 223

5. Peter Mazell, *A Section of the House of Commons Dublin*, 1767. Courtesy of the National Library of Ireland, Dublin (ET C466). 225

6. William Kent, unexecuted design for the Houses of Parliament (Design A), 1739. © RIBA Collections, London (VOS/150, fol. 17). 226

7. Unexecuted designs for the Houses of Parliament (Design D2), 1739. © RIBA Collections, London (VOS/150, fol. 20). 226

8. Isidor Stanislas Helman, after Charles Monnet, *Ouverture des Etats Généraux à Versailles le 5 Mai 1789*, 1789. Amsterdam, Rijksmuseum (RP-P-OB-63.129). 228

9. Isidor Stanislas Helman, after Charles Monnet, *Assemblée Nationale: Abandon de tous les Privilèges*, 1790. Amsterdam, Rijksmuseum (RP-P-OB-132). 229

10. Isidor Stanislas Helman, after Charles Monnet, *Journée du 1er Prairal de l'an III*, 1797. Amsterdam, Rijksmuseum (RP-P-OB-63.139). 231

11. Louis-Marie Normand, *Hémicycle de l'Assemblée Nationale*, 1837. Paris, Musée Carnavalet. 232

12. Etienne-Sulpice Hallet, *Federal Capitol*, c.1793–5. Washington, DC, Library of Congress, Prints and Photographs Division (ADE – UNIT 2461, no. 6 (D size)). 234

13. Benjamin Henry Latrobe, *United States Capitol, Washington, DC*, c.1808–9. Washington, DC, Library of Congress, Prints and Photographs Division (ADE – UNIT 2462, no. 3 (Cabinet B)). 235

14. Benjamin Henry Latrobe, *United States Capitol, Washington, DC*, 1817. Washington, DC, Library of Congress, Prints and Photographs Division (ADE – UNIT 2463, no. 2 (D size)). 236

15. Samuel Morse, *The House of Representatives*, 1822–3. © National Gallery of Art, Washington, DC (2014.79.27). 236

Hill, 'Antiquaries, Architects, and St Stephen's Chapel'

1. John Carter, *South View in the Entrance or Porch at the west end of St Stephen's chapel*, c.1790. Yale Center for British Art, Paul Mellon Collection (B1977.14.22482). 246

2.	James Basire the Younger, after William Capon, *Plan of the ancient Palace of Westminster by the late Mr. William Capon*, 1828. Yale Center for British Art, Paul Mellon Collection (B1977.14.22448).	247
3.	William Capon, *Painted Chamber*, 1799. © UK Parliament (WOA 1648).	249
4.	Isaac Cruickshank, *View of the Houses of Lords and Commons from Old Palace Yard*, 1808. Yale Center for British Art, Paul Mellon Collection (B1977.14.17696).	250
5.	John Thomas Smith, *Cotton Garden, Westminster*, published 1804. © UK Parliament (WOA 630b).	251
6.	John Thomas Smith, *East End of Painted Chamber*, from Smith, *Antiquities*, facing p. 45.	253
7.	James Basire the Younger, after Charles Alfred Stothard, *The Coronation of Edward the Confessor*, 1842. Yale Center for British Art, Paul Mellon Collection (B1977.14.22593).	254
8.	John Thomas Smith, *Views of the East side of the House of Lords*, published 1807. © UK Parliament (WOA 630a).	255
9.	John Soane, *House of Lords*. © TNA (WORK 29/17).	255

Moore, 'Temporary Accommodation and the New House of Commons'

1.	Robert William Billings, *Parliamentary & Other Offices, Courts, &c, Westminster*, principal floor plan, 1835. © PA (HC/LB/1/114/17).	265
2.	Vacher & Son, *Plan of the Temporary Houses of Parliament, & Parliamentary Buildings*, 1835. © PA (HC/LB/1/114/18).	269
3.	Robert William Billings, *The Temporary House of Commons as fitted up in 1835*. © UK Parliament (WOA 15).	270
4.	Anon., *T. Duncombe, Esq, Presenting the Petition*. © UK Parliament (WOA 80).	273
5.	Joseph L. Williams, *The New House of Commons, From the Bar*. Published in *The Illustrated London News*, 7 Feb. 1852, p. 121. © UK Parliament (WOA 6109).	277

Collins, 'The Gothic Legacy of the Chapel'

1.	Anon., *St. Stephen's Chapel looking east after the fire*, c.1834. © UK Parliament (WOA 3639).	280
2.	Robert Havell the Elder, and the Younger, *View of the House of Lords and Commons from Old Palace Yard*, 1821. © UK Parliament (WOA 1085).	284

3.	After James Wyatt, *Speaker's House in about 1800* [sic], c.1807. © UK Parliament (WOA 2873).	284
4.	Anon., *Henry VII Chapel, Westminster Abbey*. © UK Parliament (WOA 3589).	285
5.	Office of John Soane, *Approved design for the Scala Regia*, 1822. © Trustees of Sir John Soane's Museum, London (SM 71/2/72).	286
6.	William Heath, *The Destruction of the Houses of Lords and Commons by Fire*, 1834. © UK Parliament (WOA 589).	287
7.	Joseph Nash, *The House of Lords*, 1857. © UK Parliament (WOA 6281).	289
8.	Anon., *The New House of Commons, Westminster*. Published in *The Builder*, 5 Jan. 1850, opposite p. 36.	293
9.	E. Chavanne, *Interior of the House of Commons*, c.1852. © UK Parliament (WOA 1643).	296
10.	Anon., *The Prime Minister [Winston Churchill] Inspecting the Ruined House of Commons*. From the *Illustrated London News*, 17 May 1941, p. 641. © Mary Evans Picture Library.	297
11.	House of Commons chamber. © UK Parliament/Estates Archive.	299

Hallam Smith, 'St Mary Undercroft'

1.	The Chapel of St Mary Undercroft, interior looking east. © Parliamentary Estates Directorate.	302
2.	John Carter, ground plan of the undercroft of St Stephen's Chapel, c.1791–2. Published in Topham, pl. II.	303
3.	Office of John Soane, *Survey of the Palace of Westminster*, 1760–6 (part). © Trustees of Sir John Soane's Museum, London (SM 37/1/24).	306
4.	John Thomas Groves, *Plan of the late Duke of Newcastle's House in the Exchequer, since the Speaker's House [ground floor]*, 1794. © Trustees of Sir John Soane's Museum, London (SM 37/1/28).	308
5.	Thomas Chawner and Henry Rhodes, *No. 2 Ground Storey Offices of the House of Commons*, 1834. © TNA (WORK 29/22).	313
6.	J. Mackenzie, *The Crypt*, 1834. © UK Parliament (WOA 84).	315
7.	Vacher & Sons, *Plan of the Offices and Committee Rooms of the House of Commons*, 1843. © PA (HC/LB/1/114/19).	317
8.	George Moore, *St Stephen's Chapel*, 1836–7. © London Metropolitan Archives, Prints Collection (record no. 313151).	318

xviii   *Illustrations*

9. G. H. Checkley, *Westminster Palace (Houses of Parliament): Plan.*
   © Historic England Archive, Swindon (PSA01/08/00003). 319

10. Vacher & Sons, *Plan of the House of Commons, Committee Rooms & Offices,*
    1846. © PA (HC/LB/1/114/21). 321

11. Office of Works, sketch to illustrate problems with the ventilation of the
    Temporary Houses, 1846. © TNA (WORK 11/12, fol. 204). 322

12. John Wykeham Archer, *Crypt of St Stephen's Westminster,* 1852. © Trustees
    of the British Museum, London (mus. no. 1874,0314.191). 324

13. George Scharf, *View through the S. E. Window of the Crypt,* 1852.
    Yale Center for British Art, Paul Mellon Collection (B1977.14.22534). 325

14. *The Crypt Under St Stephen's Chapel.* From *The Illustrated London News,*
    5 Feb. 1859, p. 129. 327

15. Edward M. Barry, *St Stephen's Crypt,* 1863. © UK Parliament (WOA 1601). 329

Shenton and Unwin, 'From Valhalla to New Dawn'

1. Henry W. Pickersgill, *Sir Charles Barry, R.A. 1795–1860.* © UK Parliament
   (WOA 2729). 334

2. George Scharf, *Panorama of the Ruins of the Old Palace of Westminster,* 1834.
   © UK Parliament (WOA 3793). 335

3. St Stephen's Hall, Palace of Westminster. © UK Parliament/Estates Archive. 337

4. Pisan, *Interior of the Valhalla at Regensburg,* for *Magasin Pittoresque,* 12,
   Jan. 1844, p. 37. © Alamy (CWTE15). 339

5. Charles H. Sims, *King John Assents to the Magna Carta 1215.*
   © UK Parliament (WOA 2602). 341

6. Frances Rickman, *Sketch of a Ventilator in Ladies Gallery Attic in*
   St Stephen's, 1834. © UK Parliament (WOA 26). 343

7. H. K. Porters, Boston, USA, Porter's 'Easy' Bolt Clippers No. 2, *c.*1908–9.
   Principal Doorkeeper's Office, House of Commons. © Heritage Collections,
   UK Parliament. 345

8. *Suffragette Outrage in St Stephen's Hall.* Unidentified press cutting,
   June 1905. © PA (HC/SA/SJ/10/12/21). 346

9. Mary Branson, *New Dawn,* 2016. © UK Parliament (WOA S753).
   Photograph, Ms Mary Branson. 353

Every attempt has been made to trace the copyright holders of material reproduced in this book. The authors apologize for any inadvertent omissions.

List of Contributors

Tim Ayers is Professor of History of Art at the University of York. He was Co-Investigator on the AHRC-funded project 'St Stephen's Chapel, Westminster: Visual and Political Culture, 1292–1941' (2013–17), and edited the critical edition of the fabric accounts for St Stephen's Chapel (2020).

Elizabeth Biggs is a postdoctoral research fellow on the 'Virtual Record Treasury of Ireland' project at Trinity College Dublin, reconstructing the records of medieval English government in Ireland. She completed her doctorate at the University of York on 'St Stephen's College, 1348–1548' as part of the 'St Stephen's Chapel' project.

Paul Binski is Emeritus Professor of the History of Medieval Art at Cambridge University, and a fellow of the British Academy. He has written extensively on the medieval art and architecture of Westminster Palace and Abbey.

Mark Collins is Estates Historian at the Palace of Westminster, providing historical research and interpretation to inform architectural conservation. His specialist areas are the history of British architecture, and the decorative arts of the nineteenth and twentieth centuries.

John Cooper is Professor in History at the University of York and Director of the Society of Antiquaries of London. He was Principal Investigator of the project 'St Stephen's Chapel, Westminster: Visual and Political Culture, 1292–1941', which was the inspiration for this book. He is now working on an AHRC-funded project studying Henry VIII's royal progresses.

Elizabeth Hallam Smith is an Historical Research Consultant, Architecture and Heritage, at the House of Commons, specializing in the history of the Palace of Westminster. She was formerly Director of Information Services and Librarian at the House of Lords.

John Harper is investigating the relationship between liturgy, ritual, people, buildings, and furnishings, with particular emphasis on the first cathedral at Salisbury (Old Sarum) in the long twelfth century. He is Emeritus Professor at Bangor University, Honorary Professor at the University of Birmingham, and Emeritus Director of The Royal School of Church Music.

Rosemary Hill's study of Antiquarianism, *Times Witness: History in the Age of Romanticism*, was published in 2021. Her life of A. W. N. Pugin, *God's Architect* (2007), won the Wolfson

History Prize. She is a fellow of the Society of Antiquaries, the Royal Society of Literature, and a Quondam fellow of All Souls College, Oxford.

James Hillson is an art historian who specializes in architectural design practices in later medieval Europe (c.1000–1500). He is currently working as a Lecturer in Architectural History at the University of Edinburgh.

Rebekah Moore is a researcher in nineteenth-century political history. Her work has focused on the relationship between politics and parliamentary space after 1832.

The late **W. Mark Ormrod** was Professor of Medieval History at the University of York, specializing in the later Middle Ages in Britain. He published extensively on royal government and the Plantagenets, including a biography of *Edward III* (2011).

Paul Seaward was Director of the History of Parliament Trust 2001–17 and 2020–3. He is currently writing a history of Parliament as an institution, from its beginnings to the present.

Caroline Shenton was formerly Director of the Parliamentary Archives, and one chair of the 'St Stephen's Chapel' project board. She is the author of *The Day Parliament Burned Down* (2012) and *Mr Barry's War. Rebuilding The Houses of Parliament after the Great Fire of 1834* (2016).

Jane Spooner is Senior Lecturer and Head of the MA in Wall Paintings Conservation at the Courtauld Institute of Art, London. Previously, she was Historic Buildings Curator, and Head of Historic Buildings at Historic Royal Palaces, and a wall paintings conservator. Her doctoral research explored the art history of royal wall paintings in fourteenth-century England.

Murray Tremellen recently completed his Ph.D. in the Department of History of Art at the University of York. His interdisciplinary thesis explores the history of the first Speaker's House in the Palace of Westminster, from political and architectural perspectives.

Melanie Unwin was Deputy Curator of the Parliamentary Art Collection until her retirement in 2022. She was the commissioning curator of *New Dawn*, a permanent artwork by Mary Branson, which celebrates women's suffrage in Parliament, and co-curator of *Voice & Vote* (2018), a major public exhibition marking the centenary of votes for women.

Magnus Williamson is Professor of Early Music at Newcastle University, and Chairman of the British Academy series, Early English Church Music.

Acknowledgements

This book presents research conducted by, and in dialogue with, the research project 'St Stephen's Chapel, Westminster: Visual and Political Culture, 1292–1941', which was based at the University of York and funded by the Arts and Humanities Research Council (AHRC) between 2013 and 2017, in partnership with the UK Parliament and in association with the History of Parliament Trust. The Principal Investigator was John Cooper; the Co-Investigators Tim Ayers and Miles Taylor; with Research Fellow Rosemary Hill; Research Assistants James Jago, Simon Neal, and Martha Vandrei; project Ph.D. student Elizabeth Biggs; and chairs of the project board, Elizabeth Hallam Smith and Caroline Shenton. Digital modelling of the Virtual St Stephen's project was carried out by Anthony Masinton and the Centre for the Study of Christianity & Culture at the University of York. In parallel with this larger project, the Leverhulme Trust generously funded production of a critical edition, *The Fabric Accounts of St Stephen's Chapel, Westminster, 1292–1396* (2020). A follow-on project, 'Listening to the Commons: The Sounds of Debate and the Experience of Women in Parliament c.1800', also funded by the AHRC (2018), was timed to coincide with the exhibition *Voice & Vote* in Westminster Hall. The late W. Mark Ormrod was instrumental in the framing of the original project and continued to give time to it with typical energy, insight, and generosity. We dedicate this volume to his memory, as scholar, mentor, and friend.

We would like to thank the many institutions that have generously contributed to our research, and have allowed us to reproduce items in their collections. At the Palace of Westminster, the project benefited from the expertise and help of a number of current and past curators and custodians of the Palace's collections, buildings and history, some of whose contributions appear in this book. The St Stephen's Chapel project was grateful for the encouragement offered by the Speaker's Advisory Committee on Works of Art and the Lord Speaker's Advisory Panel on Works of Art, and for the support provided by the then Gentleman Usher of the Black Rod David Leakey. Access to research materials and expert advice were graciously offered by the Society of Antiquaries of London, the British Museum, and Sir John Soane's Museum. Many other people kindly gave of their time to discuss aspects of the Virtual St Stephen's reconstructions during the course of the project, including: Ann-Marie Akehurst, Jeremy Ashbee, Clare Brown, Sarah Brown, Joanna Cannon, John Crook, Lloyd de Beer, the late Kerry Downes, Robin Eagles, Anna Eavis, James Ford, Claire Gapper, Anthony Geraghty, John Goodall, John Harper, Hugh Harrison, Stuart Harrison, Alasdair Hawkyard, Malcolm Hay, Gordon Higgott, Olivia Horsfall-Turner, Paul Hunneyball, Maureen Jurkowski, Mark Kirby, Philip Lankester, Richard Marks, Dan Miles, Christopher Norton, Norbert Nussbaum, the late W. Mark Ormrod, Lisa Reilly, Paul

Seaward, Jane Spooner, Tim Tatton-Brown, Charles Tracy, Christopher Wilson, Joseph Wisdom, and Lucy Wrapson.

For help with production of the present volume, the editors would like to thank Murray Tremellen for picture research, and Laura Napran for editorial assistance. We have benefited greatly from the expert and efficient help of our publisher the Boydell Press, especially Caroline Palmer and Christy Beale. Production of the book and the creation of the index were supported by a publication grant from the Marc Fitch Fund.

List of Abbreviations

Ayers & Jurkowski	Ayers, Tim (ed.), and Maureen Jurkowski (transcr. and trans.), *The Fabric Accounts of St Stephen's Chapel, Westminster, 1292–1396* (2 vols, Woodbridge, 2020)
BAA	British Archaeological Association
BAA, *Westminster*	Rodwell, Warwick, and Tim Tatton-Brown (eds), *Westminster, The Art, Architecture and Archaeology of the Royal Abbey and Palace*, BAA Conference Transactions, 39 (for 2013), 2 parts (London, 2015)
BL	London, British Library
BM	London, British Museum
BNF	Paris, Bibliothèque nationale de France
Brayley & Britton	Brayley, Edward Westlake, and John Britton, *History of the Ancient Palace and Late Houses of Parliament at Westminster* (London, 1836)
Cannadine	Cannadine, David (ed.), *Westminster Abbey, A Church in History* (New Haven/London, 2019)
CChR	*Calendar of Charter Rolls* (6 vols, London, 1903–27)
CLR	*Calendar of Liberate Rolls* (6 vols, London, 1916–64)
CPR	*Calendar of Patent Rolls* (London, 1891–)
EHR	*English Historical Review* (London, 1886–)
GM	*Gentleman's Magazine* (London, 1731–1868)
HC	House of Commons Papers
HC Deb	House of Commons Debates
Hist Parl	*History of Parliament* (London 1936–)
Hist Parl Online	<https://www.historyofparliamentonline.org>
HKW	Colvin, H. M. (general editor), *The History of the King's Works* (6 vols, London, 1963–82)
HL	House of Lords Papers
HL Deb	House of Lords Debates

JBAA	*Journal of the British Archaeological Association* (London, 1845–)
L & P Henry VIII	*Letters and Papers, Foreign and Domestic, of the Reign of Henry VIII: Preserved in the Public Record Office, the British Museum, and Elsewhere in England* (37 vols, London, 1863–1932)
Mackenzie	Mackenzie, Frederick, *The Architectural Antiquities of the Collegiate Chapel of St. Stephen, Westminster, The Late House of Commons: Drawn from actual survey and measurements made by direction of the commissioners of her majesty's woods and works, &c.* (London, 1844)
Mr Barry's War	Caroline Shenton, *Mr Barry's War: Rebuilding the Houses of Parliament after the Great Fire of 1834* (Oxford, 2016)
ODNB	*The Oxford Dictionary of National Biography Online* <http://www.oxforddnb.com>
PA	London, Parliamentary Archives
PH	*Parliamentary History* (Gloucester, 1982–)
Pipe Roll	*The Pipe Roll Society, for the Publication of the Great Rolls of the Exchequer, commonly called the Pipe Rolls* (London, 1884–)
Port, *HoP*	Port, Michael (ed.), *The Houses of Parliament: History, Art, Architecture* (London/New Haven, 1976)
Pugin, *Letters*	Belcher, Margaret (ed.), *The Collected Letters of A. W. N. Pugin* (5 vols, Oxford, 2001–15)
RCHME	Royal Commission on the Historical Monuments of England
Riding & Riding	Riding, Christine, and Jacqueline Riding (eds), *The Houses of Parliament: History, Art, Architecture* (London, 2000)
SAL	The Society of Antiquaries of London
Smith, *Antiquities*	Smith, John Thomas, *Antiquities of Westminster: The Old Palace; St. Stephen's Chapel (Now the House of Commons)* (London, 1807)
Space and Sound	Cooper, J. P. D., and Richard A. Gaunt (eds), *Space and Sound in the British Parliament: Architecture, Access and Acoustics* (Chichester, 2019)
Topham	Topham, John, *Some Account of the Collegiate Chapel of St Stephen, Westminster; Plans, Elevations, Sections, and Specimens of the Architecture and Ornaments, of the Remaining Parts of Saint Stephen's Chapel, Westminster* (London, 1795). Additional Plates, text by H. C. Englefield (London, 1811)
TNA	Kew, Surrey, The National Archives
WAM	London, Westminster Abbey Library and Muniments
WOA	London, UK Parliament, Works of Art Collection

Introduction:
St Stephen's Chapel Westminster and its Legacies, 1292 to the Present

Tim Ayers, J. P. D. Cooper, Elizabeth Hallam Smith, and Caroline Shenton

St Stephen's Chapel and College

St Stephen's Chapel was in its day one of England's most significant and spectacular buildings. Completed in the mid fourteenth century, it was prominently situated within the Palace of Westminster on the banks of the River Thames (fig. 1). From the city of London two miles away to the east, its upper levels would have been clearly visible. Around it lay the great Palace of the Anglo-Saxon and Norman kings which had developed into the principal residence of the Plantagenets; and close by was Westminster Abbey, their magnificent and wealthy coronation and burial church.[1] Westminster was the epicentre of English royal ceremony, government and justice, and was subject to the king's will: from the late fourteenth century the monarch might at times commandeer the Abbey's chapter house and refectory for meetings of the royal council or for Parliament.

By contrast, St Stephen's Chapel, generously endowed with lands and rights, and with a college of canons founded in 1348, was there to intercede for crown and kingdom. It was never intended to rival the Abbey's monopoly over coronations or other great ceremonial occasions. Its associations with the royal family and household were more personal, and its secular (rather than monastic) constitution ordained a different set of roles for its vicars and canons. Its location meant that St Stephen's was always close to the practice of kingship, whether that meant the sanctification of royal power through liturgy and prayer, or the everyday activity of serving the monarch, collecting his revenues and seeing his justice well kept. Canons of St Stephen's included Exchequer officials and Chancery clerks, ecclesiastical and civil lawyers, royal secretaries and almoners. The last dean of the college, John Chamber, was Henry VIII's personal physician.

The first reference to a chapel dedicated to St Stephen at Westminster dates from the reign of King John. The chapel begun by Edward I in 1292, provided with a college by Edward III

---

[1] Cannadine, esp. pp. 1–133.

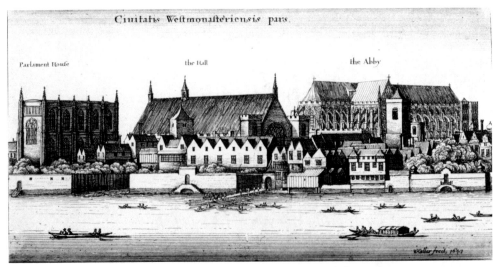

Fig. 1. Wenceslaus Hollar, *Civitatis Westmonasteriensis Pars*, 1647. Etching, on paper, 28.6 × 15.2 cm. WOA 845.

in 1348, and finished in the 1360s, perpetuated the earlier dedication. Occupying a site at the south-eastern corner of Westminster Hall, St Stephen's stood at a right angle to the Hall: its east end faced the river. This location, at a meeting point between the publicly accessible Westminster Hall and the Lesser or White Hall – which in turn led on to the Painted Chamber and other royal apartments within the privy palace – would be an important influence on the life both of the medieval chapel and of the House of Commons that followed it. An intimate space in which rulers and their households worshipped and prayers for the royal dead were sung, St Stephen's was also accessible to litigants in the Courts of King's Bench, Common Pleas and Chancery, traders with business in Westminster Hall, officials presenting their accounts at the Exchequer, and even the occasional tourist or pilgrim.

In the later Middle Ages the exterior of St Stephen's Chapel would have appeared particularly impressive to those approaching the Palace from the water, the preferred means of access. Rising above the roof of Westminster Hall, it was a slender structure of two storeys, built in the same creamy-yellow Caen limestone and pale Reigate sandstone as Westminster Abbey and the Tower of London: its eastern elevation would have glowed in the morning sun. Often regarded as an archetype of Perpendicular architecture, by the early sixteenth century it would have complemented rather than clashed with the dazzling late-flowering Gothic of Henry VII's Chapel at Westminster Abbey just to the west, and with the College's own fine, new and double-height cloister, which was in a similar panelled style.

The interior of St Stephen's was of astonishing magnificence, emblematic of the deep bonds between the English monarchy and the Church which sanctified it. Some 90 feet long by 30 feet wide, the upper chapel was divided into five bays, with a timber pulpitum between the second and third bay from the west, separating the choir in the east from the nave. The flooring and wall shafts were of polished Purbeck marble, drawing the eye up to the lofty clerestory with ten huge windows. The whole surface was a riot of colour, superbly executed, combining stonework with blue grounds, red mouldings and gilded ornaments, and stained glass and painted woodwork. Prominently featured were wall paintings of the royal family – Edward III to the north of the high altar, and Queen Philippa to the south, with their sons and daughters – along with scenes of faith maintained through tribulation which were sourced from the Old Testament. The iconography of the chapel's paintings was thus expressive of virtuous queenship as well as kingship.

St Stephen's Chapel has often been compared with the Sainte-Chapelle in Paris, the palatine chapel of the kings of France, constructed by Louis IX in the 1240s, which it was evidently intended to outshine. Both explicitly symbolized the sacred splendour of monarchy, and both were served by colleges of canons interceding for crown and kingdom through lavish liturgical cycles. Both, too, were constructed on two storeys and were adorned with decorative schemes evoking the grandeur, power and sanctity of kingship. Yet for all its splendour, St Stephen's had nothing to compare with the peerless collection of relics acquired for his Sainte-Chapelle by Louis IX. In spite of the dazzling surface ornamentation that they shared, the exquisite architecture of the Sainte-Chapelle is fundamentally French, while the innovative and evolving style of St Stephen's Chapel was very different: architectural historians have drawn attention to aspects that draw upon both French design practice and English traditions.

St George's Chapel in Windsor Castle is also often compared to St Stephen's, and they shared a founder. In 1348, at the same time as he set up his new college at Westminster, Edward III had endowed its twin organization in this other great royal residence. Based in Henry III's chapel of St Edward the Confessor, which the king rededicated to St George, the college had a role in supporting the prestigious Order of the Garter which ensured its survival through the Reformation and beyond. Likewise the chapel, which would be spectacularly remodelled from 1475 by Edward IV and the first two Tudors, endured. St George's is today the British monarch's imposing private church at Windsor, and a burial place for many members of the royal family, including Queen Elizabeth II and Philip, Duke of Edinburgh. By contrast St Stephen's is lost, gutted in the Palace fire of 1834 and subsequently demolished to make way for St Stephen's Hall in Charles Barry's new Palace of Westminster.

The high esteem and standing of St Stephen's College ensured that it attracted the donations of successive monarchs. By the time of the Reformation its lands brought in £1,000 a year, almost half the income of Westminster Abbey. But this, and its highly desirable location, made it a prime candidate for dissolution. In 1548 St Stephen's was extinguished by the boldly Protestant government of Edward VI; John Chamber surrendered his college back to the crown. Its former buildings – the upper and lower chapel, a bell-tower, a Tudor cloister, the vicars' hall and the canons' houses – were all cleared out for redevelopment. They were subsequently used for a great variety of purposes, ranging from a meeting-place for the House of Commons to a courthouse, residential and office space for the Exchequer, a wood store and a boiler room.

Before St Stephen's Chapel was handed over to secular use, an inventory of its possessions was drawn up: vestments and altar frontals, vessels for celebrating the mass and venerating the sacrament, incense boats and music books. This serves as a poignant last vision of St Stephen's College as a functioning religious community, before everything was sold and dispersed.

St Stephen's and the House of Commons

Once cleared of its sacred contents, St Stephen's did not lie empty for long: it now switched abruptly from interceding for crown and kingdom to what is today its better-known identity as the first dedicated meeting-place of the House of Commons. The decision to convert the redundant upper chapel for this purpose is not documented in the (often irregular) records kept by Edward VI's protectorate. It was a logical move, however, as the Commons was expanding both in numbers and political reach. The Commons' most recent accommodation, in the refectory of Westminster Abbey, had been demolished, and the House of Lords was already long established within the Palace of Westminster. Whoever in government took the decision, its consequences were profound. With the fitting out of St Stephen's as a debating space in 1549–50, the House of Commons acquired dedicated premises for the first time. Whether the allocation was intended as a temporary expedient or a permanent solution, in practice MPs soon came to regard St Stephen's as their own space within the royal Palace, which they occupied by right.

Renamed the 'Parliament House', St Stephen's underwent a series of major architectural and functional alterations over the next three centuries. These aimed to meet the constantly evolving requirements of MPs for a well-appointed debating chamber and to cope with a considerable expansion of their membership. With the inclusion of MPs from Scotland in 1707 and from Ireland in 1801, the Commons chamber needed to house members from the whole of the United Kingdom (until Irish independence in 1921).

From 1691, Surveyor-General of the King's Works Sir Christopher Wren undertook a well-regarded restoration and reordering of the Commons chamber, including the removal of the medieval clerestory and the construction of side galleries. The walls were panelled in oak, creating the more decorous effect depicted in Peter Tillemans's oil painting of the House of Commons in session in c.1709–14 (see Cooper, fig. 2, p. 203) Visually, this major project transformed the appearance of the old chapel and gave it a new identity. But no amount of cosmetic work would ever be able to create within this cramped site a space that could provide adequate size, comfort and facilities for the meeting-place of the Commons.

Several major schemes to replace the chamber were planned, over more than a century. But the lower House was persistently unable to agree on proposals to move to less crowded and more sanitary accommodation – sometimes, indeed, actively defeating them. St Stephen's itself experienced a series of attempts to improve its airflows and lighting, along with a controversial and damaging remodelling of its interior by James Wyatt in 1800–1 to accommodate the additional Irish members. None was successful. By 1834 the majority of MPs were of the view that the chapel needed to be completely remodelled or replaced: the fire on the night of 16 October 1834, which reduced the House of Commons and much of the rest of the old Palace to a smouldering ruin, left them no choice.

Remarkably, the lower chapel survived the fire to be restored, returned to its original use as a place of worship, and renamed as St Mary Undercroft. But the upper chapel met a different fate: though considered for renovation, the burned-out shell was instead pulled down as a prelude to the building of the new Houses of Parliament designed by Charles Barry and A. W. N. Pugin. What had once been the 'Parliament House' was replaced with the grand Victorian St Stephen's Hall, constructed above the lower chapel and of the same dimensions as its lost predecessor. Lined with statues of famous politicians who had shaped the country's imperial past, this space was designed to serve – as it still does – as a magisterial access route from the west front of the new Palace to the Central Lobby, and the Lords and Commons chambers. A magnet for tourists, lobbyists – and in the early twentieth century for suffragette protests – St Stephen's Hall today is one of the most well-trodden places in the whole of the Palace of Westminster.

The presence of the lost chapel lingered, as Barry's and Pugin's new Houses of Parliament paid court to the 'Gothic or Elizabethan' style stipulated by the Select Committee responsible for its design. This transition from the old to the new Palace of Westminster – a transmission of form and function that was consciously repeated when the Commons was once again rebuilt following its destruction in the Second World War – stands as a significant example of architecture shaping politics through the centuries, within multiple contexts and in different ways, but with an enduring thread of continuity.

Understanding St Stephen's

The phantom of St Stephen's hovers over today's political life without us always being aware of it. Even though the chamber at Westminster has been relocated once and rebuilt twice since 1834, today's House of Commons still reflects the ghostly outline of the seating arrangements of the medieval chapel. The adversarial layout of the Commons chamber, with Government and Opposition benches facing each other, has been reproduced in many Westminster-style Parliament buildings across the Commonwealth.

The name 'St Stephen's' also lived on for centuries after it ceased to be a sacred space, as a metonym for the former chapel and the area around it. 'San Steffan' is still the name for the House of Commons or Westminster in Welsh. During salvage operations at the post-fire Palace in 1834, jokes were made in the newspapers about how labourers should take care to dodge the falling masonry of the toppling building: an allusion to the fate of St Stephen, the first-century CE Christian martyr who was stoned to death. In rebuilding the Houses of Parliament, Charles Barry was sensitive enough to the collective memory of the nation to confect St Stephen's Hall as a replacement for the upper chapel. Occupying the same footprint as St Stephen's Chapel, it was a hall of memory in more ways than one.

Yet St Stephen's has also seen challenges to the status quo and to the establishment. Suffragette Emily Wilding Davison hid in a cupboard next to St Mary Undercroft for the night of the 1911 census, so that she could be recorded at the Palace of Westminster. In 1991 a plaque to her memory was attached to its wall by Tony Benn MP. Up above in St Stephen's Hall, a large canvas by the early-twentieth-century painter Vivian Forbes commemorates Thomas More in his role as Speaker of the 1523 Parliament, calmly denying a thunderstruck Cardinal Wolsey his request for an unconstitutional payment to the king. For the artists who decorated St Stephen's Hall between the two world wars, and the committee that commissioned them, the history of the space evidently spoke of resistance to untrammelled power as well as the celebration of monarchy and empire.

Since the end of the eighteenth century many scholars have sought to reconstruct, to understand and to increase our knowledge of St Stephen's Chapel. Antiquaries, including

John Carter and John Thomas Smith, made heroic efforts to record the chapel's fabric and wall paintings in the face of James Wyatt's damaging depredations, and laid the foundations for the labours of John Britton, Edward Brayley and Frederick Mackenzie, published in the decade following the 1834 fire. Since that time, many distinguished scholars have deepened our understanding of this lost building. Recently, a major collaborative research project between the University of York and the UK Parliament has brought together historians and art historians to consider the functions of the building across its long history, including the transformation from a liturgical space into a political space. As well as numerous publications,[2] the project generated a series of interactive three-dimensional visualizations of the medieval chapel, and of the Commons chamber as it looked before 1834 (fig. 2).[3] A first critical edition was also produced of the exceptionally full fabric accounts for the chapel, between 1292 and 1396.[4] Taking advantage of these new opportunities, the present book assesses the whole of the chapel's long history, considering its many different aspects – political, institutional, liturgical and art historical – in one place for the first time.

Much of the book focuses on the architecture and art of St Stephen's – in their own terms, and for what they bequeathed to the Houses of Parliament – as well as the day-to-day realities of how these buildings were accessed, used, and contested. But this study seeks not only to exhume a long-lost building. Taking advantage of the new sources uncovered and published by our research project, it also draws in the men and women who built and altered it; lived, worked, worshipped, and died in it; improved it, desecrated it, and destroyed it. From the artificers who first decorated St Stephen's Chapel to the suffragettes who found themselves protesting on its site six hundred years later, this was their building too. Among their number are architects, masons, sculptors, painters and glass-painters; priests, acolytes and choristers; auditors and officials of the Exchequer; politicians, clerks and Speakers; accountants, housekeepers, and servants. The kings and queens who worshipped in St Stephen's, and Prime Minister Spencer Perceval who was assassinated there; the antiquaries who crawled behind panelling in an attempt to record medieval wall paintings before they were destroyed; the architects and workmen who pulled down the remnants after

---

[2] Elizabeth Biggs, *St Stephen's College, Westminster: A Royal Chapel and English Kingship, 1348–1548* (Woodbridge, 2020); Elizabeth Biggs, 'Richard II's Kingship at St Stephen's Chapel, Westminster, 1377–99', in Gwilym Dodd (ed.), *Fourteenth Century England*, X (Woodbridge, 2018), pp. 157–78; Elizabeth Biggs, 'Negotiating and Creating Collegiate Statutes in the Fourteenth Century', in Gwilym Dodd and Craig Taylor (eds), *Monarchy, State and Political Culture in Late Medieval England: Essays in Honour of W. Mark Ormrod* (York, 2020), pp. 21–38; Elizabeth Biggs, '"A Cloister of Curious Workmanship": The patronage of St Stephen's Cloisters within the Palace of Westminster in the early sixteenth century', *Historical Research* 95 (2022): 309–33; Elizabeth Biggs, 'Halls of Power: Changing Political and Administrative Culture at the Palace of Westminster in the Sixteenth Century', *Journal of British Studies* 63 (April 2024); Catriona Cooper, 'The Sound of Debate in Georgian England: Auralising the House of Commons', in *Space and Sound*, pp. 60–73; J. P. D. Cooper, 'The Elizabethan House of Commons and St Stephen's Chapel Westminster', in *Space and Sound*, pp. 34–59; J. P. D. Cooper and Richard A. Gaunt, 'Architecture and Politics in the Palace of Westminster, 1399 to the Present', in *Space and Sound*, pp. 1–16; J. P. D. Cooper and James Jago, 'Picturing Parliament: The Great Seal of the Commonwealth and the House of Commons', *Antiquaries Journal*, 101 (2021), 369–89; Rosemary Hill, '"Proceeding like Guy Faux": The Antiquarian Investigation of St Stephen's Chapel Westminster, 1790–1837', *Architectural History*, 59 (2016), 253–79.
[3] https://www.virtualststephens.org.uk/explore <accessed on 4 Dec. 2023>; Tim Ayers, '"Virtual St Stephen's": The Medieval Model and the Art Historian', *British Art Studies*, 16 (June 2020), <https://doi.org/10.17658/issn.2058-5462/issue-16/tayers2> [accessed 11 Nov. 2023]; Anthony Masinton and James Jago, 'Mapping the Unknown: Using Incomplete Evidence to Craft Three-Dimensional Models of St Stephen's', *British Art Studies*, 16 (June 2020), <https://doi.org/10.17658/issn.2058-5462/issue-16/amasinton> [accessed 11 Nov. 2023].
[4] Ayers & Jurkowski.

Fig. 2. Virtual St Stephen's project, visualization of the interior of the upper chapel, facing east from the nave.

the 1834 fire and pushed them into the Thames to form the foundations of the new Palace; even the mudlarks who have gathered fragments of the former building, providing precious evidence of its stonework – all these people play a part in this biography of the building.

The book is divided into two parts covering the full chronological span of St Stephen's, from its construction and embellishment, through the processes of its conversion and destruction, to its modern appearance and meanings. The opening section introduces new research into the medieval chapel to provide perspectives on its political, institutional and art-historical significance. It begins with a study of the presence and absence of the building by Tim Ayers, presenting the surviving sources for its creation and appearance, and introducing the craftsmen who are named in the fabric accounts. The sources remain enigmatic in many ways, which has contributed to contested interpretations of the chapel's art and architecture. Since the mid twentieth century, the place of the building within the development of late medieval English architecture has preoccupied scholars, most recently in the work of Christopher Wilson and John Goodall. James Hillson here challenges ways of thinking about the design of the building. He explains how war shaped the royal finances that were available to Edward I, Edward II and Edward III in developing their visions of the chapel, over more than half a century.

The exceptionally lavish painted and glazed decoration of St Stephen's Chapel, revealed first by building work and then by the fire of 1834, was of particular interest to nineteenth-century antiquaries and scholars. From this early date, it was recognized that the fabric accounts provided rich complementary evidence for both the wall paintings and glass painting, and their respective crafts. The overall scheme of decoration across many media is surveyed here by Paul Binski, providing new interpretations of it within the thinking of Edward III and his advisers, but also in relation to the earlier decoration of the Palace. In a case study, Jane Spooner examines the precious surviving fragments of wall paintings from St Stephen's that are now housed in the British Museum. She shows how they reveal underlying themes of dynastic survival that were deeply significant to Edward III and his family.

The first section of this book also reflects on the wider place of royal foundations within the ideology of kingship, and the significance of the foundation of St Stephen's for Westminster as a royal capital. W. Mark Ormrod places St Stephen's at the centre of royal worship for the three Plantagenet Edwards, and as a stage for the performance of royal piety. Elizabeth Biggs discusses St Stephen's College as an institution, a theme unstudied for over a century until the recent research project, to bring out the political and institutional importance of St Stephen's and its people. She shows how the College continued to serve as a site of ceremonial and commemoration for the kings of England until its dissolution, and unveils the operation of this community of secular canons, including their working lives as senior administrators in royal government and the church. The sixteenth-century cloister, surviving today as one of the hidden architectural gems of the Palace of Westminster, is put back at the heart of the community that lived around it.

Two essays reflect upon the liturgical life of the chapel, identifying its particular and exceptional qualities. John Harper's chapter addresses the functions of the royal chapel that preceded Edward III's collegiate foundation, taking us back to the reign of Henry III. He establishes the character of the worship that was performed in these different kinds of institution, and the resulting requirements in their layout and furnishings. Magnus Williamson provides a new interpretation of St Stephen's in terms of its sacred music. In the last century of its operation, the College was a centre for the composition and performance of polyphony, in the presence of distinguished composers as organist-vergers, such as John Bedyngham and Nicholas Ludford, and in its choir. The performance of this music in the undercroft of St Stephen's, for the first time in five hundred years, was a memorable moment in the research project that underpins this book.

In the second section readers are introduced to the post-Reformation incarnation of St Stephen's as the debating chamber of the House of Commons – along with its lobby, doorkeepers, clerks and petitioners, its committee rooms, and the cache of parliamentary records in its roof. John Cooper pictures St Stephen's in the early Tudor period, before examining its conversion to become the habitual meeting-place of the lower House after 1548, and by the early seventeenth century an emblem of its increased authority within the parliamentary trinity of crown, Lords and Commons. Murray Tremellen focuses on Christopher Wren's remodelling of the chamber in the 1690s as a conscious act of modernization, contrasting with the appeal to history evident in both Wyatt's restoration of the Commons in 1800–1, and the Palace of Westminster as rebuilt by Barry and Pugin following the 1834 fire.

The differing political resonances of classical and Gothic styles are equally evident in Paul Seaward's study of legislative space in the eighteenth and early nineteenth centuries.

Comparing the inherited debating chambers of Westminster with the new solutions adopted by post-revolutionary France and the United States, he reveals the role of accidents and contingencies in the creation of the Victorian House of Commons, as well as the motivations of those who wanted to privilege tradition over innovation in the layout of parliamentary space. Rosemary Hill captures the excitement of antiquaries studying and sketching St Stephen's, their admiration for its surviving medieval architecture and their distress at its wanton destruction by Wyatt and ultimate demolition by Barry. Elizabeth Hallam Smith, meanwhile, presents a wholly new interpretation of one of the medieval structures that survived: the lower chapel now known as St Mary Undercroft, which endured a number of post-Reformation uses (including its reinvention as a Gothic dining room for the Speaker of the Commons) before its ultimate recovery as a place of worship for the Palace of Westminster.

Three linked chapters address the impact of the architecture and history of the old Palace of Westminster upon its post-1834 replacement by Barry and Pugin. While much was carried over, not least in the design of the House of Commons chamber, the new Palace was decidedly not a copy of the old. Rebekah Moore recovers the temporary accommodation constructed for Parliament following the fire, highlighting innovations and arguing for the long-term influence of these on the design and functionality of the new House of Commons.

Taking a longer view of the same space, Mark Collins puts the case for continuity as well as change in the layout and decoration of the replacement House of Commons. If Edward III's chapel of St Stephen was an influence on the design choices made by Barry and Pugin, so too was the early-sixteenth-century Gothic of Henry VII's Chapel in Westminster Abbey, and the slightly later cloister of St Stephen's. When the Victorian chamber was itself destroyed in a devastating air raid in 1941, Prime Minister Winston Churchill led the campaign to rebuild along similar lines once the war had ended. The result was Giles Gilbert Scott's neo-Gothic House of Commons, the form in which it appears today: commended and criticized in roughly equal measure as a home for a twenty-first-century legislature, but indisputably a symbol of British politics the world over. Returning to the site of the pre-1834 Commons chamber, Caroline Shenton and Melanie Unwin reflect on St Stephen's Hall, whose decoration with themes in British history, and use as a significant site of political activism in support of votes for women, provided it with a piquant and ironic afterlife.

Overall, the research collected here could never be the final word on such an absorbing and elusive subject. The Palace of Westminster is an exceptionally dynamic site, in which discoveries (sometimes, rediscoveries) continue to be made – witness the seventeenth-century doorway from Westminster Hall through to St Stephen's cloister and then on to the former House of Commons chamber, relocated in 2018 by Elizabeth Hallam Smith and Mark Collins through a mixture of archival detective work and close examination of the surviving fabric.[5] As the principal surviving medieval structure in the Palace, Westminster Hall understandably attracts a steady stream of art-historical and archaeological research. Interest in the whole of the site is also growing, stimulated by the Restoration and Renewal Programme which has a strong focus on conserving and preserving the fabric, archaeology

---

[5] Elizabeth Hallam Smith, and John Crook, 'Westminster Hall's Lost Stuart Door-Passage Rediscovered', *The Antiquaries Journal*, 102 (2022), 389–417.

and heritage of the Palace. Yet fundamental issues such as the scope, costs and future course of the works are dividing opinion at Westminster, and seem likely to do so for a long time yet.

So many unpredictable elements have moulded the Palace of Westminster – the changing tastes of monarchs and the rise of democratic politics, devastating fires, the varying attentions of architects and scientists, political vicissitudes, damage from bombs and protesters, most recently the impact of the global pandemic – that predicting what may happen next seems a hazardous exercise. Whatever the future holds for the Palace of Westminster and Houses of Parliament, we hope that anyone who cares about this building, its history and conservation will find inspiration in this book.

Part I

St Stephen's Chapel and College in the Middle Ages

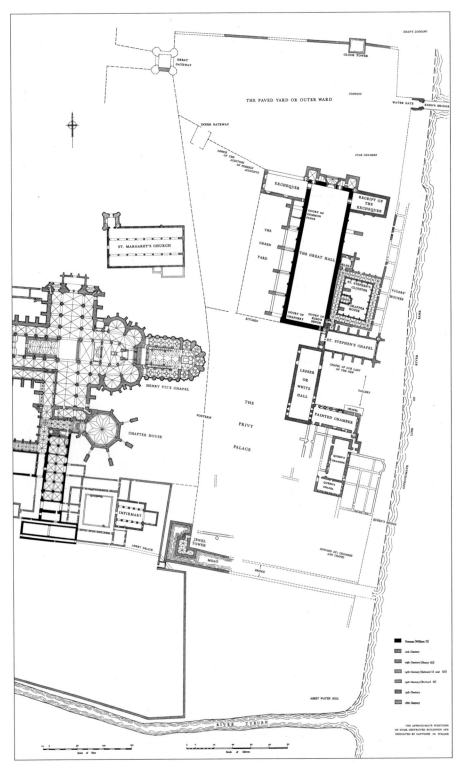

Plan of the Palace of Westminster, before 1540 (*HKW*, vols 1–2, plan III).

St Stephen's Chapel, Westminster: Presence and Absence

Tim Ayers

And so the seid Qwere [of Eton College Chapel] schall be lenger than the qwere of the Newe College at Oxford [...] And also heyer than the walles of seynt Stephenes Chapell at Westmonstre.[1]

Item, in the seide Quere on either side xxxij stalles and the rode loft there I wol that thei be made in like maner and fourme as be the Stalles and rodeloft in the chapel of saint Stephen atte Westminstre.[2]

By the mid fifteenth century, St Stephen's Chapel was something of a yardstick within the king's works, contributing to the definition of what a royal college chapel should look like, in its size and furnishings.[3] We can still recognize its distinctive profile, a rectangular building with turrets in the corners, in the chapel of Henry VI's foundation at King's College, Cambridge (figs 1–2).[4] The earliest surviving image of St Stephen's, a pen and ink drawing made probably *c.*1515–32, shows the turrets and the dominant presence of the chapel from the river. Yet today, the chapel is largely a lost building, a tantalizing absence.

St Stephen's was located in the principal residence of the Kings of England, the premier chapel within a complex that had also become the most important site of English royal government, home to the Exchequer and law-courts.[5] The first record of the dedication is

---

[1] Eton College Rolls, 39/81, fol. 2r; Robert Willis and John Willis Clark, *The Architectural History of the University of Cambridge, and of the Colleges of Cambridge and Eton* (4 vols, Cambridge, 1886), vol. 1, p. 367 (transcription). I am grateful to archivist Georgina Robinson for sending me photographs of this and the following document in the archives of Eton College (Berks.).
[2] Eton College Rolls, 39/78; Willis and Clark, *Architectural History*, vol. 1, p. 354 (transcription).
[3] The quotations are from Henry VI's instructions for his new college at Eton.
[4] John Goodall, 'St Stephen's Chapel', in BAA *Westminster*, part 2, pp. 111–19, at p. 113.
[5] For Westminster as a centre of government, see Paul Binski, *Westminster Abbey and the Plantagenets: Kingship and the Representation of Power, 1200–1400* (New Haven/London, 1995), pp. 4–9, and the essay by W. Mark Ormrod in this volume. For literature on the chapel, see J. H. Harvey, 'St. Stephen's Chapel and the Origin of the Perpendicular Style', *The Burlington Magazine*, 88:521 (Aug. 1946), 192–9; Maurice Hastings, *St Stephen's Chapel and its Place in the Development of Perpendicular Style in England* (Cambridge, 1955); J. H. Harvey, 'The Origin of the Perpendicular Style', in E. M. Jope (ed.), *Studies in Building History, Essays in Recognition of the Work of B. H. St J. O Neil* (London, 1961), pp. 134–65; *HKW*, vol. 1, pp. 510–27; John Harvey, *The Perpendicular Style, 1330–1485* (London, 1978), pp. 44–5; Christopher Wilson, 'The Origins of the Perpendicular Style and its Development to circa 1360' (Ph.D. dissertation, University of London, 1980), pp. 34–78; Christopher Wilson,

Fig. 1. *Westminster Palace and Westminster Abbey from the River Thames*, probably c.1515–32. Pen and ink, on paper, 10.1 × 17.4 cm. London, Victoria & Albert Museum, acc. no. E.128-1924. St Stephen's Chapel is shown at far right.

Fig. 2. King's College Chapel, Cambridge, built 1446–1515.

in 1205/6, but the position of the later chapel probably suggests an even earlier date for the establishment of its predecessor.[6] From 1292, the western façade stood between, and at right angles to the gable ends of two Romanesque buildings, the great hall and the lesser hall (plan, p. 12). The body of the chapel stood in parallel to the king's great chamber (Painted Chamber) to the south, and the rest of the privy palace lay beyond in that direction. It seems likely that the chapel had been here since the eleventh century, located strategically between more public and more private parts of the complex. The dedication might then be explained by the importance of St Stephen to William the Conqueror.[7] His new abbey in Caen was dedicated to this saint, and he was buried there. At Westminster, the chapel was accessible from three sides, and highly visible from inside and outside the Palace.

The chapel was rebuilt and furnished between 1292 and the 1360s under three Plantagenet kings, Edward I (1272–1307), Edward II (1307–27), and Edward III (1327–77), an extreme example of the long construction histories of many medieval buildings.[8] As discussed

---

The Gothic Cathedral: The Architecture of the Great Church, 1130–1530 (London, 1990), pp. 192–6, 198–9, 202–4, 204–5, 207; Binski, *Westminster Abbey*, pp. 176, 182–5; Paul Binski, *Gothic Wonder, Art, Artifice and the Decorated Style, 1290–1350* (New Haven/London, 2014), pp. 122–3; Goodall, 'St Stephen's Chapel'; James Hillson, 'St Stephen's Chapel, Westminster: Architecture, Decoration and Politics in the Reigns of Henry III and the Three Edwards (1227–1363)' (Ph.D. dissertation, University of York, 2015); James Hillson, 'Edward III and the Art of Authority: Military Triumph and the Decoration of St Stephen's Chapel, Westminster, 1330–1364', in Katherine Buchanan, Lucinda H. S. Dean, and Michael Penman (eds), *Medieval and Early Modern Representations of Authority in Scotland and the British Isles* (London, 2016), pp. 105–23. Studies of the chapel by James Hillson and Christopher Wilson are in progress.
[6] *Pipe Roll, 8 John*, p. 48. *HKW*, vol. 1, p. 493.
[7] Hillson, 'St Stephen's Chapel, Westminster', pp. 4–5.
[8] For the extended building period, see the essay by James Hillson in this volume.

elsewhere in this volume, the structure was repurposed after the dissolution of St Stephen's College in 1548 to become the House of Commons, and its adjacent buildings served many new uses.[9] The Commons was then gutted by the great fire that consumed much of the old Palace in 1834, and most of the medieval fabric was destroyed subsequently.[10] An exceptional number of antiquarian records and extensive fabric accounts demonstrate the extraordinary lavishness of the architecture and decoration that once existed, and that were lost at that time.[11] Today, only the undercroft remains, much restored, as the chapel for the Houses of Parliament (see Hallam Smith, fig. 1, p. 302).[12]

This essay explores the creation and presence of the chapel in the Middle Ages, to give a sense of what the building was like, drawing upon the findings of a recent major research project and a new edition of the fabric accounts.[13] It also situates the lost chapel within wider debates about medieval art and architecture. The political importance of the site, and the sensational story of the rediscovery and destruction of the medieval fabric, had already ensured the attention of both scholars and the public in the early nineteenth century.[14] The architecture was reconstructed on paper, both for scholars and the public, and building chronologies were proposed. The decoration of the building was also an object of recurring interest in relation to the involvement of Edward III as a great warrior king, and to the history of oil painting.[15]

In the twentieth century, architectural historians argued that the building occupied an important place in the sequence of styles for English medieval architecture, first defined by Thomas Rickman a century before.[16] St Stephen's has been seen as a source building for both the Decorated style, and the Perpendicular style that followed it.[17] It was also important, therefore, for those who argued that English architecture was in the vanguard of European architectural developments at this time.[18] The plentiful accounts invited study of the named craftsmen involved and the place of the chapel in the administration of the king's works.[19] More recently, St Stephen's has been reconsidered from the point of view of English kingship,

---

[9] See the essays by J. P. D. Cooper and Elizabeth Hallam Smith in this volume.
[10] Caroline Shenton, *The Day Parliament Burned Down* (Oxford, 2012).
[11] Rosemary Hill, '"Proceeding like Guy Faux": The Antiquarian Investigation of St Stephen's Chapel Westminster, 1790–1837', *Architectural History*, 59 (2016), 253–79. See also Rosemary Hill's essay in this volume. For the fabric accounts: Ayers & Jurkowski.
[12] See the contribution by Hallam Smith in this volume.
[13] 'St Stephen's Chapel, Westminster: Visual and Political Culture, 1292–1941', AHRC-funded research project, University of York, 2013–17 <https://virtualststephens.org.uk> [accessed 1 Nov. 2023]; Ayers & Jurkowski.
[14] For this, see Hill, '"Proceeding like Guy Faux"', and the essay by Hill in this volume.
[15] M. E. Roberts, 'John Carter at St Stephen's Chapel: A Romantic Turns Archaeologist', in W. Mark Ormrod (ed.), *England in the Fourteenth Century: Proceedings of the 1985 Harlaxton Symposium* (Woodbridge, 1986), pp. 202–12, at pp. 205–9, 212.
[16] Harvey, 'St. Stephen's Chapel and the Origin of the Perpendicular Style'; Harvey, 'The Origin of the Perpendicular Style'; Harvey, *The Perpendicular Style*, pp. 44–5; Wilson, 'The Origins of the Perpendicular Style and its Development to circa 1360'; Wilson, *The Gothic Cathedral*, pp. 192–6, 204–7.
[17] Wilson, *The Gothic Cathedral*, pp. 192, 204–7.
[18] Jean Bony, *The English Decorated Style, Gothic Architecture Transformed, 1250–1350* (Oxford, 1979), pp. 1–8, 62–9; Binski, *Gothic Wonder*, pp. 43–7, ch. 7 (esp. pp. 235–8); James Hillson, 'Architectural Interaction Post-Bony, Regionality, Centrality and Transformation in the English Decorated Style', in John Munns (ed.), *Decorated Revisited, English Architectural Style in Context, 1250–1400*, Architectura Medii Aevi, 9 (Turnhout, 2017), pp. 15–38.
[19] John Harvey (ed.), *English Mediaeval Architects: A Biographical Dictionary down to 1550* (London, 1954; rev. edn, Gloucester, 1984); Christopher Wilson, 'Canterbury, Michael (fl. 1275–1321), master mason' and 'Thomas Canterbury (fl. 1323–1335), master mason', *ODNB* <https://doi.org/10.1093/ref:odnb/37763> [accessed 11 Nov. 2023]. For the king's works: *HKW*, vol. 1, pp. 510–27.

royal agency, and experience of the building.[20] If the evidence has invited interpretation, the gaps have left room for many differences of opinion.

Rebuilding St Stephen's, 1292–1348

From 1292, and for over fifty years, St Stephen's was a building site, intermittently the busy home to hundreds of craftsmen and labourers, gathered partly from the nearby capital, but also from across the country. The interior of the new chapel was probably largely inaccessible to visitors, even when work had halted; materials were stored there. For the meantime, the functions of the king's chapel had been displaced to a temporary timber building at the north end of Westminster Hall, next to the Receipt of the Exchequer, and New Palace Yard beyond it, at the more public end of the Palace (plan, p. 12).[21] This was served by a community of six chaplains, comprising one of the largest royal chapels in the country.[22]

The Building

By 1348, the accounts record that the new chapel was roofed. It was a rectangular building of five bays on two storeys, comprising an upper and a lower chapel, with a turret in each corner. The materials were similar to those employed elsewhere at Westminster, in the Abbey and Palace: creamy limestone from quarries near Caen, in Normandy, and pale sandstone from quarries around Reigate (Surrey), lavishly set off with darker Purbeck marble, inside and out.[23] On the interior, the dimensions of the lower chapel were approximately 89 ft long by 28 ft wide (c.27.1 m × 8.5 m).[24] The overall height is uncertain, as the uppermost parts were removed in 1692 before accurate measurements of the structure were taken. But early representations show a building that was strikingly tall in relation to its width (fig. 1; see also Introduction, fig. 1, p. 2; Cooper, fig. 1, p. 190).

The lower chapel could be entered from the west end, but also perhaps through an elaborately carved doorway on the south side, facing the privy palace. It was a low structure in relation to its width, divided by a tripartite stone screen, between the second and third bays from the east.[25] It had a spectacular stone vault, supported on massive Purbeck wall shafts, and with figurative vault bosses (fig. 3; see also Binski, fig. 3, p. 127). In a tradition

---

[20] Binski, *Westminster Abbey*, pp. 176, 182–5; Hillson, 'St Stephen's Chapel, Westminster'; Hillson, 'Edward III and the Art of Authority'; Tim Ayers, 'Virtual St Stephen's: The Medieval Model and the Art Historian', *British Art Studies*, 16 (2020) <https://doi.org/10.17658/issn.2058-5462/issue-16/tayers2>.
[21] *HKW*, vol. 1, p. 513; Ayers & Jurkowski, vol. 1, pp. 58, 65, 67.
[22] See John Harper's essay in this volume.
[23] For the stones, see Ayers & Jurkowski, vol. 1, pp. 45–7.
[24] The building was measured by John Carter and Frederick Mackenzie: John Topham, *Some Account of the Collegiate Chapel of St Stephen, Westminster; Plans, Elevations, Sections, and Specimens of the Architecture and Ornaments, of the Remaining Parts of Saint Stephen's Chapel, Westminster* (London, 1795). *Additional Plates*, text by H. C. Englefield (London, 1811). Frederick Mackenzie, *The Architectural Antiquities of the Collegiate Chapel of St. Stephen, Westminster, The Late House of Commons: Drawn from actual survey and admeasurements made by direction of the commissioners of her majesty's woods and works, &c. accompanied by observations on the original and perfect state of the building, and a description of the plates* (London, 1844). I am grateful to James Hillson for his interpretation: lower chapel vault, wall rib to wall rib: Mackenzie, 89.040 ft × 28.562 ft (27.14 m × 8.71 m); Carter, 89.326 ft × 27.063 ft (27.23 m × 8.25 m).
[25] For the screen, see the essay by Hallam Smith in this volume. Mackenzie described several layers of flooring in the undercroft, the lowest being of Purbeck marble: Mackenzie, *Architectural Antiquities*, p. 5.

Fig. 3. George Moore, *St Stephen's Chapel Ruins, after the Fire in 1834, The West End of the Crypt under the Chapel*. Watercolour, pen and ink, on paper, 26 × 31 cm. WOA 5195.

of English decorative rib vaults, this one incorporated liernes (ribs that do not rise from the vault springers) to create kite shapes and star patterns, which can be seen in John Carter's ground plan (fig. 4; see also Hillson, fig. 5, p. 89).[26] Christopher Wilson has argued that the design was a pragmatic response to the unusual position of piers in the easternmost bay, and that it was conceived in the 1290s.[27] If so, it was among the earliest in a succession of remarkable English lierne vaults, such as those in the choirs of St Augustine's Abbey, Bristol or St Peter's Abbey, Gloucester.[28] The surviving four-light windows have tracery of the latest pattern in the 1290s, including the ogees (or double curves) that would be developed in countless English buildings in following decades. It is generally agreed that the

---

[26] The present vault was partly rebuilt in the nineteenth century: see the essay by Hallam Smith in this volume.
[27] Wilson, *The Gothic Cathedral*, pp. 195–6.
[28] Wilson, *The Gothic Cathedral*, p. 196; Christopher Wilson, 'Gothic Metamorphosed: The Choir of St Augustine's Abbey in Bristol and the Renewal of European Architecture around 1300', in Jon Cannon and Beth Williamson (eds), *The Medieval Art, Architecture and History of Bristol Cathedral: An Enigma Explored* (Woodbridge, 2011), pp. 69–147, at pp. 104–5. For a survey of English decorated vaults, see Bony, *The English Decorated Style*, ch. 5. Recently, for the development of lierne vaults, see Alexandrina Buchanan, James Hillson, and Nicholas Webb, *Digital Analysis of Vaults in English Medieval Architecture* (London/New York, 2022), pp. 62–5.

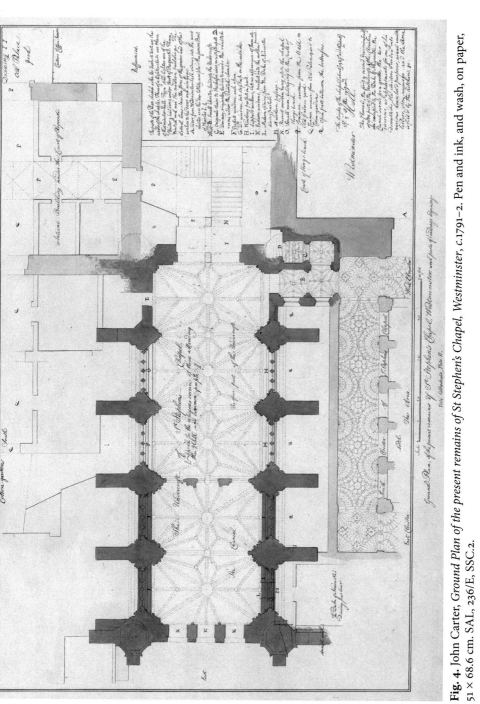

Fig. 4. John Carter, *Ground Plan of the present remains of St Stephen's Chapel, Westminster*, c.1791–2. Pen and ink, and wash, on paper, 51 × 68.6 cm. SAL, 236/E, SSC.2.

Fig. 5. John Dixon, *Eastern bay on the south* [recte *north*] *side of St Stephen's Chapel*, drawing for a plate published in 1811. Pen and ink, on paper, 94.5 × 60.3 cm. SAL, 236/E, SSC.15.

Fig. 6. Lady Chapel, Ely Cathedral, begun 1321, view towards the east.

undercroft was substantially completed by 1297, when work was suspended.[29] A reference to the protection of pinnacles, buttresses, and window jambs in 1309/10 implies that substantial progress had also been made upon the upper chapel.[30]

By contrast with the undercroft, the interior of the upper chapel was tall and brilliantly lit. The elevations were articulated with niches and arcading, of a kind that became characteristic of English buildings in the first half of the fourteenth century (fig. 5; see also Hillson, fig. 1, p. 76). The phenomenon has been called micro-architecture, because these canopies could be scaled up or down in size.[31] At St Stephen's, a delicate arcade with projecting ogee heads ran around the building, above a marble wall bench. It was topped by a battlemented cornice of quatrefoils. Directly above, the chapel was lit by five giant four-light windows on either side, with mullions running down the walls behind the arcade. Between the windows, marble wall shafts supported image niches, twelve in all, flanked by blind arcading in the spandrels of the windows, and surmounted by another substantial cornice.[32] The Lady Chapel at Ely, begun in 1321, gives some idea of the overall effect (fig. 6).[33] Micro-architecture had been a feature of French Rayonnant portal design in the thirteenth century. Wilson

---

[29] For chronologies of the building, and a later date for the insertion of the vault, see Hillson's essay in this volume.
[30] Ayers & Jurkowski, vol. 1, p. 475.
[31] François Bucher, 'Micro-Architecture as the "Idea" of Gothic Theory and Style', *Gesta*, 15:1/2 (1976), 71–89.
[32] For the cornice and heraldry, see Hillson's essay in this volume.
[33] Harvey, *The Perpendicular Style*, p. 77; Binski, *Gothic Wonder*, p. 75.

argued that its use in England was pioneered by the master mason at St Stephen's in the 1290s, playing with its component parts in new ways.[34]

Above the cornice, there was another tier of windows (a clerestory), which appears indistinctly in images of the exterior made before the upper parts of the chapel were destroyed (fig. 1; see also Hillson, fig. 18, p. 100). The clerestory is often considered to be an addition to the original design.[35] If so, it is likely that it was conceived at the same time as the vault that it would later support. This is documented to have been designed in the 1320s and, unlike the undercroft vault, it was made of wood.[36] The giant six-light east and west windows were to an unusual design, with a trefoil arch head. Early drawings and prints show an oculus or rose in the tracery (fig. 1; see also Hillson, fig. 18, p. 100).[37] If so, the design combined the rose window of great thirteenth-century churches, like Westminster Abbey and Old St Paul's Cathedral nearby in London, with the traceried window that was such a fruitful field for the creativity of contemporary masons; earlier examples include the east window of the Angel Choir at Lincoln, and the west window of the chapel of the Bishops of Ely in Holborn. As a result of all these windows, probably twenty-two at least, the interior will have been flooded with light.

The outside of the building was designed to convey an illusion of the internal structure (fig. 7).[38] Like the interior, it had elaborate cornices, suggesting levels in the elevation. These do not, however, match the actual heights of the internal structure, but rather suggest a taller lower storey, correcting the unusually squat proportions of the lower chapel. Substantial buttresses separated the bays, to support the stone vault in the undercroft, and the timber vault above. Turrets defined the corners. These too concealed the actual structure: at the north-west angle, the turret was built out over the corner of the adjoining Romanesque hall. The design responded pragmatically to the character of the existing site. The lower storey was decorated in an unusual way, with a grid of vertical panels, including shafts that ran in front of the undercroft window openings, masking them. Dating certainly from the 1290s, this feature was borrowed from the triforia of much larger thirteenth-century French churches. It is without parallel in earlier English architecture, and it would be an inspiration for many later buildings, as we shall see.

The exterior was meant to impress from all four sides. It was to be covered with figure sculpture, for which supporting brackets had been created on the eastern and western fronts, and perhaps on the buttresses. An elaborate porch or vestibule stood at the western entrance to the upper chapel, in front of a great double-doorway, with another bracket for sculpture (see Hillson, figs 20–1, pp. 105, 106).[39] This was the ceremonial entrance to the chapel, liturgically.[40] It was also the entrance for visitors, approaching between the greater and lesser halls. Stairs led up to the vestibule on the north side, and you could access the lesser hall at first-floor level, to the south, down another flight of steps (fig. 8a–b).

---

[34] Wilson, *The Gothic Cathedral*, pp. 193–4; Wilson, 'Gothic Architecture Metamorphosed', p. 98. In some respects, however, the chronology of the upper chapel design remains elusive: see Hillson's essay in this volume.
[35] Wilson, 'Origins of the Perpendicular Style', p. 42; Binski, *Gothic Wonder*, p. 42 and n. 165.
[36] Ayers & Jurkowski, vol. 1, p. 62. For an alternative date for the design, see the essay by Hillson in this volume.
[37] See Hillson's essay in this volume.
[38] Wilson, *The Gothic Cathedral*, p. 196.
[39] Goodall, 'St Stephen's Chapel', pp. 116–17.
[40] It is described as a 'galilee': Ayers & Jurkowski, vol. 2, pp. 1101–11.

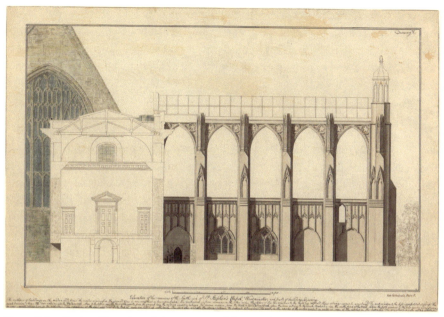

Fig. 7. John Carter, *Elevation of the remains of the South side of St. Stephen's Chapel, Westminster*, c.1791–2. Pen and ink, and wash, on paper, 51 × 68.6 cm. SAL, 236/E, SSC.5.

Fig. 8a–b. Robert William Billings, *Stairs and Passage from St. Stephen's Chapel to Cloister* and *Vestibule to St. Stephen's Chapel, Westminster*, published in Brayley & Britton, pls XVI, XXIX.

The chapel was therefore integrated with these sites for public assembly, royal ceremony, and government. At the east end of the chapel, a covered walkway connected St Stephen's to the king's great chamber and the privy palace on the south side (plan, p. 12). To the north, a doorway led into a vestry for the clergy (fig. 5). The chapel faced in multiple directions, for different users and visitors.

Masons, Carpenters, and Style

Architectural historians have identified smaller buildings, including palace chapels, as sites of particular creativity in architecture of the thirteenth and fourteenth centuries, where new ideas could be trialled for wealthy patrons.[41] The preceding analysis has suggested a number of ways in which this was true of St Stephen's. The fabric accounts also give names to the makers of the building, identifying the three master masons, and the master carpenter, who designed it and oversaw its construction. Scholarship has constructed biographies for them, identifying their ways of thinking about design through analysis of the fabric, and linking St Stephen's to buildings elsewhere.[42]

The first master mason Michael of Canterbury set up his timber lodge at Westminster in April 1292, the accounts record. Wilson has argued that his design for St Stephen's adopted three modes: for the lower chapel, the upper chapel, and the exterior.[43] Such thinking, he proposed, was then applied to buildings on a larger scale in the following decades by other masons. These famous monuments in the Decorated style include the choir of St Augustine's Abbey at Bristol, the crossing and Lady Chapel at Ely Cathedral, and the east end of Wells Cathedral (Som.).[44] For a sense of the sophistication of Michael's work, we may turn today to the gatehouse of St Augustine's Abbey, in Canterbury (fig. 9), or the chapter house and choir enclosure at Canterbury Cathedral, where he was also master mason (fig. 10).[45] Like St Stephen's, it has been argued, the gatehouse employed a different mode in each of the three levels of its elevation – a massive and relatively plain infrastructure, a richly decorated and arcaded middle storey, and panelled turrets.[46] The choir enclosure is also highly decorated, playing wittily with architectural motifs of different sizes to convey multiplicity, unity, and exclusivity. If the repeating traceried windows defined the seats of the monks, the friezes and battlements define the boundary of the community's liturgical space. The delicate mouldings, repeating arcaded motifs and strongly horizontal and battlemented cornices are found also at St Stephen's. In Michael of Canterbury, Wilson has constructed the first named English master mason as a creative personality.

---

[41] Wilson, *The Gothic Cathedral*, p. 189; Dieter Kimpel and Robert Suckale, *Die gotische Architektur in Frankreich: 1130–1270* (Munich, 1985), pp. 393–8, 399–405, 422, 428–31; Norbert Nussbaum, *German Gothic Architecture* (New Haven/London, 2000), pp. 103–10.
[42] For Michael of Canterbury, Thomas of Canterbury, William Hurley, and William Ramsey, see J. Harvey (ed.), *English Mediaeval Architects*; *ODNB*, C. Wilson, 'Canterbury, Michael (fl. 1275–1321), master mason', 'Thomas Canterbury (fl. 1323–1335), master mason', and 'Ramsey, William (d.1349), master mason' <http://www.oxforddnb.com> [accessed 13 Nov. 2023]. Christopher Wilson is working on a study of Michael of Canterbury.
[43] Wilson, *The Gothic Cathedral*, pp. 196, 199; Wilson, 'Gothic Metamorphosed', pp. 95–8.
[44] Wilson, *The Gothic Cathedral*, pp. 196–8, 198–204; Wilson, 'Gothic Metamorphosed', pp. 95–116.
[45] For the gatehouse, see Wilson, 'Gothic Metamorphosed', p. 97, illus. 4.31.
[46] Ibid., pp. 97–8.

Fig. 9. Gatehouse, St Augustine's Abbey, Canterbury, *c.*1300–8, the design attributed to Michael of Canterbury.

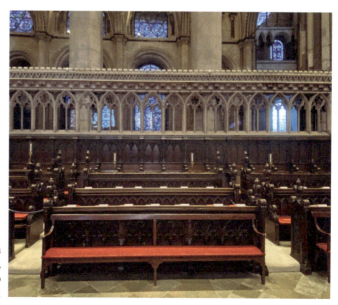

Fig. 10. Choir enclosure, north side, Canterbury Cathedral, the design attributed to Michael of Canterbury.

Fig. 11. Wenceslaus Hollar, [*Old*] *St Paul's, Chapter House*, published 1658. Etching, 20 × 29 cm. University of Toronto Libraries, Wenceslaus Hollar Digital Collection, Hollar_k_0977.

The accounts record that Michael's successor at St Stephen's (by 1323) was Thomas of Canterbury, perhaps his son. Thomas was then replaced in 1336 by William Ramsey. Scholars have debated the contributions of these masons to the chapel itself, in relation to the recorded chronology of the building and the possible evolution of the design. The lost clerestory has sometimes been attributed to Thomas and the western porch to William.[47] Interpretation of the contributions of all three master masons has revolved not only around building chronology, but also two important issues for the study of medieval architecture more generally: the role of architectural drawings, and the ways in which extended building periods may have affected architectural practice. Wilson argued that the complex design of St Stephen's presupposed drawings, and that this design could have been implemented over a period of time, as well as facilitating transmission elsewhere.[48] Others have argued that extended building periods during the Middle Ages

---

[47] For the historiography, and an attribution of these parts, see Hillson's essay in this volume.
[48] Wilson, 'The Origins of the Perpendicular Style', 40; Wilson, *The Gothic Cathedral*, pp. 140–1. No architectural drawings on parchment survive from thirteenth-century England, but they are assumed by Wilson to have been the means for transmitting designs between monuments, and across long distances. See, for example, Christopher Wilson, 'Not without Honour save in its own Country? Saint-Urbain at Troyes and its Contrasting French and English Posterities', in Alexandra Gajewski and Zoë Opačić (eds), *The Year 1300 and the Creation of a New European Architecture*, Architectura Medii Aevi, 1 (Turnhout, 2007), pp. 107–21. For drawing and groups of drawings, see Roland Recht (ed.), *Les Bâtisseurs des cathédrales gothiques* (Strasbourg, 1989), pp. 225–305; Valerio Ascani, *Il Trecento disegnato: Le basi progettuali dell'architettura gotica in Italia* (Rome, 1997); Johann Josef Böker et al., *Architektur der Gotik. Bestandskatalog der weltgrößten Sammlung an gotischen Baurissen (Legat Franz Jäger) im Kupferstichkabinett der Akademie der bildenden Künste Wien* (Salzburg, 2005); Johann Josef Böker et al.,

Fig. 12. South transept, Gloucester Cathedral, the design attributed to Thomas of Canterbury.

tended to generate an open-ended way of thinking about the design of buildings – that it was understood that each generation would add to them.[49] James Hillson makes a case for this elsewhere in the present volume.

Like Michael before them, neither Thomas of Canterbury nor William Ramsey was employed solely by the king. Ramsey became master mason at St Paul's Cathedral in London, where he was responsible for the chapter house and cloister, begun in 1332.[50] Now lost, these structures are known from a seventeenth-century print by Wenceslaus Hollar (fig. 11). The treatment of the exterior, with a grid of vertical panels that incorporates the window mullions, may be related to the exterior of the lower storey, and the interior of the upper chapel at St Stephen's.[51] Wilson identified Thomas of Canterbury as the master mason of the south transept at St Peter's Abbey in Gloucester (now the cathedral), where the murdered King Edward II was buried in 1327; rebuilding of the transept began in the early 1330s (fig. 12).[52] He related many details of the design to St Stephen's, from the grid of panelling, to details of the moulding profiles. He also identified a similar way of thinking about the new elevation, as a skin: the panelling conceals a Romanesque structure behind it, just as the shafts run over the undercroft windows of the chapel at Westminster. The south transept at Gloucester and the chapter house at St Paul's have both been identified as key buildings in the development of what has been known since the nineteenth century as the Perpendicular style.[53]

Architektur der Gotik, Ulm und Donauraum (Salzburg, 2011); Johann Josef Böker et al., *Architektur der Gotik, Rheinlande* (Salzburg, 2013); Étienne Hamon, 'Fantômes et revenants: les dessins français d'architecture gothique', *Livraisons d'histoire de l'architecture*, 30 (2015), 13–27; Buchanan et al., *Digital Analysis of Vaults*, pp. 84–91.
[49] Marvin Trachtenberg, *Building-in-Time, from Giotto to Alberti and Modern Oblivion* (New Haven/London, 2010), pp. 63–7.
[50] Harvey, *English Medieval Architects*, q.v.; Wilson, 'Ramsey, William (d.1349), master mason', *ODNB* <https://doi.org/10.1093/ref:odnb/37883> [accessed 11 Nov. 2023].
[51] Harvey, *The Perpendicular Style*, pp. 75–7. The cloister may have inspired the two-storey sixteenth-century cloister at St Stephen's, in turn, as part of an ongoing conversation between these buildings.
[52] Wilson, *The Gothic Cathedral*, pp. 204–6.
[53] On this, see Harvey, *The Perpendicular Style*, pp. 75–96; Wilson, *The Gothic Cathedral*, pp. 206–7. For the Perpendicular style, see Wilson, '"Excellent, New and Uniforme": Perpendicular Architecture, c.1400–1547', in Richard Marks and Paul Williamson (eds), *Gothic: Art for England, 1400–1547*, exhibition catalogue, Victoria & Albert Museum, London (London, 2003), pp. 98–119.

Fig. 13. The Octagon, Ely Cathedral, the design of timber vault and lantern attributed to William Hurley, after 1322.

The timber architecture at St Stephen's may also have been exceptional, to judge from the other known work of its master carpenter. The late thirteenth and fourteenth centuries saw the creation of wonders in English carpentry, such as the chapter house vault and roof at York Minster (1290s), the Octagon at Ely Cathedral (second quarter fourteenth century) and the roof of Westminster Hall (1390s). At St Stephen's, the accounts record that the roof and vault of the upper chapel were designed by the king's master carpenter William Hurley, and made between 1324 and 1326.[54] The component parts were first assembled on the ground and then stored, before installation two decades later (by Michaelmas 1346).[55] No visual evidence for the vault survives from before its destruction in 1692. Elsewhere, however, Hurley's designs were outstandingly original. He was probably responsible for the timber elements of the Ely Octagon, created after the collapse of the central tower in 1322 (fig. 13).[56] Spanning an enlarged crossing, his design creates the illusion of a tierceron vault in stone, interrupted centrally by a tall lantern whose windows flood the crossing with light, in an image of heaven presided over by Christ himself. The design of the lantern suggests knowledge of St Stephen's, in the linkage between the window mullions and the panelled dado.[57]

---

[54] Ayers & Jurkowski, vol. 1, p. 62, nos 18, 19.
[55] Ayers & Jurkowski, vol. 2, no. 37.
[56] John Maddison, 'The Gothic Cathedral', in Peter Meadows and Nigel Ramsay (eds), *A History of Ely Cathedral* (Woodbridge, 2003), pp. 127–32; Wilson, *The Gothic Cathedral*, pp. 197–8; Binski, *Gothic Wonder*, ch. 6. For a more cautious attribution, see Lynn T. Courtenay, 'Hurley, William (d.1354), master carpenter', *ODNB* <https://doi.org/10.1093/ref:odnb/42235> [accessed 1 Nov. 2023].
[57] Hastings, *St Stephen's Chapel*, p. 92; Wilson, *The Gothic Cathedral*, p. 198.

Every medieval building site brought craftsmen together. The scale of the St Stephen's project, and its long duration, gathered many hundreds to Westminster over half a century. Their names are recorded in the accounts, often with toponyms that suggest their places of origin. In the 1290s, there were sometimes over 150 masons at Westminster at one time.[58] In October 1292, they were drawn from 22 counties.[59] The project provided training in masonry and carpentry, for those making their way in these crafts, and their progress can sometimes be tracked over time in the accounts, through rises in pay and status. Given the shared experience of these craftsmen (and they were almost all men), it is inherently likely that they took away ideas about design, craft practices, and even features of the building. Richard Morris explored the career of Thomas of Witney, active at Westminster between 1292 and 1294, who became master mason at Wells and Exeter cathedrals in the first quarter of the fourteenth century.[60] Many aspects of the eastern arm at Wells have been compared to St Stephen's, including the elevation of the central vessel, in the image niches at triforium level and the visual linkage between triforium and clerestory windows.[61] St Stephen's inspired some of England's greatest buildings.

Kings and Courts

We can assess the importance of the slowly rising stone chapel for different protagonists and viewers. For Edward I, the rebuilding of St Stephen's was contemporary with a wider pattern of dynastic commemoration and celebration, especially at Westminster, in Palace and Abbey.[62] The beginning of work on St Stephen's in 1292 coincided with a major repainting of the king's great chamber, to the south of the chapel; they were accounted for together.[63] Paul Binski has argued that the work included Old Testament military subjects from the book of Maccabees.[64] At the Abbey, Edward was completing monuments for his father Henry III and wife Eleanor of Castile (d.1290).[65] Between Lincoln and Westminster, he constructed a string of crosses to mark the funeral procession of his queen. Edward was looking to similar monuments that had been set up along the funeral route of his uncle, Louis IX of France (to be canonized as St Louis in 1297). It has also often been suggested that the king's new chapel should be understood in relation to the Sainte-Chapelle, built by Louis IX in his palace on the Ile de la Cité in Paris, to house Christ's crown of thorns (see Binski, fig. 1, p. 126).[66] Both were two-storey chapels of great magnificence, and there

---

[58] Ayers & Jurkowski, vol. 1, p. 86, table 10.
[59] Ayers & Jurkowski, vol. 1, p. 76, table 3.
[60] Richard K. Morris, 'Thomas of Witney at Exeter, Winchester and Wells', in Francis Kelly (ed.), *Medieval Art and Architecture at Exeter Cathedral*, BAA Conference Transactions, 11 (for 1985) (Leeds, 1991), pp. 57–84.
[61] Wilson, *The Gothic Cathedral*, pp. 202–3.
[62] For this and what follows, see Binski, *Westminster Abbey*, pp. 104–12; Hillson, 'St Stephen's Chapel, Westminster', pp. 93–105.
[63] Ayers & Jurkowski, vol. 1, p. 59, no. 1.
[64] The relationship between chapel and great chamber is discussed in the essay by Paul Binski in this volume. For differing views on the chronology, see Paul Binski, *The Painted Chamber at Westminster*, Occasional Paper, NS, 9, SAL (London, 1986), ch. III; Christopher Wilson, 'A Monument to St Edward the Confessor: Henry III's Great Chamber at Westminster and its Paintings', in BAA, *Westminster*, part 2, pp. 152–86, at pp. 164–8; Paul Binski, 'The Painted Chamber at Westminster and its Documentation', *Walpole Society*, 83 (2021), 1–68.
[65] Binski, *Westminster Abbey*, pp. 107–9.
[66] Hastings, *St Stephen's Chapel*, p. 65; HKW, vol. 1, p. 510; Binski, *Gothic Wonder*, pp. 42–3. For a reconsideration, see Hillson, 'St Stephen's Chapel, Westminster', pp. 93–7.

are similarities in proportions and measurements. St Stephen's never had a relic of this significance, however. As Binski has argued, English royal patronage did not simply copy models elsewhere, but was eclectic and responsive to the demands of different monarchs.[67]

For the king, his family, household and court, the new chapel was to be integrated with the privy palace, the royal residence.[68] At the command of Edward II, as the accounts record, the previously mentioned two-storey covered walkway was constructed between the great chamber and the chapel in the 1320s (plan, p. 12).[69] It was a substantial structure, built of stone and with glazed windows. At this time, an oratory later known as St Mary le Pew was begun, for royal prayer, at the north end of the walkway.[70] Other places of worship within the privy palace included an oratory of St Lawrence, at the other end of Edward II's new walkway, and St John's Chapel by the queen's apartments, further south.[71]

The building accounts also document the presence and central position of St Stephen's in relation to more public parts of the Palace. They record disruptions to the work, for example, as a result of political events. In 1313, stores were disturbed by feasting arrangements, on the occasion of a Parliament.[72] Stones were damaged at the time of Philippa of Hainault's coronation, in February 1330.[73] In March 1337, a short period of work, carried out solely by the masons, coincided exactly with another meeting of Parliament, when the king was seeking consent for war with France.[74] The significance of this brief phase is now uncertain; possibly, renewed progress on the king's chapel was something of a spectacle in itself. The view from the River Thames was undoubtedly already considered to be important; the Palace was often approached by water, as discussed previously (fig. 1). In September 1333, this was the first façade to be populated with sculpture, long before the chapel had a roof. Richard of Reading was paid for making statues of St Edward the Confessor and the Pilgrim, a familiar subject at Westminster, representing a key story in the life of the royal saint enshrined in the Abbey.[75]

In the past, works of royal patronage were sometimes thought to conform to a 'court style', a term applied to St Stephen's Chapel by Maurice Hastings.[76] It has since been established that work done for the king was in many styles, and that the craftsmen concerned often worked for others, as we have seen.[77] Yet the significance of courts as sites of exchange, and the place of works created for the king within English art and architecture have continued

---

[67] Binski, *Westminster Abbey*, pp. 43, 46. For royal agency, see Hillson, 'St Stephen's Chapel, Westminster'.
[68] For the Palace, see *HKW*, vol. 1, ch. XII; Virginia Jansen, 'Henry III's Palace at Westminster', in BAA, *Westminster*, part 2, pp. 89–110.
[69] Ayers & Jurkowski, vol. 1, pp. 62, 611.
[70] C. L. Kingsford, 'Our Lady of the Pew: The King's Oratory or Closet in the Palace of Westminster', *Archaeologia*, 68 (1917), pp. 1–20; Elizabeth Biggs, *St Stephen's College, Westminster: A Royal Chapel and English Kingship, 1348–1548* (Woodbridge, 2020), pp. 47–8.
[71] *HKW*, vol. 1, pp. 498, 501–3; Ayers & Jurkowski, vol. 1, p. 58.
[72] Ayers & Jurkowski, vol. 1, p. 481.
[73] Ayers & Jurkowski, vol. 1, p. 807.
[74] Ayers & Jurkowski, vol. 1, p. 64, no. 29 (5 March to 20 April 1337). For another interpretation, see Hillson's essay in this volume.
[75] Ayers & Jurkowski, vol. 1, p. 863. For story and Abbey, Binski, *Westminster Abbey*, pp. 49, 66, 68–9, 74, figs 90, 107.
[76] J. M. Hastings, 'The Court Style', *The Architectural Review*, 105 (Jan. 1949), pp. 3–9; idem, *St Stephen's Chapel*, pp. 176–90; Robert Branner, *Saint Louis and the Court Style in Gothic Architecture* (London, 1965).
[77] H. M. Colvin, 'The "Court Style" in Medieval English Architecture: A Review', in V. J. Scattergood and J. W. Sherborne (eds), *English Court Culture in the Later Middle Ages* (London, 1983), pp. 129–39.

to preoccupy scholars.[78] Attention has been drawn to the administrators who oversaw the king's works, as the employers of the same craftspeople.[79] The most senior was the king's Treasurer, who presided over the Exchequer, which stood just a few hundred yards from St Stephen's. The building accounts reveal the personal interventions of Walter Stapeldon (1320–1, 1322–5) and William Edington (1344–56), in particular.[80] Similarities between the design of St Stephen's and the chapter house at Wells Cathedral (complete by c.1305) may be explained by the good offices of William March, Bishop of Bath and Wells (1292–1302), and Treasurer of England (1290–5).[81] We may even glimpse a reciprocal process. In 1294, March instructed the glazier of Wells to supply glass from Wells for St Stephen's. The patronage of such men, and many lesser officials, has been identified in the churches within their care, and in the monuments that they created to commemorate themselves.[82] Working relationships with craftsmen in the king's employment could be carried out into the wider world.

St Stephen's College, 1348–1548

From 1349, the chapel was furnished for a new kind of institution, a college of canons.[83] St Stephen's College was a sister community to that of St George at Windsor, both of which were established formally on 6 August 1348.[84] They were chantry foundations, intended to be powerful prayer machines for the royal family, and they occupy an important place in the history of the late medieval college in England.[85] At a time when the king was claiming the French throne, it is not a coincidence that the form of the college closely resembled that of the Sainte-Chapelle.[86] The community comprised thirty-six clerics, under a dean, who lived and worshipped at St Stephen's until 1548. The furnishings at the dissolution are described in a lengthy inventory, which records the accumulated benefactions of two hundred years.[87]

Laying Out and Furnishing the Chapel

It is not documented when the college first moved into the new building, but it may have been a decade after 1348 before the upper chapel was usable. The stalls were still being constructed in the summer of 1358, the accounts reveal.[88] In the same year, Edward III gave

---

[78] For a discussion, see Hillson, 'St Stephen's Chapel, Westminster', pp. 23–5.
[79] Binski, *Gothic Wonder*, pp. 95–7.
[80] Ayers & Jurkowski, vol. 1, pp. 13, 15, 537. For Edington, see Biggs, *St Stephen's College*, pp. 35–6.
[81] Wilson, 'Origins of the Perpendicular Style', p. 311; Tim Ayers, *The Medieval Stained Glass of Wells Cathedral*, Corpus Vitrearum Medii Aevi, Great Britain, 4 (2 vols, Oxford, 2004), vol. 2, pp. 499–500.
[82] Binski, *Gothic Wonder*, pp. 95–7.
[83] For the college, and the character of the collegiate chapel, see Biggs, *St Stephen's College*, and the essays in this volume by Elizabeth Biggs and John Harper.
[84] The foundations are discussed in essays by Biggs, Harper, and Ormrod in this volume. For Windsor, see Nigel Saul (ed.), *St George's Chapel, Windsor, in the Fourteenth Century* (Woodbridge, 2005); Steven Brindle, 'Edward III's Windsor, c.1365–77', in Steven Brindle (ed.), *Windsor Castle: A Thousand Years of a Royal Palace* (London, 2018), pp. 102–17; Nigel Saul, 'Chivalry and St George, 1327–1357', in ibid., pp. 82–93.
[85] Biggs, *St Stephen's College*, pp. 38–41. For medieval colleges, see Clive Burgess, 'An Institution for All Seasons: The Late Medieval English College', in Clive Burgess and Martin Heale (eds), *The Late Medieval English College and its Context* (Woodbridge, 2008), pp. 3–27.
[86] Biggs, *St Stephen's College*, p. 41.
[87] J. R. D. Tyssen and M. E. C. Walcott, 'The Inventory of St Stephen's Chapel, Westminster', *Transactions of the London and Middlesex Archaeological Society*, 4 (1871), 365–76.
[88] Ayers & Jurkowski, vol. 2, no. 47.

Fig. 14. Visualization of the interior of St Stephen's Chapel, looking towards the high altar from the choir stalls.

the chapel a holy water stoup, silver candelabra, and a cross; images for altars had already been bought in 1355–6.[89] The long duration of the furnishing process suggests again the shifting attention of the monarch.

The visual and documentary sources leave no doubt, however, about the magnificence of the upper chapel as it was completed by the 1360s. The recent research project brought this evidence together in a three-dimensional visualization, as a way to investigate the relationship between the parts, and to present an integrated image to the public (fig. 14; see also Introduction, fig. 2, p. 7; Harper, fig. 2, p. 67).[90] There are too many gaps in our knowledge for the virtual reconstruction to represent the interior exactly as it once looked.

---

[89] W. Mark Ormrod, *Edward III* (New Haven/London, 2011), p. 312; Ayers & Jurkowski, vol. 2, pp. 1261, 1275, 1287, 1299.
[90] <https://www.virtualststephens.org.uk> [accessed 14 Nov. 2023]; Ayers, 'Virtual St Stephen's'.

Very little is known about the form of the stained-glass windows, for example, and nothing about the painting of the clerestory or vault. Instead, the visualizations give an impression of the magnificence of the upper chapel in the 1360s, as an invitation to imagine the space, and ultimately to rethink it.

The upper chapel was divided into two parts: three eastern bays for the liturgical choir and sanctuary, and a short two-bay nave, to the west.[91] Documentary evidence of the fifteenth century records a deep timber pulpitum, or screen, that separated them.[92] In the choir, timber stalls were created for the college not once, but twice; the first set proved unsatisfactory, and was sold off to the nuns of Barking Abbey for £33 10s. 8d.[93] Made under the direction of the king's master carpenter William Hurley and his deputy William Herland, this first set was dismissed by the king's council, meeting in the chapel itself. The design clearly mattered. The second set was designed and constructed under the direction of an Augustinian canon called Edmund of St Andrew, from autumn 1355.[94] The accounts record the purchase of ceramic pots for the stalls, perhaps sounding jars to amplify the liturgy, of a kind found elsewhere.[95] Liturgical music would be one of the greatest achievements of the college in the two centuries that followed.[96] The final form of Edmund's stalls is not known for certain; our reconstruction is based upon drawings of nearly contemporary examples that were formerly in the royal chapel of St Katharine by the Tower of London.[97] But the general arrangement of them would be of lasting significance to the future layout of the House of Commons.

We must imagine a combination of colours, gilding and textures, enhancing the architecture of the chapel. Many medieval buildings were painted originally, but John Carter's records of St Stephen's, made in the 1790s, indicate an exceptional richness of colour (fig. 15).[98] Frederick Mackenzie later described the blue and red architectural elements with gilded decoration, the latter confirmed in the purchase of applied ornaments ('prints') and tens of thousands of gold-leaf foils in the accounts.[99] The red, blue, and gold were inspired by the English royal arms, which were referenced also in lions and lilies around the window arch heads, and elsewhere. On the walls, and at the altars, many sculptures are recorded, fulfilling the plan for a populated building. They were painted and decorated, too; a fragment (now lost) was drawn by John Wykeham Archer in c.1834 (fig. 16). Purbeck marble continued to be important, as an expensive, luxurious, and shining material. The floor was made from 1,200 slabs of it. The richness of the interior is comparable with the greatest surviving royal palace

---

[91] For the liturgical arrangement, see the essay by Harper in this volume.
[92] Willis and Clark, *The Architectural History of the University of Cambridge*, vol. 1, p. 354.
[93] Ayers & Jurkowski, vol. 2, p. 1227.
[94] Ayers & Jurkowski, vol. 1, p. 41.
[95] Ayers & Jurkowski, vol. 1, p. 70, vol. 2, p. 1300 ('pro [...] ollis et aliis necessariis pro stallis'). For sounding jars, see Charles Tracy, 'Choir-stalls from the 14th-Century Whitefriars Church in Coventry', *JBAA*, 150 (1997), 84–6; Alexandra Buckle, 'Fit for a King: Music and Iconography in Richard Beauchamp's Chantry Chapel', *Early Music*, 38:1 (Feb. 2010), 4.
[96] For the music of the college, see the essay by Magnus Williamson in this volume.
[97] BL, Add. MS 36402, fol. 44r. For another rendering, see Goodall, 'St Stephen's Chapel', 116, fig. 1.
[98] Smith, *Antiquities*, pp. 152–4, 156–64; Topham, pp. 8–9, 12–22; Mackenzie, pp. 28–9. For Carter's drawings, see SAL, 236E SSC.8, 10–13. For the painting of medieval architecture, see Géraldine Victoir, 'La polychromie et l'apport de son étude à la connaissance de l'architecture gothique', in Stéphanie D. Daussy and Arnaud Timbert (eds), *Architecture et Sculpture Gothiques: Renouvellement des méthodes et des regards* (Rennes, 2012), pp. 121–35.
[99] Mackenzie, *Architectural Antiquities*, pp. 28–9; Ayers & Jurkowski, vol. 1, p. 52.

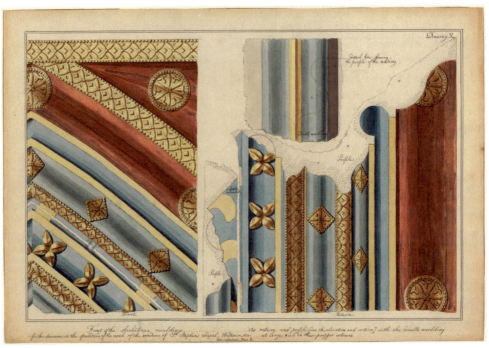

Fig. 15. John Carter, *Front of the Architrave mouldings [...] its return and profile [...] in the proper colours, showing the mouldings and spandrel of a window in the upper chapel*, c.1791–2. Pen and ink, and wash, on paper, 51 × 68.6 cm. SAL, 236/E, SSC.10.

chapels on the continent, such as the earlier Sainte-Chapelle in Paris, or the castle chapel of Christ's Passion (sometimes called chapel of the Holy Cross) at Karlštejn, in Bohemia, completed for Emperor Charles IV and consecrated in 1365.[100]

Both before and immediately after the fire of 1834, the antiquaries discovered figurative paintings everywhere they looked: on the altar wall, behind the wall arcade, and in the spandrels between the windows and on their splays. In this volume, Paul Binski surveys the iconographical scheme of the chapel, as a whole. Unusually, the lower parts of the windows had also been filled with masonry to receive narrative scenes, with explanatory verse inscriptions in Latin (fig. 5; see also Spooner, fig. 4, p. 142).[101] Some of these scenes are today in the British Museum; they are studied here by Jane Spooner. They attracted the particular attention of nineteenth-century scholars, interested in the history of oil painting. The earliest known chemical analysis of an English medieval painting, in the early 1800s, revealed that these examples had, indeed, been created in an oil medium.[102] Recently, a

---

[100] Sainte-Chapelle: Meredith Cohen, *The Sainte-Chapelle and the Construction of Sacral Monarchy: Royal Architecture in Thirteenth-Century Paris* (New York, 2015). Karlštejn: František Kavka, 'The Role and Function of Karlštejn Castle as Documented in Records from the Reign of Charles IV', in Jiří Fajt (ed.), *Magister Theodoricus, Court Painter to Emperor Charles IV*, exhibition catalogue, National Gallery Prague (Prague, 1998), pp. 15–33; Milada Studničková, 'Karlstein Castle as a Theological Metaphor', in Zoë Opačić (ed.), *Prague and Bohemia: Medieval Art, Architecture and Cultural Exchange in Central Europe*, BAA Conference Transactions, 32 (London, 2009), pp. 168–82.
[101] See the essay by Jane Spooner in this volume.
[102] Smith, *Antiquities*, pp. 223–6.

Fig. 16. John Wykeham Archer, *Fragments, St Stephen's Chapel, Westminster*, including a piece of painted and gilded sculpture, c.1834. Watercolour with body colour over graphite, on paper, 33.9 × 26.1 cm. BM, mus. no. 1874,0314.187.

new analysis has extended our knowledge of their technical sophistication, inviting further research.[103] There is more to learn about the creation and significance of these understudied works, in relation to the fabric accounts, for example. They are the most important surviving English paintings of their period.

Edward III and the King's Works at Westminster

In 1340, long before the establishment of the college, Edward III had built new royal living quarters at the south end of the Palace, re-emphasizing his commitment to Westminster.[104] Elsewhere in this volume, Elizabeth Biggs discusses the king's later presence and participation in the liturgy of St Stephen's, the engagement of subsequent Kings of England, and possible uses of the two-storey chapel. It is sometimes assumed that the royal family used the upper chapel, and that the household used the undercroft.[105] In the undercroft, there was a font, which could be used to baptize children of the king and magnates.[106] The royal family were also powerfully represented in the upper chapel, both in images and in the English royal arms, at the heart of an extended scheme of heraldry.[107] Most striking were the images of the king, his wife, and their children, beside the high altar (figs 14, 17; see also Binski, fig. 5a–b, p. 130).[108] They were to be constantly before the eyes of the college community and objects for their prayers.

The decoration took place at a time of triumph and disaster for the king. It was begun at a moment of success in his war to secure the French crown, after military victories at Crécy and the siege of Calais (1346–7); it was still continuing in 1356, the year of the battle of Poitiers. Yet, the furnishing was also begun soon after the arrival of the Black Death, which reached London in October 1348.[109] At St Stephen's, the pandemic killed the first dean of the college and the master mason William Ramsey. The king himself had already lost a daughter to it. The building accounts provide evidence for the effects of the pandemic upon the price of materials, recruitment, and the cost of labour.[110] They also throw into relief the importance of the chapel to the king. At the height of the plague, in January 1349, a veteran royal servant Walter of Weston was recalled from duties elsewhere to see the project through.[111] Work began on painting and decorating in the second half of the financial year 1348/9, and accelerated. The glazing was completed by the end of March 1352. Thereafter, work seems to have slowed as the king's attention moved elsewhere.

---

[103] Helen Howard, Lloyd de Beer, David Saunders *et al.*, 'The Wall Paintings at St Stephen's Chapel, Westminster Palace: Recent Imaging and Scientific Analysis of the Fragments in the British Museum', *British Art Studies*, 16 (2020) <https://doi.org/10.17658/issn.2058-5462/issue-16/oneobject> [accessed 1 Nov. 2023].
[104] *HKW*, vol. 1, p. 534.
[105] Goodall, 'St Stephen's Chapel', p. 112. For the varying uses of two-storey chapels, see the essay by Harper in this volume.
[106] Ayers & Jurkowski, vol. 2, appendix 3, p. 1417. See also the essay by Ormrod in this volume.
[107] James Hillson, 'Edward III and the Art of Authority: Military Triumph and the Decoration of St Stephen's Chapel, Westminster, 1330–1364', in Katherine Buchanan, Lucinda H. S. Dean, and Michael Penman (eds), *Medieval and Early Modern Representations of Authority in Scotland and the British Isles* (London, 2016), pp. 105–23.
[108] See the essay by Binski in this volume.
[109] Barney Sloane, *The Black Death in London* (Stroud, 2011), pp. 29–33.
[110] Ayers & Jurkowski, vol. 1, pp. 34–5, 48, 51, table 6.
[111] Ayers & Jurkowski, vol. 1, pp. 28–9.

Fig. 17. Richard Smirke, *Queen Philippa of Hainault*, detail from a drawing, *c.*1800, of a painting on the east wall of the chapel, made originally in the 1350s. Pencil, on paper, 52 × 32 cm. SAL, 236/E, SSC.17.3.

To complete the chapel, the instruments of royal government were tuned to a new pitch.[112] Before 1348 William of Edington, the king's capable Treasurer (1340–56), had promoted construction of the chapel, and he was key to the establishment of the college.[113] In the 1350s, he put the king's household finances on a new footing and navigated the financial consequences of the pandemic.[114] Under his leadership, directly or indirectly, old ways of controlling labour, materials, and costs were reinvigorated at St Stephen's. In the previous

---

[112] *HKW*, vol. 1, pp. 182–5.
[113] Biggs, 'The College and Canons of St Stephen's, Westminster', pp. 30–3; Ayers & Jurkowski, vol. 1, p. 13.
[114] W. Mark Ormrod, 'The English Government and the Black Death of 1348–49', in W. Mark Ormrod (ed.), *England in the Fourteenth Century: Proceedings of the 1985 Harlaxton Symposium* (Woodbridge, 1986), pp. 175–88; idem, 'The Protocolla Rolls and English Government Finance, 1353–1364', *EHR*, 404 (July 1987), 622–32; idem, 'The Politics of Pestilence: Government in England after the Black Death', in W. Mark Ormrod and Phillip Lindley (eds), *The Black Death in England* (Stamford, 1996), pp. 147–81; idem, *Edward III*, pp. 373–7.

decade, impressment and purveyance, compulsory powers of recruitment and purchase, had been used occasionally for the king's works, including at Windsor Castle.[115] They had also been used for building work during wartime, by Edward I for his Welsh castles, for example. In 1350, the king sent out his agents across southern, eastern, and midland England to recruit craftsmen for the painting and glazing of St Stephen's.[116] Subsequently, the accounts record an army of glaziers, under up to six masters.[117] There were forty of them on-site in some weeks during the autumn of 1351. In the wake of the Black Death, this kind of enlistment was brought to bear on St Stephen's in a new way. It reinforces again the importance of the chapel to Edward III.

The College in the Palace, and Visitors to St Stephen's

The establishment of the college demanded adjustments to the fabric of the chapel and the Palace. A cloister was built on the north side, on part of the former building site, accessed by a new doorway at the west end of the north wall of the chapel's undercroft.[118] By 1548, this cloister was a magnificent two-storey structure (then just recently rebuilt), parts of which survive (see Biggs, fig. 1, p. 118).[119] To provide access to the upper chapel, steps led up from the south-west corner of the cloister, within the thickness of the south-east corner of Westminster Hall, to the vestibule and western entrance (plan, p. 12; fig. 8a). The houses of the vicars ran along the river wall, to the north of the chapel. Under Richard II (1377–99), a new kitchen and a common hall were provided.[120] A stone belfry stood next to Westminster Hall, nearby. It was later claimed that this was hung with bells captured by Edward III in his French campaigns; if so, they proclaimed in a very particular way the moment of military triumph when St Stephen's was completed.[121] The dean and canons lived further north; today, the street called Canon Row still marks the site of their houses.[122] The college community lived, worshipped and died around St Stephen's; some were buried in the chapel.[123] A recent analysis of bones excavated from the undercroft has given insight into their lifestyles, including a high-status diet.[124]

---

[115] Douglas Knoop and G. P. Jones, 'The Impressment of Masons for Windsor Castle, 1360–1363', *Economic History*, 3 (Feb. 1937), 350–61; idem, 'The Impressment of Masons in the Middle Ages', *Economic History Review*, 8:1 (Nov. 1937), 57–67; Steven Brindle and Stephen Priestley, 'Edward III's Building Campaigns at Windsor and the Employment of Masons, 1346–1377', in Nigel Saul (ed.), *St. George's Chapel, Windsor, in the Fourteenth Century* (Woodbridge, 2005), pp. 203–23.
[116] Ayers & Jurkowski, vol. 1, pp. 32–3, 43, table 2.
[117] Ayers & Jurkowski, vol. 1, p. 43; vol. 2, 1155. For summaries, see L. F. Salzman, 'Medieval Glazing Accounts', *Journal British Society Master Glass Painters*, 2:3 (1928), 116–20; 2:4 (1928), 188–92; 3:1 (1929), 25–30.
[118] *HKW*, vol. 1, p. 526; Ayers & Jurkowski, vol. 1, p. 72.
[119] See the essay by Biggs in this volume.
[120] *HKW*, vol. 1, pp. 525–7; Elizabeth Biggs, 'Richard II's Kingship at St Stephen's Chapel, Westminster, 1377–99', in Gwilym Dodd (ed.), *Fourteenth Century England*, X (Woodbridge, 2018), pp. 157–77; Ayers & Jurkowski, vol. 1, p. 72 and vol. 2, nos 58–61.
[121] *CPR, 1452–61*, p. 113, 23 June 1453. For the wider significance of bells, see John Arnold, 'Resounding Community: The History and Meaning of Medieval Church Bells', *Viator*, 43:1 (Jan. 2012), 99–130.
[122] Ayers & Jurkowski, vol. 2, appendix 4, 'Reconstructing the Plan of St Stephen's College, Westminster, in the late Fourteenth Century', by John Crook.
[123] For the life of the college, see the essay by Biggs in this volume.
[124] Julia Beaumont, Jelena Bekvalac, Samuel Harris, and Catherine M. Batt, 'Identifying Cohorts Using Isotope Mass Spectrometry: The Potential of Temporal Resolution and Dietary Profiles', *Archaeometry*, 63:5 (2021), 1024–41 <https://doi.org/10.1111/arcm.12667> [accessed 1 Nov. 2023].

The chapel was accessible to many different groups during the two hundred years of its existence, beyond the king and his household, the college and administrators at Westminster. From the beginning, Edward III obtained indulgences from the pope to attract visitors to services.[125] There are occasional references to visitors and the fabric, suggesting the accessibility of the upper chapel to those attending the law-courts, the Exchequer, or Parliament. Adjacent to a door in the south end of Westminster Hall, a covered stairway (*alura*) up to the vestibule had been constructed along the gable wall in 1351.[126] A fourteenth-century visitor admired the workmanship of a screen in the chapel, 'by Westminster Hall'.[127] It was also possible to visit a devotional image in the chapel of St Mary le Pew, through the chapel itself.[128] St Stephen's registered with international visitors, too, in this palace of the Kings of England.[129] An early-fifteenth-century Bohemian itinerary describes sights to be seen in London and Westminster, including London Bridge, St Paul's Cathedral, and Westminster Abbey, but also Westminster Hall and a 'very beautiful' chapel, which must be St Stephen's.[130] The account neatly draws attention to key features of the building and its decoration: on two storeys, and painted, with gilded statues.[131] The chronicler Jean Froissart simply described St Stephen's in 1388 as 'moult belle, moult riche et moult noble'.[132]

Today, that very beautiful, rich, and noble structure remains elusive in many ways, but the fragmentary evidence is exceptionally evocative. The absent building has prompted the imaginative and intellectual engagement of scholars and the wider public, through both traditional and digital means of communication. It has invited the telling of stories about the building itself and the people who created it, the communities that lived and worked around it, and the visitors who were drawn to Westminster. The following chapters develop many of these stories. There are undoubtedly more to be told.

---

[125] For public access, see Biggs, *St Stephen's College*, pp. 46–7, and her essay in this volume.
[126] Ayers & Jurkowski, vol. 1, p. 68; vol. 2, pp. 1175, 1179, 1181, 1197, 1215, 1217.
[127] Oxford, Bodleian Library, MS Rawlinson D 1066, fol. 26v.
[128] For later use of the Pew Chapel, see Biggs, *St Stephen's College*, pp. 146–8, and her essay in this volume.
[129] For Edward III's interest in royal magnificence at Westminster, see Ormrod's essay in this volume.
[130] Prague, Archiv Pražského Hradu, Knihovna metropolitní kapituly, H.15, fol. 92v. The document is discussed in Marek Suchý, 'England and Bohemia in the Time of Anne of Luxembourg: Dynastic Marriage as a Precondition for Cultural Contact in the Late Middle Ages', in Zoë Opačić (ed.), *Prague and Bohemia: Medieval Art, Architecture and Cultural Exchange on Central Europe*, BAA Conference Transactions 32 (for 2006) (Leeds, 2009), pp. 8–21, at p. 10 and n. 19, fig. 2; Michael Van Dussen, 'A Late Medieval Itinerary to England', *Mediaeval Studies*, 76 (2014), 275–96. Van Dussen includes an edition of the itinerary, ascribing a date of c.1402–c.1413 to it (288–9). I am grateful to Christopher Wilson for drawing my attention to the reference to St Stephen's.
[131] Prague, Archiv Pražského Hradu, Knihovna metropolitní kapituly, H.15, fol. 92v: 'Ibi etiam est capella valde pulcra picta cum auro desuper et imaginibus, et subtus est alia cappella [*sic*] satis pulcra.' I am grateful to Marek Suchý for help with the transcription, which differs slightly from Van Dussen's.
[132] Besançon, Bibliothèque municipale, MS 865, fol. 363v, in Peter Ainsworth and Godfried Croenen (eds), *The Online Froissart*, version 1.5 <http://www.dhi.ac.uk/onlinefroissart> [accessed 28 May 2022]: 'Tous y vindrent, ne nul ne desobeÿ, et y ot moult de pueple, je vous dy, a Londres et a palays a Wesmoustier, et fist le roy Richart en la chappelle du palays qui est moult belle, moult riche et moult noble, royaulment en estat royal, la couronne ou chief, et fist ce jour le divin office l'arcevesque qui la messe chantoit, et fut moult voulentiers ouy, car bien sceut faire la predicacion.'

The Plantagenet Purpose: St Stephen's Chapel and English Kingship, 1272–1377

W. Mark Ormrod

This chapter explores and explains the ways in which the foundation of the chapel and college of St Stephen reflected and served the wider purposes of English kingship during the reigns of Kings Edward I, II, and III. It considers three main areas. First, it offers an overall consideration of the religiosity of the three Edwards, and of the role of religion in their performance of kingship. Secondly, it places St Stephen's Chapel within the overall pattern of royal ecclesiastical patronage and foundation over the century in question, in order to reflect on the role of royal chapels and collegiate foundations in the wider promotion of a Plantagenet ideology. Finally, it considers the place of St Stephen's within the evolution of Westminster as a royal capital. While some comment is made on the material representation of monarchy, the emphasis here is primarily on agency and activity rather than on campaigns of building, decoration, and iconography, all of which are the subject of detailed study elsewhere in this volume.

Royal Religiosity

Medieval monarchy required of its holders a public dedication to the tenets of Catholic Christendom and at least a sufficient observance of its practices as to provide evidence of a proper personal religiosity.[1] It is not easy to separate out the public and the private aspects of kingly piety, since so much of what we might regard as the personal preference of a given ruler was inevitably part of a performative strategy designed for and/or delivering an appropriate image of godliness. The most obvious public responsibilities of the king revolved around his coronation oath to uphold the liberties of Holy Church. The challenge here was to keep senior ecclesiastics sufficiently satisfied with the general purpose of royal strategy as to reconcile them to policies that were otherwise potentially or really hostile to

---

[1] For this paragraph in general, see W. Mark Ormrod, 'The English Monarchy and the Promotion of Religion in the Fourteenth Century', in Ludger Körntgen and Dominik Wassenhoven (eds), *Religion und Politik im Mittelalter: Deutschland und England im Vergleich* (Berlin, 2013), pp. 205–18.

the interests of the Church. Both Edward I and Edward III had very public confrontations with Archbishops of Canterbury – respectively Robert Winchelsey and John Stratford – who regarded their kings' heavy taxation of the clergy (in the first instance) and breach of the right of senior churchmen to defend their record in government (in the second) as direct assaults on the rights of the first estate. Stratford in particular was more than prepared to play upon the tradition of opposition to an aggressive secular arm by representing himself as a worthy successor to his predecessor at Canterbury, the martyred St Thomas Becket. In the event, none of the conflicts between state and Church during this period had the same levels of seriousness or the problematic outcomes that were associated, for example, with the Interdict under King John or the execution of Richard Scrope, Archbishop of York, under Henry IV. To a degree this was a consequence of the instinct of most ecclesiastical leaders of the period to avoid open disputes and to reconcile themselves with the king and his policies: Walter Reynolds, Archbishop of Canterbury for most of the reign of Edward II, has been said to have acted with 'excessive caution, anxious above all not to cross the king and his government' at a time when the moral compass of the state was arguably particularly awry.[2] On the other hand, none of the kings of this period chose to stretch the authority they claimed over the Church to breaking-point, and the arguments that did inevitably arise – over the patronage of ecclesiastical offices, for instance – were not such as generally to excite the wider political community into strong support for any attempted anti-establishment position on the part of senior churchmen. The statements generated at the time of Edward II's deposition to justify the forced removal of the king from the throne certainly declared him an enemy of Holy Church, but were put in such a way as made little distinction between his unreasonable treatment of clergy and laity alike.[3]

If all three Edwards had some claim to remain sufficiently on the side of the Church as to uphold their coronation oath, their acts of piety also showed clear traits designed to satisfy those in the political elite who looked for signs of inward religious sincerity in their monarchs. The records of the royal household (and specifically, of the offices of the wardrobe and the chamber) provide the most instructive guide to the yearly round of religious observances of the king and the royal family, and have been analysed extensively for Edward I and Edward III and to a more limited degree for Edward II.[4] The most important feature of these records is their comparative predictability: they reveal three successive monarchs content, in the main, to pursue the observations provided and recommended by their clerks and confessors, and disinclined to deviate from what they saw as a kingly norm. There are few hints either in the household records or in contemporary comment preserved in the chronicles to suggest that the three Edwards had anything approaching the affective piety

---

[2] Roy M. Haines, *King Edward II: Edward of Caernarfon, his Life, his Reign, and its Aftermath, 1284–1330* (Montreal, 2003), p. 337.
[3] Claire Valente, 'The Deposition and Abdication of Edward II', *EHR*, 113 (1998), 852–81, at 879–81; Seymour Phillips, *Edward II* (London, 2010), pp. 527, 530.
[4] These records have scattered over the course of seven centuries, and are now located in TNA, the British Library, and SAL. See A. J. Taylor, 'Royal Alms and Oblations in the Later Thirteenth Century', in Frederick Emmerson and Roy Stephens (eds), *Tribute to an Antiquary: Essays Presented to Marc Fitch* (London, 1976), pp. 93–125; Michael Prestwich, 'The Piety of Edward I', in W. Mark Ormrod (ed.), *England in the Thirteenth Century: Proceedings of the 1984 Harlaxton Symposium* (Woodbridge, 1985), pp. 120–8; W. Mark Ormrod, 'The Personal Religion of Edward III', *Speculum*, 64 (1989), 849–77; Malcolm Vale, *The Princely Court: Medieval Courts and Culture in North-West Europe, 1270–1380* (Oxford, 2002), pp. 236–41.

that can be seen in the cases of Henry III, Richard II, and in particular, Henry V.[5] There is a story, still contested, that Edward II survived his supposed grisly death in 1327 and became a penitent hermit in Italy; but it is noticeable that within England, the cult that developed around Edward's tomb at Gloucester Abbey was rooted very clearly in the tradition of political martyrdom rather than in any directed understanding of the inherent goodness of the individual.[6] The three Edwards were not, either by instinct or by projection, holy men.

Within this rather limited arena, a number of activities particularly stand out as indicative of royal religiosity during this period. The first is an interest in sanctified kings of the biblical and historical past. Edward I sent alms to, and Edward III visited, the shrine of the Three Kings at Cologne, the latter making the somewhat fanciful statement of his intention to be buried there.[7] Edward II's interest in the cult of the Magi is evident in the king's special offerings of gold, frankincense, and myrrh at the feast of Epiphany in 1316.[8] The fact that all three of the kings surveyed here were named from Henry III's very public devotion to Edward the Confessor does not seem to have elicited in them a particularly personal interest in the latter's shrine at Westminster Abbey; but Edward III, whose baptism was timed to coincide with the feast day of the Confessor, certainly made special alms on that anniversary every year.[9] The royal relic collection also included an appropriate array of royal paraphernalia: an inventory compiled early in the reign of Edward III included the chasuble and alb of Edward the Confessor and – interesting in the context of this volume – the blood and hair of St Stephen.[10]

The three Edwards also had an interest in English saints and in cults that could be appropriated to the English cause. Of all the pilgrimage places of England, the shrine of Becket at Canterbury was probably the site most regularly visited and patronized by kings and members of the royal family in this period.[11] In 1317 Edward II was persuaded that he was the intended recipient of a phial of holy oil miraculously bestowed on Becket by the Virgin Mary, and that he should be reanointed with the oil as supposed confirmation of his status as a champion of the Church and a supporter of the crusading ideal.[12] During the Welsh and Scottish wars, Edward I seized a number of important relics as symbols of his sovereignty, or attempted sovereignty, over those lands. One of the most important of these was the Holy Rood of Scotland, which was returned to the Scots under the terms of the treaty of Edinburgh-Northampton of 1328, but was captured again by the English at the battle of Neville's Cross in 1346.[13] Among various fragments of the True Cross in the royal collection,

---

[5] D. A. Carpenter, 'King Henry III and St Edward the Confessor: The Origins of the Cult', *EHR*, 122 (2007), 865–91; Shelagh Mitchell, 'Richard II: Kingship and the Cult of Saints', in Dillian Gordon, Lisa Monnas, and Caroline Elam (eds), *The Regal Image of Richard II and the Wilton Diptych* (London, 1997), pp. 115–24; Malcolm Vale, *Henry V: The Conscience of the King* (London, 2016).
[6] Ian Mortimer, 'The Death of Edward II in Berkeley Castle', *EHR*, 120 (2005), 1175–1214; Simon Walker, *Political Culture in Later Medieval England* (Manchester, 2006), pp. 198–222.
[7] Prestwich, 'Piety', p. 124; Ormrod, 'Personal Religion', p. 860.
[8] Vale, *Princely Court*, p. 237.
[9] Prestwich, 'Piety', p. 121; Phillips, *Edward II*, p. 64; Ormrod, 'Personal Religion', pp. 858–9.
[10] Ormrod, 'Personal Religion', p. 856.
[11] A. J. Taylor, 'Edward I and the Shrine of St Thomas of Canterbury', *JBAA*, 132 (1979), 22–8; Ormrod, 'Personal Religion', p. 858; Ben Nilson, *Cathedral Shrines of Medieval England* (Woodbridge, 1998), pp. 119, 120, 183.
[12] J. R. S. Phillips, 'Edward II and the Prophets', in W. Mark Ormrod (ed.), *England in the Fourteenth Century: Proceedings of the 1985 Harlaxton Symposium* (Woodbridge, 1986), pp. 196–201.
[13] E. L. G. Stones, 'An Addition to the "Rotuli Scotiae"', *Scottish Historical Review*, 29 (1950), 33.

the most prestigious came to be the so-called Croes Nawdd, taken in the Welsh Wars by Edward I and given eventually by Edward III to St George's Chapel, Windsor, in 1352.[14]

The most striking act of appropriation to the English cause, however, was the royal household's development of the cult of St George. Already in the Welsh campaigns of the 1280s, English infantry soldiers were wearing armbands with the cross of St George.[15] Courtly interest in the saint was well attested by the boyhood of Edward III: there was a relic of the saint in the royal collection; the king's mother, Queen Isabella, owned a statue of George decorated with pearls; and the instructional text compiled for the young king by Walter of Milemete included a striking image of a royal youth receiving the trappings of knighthood from the great patron saint of chivalry.[16] The extension of this cult is intimately bound up in Edward III's foundation of the Order of the Garter in 1348 and his refoundation of the royal chapel of Edward the Confessor at Windsor Castle into an establishment with a triple dedication: to the Confessor, the Virgin, and St George. Over the course of the second half of the fourteenth and early fifteenth centuries, George emerged as England's patron saint *par excellence*.[17]

All three Edwards were properly observant in the honouring and commemoration of the dead. Edward I's devotion to his first wife, Eleanor of Castile, generated the altogether exceptional public memorials known as the Eleanor Crosses, modelled on the *montjoies* of St Louis.[18] Other royal and aristocratic deaths were accompanied by more conventional forms of royal patronage, including the giving of alms and of cloth of gold, and (in the case at least of members of the royal household) the general costs associated with the construction of a hearse, the tolling of bells, and the provision of a collation for the attendees at the funeral.[19] In line with elite practice, the funerals of kings tended to become more elaborate affairs during the later Middle Ages, although the nature and extent of the accompanying ceremonies was always subject to practical issues such as the place of death and, in the case of Edward II, to sensitivities over the exceptional and difficult circumstances of the king's demise.[20] The funeral of Edward III seems to have been the first royal occasion on which a knight bearing the heraldic achievements of the deceased monarch entered the church

---

[14] Taylor, 'Royal Alms and Oblations', p. 119 n. 49; Juliet Vale, *Edward III and Chivalry: Chivalric Society and its Context, 1270–1350* (Woodbridge, 1983), p. 53.

[15] Michael Prestwich, *Edward I* (London, 1988), pp. 199–200.

[16] D. A. L. Morgan, 'The Banner-bearer of Christ and Our Lady's Knight: How God Became an Englishman Revisited', in Nigel Saul (ed.), *St George's Chapel Windsor in the Fourteenth Century* (Woodbridge, 2005), pp. 58–9; W. Mark Ormrod, *Edward III* (London, 2011), p. 15 and n. 71.

[17] Vale, *Edward III and Chivalry*, pp. 76–91; Hugh E. L. Collins, *The Order of the Garter, 1348–1461: Chivalry and Politics in Late Medieval England* (Oxford, 2000), 20–1; Jonathan Good, *The Cult of St George in Medieval England* (Woodbridge, 2009), pp. 68–73, 95–121; Richard Barber, *Edward III and the Triumph of England: The Battle of Crécy and the Company of the Garter* (London, 2013), pp. 178–339; W. Mark Ormrod, 'The Foundation and Early Development of the Order of the Garter in England, 1348–1399', *Frümittelalterliche Studien*, 50 (2016), 363–9.

[18] 'The Eleanor Crosses', in Jonathan Alexander and Paul Binski (eds), *Age of Chivalry: Art in Plantagenet England, 1200–1400* (London, 1987), pp. 361–6; Elizabeth M. Hallam, 'Introduction: The Eleanor Crosses and Royal Burial Customs', in David Parsons (ed.), *Eleanor of Castile, 1290–1990* (Stamford, 1991), pp. 9–21.

[19] Ormrod, 'Personal Religion', pp. 867–9; Vale, *Princely Court*, p. 241; Ormrod, *Edward III*, p. 467. See also, more generally, Jeremy I. Catto, 'Religion and the English Nobility in the Later Fourteenth Century', in Hugh Lloyd-Jones, Valerie Pearl, and Blair Worden (eds), *History and Imagination: Essays in Honour of H. R. Trevor-Roper* (London, 1981), pp. 43–55.

[20] Joel Burden, 'How do You Bury a Deposed King? The Funeral of Richard II and the Establishment of Lancastrian Authority in 1400', in Gwilym Dodd and Douglas L. Biggs (eds), *The Reign of Henry IV: The Establishment of the Regime, 1399–1406* (York, 2003), pp. 35–54; Anna M. Duch, 'The Royal Funerary and Burial Ceremonies of Medieval English Kings, 1216–1509' (Ph.D. dissertation, University of York, 2016).

in the course of the exequies and made a formal offering of the shield and, probably, the sword.[21] The innovation was a fitting tribute to a ruler whose chivalric prowess was famed throughout Christendom.

One of the most public and, to modern sensibilities, the most remarkable aspects of royal piety under the three Edwards was the performance of the ritual known as the royal touch: that is, the ritual healing by the king of persons suffering from the tubercular infection known as scrofula. The rite included the touching, or blessing, of the sufferers and the payment (by the royal almoner) to each of them of a penny. While the royal touch may already have been well established in England (and in France) by Edward I's time, it is only from his reign that we possess firm documentation of the practice.[22] The records of the royal household yield evidence that all three Edwards performed ritual healings, though it is difficult to establish any general pattern of behaviour or to interpret the numbers of persons blessed as so much evidence of the relative strength of individual rulers' adherence to the rite.[23] The most striking aspect of the data is the fact that Edward I and Edward III used the royal touch as part of their expansionist policies: the former touched for scrofula in Scotland, and the latter in Flanders (and thus, in effect, within the jurisdiction of the kingdom of France).[24] Another practice that may have begun under Edward I, but for which direct evidence survives only from Edward II and Edward III, is the placing of money before the Croes Nawdd on Good Friday to be melted down and made into cramp rings for the relief of epilepsy.[25] The various thaumaturgical powers claimed by the English monarchy by the early fourteenth century, and the willingness of individual kings to perform the associated rites, reflect powerful assumptions in contemporary culture both about the sacred quality of the royal office and about the obligations set upon each monarch to fulfil his God-given destiny.

Royal Foundations

More than in the general performance of piety, the pattern of activity under Edward I, II, and III with regard to royal foundations suggests a greater inclination on the part of the Plantagenet monarchy to pick up on new influences and opportunities and, in some cases, to be genuinely innovative. The major foundations of the three Edwards fall into three obvious categories: religious houses, university colleges, and the ecclesiastical establishments to service royal chapels.

All three Edwards established their own foundations for the monastic and/or mendicant orders. Edward I's decision to create a great new Cistercian house at Vale Royal in Cheshire, formalized in 1277, represented the most ambitious project conceived during this period, intent on nothing less than creating the largest Cistercian monastery in England. In fact, neither the flow of cash to fund the building nor the endowments set aside for the house were anything like enough to realize the initial plans, and after 1290 Edward largely gave up

---

[21] Chris Given-Wilson, 'The Exequies of Edward III and the Royal Funeral Ceremony in Later Medieval England', *EHR*, 125 (2009), 257–82.
[22] Frank Barlow, 'The King's Evil', *EHR*, 95 (1980), 3–27.
[23] Marc Bloch, *The Royal Touch: Sacred Monarchy and Scrofula in England and France*, trans. J. E. Anderson (London, 1973), pp. 56–60.
[24] Prestwich, 'Piety', p. 126; Ormrod, 'Personal Religion', pp. 862–3.
[25] Prestwich, 'Piety', pp. 126–7; Ormrod, 'Personal Religion', pp. 864–5.

his interest in the house. The Black Prince took up the project in the 1350s, though ultimately without the investment needed to complete it to the scale envisaged by the original founder.[26] New Cistercian foundations were rare in late-thirteenth- and fourteenth-century England, and Edward III's decision to found such a monastery at St Mary Graces in London in 1350 may be seen as a direct emulation of his esteemed grandfather, or else a more general expression of both kings' marked devotion to the Virgin.[27]

Edward II's patronage, by contrast, fell upon the Dominican order when he founded a friary at Kings Langley at the beginning of his reign. Kings Langley remained an important project for this monarch, not least because it became the burial place of his great friend Piers Gaveston after the latter's murder by the king's opponents in 1314. As at Vale Royal, however, the original plans were severely scaled down; the church remained unfinished at the time of Gaveston's burial there in 1315, and the conventual buildings were not to be completed until much later in the century.[28] Edward II planned a female house of Dominicans, also at Kings Langley, but this was not brought to fruition until the 1340s, when Edward III revived the project and moved its location to Dartford. Dartford was and remained the only house of Dominican nuns in England, and its apparently anomalous position is explained by practicalities. Since female houses were allowed to hold real estate, the nunnery was intended to act as a custodian of the property portfolio amassed for the male house at Kings Langley. In a more general sense, though, Kings Langley and Dartford represented the significant influence of the Dominican order upon the royal household throughout the three reigns under review, and especially in its provision of confessors to the royal family. John Woodrove, for example, was simultaneously prior of Kings Langley and Dartford, royal confessor, and supervisor of the building works at Dartford during the 1350s.[29]

Royal involvement in the foundation of colleges within the universities of Oxford and Cambridge was a new feature of the reigns of Edward II and Edward III. In 1314 Edward II was said to have vowed to found a house for twenty-four Carmelites to study at Oxford; the community was at first housed at Sheen, but by 1318 was based at the king's manor house, Beaumont Palace, by the North Gate in Oxford.[30] Edward II is remembered as founding Oriel College, Oxford in 1326, though the original scheme was that of Adam de Brome, a clerk of the royal Chancery.[31] In similar vein, the Queen's College, Oxford, began life as a hall founded by Philippa of Hainault's chaplain, Robert Eglesfield but attracted royal sponsorship from the start.[32] The most important direct act of patronage performed by

---

[26] Prestwich, *Edward I*, pp. 113–14; *HKW*, vol. 1, pp. 248–57; Anne J. Kettle, 'Houses of Cistercian Monks: The Abbey of Vale Royal', in Christopher Elrington and B. E. Harris (eds), *The Victoria County History of the County of Cheshire, Vol. 3* (London, 1980), pp. 156–65.

[27] Ormrod, *Edward III*, pp. 310–11; I. Grainger and C. Phillpotts, *The Cistercian Abbey of St Mary Graces, East Smithfield, London* (London, 2011); C. Phillpotts, 'Richard II and the Monasteries of London', in W. Mark Ormrod (ed.), *Fourteenth Century England VII* (Woodbridge, 2012), pp. 201–4. For royal adherence to the cult of the Virgin in this period, see also Elizabeth Biggs's essay in this volume.

[28] *HKW*, vol. 1, pp. 257–63; Phillips, *Edward II*, pp. 65, 67–8.

[29] *HKW*, vol. 1, p. 264; Phillips, *Edward II*, pp. 64–5; A. B. Emden, *A Survey of Dominicans in England Based on the Ordination Lists in Episcopal Registers (1268 to 1538)* (Rome, 1967), p. 486; Paul Lee, *Nunneries, Learning and Spirituality in Late Medieval English Society: The Dominican Priory of Dartford* (York, 2001), pp. 15–17.

[30] *HKW*, vol. 2, p. 987; Phillips, *Edward II*, p. 68.

[31] J. R. L. Highfield, 'The Early Colleges', in Jeremy I. Catto (ed.), *The History of the University of Oxford* (Oxford, 1984), vol. 1, pp. 237–8; Alfred B. Cobban, *The Medieval English Universities* (Aldershot, 1988), p. 129.

[32] Highfield, 'Early Colleges', pp. 238–9.

kings in this period took place at Cambridge, where Edward II established the Society of the King's Scholars in 1317. This was later subsumed into Edward III's larger 1337 foundation of the King's Hall, a body that was itself subsequently absorbed into Henry VIII's Trinity College.[33] The court and the wider reaches of royal government regarded the universities as effective training grounds for future administrators, particularly for those involved in the top levels of international diplomacy, and a strongly utilitarian emphasis is evident in the patronage provided by Edward II and Edward III to Oxford and Cambridge.[34] The reputation of these monarchs as formal founders of colleges was nonetheless significant within their own time and in the later fourteenth and fifteenth centuries in promoting a wider tradition of aristocratic and royal foundation in the two universities.

Under Edward III the crown turned itself, for the first time, to the establishment of secular colleges of canons founded and funded to service their palace chapels. There were already collegiate institutions of secular priests outside the confines of royal residences: the so-called royal free chapels, ancient foundations whose prebends did not on the whole require residence of their holders, were a particularly well established form of patronage for clerks working in the royal civil service.[35] An important change came about, however, in 1348, with the foundation of colleges of secular clergy at St George's Chapel Windsor and at St Stephen's Chapel in the Palace of Westminster. Previously, kings of England had not developed permanent and endowed establishments to staff royal chapels.[36] St George's Windsor and St Stephen's Westminster, by contrast, were properly endowed with guaranteed forms of landed income of their own – even if, in the latter case in particular, it took longer than the founder's lifetime to effect the full endowment.[37] Their staffing establishments also ran beyond a dean and twelve canons to include vicars, clerks, and boys employed as professional singers. The two chapels thus had the capacity required to guarantee an appropriately elevated level of liturgical ceremony.[38]

If there was an observable precedent for the collegiate foundations of St George's and St Stephen's, it was most likely found in France. The Sainte-Chapelle in Paris had a permanent staff of forty-three, including a dean (called the *trésorier*), twelve canons, and choristers.[39] In 1344, moreover, the heir to the throne of France, John of Normandy, had indicated his intention to found a chivalric order complete with its own clerical arm of twelve canons and

---

[33] Alfred B. Cobban, *The King's Hall within the University of Cambridge in the Later Middle Ages* (Cambridge, 1969), pp. 9–28.
[34] Jean Dunbabin, 'Careers and Vocations', in Jeremy I. Catto (ed.), *History of the University of Oxford*, vol. 1, pp. 581–96.
[35] W. R. Jones, 'Patronage and Administration: The King's Free Chapels in Medieval England', *Journal of British Studies*, 9 (1969), 1–23; Jeffrey H. Denton, *English Royal Free Chapels, 1100–1300: A Constitutional Study* (Manchester, 1970).
[36] Edward II's initiative to set up a group of clergy operating permanently at Windsor Castle was more akin to an older tradition of lodging clerks of the royal household in a semi-permanent state at the king's main places of residence, and it failed because it relied on direct funding from the crown, which proved (as so often, too, in royal ecclesiastical building works) to be unforthcoming. See A. K. B. Roberts, *St George's Chapel, Windsor, 1348–1416: A Study in Early Collegiate Administration* (Windsor, 1948), p. 5.
[37] Chris Given-Wilson, 'Richard II and his Grandfather's Will', *EHR*, 93 (1978), 320–7; Elizabeth Biggs, 'The College and Canons of St Stephen's, Westminster, 1348–1548' (Ph.D. dissertation, University of York, 2016), pp. 49–69.
[38] Ormrod, 'Personal Religion', pp. 865–6; Roger Bowers, 'The Music and Musical Establishment of St George's Chapel, Windsor in the Fifteenth Century', in Colin Richmond and Eileen Scarff (eds), *St George's Chapel, Windsor, in the Later Middle Ages* (Windsor, 2001), pp. 171–214; Biggs, 'College and Canons of St Stephen's', pp. 165–74.
[39] Biggs, 'College and Canons of St Stephen's', p. 29.

twelve supporting priests.[40] The plans for what would, in 1350, become the French Company of the Star are widely assumed to have influenced Edward III's decisions first to create a large fraternity of three hundred knights in 1344 and then, once that idea had collapsed, to found the much smaller and elitist Order of the Garter in 1348.[41] There is little to indicate, though, that the Garter in the characteristic form in which it developed – comprising the monarch and a highly elite company of twenty-four knights – had a long or coherent gestation. The membership of the order seems largely to have reflected the tournament teams that met at Windsor in June 1348 to celebrate the queen's churching after the recent birth of Prince William of Windsor.[42] Six weeks later, on 6 August, the king gave his authority for the refoundation of the chapel in the lower ward of Windsor Castle and the setting up there of the permanent college of secular clerks.[43] It was this determination to create a permanent and full ecclesiastical establishment around the annual gathering of the knights of the order on 23 April, St George's Day, that did more than anything else to turn the Garter from an event into an institution.

A similar sense of relative spontaneity surrounds the foundation of the college to support the chapel of St Stephen in Westminster Palace. The college's foundation document is dated the same day as that of St George's Chapel at Windsor. But there is reasonable evidence, recently elucidated by Elizabeth Biggs, that the decision regarding St Stephen's may have been taken some while later, perhaps in September 1348, and that the foundation deed was then backdated in order to give this college equality with its sister foundation at Windsor.[44] If this is the case, then it may also help us to understand some of the reasoning behind the decision. Edward III's chief minister, William Edington, Bishop of Winchester, who was closely involved in both foundations, may have advised that it was seemly for the king's primary and official residence of Westminster to have the same level of clerical provision as Edward's birthplace and the special place of his affection, Windsor.[45]

From the historian's perspective, the comparative novelty of the collegiate foundations at St George's Windsor and St Stephen's Westminster points the way forward to a new fashion in ecclesiastical foundations during the later Middle Ages. The religious culture brought on by the advent of the plague and the need to care for the souls of the deceased encouraged the development of chantries dedicated to the saying of masses and prayers for the founder and his or her family. Chantries took many forms, but the most elaborate of them had permanently endowed clerical staffs living according to the collegial model. It has been calculated that over seventy chantry colleges were founded in England between 1350 and the Reformation.[46] Commemoration was certainly an important motivating force

---

[40] D'A. D. J. Boulton, *The Knights of the Crown: The Monarchical Orders of Knighthood in Later Medieval Europe, 1325–1520*, 2nd edn (Woodbridge, 2000), pp. 174–5.
[41] Ormrod, *Edward III*, pp. 300–5.
[42] Vale, *Edward III and Chivalry*, pp. 76–82; Caroline Shenton, 'Philippa of Hainault's Churchings: The Politics of Motherhood at the Court of Edward III', in Richard Eales and Shaun Tyas (eds), *Family and Dynasty in Late Medieval England* (Donington, 2003), p. 110.
[43] Collins, *Order of the Garter*, p. 13.
[44] Biggs, 'College and Canons of St Stephen's', p. 33 and n. 65.
[45] For Edington's involvement at Windsor and Westminster, see Roberts, *St George's Chapel*, 149; Biggs, 'College and Canons of St Stephen's', pp. 30–3; and Elizabeth Biggs's essay in this volume.
[46] Christopher Harper-Bill, 'The English Church and English Religion after the Black Death', in W. Mark Ormrod and Phillip G. Lindley (eds), *The Black Death in England, 1348–1500* (Stamford, 1996), p. 104. See also, more

in the foundation of the Order of the Garter: the statutes of the order, probably compiled in the immediate aftermath of the first outbreak of the Black Death, set great store by the provision for the souls of deceased members of the knightly confraternity.[47] In another sense, however, the foundation at Westminster looked back in time. The letters patent of 6 August 1348 referred to the work of Edward III's predecessors in beginning the work of building the new chapel of St Stephen, and represented his own determination to bring that work to completion as an act of dynastic piety.[48] Put more specifically, the work was part of a wider preoccupation of Edward III with the achievements of his grandfather, Edward I, under whom the original decision had been taken to rebuild the chapel of St Stephen at Westminster. The creation and observation of a kind of political cult of Edward I was a defining feature of Edward III's personal religion, as more generally of his military and diplomatic ambitions.[49] The decision to set up a collegiate establishment at Westminster was therefore fixed very much in the tradition of ancestor-worship that was a recognized and regular part of royal pious practice in the later Middle Ages.

The Royal Capital

The third theme to be explored in this contribution concerns the place of St Stephen's Chapel within the wider story of the emergence of Westminster as a royal capital during the reigns of the three Edwards. The beginnings of this process are to be located in the reign of Henry III, whose great rebuilding of Westminster Abbey and construction of the Painted Chamber within the Palace of Westminster stood as very tangible signs of a new attention to royal magnificence.[50] By contrast with Henry III, Edward I and Edward II did not spend significant amounts of time at Westminster Palace; in the case of Edward II, indeed, there was a tendency when at Westminster to reside not in the main complex but at more private lodgings inside and outside the Palace precinct.[51] In institutional terms, too, the reigns of Edward I and Edward II represented one of the 'conflicting tendencies' that Thomas F. Tout identified in the history of English government: namely, the periodic removal of the principal offices of state – especially the Chancery, the Exchequer, and the Court of Common Pleas, but also the Court of King's Bench and Parliament – from Westminster to Shrewsbury and, more particularly, York during the wars in Wales and Scotland.[52] In these respects, there seems little to suggest that Edward I and Edward II continued Henry III's grand designs for Westminster.

---

generally, Clive Burgess, 'An Institution for All Seasons: The Late Medieval English College', in Clive Burgess and Martin Heale (eds), *The Late Medieval English College and its Context* (York, 2008), pp. 3–27.
[47] Ormrod, 'Personal Religion', p. 855.
[48] Paul Binski, *Westminster Abbey and the Plantagenets: Kingship and the Representation of Power, 1200–1400* (New Haven/London, 1995), p. 182.
[49] Ormrod, 'Personal Religion', pp. 871–2.
[50] *HKW*, vol. 1, pp. 494–504; Paul Binski, *The Painted Chamber at Westminster* (London, 1986).
[51] *HKW*, vol. 1, pp. 504–9.
[52] Thomas F. Tout, *Collected Papers* (3 vols, Manchester, 1932–4), vol. 3, pp. 223–75; Dorothy M. Broome, 'Exchequer Migrations to York in the Thirteenth and Fourteenth Centuries', in A. G. Little and F. M. Powicke (eds), *Essays in Medieval History Presented to Thomas Frederick Tout* (Manchester, 1925), pp. 291–300; W. Mark Ormrod, 'Competing Capitals? York and London in the Fourteenth Century', in Sarah Rees Jones, Richard Marks, and A. J. Minnis (eds), *Courts and Regions in Medieval Europe* (York, 2000), pp. 75–98.

In two very important respects, however, these reigns represented a fairly decisive orientation of the religious and ceremonial aspects of monarchy towards the Abbey and Palace of Westminster. First, the incorporation of the Stone of Scone into a new coronation chair under Edward I, the new attention given to the elevation of this ceremonial seat during the coronation of Edward II, and the placing of the chair at other times in close proximity to the shrine of Edward the Confessor all speak to a new emphasis on the permanent representation of the sacral aspects of monarchy. As Paul Binski has noted, the coronation chair's allusions to the Throne of Solomon linked back to the representation of Edward the Confessor upon the bed of Solomon in the wall paintings of the Painted Chamber. The iconographical displays at the Palace and the Abbey were thereby brought into conscious alignment and used to recharge the quasi-sacerdotal authority of English kingship.[53]

Secondly, the reigns of Edward I and Edward II were of key importance in establishing the choir of the abbey church of Westminster as the primary burial place within England both of kings and of their close relatives and friends.[54] The interment of Henry III in close proximity to the shrine of the Confessor set the precedent and tone for something that England had previously lacked: a distinct royal necropolis. Notwithstanding the burial of Edward II at Gloucester Abbey, which was the product of the unprecedented circumstances of the king's forced removal from the throne and subsequent death, and likely murder, at Berkeley Castle, Westminster Abbey had become, by 1327, *the* royal mausoleum of choice in England. In 1339 Edward III directed that the remains of his brother, John of Eltham, should be removed from their existing place of burial in Westminster Abbey and placed 'among the royals'; the prince was duly reinterred in the Chapel of St Edmund, just across the ambulatory from the arcade reserved as burial space for kings and queens.[55] In spite of his supposed intention to be buried at the shrine of the Three Kings at Cologne, Edward III seems to have been clear from the outset about the inevitability of his interment at Westminster, and was said to have declared in 1359 that he wished to be buried alongside 'that most illustrious and courageous soldier, and the most prudent statesman', Edward I.[56]

The reign of Edward III also witnessed some real and symbolic changes in the architecture and usages of the royal Palace. First among these developments, of course, was the campaign for the completion of St Stephen's Chapel in the late 1340s and 1350s. The king's works at Westminster were subsequently eclipsed, in his own time and in later historical writing, by the great campaign of rebuilding in the lower and upper wards of Windsor Castle.[57] But Edward III actually showed considerable interest in the Westminster complex. As other studies in this collection attest, the choices that the king and his craftsmen made about the decoration of St Stephen's Chapel served to project the monarch's strong sense of destiny, both for himself and for his large family of children.[58] During the second half of his reign, when he ceased to travel so extensively, Edward resided quite frequently at Westminster.

---

[53] Binski, *Painted Chamber*, pp. 96–103; Binski, *Westminster Abbey*, pp. 126–40.
[54] Binski, *Westminster Abbey*, pp. 90–120; D. M. Palliser, 'Royal Mausolea in the Long Fourteenth Century (1272–1422)', in W. Mark Ormrod (ed.), *Fourteenth Century England III* (Woodbridge, 2004), pp. 1–16.
[55] Ormrod, 'Personal Religion', p. 868 and n. 109; Binski, *Westminster Abbey*, pp. 177–9.
[56] Antonia Gransden, *Historical Writing in England, c.1307 to the Early Sixteenth Century* (London, 1982), p. 108.
[57] May McKisack, *The Fourteenth Century* (Oxford, 1959), p. 226; *HKW*, vol. 1, p. 236.
[58] For Edward's wider dynastic strategy, see W. Mark Ormrod, 'Edward III and his Family', *Journal of British Studies*, 26 (1987), 398–422.

The Plantagenet Purpose: St Stephen's Chapel and English Kingship, 1272–1377

New works were undertaken in the privy palace, most notably with the building of the Jewel Tower in the 1360s.[59] In these and other works in the Palace, Edward deployed the skills of the outstanding craftsmen Henry Yevele and Hugh Herland, who would go on to mastermind the Palace's major refurbishment under Richard II.[60]

Edward III understood the practical and symbolic importance of the Palace complex at Westminster as a site of royal authority and a backdrop to royal display. In the twelve months from December 1340, for example, during which Edward moved from the most serious political crisis of his reign to the formal reassertion of his rights and authority, he carried out some 355 ritual healings for scrofula, 257 of which were performed at the regal and sacral headquarters of Westminster.[61] During the second half of the reign in particular, many of Edward's audiences of state and diplomatic meetings were held within the Palace complex.[62] It was in this period, too, that the various elements of the king's Parliament became associated with particular rooms and spaces within the Westminster complex. The opening and closing plenary meetings of king, Lords and Commons usually took place in the Painted Chamber. In between, the Lords removed for their separate deliberations to the White Chamber. The Commons often used the Painted Chamber in the middle years of the fourteenth century, but by 1376 had shifted to the chapter house of the Abbey, and after 1395 seem to have met always in the Abbey refectory.[63] In the 1360s and 1370s we begin to get regular references to feasts held in the great hall of the Palace to mark the closing of Parliaments, to which members of the Commons as well as of the Lords were invited. More generally, the second half of Edward III's reign seems to have witnessed an increase in the ceremony and solemnity associated with meetings of Parliament at Westminster.[64] The completion of St Stephen's Chapel in the 1350s also prompted a new awareness of its capabilities as a royal space: in 1361, Edward III secured from the papacy the special privilege of baptizing and burying the children of the Kings of England.[65] A new addition to the Palace complex came in the 1360s with the building of a new belfry to house the great bell known as 'Edward of Westminster'.[66] Set in this context, the building and completion of St Stephen's Chapel can be seen as part of a wider policy of royal magnificence promoted especially at the court of Edward III and which drew both inspiration and emulation in the courts of continental Europe.[67]

---

[59] *HKW*, vol. 1, pp. 534–6.
[60] Ormrod, *Edward III*, p. 453.
[61] Ormrod, 'Personal Religion', p. 863.
[62] Ormrod, *Edward III*, p. 452.
[63] Sir Goronwy Edwards, *The Second Century of the English Parliament* (Oxford, 1979), pp. 4–7; Barbara Harvey, 'The Monks of Westminster and their Chapter House', in Warwick Rodwell and Richard Mortimer (eds), *Westminster Abbey Chapter House: The History, Art and Architecture of 'A Chapter House Beyond Compare'* (London, 2010), pp. 102–11. For the political significance of the Commons' meeting 'in the round' in the chapter house in 1376, see W. Mark Ormrod, 'The Good Parliament of 1376: Commons, *communes*, and "Common Profit" in Fourteenth-Century English Politics', in David Nicholas, Bernard S. Bachrach, and James M. Murray (eds), *Comparative Perspectives on History and Historians: Essays in Memory of Bryce Lyon (1920–2007)* (Kalamazoo, 2012), pp. 169–88.
[64] Ormrod, *Edward III*, pp. 454–5.
[65] Ormrod, *Edward III*, p. 466.
[66] *HKW*, vol. 1, p. 509.
[67] Paul Crossley, 'Architecture', in Michael Jones (ed.), *The New Cambridge Medieval History, VI* (Cambridge, 2000), pp. 235–9.

The final element in the settlement of Westminster Palace as an effective capital came with the permanent settlement there of the various offices of state. The removal of the Chancery, Exchequer, and Common Pleas from York back to Westminster in 1337–8 proved a turning point, after which these two courts sat regularly at Westminster, only moving north again in 1392–3 when Richard II used their temporary relocation to York as part of a scheme to punish the disloyalty of the city of London.[68] The Court of King's Bench continued to be itinerant, but sat more frequently at Westminster after the late 1330s; and Parliament too, though occasionally called to meet at provincial locations, was also now expected for the main part to meet at Westminster.[69] In the mid-1340s came two further indicative developments: the privy seal office no longer moved around with the king and his household, but settled more or less permanently at Westminster; and the royal council was provided, for the first time, with its own established meeting-place in the Palace, in the 'new chamber', later known as the Star Chamber.[70] The overall effect was to make Westminster Palace, as never before, *the* seat within England of royal politics, justice, finance, and public business.

It was in this context that the collegiate establishment attached to St Stephen's Chapel in 1348 came particularly into its own. Among the royal offices of state, the only one to have a structure binding its staff together into a single community was the Chancery, whose clerks were formally members of the Chancellor's household and, in theory at least, lived as a collective community in his London residence on what is now Chancery Lane. The later Middle Ages witnessed the gradual weakening of this collective, as the clerks organized themselves into smaller domestic units or (in the case of the increasing number of those who only took minor orders) married and set up households of their own.[71] Down to the end of Edward III's reign, however, these trends were not particularly evident: indeed, in some respects the great bonanza of ecclesiastical patronage that fell to the crown as a result of the Black Death of 1348–9 and subsequent outbreaks served to intensify the commitment of the civil service to clerical orders, in the expectation of gaining the handsome incomes now falling available.[72] There were already links between particular departments of government and ecclesiastical institutions in and around the capital: many of the keepers of the king's wardrobe in the thirteenth and fourteenth centuries were granted the deanery of the royal free chapel of St Martin le Grand, London; and latterly the clerks of the king's works were often rewarded with canonries there, too.[73] In the wake of the foundation of a new college of secular clerks at St Stephen's Chapel in 1348, the king's Treasurer, William Edington, hit upon

---

[68] Caroline M. Barron, 'The Quarrel of Richard II with London, 1392–7', in F. R. H. Du Boulay and Caroline M. Barron (eds), *The Reign of Richard II: Essays in Honour of May McKisack* (London, 1971), pp. 173–201; Nigel Saul, 'Richard II and the City of York', in Sarah Rees Jones (ed.), *The Government of Medieval York: Essays in Commemoration of the 1396 Royal Charter* (York, 1997), pp. 1–13; Nigel Saul, 'Richard II, York, and the Evidence of the King's Itinerary', in James L. Gillespie (ed.), *The Age of Richard II* (Stroud, 1997), pp. 71–92.
[69] Anthony Musson and W. Mark Ormrod, *The Evolution of English Justice: Law, Politics and Society in the Fourteenth Century* (Basingstoke, 1999), pp. 194–205.
[70] Thomas F. Tout, *Chapters in the Administrative History of Mediaeval England* (6 vols, Manchester, 1920–33), vol. 5, 72–3; James F. Baldwin, *The King's Council in England during the Middle Ages* (Oxford, 1913), pp. 355–6.
[71] Tout, *Collected Papers*, vol. 2, pp. 143–71; C. W. Smith, 'Some Trends in the English Royal Chancery, 1377–1483', *Medieval Prosopography*, 6 (1985), 69–94.
[72] W. Mark Ormrod, 'Accountability and Collegiality: The English Royal Secretariat in the Mid-Fourteenth Century', in Kouky Fianu and DeLloyd J. Guth (eds), *Écrit et pouvoir dans les chancelleries médiévales: Espace français, espace anglais* (Louvain-la-Neuve, 1997), pp. 76–9.
[73] Tout, *Chapters*, vol. 1, pp. 195–6, 201, 279, 297 n. 2; vol. 2, pp. 15 n. 1, 270; vol. 4, p. 155; *HKW*, vol. 1, p. 173.

the idea of using the newly available canonries of the college of St Stephen as emoluments for the principal clerks of the lower Exchequer (otherwise known as the Exchequer of Receipt). In the late 1340s Edington was introducing new checks and balances into the record-keeping of the lower Exchequer in an attempt to establish greater accountability. In the early 1350s, furthermore, he was responsible for the appointment of a number of key officers of the lower Exchequer to senior positions in the wardrobe, the great wardrobe and the chamber as part of a concerted effort to co-ordinate the income and expenditure of these financial agencies of the royal household. The key men in question – including John Buckingham, John Chesterfield, and William Rothwell – were all appointed during the same period to canonries at St Stephen's Chapel.[74] In this sense, the early stages of the college of St Stephen were intimately linked with administrative reform and, more generally, with the bureaucratic politics of Westminster Palace.

Although Edington's initial plan did not outlive his tenure as royal Treasurer, the connections between the college of St Stephen and the wider clerical community of the Westminster administration proved enduring. As Elizabeth Biggs has shown, the prebendaries of St Stephen's almost always included men employed in the Chancery and Exchequer, as well as a rather smaller tradition of links to the council and the diplomatic service, as well as the royal household. While very little is known of the conditions and atmosphere under which such individuals observed the collective domestic requirements of the college or went about their responsibilities for its management in the later fourteenth century, it is especially significant that they were (unusually in such colleges) required to be in perpetual residence, and records from the later fifteenth century indicate that this specification was still normally observed.[75] We can therefore hypothesize that the effect of the foundation of 1348 was to create, within the Palace of Westminster, an influential enclave of canons deploying their collective membership of the college of St Stephen in their daily responsibilities within individual departments of royal government. In this sense, St Stephen's Chapel may indeed be said to have been a perfect microcosm of the late medieval English state.

Conclusion

In spite of their very different personalities and records as rulers, Edward I, II, and III shared an awareness of certain of the values and expectations of their royal office and performed their religiosity in a manner generally designed to satisfy the clerical and lay clerical elites of the time. This included not only the proper observation of Catholic Christianity, but also a willingness to engage in certain public rituals that emphasized the unique qualities and powers of an anointed king. It also involved showing a proper sense of duty in the foundation of ecclesiastical institutions and support for the (often floundering) initiatives of previous rulers. Edward II and Edward III both followed new trends in their foundations, adding university halls and colleges of secular clerks to the existing royal tradition of monastic patronage. In 1348 Edward III specifically articulated his desire to revive and bring to fruition the long-standing project at St Stephen's Chapel Westminster, as an act

---

[74] W. Mark Ormrod, 'The Protocolla Rolls and English Government Finance, 1353–1364', *EHR*, 102 (1987), 624–6; Biggs, 'College and Canons of St Stephen's', pp. 31–2, 136.
[75] Biggs, 'College and Canons of St Stephen's', pp. 126–56.

of dynastic piety, reflecting his wider admiration for and commemoration of the deeds and memory of his grandfather, Edward I. It was also under the three Edwards that the Abbey and Palace of Westminster emerged as the official burial place of kings and royals, the primary headquarters of English royal government, and the ceremonial capital of England. The building of St Stephen's Chapel Westminster between the 1290s and the 1350s thus not only coincided with, but also stood as a supreme expression of, the English monarchy's institutional power and ritualized magnificence.

St Stephen's Chapel, Westminster: From a King's to a Collegiate Chapel

John Harper

When in 1348 Edward III founded the college of St Stephen in the Palace of Westminster, and of St George in Windsor Castle, he adapted liturgical spaces initially conceived as king's chapels. Chapels staffed in the thirteenth century by a small number of king's chaplains had now to accommodate a college of thirty clergy along with boy choristers and chapel officers. This chapter considers the spatial and ritual transformation of a king's to a collegiate chapel.[1] Given the loss of so much of the documentation relating to St Stephen's, it is inevitable that frequent reference has to be made to St George's. The starting point, however, is the royal chapels repaired, refurbished, and newly built, staffed, equipped, and used for worship in the reign of Henry III from his majority onwards (1227–72) – a subject that merits a full study in its own right.[2] Here, a preliminary survey of his activities provides the context for St Stephen's, a chapel that Henry III inherited and refurbished. This was the chapel known to and replaced by his son, Edward I (1272–1307). Henry himself built the new king's chapel in the lower bailey of Windsor Castle alongside his new lodgings – St Edward's Chapel, which survives in part as the Albert Memorial Chapel, east of the present St George's.[3]

Chapels in Late Medieval Royal Houses and Castles

Images of medieval monarchs generally depict them alone, or with a small number of other essential figures, belying the scale of the royal household always present with them,

---

[1] The chapter has benefited considerably from conversations and communications about the physical disposition of St Stephen's as a collegiate chapel and its use, especially with Tim Ayers, James Hillson, and Elizabeth Biggs, and from two doctoral dissertations: James Hillson, 'St Stephen's Chapel, Westminster: Architecture, Decoration and Politics in the Reigns of Henry III and the three Edwards (1227–1363)' (Ph.D. dissertation, University of York, 2015), and Elizabeth Biggs, 'The College and Canons of St Stephen's, Westminster, 1348–1548' (Ph.D. dissertation, University of York, 2016). The latter has been reworked as Elizabeth Biggs, *St Stephen's College, Westminster: A Royal Chapel and English Kingship 1348–1548* (Woodbridge, 2020), but the references here are to her thesis, which contains material omitted from the printed volume.

[2] Hillson, 'St Stephen's Chapel', pp. 434–56, lists a total of seventy royal castles and houses, containing 159 chapels, recording works ordered by Henry III in all but twenty-three chapels. To these can be added the chapel at Rhuddlan Castle (mentioned below).

[3] The evidence of this chapel, and of the later college of St George at Windsor, are important reference points for the lost building and documentation of St Stephen's. See Steven Brindle, 'The First St George's Chapel', in

from those closest to the king and in high office to the most menial of servants. Among this body were the royal chaplains, who variously served both the king and his household, and the queen and her household. These priests provided for the spiritual needs of all within the court, whether in castle, palace or hunting lodge, from the king and queen themselves to the most humble – part of a protective sacred force-field of prayer, venerated objects, devotion, and especially the daily offering of the sacrifice of the Mass enfolding king and court. Some chaplains accompanied the king and queen wherever they went; but others were a permanent presence in royal castles and houses.[4] They were not all of equal calibre: they ranged from the most highly educated and able – men with the capacity to be high-ranking administrators and lawyers in government, close to the king or based at Westminster – to those recruited by a local sheriff to serve a castle chapel, who might only have sufficient Latin literacy to recite the limited repertory of a daily Mass of the Virgin Mary or Requiem.

In some locations, the chaplains were part of a larger group of priests, monks, and nuns offering prayer for the king and his family. Before the Norman Conquest, when Winchester was a centre of government, there were three monasteries adjacent to the royal palace (Old Minster, New Minster, and Nunnaminster).[5] By the thirteenth century, the Palace of Westminster as the hub of royal administration and government was adjacent to the Benedictine abbey of St Peter and the church of St Margaret, in addition to at least four chapels within the curtilage of the Palace itself (St John, St Stephen, St Lawrence by the king's chamber, and the queen's chapel).[6] When Henry III came to the throne in 1216, the chapels of St John and St Stephen each had at least two permanently resident chaplains; and during that century there was a gradual expansion and consolidation of chaplains. This occurred both at Westminster and in the new king's chapel, dedicated to St Edward the Confessor, built by Henry III within Windsor Castle in the 1240s (fig. 1).[7] There was also another new chapel in the great park. By 1331, the chaplains of both the new castle and the new park chapels at Windsor were amalgamated as a single group: eight chaplains with two clerks based at St Edward's Chapel in the castle. And when Edward III wanted to expand the clerical body at both Westminster and Windsor, his original plan was to have a warden and twenty-three chaplains at Windsor.[8] In the final event, he chose in 1348 to found colleges within the Palace of Westminster and Windsor Castle, established by 1352 as self-governing, independently endowed, statutory institutions, each with twenty-six canons.

Nigel Saul and Tim Tatton-Brown (eds), *St George's Chapel, Windsor: History and Heritage* (Wimborne Minster, 2010), pp. 36–44; and Steven Brindle (ed.), *Windsor Castle: A Thousand Years of a Royal Palace* (London, 2018).
[4] Some castle chapels had been founded as colleges of prebendal canons (as at Bridgnorth, Dover, and Oxford), though only Bridgnorth persisted in this form. J. H. Denton, *English Royal Free Chapels, 1100–1300: A Constitutional Study* (Manchester, 1970), pp. 57–8, 119–21.
[5] Martin Biddle, '*Felix Urbs Winthonia*: Winchester in the Age of Monastic Reform', in David Parsons (ed.), *Tenth-Century Studies* (London/Chichester, 1975), pp. 123–40.
[6] The location of St John's Chapel remains uncertain: see *HKW*, vol. 1, pp. 502–3. Tim Ayers has suggested that St John's and the queen's chapel may be one and the same: see Ayers & Jurkowski, vol. 1, p. 58.
[7] Hillson, 'St Stephen's Chapel', pp. 47–8: tables of chaplains at Westminster and Windsor.
[8] A. K. B. Roberts, *St George's Chapel, Windsor Castle, 1348–1416* (Windsor, [1947]), pp. 5–6. Roberts also draws attention to the establishment by Edward II of a proto-college in the chapel of Windsor great park with dean, twelve chaplains, and four clerks – diminished to just four chaplains by the time they were brought to the king's chapel in the castle (first recorded *CPR 1313–17*, p. 11: 20 Aug. 1313).

St Stephen's Chapel, Westminster: From a King's to a Collegiate Chapel

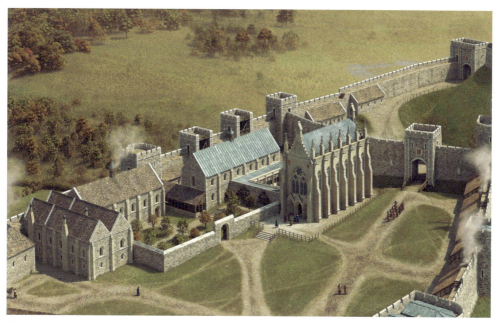

Fig. 1. Reconstruction drawing of Windsor Castle, showing the outer bailey, the chapel of St Edward the Confessor and the king's lodgings newly built by Henry III in the 1240s, by Bob Marshall.

Edward III's two collegiate foundations mark the clear separation of royal clerical provision: a substantial, permanently resident collegiate body at both Westminster and Windsor on the one hand; and an itinerant royal household chapel, resident wherever the king or queen was located at any one time, on the other. Within the itinerant body were chaplains personal to the king or queen, and those serving the household. This delineation is even clearer in the time of the Tudors: chaplains serving in the intimacy of a small chapel or oratory adjoining the king's chamber at first-floor level in the royal apartments; and a chapel for the use of the household, located on the ground floor, whose liturgy could be shared (or at least observed) by the king from a closet at first-floor level.[9] Only rarely did the king descend from the closet to the main floor of the household chapel; and even then he might be enclosed by a temporary traverse.[10]

The transition from a chapel staffed by royal chaplains to a college of clergy had implications for both the configuration of the space and the pattern of the liturgy. At both Westminster and Windsor, chapels built (or at least set out) in the thirteenth century for one purpose were adapted in the mid fourteenth century for another.

---

[9] Simon Thurley, *The Royal Palaces of Tudor England* (New Haven/London, 1993), pp. 195–205. Royal closets are still to be seen in the surviving royal household chapels at Hampton Court and in St James's Palace.
[10] Andrew Ashbee and John Harley, *The Cheque Book of the Chapel Royal* (2 vols, Aldershot, UK/Burlington, Vermont, 2000), vol. 1, pp. 94–5: a later description of royal use of a traverse in the Chapel Royal of Greenwich Palace at the christening of Princess Mary, 1605.

The Thirteenth-century Royal Chapels of Henry III

As a pious man and a great patron of the Church, Henry III initiated the complete rebuilding of Westminster Abbey, and supported and contributed funds to other foundations, including the new cathedral at Salisbury and a number of mendicant houses. He also undertook a significant building programme of his own royal chapels: repairing, refurbishing, decorating, and enriching many of the existing chapels in the royal castles and houses, including St Stephen, Westminster; and in a number of cases building new chapels, including the chapel of St Edward the Confessor, Windsor Castle. Most of these chapels are lost or completely rebuilt; and we are principally reliant on surviving royal documents for scattered and often enigmatic details of their size, disposition, furnishing, staffing, and use.[11]

In a few instances the dimensions of the new royal chapels were set down, indicating their varying scale.[12]

Date	Place	Length (ft)	Width (ft)	Area (sq ft)
1233	Hereford Castle	25	unspecified	
1237	Kempton (queen's)	30	12	360
1253	Havering (queen's)	28	14	392
1244	Sauvey Castle	40	20	800
1239	King's Cliffe	50	22	1100
1240	St Edward, Windsor Castle	70	28	1960

Some chapels were specified to be wooden (as at the castles of Rhuddlan, Rochester, and Sauvey), and some of stone (as at King's Cliffe).[13] In a number of cases these new chapels were built at first-floor level (the level of the royal chambers) – as at Clarendon (both the king's and the queen's chapels), Gillingham, and Woodstock (both king's and queen's);[14] others had both an upper and lower chapel, as at Kempton, Rochester, and Havering.[15]

At Kempton, there is delineation of function: the upper chapel, leading from the queen's chamber, intended for the queen and her immediate entourage; the lower chapel designated for the king's household. The same arrangement was made when the chapel of St Judoc, Winchester Castle was adapted for the queen (upper chapel) and the king's household (lower).[16] The same may be the case in the king's upper and lower chapels at Havering, each

---

[11] Almost all the works are discussed in *HKW*. Henry III's work at Rhuddlan is not included.
[12] *CLR 1226–40*, p. 230: 11 Sept. 1233 (Hereford); p. 262: 13 April 1237 (Kempton); p. 411: 28 Aug. 1239 (King's Cliffe); p. 439: 4 Jan. 1240 (Windsor). *CLR 1240–45*, p. 249: 7 July 1244 (Sauvey). *CLR 1251–60*, p. 119: 8 April 1253 (Havering). In the table that follows 1 ft = 0.3 m.
[13] *CLR 1240–45*, p. 104: 4 Feb. 1242 (Rhuddlan); p. 211: 4 Jan. 1244 (Rochester); p. 249: 7 July 1244 (Sauvey). *CLR 1226–40*, p. 411: 28 Aug. 1239 (King's Cliffe).
[14] Upper storey locations confirmed in *CLR 1226–40*, p. 251: 10 Jan. 1237 (Clarendon, queen's chapel). *CLR 1245–51*, p. 292: 20 June 1250 (Woodstock); p. 297: 30 July 1250 (Gillingham); p. 324, 7 Dec. 1250 (Clarendon, king's chapel).
[15] *CLR 1226–40*, p. 262: 13 April 1237 (Kempton); *CLR 1240–45*, p. 211: 4 Jan. 1244 (Rochester); *CLR 1245–51*, p. 372: 26 Aug. 1251 (Havering).
[16] *CLR 1226–40*, p. 262: 13 April 1237 (Kempton). *HKW*, vol. 2, p. 862, citing and quoting *Pipe Roll, 21 Henry III*, rot. 10d (Winchester): 28 Jan. 1237: 'fieri facias duas capellas […] unam superius ad opus regine nostre et aliam inferius ad opus familie nostre'.

of which seems to have been set out differently.[17] However, at Rochester, the new upper king's chapel (dedicated to St Margaret) appears to have been a shared space: in 1254 an external stone staircase and door were ordered 'so that strangers and others can enter the chapel without going through the middle of the king's chamber as they used to do'.[18] This suggests that what was first intended for the king and those admitted to his chamber now had wider availability. In other royal houses there appears to have been separation within the chapel: at Geddington a screen (*clausam*) was made with a central doorway,[19] and at Kenilworth Castle, a wooden wall was erected, perhaps with openwork (it is described as *lineatum*), each dividing the chapel into chancel and nave.[20] In some other chapels (whether new or old), there is reference to chancel or nave, implying a double-cell building, again allowing separation – as in the chapel of the king's new hall in Oxford, the king's lower chapel at Havering, All Saints' Chapel at Clarendon, Saint Nicholas' Chapel, Marlborough Castle (a new chancel added), and at St Peter ad Vincula within the bailey of the Tower of London.[21] The latter had two 'chancels' (St Peter and St Mary), and evidently served in part as a parish church with its own parish priest in addition to the royal chaplains.[22]

There is reference to only a limited range of furnishing in the chapels. An altar is assumed, and there was a sedilia for the use of the clergy at Mass at Nottingham Castle.[23] Additional altars are referred to in a few places, either as already present (for instance, the altars of St Nicholas and St Katherine in St Peter ad Vincula in the Tower),[24] or to be added (the altar of St Edward on the south side of the nave in Oxford,[25] and three altars in the church of St Mary in Dover Castle).[26] In a number of chapels Henry III required a font: as, for example, at St Stephen's and the queen's chapel, Westminster Palace;[27] the king's chapel, Windsor Castle;[28] All Saints' Chapel, Clarendon (*baptisterium*);[29] St Thomas's (the king's) Chapel, Winchester Castle;[30] and St Peter ad Vincula in the Tower (specified as marble with marble columns).[31] For the most part, only seats for the king and queen are specified in the king's chapels, and for the queen in her own chapels. At St Peter ad Vincula there were stalls (rather than seats) for the king and queen, before the altars of St Nicholas (on the south side) and St Katherine (on the north), near the entrance to the chancel of St Peter.[32] This may suggest a

---

[17] *CLR 1245–51*, p. 372: 26 Aug. 1251.
[18] *CCR 1253–54*, p. 285: 18 Dec. 1254, 'quod extranei et alii libere possint ingredi capellam illam et quod non transeant per medium camere regis sicut facere consueverunt'. *CLR 1251–60*, pp. 290–1: 8 May 1256 (payment).
[19] *CLR 1251–60*, p. 21: 27 Jan. 1252. There were seats (presumably for king and queen) on each side of the doorway.
[20] *CLR 1240–45*, p. 31: [26 Feb.] 1241.
[21] *CLR 1226–40*, p. 176: 15 April 1230 (Marlborough – also *HKW*, vol. 2, p. 735); pp. 452–3: 21 Feb. 1240 (St Peter ad Vincula). *CLR 1245–51*, p. 119: 28 April 1247 (Oxford); p. 372: 26 Aug. 1251 (Havering). *HKW*, vol. 2, p. 915 (Clarendon).
[22] *CLR 1226–40*, pp. 452–3: 21 Feb. 1240; p. 427: 2 Nov. 1239 (when the priest was compensated for damage to the church).
[23] *CLR 1240–45*, p. 252: 16 July 1244.
[24] *CLR 1226–40*, p. 453: 21 Feb. 1240.
[25] *CLR 1245–51*, p. 119: 28 April 1247.
[26] *CLR 1245–51*, p. 112: 15 March 1247.
[27] *CLR 1226–40*, p. 478: 5 July 1240.
[28] Extant in part. Pamela Tudor-Craig, 'The Fonts of St George's Chapel', in N. Saul (ed.), *St George's Chapel Windsor in the Fourteenth Century* (Woodbridge, 2005), pp. 151–64, especially pp. 156–61.
[29] *CLR 1245–51*, p. 296: 30 July 1250.
[30] *HKW*, vol. 2, p. 637.
[31] *CLR 1240–45*, p. 15: 10 Dec. 1240.
[32] *CLR 1226–40*, p. 453: 21 Feb. 1240. Howard Colvin suggests that these stalls were outside the chancel at the eastern end of the nave (*HKW*, vol. 2, p. 715), but this would seem to be less typical. If the altars of St Nicholas

different provision from elsewhere. In most places there is no reference to other seating;[33] but forms were ordered for the king's and queen's chambers and chapels at Geddington;[34] four forms (*formas*) were also ordered for the new chapel by Oxford Castle;[35] and stalls, benches, and prie-dieux are listed in St Leonard's, one of three chapels at Ludgershall Castle.[36]

Henry III evidently expected each chapel to be staffed by at least one chaplain. Prayer for the king and his family was to be offered in all royal houses and castles if possible; and at Dover Castle there was an instruction for a chaplain to recite the prayer *Salus populi* daily against the sudden death of the king and his relatives.[37] There are specific directives to royal officials (most often sheriffs) to provide a chaplain – for instance, in 1244–5 at the royal houses of Hodsock and King's Cliffe, and in the royal castles of Canterbury, Devizes, Hereford, Nottingham (two chapels), Rockingham, Sauvey, and York.[38] Often the directive is accompanied by an instruction to provide chalice, missal, and a set of vestments – the essential equipment for a priest to say Mass. In contrast with the valuable ritual objects at Westminster or Windsor, for instance, these were functional acquisitions: in 1253 a chalice for Rochester was to be of 'average price', and the cost of this, the vestments, altar cloths, missal, and antiphonal was not to exceed five pounds.[39]

In some instances, other books are specified (but only as single copies): in 1251 a missal, gradual, breviary, antiphonal, psalter, hymnal, and troper, for Nottingham Castle – a suite of books for both Mass and Office;[40] and in 1255 a missal and gradual with troper to be obtained for Clipstone without delay (an order of 1251 having not been fulfilled).[41] Exceptionally, in 1239, a missal, gradual, breviary with antiphonal, lectionary, psalter, collectar, capitulary, and hymnal were listed for Sherborne Castle, but then amended simply to missal (with another for Corfe Castle).[42] In 1242, a combined missal with gradual and antiphonal in one volume was to be sent to Rhuddlan Castle for the new chapel, suggesting a selective body of material rather than full provision.[43] Such selective provision may have included Mass of the Blessed Virgin Mary, required to be recited at St Peter ad Vincula in the Tower of London,[44] and at the castle chapels of Dover[45] and Dublin,[46] for instance. It is not always possible to tell whether this Mass of the Virgin Mary was to be a daily observance (as was

---

and St Katherine were within the chancel (for the use of royal chaplains, while the high altar was for the parish priest), the stalls might be in the more usual place at the west end of the chancel.

[33] It would be rare for a nave to have seating for the people at this time.
[34] *CLR 1251–60*, p. 21: 27 Jan. 1252.
[35] *CLR 1226–40*, p. 14: 20 Jan. 1227.
[36] *HKW*, vol. 2, p. 736, citing *Pipe Roll, 16 Henry III*, rot 16.
[37] *CLR 1245–51*, p. 54: 23 May 1246. From the context this seems more likely to be the collect, rather than the Mass *Salus populi*.
[38] *CLR 1240–45*, p. 249: 7 July 1244 (King's Cliffe and Sauvey); p. 255: 23 July 1244 (Hodsock, Devizes, and Nottingham); p. 257: 6 Aug. 1244 (York); p. 263: 2 Sept. 1244 (Nottingham second chapel, and Rockingham), 6 Sept. 1244 (Canterbury); p. 296: 15 April 1245 (Hereford).
[39] *CLR 1251–60*, p. 133: 4 June 1253.
[40] *CLR 1251–60*, p. 11: 12 Dec. 1251. For explanations of the liturgical books, see John Harper, *The Forms and Orders of Western Liturgy* (Oxford, 1991) or Eric Palazzo, *A History of Liturgical Books from the Beginning to the Thirteenth Century* (Collegeville, MA, 1998).
[41] *CLR 1251–60*, p. 235: 3 Aug. 1255 (earlier order *CLR 1251–60*, p. 12: 13 Dec. 1251).
[42] *CLR 1226–40*, p. 367: 20 Feb. 1239.
[43] *CLR 1240–45*, p. 121: 24 April 1242.
[44] *CLR 1226–40*, p. 499: 15 Oct. 1240.
[45] *CLR 1240–45*, p. 173: 3 March 1243.
[46] *CCR 1242–47*, p. 514: 17 Sept. 1242.

becoming increasingly common by this time), or the older custom of weekly Mass recited on Saturday (or another available day). In the king's chapel of his new hall at Oxford, tapers were to burn during the Saturday Mass of the Blessed Virgin Mary.[47] The instruction at Dublin, however, is unambiguous: each day one chaplain is to recite Mass of St Edward the Confessor, and the other Mass of the Blessed Virgin Mary; on Saturday fifteen tapers are to burn, and on other days four.[48]

The priority was the offering of daily Mass, surrounding king, family, kin, and country, with the sacrifice and intercessions. However, later payments may suggest the observance of the daily Office services. Acquisition of a breviary (often named 'porteous') occurs more often after 1250 – as for the chapels at Kempton (1256) and Winchester (1259), the latter to be a full noted breviary (*plenarium portehors bene notatum*).[49] These were residences used by Henry and his queen, and the observance of the sung Office may have been limited to those times when the royal household was present, bringing the additional resources of the household chaplains and clerks.

It is impossible to know whether a chaplain in a royal house or castle offered daily Mass alone, or with assistance from others who might sing the chant, drawn from other household staff. A gradual was ordered for Clipstone, Nottingham, and Winchester, suggesting this may have been the case at least at some times.[50] The provision of a single set of vestments implies a simple pattern of ritual. Even where there were several chaplains, sufficient to celebrate the Mass with priest, deacon, and subdeacon and full ritual (as at both St John's and St Stephen's Chapels in Westminster Palace), the predominance of records of chasubles over dalmatics and tunicles suggests that Mass with a single priest may have been more common.[51] Nevertheless, full ritual must have been observed at St Stephen's, at least when the king and queen were in residence, as the large number of copes acquired there may suggest.[52] Certainly, the orders for fifteen surplices for Easter 1237, and fifty for Christmas 1240 indicate the presence of significant numbers of clergy in St Stephen's Chapel at those feasts, most likely including members of the royal household chapel.[53] The repair of five copes (also before Easter 1237)[54] may be associated with the five clerks of the household chapel remunerated for singing *Christus vincit* at the crown-wearing ceremony, observed on many occasions during the reign wherever the king was resident.[55]

If there is little indication of the furnishing of the royal chapels, the detailed descriptions of the vestments acquired principally for the king's chapel in Westminster confirm the

---

[47] *CLR 1240–45*, 220: 25 Feb. 1244.
[48] *CCR 1242–47*, p. 514: 17 Sept. 1242.
[49] *CLR 1251–60*, p. 339: 10 Nov. 1256; p. 478: 1 Oct. 1259.
[50] *CLR 1245–51*, p. 237: 31 May 1249 (Winchester); *CLR 1251–60*, p. 11: 12 Dec. 1251 (Nottingham, together with a Troper, in addition to books for the Office); p. 235: 3 Aug. 1255 (Clipstone).
[51] These vestments are specific to certain ranks of clergy at the Mass: the priest wears a chasuble, the deacon a dalmatic, and the subdeacon a tunicle. (There are more elaborate seasonal regulations of liturgical dress, but this is a basic classification.)
[52] *CLR 1226–40*, p. 322 (1238), p. 438 (1240). *CLR 1241–45*, pp. 22, 25 (1241), pp. 286, 307 (1245).
[53] *CLR 1226–40*, p. 261: 3 April 1237. *CLR 1240–45*, p. 15: 13 Dec. 1240.
[54] *CLR 1226–40*, p. 270: 19 May 1237.
[55] Payments of 25 shillings for singing *Christus vincit* are common in the Calendar of Liberate Rolls, most often to five clerks of the king's chapel (in this case the household chapel travelling with the king). The original pattern was for crown-wearing at Christmas, Easter and Pentecost (as from Christmas 1227 to Easter 1230 – *CLR 1226–40*, pp. 14, 27, 39, 69, 79, 87, 115, 128, 139, 164, 177); in the Calendar of Liberate Rolls payments increase to seven or more crown-wearings after 1233.

richness of the fabrics and their opulent decoration.[56] These are paralleled by the orders for ritual objects in precious metals: for instance, in 1242 for gilded censers, tabernacle, ferrules for processional crosses, and morses for copes;[57] in 1244 for silver altar lecterns (for the missals), and in 1246 for gilded double candlesticks.[58] No less detailed are the instructions for carved and painted images and for other paintings to be provided not only at Westminster but in other royal houses and castles frequented by the king and queen. They point both to the visual dynamic of the chapels, and to iconographical (and therefore devotional) preferences, for in a number of instances the paintings are close to the royal seats. Frequent subjects are the Crucifixion (with the Virgin Mary and St John), in some cases on a painted rood beam, Christ in Majesty, the Virgin Mary and child Jesus, the Evangelists, and saints to whom the chapels or altars are dedicated. St Nicholas and St Katherine often occur, especially earlier in the reign, but St Edward the Confessor and the newly canonized St Edmund of Canterbury became increasingly favoured.

The chapels of Henry III, Eleanor of Provence, and their first son Prince Edward, served each of them directly (as places to pray and hear Mass) and indirectly (as places where prayer and especially Mass were offered in a constant round for their well-being). They also served their individual households, whose members would have expected to hear Mass at least on Sundays and major holy days (at least a hundred days in the year). In some royal residences one or two chapels had to serve; but in others there were at least three chapels (as at Clarendon, Windsor, and Winchester Castle) or even as many as six (as seems to have been the case at Woodstock by the end of the reign). There must have been considerable contrast between those times when the king and queen were in residence with a large retinue needing to be served by the chapels, and those times when a permanent skeleton staff maintained the palace, house, or castle. Such variously sized chapels must have demanded different solutions when numbers were high.

The evidence of the disposition, staffing, and equipping of the royal chapels may be far from comprehensive; but taken together it provides a basis for a better understanding of the likely nature and use of the two king's chapels transformed by Edward III into the liturgical and ritual spaces of the new colleges of St Stephen, Westminster, and St George, Windsor.

The New Chapel of St Edward the Confessor, Windsor Castle

Henry III's new chapel in the lower bailey at Windsor (fig. 1) was to be 70 ft (21.34 m) long and 28 ft (8.53 m) wide; that is to say, larger than the new chambers also built in the lower bailey for the king (60 ft by 28 ft or 18.29 × 8.53 m) and queen (40 ft or 12.12 m long),[59] but a little smaller in floor area and length than the king's great Painted Chamber at Westminster (80 ft 6 in or 24.45 m long and 26 ft or 7.92 m wide).[60] While the chapel was a single-cell rectangular building, with western entrance porch, it is apparent that it was divided into

---

[56] E.g. the order for vestments, 10 April 1238 (*CLR 1226–40*, p. 322).
[57] A portable censer (on chains) is used for incense; a tabernacle contains the consecrated bread and wine from the Mass in readiness for emergency use, and as a focus for devotion; a ferrule is the cap on the end of a staff (here the staff of a processional cross); and a morse is the decorated clasp for a cope.
[58] *CLR 1240–45*, p. 120: 24 April 1242; p. 228: 15 April 1244. *CLR 1245–51*, p. 77: 30 Aug. 1246.
[59] *CLR 1227–40*, p. 440: 4 Jan. 1240.
[60] *HKW*, vol. 1, p. 495; Brindle, 'The First St George's Chapel'.

St Stephen's Chapel, Westminster: From a King's to a Collegiate Chapel 63

chancel and nave; and the king's seat was to be placed at the western end of the chancel: 'in capella illa pulcherrima sedes regis fieri faciat inter cancellum et navem capelle'.[61] The requirements for wall paintings of the Old and New Testaments, four gilded figures, and a panelled and painted ceiling to give the impression of stone vaulting are set out in the Close Rolls;[62] a fragment of the marble font (in which Prince Edward was baptized) survives;[63] but little else is known of the furnishing or decoration.

A direction for the warden of the castle to find four chaplains was issued in November 1248.[64] Payments to four chaplains were certainly dated from Michaelmas 1249 (just before the last payments to William the painter for decoration of the chapel).[65] The dates of the initial acquisition of books and vestments corresponds with the recruitment of the four chaplains who formed the regular core staff of what was now referred to as the king's 'great chapel'. There are two orders for books (1249 and 1251), so close in content as perhaps to represent one duplicated list.[66] Just possibly, however, the first list represents existing, corrected books from Westminster transferred to Windsor ('De libris emendis et ponendis in capella de Windles'), and the second list represents newly made books which take their place.

May 1249
one missal
two graduals with troper
one breviary of the Use of Salisbury
two antiphonals,
    with collectar, capitulary, and hymnal
two psalters

May 1251
one missal[67]
two graduals with troper
one breviary,
    with collectar, capitulary, and hymnal
two antiphonals
two psalters

The usual number of chaplains in the new chapel was four; thus, this list of books would amply supply their needs to sing both Mass and Office.

The provision of just one missal and one chalice suggests that there was only one altar; though here, as elsewhere, what is listed in the records may not identify all that was found in

---

[61] *CCR 1237–42*, p. 4: 25 Sept. 1242.
[62] *CCR 1237–42*, p. 514: 25 Sept. 1242; *1242–47*, p. 20: 10 April 1243; p. 39, 20 Aug. 1243. The work was completed some years later, as payments in 1248–9 to William the painter, monk of Westminster, attest (*CLR 1245–51*, pp. 178, 187, 203, 255: 24 March, 11 June, 16 Oct. 1248; 14 Oct. 1249).
[63] Pamela Tudor-Craig, 'The Fonts of St George's Chapel'.
[64] *CLR 1245–51*, p. 208: 2 Nov. 1248.
[65] *CLR 1245–51*, p. 255: 14 Oct. 1249 (payments to William the painter); p. 278: 11 Feb. 1250 (chaplains' payment, backdated to Michaelmas 1249).
[66] *CCR 1247–51*, p. 162: 15 May 1249; p. 447: 21 May 1251.
[67] This may be the missal purchased from Laurence of Westminster, king's chaplain, for the king's chapel in Windsor. The record is dated 19 Oct. 1251, but may be retrospective (*CLR 1245–51*, p. 381).

the chapel. (The same order required four towels and four altar cloths, suitable for rotation at a single altar.)[68] The orders for vestments (1248–52) also provided for a group of four chaplains. The order made in 1248 may have been from existing stock:

> three sets of [mass] vestments 'sufficiently decent' (*satis decentia*),
>   with dalmatic and tunicle,
> four choir copes (possibly for festal rather than everyday use).[69]

Vestments in the two orders made in 1251 were probably specially made, and of richer quality:

> one silk chasuble with gold-apparelled alb and amice, and dalmatic and tunicle,
> one chasuble with orphreys, one dalmatic and one tunicle, also with orphreys,
>   all in Roman style (*modo Romano*), as personally prescribed by the king,
> two silk copes (one saffron in colour),
> one embroidered cope.[70]

There followed, in 1252, an order for a chasuble (with apparelled alb and other necessaries) for use on ferial days.[71]

Incomplete as these details may be, they are sufficient to indicate certain key features about the new chapel. It was a single space, divided (presumably by a screen) into chancel and nave. The king's seat (and perhaps a seat for the queen) was set at the western end of the chancel. There was one altar at the east end. The nature of the books confirms that the chaplains were expected to recite both Mass (missal and graduals) and Office (breviary, antiphonals, psalters) in the chapel; but the number of books (and vestments) suggests that there were not usually large numbers of clergy present. Given the provision of graduals and antiphonals it appears that the services were chanted. Moreover, the inclusion of tropers suggests that tropes were still sung at Mass (a practice less common by the mid thirteenth century, and largely absent from Salisbury books of the time). The full suits of vestments suggest the solemn celebration of Mass with priest, deacon, and subdeacon at least on Sundays and feast days; and though only a chasuble was ordered for ferial days, there may still have been deacon and subdeacon but vested only in albs. The copes may have been intended for the blessing of salt and water, and the sprinkling of altar and those present every Sunday before the principal Mass. They will also have been suitable for use at the Office on feast days when the officiant wore a cope. The absence of processionals (as at other chapels where books are listed) suggests that processions were not a regular feature of the liturgy: the chapel was small (by comparison with Salisbury Cathedral) and not configured for processions. However, the order for two red banners and a small banner for the processional cross may indicate occasional processions,[72] as perhaps at Rogationtide when the chaplains may have processed to another chapel within the castle for Mass. On a daily basis, there

---

[68] *CCR 1247–51*, p. 447: 21 May 1251.
[69] *CCR 1247–51*, p. 132: 9 Dec. 1248.
[70] *CCR 1247–51*, p. 445: 17 May 1251.
[71] *CCR 1251–53*, p. 268: 29 Oct. 1252.
[72] *CCR 1247–51*, p. 447: 24 May 1251.

St Stephen's Chapel, Westminster: From a King's to a Collegiate Chapel 65

will usually have been at least four Masses (one celebrated by each chaplain). Given the practice recorded at other chapels, these may perhaps have been Mass of St Edward (to whom the chapel was dedicated, and as at Dublin), of the Virgin Mary (as in other castles noted above), a Mass for the king and his family (perhaps *Salus populi*) or his ancestors (a Requiem), and Mass of the day.

When the king was in residence there were additional clergy available: the chaplains and clerks of the king's household who accompanied the king on his itineraries. The placing of the king's household chaplains and clerks in a building near the chapel, with a wicket gate leading to it, confirms that the chapel was used by the household, and not exclusively by the king's immediate entourage.[73] Ritually and musically the presence of the household chaplains and clerks must have transformed the resource of the chapel, especially when the king was resident at Windsor for any of the great liturgical feasts (e.g. Christmas or Easter). Furthermore, it was evidently in a busy part of the castle that needed to be sealed off: a ten-foot wall was built between the king's lodgings and the western galilee porch of the chapel; and a wooden barrier was created around the porch to prevent horses from gaining access.[74] What was a large space for a small group of chaplains when the king was not in residence must have been packed when the household arrived.

The Former Chapel of St Stephen, Westminster Palace

Notwithstanding the lack of physical evidence or written details of the chapel of St Stephen known to Henry III, tentative suggestions can be put forward, drawing on the pattern and provision at Windsor – always accepting that such evidence is far from complete. St Stephen's was a single-cell, rectangular building. The floor of the chapel may have been lower than that of the greater and lesser halls, and of the Painted Chamber, since one royal order refers to the descent from hall to chapel.[75] This order was for a painting of the Virgin Mary placed behind the king's seat, visible on entering the chapel from the direction of the hall; given the layout of Windsor, this suggests that there was some form of screen behind the king's seat (and implicitly that of the queen on the other side). Thus the chapel, as at Windsor, may have been divided at least nominally into chancel and nave. The king's seat will have been on the south side, the queen's on the north (as specified at Kenilworth Castle).[76] Both king and queen will have faced the altar. To the right of the king's seat was a picture of the Crucifixion, and this was matched by another picture of the Crucifixion (with the Virgin Mary and St John) to the left of the queen's seat.[77] At the west end, above the main doorway, was painted a doom (Last Judgement), one of a series of wall paintings ordered by the king.[78] At the eastern end, there was a painted image of St Stephen above

---

[73] *CLR 1251–60*, p. 505: 25 May 1260.
[74] *CLR 1245–51*, p. 296: 20 July 1250.
[75] *CCR 1242–47*, p. 287: 7 Feb. 1245, 'sicut intratur in capella decendendo de aula'. Tim Ayers has raised the possibility that, rather than a chapel at a lower level, such a descent may have been from the dais at the south end of the hall, where there was a later doorway (private communication, 30 Oct. 2017).
[76] *CLR 1240–45*, p. 31: [26 Feb.] 1241.
[77] *CCR 1234–37*, p. 484: 7 Feb. 1236.
[78] *CCR 1237–42*, p. 149: 29 Oct. 1239 (doorway); *CCR 1247–51*: 13 Aug. 1250 (doom, together with other wall paintings).

the altar.[79] The altar itself stood on at least one marble step.[80] As at Windsor there is no reference to further altars; but there was a marble font, which may well have been in the nave, as in other churches.[81] In addition to the principal door at the west end, there was a second door, most likely in the south wall of the chancel, leading to the garden between the chapel and Painted Chamber. Opposite it (on the north wall) was a painting of a king and queen – a royal presence even when they were not themselves in residence.[82]

This is the chapel that Edward I knew well from childhood, and which would inevitably have served as the spatial and ritual reference when he set out to rebuild it on a grander scale – the chapel which his grandson Edward III transformed into a collegiate chapel, along with Henry III's chapel at Windsor. Whatever its earlier form, St Stephen's was now planned as a double chapel. It is not certain whether the impressive double chapel of Sainte-Chapelle in Paris informed or influenced Edward I's new building.[83] He would in any case have been familiar with the provision and distinct uses of upper and lower chapels in a number of the royal houses in which he was brought up.

From a King's to a Collegiate Chapel

The Liturgical Space

The transition of both St Stephen's Westminster, and St Edward's Windsor Castle, from king's to collegiate chapel effected by Edward III in the mid fourteenth century had significant implications for both the disposition of the space and the liturgical pattern of the day. The statutes of 1352 and the inventory of 1384/5 surviving at Windsor offer substantial evidence of the new liturgical pattern;[84] and the disposition of the new, larger, later fifteenth-century chapel of St George points towards the likely reconfiguration of the smaller, earlier chapel. At Westminster Edward III inherited an incomplete chapel: the new building begun by Edward I was larger than that used by Henry III, but – as at Windsor – it was a chapel initially intended principally for the king and his chaplains, a chapel where Mass was the dominant liturgy. A new dimension at St Stephen's was the provision of both lower and upper chapels, an arrangement adopted in some of Henry III's chapels, as at Kempton and Winchester, where – in more modest buildings – the upper chapel was designated for the queen, and the lower chapel for the king's household. Such separation may perhaps have been part of the original plan at St Stephen's as conceived by Edward I – though not for king and queen. It may be (as at Sainte-Chapelle) that the upper chapel was for the king and those close to the king, with his personal chaplains; and the lower chapel for the larger household, including the household chaplains and clerks. This cannot be established.

---

[79] *CCR 1231–34*, pp. 9–10: 4 Dec. 1231; p. 207: 12 April 1232.
[80] *CCR 1237–42*, p. 26: 10 Feb. 1238.
[81] *CLR 1226–40*, p. 478: 5 July 1240.
[82] *CCR 1242–47*, p. 287: 7 Feb. 1245.
[83] On the building of the new chapel, see Tim Ayers' essay in this volume.
[84] Galley proofs of a transcription and translation of the statutes made by J. N. Dalton (1895) are kept in St George's Chapel Archives and Chapter Library, Windsor Castle. A transcription and translation of the inventory appear in Maurice F. Bond, *The Inventories of St George's Chapel, Windsor Castle, 1384–1667* (Windsor, 1947), pp. 31–83.

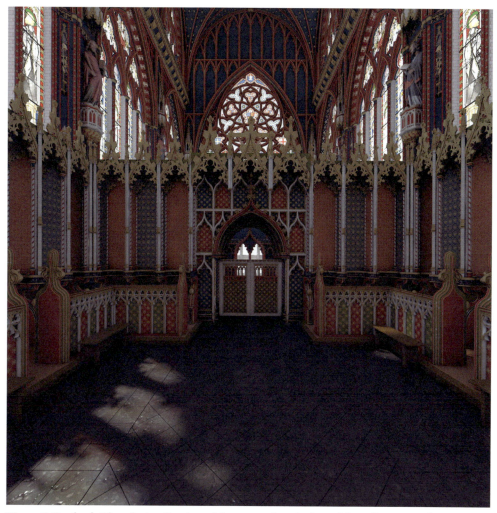

Fig. 2. St Stephen's Chapel, visualization of the upper chapel adapted for collegiate use by Edward III, showing the western stalls and pulpitum.

The adaptation of the chapels at Westminster and Windsor to accommodate a college of canons with their vicars and clerks demanded significant physical changes. Instead of what were probably relatively open spaces for Mass and occasional ritual and ceremonial events, these became spaces where a substantial body of clergy could gather in the choir to sing the eight services of the daily Office as well as three sung Masses (fig. 2). In addition to the royal seats, there was need for stalls for the clergy; a pulpitum with upper floor large enough to accommodate the Gospel ritual (replacing the screen dividing chancel and nave); and sufficient altars to enable each priest to celebrate Mass daily (probably five or more Masses at each subsidiary altar). St George's Chapel had additionally to accommodate both the knights of the Order of the Garter and the poor knights.

While there are rich and prolific accounts for the building, furnishing, and decoration of the upper chapel of St Stephen, they give few indications of the exact disposition of the space and furnishing.[85] Evidence for the upper chapel has to be tentatively pieced together from the remaining lower chapel, which defines the original floor area; the descriptions, drawings and plans published between 1795 and 1844 (before and after the fire of 1834), which provide a record of what survived after alterations and fire (including conjectural reconstructions of the original building);[86] and the inventory of chapel goods taken at the time of the dissolution of the college in 1548, which supplies a list and summary description of the movable objects remaining in the upper and lower chapels, the vestries, and the chapel of St Mary le Pew when the commissioners visited.[87] To this evidence can be added the surviving vocal polyphony found in the so-called Caius Choir Book, probably representing part of the chapel repertory in the 1530s;[88] at least some of the extant compositions of Nicholas Ludford (verger and organist from 1527 to 1548); and perhaps – from the mid fifteenth century – the mass settings of John Bedyngham (verger and organist c.1456–9).[89] These repertories are discussed in Magnus Williamson's chapter.[90]

The transformed chapel may have been lofty, but at floor level the three eastern bays formed an intimate space for so substantial a college community (fig. 2) – let alone the crowding that must have been inevitable on great feasts when the court was in residence. Of surviving late medieval collegiate chapels, that of Magdalen College, Oxford, offers a more appropriate comparison than the great chapel of King's College, Cambridge. There was no spacious presbytery (as at King's or next door in Westminster Abbey): at St Stephen's it can have occupied no more than the first eastern bay, leaving a further two bays to accommodate the collegiate stalls and royal seats.

The presbytery will have been much as in any king's chapel: a high altar most likely against the eastern wall,[91] with piscina and sedilia adjacent on the southern wall. There may also have been a movable lectern on the north side of the altar, from which to recite the Gospel at Mass on those days when the choir was not ruled. A door in the north wall opened onto the vestry, and another on the south to an oratory and then on to the passageway (*alura*) leading to the king's Painted Chamber in the privy palace. It could be expected that the presbytery was at least one step higher than the choir; and there may have been three further steps for priest, deacon, and subdeacon before the altar.[92]

---

[85] Ayers & Jurkowski, *passim*.
[86] For a review of these publications, see Rosemary Hill, '"Proceeding like Guy Faux": The Antiquarian Investigation of St Stephen's Chapel Westminster, 1790–1837', *Architectural History*, 59 (2016), 253–79.
[87] J. R. Daniel Tyssen and Mackenzie E. C. Walcott, 'The Inventory of St Stephen's Chapel, Westminster', *Transactions of the London and Middlesex Archaeological Society*, 4 (1871), 365–76 <http://www.lamas.org.uk/archives/transactions/transactions-volo4fs.html> [accessed 14 Nov. 2023].
[88] Cambridge, Caius College Library, MS 667/760. David Skinner, 'Discovering the Provenance and History of the Caius and Lambeth Choirbooks', *Early Music*, 25 (1997), 245–66.
[89] David Skinner, ed., *Nicholas Ludford I, II*, Early English Church Music, 44, 45 (London, 2003, 2005). *Nicholas Ludford, Collected Works, I: Seven Lady-Masses*, ed. John D. Bergsagel, Corpus mensurabilis musicae, 27 ([Rome], 1963). Gareth Curtis and David Fallows (eds), *Fifteenth-Century Liturgical Music IX: Mass Music by Bedyngham and his Contemporaries* (London, 2017). Biggs, 'College and Canons' has extracted details from the obit book (BL, Cotton MS Faustina B VIII), and wills of canons, mostly from the later fifteenth century; see especially chapter 8, pp. 157–81.
[90] See pp. 171–85.
[91] At Windsor there was evidently a small private altar behind the principal altar: Bond, *Inventories*, p. 45, item 82.
[92] The questions of the disposition of the reordered chapel were central to the virtual reconstruction of the interior undertaken as part of the research project: <https://www.virtualststephens.org.uk/explore> [accessed 14 Nov. 2023]. In this case, the project team placed the royal stalls at the eastern end of the chapel, nearest the *alura*.

St Stephen's Chapel, Westminster: From a King's to a Collegiate Chapel

The choir space needed to accommodate the king and queen, and at least thirty-six members of the college. The detailed accounts of the stalls give no indication of their design or layout, but there must have been at least two royal stalls and twenty-six stalls for the canons and vicars. There may have been a further four stalls for the clerks.[93] The six choristers (who rarely sat in the liturgy) are likely to have shared two benches placed in front of the stalls; and the verger and his assistant(s) may not have had seating in choir. Whether there was simply one row of stalls on either side, or additional under-stalls it is impossible to know; but, on the basis of earlier practice and of the arrangement at Windsor, the stalls for king and queen may have been at the western end on either side of the entrance to the choir, facing east.[94] The dean and canons will have sat on either side of the chapel in seniority order, with the dean and most senior canon closest to the royal stalls, and the vicars nearer to the altar.[95] The four clerks may have been accommodated at the eastern end of the stalls, or in under-stalls (as may, perhaps have been the most junior vicars). This was a relatively compact liturgical space to accommodate the enlarged clerical community – significantly smaller than the choir and presbytery of a cathedral, collegiate church, or monastery of comparable numbers. It is impossible to be sure of the relative proportions of the presbytery (which needed to allow space for the ritual actions and movements of three clergy and at least four servers at Mass), to the choir (which now needed to include seating for at least thirty-six persons).

There was little need for movement in choir during either Mass or Office: each person in the lateral stalls needed sufficient space to stand or sit facing across the chapel, and to stand or kneel facing the altar (required during most prayers and for much of the Mass). The stalls will have had misericord seats and book desks.[96] It is likely that there was at least one lectern in the middle of the chapel at the presbytery step (facing the altar), where readings, responsories, and prayers were recited at some services, and possibly another lectern – again in the middle of the chapel but towards the western end – to be used by the rulers of the choir on Sundays and a significant number of saints' days and other observances when the choir was ruled.[97]

The pulpitum stood across the chapel at the western end of the choir, between the third and fourth bays of the chapel. In giving directions for his new chapel to be built at Eton College, Henry VI referred to the pulpitum at St Stephen's, suggesting that the loft was twelve

---

[93] This would total thirty-two stalls, the number that Henry VI specified for the chapel of his new college at Eton in the 1440s, when he cited St Stephen's as his model: 'in the saide Quere oon either side xxxii stalles and the rode loft, I wol that they be made in like maner and fourme as be the stalls and rodeloft in the chappell of saint Stephen atte Westminster, and of the lengthe of .xxxii. fete and in brede clere .xii. fete of assise'. Robert Willis and John Willis Clark, *The Architectural History of the University of Cambridge and of the Colleges of Cambridge and Eton* (4 vols, Cambridge, 1886), vol. 1, p. 354.
[94] This was the case at Windsor, where there were stalls for the king and prince at the western end of the choir. An additional pew for the queen was required at the eastern end of the north stalls, since she could not take a place within the stalls of the Order of the Garter. Brindle, 'The First St George's Chapel', p. 39.
[95] In his will of 1381, Adam Chesterfield refers to the small chapel opposite the vicars' stalls (i.e. that on the south side of the presbytery, through which access was gained to the *alura* leading to the privy palace). Biggs, 'College and Canons', p. 167, note 56, citing BL, Cotton MS Faustina B III, fol. 10v.
[96] In 1421, Robert Foulmer bequeathed his missal for use of his successors, requiring it to be chained to his stall (BL, Cotton MS Faustina B III, fol. 21v). I am grateful to Elizabeth Biggs for this detail.
[97] The building accounts for 1351 refer to the making of capitals and bases for the ambos: 'Die lune xix die Decembris Thome Tournour pro iiij paribus de chapitrals et bassis emptis pro ambobus capelle xij d.' (Ayers & Jurkowski, vol. 2, no. 40).

feet deep, and that it was large enough not only for ritual use but also to accommodate an organ. The lower part of the pulpitum may have been less deep, but Henry VI's third set of directions for Eton implies that this was not less than six feet, in order to accommodate an internal stairway.[98] On days when the choir was ruled, the lessons at Matins were recited from the centre of the pulpitum (facing towards the altar), as were the Epistle, solo sections of Gradual and Alleluya, and Gospel at Mass. For the Gospel, deacon (as reader), subdeacon, two candle-bearers, thurifer, and (on certain days) cross-bearer needed to stand on the pulpitum. There was an eagle lectern which will have stood on the north side of the pulpitum facing north, for the deacon to recite the Gospel.[99]

Beyond the pulpitum was the nave, where there will have been fewer fixed furnishings. It is apparent from the 1548 inventory that there were two nave altars, one on each side of the pulpitum (see Introduction, fig. 2, p. 7). Their dedications are unknown; St George and St Barbara (who along with St Stephen and the Virgin Mary were represented by statues listed in 1548) are possible candidates. There may have been at least one step before the two side altars, possibly extending across the full width of the chapel; but there is no definitive evidence for this or the presbytery step in the chancel.

The lower chapel, dedicated to the Virgin Mary, occupied the same floor space as the upper chapel, and was unambiguously divided into chancel and nave by steps between the second and third bay from the east (see Ayers, fig. 4, p. 19; Hillson, fig. 1, p. 76).[100] This seems to have been the space for members of the household to attend Mass before work: in 1381 Adam Chesterfield, a canon, bequeathed a missal for Morrow Mass in this chapel (the earliest Mass said before work each day).[101] There was also a font.[102] The limited vestments and 'old' organ listed in the 1548 inventory suggest that the lower chapel was little used by that time except for burials; and this may be another pointer to its earlier use as a household chapel. At Windsor, after the founding of St George's College, the king's apartments were moved back to the upper bailey; and while the new college used the remodelled king's chapel, the royal household occupied the chapel adjacent to the great hall in the upper bailey. At Westminster no such arrangement could prevail. The lower chapel (as at Kempton and Winchester in the thirteenth century) may therefore have served as the royal household chapel until 1512, when the fire in the royal apartments forced the king to use other royal houses in or near London – Blackfriars, Richmond and, after the fall of Wolsey, Whitehall. There were occasions when both the college clergy and the royal household chapel gathered together in the upper chapel for special occasions in the presence of the king;[103] but in the main their nature and regular functions were separate and distinct. The lower chapel was

---

[98] In the third version of Henry VI's 'will' (for an enlarged foundation), he defined the purpose of the rood loft: 'for redyng and syngyng and for the Organs and other manere observance there to be had after the Rewles of the Churche of Salesbury', also stating that the base of the rood loft was to be six feet deep (to allow for the internal staircase to the loft). Willis and Clark, *Architectural History*, vol. 1, p. 366. At Windsor there was also an altar on the pulpitum: Bond, *Inventories*, p. 45, item 81.
[99] In 1359 the building accounts record 'unius aquile pro lectrino' (Ayers & Jurkowski, vol. 2, no. 53).
[100] As shown in the drawings undertaken by Carter in the 1790s.
[101] Biggs, 'College and Canons', p. 139, note 87, citing BL, Cotton MS Faustina B III, fol. 10r.
[102] Biggs, 'College and Canons', p. 249. In 1484 William Chauntre was buried between the font and the west door of the lower chapel. TNA, PROB 11/7/276.
[103] These include the crown-wearing of Richard II, Henry V at Candlemas in 1415, and Mass on the morning after the wedding of Henry VII and Elizabeth of York in January 1486, for example.

less than a third of the height of the exceptionally lofty upper chapel; its floor space was ample for a household chapel, and larger than some of the other spaces where it officiated. If so, the Chapel Royal would have brought their own vestments, books, and ritual objects, thus accounting for their absence in the inventory.[104] Practice may have changed across the two centuries, not least as the personnel of the Chapel Royal expanded in numbers.[105] There is no clear-cut answer regarding either shared usage or the combination of college and chapel forces when the king was in residence. The upper chapel offered ready access to both the great hall and the royal apartments, and was thus a natural religious hub for the Palace. The building of cloisters on two levels, interconnected by a stairway, may suggest some integration in the use of the two chapels.[106]

Ritual and Music

The clerical body of St Stephen's College was divided into two parts with distinct working emphases. The dean and canons were often king's clerks, occupied in government administration and the law, much like the earlier royal chaplains. The vicars were specialists in the liturgy, were required to be competent singers and musicians,[107] and were assisted by the four clerks and the six choristers. If the pattern at Windsor was duplicated at St Stephen's then two of the clerks will have been deacon and subdeacon (Gospeller and Epistoler), and two will have been in minor clerical orders. The duties of the choristers will have been predominantly ritual rather than musical. In the second half of the fifteenth century, the musical standing and expectations of both clerks (now generally lay singers) and choristers increased significantly, and the verger who served effectively as chapel administrator in the fourteenth century then took on a new identity as organist.

In the absence of surviving evidence for St Stephen's, the statutes and earliest inventory of the sister college of St George provide an indication of the pattern of services and ritual in the decades after foundation. The extent and opulence of the books, vestments, vessels, relics, hangings, linen, and other ritual objects listed in the inventory of 1384/5 are witness to the richness of these chapels. The books in choir at St George's make full provision for

---

[104] Alternatively, they may have been removed at the dissolution of the college, since they were not college property.
[105] In the second half of the fourteenth century the royal household chapel numbered fifteen or sixteen: most often a dean, thirteen chaplains, and two clerks are listed, but from 1376/7 the lists do not separate chaplains and clerks. Roger Bowers, 'Choral Institutions within the English Church: Their Constitution and Development 1340–1500' (Ph.D. dissertation, University of East Anglia, 1975), p. 3027. The Chapel Royal is not the principal focus of this essay, but has some bearing here. In addition to the work of Roger Bowers, see Ian Bent, 'The English Chapel Royal before 1300', *Proceedings of the Royal Musical Association*, 90 (1963–4), 77–95; Fiona Kisby, 'The Royal Household Chapel in Early Tudor London, 1485–1547' (Ph.D. dissertation, Royal Holloway, University of London, 1996); Andrew Wathey, 'The English Chapel Royal: Models and Perspectives', in Tess Knighton, Juan José Carreras, and Bernardo García García (eds), *The Royal Chapel in the Time of the Habsburgs: Music and Ceremonial in the Early Modern European Court* (Woodbridge, 2005), pp. 23–8. On the ritual practice of the Chapel Royal in the mid fifteenth century, see Walter Ullmann (ed.), *Liber Regie Capelle*, Henry Bradshaw Society, 92 (1961, repr. Woodbridge, 2010).
[106] Biggs, 'College and Canons', pp. 157–81.
[107] At Windsor, statute 13 demands that no vicar should be admitted unless he is vocally able and musically competent – regardless of other learned or other qualities he may offer: 'nisi modulandi competens habeat instrumentum et cantus scienciam competentem, eciam si sciencia seu quavis virtutum prerogativa ditetur'. The phrase 'cantus scienciam' may indicate knowledge of techniques of improvised polyphony. And statute 33 establishes that one vicar was both master (*magister*) and instructor (*informator*) of the choristers.

Mass and Office, as well as for pastoral services (a manual) and processions.[108] Some canons may additionally have owned their own books; otherwise it would appear that two clerics shared each book in the stalls. The daily liturgical pattern set out in the early Windsor statutes derived from the Use of Salisbury, to be followed as far as the place and the people available allowed.[109] Matins (with Lauds and the first part of Prime) was sung in the early morning (to finish before dawn in winter,[110] and begin at dawn in summer). A meeting of chapter followed (beginning with the conclusion of Prime). There were three Masses sung in choir: of the Virgin Mary and of the Dead,[111] undertaken by the vicars on a rota basis, and of the day (with all available present). There is no mention of the lesser Hours of Terce, Sext, and None: these may have been sung before or after the Masses, or recited privately. The liturgical day will have concluded in the later afternoon with Vespers and Compline. The warden and canons were expected to celebrate at the principal Mass on double feasts (probably including Sundays as well as holy days, but not on work days).[112] All these services took place in the choir and presbytery, and all the sung Masses were celebrated with priest, deacon, and subdeacon, assisted by four servers.[113]

On this basis, at St Stephen's on Sundays and holy days (about a hundred days in the year), the dean, those canons in residence, vicars, clerks, and choristers will have been in chapel for both Office and the principal Mass. On work days (about 250 days), the canons may only have been at Matins, Lauds, Vespers, and Compline at most, and said their own Mass privately:[114] the remaining collegiate Masses will have been undertaken by the vicars and clerks, with the choristers attending at least the principal Mass in addition to Lauds and Vespers. Such a constant round of sung prayer must have been in marked contrast to the liturgy of the pre-collegiate chapel (focused principally on the Mass), both in the numbers of clergy and in the extent of services.

In the Windsor inventory of 1384/5 there is only one likely indication of polyphonic music – a roll given by John Aleyn (d.1373), canon of Windsor, former member of Edward III's

---

[108] Bond, *Inventories*, pp. 32–5. For the Office: ten noted breviaries (another of little worth), four antiphonals, lectionary (in two volumes), two collectars (one in two volumes). For the Mass: eight missals, six graduals (as a set 'de una simil nota', and two more old), two books of solo verses for Gradual and Alleluya (one in the pulpitum), an Epistle book, a Gospel book (and one old). For processions: six processionals (noted as being 'defectiva in littera'). Other liturgical books: ordinal, manual, book of Lenten collation readings. One roll of [polyphonic] music, presented by the canon (and composer) John Aleyn (d.1373). Later additions and deletions in the inventory are excluded here.

[109] Statute 21: 'Item statuimus et ordinamus quod usus et consuetudo psallendi et dicendi seu celebrandi divinum officium ministrandique in choro et altari seu circa illud celebrandique seu dicendi missas de die ac de beata Maria virgine necnon defunctis, tam celebrando et legendo quam cantando stando et sedendo in choro et extra ipsum, qui in ecclesia Sarum serventur in capella observentur antedicta, secundum loci congruenciam et exigenciam personarum.'

[110] i.e. from Michaelmas to the beginning of March.

[111] On days when the principal Mass of the day was of the Virgin Mary or of the Dead, then the Mass *Salus populi* (for the king and his family) was sung instead.

[112] Windsor statutes 25 and 27.

[113] Windsor statute 28. The servers may have been four of the choristers, or perhaps the two junior clerks in minor orders and two choristers. In the Use of Salisbury, one or two choristers were additionally required to sing the verse of the Gradual (either at the choir step or from the pulpitum).

[114] Each priest needed to celebrate Mass daily. Three will have been able to do this at the three collegiate Masses at the principal altar – Mass of the Virgin Mary, Requiem Mass, Mass of the day – but up to twenty-three will have needed to say Mass each morning using the two lesser altars in the nave, and at altars in the oratory, chapel of St Mary le Pew, and even perhaps in the vestry or on the pulpitum, as well as at altars in the lower chapel when it was available.

household chapel, and composer.[115] The text of Aleyn's ceremonial motet *Sub Arturo* names a series of composers and singers, some of whom served as canons of Windsor or St Stephen's or members of the royal household chapel (or a combination of two or three of these). Among them are John de Corby (d. ?c.1381) and William Tiddeswell (d.1363/4), both canons of St Stephen's.[116] All this confirms the presence of some of the best musicians of their time from the early years of St Stephen's, men well able to compose and perform polyphony (improvised as well as written-down).[117] Nevertheless, the chant will have represented the greater majority (and often all) of the music for Mass, Office, and processions at both St George's and St Stephen's from the decades following the foundation of the two colleges up to 1548. Polyphonic elaboration here, as in many other collegiate foundations and in monastic Lady Chapels, proliferated from the second half of the fifteenth century onwards; at St Stephen's, this is confirmed in the 1548 inventory by the listing of three organs and three great choirbooks containing pricksong (choral polyphony).[118]

In so small a chancel and nave, the full ritual of the late medieval Use of Salisbury could not be undertaken on the same scale as in Salisbury Cathedral itself; as, for instance, the procession on the patronal feast of St Stephen (26 December). At Salisbury all the deacons left the choir towards the end of Vespers on Christmas Day, put on silk copes, and then processed through the choir leaving through the north choir door to go to the altar of St Stephen at the eastern end of the south choir aisle. There they sang an abbreviated form of first Vespers of St Stephen before processing back into the choir. At St Stephen's Westminster, there were probably few deacons (since canons and vicars were intended to be priests) and the processional route would have been very short – a few feet from choir to high altar. Therefore, it may well have been in the sonic ceremonial of elaborate polyphony that such an observance was expressed. In the final decades of the college's life, the polyphonic compositions of Nicholas Ludford and other works found in the Caius Choirbook are indicative of this choral prowess.[119] The Caius Choirbook includes four of Ludford's large-scale works; among them is the Mass *Lapidaverunt Stephanum* (based on a plainsong psalm antiphon sung at Lauds on St Stephen's day) which must surely have been intended for the chapel's patronal feast day (see Williamson, fig. 3, p. 179).[120]

While the style, scale, and elaboration of the extant polyphonic music used especially on feast days in the last decades of the college of St Stephen's may have been significantly different from any polyphony sung in the fourteenth century, the books, vestments, vessels, hangings, and ritual objects in St Stephen's Chapel listed in the 1548 inventory confirm a pattern of work day, holy day, and seasonal ritual observance according to the Use of

---

[115] Bond, *Inventories*, p. 25, item 26.
[116] Brian Trowell, 'A Fourteenth-Century Ceremonial Motet and Its Composer', *Acta Musicologica*, 29 (1957), 65–75. Andrew Wathey, 'The Peace of 1360–1369 and Anglo-French Musical Relations', *Early Music History*, 9 (1990), 129–74; especially 170, 173–4.
[117] Additionally, the vicars were musically competent, and there was an organ stored in the upper vestry of St Stephen's throughout the building works (and evidently gradually deteriorating): it is listed in the building accounts for St Stephen's between 1326/7 and 1356/7 (Ayers & Jurkowski, nos 21, 23, 37, 46, 50, 52).
[118] See Magnus Williamson's contribution in this volume; Roger Bowers, 'Choral Institutions', especially parts 5 and 6.
[119] Cambridge, Caius College Library, MS 667/760. Skinner, 'Discovering the Provenance and History of the Caius and Lambeth Choirbooks'.
[120] David Skinner (ed.), *Nicholas Ludford II: Five and Six-Part Masses and Magnificat*, Early English Church Music, 45 (London, 2005), pp. 1–47.

Salisbury comparable with that represented by the contents of the 1384/5 inventory at St George's Windsor, over 150 years earlier.[121] Furthermore, the chantry certificate of 1548 establishes that the 'late college of St Stephen' was almost fully staffed, and apparently flourishing at its dissolution.[122] There may have been a change of emphasis in the musical life of the chapel, from the later fifteenth century drawing on the expertise of lay singers as clerks and on the newly identified musical potential of boy choristers; but the underlying liturgical pattern seems to have been much as it was first envisaged in the mid fourteenth century. It was at that time, in the transition from a king's to a collegiate chapel, that the radical changes to the space, furnishings, and liturgy took place, recorded or at least implicit in the extensive records of the programme of building and decoration undertaken by Edward III.

---

[121] Tyssen and Walcott, 'Inventory', *passim*. Unsurprisingly by this date, no relics are listed. There are books for the Office: seventeen antiphonals, three psalters, one responsorial, two lectionaries; and for the Mass: four missals, ten graduals, three books of Epistles and Gospels. No breviaries or processionals are listed, but these may have been owned individually. Among the vestments are twenty-one sets of Mass vestments (chasuble, dalmatic, and tunicle), 113 copes, eleven pairs of altar hangings for the main altar, and three double pairs for the two altars in the nave. One set of vestments includes a cope for a child, no doubt for the feast of Holy Innocents (28 Dec.), when the boy bishop (one of the choristers) presided at the liturgy (though not at Mass). The twenty-five chasubles listed in the chapel of St Mary le Pew were probably primarily intended for a single priest to say Mass.

[122] There was almost a full statutory complement, with dean, eleven canons (not twelve, since John Crayford or Crawford had died in August 1547), eleven vicars (not thirteen), four clerks, seven choristers (not six), and three officers. In addition, there were four chantry chaplains. C. J. Kitching (ed.), *London and Middlesex Chantry Certificate 1548*, London Record Society, 16 (Woodbridge, 1980), no. 190.

War, Politics, and Architecture: Iterative Design at St Stephen's Chapel, 1292–1348

James Hillson

On Monday 28 April 1292, the first roll of expenses was recorded for the new works at St Stephen's Chapel in Westminster.[1] Over the next five decades, the preceding chapel was replaced by an entirely new two-storey structure on an impressive scale, remarkable for its variety of ornament and diversity in style (fig. 1). The broad, heavy motifs and stocky piers of the lower chapel contrasted sharply with the slender shafts, intricate details, and intense decoration of its upper chapel counterpart. Ogee (or double curved) arches bent and flexed, emerging from an articulating framework of responds (the engaged columns that support an arch) and crenellated cornices that compartmentalized the building's forms within a cage of vertical and horizontal lines.[2] Though many aspects of the chapel's appearance remain lost, the surviving details suggest a careful balancing act on the part of the designers, the stylistic coherence of its disparate elements being conveyed by the playful interaction of layers, levels, divisions, and planes. Yet how accurate is this impression of stylistic conformity at St Stephen's? Does the apparent coherence of the chapel's forms indicate a focused and singular design, or does the diversity of its decoration suggest a more iterative process of conception was at work?

The task of interpreting the design of St Stephen's is complicated by its prolonged and frequently disrupted building history.[3] Begun during the reign of Edward I (under way 1292–7) under the direction of Master Michael of Canterbury (1292–1322), St Stephen's saw two changes of patron (Edward II (1320–6) and Edward III (1331–66)), as well as the input of at least four additional master masons (Thomas of Canterbury (1323–35), William Ramsey

---

[1] TNA, E 101/468/6, rot. 2 (Ayers & Jurkowski, vol. 1, pp. 96–101).
[2] For the role of linearity in architectural design, see James Hillson, 'Linearity and the Gothic Style: Architectural Conception in England and France, 1200–1400', in Julian Luxford (ed.), *Tributes to Paul Binski: Medieval Gothic: Art, Architecture and Ideas* (Turnhout, 2021), pp. 62–75.
[3] For a more detailed version of the arguments and chronology presented in this article, see James Hillson, *St Stephen's Chapel, Westminster: Architecture and Politics under the Plantagenets (1227–1363)* (Turnhout, forthcoming). An earlier iteration of these arguments can be found in the author's doctoral thesis, 'St Stephen's Chapel, Westminster: Architecture, Decoration and Politics in the Reigns of Henry III and the Three Edwards (1227–1363)' (Ph.D. dissertation, University of York, 2015).

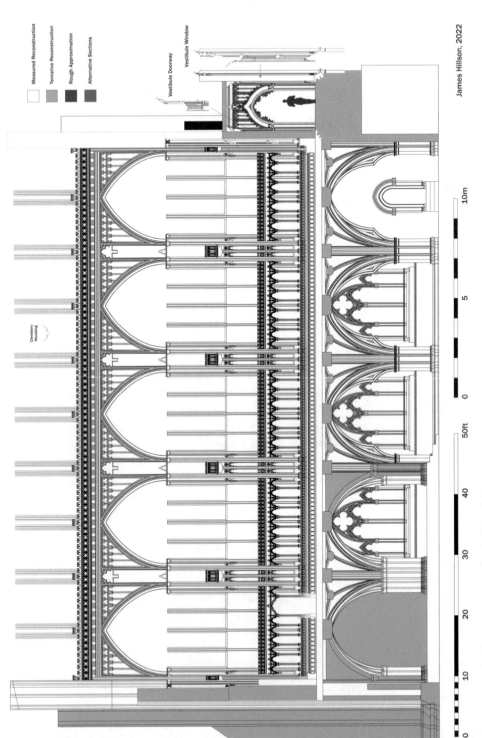

Fig. 1. Longitudinal section, St Stephen's Chapel, Westminster, 2022.

(1337–48), Philip de Cherde (1340s), and John Box (c.1350–3)) and three master carpenters (William Hurley, William Herland, and Edmund of St Andrew), not to mention dozens of other master craftsmen, subordinates, and specialists.[4] With so many agents involved in the chapel's construction, any attempt to attribute its design to specific individuals is necessarily tentative. Over a period of more than fifty years, the creators of St Stephen's would have been presented with many opportunities to change the direction of their design, whether it be minor decorative details or major structural elements.

The problem of design attribution is further exacerbated by the near-total loss of the chapel's material fabric. Following its destruction by fire in 1834 and subsequent demolition, the St Stephen's of the thirteenth and fourteenth centuries is accessible only through the few antiquarian texts and images that survive from the late sixteenth to early nineteenth centuries.[5] The appearance of the building which they record had already departed considerably from its medieval origins, after over three centuries of increasingly intrusive interventions into its extant fabric. Consequently, the image of St Stephen's which comes down to us is not the coherent vision of a lost original, but a palimpsest of multiple, limited viewpoints, each showcasing the effects of numerous medieval and post-medieval renovations, differing degrees of access, varying accuracy in recording methods and the occasional touch of outlandish invention.

Given the inherent difficulties presented by the visual and documentary evidence, it is unsurprising that disagreement has long been the leitmotif of interpretation for the chapel's design and construction history. The building's remarkable diversity in form has led many previous scholars to attribute its appearance to the influence of multiple designers, each operating in a distinctive stylistic mode. Relying extensively on the arguments advanced by the antiquarian Frederick Mackenzie in 1844, in 1906 the architect William Richard Lethaby suggested that the lower chapel was started under Edward I (1292–7), but that its completion was delayed into the 1320s.[6] The upper chapel, by contrast, was placed within the reigns of Edward II and Edward III, its divergent form being attributed to a change in designer as well as a corresponding shift from English Decorated towards the nascent Perpendicular style.[7] This set the tone of scholarship over the subsequent fifty years, which tended to identify the upper and lower chapels as discrete stylistic units, each conceived under different patrons and master masons. John H. Harvey self-consciously adopted Lethaby's chronology in a series of books and articles published from 1944 to 1946, elaborating his stylistic arguments in response to the provocative challenges presented by J. Maurice Hastings.[8] Though Hastings accepted the formal disparities between the upper

---

[4] John H. Harvey, *English Mediaeval Architects: A Biographical Dictionary down to 1550*, rev. edn (Gloucester, 1987), pp. 31, 45–6, 46–7, 137–41, 142–3, 154–5, 242–5, 265; Christopher Wilson, 'The Origins of the Perpendicular Style and its Development to circa 1360' (Ph.D. dissertation, University of London, 1980), pp. 27–258; Ayers & Jurkowski, vol. 1, pp. 32–44.
[5] For the chapel's destruction by fire, see Caroline Shenton, *The Day Parliament Burned Down* (Oxford, 2012). For the antiquarian sources relating to the chapel, see Topham; Smith, *Antiquities*; Brayley & Britton; Mackenzie; Rosemary Hill, '"Proceeding like Guy Faux": The Antiquarian Investigation of St Stephen's Chapel Westminster, 1790–1837', *Architectural History*, 59 (2016), 253–79.
[6] William Richard Lethaby, *Westminster Abbey and the Kings' Craftsmen: A Study of Mediæval Building* (London, 1906), pp. 180–2, 188–96.
[7] Lethaby erroneously introduced an additional phantom master mason, Walter of Canterbury, between Michael and Thomas, further complicating the chapel's attribution.
[8] Harvey first put forward his arguments in John H. Harvey, *Henry Yevele c.1320 to 1400: The Life of an English Architect* (London, 1944), pp. 6–7. This was challenged by Hastings in his review of the book (J. Maurice Hastings,

and lower chapels which Harvey and Lethaby identified, he questioned their chronology, proposing that the lower chapel was entirely completed c.1292–7, with the upper chapel being identified as the proto-Perpendicular product of a developing 'Court style of London'.[9]

By contrast, more recent scholars have tended to emphasize unity of conception in the chapel's design. The first movement towards this new consensus was made by the architectural historian Howard Colvin in his exhaustive and monolithic *The History of the King's Works* (1963–82).[10] Colvin presented a revised building chronology in which the upper chapel was begun during the reign of Edward I, overturning the traditional assumption that stylistic distinction was necessarily linked to a change in designer. This new theory was expanded by Christopher Wilson in his doctoral thesis of 1980.[11] Whereas previous scholars had argued that the upper and lower chapels were the result of several design phases, Wilson proposed that they were primarily the product of a single designer operating in multiple, simultaneous stylistic modes. Attributing the majority of the chapel's motifs to the hand of its first master mason, Michael of Canterbury, Wilson argued that an authoritative initial design was produced during the 1290s, its forms being transmitted to future generations through the media of lost drawings and a large number of prefabricated components placed in storage before the hiatus of 1297–1320. Over the course of his academic career, Wilson has continued to build on this hypothesis, proposing that the status of St Stephen's as an 'architectural one-off' firmly establishes the position of Master Michael as one of the most innovative and influential designers in the history of European architecture.[12]

While the impact of St Stephen's Chapel on the architecture of fourteenth-century England is difficult to deny, the question of its design attribution remains open-ended. Though many aspects of the revised chronology presented by Wilson are strongly supported by the available visual and documentary evidence, the concept that an initial design by a single master could possess sufficient inertia to carry it unchanged through several generations of patrons and designers is more problematic. Throughout the history of building in Europe during the thirteenth and fourteenth centuries, the consistent pattern identified by the majority of architectural historians is not one of design persistence, but rather of continuous and iterative design change.[13] Surviving architectural drawings seldom relate

---

'Perpendicular Fantasies: Henry Yevele, the Life of an English Architect', *The Architectural Review*, 98 (March 1945), 92), which occasioned an exchange of letters published in the *Architectural Review* (John H. Harvey, 'Letter: Perpendicular Fantasies', *Architectural Review*, 98 (May 1945), liv; J. Maurice Hastings, 'Letter: Perpendicular Fantasies', *Architectural Review*, 98 (May 1945), liv–vi), and Harvey's 1946 article (Harvey, 'St Stephen's Chapel and the Origin of the Perpendicular Style', *The Burlington Magazine*, 88 (1946), 192–9). For Hastings' response, see J. Maurice Hastings, *St Stephen's Chapel and its Place in the Development of Perpendicular Style in England* (Cambridge, 1955).
[9] Hastings, *St Stephen's*, pp. 1–4, 176–90.
[10] *HKW*, vol. 1, pp. 510–33.
[11] Wilson, 'Origins', pp. 27–258.
[12] Christopher Wilson, *The Gothic Cathedral: The Architecture of the Great Church, 1130–1530* (London, 1990), pp. 191–223; Wilson, 'Gothic Metamorphosed: The Choir of St Augustine's Abbey in Bristol and the Renewal of European Architecture around 1300', in Jon Cannon and Beth Williamson (eds), *The Medieval Art, Architecture and History of Bristol Cathedral: An Enigma Explored* (Woodbridge, 2011), pp. 69–147.
[13] For selected examples, see John James, *The Template-Makers of the Paris Basin: Toichological Technique for Identifying the Pioneers of the Gothic Movement* (Leura, 1989); Richard K. Morris, 'European Prodigy or Regional Eccentric? The Rebuilding of St Augustine's Abbey Church, Bristol', in Laurence Keen (ed.), 'Almost the Richest City': Bristol in the Middle Ages (London, 1997), pp. 41–56; Stephen Murray, *Building Troyes Cathedral: The Late Gothic Campaigns* (Bloomington, 1987); Murray, *Notre-Dame, Cathedral of Amiens: The Power of Change in Gothic* (Cambridge, 1996); Dany Sandon, *La Cathédrale de Soissons: Une architecture en mutation* (Paris, 2000); Alain

directly to the finished forms of extant buildings, and may well have served more as starting points for further discussion than binding intentions for future works.[14] Furthermore, the identification of an early date for the more innovative features at St Stephen's elides deeper uncertainties regarding the wider narrative of architectural style during the decades on either side of 1300. There are few buildings with clear dates of conception or construction during this period, and the relative sequence of the motifs they incorporate cannot therefore be established with any degree of certainty. Though it has often been used as a stationary point within this stylistic narrative, St Stephen's Chapel is no exception, as despite the survival of copious building accounts and extensive visual records there remain serious gaps in our knowledge regarding its form, construction sequence, and conception process. Style alone is no certain guide to the relative chronology of a building, and it only takes the slightest shift of emphasis for a pioneering innovation to be recast as a subtle deviation from an established theme.

With such obstacles in mind, it is clear that any attempt to reconstruct the chapel's design and construction process relies more on the underlying principles of the scholars themselves than the internal evidence provided by the building. In identifying St Stephen's largely as the product of a singular and coherent design conceived during the 1290s, Wilson reveals a set of fundamental assumptions regarding the functionality of drawings within medieval architectural practice, as well as the prominence of royal workshops as driving centres for revolutionary artistic change. A pattern of stylistic development is established wherein the 'rapid emergence of influential exemplars' alternates with 'intervening periods in which the innovations of those models were assimilated',[15] a principle which was equally applied whether that model was disseminated in stone or on parchment. The impact of contemporary events on the chapel's progress are framed as interruptions to the realization of Michael of Canterbury's initial scheme, with the few subsequent changes being presented as disruptive to the integrity of the original design.

Villes, *La Cathédrale Notre-Dame de Reims: chronologie et campagnes de travaux* (Joué-lès-Tours, 2009); Marvin Trachtenberg, *Building-in-Time: From Giotto to Alberti and Modern Oblivion* (New Haven/London, 2010); Villes, 'La construction d'un chef-d'oeuvre gothique', in Thierry Jordan (ed.), *Reims: la grâce d'une cathédrale* (Strasbourg, 2010), pp. 51–72; Alexandrina Buchanan, James Hillson, and Nicholas Webb, *Digital Analysis of Vaults in Medieval English Architecture* (London/New York, 2022), pp. 83–246.

[14] James Hillson, 'Villard de Honnecourt and Bar Tracery: Reims Cathedral and Processes of Stylistic Transmission, ca. 1210–40', *Gesta*, 59 (2020), 169–202; Hillson, 'Linearity', pp. 62–75; Buchanan, Hillson, and Webb, *Digital Analysis*, pp. 84–113. For alternative views on the role of drawing in communicating architectural designs, see Franklin Toker, 'Gothic Architecture by Remote Control: An Illustrated Building Contract of 1340', *The Art Bulletin*, 67:1 (1985), 67–95; Wolfgang Schöller, 'Le Dessin d'Architecture a l'Époque gothique', in Roland Recht (ed.), *Les Bâtisseurs des Cathédrales gothiques* (Strasbourg, 1989), pp. 227–36; Werner Müller, 'Le Dessin Technique a l'Époque gothique', in Recht, *Bâtisseurs*, pp. 237–54; James, *Template-Makers*, pp. 190–204; Roland Bechmann, *Villard de Honnecourt: La pensée technique au XIIIe siècle et sa communication* (Paris, 1993), pp. 52–7; Michael T. Davis, 'On the Drawing Board: Plans of the Clermont Ferrand Terrace', in Nancy Y. Wu (ed.), *Ad Quadratum: The Practical Application of Geometry in Medieval Architecture* (Aldershot, 2002), pp. 183–204; Arnold Pacey, *Medieval Architectural Drawing: English Craftsmen's Methods and their Later Persistence (c.1200–1700)* (Stroud, 2007), pp. 33–58; Johann Josef Böker et al., *Architektur der Gotik: Bestandskatalog der weltgrößten Sammlung an gotischen Baurissen (Legat Franz Jäger) im Kupferstichkabinett der Akademie der bildenden Künste Wien mit einem Anhang über die mittelalterlichen Bauzeichnungen im Wien Museum Karlsplatz* (Salzburg, 2005); Michael T. Davis, '"Ci poes vos veir": Technologies of Representation from Drawing to Digital', in Robert Bork (ed.), *New Approaches to Medieval Architecture* (Farnham, 2011), pp. 219–34; Robert Bork, *The Geometry of Creation: Architectural Drawing and the Dynamics of Gothic Design* (Aldershot, 2011).

[15] Wilson, 'Gothic Metamorphosed', p. 80.

An alternative approach is to consider the design of St Stephen's not as a singular historical moment, but rather as a continuous historical process corresponding to a wide range of contemporary events. This chapter explores such a possibility by establishing two principles of its own. First, that political events and their consequences had direct, tangible effects on the chapel's construction progress. Secondly, that such effects enabled an iterative approach to architectural design distributed across fifty years of frequently interrupted works, with the final building reflecting the input of multiple discrete agents. Focusing on the impact of royal finances, civil unrest, and continental warfare on the English monarchy between the 1290s and 1340s, this chapter considers the potential consequences of these political events for the chapel's form and structure. In the process, it suggests that breaks in construction enabled significant, lasting changes to architectural designs, even in situations where they were not necessitated by historical circumstances. The design of St Stephen's was not isolated from contemporary events, but rather was continuously reimagined in response to political change, reflecting over half a century of influences from a diversity of sources.

Edward I (1292–7)

While the 1292–7 building campaign at St Stephen's is well represented by the extant documentary records, the nature, extent, and rate of progress of the works are difficult to quantify. Unlike the particulars of account recorded in subsequent reigns, the accounts from this period are relatively sparse on details.[16] Stone and other building materials tend to be recorded in general terms, with few indicators of their intended location, purpose, or form. Starting in the week of 28 April and continuing up to July 1292, foundations consisting of trenches partially filled with chalk and gravel were dug with wooden piles driven in deep to stabilize the marshy ground.[17] Masons were employed to cut stones from the second week onwards and from June 1292 stone-layers joined the workforce, perhaps indicating that they began to raise the walls as soon as the foundations were completed.[18] Works continued up to the week of 4 July 1297 when they were curtailed abruptly, with the remaining materials being stored in wooden houses built specifically for the purpose.[19]

The limitations of the documentary records make it difficult to assess how much of the chapel was completed during this time. From the end of October 1292, Spanish iron was being imported in large quantities, presumably for the tie bars of the lower chapel windows, and in March 1293 six marble columns of five feet were purchased, a length which corresponded to those adorning the flanking piers (fig. 2).[20] From this it can be inferred that the walls of the lower chapel were in an advanced state of completion. This supposition is further reinforced by the regular purchase of stone in feet, which could imply the presence of the

---

[16] The documents relating to St Stephen's are largely held in TNA, consisting of dedicated particulars of account (E 101), pipe rolls (E 372), issue rolls (E 403) and jornalia rolls (E 405/1). See Ayers & Jurkowski, vol. 1, pp. 15–27.
[17] TNA, E 101/468/6, rot. 2, 4, 4d, 8b, 9a, 80, 81, 81d (Ayers & Jurkowski, vol. 1, pp. 96–121). An archaeological investigation was conducted in 1992–4 beneath the present nineteenth-century iteration of the lower chapel which revealed the holes left by decayed wooden piles. Chris Thomas, 'St Stephen's Chapel, Palace of Westminster SW1: City of Westminster: An Archaeological Watching Brief' (unpublished report, Museum of London Archaeology Service, 1994).
[18] TNA, E 101/468/6, rot. 9a (Ayers & Jurkowski, vol. 1, pp. 132–5).
[19] TNA, E 405/1/11, m. 5, 11 (Ayers & Jurkowski, vol. 1, pp. 460–1).
[20] TNA, E 101/468/6, rot. 16, 29 (Ayers & Jurkowski, vol. 1, pp. 164–5, 208–9).

Fig. 2. Frederick Mackenzie, *St Stephen's Chapel, one of the Windows of the Chapel of St Mary in the Vaults*, c.1844. Ink and wash drawing, 61.5 × 73.5 cm. TNA, WORK 29/765.

continuous vertical or horizontal mouldings found in many of the building's decorative details. In addition, there is some evidence that parts of the upper chapel were under way at this time. On 17 August 1293 payment was made for ten feet of a marble *tabula*, perhaps referring to the flat surface of the Purbeck marble seat which encircled the interior of the upper chapel.[21]

Further information is provided by two pieces of evidence: one documentary, the other material. The first is the account for repairs undertaken in 1309, which records the employment of three plumbers to cover the window jambs, pinnacles, and buttresses of the chapel with lead and build a wall beneath the porch.[22] As lead was conventionally used

---

[21] TNA, E 101/468/6, rot. 37 (Ayers & Jurkowski, vol. 1, pp. 252–3). See Louis F. Salzman, *Building in England Down to 1540* (Oxford, 1952), p. 106. The material of the seat in the upper chapel at St Stephen's is recorded on a drawing by John Carter (SAL, 236E, SSC.8).

[22] TNA, E 101/468/21, fol. 109v (Ayers & Jurkowski, vol. 1, pp. 474–5).

Fig. 3. John Dixon, *Eastern bay on the south* [recte *north*] *side of St Stephen's Chapel*, detail of upper cornice showing heraldic shields, published 1811. Pen and ink, on paper, 94.5 × 60.3 cm. SAL, 236E, SSC.15.

to seal the terminations of finished architectural components (with reeds being used for incomplete elements), it can be inferred that at least some of the buttress terminations at St Stephen's had been completed and installed by this time. This could potentially take the height of some bays of the chapel right up to the level of the upper cornice, a possibility which is further supported by the second piece of evidence – a sequence of heraldic shields that lay directly underneath the cornice (fig. 3).

Recorded in a series of drawings by John Carter in 1791–2, the stone shields are difficult to date precisely (fig. 4).[23] Two remain unidentified, but the remainder consist of the arms of Castile-León, France, Geoffrey de Geneville, Strathbogie, Edward the Confessor, Edmund the Martyr, and the ancient arms of Anjou, attributed retrospectively to Geoffrey Plantagenet.[24] It is extremely unlikely that the arms of Strathbogie were carved in the 1290s. John de Strathbogie was a Scottish earl who took up arms against England in the war of 1296, and was imprisoned in the Tower between May that year and July 1297.[25] By contrast, his son David II

---

[23] For earlier iterations of the discussion of these arms, see James Hillson, 'Heraldry, Time and the King's Two Bodies: the Palace and Abbey at Westminster, 1253–1363', in Torsten Hiltmann and Miguel Metelo de Siexas (eds), *Heraldry in Medieval and Early Modern State Rooms* (Ostfildern, 2020), pp. 29–52.
[24] John W. Papworth, *An Alphabetical Dictionary of Coats of Arms* (London, 1874), 684; G. J. Brault, *Rolls of Arms; Edward I (1272–1307)* (2 vols, Woodbridge, 1997), vol. 1, pp. 148, 239–40, 404–5. D. Hubert et al., *Dictionary of British Arms: Medieval Ordinary* (4 vols, Woodbridge, 1992–2014), vol. 1, pp. 245–6; vol. 2, pp. 110, 216–17; vol. 3, pp. 32, 182–3, 243–4; vol. 4, pp. 47–8, 161, 279. The attributed arms of Anjou are similar to those of Navarre, but differenced by a chief argent. This attribution is testified in Francis Sandford and Samuel Stebbing, *A Genealogical History of the Kings and Queens of England* (London, 1707), p. 34.
[25] Sir James Balfour Paul (ed.), *The Scots Peerage* (Edinburgh, 1904), vol. 1, pp. 426–7.

War, Politics, and Architecture: Iterative Design at St Stephen's Chapel, 1292–1348

Fig. 4. John Carter, *Some of the most remarkable Blockings in the frize of the entablatures over the windows of St Stephen's in their propper colours. (Drawn nearly half the size of the originals.)*, c.1791–2. Pen and ink wash, on paper, 37.3 × 55 cm. SAL, 236E, SSC.12–13.

(incumbent 1307–26) was a loyal supporter of the English cause, holding lands in England after his Scottish possessions were stripped by Robert the Bruce in 1314.[26] While this would make him a far more likely candidate for commemoration, it does not necessarily follow that the shields were completed under Edward II (1320–6). This is indicated by the presence of Geoffrey de Geneville (from the English branch of the Joinville family), whose death without heirs in 1314 left his arms to be inherited by his daughter Joan, the wife of Roger Mortimer.[27] Mortimer, the future architect of Edward II's deposition in 1327, rebelled against the king in May 1321 and was imprisoned from 22 January 1322 until his escape to France in August 1323.[28] His wife similarly suffered house arrest at Edward's hands in 1322, and the seizure of her possessions and more formal imprisonment from April 1324 onwards.[29]

While it is therefore possible the shields were cut between November 1320 and May 1321, when over £200 was assigned to the works at Westminster and the Tower of London,[30] it is more likely that the cutting of the shields was split over two periods. A 1290s context for the arms of Geneville is far more plausible, as Geoffrey had been the effective lieutenant of

---

[26] Paul, *Scots Peerage*, pp. 428–30; Fiona Watson, 'Strathbogie, David, styled tenth Earl of Atholl (d.1326)', *ODNB* <http://www.oxforddnb.com/view/article/54330> [accessed 30 Aug. 2015].
[27] Michael Prestwich, *Edward I* (London, 1988), pp. 13–14, 52, 413–21; Robin Frame, 'Ireland and the Barons' War', in P. R. Coss and S. D. Lloyd (eds), *Thirteenth Century England: 1: Proceedings of the Newcastle upon Tyne Conference 1985* (Woodbridge, 1986), pp. 161–4.
[28] Ian Mortimer, *The Greatest Traitor: The Life of Sir Roger Mortimer* (London, 2004), pp. 99–149.
[29] Mortimer, *Greatest Traitor*, pp. 120–1, 126, 135–6.
[30] See note 60.

the king in Ireland since the reign of Henry III.[31] During the crisis of 1297, when Edward I's Marshal Roger Bigod and Constable Humphrey de Bohun refused to tally the forces attending the muster of 7 July, it was Geoffrey who replaced Bigod as Marshal, a strong indication that he was considered a trusted supporter and safe pair of hands during a time of political unrest.[32] Such a date is further indicated by the inclusion of the arms of Castile–León, referring in all probability to Edward I's first wife, Eleanor of Castile, whose death in 1290 was commemorated by a variety of monuments throughout the subsequent decade.[33] Yet, though the arms of France could refer to the king's second wife, Margaret of France, it is improbable that this would have been carved during the 1290s. From 1294 to 1299 England was at war with France, and Edward was only to marry Margaret after its conclusion as one of the conditions of peace. A similar argument holds true for Edward II's wife, Isabella of France as, though her marriage was agreed at the same time as Margaret's, it was not to occur until January 1308.[34] Together, these observations suggest that some of the shields were at least cut (if not necessarily installed) by 1297, whereas others were executed during the 1320–6 campaigns.

By July 1297 it would therefore be reasonable to assume that the walls of the lower chapel were largely completed, with further works being completed to a variable height and indeterminate level of detail within the upper chapel. Though some of the buttresses may have reached the height of the upper cornice (including presumably the window jambs, though not necessarily the arches above), it is unlikely that extensive works were completed at this high level. A more pressing problem is why the project ceased so suddenly. The conventional assumption, advanced by Colvin, is that the reasons were financial, specifically the diversion of funds towards warfare in Scotland and France.[35] In January 1296 Edward I issued a *memorandum* to the Exchequer stopping all building works excepting those in Wales (presumably the castles then under construction) and the painting of his chambers at Westminster.[36] Curiously, this order does not seem to have applied to the chapel, though it is notable that works on the paintings were recorded within the particulars of account for the chapel. However, by April 1295 the number of masons employed at the chapel had already dropped by over 85% from its high point in the previous August, and numbers remained at this level for the remaining duration of operations.[37] No further orders of stone were recorded, and construction continued only until the issuing of a second *memorandum* on 4 July 1297, whereupon it stopped entirely.[38]

---

[31] Prestwich, *Edward I*, pp. 13–14, 52; Robin Frame, 'Ireland and the Barons' War', in P. R. Coss and S. D. Lloyd (ed.), *Thirteenth Century England: 1: Proceedings of the Newcastle upon Tyne conference 1985* (Woodbridge, 1986), pp. 161–4.
[32] Prestwich, *Edward I*, pp. 413–21.
[33] David Parsons (ed.), *Eleanor of Castile 1290–1990: Essays to Commemorate the 700th Anniversary of her Death: 28 November 1290* (Stamford, 1991); Paul Binski, *Westminster Abbey and the Plantagenets: Kingship and the Representation of Power 1200–1400* (New Haven/London, 1995), pp. 107–10; Carsten Dilba, *Memoria Reginae: Das Memorialprogramm für Eleonore von Kastilien* (Hildesheim, 2009).
[34] Seymour Phillips, *Edward II* (New Haven/London, 2011), pp. 132–4.
[35] *HKW*, vol. 1, p. 512.
[36] The *memorandum* was issued to the Treasurer, Barons, and Chamberlains of the Exchequer 'derechef decesser de totes maneres de oueraignes suue le oureaigne de Gales e les peintures des chaumbres de Wesmoster deuisees' (TNA, E 159/6, rot. 11d). *HKW*, vol. 1, pp. 380 (n. 1), 512.
[37] See Hillson, 'St Stephen's', pp. 76–7; Ayers & Jurkowski, vol. 1, p. 86.
[38] 'Memorandum quod iiij die Julii [1297] dominus Rex mandavit per Johannem de Drokenesford custodem Garderobe sue quod operaciones Westm' cessarent decetero quousque aliud duxit ordinandum' (TNA, E 405/1/11, m. 5). *HKW*, vol. 1, p. 512.

The timing of the cessation of the works in relation to political events is highly revealing. Despite the date of the king's first *memorandum*, the first great financial surprise of the reign came not in 1296, but in 1294. The outbreak of war with France in March 1294 over the status of the English lands in Gascony was a sudden surprise for Edward I, who had remained committed to finding a peaceful solution to the escalating tensions right up to this moment.[39] The requirements of a war economy necessitated building up a large reserve of cash to finance a planned invasion of France, the defence of Gascony, and vast negotiated payments to continental allies, many of which were due for Christmas that year.[40] Meeting these obligations was made even more difficult by the outbreak of a Welsh rebellion at the end of September, necessitating the postponement of the French invasion and the redirection of most of his remaining funds towards preparations on this new front.[41]

Surprisingly, work at St Stephen's was apparently unaffected during this period, with no sign of change to the provision of labour or materials. This aptly demonstrates the king's capacity to finance building significantly beyond the limitations of his budget, even at times when his funds were severely constrained. This was made possible by the close relationship which Edward I established between the Exchequer and Italian banking firms, in particular the Riccardi of Lucca.[42] First established in the early 1270s when the future king was on crusade, Edward's reliance on the Riccardi soon developed into a system of continuous rolling loans to be repaid by future income from customs and other sources of revenue.[43] Whereas taxes, customs, duties, and the like were comparatively slow to gather and thus difficult to tap into for immediate monetary demands, such loans provided instant coinage in large quantities whatever the king's financial situation might be. Not only were the Riccardi essential to the support of Edward I's government, they were also instrumental in supplying cash for the ongoing works at St Stephen's, with records showing the advances of £400 in July 1292, £680 in August, and £275 6s. 8d. for February and March 1295.[44]

It was not until the banking system faltered that the impact of the king's pressured finances began to be felt in the works at St Stephen's. The arrest of the Riccardi on 28 October 1294, following their failure to supply Edward with the resources he required, resulted in a sudden curtailment of the king's financial flexibility.[45] It is therefore unsurprising that during the period between the first week of October 1294 and third week of April 1295 the number of masons on site fell dramatically.[46] Whereas other aspects of the king's finances could still be managed by trading against his future income, his ongoing architectural patronage was reliant on immediate cash supply.[47] Though a modicum of financial stability was regained through the lay and clerical taxes instituted in November–December 1295 and November

---

[39] Prestwich, *Edward I*, pp. 377–81.
[40] Michael Prestwich, *War, Politics and Finance under Edward I* (London, 1972), p. 157; Prestwich, *Edward I*, pp. 386–91.
[41] Prestwich, *Edward I*, p. 225; Prestwich, *War, Politics and Finance*, pp. 165–6.
[42] Richard W. Kaeuper, *Bankers to the Crown: The Riccardi of Lucca and Edward I* (Princeton, 1973).
[43] Kaeuper, *Bankers*, pp. 79–83.
[44] Kaeuper, *Bankers*, p. 102; TNA, E 372/143, m. 35d (Ayers & Jurkowski, vol. 2, p. 1407).
[45] Prestwich, *War, Politics and Finance*, p. 151.
[46] Ayers and Jurkowski, vol. 1, p. 86.
[47] At St Stephen's goods were apparently paid for on arrival and were often imported from abroad. The 1290s alone saw Spanish iron, French stone from Caen and Boulogne, and Baltic timbers, albeit the latter were often purchased from suppliers based in London. See TNA, E 101/468/6 (Ayers & Jurkowski, vol. 1, pp. 95–401).

1296, the short-term effects of these were limited.[48] With the opening of a third front in Scotland in October 1295, the issuing of a *memorandum* to reduce architectural expenditure in January 1295 is scarcely surprising and can be considered a marker of the continuing deterioration of his spending power. By mid-1297, the worsening financial situation had forced the king to take extraordinary measures in raising revenues, seizing wool supplies and pressuring his earls and the clergy to the point of open rebellion.[49] Without readily available cash loans, continuing the works at St Stephen's became untenable and it is likely no coincidence that the August 1297 muster for the invasion of France was paralleled by a decisive break in construction.[50]

It is worth noting, however, that works at St Stephen's were continued long past the point of pragmatism. War and financial disaster alone were not sufficient to trigger a hiatus, and it was only with the total exhaustion of his finances that Edward was willing to abandon his cherished architectural projects. Though the chapel appears to have survived intact the fire which broke out in the Palace of Westminster in 1298,[51] construction was not to be resumed until long after the king's death. Successive campaigns in Scotland conducted in 1301–2, 1303–5, and 1306–7 provided near-continuous drains on Edward's resources, and the unpaid debts of the 1290s and 1300s resulted in an increasing deficit which made returning to the works impossible.[52] For the remainder of Edward I's reign, St Stephen's remained an abandoned building site, quietly mouldering in a partially ruined Palace dotted with ageing stores of wood and stone.

Edward II (1320–2; 1323–6)

By the time of his death in 1307, the cumulative debts of Edward I may have totalled as much as £200,000.[53] This enormous sum continued to be an unshakeable burden throughout the first decade and a half of his son's reign, necessitating a series of hard decisions regarding the king's ongoing architectural projects. From as early as 1307, it is clear that Edward II recognized that St Stephen's was likely to remain unfinished for the foreseeable future. Though a series of repair works were conducted at Westminster from 1307 to 1311, these barely touched on the chapel itself and instead focused on renovating the temporary chapel of St Stephen's by the Receipt, presumably with the intention of acting as a long-term replacement.[54] The frugality of this approach was in part a reflection of the constant drain on his financial resources during this period. Wars, civil and foreign, were a regular occurrence, forcing Edward to supplement his income through extensive loans.[55] There were therefore few opportunities for Edward to repay his father's debts, a problem exacerbated by the Ordinances imposed on him by his barons in 1311, which further limited his capacity to meet

---

[48] Prestwich, *Edward I*, pp. 405–6.
[49] Prestwich, *Edward I*, pp. 412–24.
[50] Prestwich, *Edward I*, pp. 423–5.
[51] *HKW*, vol. 2, pp. 1041–4.
[52] Prestwich, *Edward I*, pp. 517–55.
[53] Prestwich, *War, Politics and Finance*, p. 221.
[54] TNA, E 101/468/21, fol. 106r (Ayers & Jurkowski, vol. 1, pp. 470–1). For the location of this chapel, see *HKW*, vol. 1, p. 503 n. 10; pp. 505–7, 513 n. 9, Hillson, 'St Stephen's', p. 139.
[55] Seymour Phillips, *Edward II* (New Haven/London, 2011), pp. 217–19, 251–2, 342–4, 419–22.

his financial obligations.[56] Even as late as the 1320s, approximately £60,000 of Edward I's debt was still outstanding, and it was not until the restrictions of the Ordinances were removed in May 1322 that Edward was able to begin the process of financial recovery.[57] On 21 September 1323 he instructed the Treasurer and Barons of the Exchequer to 'serve us in such a way that we should become rich', and by 1325 the treasury (which had only £1,195 in its possession in early May 1322) had grown to contain nearly £62,000, almost exactly a year's income.[58]

Work at St Stephen's may have resumed as early as March 1319 under the direction of Michael of Canterbury, though their extent is once again unclear. The earliest set of accounts, extending from Michaelmas 1319 to December 1322, consist of a sparse and ambiguously worded list of *liberaciones* made to John de Ditton, the clerk of the king's works at the Palace of Westminster and Tower of London.[59] Funds were set aside for both sites in general terms, and it is not clear what proportion was to be directed to St Stephen's. On 7 November 1320 the first relevant entry indicates that £200 were to be released for works at Westminster, the Tower and the chapel together, a payment which was only fully completed on 25 May 1321.[60] A similar ambiguity can be found in the order issued on the immediately preceding 18 May for £1000 towards 'the aforesaid works'.[61] Stones were purchased for works in the Palace and chapel the following 1 July, but while the final payment of 23 December 1321 does indicate that the £1000 was 'for the works of the new chapel of St Stephen', the accuracy of this statement remains open to interpretation.[62] By the close of the works at the end of 1322, £131 5s. 2d. still remained to be paid out from the Exchequer, and there is no evidence that this obligation was ever met.[63]

With so many uncertainties surrounding this period of the project, quantifying what Edward II achieved between 1320 and 1322 is therefore extremely difficult, perhaps approachable only by comparison with the periods that preceded and succeeded it. By November 1323 the site was already under the direction of a new master mason, Thomas of Canterbury,[64] and the associated accounts start to provide a far more detailed record of the building process. On 23 April 1324 wood was purchased from the Bishop of Exeter for a new scaffold on the north side of the chapel,[65] raising the possibility that the preceding

---

[56] Phillips, *Edward II*, p. 419.
[57] Michael Prestwich, *Plantagenet England 1225–1360* (Oxford, 2005), pp. 175–7.
[58] 'mettez votre peine qe nous soioms riches' (TNA, E 159/97, m. 17; translation in Natalie Fryde, *The Tyranny and Fall of Edward II 1321–26* (Cambridge, 1979), p. 94). For the valuation of the Treasury, see Phillips, *Edward II*, pp. 419–20.
[59] TNA, E 101/469/3 (Ayers & Jurkowski, vol. 1, pp. 495–503).
[60] 'Eidem Johanni [de Ditton'] c s. liberati eidem vij die Novembris [1320] per manus proprias viz. tam super operacionibus palacij Westm' et Turris London' quam capelle sancti Stephani infra palacium predictum super breve de liberate continens cc li. sibi liberandas super operacionibus predictis cuius data est apud Westm' v die Novembris anno xiiij' (TNA, E 101/469/3, m. 1; Ayers & Jurkowski, vol. 1, p. 499).
[61] 'Eidem Johanni super aliud breve de liberate continens m^l li. sibi liberandas super operacionibus predictis cuius brevis data est apud Westm' xviij die Maij anno xiiij [1321] L marce liberate eidem xxv die Maij per manus proprias in parte solucione brevis predicti' (TNA, E 101/469/3, m. 1; Ayers & Jurkowski, vol. 1, p. 499).
[62] 'Eidem primo die Julij [1321] xj li. vj d. per manus Ricardi de Bray recipienti denarios pro lapidibus emptis de eodem pro operacionibus palacij et capelle predicte' (TNA, E 101/469/3, m. 1; Ayers & Jurkowski, vol. 1, pp. 496–7).
[63] TNA, E 101/469/3, m. 1d (Ayers & Jurkowski, vol. 1, pp. 502–3).
[64] TNA, E 101/469/8 (Ayers & Jurkowski, vol. 1, pp. 506–7).
[65] 'Die lune xxiij die Aprilis [1324] domino Waltero Exoniensis Episcopo pro lxj peciis fraccini longitudinis xlij pedum et pro cccc peciis alni longitudinis xxxviij pedum pro scaffoto capelle ex parte boriali faciendo in boscis manerij sui de Henle iuxta Gyldeford emptis vj li. xiij s. iiij d.' (TNA, E 101/469/8, m. 3; Ayers & Jurkowski, vol. 1, pp. 536–7).

period of works had focused more on raising the upper chapel walls on the south side. Buttresses and piers were raised to the requisite height, the window arches were closed, decorative spandrels were inserted above and crenellated cornices laid out down the full length of the upper chapel, establishing a framework within which decorative details could be installed.

This interpretation is further supported by the evidence for works on the upper chapel windows. From April to November 1324 iron was periodically bought for window bars, in April and May that year Caen stone 'mold pieces' were imported (in all probability for the mouldings of the window frames) and from April 1325 onwards Reigate stone 'mould' or 'form pieces' were purchased, indicating the start of work on the window tracery.[66] Hundreds of feet of Purbeck marble were bought for columns, indicating that many of the shafts surrounding the upper chapel interior were finally being cut and prepared for installation. From March to November 1325, work began on a new intervention to the structure, a two-storey gallery or *alura* with at least twenty-four casemented windows and elaborate cresting on its exterior.[67] Though the *alura* had been all but obliterated by the time antiquarian records began during the 1790s, both documents and the few records of its material fabric suggest that it extended between the east end of St Stephen's and the Painted Chamber to the south, incorporating an oratory which directly adjoined the chapel's south-easternmost bay (fig. 5). This would later come to be known as the chapel of St Mary le Pew, the location of a miracle-working statue of the Virgin.[68] At the same time, work began on the chapel roof under master carpenter William Hurley and his subordinate William de Underdown, lasting from March to November 1325.[69] An inventory compiled in 1332 tallies the completed timbers and wooden components, including some intended for the *vosura* or vault.

While such observations give some indication of the progress of the works at St Stephen's, in combination with the visual evidence provided by antiquarian drawings they also have potential implications for the development of its design. On the south side of the upper chapel exterior, the intersection between the *alura* and the east end was marked by a doorway which was cut indifferently through the continuous mullions that extended down over the lower chapel windows (fig. 6). This corresponded to a depressed ogee-arched entrance on the upper chapel interior, breaking up the blind arcading which originally encircled the building in a uniform sequence of projecting ogees (fig. 7). A second, near identical entrance appeared on the north side, probably leading to the adjoining two-storey vestry (a lock for which was bought at the start of May 1324) (fig. 8).[70] The closest comparisons to these archways are

---

[66] TNA, E 101/469/8, m. 2, 3, 6, 9, 12 (Ayers & Jurkowski, vol. 1, pp. 533–605). For comparable examples of accounts recording ironwork for use as through-bars at Merton College, Oxford in the 1290s, see Tim Ayers, *The Medieval Stained Glass of Merton College, Oxford, CVMA Great Britain* (Oxford, 2013), p. 5; Salzman, *Building in England*, pp. 110, 291–2.
[67] TNA, E 101/469/8, m. 13–19 (Ayers & Jurkowski, vol. 1, pp. 608–53), E 101/469/10, m. 1–3 (ibid., vol. 1, pp. 682–701).
[68] For the chapel of St Mary le Pew, see Smith, *Antiquities*, pp. 101, 123–4, 222; *HKW*, vol. 1, p. 517; Charles Lethbridge Kingsford, 'Our Lady of the Pew: The King's Oratory or Closet in the Palace of Westminster', *Archaeologia*, 68 (1917), 1–20; Elizabeth Biggs, 'The College and Canons of St Stephen's, Westminster, 1348–1548' (Ph.D. dissertation, University of York, 2016), pp. 58, 76–7, 85–6, 94–5; Biggs, *St Stephen's College, Westminster: A Royal Chapel and English Kingship 1348–1548* (Woodbridge, 2020), pp. 47–8.
[69] For William de Underdown, see Harvey, *English Mediaeval Architects*, p. 305.
[70] TNA, E 101/469/8, m. 3 (Ayers & Jurkowski, vol. 1, p. 539).

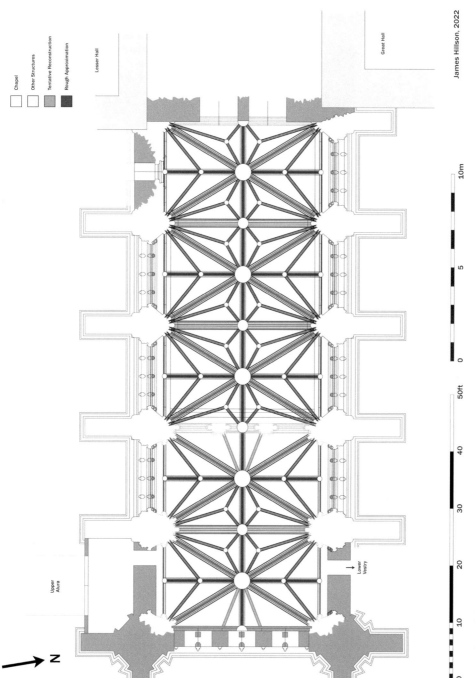

Fig. 5. Plan of the lower chapel, St Stephen's Chapel, Westminster, 2022.

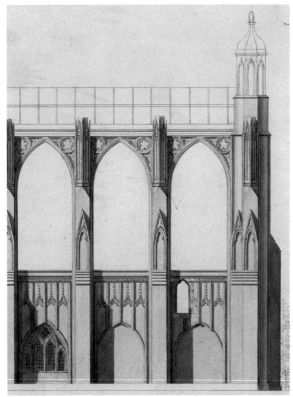

Fig. 6. John Carter, *Elevation of the remains of the South side of St Stephen's Chapel, Westminster, and parts of the buildings adjoining*, detail showing doorway cut into the upper chapel's easternmost bay, c.1791–2. Pen and ink and wash, on paper, 51 × 68.6 cm. SAL, 236E, SSC.5.

provided by the early-fourteenth-century works at Exeter Cathedral, specifically the upper register of the pulpitum (c.1317–25) and the external doorway to the Grandisson Chapel on the south side of the west front's central portal (c.1328–30) (figs 9–10).[71] Consequently, it is entirely plausible that both entrances as well as the vestry and *alura* were additions of the 1320s, representing new interventions into the chapel's design.

Similar observations can be made regarding the projecting ogees of the blind arcade. Such a feature was apparently unique to the upper chapel, appearing only at dado level and in the heads of the rectangular panels adorning the adjoining piers. While ogee arches were employed at St Stephen's during the 1290s, this particular variety appears to be paralleled exclusively by later monuments. Comparisons have been drawn with the examples found in the tomb of Thomas II Berkeley at St Augustine's, Bristol, which has traditionally been dated to c.1307–9 and has even been placed as late as the early 1320s (fig. 11).[72] The same type of arch can be found in the sedilia of the Lady Chapel at Wells Cathedral, which has

[71] Veronica Sekules, 'The Liturgical Furnishings of the Choir of Exeter Cathedral' in Francis Kelly (ed.), *Medieval Art and Architecture at Exeter Cathedral* (London, 1991), pp. 172–9; Richard K. Morris, 'Thomas of Witney at Exeter, Winchester and Wells' in idem, p. 65. Both structures have been attributed to Master Thomas of Witney, who was probably the 'Thomas de Wytteneye' employed as a mason at St Stephen's between Oct. 1292 and Sept. 1294 (Harvey, *English Mediaeval Architects*, pp. 338–41). However, this does not necessarily mean that the direction of influence went from St Stephen's to Exeter – the reverse was equally possible.
[72] For St Augustine's, Bristol, see Richard K. Morris, 'European Prodigy or Regional Eccentric?', pp. 45–6; Wilson, 'Gothic Metamorphosed', pp. 73–5, 99–101. Wilson proposes an earlier date of conception around 1298.

War, Politics, and Architecture: Iterative Design at St Stephen's Chapel, 1292–1348   91

Fig. 7. John Thomas Smith, *Part of the South side of the same Chapel*, detail, from Smith, *Antiquities*, facing p. 153. WOA 3129.

Fig. 8. John Dixon, *Eastern bay on the south [recte north] side of St Stephen's Chapel*, detail of dado arcading showing doorway to the upper vestry, published 1811. Pen and ink, on paper, 94.5 × 60.3 cm. SAL, 236E, SSC.15.

Fig. 9. Detail of blind arches, pulpitum, c.1317–25, Exeter Cathedral.

Fig. 10. Doorway to Grandisson Chapel, c.1328–30, west front, Exeter Cathedral.

been dated variously to c.1306–19 and c.1323–6 (fig. 12).[73] A later date is further supported by the recorded fabric of the arcading itself, where close observation reveals that the projecting ogees were overlaid onto a set of simple pointed trefoils, the tips of which would have remained just visible underneath the ogee points (fig. 13). These underlying arches were recorded in more detail by the antiquarians John Thomas Smith and John Carter (figs 7, 14), and may well be the remnant of an earlier phase of design at St Stephen's. While none of the other buildings that have been attributed to Michael of Canterbury employ a projecting ogee of this kind, a projecting trefoil is displayed prominently on the street side of St Augustine's gatehouse in Canterbury (c.1300–8), which bears a number of stylistic similarities to his work at St Stephen's (fig. 15).[74] It is therefore entirely plausible that the upper chapel's dado arcade originally consisted of a series of pointed trefoils, projecting or otherwise, with the intersection of the *alura* during the 1320s prompting the transition to a more recently developed architectural form.

Further evidence for active design work during the 1320s is provided by the building accounts. Works relating to the *trasura* or tracing house were conducted on three separate occasions (November 1323, February 1324, and January 1325), and the entries include numerous references to new templates being cut for various purposes.[75] One of the major

---

[73] For the sedilia at Wells, see Cameron, *Sedilia*, pp. 141, 156–7; Peter Draper, 'The Sequence and Dating of the Decorated Work at Wells' in Peter Draper and Nicola Coldstream (eds), *Medieval Art and Architecture at Wells and Glastonbury* (Leeds, 1981), pp. 18–29, at pp. 20–2.

[74] Examples of buildings attributed to Michael of Canterbury include the Peckham tomb, Canterbury (1292–3), the Aveline de Forz (1292–3) and Crouchback tombs (1297), Westminster, the Louth tomb, Ely Cathedral (1298), Westminster Abbey cloister (c.1298), the Eastry screen (1304–5) and chapter house of Canterbury Cathedral (1300–5), and St Augustine's gatehouse, Canterbury (1300–8) (Harvey, *English Mediaeval Architects*, pp. 45–6; Wilson, 'Origins', pp. 27–111).

[75] Within the accounts there is some ambiguity as to whether the term *trasura* referred to a building, drawing board, or plaster drawing surface. See TNA, E 101/469/8, m. 1, 2, 10 (Ayers & Jurkowski, vol. 1, pp. 506–7, 522–3,

Fig. 11. Detail of interior, tomb of Thomas II Berkeley, c.1307–9/1320s, Bristol Cathedral (St Augustine's Abbey).

Fig. 12. Detail of sedilia canopies, Lady Chapel, c.1323–6, Wells Cathedral.

Fig. 13. Frederick Mackenzie, *St Stephen's Chapel*, detail of upper chapel dado arcading, *c*.1844. Ink and wash, on paper, 61.5 × 66 cm. TNA, WORK 29/766.

Fig. 14. John Carter, *Elevation and plan of the lower part of the columns […]; their bases & surbases, the marble seat running around the building; part of the impost of the windows [etc.] of St Stephen's Chapel*, detail of upper chapel dado arcading, *c*.1791–2. Pen and ink wash, on paper, 38 × 55.3 cm. SAL, 236E, SSC.8.

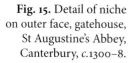
Fig. 15. Detail of niche on outer face, gatehouse, St Augustine's Abbey, Canterbury, c.1300–8.

features being designed during this period was the 'tabernacles' (*tabernaculi*), probably the canopies intended to adorn the inner faces of the upper chapel piers.[76] Though the exact appearance of these complex and labour-intensive creations is entirely lost, what little is known about their form suggests that they would have had a significant impact on the visual articulation of the chapel's interior. The concave faces and Y-tracery panels of the consoles which sat beneath them represented new departures in the chapel's formal repertoire (fig. 16), and it would not be surprising if similar developments appeared in the canopies above.[77] Further details are provided by the inventory conducted in 1346, which associates the tabernacles directly with a set of Purbeck marble columns.[78] These are described as emerging both from the *sources* or bases underneath the tabernacles and 'out of each side of the tabernacles' ('ex utraque parte tabernaculorum') above, suggesting some kind of continuous shaft linking all levels of the elevation. Corresponding to the

---

588–93). For templates, see E 101/469/8, m. 1, 2, 4, 8, 10–15 (ibid., pp. 514–15, 528–31, 548–9, 580–1, 594–623). For the role of templates in architectural design and construction, see Lon R. Shelby, 'Medieval Masons' Templates', *Journal of the Society of Architectural Historians*, 30:2 (1971), 140–53; James, *Template-Makers*; Hillson, 'Villard', pp. 182–3, 196–7, Hillson, 'Linearity', pp. 68–9; Buchanan, Hillson, and Webb, *Digital Analysis*, pp. 87–90, 176–202.
[76] The very first entry of the accounts, on 21 Nov., records the purchase of six boards for a *trasura* explicitly for the purpose of designing the tabernacles (TNA, E 101/469/8, m. 1; Ayers & Jurkowski, vol. 1, pp. 506–7).
[77] The form closely resembles the examples found in some windows in the easternmost bays of the Lady Chapel at St Augustine's Abbey, Bristol, possibly dating from 1298 to 1316.
[78] TNA, E 101/470/16, m. 1 (Ayers & Jurkowski, vol. 2, pp. 1049–57).

Fig. 16. John Thomas Smith, *Sculpture and Painted Glass from St Stephen's Chapel*, published 1800. Coloured line engraving, 16.4 × 25.1 cm. WOA 1492b.

capitals which Frederick Mackenzie recorded atop the upper cornice, these concave-faced octagonal responds may have been intended to provide a springing point for the wooden vault above, providing a cohesive link between all new and old elements of the upper chapel's design.[79]

If such an interpretation is correct, then a significant set of alterations to the design of St Stephen's had occurred. The 1320s would have seen the introduction of projecting ogees, Y-tracery and a new form of scalloped octagonal profiles in its shafts and consoles, and it is quite possible that these were not the only changes to be instituted during this period. Tracery was an element which could be readily modified at any stage of the design, and in the absence of any evidence for the appearance of the upper chapel's north and south windows it is plausible (though of course unprovable) that they represented a later stage of development. Whatever the case, the alterations of the 1320s should not be seen as jarring and incongruous interventions into an established building, but rather as carefully integrated additions to a cumulative design developed by iteration. Whether such modifications should be attributed to Michael of Canterbury, Thomas of Canterbury, or some combination of

---

[79] In this it may have been following the intentions of Michael of Canterbury to terminate the building's masonry at upper cornice level. If this is correct, the arrangement of the roof and vaulting was probably similar to that at St Etheldreda's Chapel, Holborn (1284–6), Merton College Chapel, Oxford (*c.*1286–97), and the chapter house at Canterbury Cathedral (1304–5).

the two, the evidence suggests that the designers of the 1320s were not passively completing an established plan of the 1290s, but actively reinvigorating it in response to more recent architectural developments.

Works ceased abruptly in the week following 26 November 1325, and by March 1326 the site had been completely shut down.[80] Though the north and south walls were structurally complete and their decoration was beginning to take shape, large portions of the scheme were left unfinished. The east and west ends were still open to the elements, the roof was placed in storage and the inventory taken in 1332 records many incomplete and uninstalled elements from all levels of the chapel's fabric (including the new tabernacles).[81] However, the suddenness of the closure does not appear to have been prompted by financial constraints as it had been in 1297. Since the Statutes of York in 1322, the vitality of royal finances had improved dramatically, and even the impressive expenditure of approximately £65,000 on the War of Saint-Sardos (1324–5) had no appreciable effect on the progress of construction.[82]

What changed in November 1325 was the threat of civil war backed by foreign invasion. Edward's relationship with his wife Isabella had, by all accounts, been deteriorating for some time.[83] In March 1325 she was sent to France to conduct peace negotiations, but her refusal to return made her a focal point for opposition to the king. By early November, the threat posed by her open association with the hostile community of English émigrés led by Roger Mortimer had become clear, all the more so because she retained the king's twelve-year-old son, the future Edward III, in her custody.[84] Surviving letters sent from Edward II and his bishops to Isabella reveal growing fears of foreign invasion, a reality which was further emphasized by a series of jumpy mobilization orders for England's naval defences.[85]

Given its close proximity to the cessation of works at St Stephen's, the growing threat of foreign invasion was the most likely cause of the hiatus. As Edward II already possessed a plentiful cash supply, the reason for such a break was probably not a forced reduction in expenditure, but rather the increase in fiscal flexibility which it offered. Facing threats of invasion by Robert the Bruce from Scotland, Charles IV of France in Gascony and his own wife and son in England, Edward II could not be certain where his enemies would strike first. Whereas conducting campaigns against a defined enemy on foreign soil could be planned for and budgeted in advance, the unpredictability of defending against civil unrest and external invaders would have necessitated the rapid mobilization of funds and manpower at short notice. As the campaign at St Stephen's had reached a logical stopping point, it would have been a reasonable response to close down the works until the crisis had passed.[86]

---

[80] TNA, E 101/469/10, m. 3–5 (Ayers & Jurkowski, vol. 1, pp. 696–709).
[81] TNA, E 101/469/11, m. 1d (Ayers & Jurkowski, vol. 1, pp. 804–11).
[82] Fryde, *Tyranny*, pp. 94, 105; Phillips, *Edward II*, pp. 419–20.
[83] Phillips, *Edward II*, pp. 471–86; Alison Weir, *Isabella: She-Wolf of France, Queen of England* (London, 2005), pp. 163–4, 169–70, 173–7.
[84] Phillips, *Edward II*, pp. 485–8; W. Mark Ormrod, *Edward III* (New Haven/London, 2011), pp. 31–41.
[85] CChR 1323–27, p. 580; Wendy R. Childs (ed.), *Vita Edwardi Secundi: The Life of Edward II* (Oxford, 2005), pp. 244–7.
[86] The works at St Stephen's usually shut down temporarily over Christmas, as they had in 1324 (Ayers & Jurkowski, vol. 1, pp. 586–9).

Edward III (1331–5; 1337; 1342–3; 1347–8)

Though it could be considered a conclusion to the crisis, the deposition of Edward II by Isabella and Mortimer in January 1327 did not result in an immediate resumption of works at St Stephen's. The treasure which the former king had so carefully built up throughout the 1320s was rapidly expended by the new regency, and architectural patronage was not a priority for public spending.[87] Their royal ward, Edward III, appears to have taken a different approach. A mere eight months after he assumed his majority in a bold *coup d'état* in October 1330, the new king reinitiated works on the chapel.[88] Still under the leadership of Thomas of Canterbury, the first campaign of the reign (1331–5) was focused on finishing the east end and adding a new feature to the north and south walls – the clerestory.

The appearance of the east end can be reconstructed in some detail. Framed by piers that closely emulated those of the flanking walls, the great east window adopted a unique pointed trefoil shape, its cusps decorated with blind tracery on the interior (fig. 17). Though its tracery did not survive to be recorded by antiquarians, its six-light structure was testified by the bases of the remaining mullions. Some indication of its form is provided by an engraved frontispiece to John Nalson's *An Impartial Collection of the Great Affairs of State* (published 1682–3) (fig. 18), which depicts a central oculus containing one cinquefoil encircled by five others.[89] A similar contemporary design is provided by the window of St Anselm's Chapel in Canterbury Cathedral, dating to *c*.1336, which may well represent a response to the east window at St Stephen's.[90]

On the exterior, the spandrels to either side of the east window consisted of two niches containing large sculptures of St Edward the Confessor and St John the Evangelist disguised as a pilgrim (fig. 19).[91] This iconography had a long tradition in Plantagenet artistic patronage, and was represented nearby on the interior of the south transept at Westminster Abbey (*c*.1253) and the Painted Chamber in the Palace of Westminster (1263–72), the latter of which was connected via the *alura* to the chapel's south side.[92] Above this level was a blind arcade of low proportions, matched on the interior by a set of rectangular panels coating the wall surface as it was extended to incorporate the clerestory. Far less is known about the appearance of this latter feature. Its complete destruction by Christopher Wren in the renovations of the 1690s has prevented any detailed record of the clerestory's appearance,

---

[87] Fryde, *Tyranny*, pp. 105, 207–27; Ormrod, *Edward III*, pp. 64–6.
[88] For Edward III's *coup d'état*, see Ormrod, *Edward III*, pp. 90–7; Richard Barber, *Edward III and the Triumph of England: The Battle of Crécy and the Company of the Garter* (London, 2013), pp. 59–66; Ian Mortimer, *The Perfect King: The Life of Edward III Father of the English Nation* (London, 2008), pp. 80–7.
[89] See John Nalson, *An Impartial Collection of the Great Affairs of State* (London, 1682–3). John Hawkins and John Thomas Smith were the first to identify the architectural significance of this image and discuss its implications in print (Smith, *Antiquities*, pp. 145–8).
[90] This connection was first made by Christopher Wilson in his doctoral thesis (Wilson, 'Origins', pp. 73, 126).
[91] TNA, E 101/469/12, m. 25 (Ayers & Jurkowski, vol. 1, pp. 862–3). For the story of Edward and St John the Evangelist, see Aelred, *The Life of Saint Edward, King and Confessor*, trans. Jerome Bertram (Guildford, 1990), pp. 95–8.
[92] For Henry III's use of the iconography, see Tancred Borenius, 'The Cycle of Images in the Palaces and Castles of Henry III', *Journal of the Warburg and Courtauld Institutes*, 6 (1943), 40–50, at 48–9; Paul Binski, *The Painted Chamber at Westminster* (London, 1986), p. 40; Binski, *Westminster Abbey*, pp. 49, 63–6; *CLR 1226–40*, p. 453; *CLR 1245–51*, pp. 177, 186, 192, 342; *CLR 1251–60*, pp. 57, 95; *CLR 1260–67*, p. 21.

Fig. 17. John Carter, *Section of the Remains of the East End of St Stephen's Chapel Westminster, and part of an ancient building adjoining*, view towards east, c.1791–2. Pen and ink wash on paper, 36.8 × 54.5 cm. SAL, 236E, SSC.6.2.

Fig. 18. R. W., *Frontispiece*, c.1682–3, published in John Nalson, *An Impartial Collection of the Great Affairs of State* (London, 1682–3).

and all that remained were the traces of a moulding from the window frame recorded by Frederick Mackenzie in 1844.[93]

Work began in May 1331, focusing on the east end and the new clerestory windows. Form pieces were bought for the clerestory from April 1332 onwards, but those for the east gable were only purchased from the end of September, following on from the installation of the mullions in August.[94] On 19 July 1333, 'according to ancient custom' the masons were given a special payment called *arcagium* for closing the east window arch, suggesting that this

---

[93] Mackenzie, p. vii.
[94] TNA, E 101/469/11, m. 6, 7, 8 (Ayers & Jurkowski, vol. 1, pp. 774–5, 780–1, 784–5, 796–7).

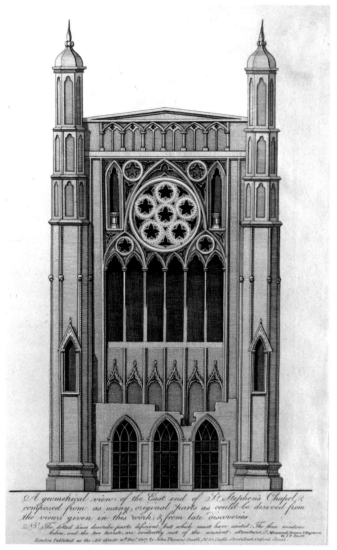

Fig. 19. John Thomas Smith, *A geometrical view of the East end of St Stephen's Chapel*, published 1807. Monochrome line engraving, 35.8 × 24.4 cm. WOA 1903.

portion of the chapel's front was nearing completion.[95] In August 1333 a reference was made to works on the two eastern towers, which continued up to the closure of works which lasted from 28 November 1334 to the week starting 23 January 1335.[96] The project had been slowing since May 1333 when the number of working masons dropped by around half,[97] a development which coincided with a significant change in circumstances for the king's finances.

---

[95] 'Item liberati predictis cementariis pro arcagio eorum die quo magna gabla perclusus [sic] fuit quod habere debent de antiquo consuetudine vj d.' (TNA, E 101/469/12, m. 23; Ayers & Jurkowski, vol. 1, pp. 852–3).
[96] TNA, E 101/469/12, m. 23–5, E 101/469/17, m. 3, E 101/470/15, m. 3–11 (Ayers & Jurkowski, vol. 1, pp. 856–65, 880–3, 898–937).
[97] For a tabulation of these figures, see Ayers & Jurkowski, vol. 1, p. 86.

Though it had been a highly successful campaign, the invasion of Scotland which Edward III conducted in 1332–3 had been more expensive than anticipated. The difficulties he encountered in financing the war are demonstrated by his attempts to generate income from extraordinary sources, such as the wool subsidies raised in January and June 1333.[98] With the outbreak of further conflict in Scotland in July 1334, the pressure on Edward III's finances only increased. Fresh taxes and a new wool subsidy were granted at the Parliament of September 1334 and from Michaelmas onwards Edward began to draw on the Bardi of Florence for regular loans.[99]

Though the muster order at Newcastle for the following November coincided closely with the closure of works at St Stephen's,[100] it was not necessarily its ultimate cause. As his negotiations with the Bardi demonstrated, the king would still have been able to extend construction through loan financing, much as his grandfather had during the 1290s. The cessation therefore illustrates a degree of caution in the monarch's architectural patronage, perhaps prompted by the example of his predecessors whose financial imprudence had resulted in near insurmountable war debts. Another key difference was the heightened threat of French intervention. After Philip VI of France granted asylum to the deposed King David II of Scotland in May 1334, Edward's attempts to negotiate a lasting peace settlement fell apart, and the consequent hardening of French attitudes made foreign invasion a real possibility.[101] Premature warnings of imminent attack were being sent to Edward III as early as the following October,[102] and under the circumstances increased financial flexibility must have been eminently desirable.

In such an uncertain political environment, it is unsurprising that the ongoing works at St Stephen's were sacrificed to political pragmatism. Tensions continued to rise throughout 1335 and 1336 in response to piracy, coastal raids, and regular invasion scares,[103] presenting the king with few opportunities for resuming construction. When the works reinitiated in March 1337, it was under the direction of a new master, William Ramsey, and lasted very briefly. For six weeks masons were employed cutting stones, but by April they were placing them in storage and abandoning the work. Consequently, the episode has all the appearance of an abortive and abruptly curtailed testing of the waters, not a cohesive campaign. The reason for this may have been the sudden escalation in financial demands arising from the securing of new alliances in France, the Empire, and the Low Countries (especially Flanders) at this time. By April 1337 Edward and his advisers knew that they needed £124,000 by the end of the year for the first instalment to his allies alone, and it seems likely that they shifted their priorities accordingly.[104]

---

[98] Ormrod, *Edward III*, pp. 147–63; Jonathan Sumption, *Hundred Years War, Volume 1: Trial by Battle* (2 vols, London, 1990), vol. 1, pp. 140–1; F. R. Barnes, 'The Taxation of Wool, 1327–1348', in George Unwin (ed.), *Finance and Trade under Edward III* (Manchester, 1918), pp. 137–77, at pp. 140–1.

[99] From 1332 to 1334 Edward III had resisted calling on the services of the Bardi. Barnes 'Taxation', p. 141; Ephraim Russell, 'The Societies of the Bardi and the Peruzzi and their Dealings with Edward III, 1327–1345', in George Unwin (ed.), *Finance and Trade under Edward III* (Manchester, 1918), pp. 93–135, at pp. 104–6.

[100] Ormrod, *Edward III*, pp. 164–5; Sumption, *Hundred Years War*, p. 141.

[101] Sumption, *Hundred Years War*, pp. 135–9; Michael A. Penman, *David II, 1329–71* (East Linton, 2004), pp. 52–3.

[102] Sumption, *Hundred Years War*, p. 138.

[103] Sumption, *Hundred Years War*, pp. 145–8, 155–8, 163–8; Ormrod, *Edward III*, pp. 173–4; Mortimer, *Perfect King*, pp. 124–6, 130–2.

[104] Edmund Boreslav Fryde, 'Financial Resources of Edward III in the Netherlands, 1337–40 (2nd Part)', *Revue Belge de Philologie et d'histoire*, 45 (1967), 1142–1216, at 1146–8; Ormrod, *Edward III*, pp. 190–4.

The burden of these alliances continued to affect the king's finances well into the early 1340s; they further deteriorated due to a growing scarcity of coinage, loans secured at crippling interest rates, and the collapse of his primary financiers, the banking houses of the Bardi and Peruzzi.[105] However, it was around this time that work on the chapel resumed. Though detailed particulars of account for this period do not survive, other records show that expenditure on the chapel restarted at some point between October 1340 and May 1341.[106] Without precise dates, it is difficult to assess what the catalyst may have been. The summer of 1340 had seen two major victories against the forces of Philip VI, the first at sea in the battle of Sluys and the second on land at the siege of Tournai.[107] With the granting of a nine-month truce and the high expectations of a new tax granted the preceding March,[108] it is certainly possible that the king's finances seemed secure enough to reinitiate the works at this time. However, when the tax fell drastically short of its initial assessment, the young king began to quarrel bitterly with his ministers, precipitating a political crisis which continued right up to the Parliament of April 1341.[109] During this period the king continued to organize tournaments and other displays of courtly splendour, and it is conceivable that the resumption of works represented a similar public show of confidence.[110] By January 1341 the king's finances had already begun to improve, providing an influx of resources which could have been used for architectural works.[111]

Works at St Stephen's apparently continued down to late 1343, with particulars of account surviving for September 1342 to December 1343.[112] During the latter period the focus shifted to the west end of the chapel, as indicated by the pentice being constructed on this site between October 1342 and January 1343, and the structural ironwork bought for the west gable the following 25 August.[113] The appearance of the great west window and the gable above it are entirely unknown, though Mackenzie noted that the western piers corresponded exactly with their counterparts at the east end.[114] Minor works were also conducted on the tabernacles which had long lain in storage, suggesting that the decorative details of the upper chapel may have been finalized at this time.[115]

The gap in records between 1343 and 1347 is more difficult to quantify.[116] One potential explanation is the absence of its master mason. By February 1344 William Ramsey had been diverted to construct the hastily conceived Round Table building at Windsor Castle, where

---

[105] Edmund Boreslav Fryde, 'The Financial Policies of the Royal Governments and Popular Resistance to them in France and England c.1270–c.1420', *Revue Belge de Philologie et d'Histoire*, 57 (1979), 824–60, at 839–40; Fryde, 'Financial Resources', p. 1159; Ormrod, *Edward III*, pp. 111–18, 179–211.
[106] TNA, E 101/470/10, E 372/189, rot. 49–49d (Ayers & Jurkowski, vol. 2, pp. 1003–11, 1113–17).
[107] Ormrod, *Edward III*, pp. 221–7.
[108] Ormrod, *Edward III*, pp. 227–8.
[109] Ormrod, *Edward III*, pp. 242–46.
[110] Juliet Vale, *Edward III and Chivalry: Chivalric Society and Its Context 1270–1350* (Woodbridge, 1982), p. 173.
[111] The resolution of the crisis of 1341 exacted several significant concessions from Parliament, including a substantial wool subsidy which proved to be one of the largest tax yields of the entire period. At the same time, the great continental alliance which Edward III had negotiated started to unravel, freeing the king from his most onerous financial obligations. Ormrod, *Edward III*, pp. 235, 239–46, 257–60; Fryde, 'Financial Policies', pp. 840–1.
[112] TNA, E 101/470/13 (Ayers & Jurkowski, vol. 2, pp. 1013–39).
[113] TNA, E 101/470/13, m. 1, 6 (Ayers & Jurkowski, vol. 2, pp. 1014–23, 1037).
[114] Mackenzie, p. 19.
[115] TNA, E 101/470/13, m. 3 (Ayers & Jurkowski, vol. 2, pp. 1022–3).
[116] Ayers & Jurkowski, vol. 2, pp. 65–6.

he headed an enormous workforce which peaked at 720 men in the first week of March.[117] The scale of this enterprise marked a drastic shift of priorities away from St Stephen's Chapel by Edward III, but on the following 27 November the works at Windsor stopped abruptly. A reason for this was recorded by the chronicler Thomas Walsingham, writing in the 1380s, who stated that: 'The weekly expenses were at first a hundred pounds, but afterwards because of news which the king received from France, this was cut back to nine pounds because he needed a great deal of money for other business.'[118]

What that news was specifically is unclear, though it is possible that the recent failure of negotiations between the English and French parties organized by the pope in Avignon had caused the king to re-evaluate the resources that would be required to bring the war to a profitable close.[119] However, this does not mean that works at St Stephen's were necessarily abandoned at this time. The inventory made in 1346 indicates that almost all of the components stored in 1332 had been expended, including those relating to the tabernacles and the wooden roof and vault made during the 1320s.[120] While it is probable that the majority of these were installed between 1340 and 1343, it is nonetheless possible that at least some were completed over the succeeding three years.

Another feature which may have been built during the 1340s was the lower chapel's lierne vault (fig. 5). While this has long been considered one of the more innovative features of the chapel's original design, there is little evidence that such a vault was installed at this early point in the building's history. The repeated renovations of St Stephen's by the Receipt in the 1320s and 1340s suggest that the lower chapel had remained unused throughout the construction process, and it apparently remained unfinished until the tiling of its floors during the 1350s and 60s.[121] A 1340s date is further suggested by the vault's keystones, which featured figurative bosses depicting the martyrdoms of Sts Stephen, John the Evangelist, Katherine, Margaret, and Lawrence.[122] Recorded by John Carter during the 1780s (see Binski, fig. 3, p. 127), the clothing of the male figures reflected a dramatic change in style within English figurative arts that occurred during the early to mid-1340s, suggesting that the sculptures at least were the product of this later period.[123] A 1340s date is further confirmed by an inventory of Exchequer records from 1346–7 which included a lost contract with Master Philip de Cherde, mason, 'about the vault of the chapel of St Stephen, Westminster'.[124] The

---

[117] Julian Munby, 'The Windsor Building Accounts', in Julian Munby, Richard Barber, and Richard Brown (eds), *Edward III's Round Table at Windsor: The House of the Round Table and the Windsor Festival of 1344* (Woodbridge, 2007), pp. 44–52 and Appendix, at pp. 46–7, 198–236.
[118] Translated in Richard Barber, 'The Round Table Feast of 1344', in Julian Munby, Richard Barber, and Richard Brown (eds), *Edward III's Round Table at Windsor: The House of the Round Table and the Windsor Festival of 1344* (Woodbridge, 2007), pp. 38–43, at p. 41.
[119] Ormrod, *Edward III*, pp. 260–1.
[120] See note 78.
[121] For the 1340s renovations of St Stephen's by the Receipt, see TNA, E 101/470/10, m. 1 (Ayers & Jurkowski, vol. 2, pp. 1004-7). For the paving of the chapel, see TNA, E 101/471/6, m. 15; E 372/197, rot. 47, m. 2, E 372/206, rot. 46, m. 1–2 (Ayers & Jurkowski, vol. 2, pp. 1184–5, 1334–5, 1358–61).
[122] For a full discussion of these, see James Hillson, 'Edward III and the Art of Authority: Military Triumph and the Decoration of St Stephen's Chapel, Westminster 1330–64', in Kate Buchanan, Lucy Dean, and M. Penman (eds), *Medieval and Early Modern Representations of Authority in Scotland and Northern Europe* (London/New York, 2016), pp. 105–23; Hillson, 'St Stephen's', 86–7.
[123] For the stylistic dating of clothing in the fourteenth century, see Stella Mary Newton, *Fashion in the Age of the Black Prince: A Study of the Years 1340–1365* (Woodbridge, 1980).
[124] 'Item indentura inter thesaurarium et camerarium de scaccario et magistrum Philippum de Cherde mason de fousura capelle Sancti Stephani Westm' remanent in parva cista duarum cerurarum' (Sir Francis Palgrave,

Fig. 20. John Carter, *Elevation of the remains of the West Front of St Stephen's Chapel, Westminster, and parts of buildings adjacent*, c.1791–2. Pen and ink wash, on paper, 37.7 × 55.3 cm. SAL, 236E, SSC.4.

Fig. 21. Frederick Mackenzie, *Vestibule of St Stephen's Chapel*, details of interior, c.1844. Ink and wash, on paper, 58.5 × 76 cm. TNA, WORK 29/767.

most probable solution is that the lower chapel vault was constructed at some point during the early to mid-1340s, built under contract at a time when the attention of William Ramsey may have been occupied by the new and demanding architectural project at Windsor.

The Crécy campaign of 1346–7 marked a dramatic shift in royal fortunes. Its cost had been approximately half that of the military campaigns of 1338–40, and its success would have greatly reduced the political and financial pressures on the king.[125] In the interim, the king's Round Table project had been quietly dropped, leaving his masons free to return to the chapel in earnest. It is perhaps no coincidence that accounts resumed on 15 October

---

The Antient Kalendars and Inventories of the Treasury of his Majesty's Exchequer (3 vols, London, 1836), vol. 1, p. 164).
[125] Resources did continue to be diverted to the siege of Calais throughout this period of construction, including masons and carpenters. Ormrod, *Edward III*, p. 297; Ralph Anthony Kaner, 'The Management of the Mobilization of English Armies: Edward I to Edward III' (Ph.D. dissertation, University of York, 1999), p. 159.

1347, just three days after the king's triumphant return to England.[126] The focal point of these works seems to have been the wooden vault, as well as the chapel's subsidiary structures. Between October 1347 and August 1348, a team of carpenters under Master William Hurley were employed to work on the *celura* or *vousura* ('vault') at St Stephen's, including cutting boards or planks and carving bosses.[127] It is therefore likely that the vault components listed as expended in the 1346 inventory largely constituted a framework for supporting a network of boards, ribs, and bosses, the latter being completed 1347–8.

At the same time, masons were recorded working on a sizeable undertaking. An identity for this project is suggested by a reference on 30 June 1347 to a purchase of Kentish ragstone for a 'new house called the galilee between the great hall and lesser [illegible] of the new chapel'.[128] As the term 'galilee' was often used to describe the porches adjoining the west end or transept of a major church,[129] it is therefore likely that this referred to the porch or vestibule located between the great and lesser halls at Westminster (figs 20, 21). Though the lower storey of this building may have been begun in the 1290s, the upper was an impressively decorated and stylistically distinct structure, its principal point of similarity with the extant works being the blind panels of Y-tracery surrounding the interior. These closely resemble the tracery of the consoles underlying the tabernacles in the upper chapel, suggesting a deliberate attempt to echo the forms of the existing building. However, the overall appearance of the upper vestibule represented a significant departure from the established formal repertoire of the building, enabling Ramsey to make his own idiosyncratic addition to the ongoing works.

Conclusions

On 6 August 1348 letters patent were issued for the foundation of St Stephen's College.[130] While there was still much left to be done before the chapel was ready for regular use, its architectural fabric had been largely completed, its form reflecting the cumulative input of multiple generations of patrons and designers. The addition of the *alura*, tabernacles, and clerestory under Thomas of Canterbury, and the new vestibule under William Ramsey, were substantial changes to the appearance and functionality of the building, and together with the potential for further alterations to the upper chapel's blind arcading and window tracery or the lower chapel vault, it is very unlikely that the chapel of the 1340s represented the undiluted intentions of its initial designers during the 1290s. From the reigns of Edward I to Edward III, design change was a constant feature of the works at St Stephen's, the form of the building being developed gradually and continuously in response to the creative input of a wide variety of patrons and craftsmen.

The pattern of cessations and resumptions during this period strongly supports the hypothesis that political events could serve as an indirect catalyst for stylistic change. By investigating the historical context of the hiatuses of 1297–1320, 1326–31, 1335–7, 1337–40,

---

[126] TNA, E 101/470/18, m. 1 (Ayers & Jurkowski, vol. 2, pp. 1060–1).
[127] TNA E 101/470/18 (Ayers & Jurkowski, vol. 2, pp. 1060–111).
[128] TNA E 101/470/18, m. 11 (Ayers & Jurkowski, vol. 2, pp. 1100–1).
[129] For examples, see the Galilee Chapel at Durham Cathedral and Galilee porch at Ely Cathedral. There was also a galilee porch on the south transept at Lincoln Cathedral.
[130] CPR 1348–50, p. 147; Biggs, 'College and Canons', pp. 23–54; Biggs, *St Stephen's College*, pp. 29–33.

and 1343–7, it has been possible to demonstrate a close relationship between architectural progress and political circumstances, identifying the instrumental roles of bankruptcy and the threat of foreign invasion in interrupting the ongoing works. Through prolonging the construction of St Stephen's, such events had the practical effect of exposing the project to over fifty years of changing historical circumstances. Patrons passed away, masters and craftsmen were replaced, and the artistic context of the building developed, exposing its designers to a continuously shifting environment which actively encouraged them to explore new directions in architectural conception. Throughout the building's complex history, its designers were never isolated from the political realities in which they operated, but rather embraced the opportunities which the situation provided to reimagine the chapel's architectural form.

To propose an iterative design process of this kind is not to denigrate the creative prowess of the chapel's designers. Though the chronology outlined above represents a significant redating of several features that are traditionally identified as the more precocious aspects of the building's design, this does not relegate St Stephen's to the position of a repository for external innovations. Instead, it acknowledges that creativity in the thirteenth and fourteenth centuries was not a close-ended process with a definitive design outcome, but an open-ended discussion which continued across multiple generations of patrons and craftsmen. Operating within an iterative system of conception enabled the designers of St Stephen's to respond creatively to the latest developments in architectural ideas, continuously revising, improving, or updating the chapel's form and function over a period of five decades. From 1292 to 1348 and beyond, the chapel was never treated as a fixed solution to a specific architectural problem, but rather as a constantly expanding work in progress, realized stage by stage through an iterative process of design.

St Stephen's College, 1348 to 1548

Elizabeth Biggs[1]

St Stephen's Chapel was a newly completed if undecorated building when Edward III issued letters patent dated 6 August 1348 founding a secular college made up of a dean, twelve canons, thirteen vicars, four clerks, and six choristers.[2] On the same day, he also founded St George's College, Windsor to be the home of the Order of the Garter.[3] Edward promised St Stephen's College an endowment worth £500 yearly with any shortfall to be made up by the Exchequer. Two hundred years later, at the dissolution of the college, its landed estate was worth about £1,000 each year.[4] St Stephen's College was to remain in possession of the chapel and its two subsidiary chapels, St Mary Undercroft and St Mary le Pew, as well as substantial landed interests in London and Westminster, and other parts of England until the sixteenth century. However, the canons could not ultimately escape the changing theology of the Edwardian Reformation, and in 1548 St Stephen's was one of the first victims of the Second Chantries Act, which abolished almost all commemorative foundations and activity, except St George's College, which remains the sole survivor of its type.[5] St Stephen's was a small, autonomous but very visible part of the Palace, situated on the busy Thames waterfront (see Ayers, fig. 1, p. 14). This essay examines St Stephen's College within its Westminster context and serves as a summary of the institutional history of this important building before it became the House of Commons in the years after 1548.

St Stephen's has been well-discussed as a building, but not as an institution. The last attempt to write the history of St Stephen's College was made by the anonymous contributor to the Victoria County History volume on London, edited by William Page in 1909.[6] Patricia Croot discusses its presence as a royal college with a significant landed estate in Westminster in the 2009 Victoria County History.[7] The college was briefly discussed as a contributor to the

---

[1] I am grateful to the late W. Mark Ormrod for his comments on an earlier draft of this essay and to the Arts and Humanities Research Council for the Ph.D. studentship, as part of the 'St Stephen's Chapel' project (2013–17), that made my research on St Stephen's College possible.
[2] *CPR 1348–50*, p. 147. Where possible I have referenced the relevant calendar instead of the manuscript for ease of reference.
[3] *CPR 1348–50*, p. 144.
[4] TNA, SC 12/6/62.
[5] Discussed in Alan Kreider, *English Chantries: The Road to Dissolution* (Cambridge, MA, 1979).
[6] 'Colleges: Royal Free Chapel of St Stephen, Westminster', in William Page (ed.), *A History of the County of London: Volume 1, London Within the Bars, Westminster and Southwark* (London, 1909), pp. 566–71.
[7] Patricia Croot, 'Landownership in Westminster', in Patricia Croot et al. (eds), *A History of the County of Middlesex: Volume 13: City of Westminster Part 1* (London, 2009), pp. 66–8.

development of the Palace of Westminster as a series of buildings and building campaigns by Howard Colvin.[8] Ralf Lützelschwab has examined its dispute with Westminster Abbey in the late fourteenth century as an episode in urban relations.[9] Others have noted in passing its canons as having a Westminster point of view, such as all those Hicks identifies as possible continuators of the Crowland Chronicle in 1483.[10] Beyond these episodes, the college has never fully been set into its Westminster context as part of the Palace, in part due to the loss of its archives in the Reformation. There are several larger overlapping historiographies to which St Stephen's contributes. The peculiarities of Westminster as an urban manor in the Middle Ages and into the early modern period have been examined by Gervase Rosser and Julia Merritt.[11] Simon Thurley's work on Whitehall and the Tudor royal palaces more generally provides important context for St Stephen's in the sixteenth century.[12]

Edward III's foundation of 1348 thus marked an entirely new departure for St Stephen's Chapel. Instead of a group of chaplains employed solely to look after the chapel in the king's absence, an ecclesiastical foundation on a slightly smaller scale than that of the secular cathedrals was to maintain the liturgy continually.[13] Like its sister college of St George's Windsor, St Stephen's would be an independent foundation, with its own endowment, lands, and religious purposes. The college was to serve as a chantry, one of the earliest such foundations in England. It was to pray for the king, for his progenitors' souls and, unusually, for his successors.[14] Edward was carefully setting up a dynastic foundation, tied to the kingship of England as well as to the history of his own family.[15] The lavishness of the scale of the foundation was matched in the liturgy that visitors and the household would see. St Stephen's was to celebrate the liturgy as at the cathedral church of Salisbury, often referred to as the Sarum Use, in an elaborated musical form, 'cum nota', and had the musical specialists in the four lay clerks to do so.[16] The statutes of St Stephen's, which would offer specifics of practice, do not survive. We have to look to the statutes of its sister college St George's Windsor, which were also written under the auspices of William Edington, Bishop of Winchester, to see what was intended liturgically at St Stephen's. Edington oversaw the statutes for St Stephen's, finally sealed in 1355.[17] A single 'clausule' from the St Stephen's statutes in a record at Westminster Abbey states that any offerings made at St Stephen's when the king was present belonged to the college.[18] This record suggests that the king was expected to be a regular participant in the college's liturgy. The liturgy was probably also specialized around royal interests and display. In the statutes of

---

[8] *HKW*, vol. 2, pp. 510–27.
[9] Ralf Lützelschwab, 'Verletzte Eitelkeiten? Westminster Abbey und St Stephen's, Westminster – Mönche und Kanoniker im Konflikt', in J. Oberste (ed.), *Pluralität – Konkurrenz – Konflikt: Religiöse Spannungen im städtischen Raum der Vormoderne* (Regensburg, 2013), pp. 81–100.
[10] Michael Hicks, 'Crowland's World: A Westminster View of the Yorkist Age', *History*, 90 (2005), 172–90.
[11] Gervase Rosser, *Medieval Westminster 1200–1540* (Oxford, 1989); J. M. Merritt, *The Social World of Early Modern Westminster: Abbey, Court, and Community 1525–1640* (Manchester, 2005). There is no full study of Westminster Palace specifically across this period.
[12] Simon Thurley, *The Royal Palaces of Tudor England: Architecture and Court Life, 1460–1547* (New Haven, 1993), and idem, *Whitehall Palace: An Architectural History of the Royal Apartments, 1240–1698* (New Haven, 1999).
[13] *CPR 1348–50*, p. 147. See John Harper's essay in this volume.
[14] *CPR 1348–50*, p. 147.
[15] See W. Mark Ormrod's essay in this volume.
[16] *CPR 1348–50*, p. 147.
[17] WAM 18431.
[18] WAM 18431.

St George's, daily prayers were to be offered for the king 'that now is' ('id nunc est'), for Edward III and his wife, Philippa of Hainault, in addition to their eldest son, the Black Prince.[19] There was also to be a daily Office of the Dead and a daily Office of the Virgin, usually known as the Lady Mass. The additional offices reflected Edward's own interests in Marian devotion, as well as the colleges' ecclesiastical purpose to remember the dead in purgatory.

Queenship and devotion to the Virgin were key parts of the new foundation. Its dedication was to God, St Stephen, and the Virgin Mary.[20] Mary was to receive special emphasis at the new foundation in the liturgy, through the veneration of relics, and in the decoration of the chapel. From the statutes of St George's, we know that there was to be a Lady Mass daily, perhaps celebrated in St Stephen's at one of its two Marian altars: in the oratory of St Mary le Pew or in the undercroft chapel. This observance reflected Edward III's own strong interest in Marian devotion, seen for example, in his 1350 foundation of the Cistercian abbey of St Mary Graces in London as thanksgiving for surviving a sea-crossing in 1347.[21] Edward also gave a cult image of the Virgin to the small oratory of St Mary le Pew, which became a fairly significant pilgrimage destination. The image received reasonably high levels of offerings. In the 1390s, five hundred marks worth of offerings in the chapel were stolen.[22] The cult received royal support throughout its existence, particularly notably from Margaret of Anjou and Elizabeth of York.[23] The third way in which Mary was emphasized at St Stephen's was in the altar-wall murals of the upper chapel, which survive in antiquarian drawings of the remnants *c.*1800 (see Binski, fig. 5a–b, p. 130).[24] In these, St George is shown presenting the king and his sons to Mary, seated with her infant son above them.[25] This impression of strong Marian and maternal resonances is reinforced by the wording of the foundation charter, in which Edward noted that the college was founded in honour of the Virgin, 'who has been a better mother' (*melior mater*); 'to me' is implied.[26] This wording hints at some of the familial relationships that might lie behind the foundation of the college, as well as the importance of the royal women in its creation.[27] Edward's own mother, Isabella of France, was commemorated in St Mary le Pew with masses from 1369, along with his wife, Philippa of Hainault, who died in that year.[28] Both women may also be seen in the altar-wall murals, on the south side of the high altar paralleling Edward and

---

[19] Windsor, St George's College Archives, XI D 20, as transcribed by J. N. Dalton.
[20] *CPR 1348–50*, p. 147.
[21] Ian Grainger and Christopher Phillpotts, *The Cistercian Abbey of St Mary Graces, East Smithfield, London* (London, 2011), p. 7.
[22] The evidence concerning this chapel is summarized in C. L. Kingsford, 'Our Lady of the Pew: The King's Oratory or Closet in the Palace of Westminster', *Archaeologia*, 68 (1917), 1–20; for the theft of offerings see *CPR 1392–96*, p. 244.
[23] 'The Household of Margaret of Anjou 1452–53 II', ed. Alec R. Myers, *Bulletin of the John Rylands Library*, 40 (1957), 423; N. H. Nicholas (ed.), *Privy Purse Expenses of Elizabeth of York etc.* (London, 1830), pp. 2–3, 22–3, 78.
[24] The fullest discussion is Emily Howe, 'Divine Kingship and Dynastic Display: The Altar Wall Murals of St Stephen's Chapel, Westminster', *Antiquaries Journal*, 81 (2001), 259–304; see also James Hillson, 'St Stephen's Chapel, Westminster: Architecture, Decoration and Politics in the Reigns of Henry III and the Three Edwards (1227–1363)' (Ph.D. dissertation, University of York, 2015), pp. 198–202.
[25] See Paul Binski's essay in this volume.
[26] *CPR 1348–50*, p. 147.
[27] Caroline Shenton, 'Philippa of Hainault's Churchings: The Politics of Motherhood at the Court of Edward III', in Richard Eales and Shaun Tyas (eds), *Family and Dynasty in Late Medieval England: Proceedings of the 1997 Harlaxton Symposium* (Donington, 2003), pp. 105–21, particularly pp. 120–1.
[28] *CPR 1367–70*, p. 325.

his sons on the north side.[29] The dynastic ambitions of the college and of Edward himself depended on his female relatives and was carried out in relation to the most maternal aspect of the Virgin. Unlike at Greyfriars, London, where a series of queens asserted their own identities as French queens, at St Stephen's they were cast as supporting characters to male and English dynastic ambitions.[30]

The location of the college was also important. As a consequence of its site at the heart of the Palace, the college was associated with the administrative and court activities that surrounded it. It provided housing for its canons, who were both priests and senior administrators throughout its existence. The first canons can be associated with the Exchequer and in particular with the treasurer, William Edington, who also oversaw the college's statutes.[31] Roger Chesterfield, canon from 1351 to his death in 1367, was an Exchequer clerk until 1356.[32] In that year, when Edington became Chancellor, Chesterfield was parachuted into Chancery as a clerk of the first form to help Edington in his efforts at reforms there.[33] For the rest of the Middle Ages, St Stephen's was to remain the home of royal administrators who used it as a base for their working lives in the Palace of Westminster. Robert Mouter was granted a canonry in the 1450s so that he would have a place to store the records of the hanaper. As keeper of the rolls, he would otherwise have had to hire a house in the vicinity for this purpose.[34] The hanaper was one of the departments of Chancery, based in the area around the great hall, just to the north of the college's own site. Having a house nearby on Canon Row would make Mouter's working arrangements much easier and make access to the records needed for tracking financial business possible for his colleagues. Other royal service was also represented at St Stephen's. A series of Deans of the Chapel Royal, including Richard Sampson, Dean of the Chapel Royal from 1520, held canonries, which would keep them close to the king and to the centre of ceremonial, particularly at Westminster Abbey.[35]

St Stephen's also had strong links with the wider English Church, particularly to bishops with connections to royal administration and politics. Canons who went on to the episcopate included William Wykeham, the powerful fourteenth-century administrator and founder of New College, Oxford.[36] William Aiscough, Henry VI's confessor and personal friend, who was murdered in 1450, was also a canon before becoming Bishop of Salisbury.[37] William Lyndwood, Bishop of St David's in the mid fifteenth century, is not known to have been a canon of St Stephen's, but the college clearly had meaning for him. When he died in 1446, he asked to be buried in St Stephen's, where he had been made a bishop in 1442, and founded a chantry of two priests who would pray for him in perpetuity. In addition, he gave six

---

[29] The identification of Isabella in the altar-wall murals has been made by James Hillson based on the crowns worn by the first two women, Hillson, 'St Stephen's Chapel, Westminster', pp. 178–9.
[30] Laura Slater, 'Defining Queenship at Greyfriars London, c.1300–58', *Gender & History*, 27:1 (April 2015), 53–76.
[31] For full details see Elizabeth Biggs, *St Stephen's College, Westminster: A Royal Chapel and English Kingship, 1348–1548* (Woodbridge, 2020), pp. 35–6.
[32] For his canonry, *CPR 1350–54*, pp. 54–5, and *CPR 1367–70*, p. 24; John Christopher Sainty, *Officers of the Exchequer* (London, 1983), p. 195.
[33] Bertie Wilkinson, *The Chancery Under Edward III* (Manchester, 1929), p. 167.
[34] *CPR 1441–46*, p. 413.
[35] Discussed in Biggs, *St Stephen's College*, pp. 120, 157–8.
[36] Wykeham became a canon in April 1363, *CPR 1360–63*, p. 323.
[37] *CPR 1436–41*, pp. 26, 183.

hundred marks towards work on the cloisters.[38] Lyndwood's major achievement was the harmonization of Roman canon law with English provincial practice in the church courts known as the *Provinciale*. It became the standard guide to the peculiarities and customs of English canon law for the rest of the Middle Ages and into the sixteenth century.[39] He left his personal manuscript of the *Provinciale* to be chained in the vestry of St Stephen's as the proof-text, and clearly expected lawyers to come to the chapel if there were disputed readings in other copies.[40] His chantry was still active at the dissolution.[41] In 1852, a body and crozier presumed to be his were found by workmen taking down the walls of St Mary Undercroft after the 1834 fire which destroyed the medieval Palace.[42]

St Stephen's was shaped by the changing dynastic fortunes of the English kings. While St Stephen's moved seemingly easily as an institution from Plantagenet to Lancastrian to Yorkist regimes, individual canons were not quite so fortunate. At moments of regime changes, many sought to have their positions at the college confirmed by the new ruler to minimize the effect of political change on their revenues and status.[43] Some, however, were unlucky. Under Richard II, Nicholas Slake had the king's confidence, building up a series of prebends, including the deaneries of St Stephen's and Wells Cathedral. He might reasonably have expected to reach the episcopate by the end of the 1390s. The Merciless Parliament, however, destroyed those hopes in 1388. Slake was among those who were censured and imprisoned by the Commons and he was removed from the deanery of the Chapel Royal.[44] Worse still was to come, however, when Richard was deposed in 1399. Under Henry IV, Slake retained his current deaneries and other preferments, but was not to be offered any new roles. In addition, he was to struggle to retain control at Wells.[45]

At the next moment of regime change in 1460, Edward IV did not immediately rush to deprive Lancastrian royal servants in favour of his own priests. By the time of the Readeption crisis of 1470–1, however, enough prebends had become vacant for Edward's men to be the dominant force within the college.[46] Ralph Makerell, Margaret of Anjou's chancellor and key Lancastrian negotiator, was rewarded with a prebend in 1470 by the restored Henry VI, and shortly afterwards Richard Neville, Earl of Warwick was given the right to present his own candidate to the next vacant prebend.[47] Canonries at St Stephen's were clearly seen as appropriate rewards for the men who had made Henry VI's return to power possible. Similarly in 1485, when Henry VII took the throne at Bosworth, he almost immediately replaced Richard III's close counsellor William Beverley with his own

---

[38] His will is printed in John Prior et al., 'Report of the Committee Appointed by the Council of the Society of Antiquaries to Investigate the Circumstances Attending the Recent Discovery of a Body in St Stephen's Chapel, Westminster', *Archaeologia*, 34 (1851–2), 418–20.
[39] Discussed in Richard H. Helmholz, 'Lyndwood, William (c.1375–1446)', *ODNB* <https://doi.org/10.1093/ref:odnb/17264> [accessed 11 Nov. 2023].
[40] Prior, 'Discovery of a Body', p. 419.
[41] There were wages of £7 8s. 8d. in 1548 for two chantry priests, TNA, SC 12/6/62.
[42] Prior, 'Discovery of a Body', p. 415.
[43] For example, at the start of Henry IV's reign, *CPR 1399–1401*, pp. 26, 137, 363.
[44] *The Chronica Maiora of Thomas Walsingham, 1376–1422*, trans. David Preest, ed. James G. Clark (Woodbridge, 2005), pp. 261–3.
[45] For a summary of his career, see Biggs, *St Stephen's College*, p. 94; for Wells see TNA, KB 9/187/43.
[46] In the calendars of patent rolls covering Edward IV's first reign, there were eight direct grants of prebends and four grants of the right to present to the next vacant canonry, although there is no evidence of whether these rights were exercised, *CPR 1461–67*, pp. 6, 19, 78, 322, 357, 469, 539, 543; *CPR 1467–77*, pp. 106, 111, 180.
[47] *CPR 1467–77*, pp. 235, 244.

chaplain and almoner, Christopher Urswick, who had been in exile with him.[48] We should not, however, push this political association too far. Thomas Barowe began his career in Chancery under Richard III in 1483, and seemingly moved smoothly into Henry VII's service with no appreciable ill effects. Certainly, he remained active in administration and at St Stephen's until his death.[49] When he died in 1494, he left gifts to James Tyrell and others who had strongly supported Richard III, which suggests that he remained committed to Yorkist friends.[50] St Stephen's was marked by the political fortunes that surrounded it although not controlled by them.

By the end of Edward III's reign the college's statutes had been completed and the college was fully staffed and operational. Yet the foundation was not fully complete, as a result of an emerging dispute over rights and privileges within Westminster. In 1349 Pope Clement VI had granted St Stephen's the rights of a royal free college.[51] The royal free colleges in the twelfth century had fought to be seen as independent from the diocesan authorities, as well as to function as exempt deaneries outside the usual structures of the Church.[52] The deans of the free chapels exercised their rights to baptize, marry, and bury those who lived within their peculiar, as well as to be sued only in the king's Court of Chancery rather than in the ecclesiastical courts. The first deans of St Stephen's seem to have interpreted the papal mandate as applying to the whole of the Palace of Westminster as if it were a deanery. In particular, William Sleaford, the fourth dean, proved wills and buried royal servants.[53] However, these rights infringed on the cherished privileges of Westminster Abbey to have its own exempt deanery, granted in 1222, within the area in which the Palace stood.[54] The Abbey, as the older institution, believed that its privileges and rights took precedence, which would mean that St Stephen's was subject to the Abbey's jurisdiction and subordinate to the parish church of St Margaret's. If so, St Stephen's would need permission to hold baptisms, weddings, and funerals. Any financial payments made to the college would need to be partially handed over to the Abbey. In 1375 Westminster Abbey opened a case against St Stephen's in front of papal judges delegate in England.[55] Edward III promptly stopped that case through a writ of *prohibitio*, pointing to the right of St Stephen's to be sued only before the Chancery.[56] On Edward's death in 1377, the Abbey tried again, launching a dispute that was to last for twenty years and be fought in a variety of courts, both royal and papal, until an agreement was reached in 1394.[57] The terms of that agreement left the Dean of St Stephen's with jurisdiction over the college's own members only and able to carry out baptisms, marriages, and funerals for the royal family. This settlement was never seriously challenged again after 1394.

---

[48] *CPR 1485–94*, p. 24.
[49] Jonathan Hughes, 'Barowe, Thomas (d.1499)', *ODNB* <https://doi.org/10.1093/ref:odnb/17264> [accessed 11 Nov. 2023].
[50] TNA, PROB 11/11/672.
[51] *Petitions to the Pope 1342–1419*, ed. W. H. Bliss (London, 1896), p. 188.
[52] J. H. Denton, *English Royal Free Chapels 1100–1300: A Constitutional Study* (Manchester, 1970), p. 92.
[53] WAM 18453.
[54] Lützelschwab, 'Verletze Eitelkeiten?', pp. 85–6.
[55] WAM Muniment Book 12, fol. 34v.
[56] WAM Muniment Book 12, fols 34v–35r.
[57] For a summary see Biggs, *St Stephen's College*, pp. 56–8; TNA C66/341, mm. 24–6; published in Ayers & Jurkowski, vol. 2, appendix 3, pp. 1409–20.

The other area left seemingly unresolved at Edward III's death was the designation of space allocated to the college within the Palace of Westminster. In the foundation charter of 1348 the college had been given the inn of the Earl of Kent, on the north side of New Palace Yard.[58] The canons also seem to have been using the area between the great hall, the chapel, and the river. The first cloister belonging to the college appears to have been on the site of the subsequent cloisters, and thus would have been in this part of the Palace precinct. The king's workmen began to build a cloister for the college in October 1355, and this work seems to have prompted concerns about whether St Stephen's was entitled to the relevant space.[59] In 1356 the college petitioned to have the situation clarified and was formally licensed to control the area it had already been using; the grant was backdated to 1355 to ensure that the cloister was demonstrably the college's own.[60] The grant says that the land was given to be used for a cloister and other necessary houses ('maisons busoigenables et necessa[i]r[e]s').[61] The canons were evidently living in houses on this site, close to the chapel and their work in the Palace.

By the 1380s, the housing had become inadequate, probably due to changing expectations of collegiate housing. In the fourteenth century at St George's Windsor, each canon had shared his house with his vicar, who was seen very much as his deputy. In 1409, however, a new cloister for the vicars was built and they were given their own separate houses and communal spaces.[62] At Westminster, this process of enhancing the position of the vicars is less clear but also seems to have happened slightly earlier: by 1394 the canons were certainly living in new houses along the river on Canon Row, to the north of New Palace Yard, while the vicars had their houses on the eastern range of the cloister after 1384/5.[63] The site of the Canon Row houses has been reconstructed from the 1394 composition by John Crook.[64] In 1396, the status of the vicars was further enhanced by the creation of a sub-college for them, with riverfront gardens and a financial endowment as well as a common vicar's hall in the north range of the cloister.[65]

In addition, St Stephen's continued to be used by the king and his advisers. Every English king, with the sole exceptions of Edward V and Richard III, acknowledged St Stephen's College and its place within their Palace by endowing yearly memorial services for themselves.[66] Even Henry VIII added himself to the chapel's round of services, drawing on the resources of the Court of Augmentations to pay for his obit.[67] The Brut Chronicle called St Stephen's 'the king's chief chapel in his palace' in 1445 when it was used as the venue for the trial of the king's aunt, Eleanor Cobham, Duchess of Gloucester, for treasonable

---

[58] CPR 1348–50, p. 147.
[59] TNA, E 101/471/16 m. 2; published in Ayers & Jurkowski, vol. 2, no. 46.
[60] The petition is TNA, SC 8/247/12304; the grant is calendared in CChR 1341–1417, pp. 133–4.
[61] TNA, SC 8/247/12304.
[62] Tim Tatton-Brown, 'The Constructional Sequence and Topography of the Chapel and College Buildings', in Colin Richmond and Eileen Scarff (eds), *St George's Chapel, Windsor in the Late Middle Ages* (Windsor, 2001), p. 28.
[63] TNA E 364/24 rot. C m. 1; translated in Ayers & Jurkowski, vol. 2, no. 60.
[64] Ayers & Jurkowski, vol. 2, Appendix 4 (John Crook, 'Reconstructing the Plan of St Stephen's College, Westminster in the late Fourteenth Century'), pp. 1421–6.
[65] CPR 1392–96, p. 669; payments for a vicars' hall were made in 1389–94, TNA E 101/473/6 m. 1, printed in Ayers & Jurkowski, vol. 2, no. 58.
[66] BL, Cotton MS Faustina B VIII, fols 2r–7r.
[67] TNA, SC 12/6/62.

necromancy.[68] The use of the chapel allowed Henry VI and his council to circumvent many of the jurisdictional issues of trying the wife of a peer for this crime. Necromancy was tried in the church courts, while treason was the domain of the royal courts. St Stephen's was both royal and ecclesiastical. It was thus a suitable venue for a case that also had political and dynastic implications. Bishops who were also members of the king's council were the judges, further blurring the lines between ecclesiastical and secular jurisdiction. The citation of Eleanor by the Archbishop of Canterbury was recorded in the patent rolls, for example.[69] It did not say whether the archbishop was sitting as the head of the English church courts or whether he was acting as a deputized member of the privy council in the royal courts. Eleanor was made to do public penance and spend the rest of her life under house arrest.

The chapel seems to have been used for at least some liturgical services by the court when at Westminster. In 1415 Henry V was present on 2 February as Archbishop Chichele celebrated Candlemas in St Stephen's Chapel. Chichele was then called upon to adjudicate a dispute between the college and Westminster Abbey over the high level of offerings given. He solved the problem by giving the money to the vicars of St Stephen's, not to the common fund.[70] In 1483 Edward IV died unexpectedly at Westminster. His body lay in state in St Stephen's until funeral arrangements were made and he could be transported ceremoniously to Windsor, where he had requested burial in his refounded St George's Chapel.[71] The records are unclear, but it is possible that earlier in 1483 Edward had used St Mary Undercroft as the venue for his younger son's marriage to Anne Mowbray. As both Richard, Duke of York, and Anne were under ten years old, the chapel may have been chosen as a quieter venue than the usual royal wedding sites of Westminster Abbey or St Paul's Cathedral.[72] In 1501, when Henry VII's eldest son, Prince Arthur, married Katherine of Aragon, the canons of St Stephen's found themselves hosting the Spanish ambassadors, but did not have their chapels used for any of the ceremonies.[73] St Stephen's was a royal chapel and college, and thus available for use for services and sacraments for late medieval kings but also as a resource in Westminster that could be turned to practical use.

The visibility of royalty at Westminster depended on access by spectators, whether in public processions, major events such as tournaments, or in the more restricted surroundings of the Palace itself. St Stephen's was always intended to be at least somewhat open to visitors to Westminster. The cult statue of the Virgin Mary in the chapel of the Pew has been mentioned above. Pilgrim access to that chapel as well as St Stephen's more generally through Westminster Hall was granted in 1356, formalizing the college's openness to visitors.[74] Additionally, in the 1350s and 1360s Edward III obtained for the college two

---

[68] *The Brut or the Chronicle of England*, ed. Frederick W. D. Brie, Early English Text Society, 131 and 136 (2 vols, London, 1906–8), vol. 1, p. 478; Ralph A. Griffiths, 'The Trial of Eleanor Cobham', in idem, *King and Country: England and Wales in the Fifteenth Century* (London, 1991), pp. 233–52; M. B. Nolan, 'Necromancy, Treason, Semiosis, Spectacle: The Trial of Eleanor Cobham, Duchess of Gloucester', *Proteus*, 13:1 (1996), 7–11.
[69] *CPR 1436–41*, p. 559.
[70] E. F. Jacob (ed.), *The Register of Henry Chichele, Archbishop of Canterbury, 1414–1443*, Canterbury and York Society, 42, 45, 46, 47 (4 vols, Oxford, 1937–47), vol. 4, pp. 111–12.
[71] James Gairdner (ed.), *Letters and Papers Illustrative of the Reigns of Richard III and Henry VII* (2 vols, London, 1861–3), vol. 1, p. 4.
[72] Rosemary Horrox, 'Richard, duke of York and duke of Norfolk (1473–1483)', *ODNB* <https://doi.org/10.1093/ref:odnb/23504> [accessed 11 Nov. 2023].
[73] BL, Royal MS 14 B XXXIX, fol. 5.
[74] TNA, SC 8/247/12304.

sets of indulgences.[75] The first set was to be specified by the Archbishop of Canterbury or the Bishop of Winchester. The feasts and durations of those indulgences are not known. The second set, however, allowed seven years of remission of sins to those who visited at the principal feast days of Christmas, Easter, Pentecost, Corpus Christi, Sts Peter and Paul, and St Stephen, thus encouraging those who visited the Palace to also attend services in the chapel. In addition, in 1476 Anthony, Lord Rivers obtained the major indulgence of Scala Coeli for St Mary le Pew, which gave significant remission of sins to those who had masses said in the chapel, as if they had sent for masses to be said in Rome at the church of Santa Maria Scala Coeli.[76] London and Westminster wills from the sixteenth century show individuals taking up the Scala Coeli indulgence at St Stephen's, before it was moved to a chapel also called St Mary le Pew within Westminster Abbey, possibly at the instigation of Lady Margaret Beaufort around 1504.[77]

There is also direct evidence that visitors to the Palace made use of St Stephen's Chapel as a place of worship. During the early years of the sixteenth century, Sir John Selake complained to the Chancellor, Cardinal Wolsey, that he had been forced out of a service in St Stephen's by armed men.[78] He had gone to hear mass before attending a case in Westminster Hall, but was taken to answer to Sir Giles Capel in relation to another case. Visitors might not only visit for services, but also for much more worldly reasons. In 1520, a group of men from Oxfordshire with no apparent connection to the college agreed to a land transaction in Horspath where the yearly rent was to be paid over the font in the lower chapel of St Stephen's, that is, St Mary Undercroft.[79] This agreement implies that the lower chapel was easily accessible to members of the general public.

Henry VIII's reign marked multiple new departures for Westminster and for St Stephen's. It brought two new palaces to the manor, a sea-change in religion, and also a new cloister for the college (fig. 1).[80] The conventional view, espoused by David Starkey among others, is that a fire in the winter of 1512/13 led Henry VIII to abandon Westminster in favour of Greenwich, Bridewell, and Richmond in the London area, and then to create first the new palace and hunting park of St James' in Westminster from 1520 and then the great new palace of Whitehall after 1529.[81] The idea of abandonment is, however, something of an exaggeration, as suggested by the building of a new cloister for St Stephen's College. The fire, while clearly damaging the Palace, was not nearly as devastating as that of 1298, which had not stopped the Palace from functioning.[82] Westminster was far more than simply the king's house. By the early sixteenth century it had been the seat of government for over two centuries. The courts and other administrative offices based in the Palace continued

---

[75] In 1349, W. H. Bliss (ed.), *Petitions to the Pope 1342–1419* (London, 1896), p. 188; confirmed in 1354, W. H. Bliss et al. (eds), *Calendar of Papal Registers Relating to Britain and Ireland 1198–1494* (14 vols, London, 1893–1960), vol. 3, p. 538; and confirmed again in 1361, *Petitions to the Pope*, p. 372.
[76] *Calendar of Papal Registers*, vol. 13, p. 498.
[77] Nigel Morgan, 'The Scala Coeli Indulgence and the Royal Chapels', in Benjamin Thompson (ed.), *The Reign of Henry VII* (Stamford, 1995), pp. 93–101.
[78] TNA, C 1/442/7 and C 1/442/8.
[79] TNA, E 40/3184.
[80] John Stow, *A Survey of the City of London Reprinted from the Text of 1603*, ed. C. L. Kingsford (Oxford, 1908), p. 121.
[81] David Starkey, 'Court, Council, and Nobility in Tudor England', in Ronald G. Asch and Adolf M. Birke (eds), *Princes, Patronage, and the Nobility: The Court at the Beginning of the Modern Age* (Oxford, 1991), p. 180.
[82] Stow, *Survey*, p. 173.

Fig. 1. Anthony Salvin, *Topographical view of the Cloisters looking south west after the fire of 1834 with the oratory in the foreground and the ruins of St Stephen's Chapel in the background*, inscribed 'Back of Speaker's House', 1834. Pencil and brown wash, on paper, 28.9 × 21.4 cm. PA, GB-061, SAL/1.

to be operational. Indeed, in the 1530s the new courts set up to deal with the Reformation, First Fruits and Tenths, and Augmentations, were given space within the old Palace.[83] The Parliament of 1515 was held at Westminster, although it was begun with high ceremony at Blackfriars.[84] More importantly, there was no particular shift in Henry VIII's behaviour. Before 1512, he had only come to Westminster for very public and ceremonial occasions, and he continued to do so after 1513: for example, he was present at a set of tournaments in 1515 in New Palace Yard.[85] The new cloister, two-storied, as opposed to the earlier single-storey cloister, may in part have been intended to facilitate access through the Palace to the Court of Star Chamber, just to the north. It was also to prove useful to Henry himself. In 1533 he had a gallery cut through from the new upper walkway into Westminster Hall so that he could watch the coronation feast of his second wife, Anne Boleyn.[86] As part of that feast, the cloister walkways were furnished sumptuously with statues and wall hangings. The Palace was, then, still very much in use after 1512/13.

The surviving cloisters are something of an enigma. There are no extant building accounts relating to their construction, despite their presence within the king's Palace. Unhappily, the royal building accounts for Westminster before 1530 do not survive. The Elizabethan antiquary John Stow tells us that the cloister was built at the charge of John Chamber, the last dean, at a cost of 11,000 marks.[87] The first depictions of it come from the 1590s in the context of its post-Reformation reuse.[88] Chamber certainly oversaw its completion, as he was dean of the college from 1514, but it is less certain that it was begun at his instigation.[89] The beginning of construction is completely unknown. The cloister was completed at some point in the period between 1515 and 1527, judging from the surviving roof bosses in the lower walkways. One boss shows the arms and cardinal's hat of Thomas Wolsey. Wolsey, who had been Dean of St Stephen's from 1512 to 1514, became cardinal-legate of England in 1515 and so provides us with our starting point for the building's completion (fig. 2).[90] The end point is given by the presence of the castle of Castile and the pomegranate badge of Katherine of Aragon (fig. 3). By 1527 the divorce case had begun and the representation of Katherine's badges would have been exceedingly impolitic within a royal palace, particularly in a space that the king himself used. Her pomegranate and castle badges are the most prevalent imagery in the surviving fabric of the lower cloister.[91] The cloister's design has striking parallels with what Wolsey intended to build at his new foundation of Cardinal College, Oxford, later Christ Church, including the pattern of the springers.[92] The presence

---

[83] W. C. Richardson, *History of the Court of Augmentations 1536–1554* (Baton Rouge, 1961), pp. 46–7.
[84] *L & P Henry VIII*, 1513–14, no. 2590.
[85] *L & P Henry VIII*, 1517–18, no. (1.10) at p. 1444 and no. (3.9) at p. 1454.
[86] H. Ellis (ed.), *Hall's Chronicle, Containing the History of England during the Reign of Henry IV and the Succeeding Monarchs to the End of the Reign of Henry VIII* (London, 1809), pp. 804–5; payments for the work are in Oxford, Bodleian Library, MS Rawlinson D 775, fols 175r, 190r, and 192v.
[87] Stow, *Survey*, p. 121.
[88] Hatfield House, Cecil Papers, 24/61 (112) and 24/62 (113)); Figures 1 and 2.
[89] *L & P Henry VIII*, 1513–14, no. 3499 (54).
[90] S. M. Jack, 'Wolsey, Thomas (1470/71–1530)', *ODNB* <https://doi.org/10.1093/ref:odnb/29854> [accessed 11 Nov. 2023].
[91] Elizabeth Biggs, '"A Cloister of Curious Workmanship": The Patronage of St Stephen's Cloisters within the Palace of Westminster in the Early Sixteenth Century', *Historical Research*, 95:260 (2022), 309–33.
[92] John Newman, 'Cardinal Wolsey's Collegiate Foundations', in S. J. Gunn and P. G. Lindley (eds), *Cardinal Wolsey: Church, State and Art* (Cambridge, 1991), p. 111.

Fig. 2. Arms of Thomas Wolsey, as Cardinal Archbishop of York, boss in the fourth bay of the east walk, St Stephen's cloisters, Westminster. RCHME survey of the Palace, c.1925.

Fig. 3. Badge of Katherine of Aragon, showing the castle of Castile, boss in the second bay of the north walk, St Stephen's cloisters, Westminster. RCHME survey of the Palace, c.1925.

of Thomas Larke among the college's canons, from 1511, is suggestive.[93] Larke oversaw many of Wolsey's building projects, including the royal delegated efforts at Windsor and Cardinal College. In addition, from 1517 onwards, he oversaw the royal works at Bridewell Palace. If we see the rebuilding of the cloister as a collaboration between the king and the college to renew an important thoroughfare within the Palace in the 1510s, then Larke would be an ideal appointment to oversee the work. He knew the masons and the patrons as well as being one of the college's own chapter, and so was able to liaise between all parties. Even if the cloister was started slightly later, under Chamber, Larke's highly experienced presence in the stalls would have probably been drawn on to help oversee the building work.

The college on the eve of the Reformation was still part of a vital and well-respected tradition. The cloister was complete and the college was at full strength. The imperatives of Henry VIII's divorce brought new theological challenges that the canons were not necessarily able to meet. It is notable that Stephen Gardiner did not canvass any of the canons over the divorce case in 1529.[94] Instead, the canons were men such as Pietro Carmeliano and Andreas Ammonias, the king's secretaries, whom he had inherited from his father.[95] These men were cautious intellectuals sympathetic to Erasmus's call for reform within the Church and had been trained usually in law rather than theology. A Dr Benet, probably William Benet, was a canon in 1528, when he is mentioned in a fellow canon's will. A William Benet was among those who supported Katherine of Aragon through the doctrinal and personal difficulties of the divorce case in the late 1520s until the 1533 break with Rome.[96] Change at St Stephen's came in 1530 with the appointment of Edward Lee as a canon.[97] Lee would quickly be promoted for his work on the divorce case and by 1531 was the reforming Archbishop of York. After this point, the men appointed as canons of St Stephen's were often engaged on the business of the Reformation; indeed the canonries often became a stepping stone for men who would go on to lead the English Church as bishops. These men reflected the eclecticism of the Henrician Reformation, particularly since the king continued to exercise his right to present to the prebends. Nicholas Heath, at that time very much an evangelical, and Thomas Thirlby, one of the more conservative bishops, were both canons at the same time.[98] Others seem to have deliberately stayed away from religious controversy entirely. Thomas Day was called a king's chaplain on his appointment to the college in 1543, and lived into Elizabeth's reign, but seems to have left no trace of his theological leanings.[99]

Divergent viewpoints among the canons did not always stop the college from acting in response to the demands of the Reformation. Even evangelical canons allowed the image in St Mary le Pew to remain until a 1545 order from the privy council to remove it, nine years

---

[93] Larke's work is discussed in *HKW*, vol. 3, p. 189; for Bridewell see *HKW*, vol. 3, p. 15; he was appointed canon in 1511, *L & P Henry VIII, 1509–13*, no. 960 (50).
[94] *L & P Henry VIII, 1531–32*, no. 6 (18).
[95] Carmeliano was appointed in 1493 in *CPR 1485–94*, p. 412; for his career see J. B. Trapp, 'Carmeliano, Pietro (c.1451–1527)', *ODNB* <https://doi.org/10.1093/ref:odnb/4699> [accessed 11 Nov. 2023]; Ammonias had come to the college in 1512, *L & P Henry VIII, 1509–13*, no. 1083 (1); for his career see Trapp, 'Ammonius, Andreas [Andrea della Rena] (*bap.* 1476, *d.*1517)', *ODNB* <https://doi.org/10.1093/ref:odnb/447> [accessed 11 Nov. 2023].
[96] TNA, PROB 11/27, D. F. Logan, 'Benet, William (*d.*1533)', *ODNB* <https://doi.org/10.1093/ref:odnb/2090> [accessed 11 Nov. 2023].
[97] *L & P Henry VIII, 1529–30*, no. 6506, see also C. Cross, 'Lee, Edward (1481/2–1544)', *ODNB* <https://doi.org/10.1093/ref:odnb/16278> [accessed 11 Nov. 2023].
[98] Heath was a canon in 1539 and Thirlby was a canon from 1537 to *c.*1540.
[99] A. B. Emden, *A Biographical Register of the University of Oxford, 1501–1540* (Oxford, 1974), p. 165.

after the 1536 Injunctions had abolished all such images.[100] In other ways the college fell into line. Commemoration of and prayers for the dead were increasingly de-emphasized within the wider Church.[101] At some point between 1542 and 1547 John Chamber founded a set of alms rooms in St Stephen's Alley, which for the first time gave the college a purpose within the emerging religious priorities of the Reformation.[102] From then onwards St Stephen's had a charitable mission, caring for eight people in need. The rooms survived the college and were still being used as a reward for retired soldiers and royal servants until at least the early eighteenth century.[103] The educational side of St Stephen's can be seen in the provision of weekly preaching in 1547. Thomas Thirlby ordered that priests in his diocese should attend the weekly sermon at St Stephen's as part of their ongoing pastoral education, unless they were already preaching themselves at that time.[104] The presence of this sermon at St Stephen's is a reflection of the ongoing presence in the choir stalls of the king's chaplains. Thirlby was himself among the conservatives in Henry VIII's reign and so may have relied on his former colleagues to help maintain religious moderation and conservatism within his diocese.[105] These two efforts at making St Stephen's fit into the wider trends of the period were not successful. The alms rooms did not obscure the fundamental purpose of St Stephen's, to pray for the royal dead including, in 1547 and 1548, Henry VIII himself. Edward VI and his advisers valued other things, including the college's wealth, rather than its continued existence.

The last days of the college must have come as something of a surprise to the canons and vicars. On 24 December 1547 the Second Chantries Act passed through the House of Lords, and received royal assent.[106] This act was fundamentally to reshape the English Church by dissolving all provision for prayers for the dead. The Second Chantries Act mandated that by Easter 1548 commissioners were to account for all chantries and colleges within each shire, and the wealth of the chantries was to be administered by the Court of Augmentations in the king's name from Easter onwards. In the chantry returns for Middlesex, St Stephen's is listed as the 'late college', which suggests that the college may have served as a test case for the commissioners.[107] Its wealth was considerable and its land holdings very dispersed, and so if the court could deal with St Stephen's, it could have confidence that it would be able to manage the wealth of the chantries more generally. At some point between 25 December 1547 and 27 March 1548, the date of Easter that year, the dean and canons of St Stephen's formally surrendered their property to the king's commissioners and received pensions in return.[108] Some, like John Chamber, remained in Westminster and did not seek other positions. Others sought careers elsewhere in the Church, but all had to choose whether

---

[100] *L & P Henry VIII, 1545 Part 2*, no. 645.
[101] Peter Marshall, *Beliefs and the Dead in Reformation England* (Oxford, 2002), p. 47.
[102] *L & P Henry VIII, 1542*, no. 71 (35); and TNA, SP 46/128, fol. 208.
[103] The last trace I have found for them is in 1708, in TNA, PC 1/2/79.
[104] W. H. Frere and W. McClure Kennedy (eds), *Visitation Articles and Injunctions of the Period of the Reformation: Vol. 2 1536–1558* (London, 1910), pp. 131–4.
[105] See C. S. Knighton, 'Thirlby, Thomas (c.1500–1570)', *ODNB* <https://doi.org/10.1093/ref:odnb/27184> [accessed 11 Nov. 2023].
[106] 1 Edw. 6 c.14; *Journals of the House of Lords*, vol. 1 (1509–1577), pp. 312–13.
[107] C. J. Kitching (ed.), *London and Middlesex Chantry Certificate 1548*, London Record Society, 16 (Woodbridge, 1980), pp. 79–80.
[108] The surviving pensions list is from 1554, BL, Add. MS 8102.

to accept the changing doctrines of the English Church or be deprived of their benefices or posts. The lands and wealth of St Stephen's enriched men such as Anthony Denny and Walter Mildmay, while the college's buildings were repurposed as the House of Commons and as administrative buildings.[109]

St Stephen's College was for two hundred years an ecclesiastical institution at the heart of the most important royal palace in England. Once its position in relation to Westminster Abbey had been settled in the late fourteenth century, the chapel did not serve any immediate parochial function for the Palace community, but it still offered services to that community, not least in providing homes for senior administrators who needed to be based close to their places of work. It had inherited an older role as a palace chapel in an extremely visible part of the Westminster Palace complex. As such it took part in the wide variety of activities that surrounded the king and his court, including liturgy and public worship, when they were present in the Palace. The importance of Westminster stems from its constant administrative and legal usage, even when the court itself was absent; in turn this lent the institutional presence of the college added significance. Beyond the king's personal presence, St Stephen's projected an image of royal power and piety even in his absence. Visitors were impressed by the college's liturgy and its visual splendour. Yet, the college also adapted to the changing usages and personnel of Westminster, particularly as the composition of the administrative personnel that surrounded it changed and once Henry VIII chose not to use Westminster as a residence, but only as a place of highly visible royal ceremonial. Each generation of canons and other staff had to make the college their own, but they also continued to value and to add to its purpose as a commemorative foundation for the Kings of England. The Reformation started a new period for St Stephen's Chapel, but did not necessitate its destruction. The new usages of the college's buildings from 1548 continued to place the chapel, if not the college, at the heart of Westminster and of governance.

---

[109] Discussed in Biggs, *St Stephen's College*, pp. 206–9. See also the essays by J. P. D. Cooper and Elizabeth Hallam Smith in this volume.

The Imagery of St Stephen's Chapel: An Overview

Paul Binski

So little of the decoration of St Stephen's Chapel survives that it is now hard to appreciate its standing as one of England's most lavishly adorned medieval buildings. In essence the chapel was an instance of the late-medieval intensification of effects in moderately sized but complex and artistically accomplished chapel spaces which survive in Rome (the Sancta Sanctorum), Paris, Karlštejn (Bohemia), Padua, Ely, and elsewhere. Its programme evolved between the 1290s and 1350s. An initial impetus was provided by its precursor in the Palace, adorned for Henry III with images of the twelve Apostles, a Last Judgement, an image of the Virgin Mary, and Bible scenes drawn from the Book of Daniel. In turn, these themes may have been prompted by the greatest palace chapel erected in the thirteenth century, the Sainte-Chapelle in Paris built for Louis IX in the 1240s, to which Edward I's new project is often deemed to have been a response, and which Henry also imitated at Westminster Abbey. Like its Westminster successor, that in Paris had two storeys and prioritized stained glass, sculpture, and 'micro-architecture'. It was witnessed by Henry III in 1254 and Edward II in 1313.

Earliest Evidence

In 1292 the new St Stephen's was begun in honour of the Virgin Mary and St Stephen, and in 1348 the letters patent for its refoundation as a college repeated this dedication, which will have been that of its high altar, and specified a staff of twelve canons.[1] From this dedication the programme was unfolded by its designers. The new building was dominated by traceried windows and stained glass, the design establishing a texture of small-scale complexity eventually enhanced by the painted images (see Ayers, fig. 5, p. 20). Planned with five bays, the divisions between its windows and at its interior corners allowed twelve prominent canopied image niches which were probably filled with statues of the Apostles,

---

[1] Ayers & Jurkowski, vol. 1, p. 96; William Dugdale, *Monasticon Anglicanum* (6 vols, London, 1817–30), vol. 6, pp. 1349–50; in addition see Ernest William Tristram, *English Wall Painting of the Fourteenth Century* (London, 1955), pp. 48–54, 206–19; Paul Binski, *Westminster Abbey and the Plantagenets: Kingship and the Representation of Power 1200–1400* (New Haven/London, 1995), pp. 182–5; Emily Howe, 'Divine Kingship and Dynastic Display: The Altar Wall Murals of St Stephen's Chapel, Westminster', *Antiquaries Journal*, 81 (2001), 258–303.

Fig. 1. Sainte-Chapelle, Paris, north wall arcade, c.1248.

as in the Sainte-Chapelle, also refounded in 1318 with twelve canons (fig. 1).[2] The Apostles were sited high between the windows below where, ordinarily, the cones of a vault would be found, a vault having been omitted in the design of the elevation. The vertical spaces between the window spandrels were instead occupied by tall, possibly two-tier, canopies.[3] As a result the Apostles were placed about 20 ft (*c.*6 m) from the pavement, much higher than in the Sainte-Chapelle and more like those in the choir of Cologne Cathedral. Images in a similar position were to be found in the chapel of the Bishop of Ely in Holborn, in use by *c.*1286 (fig. 2).

Whatever else Edward I may have required in the upper chapel in 1292, the next evidence for figurative work is the carved bosses of the lierne vault in the lower chapel, recorded by John Carter, *c.*1786 (fig. 3). As reproduced in the nineteenth-century versions, which survive today, they show the martyrdoms of Sts Stephen, John, Katherine, Margaret, and Lawrence, and seem to have dated to no earlier than about 1330. This succinct and probably original focus on locally celebrated martyrs resembles the fuller scheme of martyrdoms of saints painted in the medallions of the upper chapel of the Sainte-Chapelle.[4] Since St Stephen's lower chapel, like the Sainte-Chapelle's, was dedicated to the Virgin Mary, it was appropriate

---

[2] The tabernacles did not house angels, as suggested in *HKW*, vol. 1, p. 517. Stubs of the Apostle figures are visible in an image of the Long Parliament in session in 1640 (Duchy of Cornwall Records).
[3] *HKW*, vol. 1, p. 521 n. 5.
[4] For the bosses, see the essay by James Hillson in this volume; for the Sainte-Chapelle, see Robert Branner, 'The Painted Medallions in the Sainte-Chapelle in Paris', *Transactions of the American Philosophical Society*, 58:2 (1968), 1–42.

The Imagery of St Stephen's Chapel: An Overview

Fig. 2. Chapel of the Bishops of Ely, Holborn, London, c.1286.

Fig. 3. John Carter, *Six Bosses on the Vaulting of the Undercroft and Cloisters of St Stephen's Chapel*, c.1786, published in John Carter, *Specimens of the Ancient Sculpture and Painting, now remaining in this Kingdom* (London, 1780, 1787), facing p. 26.

that a sculpted image of her, inlaid with glass gems, was supplied for it in 1355.[5] Images of two important Westminster saints, John the Evangelist and Edward the Confessor, were provided in 1333 for two niches framing the east window of the chapel (see Hillson, fig. 19, p. 101).[6]

Edward III's Chapel

By the 1340s St Stephen's was thematically in line with the Sainte-Chapelle. But Edward III was gradually to take its art in a new direction. In 1348 the chapel became a collegiate church.[7] The original plan to seat the king and his family with the *capella regis* in the upper chapel was thus formalized with new choir stalls and a pulpitum screen marking off the east end as a joint court and collegiate enclosure. St George's heraldry and image displaced that of St Edward the Confessor, to suit Edward III's thinking. Edward also laid greater stress on painted imagery than can have been intended in 1292.

The High Altar and East Wall

This was true of the high altar of the upper chapel. As planned in 1292, the east wall had a large window set low over the high altar (see Hillson, fig. 17, p. 99), permitting a low retable but allowing no space for the tall sculpted or painted altarpiece developing in Europe at this time, as on the high altar of St Paul's Cathedral. In fact there is no record of Edward III's altarpiece, which would have corresponded to the altar table approximately 12 ft (c.1.8 m) wide, larger than that of the nearby Abbey and in keeping with the trend in the fourteenth century to wider altars. Its marble altar slab was supplied in 1350.[8] Its dedication shows that the high altar could have included St Stephen with the Virgin Mary and St Lawrence, also a deacon, as standing sculpted images. This choice would have corresponded to the dedications of the chapels along the *alura* or passage to the Painted Chamber with its chapel of St Lawrence, including the chapel of St Mary le Pew. A large image of Stephen, apparently very finely finished with enamelled detail and so possibly for the main altar, was being made from 1352.[9] The fact that fine images were being supplied for both the lower and upper chapels suggests that before the 1350s neither was in operation liturgically.

Our uncertainty about the chapel's high altar imagery, and about the relics held by the chapel, limits a full understanding of the wall paintings introduced around it from 1351. By mid-1350, painting with gold and colours had begun on the new wooden vault, raised with carved bosses over the clerestory by 1348.[10] The scaffolding needed for this operation remained in place in order that the upper walls, starting with the elaborate cornice or *tabulamentum* which crowned the side elevation, might be painted and the east wall primed

---

[5] Ayers & Jurkowski, vol. 2, pp. 1261, 1275.
[6] Ayers & Jurkowski, vol. 1, p. 863.
[7] See the essays by Elizabeth Biggs and John Harper in this volume.
[8] Ayers & Jurkowski, vol. 2, p. 1408.
[9] Ayers & Jurkowski, vol. 2, pp. 1186, 1222, 1286, 1318.
[10] Ayers & Jurkowski, vol. 2, p. 1334 (I take 'fourura' to be *fousura*, 'vault'); *HKW*, vol. 1, p. 519.

Fig. 4. Richard Smirke, *Figures of Angels which were probably continued round the whole of St. Stephen's Chapel*, c.1800. Pen and ink wash, on paper, 49.2 × 63 cm. SAL, 236/E, SSC.18.2.

in June 1351.[11] The content and layout or *ordinatio* of the paintings was provided by the master, Hugh of St Albans.[12] Uncertainty surrounds a number of aspects of the figurative decoration, for example the exact location and form of the twenty angel-images supplied for 'tabernacles' by a stone carver, William of Patrington, in May 1352.[13] Possibly, as in the choir at Cologne already witnessed by Edward III, some of these were positioned on or within the tall canopies over the Apostle statues.[14]

That angelic protection was deemed important by the patron and Hugh of St Albans is suggested by the richly finished painted angels holding large cloths at waist height within the seating arcade on the side walls (fig. 4). In appearance these correspond to the angels with cloths of honour behind the Virgin Mary in central Italian panel paintings, or Italian tomb effigies. The formal presence of Mary and Stephen at the altar is implicit in the two tiers of images which filled the corresponding arcading on the east wall to either side of the main altar. Known from copies by Richard Smirke (fig. 5a–b), these were very finely executed on

---

[11] Ayers & Jurkowski, vol. 2, p. 1128.
[12] Ayers & Jurkowski, vol. 2, pp. 1132, 1136, 1140, 1194.
[13] Ayers & Jurkowski, vol. 2, pp. 1220 and 1195.
[14] Ayers & Jurkowski, vol. 2, p. 1194.

Fig. 5a. Richard Smirke, *Edward III and his Sons, Led by St George*, c.1800, reconstruction of paintings on the east wall of the chapel, made originally in the 1350s. Tempera and gold leaf, on paper, 83 × 116 cm. SAL, 236/E, SSC.29.

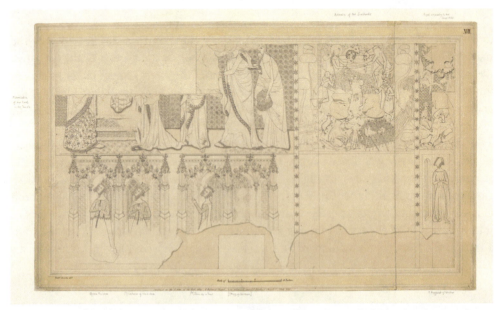

Fig. 5b. Richard Smirke, *Philippa of Hainault and her Daughters*, beneath the *Presentation in the Temple*, c.1800, after a painting on the east wall of St Stephen's Chapel, to the south of the altar, made originally in the 1350s. Pen and ink, on paper, 42.2 × 72 cm. SAL, 236/E, SSC.17.7.

quite a small scale, the figures around 18 in (46 cm) in height.[15] They depicted a devotional audience before the altar consisting of Edward III and his oldest sons kneeling within the arcading on the altar's proper right and sponsored by St George, beneath a representation of the Adoration of the Magi, opposite Queen Philippa and their daughters without sponsor, beneath scenes of the Presentation in the Temple, the Nativity, and the Annunciation to the Shepherds.

The novelty of this part of the scheme is worth stressing. Angels holding cloths of honour were certainly an innovation in English art. Even rarer anywhere at a date in the 1350s are images of royal families shown as collective full-length kneeling figures. Though small, these images should be counted as the first recorded English royal painted portraits. Their kneeling position was the norm for patronal figures before or below images, as in the case of Edward III kneeling within an arcade at the base of the Jesse Tree east window now in St Mary's, Shrewsbury, probably of the 1340s. French and Bohemian instances from the courts of Charles V and the Emperor Charles IV are later. The Wilton Diptych painted for Richard II in the 1390s shows him sponsored, not led, before the Virgin Mary by St John the Baptist, St Edmund, and St Edward. Edward III's presence beneath the Magi implies his personal devotional preference, since the custom was developing of depicting royal patrons actually in the guise of the Three Magi.[16] Edward's devotions included the cultivation both of the cult of the Virgin Mary and of the Three Magi, whose relics were in Cologne Cathedral, a building of relevance to St Stephen's. He was vicar-general of the Empire and had himself paid homage to the Magi there in 1338.[17] The representation of the royal family approaching the Virgin Mary with the Magi is structurally similar to an illustration in the *Codex Balduineus* made during the reign of Emperor Henry VII (fig. 6), showing him with his consort in devotion before the relics of the Magi in Cologne around 1340.[18] The cult of the Epiphany reached its peak in the reign of Richard II, born on the feast of the Epiphany.

That the east wall imagery was deliberately arranged both for liturgical and personal reasons is implied by its *ordinatio*. Thus the male side corresponds to Epiphany, 6 January; the dedication of the high altar to Stephen, 26 December; and the female side to the Purification (Candlemas), 2 February, Edward III having been crowned on its eve, 1 February 1327. The Presentation in the Temple is accordingly reversed with Simeon standing to the left facing south, with the Nativity and Annunciation to the Shepherds out of their conventional order, also working south. The Presentation, centred with the Epiphany, was thus significant for both Edward and Philippa. The line-up of children by gender is familiar from dozens of late-medieval funerary representations, but the keynote here is certainly Edward III's emphasis on family itself, as is apparent too on his tomb completed in the 1380s in the Abbey with small figurines of his children (fig. 7).[19]

---

[15] Tristram, *English Wall Painting*, p. 207, citing Topham; Howe, 'Divine Kingship'.
[16] W. Mark Ormrod, 'The Personal Religion of Edward III', *Speculum*, 64:2 (1989), 849–77; Binski, *Westminster Abbey*, p. 183; Olga Pujmanová, 'Portraits of Kings Depicted as Magi in Bohemian Painting', in Dillian Gordon et al. (eds), *The Regal Image of Richard II and the Wilton Diptych* (London, 1997), pp. 247–66.
[17] Ormrod, 'Personal Religion', pp. 857, 860, 865–6.
[18] Pujmanová, *Portraits of Kings*, p. 251; see Ferdinand Seibt et al. (eds), *Kaiser Karl IV: Staatsmann und Mäzen* (Munich, 1978), p. 52 fig. 7 (after Koblenz, Landeshauptarchiv MS 1C, 1, fol. 5).
[19] Binski, *Westminster Abbey*, pp. 195–9.

Fig. 6. Emperor Henry VII and his consort in devotion before the relics of the Three Magi in Cologne Cathedral. From the *Codex Balduineus*, 1340. Koblenz, Landeshauptarchiv, I C, no. 1, fol. 5r.

Fig. 7. Tomb of Edward III, c.1386, Westminster Abbey.

The Glass and Side Wall Paintings

Virtually nothing is known about the content of the glass in the twelve large upper chapel windows. In keeping with the 1292 plan, the glazing was intended to be the chapel's most splendid feature, the 'days' of the windows filled either with narrative scenes or more probably standing figures under canopies aligned with the Apostle statues to either side. The north and south walls alone provided for at least forty such figures; but after that, all is conjecture. Whether the east window functioned as some sort of reredos is unknowable. An appropriate starting point for the 'staffage' of the side windows might be provided by St Stephen's own words in his profession of faith preceding his death in Acts 6–7 and Hebrews 11, giving an epitome of the Old Testament from Abraham to King Solomon.

There is another reason for thinking the Old Testament was important. Before any glass was inserted, the curious decision was taken to block the lower quarter of each side window with masonry, to be painted (see Ayers, fig. 5, p. 20; Spooner, fig. 4, p. 142). The addition of an illuminated clerestory had increased light levels sufficiently to allow this radical undoing of the Rayonnant practice of maximum extension of window surface, possibly because small painted narratives with texts were thought preferable to narratives in stained glass at the base of the windows. The Sainte-Chapelle had already authorized this combination by placing painted martyrdom scenes beneath its windows (fig. 1), the martyrs in its case being particular to Paris. This expedient created space for at least eight and up to sixteen scenes at the bottom of each window, in two layers, accompanied by substantial panels of Gothic text. Of these, the content of very few is known for certain: fragments from the stories of Job and Tobit survive in the British Museum – the only images which do remain from the Chapel – while early authorities also mention Jonah, Daniel, Jeremiah, Judith, Susanna, Bel and the Dragon, the Acts of the Apostles, and the Ascension of Christ, but without clear authority bar one: a recorded fragment of masonry showing part of the legend of St Eustace.[20]

The obvious basis for this choice was the Old Testament glass of the Sainte-Chapelle in Paris which places the Books of Job and Tobit near the high altar. In St Stephen's, Job and Tobit occupied the easternmost bays to the north and south respectively (see Spooner, figs 1–3, pp. 138–40). From a collegiate perspective there was an ancient tradition of depicting the holy achievements of saintly men and women such as Job, Tobit, Judith, Esther, and the martyrs, recorded as early as the verses of Paulinus of Nola in the Early Christian period.[21] In the temporal of the church year, readings from Job, Tobit, and Judith were grouped together in September and October. The sixteenth-century typological biblical glass of King's College, Cambridge, a building generally in the same tradition as St Stephen's, contains similar episodes; and the fact that Job and Tobit's murals are accompanied by Latin verses also suggests a clerical – and so probably collegiate – audience.[22]

If so, the objective in part was to take Stephen's martyrdom, and that of other Christian and Old Testament worthies, as an occasion to rehearse the biblical story of suffering borne nobly, of *patientia*: the pictures were an explication of the basic liturgical fact of the chapel, its dedication to a protomartyr. Job, central to the Office of the Dead, was the greatest instance of loss; Tobit, deprived of his sight, was also associated with the care for the dead.[23] Indeed St Stephen was regarded as a 'new Job'.[24] A keynote of such patience is restoration, since both Job and Tobit, like all martyrs, gained their reward.

This leads us to a second dimension of these pictures, their familial and chivalric character. Grouped with the royal family at the high altar, Job and Tobit's stories are focused on the tribulations and rewards of the family, and include the destruction of Job's children, and Tobit's wedding: again, themes perhaps personal to Edward III and Philippa. Westminster Palace's murals had long reflected on the insecurities of kingship and dynasty. Henry III decorated his chapels and chambers with salutary stories of Joseph and Daniel about the frailties of power: his choice of Nebuchadnezzar, who lost everything, for pictures in the old St Stephen's Chapel, is relevant. It should be recalled that the new chapel was connected by a passage to the most spectacularly decorated chamber in the kingdom, the Painted Chamber, adorned with copious narratives drawn from the Old Testament's accounts of the

---

[20] See the material assembled in Tristram, *English Wall Painting*, pp. 206–19, and the essay by Jane Spooner in this volume.
[21] Carmina 28: see R. C. Goldschmidt (ed.), *Paulinus' Churches at Nola: Texts, Translations, and Commentary* (Amsterdam, 1940).
[22] For King's College, see Hilary Wayment, *The Windows of King's College Chapel Cambridge* (London, 1972), pp. 48–50, 79–80; the inscriptions are discussed in V. Agrigoroaei, 'Le manuscript lat. 15675 de la Bibliothèque nationale de France, source des inscriptions de la chapelle Saint-Étienne de Westminster', *Convivium*, 4:2 (2017), 194–201.
[23] For Job and Tobit, see Lawrence L. Besserman, *The Legend of Job in the Middle Ages* (Cambridge MA, 1979), pp. 5–40.
[24] Andreas Hoeck, 'Harvest-Herald-Hero: Stephen's Burial and the Church's Early Hermeneutics of Martyrdom', *Scripta Fulgentina*, 26:51–2 (2016), 7–27, at 13–14.

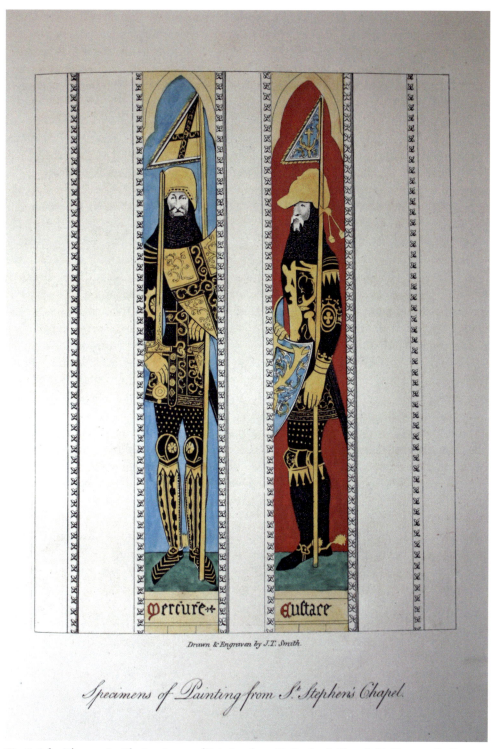

Fig. 8. John Thomas Smith, *Specimens of Painting from St. Stephen's Chapel, St. Mercure, St. Eustace*, from Smith, *Antiquities*, facing p. 244. Coloured line engraving, 20.9 × 16 cm. WOA 1490c.

sordid downfalls of tyrannical rulers and, like those in the chapel, adorned with clear Gothic inscriptions, though in court French.[25] One such story concerned Sennacherib, slaughtered by his own family: Tobit was exiled by Sennacherib. The images in the chapel may very well have extended this bleak commentary into the domain of those who, unlike tyrants, suffer undeservedly but who are restored. Such a connected display of Old Testament narrative would have been hard to match in Europe.

The Painted Chamber topics were also strongly warlike, including virtuous soldiers and leaders such as Judas Maccabeus: St Stephen was regarded as another Maccabee.[26] Suffering borne nobly was also a chivalric virtue, and it cannot be coincidental that the chapel was dedicated with full-length murals of military martyrs such as Eustace and Mercurius (fig. 8), complimenting St George at the altar, together with their stories, as well as copious heraldic shields.[27] The objectives of the Order of the Garter, founded in 1348, were fundamentally religious, for together with the protomartyr Stephen the knights too were 'athletes' of Christ who knew physical suffering.

Though the origins of the decoration of St Stephen can with certainty be traced to the 1290s, Edward III without doubt created the scheme we now know, as a full working-out of the cults of Stephen and the Virgin Mary, tracing the themes of suffering patiently endured through biblical and chivalric example. Like the Sainte-Chapelle, the scheme was 'about' martyrdom and can in this sense be understood as a programme, albeit an evolving one. The various styles of the paintings – for several teams were at work – demonstrated the complex taste of Edward's court. Some of the paintings, notably the Presentation in the Temple, Nativity, and Annunciation to the Shepherds, seem to have been closely related to the Job and Tobit pictures in their use of numerous tricks of coloration and perspective derived from central Italian painting. Likely precursors for the images of Edward's family leading inwards towards the high altar are to be found in the predellas of Tuscan panel paintings. The format of the Bible pictures with panels of text closely resembles that of some Italian illuminated Bibles of the period.[28] It must be relevant that the master of the painters, Hugh of St Albans, possessed an Italian (i.e. 'Lombard') polyptych in his London workshop which appears to have been sold on by his widow to the Abbot of St Albans at double its value.[29] By such means Italy had come to London. Whatever his men were studying, however, it is clear that this large workforce of painters assimilated and adapted new ideas quickly, in a fashion typical of the short-lived but intense court projects of the time.

---

[25] See most recently Paul Binski, 'The Painted Chamber at Westminster and its Documentation', *The Walpole Society*, 83 (2021), 1–68.
[26] Hoeck, 'Harvest-Herald-Hero', pp. 24–5.
[27] Smith, *Antiquities*, cited in Tristram, *English Wall Painting*, p. 219, enumerates at least 32 'knights'.
[28] E.g. BL, MS Add. 15277, see Otto Pächt, 'A Giottesque Episode in English Mediaeval Art', *Journal of the Warburg and Courtauld Institutes*, 6 (1943), 51–70, at 61, n. 3 and pl. 17b.
[29] See Paul Binski and Helen Howard, 'Wall Paintings in the Chapter House', in W. Rodwell and R. Mortimer (eds), *Westminster Abbey Chapter House: The History and Architecture of 'a chapter house beyond compare'* (London, 2010), pp. 184–208, at pp. 195–6.

The Iconography of the
St Stephen's Chapel Painting Fragments

Jane Spooner

This chapter focuses on the unique and understudied surviving mural fragments from St Stephen's Chapel that are preserved today in the British Museum. They were originally part of an all-encompassing decorative scheme, which also included stained glass and figurative sculpture.[1] Painters from around the country were impressed to work on the chapel on the orders of Edward III between 1350 and 1363, and the scheme was probably complete by 1365.[2] Hugh of St Albans was the first master painter, but many other artists were involved.[3]

Today, only the chapel's heavily restored undercroft and a few painted stone fragments from the upper chapel survive. Some of these are on display in the Medieval Europe Gallery at the British Museum, and others are kept in store there.[4] It is not known exactly at what point between 1350 and 1365 the paintings were completed. They were originally wall paintings, positioned beneath the windows in the north-easternmost and south-easternmost bays of the chapel, and they depict painted scenes and texts derived from the Books of Tobit and Job (figs 1–3).[5]

The Job and Tobit cycles were not the only subjects once depicted on the walls of St Stephen's Chapel. Nothing survives of the murals west of the chancel area, although it is surmised from antiquarian records that there were paintings there.[6] John Thomas

---

[1] For a survey of the imagery, see the essay by Paul Binski in this volume.
[2] As a source for the painters' work, and for a discussion of the chapel's craftsmen and materials, see Ayers & Jurkowski.
[3] Jonathan Alexander and Paul Binski (eds), *Age of Chivalry: Art in Plantagenet England* (exhibition catalogue, London, 1987), pp. 498–9, no. 680 (by David Park). For more information about artists, materials and workshop practice, see Jane Spooner, 'Royal Wall-paintings in England in the Second Half of the Fourteenth Century' (Ph.D. dissertation, Courtauld Institute of Art, 2017).
[4] I am grateful to Lloyd de Beer, joint Keeper of Medieval Collections at the British Museum, for arranging close access to the fragments on display and in store. For an account of their entry into the museum collection, see Helen Howard, Lloyd de Beer, David Saunders *et al.*, 'The Wall Paintings at St Stephen's Chapel, Westminster Palace: Recent Imaging and Scientific Analysis of the Fragments in the British Museum', *British Art Studies*, 16 (2020) <https://doi.org/10.17658/issn.2058-5462/issue-16/oneobject>.
[5] BM, mus. no. 1814, 0312.2. Besides the wall paintings, fragments of painted, carved, architectural detailing also survive in the museum's collection.
[6] H. C. Englefield in Topham, p. 17. Englefield's text is reproduced in E. W. Tristram, *English Wall Painting of the Fourteenth Century* (London, 1955), pp. 206–17. There is a rich and complex history of antiquarian recording and interpretation of the architectural and decorative schemes at St Stephen's Chapel. See the essay by Rosemary

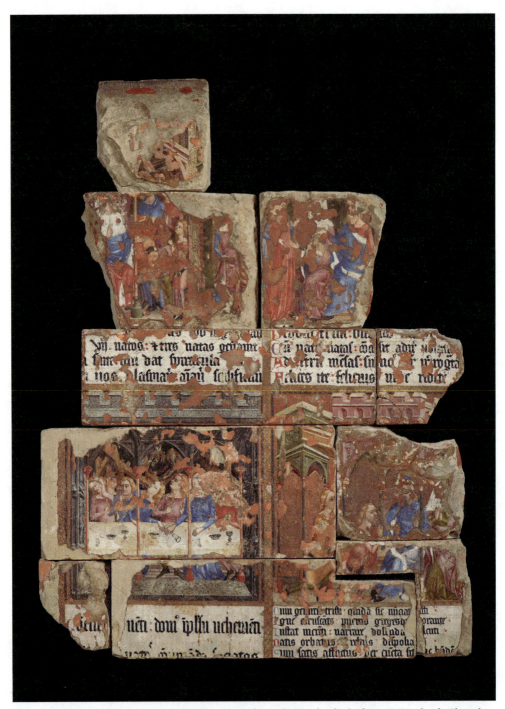

Fig. 1. Wall painting fragments, depicting scenes from the Book of Job, from St Stephen's Chapel, max. height 118 cm. BM, mus. no. MME 1814, 0312.2.

Fig. 2. Wall painting fragments, depicting scenes from the Book of Tobit, from St Stephen's Chapel. BM, mus. no. MME 1814, 0312.2.

Smith, publishing with John Hawkins, observed a painted fragment depicting a scene of the martyrdom of St Eustace and his family in a brazen bull. They also noted a mutilated example of an episode from *Susanna and the Elders*.[7] The St Eustace lost fragment was originally a wall painting, positioned beneath the window in the westernmost bay of the south wall, and Smith drew and etched it, shown among rubble dumped in the Cotton Garden at Westminster (see Hill, fig. 5, p. 251). Much later, the antiquaries Edward Westlake Brayley and John Britton added 'the ascension of Christ and the miracles and martyrdom of the Apostles' to the list of depicted subjects.[8] If the antiquaries are correct, then it seems that there was potentially a cycle of Old Testament paintings, with additional New Testament and martyrdom scenes. Without further evidence, it is hard to speculate on the nature of the whole window wall painting scheme beyond suggesting that there was a loosely typological theme to the choice of subjects. All of the Old Testament heroes,

---

Hill in this volume, and her article, '"Proceeding like Guy Faux": The Antiquarian Investigation of St Stephen's Chapel Westminster, 1790–1837', *Architectural History*, 59 (2016), 253–79.
[7] Smith, *Antiquities*, pp. 84, 153–4; Englefield in Topham, p. 22, as in Tristram, *English Wall Painting*, p. 217.
[8] Brayley & Britton, p. 433.

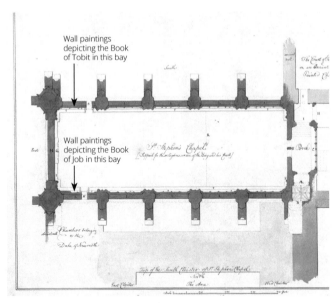

Fig. 3. Detail of John Carter, *Plan of the present remains of St Stephen's Chapel, Westminster, and parts of buildings adjoining*, with arrows indicating location of the wall paintings, c.1791–2. Pen and ink, on paper, 37.5 × 55.4 cm. SAL, 236/E, SSC.3.

Christ in the New Testament, and the saints, undergo trials of faith and display remarkable courage.[9]

By examining here the original context of the British Museum fragments in detail, and the potential iconographic sources for the surviving Job and Tobit paintings it will become clear that the way in which these two Old Testament books were artistically interpreted was far from standard. The fragments subtly reinforce the more overtly Plantagenet-orientated paintings which were on the chapel's altar wall.[10] Indeed, it will be demonstrated that the Job and Tobit themed wall paintings may have had a personal resonance for the royal family, particularly Edward III and Queen Philippa.

The Scheme's Artists

A variety of different hands have been detected on the sill paintings, but beyond that, no specific authorship can be determined.[11] What are recorded, however, are the names of a considerable number of artists involved in some way in the St Stephen's Chapel scheme, and indications of how they were recruited. In a warrant of 18 March 1350, Master Hugh of St Albans was assigned by Edward III to impress 'as many painters and other workmen as may be required' for the works in the chapel, 'in any places it may seem expedient, either within liberties or without, in the counties of Kent, Middlesex, Essex, Surrey and Sussex'.[12] John Athelard was appointed to do likewise in Lincolnshire, Northamptonshire,

---

[9] For an assessment of the overall scheme, see the essay by Binski in this volume.
[10] For a detailed examination of the iconography of the altar wall, see Emily Howe, 'Divine Kingship and Dynastic Display: The Altar Wall Murals of St Stephen's Chapel, Westminster', *Antiquaries Journal*, 81 (2001), 259–304. See also the essay by Binski in this volume.
[11] Amanda Simpson, *The Connections between English and Bohemian Painting during the Second Half of the Fourteenth Century* (New York/London, 1984), p. 166. See also Howard, de Beer, Saunders et al., 'Recent Imaging'.
[12] Brayley & Britton, pp. 170–1. Also see *CPR 1348–50*, vol. 8, p. 481 and Ayers & Jurkowski, vol. 1, pp. 42–3, 75.

Oxfordshire, Warwickshire and Leicestershire; and Benedict Nightingale in Cambridgeshire, Huntingdonshire, Norfolk and Suffolk.[13] Another warrant for the impressment of painters by Hugh of St Albans was issued in 1352.[14] This practice continued into the next decade. In 1363, painter William of Walsyngham was commanded to impress yet more artists, this time from London.[15] From this widespread search it is obvious that a huge complement of artists was required to carry out what was to become the most ambitious decorative scheme of fourteenth-century England. It appears from the accounts of the clerks of the works responsible for Westminster and the Tower of London, that painting at St Stephen's Chapel began on site in earnest in 1351. These accounts are astonishingly detailed in the naming of artists, itemizing their wages, and the listing and costing of materials.[16]

Considerable time and effort was spent on the drawing and setting out of the painted scheme in St Stephen's Chapel in the years 1351–2. For example, in 1352, Hugh of St Albans, the first master of the painter's workshop at St Stephen's, and John de Coton, were each paid a comparatively high daily wage of 12*d.* for six days of 'painting and drawing diverse designs for images'.[17] Less senior artists, such as William Maynard, spent time on 'painting angels and tabernacles', for which he was paid 9*d.* per day.[18] For the execution of the scheme, numerous painters were employed to prime, paint, and gild the walls and sculpture, while others ground the pigments. Unusually, a female painter, Alice Couper, was employed. She was paid a daily wage of 6*d.* alongside fellow male painters for 'painting and laying gold' in the chapel.[19] Most of the artists were English, but a few of the less well-paid ones were possibly Flemish, such as Lowen Tassyn, Janyn Godmered, Nicholas Bruges, and Giles Flemyng.

The British Museum Fragments

To return to the surviving wall painting fragments – they were painted in oil on blocks of Reigate stone about 5 cm (2 in) thick – a calcareous sandstone of greenish-grey appearance.[20] This stone was ubiquitous at Westminster; the building accounts for St Stephen's record its purchase in large quantities.[21] It is clear that certain scenes on the fragments were originally adjacent to each other because they were painted across ashlar blocks, which evidently fitted together (figs 1–2). The disposition of the painted scenes was not, therefore, dictated by the coursing of the stones. The paintings are highly finished in rich, saturated colours applied in oil paint, and are embellished with gilt tin-relief patterns. The episodes from the Books of Job and Tobit are depicted within rectangular compartments, with painted inscriptions beneath each one.

---

[13] *CPR 1348–50*, vol. 8, p. 481, and Ayers & Jurkowski, vol. 1, pp. 42–3, 75.
[14] *CPR 1350–54*, vol. 9, p. 308, and Ayers & Jurkowski, vol. 1, pp. 42–3, 75.
[15] Brayley & Britton, p. 186. Also *CPR 1361–64*, vol. 12, p. 345, and Ayers & Jurkowski, vol. 1, pp. 42–3, 75.
[16] See Ayers & Jurkowski.
[17] Ayers & Jurkowski, vol. 2, pp. 1152–3.
[18] Ayers & Jurkowski, vol. 2, pp. 1196–7.
[19] Ayers & Jurkowski, vol. 2, pp. 1196–7.
[20] Peter van Geersdaele and Lesley Goldsworthy, 'The Restoration of Wallpainting Fragments from St Stephen's Chapel, Westminster', *The Conservator*, 2:1 (1978), 9–12.
[21] Ayers & Jurkowski, vol. 1, p. 46.

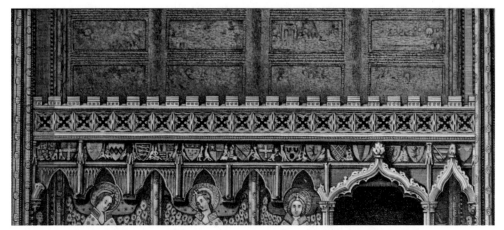

Fig. 4. John Thomas Smith, *Part of the South side of the same Chapel*, detail (for full image, see Hillson, fig. 7, p. 91), showing the easternmost bay, St Stephen's Chapel. Engraving, from Smith, *Antiquities*, facing p. 153.

The original location is recorded in John Thomas Smith's engraving of 1807 (fig. 4). It shows that they were positioned beneath the windows in the easternmost bay, the chancel area, of St Stephen's Chapel. Recognizable elements of the Tobit-painted scheme can be perceived in Smith's engraving of the bay's south wall, above the dado frieze. John Dixon's masterly architectural drawing of the north wall's easternmost bay demonstrates the original location of the Job cycle, on the flat expanses of wall beneath the window (see Ayers, fig. 5, p. 20).

There is a degree of uncertainty about the number of pictorial scenes per window bay, and their exact arrangement. According to Englefield, within each bay of the north and south elevations, the walls beneath the windows were painted with eight roughly square-shaped compartments containing painted scenes in each bay. He claimed that the compartments were arranged in two rows and that each row held four compartments.[22] This arrangement is reflected in Smith's engraving of the south wall (fig. 4). However, research by Tim Ayers and Anthony Masinton contradicts this view.[23] There may have been sixteen scenes per whole painted window wall, comprising eight scenes in each of two rows.[24] Given the many episodes in the Books of Job and Tobit, and their potential for the creation of numerous illustrations, this is entirely plausible.

The position of the scenes, and their small size, means that they would not have been particularly visible from the floor. Englefield wrote of them:

---

[22] Englefield in Topham, pp. 17–18, as in Tristram, *English Wall Painting*, p. 211.
[23] Tim Ayers, pers. comm. I am grateful to Professor Ayers for sharing this research. Ayers and Anthony Masinton established that the area between each mullion was about 3 ft wide, and that while the height of the fragments' painted scenes and the inscriptions varied, a double row would have been about 124 cm high (4 ft high). This would have left some space above the top row. Measurements of the painted fragments were kindly provided by the aforementioned Lloyd de Beer, and are not currently available on the St Stephen's Chapel wall paintings entry in the BM Collections Online website: <https://www.britishmuseum.org/collection/object/H_1814-0312-2> [accessed 15 Nov. 2023].
[24] Tim Ayers, 'Virtual St Stephen's: The Medieval Model and the Art Historian', *British Art Studies*, 16 <https://doi.org/10.17658/issn.2058-5462/issue-16/tayers2/p34> [accessed 15 Nov. 2023].

Fig. 5. Detail, wall painting fragment of the *Muting/Blinding of the Swallows* (left) and *Tobit Dejected* (right), from the Book of Tobit. BM, mus. no. MME 1814, 0312.2.

> The paintings are very carefully and minutely finished; so much so, indeed, that at the distance of ten feet from the ground, which is the elevation of the bottom of the lowest range of pictures, much of the detail must have been lost. The general size of the pictures is about a foot in height.[25]

Of the museum fragments painted with scenes from the Book of Tobit, from the south wall, four episodes of the story are shown as 'double' scenes within two compartments. One compartment shows Tobit being blinded, adjacent to a scene of him sitting blind and dejected (fig. 5). An 'orphan' inscription, missing its accompanying illustration of one of Tobit's acts of charity, also survives (fig. 6).[26] Englefield judged from the inscription that the lost imagery was of Tobit burying the executed bodies of his fellow Israelites, abandoned outside the walls of Nineveh. This image-less inscription adjoins that for the scene of Tobit's blinding by swallow dung. Another, very damaged, compartment depicts a nuptial feast at Tobit's house (fig. 7). The other double-scene compartment depicts the angel Raphael (disguised as Azarias) at Tobit's door, and also ascending heavenwards (fig. 8).

Of the compartments painted with the Book of Job, all shown in single scenes, one depicts the patriarch speaking to his sons, and another shows him and his wife conversing with their

---

[25] Englefield in Topham, pp. 17–18, as in Tristram, *English Wall Painting*, p. 211.
[26] Englefield in Topham, p. 18, as in Tristram, *English Wall Painting*, p. 212.

Fig. 6. Detail, inscriptions beneath the *Muting of the Swallows*, in a scene from the Book of Tobit, St Stephen's Chapel. BM, mus. no. MME 1814, 0312.2. The inscription on the left has no surviving picture connected with it.

Fig. 7. Detail, scene depicting the *Nuptial Feast of Tobias and Sara*, from the Book of Tobit, St Stephen's Chapel. BM, mus. no. MME 1814, 0312.2.

daughters (figs 9–10). Other compartments show the destruction of Job's children (fig. 11); a messenger informing Job and his wife of the death of their children (fig. 12); Sophar the Naamathite speaking to Job (fig. 13); and Elihu speaking with the afflicted Job (fig. 14). Another 'orphan' inscription, with no surviving picture, tells how Job triumphed over his adversity.[27]

The layout of the imagery and inscriptions is generically reminiscent of the *Biblia Pauperum* picture books, with their large illustrations of Old and New Testament scenes accompanied by explanatory texts.[28] The wall paintings' pictorial compartments and inscriptions are divided from each other by embossed and gilt borders. The painted architecture

[27] Englefield in Topham, p. 18, as in Tristram, *English Wall Painting*, p. 212.
[28] E. A. Livingstone (ed.), *The Oxford Concise Dictionary of the Christian Church*, rev. 2nd edn (Oxford, 2006), p. 71. *Biblia Pauperum* were 'picture books which have upon each page a set group of figures illustrating a New

Fig. 8. Detail, two scenes from the Book of Tobit, *Azarias/Raphael at the Door of Tobit's House* (left) and *Raphael Ascending* (right), in a wall painting fragment from St Stephen's Chapel. BM, mus. no. MME 1814, 0312.2.

Fig. 9. Detail, scene of *Job Instructing his Sons*, from the Book of Job, St Stephen's Chapel. BM, mus. no. MME 1814, 0312.2.

The Iconography of the St Stephen's Chapel Painting Fragments

Fig. 10. Detail, scene of *Daughters Asking Permission to Attend a Feast*, from the Book of Job, St Stephen's Chapel. BM, mus. no. MME 1814, 0312.2.

Fig. 11. Detail, wall painting fragment depicting the *Destruction of Job's Children*, from the Book of Job, St Stephen's Chapel. BM, mus. no. MME 1814, 0312.2.

within the scenes is closely derived from Tuscan art, with pinkish tones, similar forms, and empirical two-point perspective.[29] The scale of the architecture is much smaller than that of the figures. The eye-catchingly decorative gilt and relief-work backgrounds of some of the scenes contradict the three-dimensional illusionism of the painted architecture. The inscriptions are painted in black on a white background, and change in scale, depending on the amount of text that was included.

Careful examination demonstrates how close the inscriptions are to manuscript text. The initials are expressed in red or blue paint. The script is of 'Gothic bookhand', or *textualis formata* form, where every detail of the script is stylized, and the top and base of each stroke is squared, with extremes of thickness and thinness.[30] The inscription script is almost

---

Testament antitype. These are flanked by two corresponding Old Testament types, with short explanatory texts from the Bible and mnemonic verses.'
[29] Simpson, *Connections*, p. 165.
[30] The description of *textualis formata* employed here was originally used to describe the text of the Metz Pontifical (Cambridge, Fitzwilliam Museum, MS 298), dated 1303–16. Stella Panayotova and Teresa Webber,

The Iconography of the St Stephen's Chapel Painting Fragments

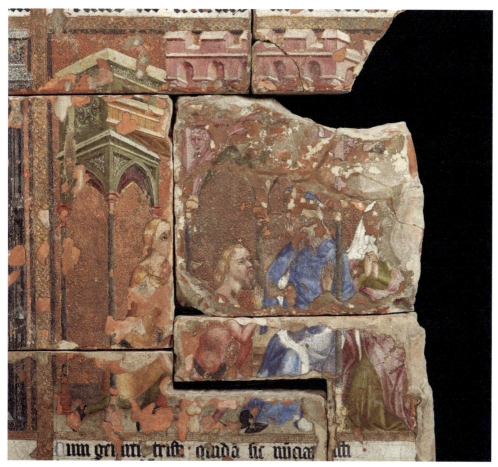

Fig. 12. Detail, wall painting fragment depicting the *Messenger of Misfortune*, from the Book of Job, St Stephen's Chapel. BM, mus. no. MME 1814, 0312.2.

certainly executed with black paint and a brush rather than with ink or a feather quill, although it is clearly intended to exactly replicate calligraphy. The ruled setting-out lines for the text are still very visible, and show how the letter-painter worked to keep the letters in the desired scale and shape. All of the surviving inscriptions beneath the Books of Job and Tobit paintings were transcribed and published in 1811. The ones beneath the Tobit scenes are in unrhymed verse, whereas those beneath Job's are in Leonine rhyme.[31] The inscriptions remain elusively eccentric, but are loosely based on the Vulgate. Much of the Vulgate's Book of Job was written in Leonine hexameters, whereas the Book of Tobit was not.[32]

'Making an Illuminated Manuscript', in Paul Binski and Stella Panayotova (eds), *The Cambridge Illuminations: Ten Centuries of Book Production in the Medieval West* (London and Turnhout, 2005), pp. 23–36, at pp. 30–1.
[31] Englefield in Topham, pp. 18–19, as in Tristram, *English Wall Painting*, pp. 212–16.
[32] Philologist Vladimir Agrigoroaei has concluded that the Job paintings' inscriptions may ultimately be derived from an unknown manuscript of Gregory the Great's *Morals on the Book of Job*, which also influenced an illuminated manuscript in Paris, Bibliothèque nationale de France (latin 15675). He has also suggested that the Tobit paintings' inscriptions were derived from Peter Riga's poem *Aurora*. See V. Agrigoroaei, 'Le manuscrit lat. 15675

Fig. 13. Detail, wall painting fragment depicting *Sophar the Naamathite*, from the Book of Job, St Stephen's Chapel. BM, mus. no. MME 1814, 0312.2.

The Iconography of the St Stephen's Chapel Painting Fragments 151

Fig. 14. Detail, wall painting fragment depicting *Elihu and Job*, from the Book of Job, St Stephen's Chapel. BM, mus. no. MME 1814, 0312.2.

Fig. 15. Scenes from the legend of Pope Sylvester, c.1332–49. Wall paintings on the inner side of the choir enclosure, Cologne Cathedral.

The use of inscriptions to label or explain scenes in murals was not novel at Westminster. The wall paintings of 1292–7 in Westminster's Painted Chamber, depicting scenes from the Old Testament Books of Maccabees, Judges and Kings, were augmented by painted inscriptions in French.[33] Inscriptions played a part in high-status fourteenth-century mural-painting schemes elsewhere, in Italy, Bohemia, Flanders, Avignon and Cologne. The manuscript-like appearance of the St Stephen's Chapel inscriptions is very unusual, however. The closest surviving parallels are the painted inscriptions on the Cologne choir enclosure, where they are positioned directly beneath large-scale scenes (fig. 15). Like the St Stephen's inscriptions, they describe the scenes immediately above them, are written on incised lines, and are also in Latin. Their emulation of manuscript text is more sophisticated than that at St Stephen's Chapel. Edward III visited Cologne in 1338, where he was inducted as a vicar-general of the Holy Roman Empire.[34] It is possible that he would have seen these murals painted on the interior faces of the choir enclosure in the cathedral. Its six stone screens were installed in 1304, and the paintings were probably executed before 1322, with later additions completed by 1380.[35]

That manuscript-like text on the wall paintings of St Stephen's was considered successful at Westminster was demonstrated by the later application of inscriptions of passages from the Book of Revelation in the chapter house's Apocalypse mural scheme at Westminster Abbey, after 1372.[36] By closely emulating a picture Bible, or a prayer book, the inscriptions in St Stephen's Chapel and the Abbey's chapter house lent the wall-painted scenes the same level of authority that they would have received in a real Bible or prayer book. This sense of authority would have been particularly important to the canons of St Stephen's and the monks of the Abbey.

Hybrid Styles and Antecedents

Stylistically, the paintings are a blend of illusionistic Tuscan-style architecture, with gilded anti-illusionistic relief-work backgrounds, and oversized figures. The exquisite scene of the *Messenger of Misfortune* (fig. 12) has a rare delicacy and finely modelled drapery, such as that found in Parisian manuscript illumination by the workshop of Jean Pucelle. By contrast, in the adjacent scene of the *Destruction of Job's Children*, the figures have an Italianate robustness (fig. 11). As Paul Binski and David Park observe, such differences emphasize the

---

de la Bibliothèque nationale de France, source des inscriptions de la chapelle Saint-Étienne de Westminster', *Convivium*, 4:2 (2017), 194–201.
[33] Alexander and Binski, *Age of Chivalry*, p. 341, nos 330–9 (by Paul Binski). Also see Paul Binski, *The Painted Chamber at Westminster*, Occasional Paper, NS, 9, SAL (London, 1986); Paul Binski, 'The Painted Chamber at Westminster and its Documentation', *Walpole Society*, 83 (2021), 1–68.
[34] W. Mark Ormrod, 'The Personal Religion of Edward III', *Speculum*, 64: 4 (1989), 849–77, at 856, 858, 860–1.
[35] Brigitte Corley, *Painting and Patronage in Cologne 1300–1500* (London, 2000), pp. 56–7.
[36] Helen Howard, 'Technology of the Painted Past: Recent Scientific Examination of the Medieval Wall Paintings of the Chapter House of Westminster Abbey', in Robert Gowing and Adrian Heritage (eds), *Conserving the Painted Past: Developing Approaches to Wall Painting conservation, Post-prints of a Conference Organised by English Heritage London 2–4 December 1999* (London, 2003), pp. 17–26, at pp. 18, 23. Also see Paul Binski and Helen Howard, 'Wall Paintings in the Chapter House', in Warwick Rodwell and Richard Mortimer (eds), *Westminster Abbey Chapter House: The History, Art and Architecture of 'a chapter house beyond compare'* (London, 2010), pp. 184–208, at pp. 184, 195.

hybrid style of the paintings, and indicate different hands at work.[37] This is confirmed by the differing technique of the paintings, revealed in recent scientific analysis.[38]

Regarding the question of the transmission of influence from the art and architecture of other countries, besides Cologne, St Stephen's patron Edward III travelled to Paris and the Low Countries as a child and a young man, and of course fought in France later in his military career.[39] Many of his closest advisers travelled to and from the papal court at Avignon, there witnessing the work of Tuscan artists, especially Simone Martini and Matteo Giovanetti (from Viterbo, but painting in a Sienese tradition).[40] Portable works of art such as Italian illuminated manuscripts, panel paintings and ivories were bought and sold, and entered the collections of the court circle and the royal family, such as Edward's mother, the dowager Queen Isabella.[41] An inventory of Isabella's belongings made at her death in 1358, records up to ten panel paintings, three of which were specifically referred to as 'tabule de opere Lumbardorum'.[42] Edward III may have inherited his mother's taste for Italian art, and her possessions could have inspired some of the Italianate features apparent in the St Stephen's Chapel paintings. Commenting on the paintings, Otto Pächt felt they could pass for the work of a provincial follower of Simone Martini, were it not for the generally English names of the artists.[43] Binski and Park have demonstrated that there was some East Anglian precedent for Tuscan influence in English wall painting, at Prior Crauden's Chapel in Ely.[44] Benedict Nightingale's impressment of Cambridgeshire artists allows for the possibility of a connection between painters working at Ely, and those at St Stephen's Chapel.

At least one artist connected with St Stephen's Chapel had knowledge of Italian painting. Artist 'Hugh Peyntour', usually assumed to be Master Hugh of St Albans bequeathed, in 1368, to his wife a 'table of six pieces of Lumbardy', worth £20.[45] This was probably a polyptych altarpiece. 'Lumbardy' did not specifically mean the region known today as Lombardy: in fourteenth-century England it was a term used to cover all areas of the Italian peninsula.

---

[37] Paul Binski, *Westminster Abbey and the Plantagenets: Kingship and the Representation of Power 1200–1400* (London/New Haven, 1995), p. 184; Alexander and Binski, *Age of Chivalry*, pp. 498–9, no. 680 (by David Park).
[38] Howard, de Beer, Saunders et al., 'Recent Imaging'.
[39] Many aspects of Edward III's kingship are published by Ormrod. His most comprehensive publication is a large monograph: W. Mark Ormrod, *Edward III* (London/New Haven, 2011).
[40] See Paul Binski, *Gothic Wonder* (London/New Haven, 2014) for the most recent, and detailed, analysis of the influence of Tuscan and Avignonese art on the patronage of English high-status individuals, including the monarchy: Binski, *Gothic Wonder*, pp. 250–60 and 332–4 on the visits and patronage of Bishops John Grandisson, William Ayermin and Anthony Bek. For information on Edward III's cousin, Henry of Grosmont, Duke of Lancaster, who visited Avignon, see Nigel Saul, 'St George's Chapel and the Foundation of the Order of the Garter', in Nigel Saul and Tim Tatton-Brown (eds), *St George's Chapel Windsor: History and Heritage* (Stanbridge, 2010), pp. 44–51, at p. 49. For information on Simone Martini and Matteo Giovanetti in Avignon, see Dominique Vingtain, *Avignon Le Palais des Papes* (Saint-Léger-Vauban, 1998), p. 285. Also Dominique Vingtain, 'Sienese Painters in Avignon during the Fourteenth Century', in Mario Scalini and Anna Guiducci (eds), *Paintings from Siena: Ars Narrandi in Europe's Gothic Age* (Brussels/Cinisello Balsamo, 2014), pp. 69–83, at pp. 72, 76–7.
[41] Juliet Vale, *Edward III and Chivalry: Chivalric Society and its Context, 1270–1350* (Woodbridge, 1982), p. 52.
[42] Vale, *Edward III and Chivalry*, p. 52.
[43] Otto Pächt, 'A Giottesque Episode in English Mediaeval Art', *Journal of the Warburg and Courtauld Institutes*, 6 (1943), 51–70, at 57.
[44] Paul Binski and David Park, 'A Ducciesque Episode at Ely: The Mural Decorations of Prior Crauden's Chapel', in W. Mark Ormrod (ed.), *England in the Fourteenth Century: Proceedings of the 1985 Harlaxton Symposium* (Woodbridge, 1986), pp. 28–41, at p. 41. Also see Binski, *Gothic Wonder*, p. 225.
[45] R. R. Sharpe (ed.), *Calendar of Wills in the Court of Husting* (2 vols, London, 1890), p. 106. Also see John H. Harvey, 'Some London Painters of the Fourteenth and Fifteenth Centuries', *The Burlington Magazine*, 89 (1947), 303–5, at 303.

Assuming that Hugh already owned the painting while working at St Stephen's Chapel, it could have been used as a model, and an exemplar of Italian style for himself and his team of artists.

In the St Stephen's Job cycle of paintings, Amanda Simpson noted similarities in the rendering of architectural elements with works by Pietro Lorenzetti of 1329, and by Giovanni da Milano. The barley-sugar columns framing the scene of Job's daughters were 'by this date, a standard feature of Italian painting', appearing in frescoes attributed to Simone Martini, painted *c.*1317–19, in the Lower Church at Assisi.[46] Robert Gibbs demonstrated that the elaborate three-bay setting for the *Destruction of Job's Children* was ultimately derived from Giotto's paintings in the Lower Church at Assisi, executed *c.*1315–20.[47] Gibbs suggested that the Westminster artists could have encountered Giotto's forms through intermediary artworks such as by the Lorenzetti brothers, or portable paintings by unknown hands.[48] Such paintings could have been those owned by Hugh of St Albans and Queen Isabella. 'Giottesque' expressiveness can also be perceived in the St Stephen's Chapel paintings. The emotion of Job's wife, wringing her hands at the news of her children's death, and the naturalistic comforting by Tobit's wife of her husband as he is blinded, owe a debt to Italian art.

Audience and Iconography

Given the small scale of the wall painting fragments, and the difficulty of 'reading' the images and the texts beneath them, a question arises about the intended audience for the window wall paintings. They were certainly installed after the foundation of the college of canons. Adjacent to the altar wall, in the sanctuary, the Job and Tobit cycles would have been visible to the clergy who served the high altar. There was also a king's closet in this eastern bay, 'on the south side of the new chapel by the high altar', which is known from an account for the leading of its roof in 1348.[49] Was the king able to view from there the altar wall, and the Job cycle on the north wall opposite? Perhaps the iconography of the surviving Job and Tobit cycles can indicate more about the intended audience for these paintings, and what might have originally been understood by the variety of scenes. What follows is a detailed exploration of this understudied iconography.

The Books of Job and Tobit

The surviving fragments depicting subjects from the Old Testament Books of Job and Tobit faced each other in the easternmost bay adjacent to the altar wall (see fig. 3). Their positions suggest an iconographic relationship with each other, and also with the altar-wall subjects. To appreciate the meaning of the Job and Tobit murals, it is important to understand how

---

[46] Simpson, *Connections*, p. 164.
[47] Robert Gibbs, 'The Three-Bay (or Five-Bay) Interior and the Apsidal Interior from Giotto to Van Eyck: a Westminster Episode', in John Mitchell and Matthew Moran (eds), *England and the Continent in the Middle Ages: Studies in Memory of Andrew Martindale, Proceedings of the 1996 Harlaxton Symposium* (Stamford, 2000), pp. 175–85.
[48] Gibbs, 'Three-Bay (or Five-Bay) Interior', p. 184.
[49] Ayers & Jurkowski, vol. 2, no. 38, m. 10 (w/b 19 May 1348), p. 1091. Also see Smith, *Antiquities*, p. 204 and C. L. Kingsford, 'Our Lady of the Pew: The King's Oratory or Closet in the Palace of Westminster', *Archaeologia*, 68 (1917), 1–20, at 7.

they were perceived in the fourteenth century. This necessarily connects with textual sources of the Old Testament stories, and their artistic interpretive traditions.

In the Book of Job, God gives Satan permission to test wealthy Job's exemplary faith. Satan inflicts upon him the loss of possessions, wealth, health, and family, a hideous skin disease, and the condemnation of his friends. Job questions God, but ultimately does not lose faith. Eventually he is restored to happiness, a long life, riches, and a new family of children.[50] The story of Job's life was used as a prologue and epilogue to the heart of the Vulgate Book of Job, which is essentially a long poem on the need to remain faithful to God, whatever tribulations must be endured. It takes the form of a lengthy discourse between Job, his friends, and God himself.

Inspired by the moralistic possibilities within the Book of Job, Gregory the Great wrote *Morals on the Book of Job* in the sixth century.[51] A homiletic commentary, it continued to be influential throughout the Middle Ages. The history of Job also appeared in the *Golden Legend* – a highly influential collection of saints' hagiographies and histories of Old Testament heroes written by Jacobus de Voragine c.1260.[52] By the fourteenth century, the story of Job was also known through an appendix to the Greek Septuagint version of the Bible. Known as the *Testament of Job*, this presented Job as a king, and his friends also as kings.[53] Although the *Testament of Job* was suppressed in the Western Church, it continued to be influential in the Byzantine tradition, and aspects of the *Testament* permeated Western iconography.[54] The main distinction between the Vulgate and the *Testament* is that the latter placed greater emphasis upon the personal narrative of Job's life story. In the *Testament*, Job became the narrator, telling his second family of children of his trials.

The Old Testament Book of Tobit tells the story of a father and son, during the period of the Babylonian exile of the Jews. Part of the Apocrypha, it appeared in the Greek Septuagint and in the Latin Vulgate versions of the Bible. In the Vulgate, both generations were called Tobias. To avoid confusion, the father is called Tobit here, and his son, Tobias. Both Job and Tobit were included in Peter Riga's popular late-twelfth-century poem *Aurora*, and the latter in Matthew of Vendôme's epic *Tobias*, also from the same period.[55] The history of Tobit, like Job's, also appeared in the later *Golden Legend*.[56]

Tobit was a wealthy Jewish man exiled in Nineveh. His story, like Job's, was one of personal suffering and redemption through pious actions and unquestioning faith, and he was considered to be a second Job. Tobit performed charitable acts, such as distributing alms, and burying his dead fellow Jews. Falling asleep in his garden, Tobit was blinded by swallow dung falling into his eyes, and subsequently afflicted by poverty and shame. He sent Tobias

---

[50] *The Bible, Douay-Rheims, Old Testament – Part 1* <http://www.gutenberg.org/cache/epub/1609/pg1609-images.html> [accessed 15 Nov. 2023].
[51] Gregory the Great, *Morals on the Book of Job*, eds J. Parker and J. Rivington (3 vols, 8 parts, Oxford, 1844–50).
[52] Jacobus de Voragine, *The Golden Legend*, Englished by William Caxton 1483, I IntraText Edition CT, Copyright Èulogos 2007: <http://www.intratext.com/ixt/ENG1293/_PX.HTM> [accessed 15 Nov. 2023].
[53] Samuel Terrien, *The Iconography of Job through the Centuries: Artists as Biblical Interpreters* (University Park, 1996), pp. xxxi–xxxv. See also *The Testament of Job*, trans. M. R. James, Apocrypha Anecdota, 2 (Cambridge, 1897) <http://wesley.nnu.edu/sermons-essays-books/noncanonical-literature/noncanonical-literature-ot-pseudepigrapha/testament-of-job/> [accessed 15 Nov. 2023].
[54] K. Meyer, 'St Job as a Patron of Music', *The Art Bulletin* 36:1 (1954), 21–31, at 23.
[55] A. G. Rigg, *A History of Anglo-Latin Literature, 1066–1422* (Cambridge, 1992), p. 156.
[56] Voragine, *Golden Legend*.

to recover money lent to a kinsman. Tobias set forth with a companion – the mysterious Azarias – who was a disguised Archangel Raphael. On the way, Tobias caught a giant fish, and Azarias instructed him in its magical properties. Tobias met and married kinswoman Sara, who was possessed by a demon which had killed her previous seven husbands on their wedding nights. Tobias and Sara prayed and drove out the demon. After feasting they returned to Nineveh, and Tobias cured Tobit's blindness with the fish's gall. A nuptial feast was held in Tobit's house. Raphael revealed his angelic identity and ascended to heaven.[57] The Book of Tobit taught of the importance of charity, of remaining faithful despite personal hardship, and belief in the power of prayer as an aid to divine intervention.

Job and Tobit in Context

There was a long tradition of artworks depicting Job and Tobit, which drew on these different textual sources, and which became influential in their turn. Byzantine manuscripts, twelfth-century capital sculpture, thirteenth-century portal sculpture and stained glass, the *Bibles moralisées* of the French court, and fourteenth-century Tuscan wall and panel paintings referenced the iconography of Job and, to a lesser extent, Tobit, in different ways.[58] The Book of Tobit really gained in popularity from the early fifteenth century onwards.[59]

Job and Tobit appear rarely in surviving or recorded English murals. Old Testament Books had provided the subjects of important royal wall painting schemes in the thirteenth century, including those in the Painted Chamber at Westminster Palace. There were also Old and New Testament mural schemes painted for Henry III at Winchester and Windsor Castles.[60] It is unknown whether Job and Tobit appeared there. Italian antecedents are more common. According to St Paulinus, the walls of part of the church of St Felix at Cimitile in Italy were painted c.400–3 CE, with Job and Tobit scenes.[61] An early example of the pairing of these two figures.

The Old Testament cycle of frescoes by Bartolo di Fredi in the Collegiata of San Gimignano includes the misfortunes of Job. The frescoes date to 1367, so were painted after the St Stephen's Chapel scheme. While on a larger scale than the St Stephen's paintings, Bartolo's murals are comparable in that the architecture is similarly perspectival, and the figures are on a larger scale than the buildings. Satan throws the house down onto the children's heads in a dramatic *Destruction of Job's Children* scene (fig. 16). While it is unlikely that the artists from the Italian and English mural projects knew about each others' work, the similarities suggest that they may have had a pictorial common source for depicting the Job story. Millard Meiss traced Italian examples of the Job subject, post 1348, and connected the choice of topic with the tribulations suffered by Tuscans in the aftermath of the plague.[62]

---

[57] The Bible <http://www.gutenberg.org/cache/epub/1609/pg1609> [accessed 15 Nov. 2023].
[58] Yves Christe, 'La Bible du Roi: L'histoire de Job dans les Bibles Moralisées et les vitraux de la Sainte Chapelle', *Cahiers de Civilisation Médiévale*, 47 (2004), 113–26, at 113.
[59] Philip J. Earenfight provides a useful survey of Tobit imagery in Western art up to 1350: Philip J. Earenfight, 'The Residence and Loggia della Misericordia (Il Bigallo)' (Ph.D. dissertation, University of New Jersey, 1999), pp. 247–67. I am grateful to Dr Federico Botana for this reference.
[60] C. Michael Kauffmann, *Biblical Imagery in Medieval England, 700–1550* (London, 2003), p. 197.
[61] Beat Brenk, 'The Sainte Chapelle as a Capetian Political Program', in Virginia Chieffo Raguin, Kathryn Brush, and Peter Draper (eds), *Artistic Integration in Gothic Buildings* (Toronto, 1995), pp. 195–213, at p. 212, note 57.
[62] Millard Meiss, *Painting in Florence and Siena after the Black Death* (Princeton, 1951), p. 68.

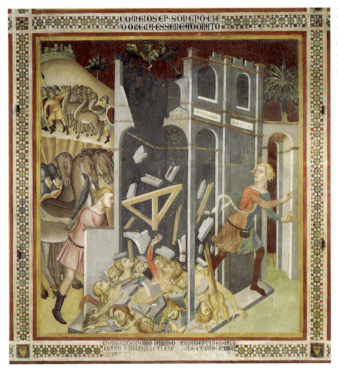

Fig. 16. *Destruction of Job's Children*, detail from a cycle of the Book of Job, wall painting by Bartolo di Fredi, Collegiata, San Gimignano.

Scholars have challenged Meiss's conclusions.[63] England also suffered from the plague in 1348, and the royal family experienced their own bereavements as a result. Despite this, and the decimation of the English population, Mark Ormrod found that the English royal coffers and administration were relatively unaffected by the disaster.[64] The inclusion of Job within St Stephen's Chapel was probably not specifically related to the Black Death of 1348.

A fragmentary Tobit cycle of wall paintings at the Bigallo in Florence also bears limited comparison with the slightly earlier St Stephen's Chapel scheme. It features similar Sienese-style architectural settings, with rectangular compartments housing episodes from the Book of Tobit.[65] Again, there is no provable relationship with St Stephen's Chapel.

Job and Tobit in French Royal Art

If wall painting antecedents are somewhat unsatisfactory, Job and Tobit do feature significantly in thirteenth-century stained glass and manuscripts associated with the French royal family. Examples include the windows of the Sainte-Chapelle in Paris, installed around

---

[63] Diana Norman, 'Change and Continuity: Art and Religion after the Black Death', in Diana Norman (ed.), *Siena, Florence and Padua: Art, Society and Religion 1280–1400* (2 vols, New Haven/London, 1995), pp. 177–95, at p. 195.
[64] W. Mark Ormrod, 'The English Government and the Black Death of 1348–9', in W. M. Ormrod (ed.), *England in the Fourteenth Century: Proceedings of the 1985 Harlaxton Symposium* (Woodbridge, 1986), pp. 175–88.
[65] Earenfight, 'Residence and Loggia della Misericordia', pp. 280, 283–6. See a reproduction of one of the frescoes in Federico Botana, *Learning Through Images in the Italian Renaissance* (Cambridge, 2020), fig. 2.11.

the late 1240s, and the Parisian *Bibles moralisées*, of the 1220s and 30s.[66] While Job and Tobit imagery was current in a variety of media in the medieval period, it is argued here that its presence in St Stephen's Chapel was a sign of the transmission and development of Capetian-sponsored typological and moralizing iconography exhibited in stained glass and biblical manuscript illumination. Capetian iconographic programmes relied heavily on the Books of the Old Testament, and included Job and Tobit. Such iconographic schemes were over a century old by the time St Stephen's was decorated, but they would have had a resonance for an English king with Capetian blood in his veins – blood which justified his claim to the throne of France.

In general conception, the decoration of St Stephen's Chapel was similar to Louis IX's Sainte-Chapelle, consecrated in 1248. They were both extravagantly ornamented with stained glass, murals, and sculpture. They both included depictions of their patrons, and royal heraldry, at strategic points throughout the decorative scheme. Both royal chapels bore narrative cycles of Old and New Testament books, scenes of saints' martyrdoms, and sculptures of angels and the Apostles. The interior decoration of both chapels was scintillating and jewel-like, and blurred the boundaries between architecture, painting, glass, enamel, and metalwork. For example, the Sainte-Chapelle had murals in medallions depicting saints' martyrdoms (see Binski, fig. 1, p. 126). These were framed with glass and had gilded backgrounds, making them appear enamel-like.[67] Smith records that at St Stephen's Chapel, elaborately carved stone brackets for sculptures were adorned with glass inserts, to similar effect.[68] This technique was also apparent in the thirteenth-century Westminster Retable, which once adorned the high altar of the nearby Abbey.[69] St Stephen's Chapel does not slavishly copy the Sainte-Chapelle, however.[70] While both were royal palace chapels, the Sainte-Chapelle was built and ornamented to house the relics of the Passion, whereas St Stephen's had no great relic. The latter was decorated after it became a collegiate chapel. The interior of the Sainte-Chapelle was dominated by magnificent stained-glass windows. At St Stephen's Chapel, while the stained glass must have played a significant part in the iconographic programme, mural paintings were of equal, if not greater, importance.

Both the Parisian glass and the Westminster murals featured Old Testament cycles, and placed the Books of Job and Tobit in proximity to each other. In the Sainte-Chapelle, the window illustrating the Book of Tobit was in a similar position to its mural counterpart in Westminster – at the south-eastern end of the chapel. The Book of Tobit was coupled with that of Jeremiah, and the Books of Judith and Job were in the window next to it.[71] Yves

---

[66] John Lowden, 'The Royal Manuscript as Idea and Object', in Scott McKendrick, John Lowden, and Kathleen Doyle (eds), *Royal Manuscripts: The Genius of Illumination* (London, 2011), pp. 18–41, at p. 34.
[67] Robert Branner, 'The Painted Medallions in the Sainte-Chapelle in Paris', *Transactions of the American Philosophical Society*, 58:2 (1968), 1–42. For more recent research on the painted medallions, see Emily Guerry, *The Wall Paintings of the Sainte-Chapelle: Passion, Devotion, and the Gothic Imagination* (London, 2018).
[68] Smith, *Antiquities*, pp. 156–7.
[69] Binski, *Westminster Abbey*, pp. 152–67. For an in-depth examination of different aspects of the Westminster Retable, see Paul Binski and Ann Massing (eds), *The Westminster Retable: History, Technique, Conservation* (London, 2009).
[70] For other aspects of the relationship between the Sainte-Chapelle and St Stephen's Chapel, see the essays by Ayers, Binski and Hillson in this volume.
[71] Louis Grodecki, *Sainte Chapelle* (Paris, 1979), pp. 65–6. Also see Jean-Michel Leniaud and Françoise Perrot, *The Sainte Chapelle* (Paris, 2007), pp. 121–201.

Christe demonstrated that several of the Sainte-Chapelle's scenes from the Book of Job were derived very closely from thirteenth-century *Bibles moralisées*. He also identified that the depictions of the *Destruction of Job's Children* in the *Bibles*, and also in the Sainte-Chapelle's window, ultimately derived from Byzantine art.[72]

A number of significant parallels can be drawn between the iconographic schemes at the Sainte-Chapelle and St Stephen's Chapel. Beat Brenk has argued for an integrated approach to understanding the iconographic programme of the Sainte-Chapelle, and demonstrated that the stained glass, sculpture, and wall paintings interacted with each other, culminating in a uniquely Capetian view of the story of Salvation, centring on Louis IX's acquisition of the Crown of Thorns relic.[73] Capetian and Castilian heraldry provided the setting for the Old Testament stories at the Sainte-Chapelle. This heraldry is particularly prominent in windows depicting the Books of Esther and Numbers, directly above wall niches which may have been used by Louis IX, and his wife or mother.[74] The stained-glass iconography presented behavioural models, such as Esther's role as wise counsellor to her husband Ahasuerus, which may have been intended to suggest the wise counsel of the dowager queen, Blanche of Castile.

Some of the Sainte-Chapelle's many wedding and banqueting scenes appear in the Job and Tobit windows. Brenk commented that these were designed to 'represent kingship as an hereditary institution, responsible for continued prosperity and power. Royalty celebrates its splendour with a banquet.'[75] At St Stephen's Chapel, it is not possible to draw such broad conclusions, given the many gaps in our knowledge, when interpreting the murals. However, in one surviving banqueting scene, that of the homecoming nuptial feast of the recently married Sara and Tobias, the single episode occupies a whole rectangular compartment, and takes place within a room strikingly decorated with rose-patterned textiles (see fig. 7). Among so many painted scenes in St Stephen's, most of which depicted buildings or gilded tin-relief patterns as background to the action, this scene would have stood out, and been particularly eye-catching. The feast, seven days in duration, took place upon the return of Tobias with his bride to Tobit's home (Tobit 11.20–1). The Bible also records a great nuptial feast at Sara's parents' house, and it is likely that this other feast was represented on a now-lost window wall painting. Such scenes celebrated the magnificence of the host, and also the promise of fecundity in the bridal couple. The fragments surviving from the Job cycle certainly place an emphasis on the importance of family gatherings, with depictions of Job and his family, and a feasting scene tragically ending with the children's death, featured there too.

Alyce Jordan reflected upon the way in which marriage and procreation were prominent themes in the Sainte-Chapelle windows.[76] She observed that the organization of the historical narratives created a form of genealogy, and that they articulated the belief that royal dynasties were perpetuated by a lineage of virtue. The Old Testament leaders in the

---

[72] Christe, 'La Bible du Roi', pp. 122–3, figs 6–7. The main source was a manuscript: Vatican City, Biblioteca Apostolica Vaticana, MS Vat. gr. 749, fol. 20r. Christe also explored the different interpretations of the events in the Book of Job in the Latin Vulgate, the *Testament of Job*, and Gregory's *Morals on the Book of Job*, and how these can be perceived in the glass of the Sainte-Chapelle. See Gregory the Great, *Morals*.
[73] Beat Brenk, 'The Sainte Chapelle as a Capetian Political Program', in Virginia Chieffo Raguin, Kathryn Brush, and Peter Draper (eds), *Artistic Integration in Gothic Buildings* (Toronto, 1995), pp. 195–213.
[74] Brenk, 'Sainte Chapelle', pp. 198, 203.
[75] Brenk, 'Sainte Chapelle', p. 199.
[76] Alyce Jordan, *Visualizing Kingship in the Windows of the Sainte Chapelle* (Turnhout, 2002), p. 18.

stained glass represented exemplars for Louis IX, who was the virtuous descendant of his biblical forebears.[77] The proximity of the St Stephen's Chapel Job and Tobit sill paintings to the altar wall, with its depictions of the family of Edward III, and also the *Nativity* and *Infancy of Christ*, could be read similarly. Emily Howe examined the way in which the otherwise conventional subject matter of the altar wall, with its emphases on Marian and Christological subjects, was combined with depictions of the king and his family. She convincingly concluded that the wall paintings were 'a statement of Plantagenet prosperity and a promise of future stability'.[78] Howe also concluded that the window wall paintings were introduced as an afterthought, as a concession to the newly installed canons. However, given the family-focused content of the Job and Tobit murals, it is proposed here that they instead amplified the themes of the altar wall. In the same way that Esther may have been a model for Blanche of Castile in the Sainte-Chapelle's windows, Job and Tobit were exemplars for Edward and his family. Job and Tobit were both models for virtuous and wise fathers. Their suffering and forbearance prefigured that of Christ, but their rewards were long lives, prosperity, and the survival of their descendants (a second family in Job's case) for generations to come.

Like the Capetian stained glass of the Sainte-Chapelle, the royal *Bibles moralisées* also provide fruitful comparison with the wall paintings of St Stephen's Chapel. The *Bibles moralisées* were extended picture Bibles with a vast arsenal of illustrations portraying the events of the books of the Old and New Testaments.[79] They were on a large scale, with eight medallions of images accompanied by biblical texts in either French or Latin, on every page.[80] First made for the royal house of Capet, patrons included Louis VIII, Blanche of Castile, and Louis IX. The *Bibles* seem to have remained exclusively royal manuscripts, and were commissioned for, or were given as gifts by, the royal family. For example, a *Bible moralisée* may have been given to Eleanor of Provence, Queen of England, as a wedding gift in 1236.[81] John Lowden has demonstrated that at least two still-extant *Bibles moralisées* were either present, or indeed made, in England around 1265–75.[82] *Bibles moralisées* continued to be produced into the late fifteenth century. The English royal family of the fourteenth century, therefore, could have either seen and inherited earlier examples owned by their predecessors, or even had new ones made. This was certainly the case in France. A *Bible moralisée* (Paris, BNF, Fr. 167) was made for King Jean II ('John the Good') by 1355 – the year before his capture at the battle of Poitiers and his long imprisonment in England. Jean's *Bible* is generally acknowledged to be a copy of another of *c*.1233 (Oxford, Bodleian Library, MS Bodley 270b). It is useful here, as an example of

---

[77] Jordan, *Visualizing Kingship*, pp. 19–20, 28.
[78] Howe, 'Divine Kingship', p. 287.
[79] Christe, 'La Bible du Roi', pp. 120–3. For an overview of the *Bibles moralisées*, and a detailed case study, see John Lowden, *The Making of the Bibles moralisées*, 2 vols: Vol. I: *The Manuscripts: The Making of the Bibles moralisées*; Vol. II: *The Book of Ruth* (University Park, 2000).
[80] Lowden, 'Royal Manuscript', p. 34.
[81] John Lowden, 'The Apocalypse in the Early Thirteenth-Century Bibles moralisées: A Reassessment', in Nigel Morgan (ed.), *Prophecy, Apocalypse and the Day of Doom, Proceedings of the 2000 Harlaxton Symposium* (Donington, 2004), pp. 195–219, pp. 203–7.
[82] Lowden, *Making of the Bibles Moralisées*, Vol. I, pp. 189–91. Lowden demonstrates that the *Bible moralisée* BL, Add. MS 18719 was a direct copy made in England, of the 'Oxford, Paris, London' *Bible moralisée*. This is so called because parts of it are now in different libraries: Oxford (Bodleian, MS Bodley 270b); Paris (BNF, MS Lat. 11560); and London (BL, Harley MS 1527).

a fourteenth-century stylistic 'update' of an older specimen, and is roughly contemporary with the decoration of St Stephen's Chapel.

The sufferings of Job and Tobit, paralleled with the sufferings of Christ, fitted well with the moralizing character of the French Bibles. The inscriptions for the *Bibles moralisées* were, like those beneath the St Stephen's Chapel murals, not strictly scriptural, but instead served an explanatory function. Harvey Stahl notes that the *Bibles moralisées* manuscripts presumed an audience that 'saw the Bible as a kind of historical handbook and living guide that rewarded verse by verse study'.[83] The same could be said of the St Stephen's wall paintings: they presented a model for the royal family, with Job as an exemplar for Edward III, instructing his children in suitable behaviour.

These distinctly French royal forms of biblical storytelling, known to have been in the possession of the English royal family, are likely to have influenced the choice and form of subjects depicted on the north and south walls of St Stephen's Chapel. Indeed, it has been convincingly demonstrated elsewhere that the Capetian *Bibles* influenced art in Westminster Abbey,[84] and in the Painted Chamber of the Palace.[85]

The Books of Job and Tobit in the British Museum Fragments

The iconographic sources for the St Stephen's Chapel fragment paintings have not been explored in depth before now. A close examination of the iconography depicted on the individual British Museum mural fragments reveals similarities with that in the *Bibles moralisées*. There are differences too, and these sometimes reflect the influence of textual sources, an Italianate expressiveness, or individual decisions made by the artists or designers of the iconographic scheme. Intriguingly, some divergences seem to indicate a specific interpretation of events in the Books of Job and Tobit, which imply sympathy with the dynastic concerns of the royal patron. Here, a detailed comparison between the fragments and textual and pictorial sources is undertaken, in order to note points of contact and divergence, and to interpret what these might mean. Comparison is made with two generations of *Bibles moralisées*, which are similar to each other iconographically speaking, although stylistically different. If the St Stephen's Chapel artists had access to a *Bible moralisée*, it may have been a thirteenth-century one owned by the English royal family, or it may have been a now-unknown fourteenth-century version perhaps stylistically similar to that commissioned by Jean II of France.

The close examination of the iconography of the painted fragments begins with those depicting scenes of Job interacting with his children (figs 9–10). There is no mention in the textual sources of Job instructing his children. His daughters asking permission to attend a feast is similarly absent. Englefield identified these two wall-painted scenes, based on their appearance and the explanatory inscriptions beneath.[86] The Vulgate (Job 1.4–5) merely states: 'And his sons went and made a feast by their houses, every one in his day. And sending, they

---

[83] Harvey Stahl, *Picturing Kingship: History and Painting in the Psalter of St Louis* (University Park, 2008), p. 163.
[84] M. A. Michael, 'The Bible Moralisée, the Golden Legend and the Salvator Mundi: Observations on the Iconography of the Westminster Retable', *The Antiquaries Journal*, 94 (2014), 93–125, at 101–9.
[85] Paul Binski, *The Painted Chamber at Westminster* (London, 1986), pp. 89, 90–1.
[86] Englefield in Topham, p. 17, as in Tristram, *English Wall Painting*, pp. 210–11.

Fig. 17. Detail, manuscript illumination, of *Job Instructing his Children*, in a *Bible Moralisée*, c.1233. Oxford, Bodleian Library, Bodley 270b, fol. 204r.

called their three sisters, to eat and drink with them.'[87] Instead, the *Bibles moralisées* provide a pictorial source for the *Instruction* scene (figs 17, 9). Job, wearing clothing which could have graced the king himself – a blue mantle with a short fur shoulder-length cape – is depicted seated and clearly instructing his numerous offspring – boys on one side, and girls on the other. However, the *Bibles* provide no pictorial source for the scene of the *Daughters Asking Permission to Attend a Feast* (fig. 10). The inclusion of this unique scene at St Stephen's may have reflected what was thought proper within the family of Edward himself, and was also an opportunity to depict another scene of family interaction. It is notable that Job's wife sits beside him, perhaps in recognition of Queen Philippa's role beside Edward.

The textual sources differ in their treatment of the cataclysmic moment when Job's children are killed at their banquet. The Vulgate (Job 1.19) describes how 'A violent wind came on a sudden from the side of the desert, and shook the four corners of the house, and it fell upon thy children, and they are dead.' In the *Testament*, Job describes Satan's actions: 'he [Satan] went and threw the house upon my children and killed them' (*Testament of Job* 4.19–20).[88] The St Stephen's Chapel scene of the *Destruction of Job's Children* (fig. 11) appears to follow the *Testament* version of events exactly, with Satan the instigator of the destruction. The *Bibles moralisées* depict the collapsing house and the children's death, but Satan is not shown (fig. 18).

The St Stephen's *Messenger of Misfortune* scene (fig. 12) closely follows the Vulgate text, in that messengers arrive and tell Job and his wife of the loss of their children and property. The couple sit within battlemented, Tuscan-style architecture. The kneeling messengers are

---

[87] *The Bible* <http://www.gutenberg.org/cache/epub/1609/pg1609> [accessed 5 Dec. 2023].
[88] M. R. James, *Testament of Job* <http://wesley.nnu.edu/sermons-essays-books/noncanonical-literature/noncanonical-literature-ot-pseudepigrapha/testament-of-job/> [accessed 15 Nov. 2023].

Fig. 18. Detail, manuscript illumination, of the *Destruction of Job's Children*, in a *Bible Moralisée*, c.1349–55. BNF, Fr.167, fol. 103v.

painted in exquisite detail. All the figures are portrayed very naturalistically, with anxious expressions in the case of the kneeling messengers, and Job and his wife recoiling in horror. Job holds up his hands as if to ward off the news, and his wife wrings her hands in despair. Scenes of the messengers in the *Bibles moralisées* are similar, in that Job is seated and gestures in distress, but he is alone, without his wife by his side (fig. 19). The St Stephen's Chapel interpretation is more expressive than that in the *Bibles*, demonstrating the effect of the terrible news on two parents, and in so doing, it more effectively communicates emotional impact. The unusual inclusion of Job's wife as a figure who shares equally in Job's grief is, by implication, more sympathetic to the spouse's role. This, and the unprecedented *Daughters Asking Permission* representation of Job's wife, places emphasis on the unity of his family, and functions as an antetype for the royal family themselves, who are depicted on the altar wall.

The two surviving scenes of afflicted Job and his friends (figs 13–14) show him naked, and seated on a rocky landscape rather than on the scriptural dunghill. His friend Sophar the Naamathite (fig. 13) sits in front of an elaborate building in a rocky landscape and reproves Job. Job responds animatedly, gesturing towards his friend. In the Vulgate, Sophar delivers a long monologue of reproof, and invites Job to repentance (Job 11.1–20; Job 20.1–29), while his role in the *Testament* is limited to offering his physician to help Job.

The next St Stephen's Chapel scene (fig. 14) depicts a youthful Elihu, gesturing towards Sophar and addressing him and one of the other friends. St Stephen's Elihu accords with the character in the Vulgate, which also makes much of his youth; he expresses anger that his

Fig. 19. Detail, manuscript illumination, of the *Messenger of Misfortune*, in a *Bible Moralisée*, c.1349–55. BNF, Fr.167, fol. 104r.

elders have not said anything sensible. This sentiment is reflected in the inscription beneath the wall painting. Elihu berates Job for not fearing God as he should, and proclaims the greatness of God (Job 32–7). There are many representations of Job with his friends, and of his lamentation, in the *Bibles moralisées*. The *Bibles*' depictions of Job dejected, with his head on his hand (for example, see fig. 20), are echoed in the *Elihu* wall painting. In the *Bibles*, however, the graphic contents of the friends' discussions are depicted around them, as if their spoken words have come to life and are being enacted before their eyes (also fig. 20). The St Stephen's scenes rely instead on the inscriptions beneath them to describe the content of the conversations. In this, the St Stephen's depictions of Job afflicted accord more closely with the *Testament*'s brevity on the friends' discourse, rather than the more loquacious Vulgate. This implies that the chief concern of the artists or designer of the St Stephen's Job cycle was the example set by the events of Job's life, and not the extended spiritual discourse put forward in the Vulgate. A further implication is that the imagery of the Job cycle was not, therefore, particularly clerical in character, despite being in a collegiate chapel.

Throughout the St Stephen's Chapel cycle, it is clear that Job was a regal figure, who retained his faith in the face of great adversity and was eventually richly rewarded. It is known that his redemption and triumph were also depicted, from the survival of an inscription explaining a lost scene depicting this.[89] The Job cycle functioned typologically as an antetype

---

[89] Englefield in Topham, p. 18 as in Tristram, *English Wall Painting*, p. 212.

Fig. 20. Detail, manuscript illumination, of *Job's Comforters*, in a *Bible Moralisée*, c.1349–55. BNF, Fr.167, fol. 108r.

of the eventual flagellation and mocking of Christ, but was also an exemplar of a king who triumphed over adversity, with a large family of descendants to succeed him. That Job was also conceived in the St Stephen's scheme as an antetype for Edward III himself can be demonstrated by his position next to the altar wall, with its meticulous depiction of the royal family.

Moving on to the Tobit scenes, an 'orphan' inscription fragment (fig. 6), without a painted picture, demonstrated his piety in burying his dead countrymen.[90] In its original position, this was immediately adjacent to the inscription describing Tobit's blinding by the 'muting' (dung falling into his eyes) of the swallows. The *Blinding* picture survives and is coupled with another fragmentary scene in a single compartment (fig. 5). In the Vulgate, the burial and blinding episodes also follow on from each other (Tobit 2.10–11): 'Now it happened one day that being wearied with burying, he came to his house, and cast himself down by the wall and slept. And as he was sleeping, hot dung out of a swallow's nest fell upon his eyes, and he was made blind.'[91] In the St Stephen's Chapel *Blinding* scene, Tobit's wife Anna embraces him in the moment that the dung falls into his eyes. She is clearly trying to help him, as he raises his hands to his eyes in distress. This act of wifely concern is highly unusual, and is not described in the Vulgate, the textual source. Nor is it represented in the *Golden Legend*. The *Bibles moralisées* (fig. 21) instead show Anna spinning wool to earn money, turned away from Tobit.

[90] Englefield in Topham, p. 18 as in Tristram, *English Wall Painting*, p. 212.
[91] *The Bible* <http://www.gutenberg.org/cache/epub/1609/pg1609-images.html> [accessed 15 Nov. 2023].

Fig. 21. Detail, manuscript illumination, of the *Muting of the Swallows*, in a *Bible Moralisée*, c.1349–55. BNF, Fr.167, fol. 95r.

The next scene within the same compartment depicts Tobit sitting dejectedly. He wears a blue cloak, ornamented with a distinctive 'T' brooch (fig. 5). It helps to distinguish Tobit in this and in two later scenes. The English royal family also owned letter-shaped brooches. In 1362, for instance, Edward III owned letter 'B' and 'R' brooches, set with jewels and pearls.[92] Tobit's high status is demonstrated by his brooch, just as that of Job is conveyed by his fur shoulder-length cape in the *Instruction* scene on the north wall.

An infrared reflectogram, reproduced here as an image (fig. 22 – compare with fig. 5) has shown that the doorway or wall separating the scene of Tobit's blinding from that of his later dejected self was originally wider.[93] There are two possibilities: either that the figure of Anna was a later addition to a completed painting, or, more likely, that a decision was made during the execution of the scene to give her greater prominence than originally planned. The infrared image shows that the architectural division was reduced so that more of Anna's

---

[92] Ronald Lightbown, *Mediaeval European Jewellery* (London, 1992), p. 187. A photograph of an early-fourteenth-century German silver-gilt letter 'E' brooch is reproduced in pl. 56, indicating what a real letter brooch of the period looked like.

[93] I am grateful to Helen Howard, Lloyd de Beer and David Saunders for permission to use the IR reflectogram image. This and other infrared reflectogram images are discussed by Howard, de Beer and Saunders in the previously cited 'Recent Imaging'. Their article includes an explanation of how infrared allows underdrawing in carbon black, and pentimenti, to be clearly seen. See <https://doi.org/10.17658/issn.2058-5462/issue-16/oneobject/p21> and <https://doi.org/10.17658/issn.2058-5462/issue-16/oneobject/figure12> [accessed 15 Nov. 2023]. This article also explores the history of the wall painting fragments as part of the collection at the British Museum.

Fig. 22. Infrared reflectogram of the *Muting of the Swallows* and *Tobit Dejected*, scenes on a wall painting fragment from St Stephen's Chapel.

body could be depicted. Her figure was eventually given as much prominence as Tobit's. Anna's significance was therefore considered worthy of increased emphasis in the scene. The artist or designer of the St Stephen's scene has unusually chosen to depict a moment of wifely concern, and a desire on Anna's part to help and comfort her husband.

The proximity of the Tobit story to the south side of the altar wall, which depicts Queen Philippa and her daughters, may account for the decision to focus upon a representation of a virtuous and sympathetic wife. The emphasis upon Tobit's wife, and the possible correlation between her story and Philippa's own role, is paralleled by earlier unconventional embellishments of the queen's clothes and chamber textiles during specific royal rituals and ceremonies.[94] Caroline Shenton has argued that the domestic intimacy of unusual designs on the queen's textiles show that churching ceremonies were not only splendid public celebrations, but also personal, family occasions, which manifested Edward's devotion to his queen.[95] The decision to position Philippa opposite himself, worshipping with their family at the feet of the Virgin and Child on St Stephen's altar wall, expressed Edward's devotion to his wife, and promoted her position.[96] It is argued here that Philippa's personal role in the royal family was also expressed through the character of Tobit's wife, Anna, as she was represented in the chapel's window wall paintings.

---

[94] Caroline Shenton, 'Philippa of Hainault's Churchings: The Politics of Motherhood at the Court of Edward III', in Richard Eales and Shaun Tyas (eds), *Family and Dynasty in Late Medieval England, Proceedings of the 1997 Harlaxton Symposium* (Donington, 2003), pp. 105–21, at p. 112.
[95] Shenton, 'Philippa of Hainault's Churchings', pp. 113, 120.
[96] Shenton, 'Philippa of Hainault's Churchings', p. 121.

The St Stephen's depiction of the homecoming nuptial feast of Tobias and Sara is relatively conventional, besides the striking depiction of the rose-decorated room (fig. 7). Nuptial feasts were depicted in the *Bibles moralisées* and were standard and similar in layout to that at St Stephen's. The unusual rose-adorned background may be a personalized reference to rose-based interior decoration favoured by Edward III and his family. His daughter Princess Joan had a rose-patterned worsted wall hanging included in her trousseau, and Edward had an entire room painted with roses in 1365–6 at Windsor Castle.[97] With its floral motifs, the interior depicted in the St Stephen's Chapel feast scene associated the biblical episode with royal contemporary life: it clearly evokes a room adorned with rose-decorated textile wall hangings.

The final surviving fragment is another 'coupled' scene, depicting Raphael (known as Azarias, when disguised) prior to revealing his true self to Tobit and Tobias, and then Raphael ascending to heaven (see fig. 8). Tobit appears twice, maybe even three times in the painting. Half of the picture illustrates Tobit's house. Tobit and Tobias stand at the doorway. Tobias offers money from his purse to Azarias, who leans on a walking stick. Azarias/Raphael is distinguished by his gilded halo, which is decorated with Italianate, black-painted rays and circles. The scene closely follows the Vulgate version of events (Tobias 12.5–6). The 'coupled' scene next to it depicts the moment when Azarias reveals his true identity:

> 'For I am the angel Raphael, one of the seven, who stand before the Lord.' And when they [Tobias and his family] had heard these things, they were troubled, and being seized with fear they fell upon the ground on their face. And the angel said to them 'Peace be to you, fear not.' (Tobias 12.15–17)

The angel's ascension is witnessed by two men (one of whom resembles Tobit) through the windows of the house. The background to this whole scene is formed of gilded tin-relief diaper pattern, and helps to signify Raphael's glory, and his ascension heavenwards. The right half of the picture depicting the ascending Raphael is unfortunately very damaged. In the foreground, blue-clad Tobit can be seen kneeling and praying, looking towards the angel. Raphael's wings and halo are gilded and resplendent. The representation of this subject matter in the *Bibles moralisées* bears little comparison with the chapel's wall painting. The artists of the St Stephen's mural have particularly revelled in the miraculous nature of the story, and the opportunity to use rich materials occasioned by the angel's glory.

It is not known what the next scene in the Tobit cycle was at St Stephen's Chapel, but in the Vulgate, he sings a hymn of thanksgiving, praising God, and filled with joy about his descendants entering the Heavenly Jerusalem (Tobit 13.11–23). The hymn includes praises such as: 'Thou shalt shine with dazzling brightness, for all the ends of the world to worship thee' (Tobit 13.13), and 'happy I count myself, if any posterity of mine is left to see Jerusalem in her splendour. Sapphire and emerald Jerusalem's gates shall be, of precious stones the wall that rings her round; shining white and clean the pavement of her streets; no quarter

---

[97] N. Nicolas, 'Observations on the Most Noble Order of the Garter', *Archaeologia*, 31 (1846), 1–163, at 54; Steven Brindle and Brian Kerr, *Windsor Revealed: New Light on the History of the Castle* (London, 1997), p. 45. Also see Steven Brindle (ed.), *Windsor Castle: A Thousand Years of a Royal Palace* (London, 2018), pp. 115–17. For a detailed investigation and discussion of the unique rose-decorated room at Windsor Castle, see Spooner, 'Royal Wall-paintings', chapter 2, pp. 184–230.

of her but shall echo the Alleluia-chant of praise' (Tobit 13.20–2).[98] Such a song must also have reflected the magnificent interior of St Stephen's Chapel itself. It is inconceivable that such a glorious episode was not depicted in the Tobit cycle at St Stephen's, and it would have echoed the polyphony of the chapel's canons, in spirit.

Conclusion

Close examination of the wall painting fragments' iconography has revealed that underlying themes of family and dynastic survival occasionally contradict straightforward biblical interpretation, and traditional pictorial prototypes for the Books of Job and Tobit. Choices made by the St Stephen's Chapel artists, or the wall painting scheme's designer, demonstrate that the pictorial scenes were carefully tailored to suit a royal family-focused agenda, the culmination of which was the altar-wall paintings. The inscriptions beneath the window wall painting scenes reinforced the iconographic programme, and aided the canons, vicars and choristers in their prayers for the royal family.

The underlying theme in the Job and Tobit stories, of maintaining faith in the face of great adversity, perhaps also had a personal resonance for Edward III. His reign began in the most inauspicious of circumstances, and he had endured disappointment and loss. Like Job and Tobit, his fortunes changed for the better, especially during the years of the decorative programme at St Stephen's Chapel. Job and Tobit, as depicted in the chapel, presented examples of the endurance of faith and married love in the face of hardship, which ultimately led to their redemption, long life, and large families. Typologically, their stories prefigured that of Christ's journey of suffering and Resurrection, but they were also antetypes for the English king's own life. In the chapel, the close physical proximity of Job and Tobit to each other, and to the altar-wall paintings, reinforced their message and their dual typology.

By using iconographic themes which the French Capetian monarchy had formerly favoured in stained glass and illuminated Bibles, St Stephen's Chapel's decorative scheme claimed descent from them. The scheme intimated Edward's own claim to the throne of France, the acquisition of which seemed, within the period of the execution of the Westminster mural scheme, to be in sight.

---

[98] *The Bible*, <http://www.gutenberg.org/cache/epub/1609/pg1609-images.html> [accessed 15 Nov. 2023].

Performing Spaces:
The Art of Polyphony Within and Beyond St Stephen's

Magnus Williamson

John Harper has traced the transformation of St Stephen's from royal chapel to collegiate foundation in the fourteenth century elsewhere in this volume. This chapter will investigate the polyphonic tradition of St Stephen's in the century preceding its dissolution, and will look beyond the chapel itself towards the neighbouring and interdependent institutions, particularly Westminster Abbey and the royal palace, and outwards towards London and beyond. Why polyphony? Around its kernel of universal obligations, medieval religion comprised a wide margin of discretionary practices: polyphonic music belonged almost entirely within this discretionary realm. Canon law required that all churches, regardless of status or income, maintain a stock of service books and to sustain the singing of choir chants at Mass and, at least, the daily Office – most importantly, Matins, Lauds, Vespers, and Compline. The singing of polyphony was regulated within the Customaries of some of the greater churches, assumed within the statutes of many late-medieval collegiate foundations and, by 1500, cultivated by a growing number of ambitious parish churches; but its canonical status remained discretionary and supplementary. Polyphony also prospered in the more loosely prescribed areas of voluntary religion, exemplified by the Marian anthem. Late-medieval polyphony is therefore an index of material prosperity and ceremonial ambition.

Its informal status also made composed polyphony institutionally adaptable and geographically mobile. Right until the 1540s, the regional liturgies of Hereford and York resisted the ever-encroaching Sarum Use, while the monastic orders maintained their own distinctive ritual traditions: chants particular to these uses were ipso facto territorially circumscribed. Conversely, even when seemingly tethered to a regional use by virtue of its text or cantus firmus, polyphony could escape its place of origin. This is exemplified by a mid-fifteenth-century English setting of the antiphon *Asperges me*, albeit one with no known links to St Stephen's. It survives in four manuscripts: one at Canterbury Cathedral (Benedictine), another now at Beverley but possibly from the Percy household at Leconfield (Yorks.), a third in the British Library, origins unknown (but probably from a southern institution adhering to Sarum Use), and the fourth now at Arundel Castle but undoubtedly originating within the chapel of St Mary and Holy Angels, York Minster (York Use).[1] For some reason, probably not its intrinsic musical merits, this setting of *Asperges* migrated to institutions using several different liturgical customs, from Kent to Yorkshire, even though its cantus firmus belonged to Sarum Use (the York melody is quite different).

Such mobility was not inevitable, and it may not even have been typical. Beyond the social status and mobility of its creator, the portability of a polyphonic composition depended upon several factors: chiefly, whether it originated in, or entered the repertory of, a well-networked institution (particularly in the metropolis), a magnate household, or one of the university colleges. By virtue of its location and connections, polyphonic repertories composed at St Stephen's belonged to the first two of these categories, and enjoyed privileged access to the third. The chapel's very close proximity to the royal palace and law-courts of Westminster also enabled its musical repertories to participate in the economy of high-status gift-giving, patronage and exchange, whether of the sound objects themselves or the books into which they were copied. The physical location of St Stephen's is therefore central to our understanding of the chapel's musical tradition.

Location

St Stephen's was but one of several choral foundations in early Tudor Westminster. The vill comprised no fewer than four of the institutional types chiefly associated with polyphonic music before the Reformation (fig. 1): the Benedictine monastery of St Peter, which sustained parallel cycles of daily worship in monks' quire and Lady Chapel; St Stephen's, a collegiate foundation of 1348 within a pre-existing chapel; Westminster Palace, a royal residence with autonomous spiritual provision and, under the Tudors, a growing number of secular ensembles of singers and instrumentalists; and St Margaret's, a parish church with its own musical tradition, funded by the parish's recurrent income and a devotional confraternity. A short boat trip down the Thames to London Bridge would have comprehended all of the remaining types of institution promoting liturgical music: the residences of episcopal and aristocratic households; friaries; hospitals; grammar schools; St Paul's, the great secular cathedral of the old foundation; and even the musically staffed bridge chapel of St Thomas, along with some further 160-odd parishes, several of which maintained permanent polyphonic choirs and nearly all of which would have had an organ or two. St Stephen's was among the most prestigious victims of the dissolutions of 1535–48, but its loss merely exemplified the shrinkage of a once-diverse pool of polyphonic choirs, in terms of both number and variety: after 1559 Westminster 'Abbey' was an anomalous survivor of the mid-century purge of collegiate churches.

Late medieval London and Westminster presented singers with varied and abundant opportunities. The capital's community of parish clerks was given collective identity by the incorporation in 1442 of the Fraternity of St Nicholas to regulate their activities and protect their livelihoods; its membership included parish singers, alongside clergy and 'lay'

---

[1] Possibly by Symon Benet. Gareth Curtis and Andrew Wathey, 'Fifteenth-Century English Liturgical Music: A List of the Surviving Repertory', *Royal Musical Association Research Chronicle*, 27 (1994), pp. 1–69, at p. 54 (no. O58). See Margaret Bent and Andrew Wathey (eds), *Fragments of English Polyphonic Music c.1390–1475: A Facsimile Edition*, Early English Church Music, 62 (London, 2022).

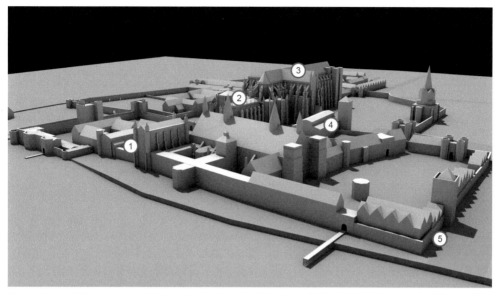

Fig. 1. View of the Palace of Westminster, showing St Stephen's Chapel (1), Henry VII's Chapel (2), Westminster Abbey (3), St Margaret's (4), the Deanery (5).

members (i.e. non-musicians) from London and beyond, affording its members a measure of social reach.[2] The parish clerks led worship and processions in their respective parishes, but convened *en masse* for general processions; through such encounters written repertories might change hands and performing practices be refined and adapted through the exchange of ideas. In 1522 the Fraternity's membership included gentlemen of the Chapel Royal, a singer in the late Margaret Beaufort's chapel, a future fellow of Fotheringhay College (Northants.), a clerk of St Thomas's Chapel, London Bridge, various senior London clergy including the ageing pluralist and one-time Dean of York and Windsor (Christopher Urswick), and a musician who featured prominently as organist-verger of St Stephen's in its final decades: Nicholas Ludford.[3] Late medieval London was in effect the clearing house for a national musical tradition, and St Stephen's links to court and metropolis put it at the heart of this network with national and, with a fair geopolitical wind, international reach.

The Pioneer Generation: John Bedyngham

If we measure this reach in terms of the circulation of music beyond its point of origin, by far the most internationally important singer of St Stephen's was John Bedyngham, the college's verger-cum-organist under Henry VI. Bedyngham was among the earliest recorded members of the Fraternity of St Nicholas. The guild's bede roll, begun in February 1449, includes his name along with those of the older composer, Nicholas Sturgeon, a canon

---

[2] On London, see Richard Lloyd, 'Provision for Music in the Parish Church in Late-Medieval London' (Ph.D. dissertation, Royal Holloway, 2000). The early history of the confraternity is discussed in N. W. James and V. A. James (eds), *The Bede Roll of the Fraternity of St Nicholas*, London Record Society, 39 (2 vols, London, 2004), vol. 1, pp. xiv–xviii.
[3] *Bede Roll*, vol. 1, pp. 274–5.

of St Stephen's and one-time subdean of the Chapel Royal.[4] The fraternity's priest members also included at least four monks of Westminster, including a future abbot.[5] At this time, Bedyngham was either in the employ of the Abbey or otherwise associated with it: a John Bedyngham or Bethyngham was granted an annual livery allowance of 13s. 4d. by the abbot and convent in 1440 which he last collected in 1453/4;[6] and a John Bedyngham, 'Gentilman' of Westminster, was subject to litigation in Common Pleas in March 1453.[7] The composer was at St Stephen's, however, by 1456 when he described himself as 'verger of your Chapell of saint Stephen within your paloys of Westminster' when interceding with Henry VI on behalf of a cousin in Ilchester gaol;[8] in legal transactions of January 1457 and March 1458, he again described himself as verger of St Stephen's; by May 1459 he had died.[9]

Bedyngham belonged to a pioneer generation of church musicians who came of age in the second quarter of the fifteenth century. Increasingly skilled in reading, singing, teaching, improvising, and composing polyphony, these practitioners participated in a continent-wide transformation in the distribution and character of polyphonic song. They took holy orders less readily than had their predecessors, while the musical culture which they helped to propagate was closely allied to the general increase in educational provision that accelerated under Pope Eugenius IV.[10] The mid-century reform of London's Hospital of St Anthony, for instance, enhanced its role as a school while simultaneously equipping it with a choir staffed by men and boys trained by a specialist instructor.[11] New foundations took account of these changes in their composition and governance, while pre-existing foundations were reconstituted or re-endowed, or adapted existing funds or posts towards the needs of musicians.

Bedyngham's official post at St Stephen's, verger, was unusual. The lost statutes of St Stephen's most probably mirrored those for St George's, Windsor, which had originally provided for a traditional verger or *virgebaiulus*: a functionary who maintained the chapel and assisted its clergy. This is how the post remained at St George's, even as that community was reconstituted and its physical fabric transformed by Edward IV in the 1470s. Perhaps the most conspicuous of Edward's changes at Windsor was to increase the number of choir singers: from the 1348 complement of four clerks and six choristers to thirteen apiece,

---

[4] *Bede Roll*, vol. 1, pp. 2, 6; Elizabeth Biggs, 'The College and Canons of St Stephen's, Westminster, 1348–1548' (Ph.D. dissertation, University of York, 2016), p. 321. Sturgeon was a member of the Chapel Royal 1413–52 (subdean from 1428), canon St Stephen's 1439–42, precentor of St Paul's Cathedral from 1442, and holder of numerous other benefices; in 1442 he had been commissioned by the king's council to select six English singers for the chapel of the Emperor Friedrich III (Margaret Bent, 'Sturgeon, N.? [Nicholas]', *Grove Music Online* <https://doi.org/10.1093/gmo/9781561592630.article.27030> [accessed 16 Nov. 2023].
[5] *Bede Roll*, vol. 1, pp. 1–2 (Robert Walsingham, William Chertsey, Edmund Down, George Norwich); Reginald Collier, prior of St Bartholomew's, was a member of the Assumption Guild in St Margaret's, Westminster.
[6] G. Curtis and D. Fallows, with T. Symons (eds), *Fifteenth-Century Liturgical Music IX: Mass Music by Bedyngham and his Contemporaries*, Early English Church Music, 58 (London, 2017), p. xi, citing WAM 19692–19705.
[7] TNA, E 40/768, rot. 404 dorse.
[8] Curtis, Fallows, and Symons, *Fifteenth-Century Liturgical Music IX*, p. xi, citing TNA, C 81/1478/25.
[9] *Bede Roll*, vol. 1, p. 51.
[10] On the emergence of trained polyphonic singers in the fifteenth century, see Reinhard Strohm, *The Rise of European Music 1380–1500* (Cambridge, 1993) and Roger Bowers, 'Choral Institutions within the English Church: Their Constitution and Development 1340–1500' (Ph.D. dissertation, University of East Anglia, 1975).
[11] Bowers, 'Choral Institutions', pp. 5081–95; Rose Graham, 'The Order of St Antoine de Viennois and its English Commandery, St Anthony's, Threadneedle Street', *Archaeological Journal*, 84 (1927), 341–406; on a near identical mid-century case, see Anne F. Sutton, 'The Hospital of St Thomas of Acre of London: The Search for Patronage, Liturgical Improvement, and a School, under Master John Neel, 1420–63', in C. Burgess and M. Heale (eds), *The Late Medieval English College and its Context* (York, 2008), pp. 199–229.

matching the number of canons and vicars, also thirteen each. This brought St George's into line with contemporary musical developments, which required trained adult singers, organ players, and instructors skilled in teaching boys chant, polyphonic notation, various methods of improvisation and, for the most capable, organ-playing.[12]

There was no systematic remodelling at the more advantageously located St Stephen's, which benefited from high levels of term-time residency among its senior clergy, and where the need for a larger choir was offset by the college's institutional partnership with the Chapel Royal.[13] Instead, a new musical post was created for St Stephen's through the simple expedient of paying the verger's salary to an experienced musician rather than a general administrator.[14] Bedyngham is the first known occupant of the newly repurposed office. Relative to its size, his compositional output is remarkably varied and well travelled. A relatively small core of Latin polyphony comprises two Masses for three voices (*Dueil angoisseux* and *Sine nomine*), and three motets for two or three voices copied as mensural curiosities by John Baldwin in the 1590s.[15]

The Mass *Dueil angoisseux* neatly encapsulates the geopolitics of English music during the second quarter of the fifteenth century. The Mass is loosely but unmistakably based on the polyphonic setting of Christine de Pisan's ballade by the Burgundian composer Binchois (Gilles de Bins). Binchois had personally encountered the English while working at Mons, and before he entered the service of Philip the Good: according to a legal deposition made three years after the event, Binchois had been instructed by William de la Pole, Earl of Suffolk, to write the lost song *Ainsi que a la foiz m'y souvient* in 1424. The tenor of Binchois's rondeau *Vostre tres doulx regart plaisant* circulated in England for several decades as raw material for improvised polyphony and basse danses,[16] as did other continental song tenors.[17] The traffic was two-way: the dominant theme in histories of mid-fifteenth-century music is the ubiquity of English polyphony in continental sources. Bedyngham typifies this trend,

---

[12] Roger Bowers, 'The Music and Musical Establishment of St George's Chapel in the 15th Century', in Colin Richmond and Eileen Scarff (eds), *St George's Chapel, Windsor, in the Late Middle Ages*, Historical Monographs relating to St George's Chapel, Windsor Castle, 17 (Windsor, 2001), pp. 171–213, at pp. 198–212. Jane Flynn, 'The Education of Choristers in England during the Sixteenth Century', in J. Morehen (ed.), *English Choral Practice 1400–1650*, Cambridge Studies in Performance Practice (Cambridge, 1995), pp. 180–99.
[13] Biggs, 'College and Canons', pp. 159–60, 175, and 234–6.
[14] Roger Bowers, 'Choral Institutions', pp. A036–A038. Bowers suggests that St Stephen's influenced the anomalously conflated post of organist-cum-verger briefly contemplated at Tattershall College in the mid-1450s; that the postholder received a lower salary than his lay clerk colleagues (£6 1s. 8d., as against £6 13s. 4d.) suggests, however, that this person may instead have been intended to blow, rather than play, the organ. The abbreviated wording in the Tattershall document is ambiguous ('*pro feodo virgebaculi et orgon*': Maidstone, Kent History and Library Centre, U1475 Q/20).
[15] Curtis, Fallows, and Symons, *Fifteenth-Century Liturgical Music IX*, pp. 1–76; *Secular Polyphony 1380–1480*, Musica Britannica, 97 (London, 2014), pp. 110–11, 113–17 (from BL, RM 24.d.2).
[16] The tenor was added in the late fifteenth century, in stroke notation and with the title 'VOTRE', to the flyleaves of BL, MS Harley 1512 (a Sarum Breviary belonging to the Apsley family of Sussex); around 1500 Binchois' tenor was copied, along with an ostinato counterpoint, into BL, Add. MS 5665 (the 'Ritson MS', fol. 144v, where the tenor is headed '*Votre trey dowce regaunt plesaunt*'); the text was copied into BL, Lansdowne MS 380 around 1500, perhaps for the education of a Bristol woman, and still lingered in the collective memory when John Skelton misquoted its incipit in *Magnyfycence* (Theodor Dumitrescu, *The Early Tudor Court and International Musical Relations* (Aldershot, 2007), pp. 20, 161–3; Kathleen Sewright, 'An Introduction to British Library MS Lansdowne 380', *Notes*, 2nd ser., 65:4 (2009), 633–736). See also Peter Wright, 'Binchois and England: Some Questions of Style, Influence, and Attribution in his Sacred Words', in Andrew Kirkman and Dennis Slavin (eds), *Binchois Studies* (Oxford/New York, 2000), pp. 87–118.
[17] See also n. 49 below.

Fig. 2. John Bedyngham's rondeau, *Mi verry joy* in its French form, *Mon seul plaisir*, published c.1470–80. Parchment, each page 22 × 16 cm. BNF, Rothschild 2973 ('Chansonnier Cordiforme'), fols 44v–45r.

as his songs and Masses are found almost exclusively in manuscripts copied in mainland Europe. The rubbing of stylistic shoulders between English and continental musicians is further reflected in the number of disputed attributions. The text of the rondeau *Mon seul plaisir* was penned in the Tower of London by Charles d'Orléans: a three-voice polyphonic setting of this text, once attributed to the leading European composer, Guillaume Du Fay, may rather have been composed by Bedyngham; indeed, the music may originally have been intended for the English translation, *Mi verry ioy and most parfit plesere*, which it fits rather better than the French (fig. 2).[18]

Between Bedyngham's death in 1459/60 and the arrival of Nicholas Ludford in the 1520s we have little more than a smattering of names as evidence of the musical tradition of St Stephen's. These have been recovered by David Skinner and Elizabeth Biggs: Walter Martin (clerk, 1458) and Robert Walby (sacristan, 1471) play cameo roles in testamentary records.[19] William Kirton, verger of St Stephen's, was possibly Bedyngham's direct successor. Kirton died sometime before 1473 when one Walter Mettingham requested burial next to his grave in St Mary Undercroft; but nothing else is known about this shadowy figure,

---

[18] David Fallows, 'Words and Music in Two English Songs of the Mid-15th Century: Charles d'Orléans and John Lydgate', *Early Music*, 5 (1977), pp. 38–43; idem, *Secular Polyphony*, pp. 66–83.
[19] TNA, PROB 11/4/159 and PROB 11/6/47 (Biggs, 'College and Canons', p. 244).

nor do we know the names of his immediate successors.[20] During Kirton's tenure at St Stephen's, the neighbouring Abbey's Lady Chapel choir was the object of intensive development under the dynamic auspices of Abbot John Estney;[21] the parish church of St Margaret was also actively cultivating the singing of polyphony by 1474/5 and its organ was played in 1478/9 by Matthew Mettingham (perhaps the son of Kirton's friend, Walter Mettingham).[22]

Tudor Sources

By 1480, therefore, St Stephen's was home to one of several Westminster choirs, including the periodically present Chapel Royal. We can assume some degree of co-operation and interaction between these choirs; Roger Bowers has detected as much between the Abbey's Lady Chapel choir and the adjacent parish of St Margaret, itself a dependency of the monastery.[23] St Stephen's enjoyed an even closer kinship with the royal household and its chapel choir, not least in the transformational middle decades of the fifteenth century: between the 1440s and the 1520s Deans of the Chapel Royal were frequently, perhaps normatively, also canons of St Stephen's; and the king's regular residencies at this, his principal historic palace, almost certainly entailed Chapel Royal attendance in St Stephen's, the largest sacred space in the Palace complex.[24] So it made sense for members of the Chapel Royal to seek lodgings in Westminster.[25] Among a number of royal musicians living in Westminster, the composer John Sheppard was buried in St Margaret's in December 1558;[26] Fiona Kisby has identified fourteen Chapel Royal gentlemen among the Henrician parishioners of St Margaret's;[27] and the organist and choir-trainer Henry Abyndon, a long-lived contemporary member of Bedyngham's pioneer generation, achieved a measure of social standing in the parish.[28]

Although his music was less well travelled than Bedyngham's, Nicholas Ludford is much the most important Tudor singer working at St Stephen's. He may have belonged to a local family: Ludfords appear in the churchwardens' accounts of St Margaret's in the 1460s and 1470s, and the composer John Ludford, possibly his father, joined the London Fraternity of

---

[20] Biggs, 'College and Canons', p. 244, citing *CCR 1468–76*, pp. 357–8. An ostinato keyboard setting of the Compline antiphon *Miserere* attributed to 'Kirton' in BL, Add. MS 29996 was probably the work of William Kyrton, who was lay clerk at Winchester College in the 1540s (John Caldwell (ed.) with David Mateer, *Early Tudor Organ Music, I*, Early English Church Music, 65 (London, 2023), p. xviii; Winchester College Muniments 22199 (1541/2) and 22201 (1543/4)).

[21] Roger Bowers, 'The Musicians and Liturgy of the Lady Chapels of the Monastery Church, c.1235–1540', in Tim Tatton-Brown and Richard Mortimer (eds), *Westminster Abbey: The Lady Chapel of Henry VII* (Woodbridge, 2003), pp. 33–58, at pp. 47–9.

[22] Fiona Kisby, 'Music and Musicians of Early Tudor Westminster', *Early Music*, 23 (1995), pp. 223–40, at p. 226; Biggs, 'College and Canons', p. 249.

[23] Bowers, 'Musicians and Liturgy', p. 47.

[24] Biggs, 'College and Canons', pp. 176–80.

[25] F. Kisby, 'The Royal Household Chapel in Early-Tudor London, 1485–1547' (Ph.D. dissertation, Royal Holloway, 1996), pp. 348–54.

[26] M. Williamson (ed.), *John Sheppard III: Hymns, Psalms, Antiphons and other Latin Polyphony*, Early English Church Music, 54 (London, 2012), pp. xi–xvi.

[27] Kisby, 'Music and Musicians', p. 234.

[28] Kisby, 'Music and Musicians', p. 228. Abyndon had fledged professionally in the household of Humphrey, Duke of Gloucester, on whose death he transferred to Eton College as organist; he was in the Chapel Royal from 1451 (master, 1455–78), then succentor of Wells Cathedral. After his burial in St Margaret's in 1497, Abyndon cantarists served there for the next twenty years.

St Nicholas in 1495.[29] Nicholas was in Westminster by 1517, and joined London's St Nicholas Fraternity in 1521. He was probably in the employ of St Stephen's at the time of the 1524 lay subsidy, and was appointed as verger and organist at St Stephen's in September 1527.[30] He probably lived in Westminster until his death during the influenza epidemic of 1557.[31] A Westminster provenance can therefore be assumed for his entire surviving output which comprises exclusively Latin church music.

The Caius and Lambeth Choirbooks, which contain Ludford's large-scale Masses (fig. 3), Magnificats, and motets mainly in six parts, were both copied in the late 1520s by the same scribe working under the auspices of Edward Higgons, Master of Trinity College, Arundel and a canon of St Stephen's.[32] His weekly cycle of seven Lady Masses (see below) never travelled beyond Westminster during Ludford's lifetime. The Peterhouse partbooks, containing a pod of his five-part Masses and motets, are believed to have been copied in Oxford for use at Canterbury's new foundation cathedral around 1540.[33] There is evidence, however, that Ludford's location in Westminster, surrounded by visitors and incomers of various nationalities, enabled his music to travel beyond south-east England, albeit less far afield than Bedyngham's had. We know, for instance, that polyphony for the new English Litany was copied by the 'chaunter of Westmynster' in the summer of 1544 for use at Durham Cathedral.[34] Twenty years earlier, a fragmentary Mass *Le Roy* attributed to 'Ludford', probably Nicholas, was copied into a choirbook along with a Mass *Sancte Cuthberte* by Thomas Ashwell, who worked at Durham Cathedral from 1513.[35] Ashwell's Mass was composed in response to his contractual obligations as the cathedral priory's lay cantor, so this was probably a Durham manuscript, with Ludford's *Le Roy* Mass imported from the south. Other composers such as John Taverner (d.1545) also used the *Le Roy* melody as cantus firmus in their Masses; its origins are uncertain, although its name hints at royal origins.

We can find the traces of the Tudor court calendar in the cantus firmi he chose for his large-scale festal Masses, whose parent feasts overlap with key crown-wearing occasions, processions, and wearing-of-purple: St Stephen, Candlemas, and the Assumption. The presence of royal listeners is suggested more palpably in the lone surviving voice-part of *Salve regina pudica mater*.[36] Although easily overlooked, this belongs to a corpus of royal set

---

[29] Ludford's career was thoroughly researched in the 1990s by Fiona Kisby and David Skinner: Kisby, 'Music and Musicians'; David Skinner, 'Nicholas Ludford (c.1490–1557): A Biography and Critical Edition of the Antiphons, with a Study of the collegiate Chapel of the Holy Trinity, Arundel, under the Mastership of Edward Higgons, and a History of the Caius and Lambeth Choirbooks' (D.Phil. thesis, Oxford University, 1995); idem, 'At the mynde of Nycholas Ludford: New Light on Ludford from the Churchwardens' Accounts of St Margaret's, Westminster', *Early Music*, 22 (1994), 393–413; idem (ed.), *Nicholas Ludford, I: Mass* Inclina cor meum *and Antiphons*, Early English Church Music, 44 (London, 2003), pp. ix–xvii.
[30] TNA, E 179/238/98, m. 4, with goods valuation of £10. Kisby, 'Music and musicians', p. 233 (citing WAM 23152); Skinner, 'At the mynde', 395 (citing TNA, E 40/13426).
[31] J. S. Moore, 'Jack Fisher's "Flu": A Visitation Revisited', *Economic History Review*, 46 (1993), 280–307.
[32] Cambridge, Gonville & Caius College, MS 676/760; London, Lambeth Palace, MS 1; David Skinner, 'Discovering the Provenance and History of the Caius and Lambeth Choirbooks', *Early Music*, 25 (1997), 235–66.
[33] Cambridge, Peterhouse, MSS 40–1 and 31–2.
[34] Andrew Johnstone, 'Thomas Tallis and the Five-part English Litany of 1544: Evidence of "the notes used in the king's majesty's chapel"', *Early Music*, 44 (2016), 219–32. The chaunter in question was most probably Ellis Peacock, precentor of Westminster Cathedral.
[35] BL, Add. MS 30520B (stray leaf from a lost choirbook of c.1520). The *Le Roy* melody was one of several 'squares' used by Ludford elsewhere, in his three-part Lady Mass settings (see below); F. Ll. Harrison, *Music in Medieval Britain*, 2nd edn (London, 1963), 429–30.
[36] BL, Harley MS 1709, fols 9r–11v (in Skinner, *Nicholas Ludford*, pp. 95–8).

Fig. 3. Nicholas Ludford, Mass *Lapidaverunt Stephanum*, late 1520s. Parchment, each folio 71.5 × 48 cm. Cambridge, Gonville & Caius College, MS 667/760, fols 80v–81r.

pieces from Henry VIII's early reign. Some of these are based on the tetrachord F G A B-flat A which Nick Sandon has suggested could be a solmization of 'God save King Harry' (using the hexachord syllables sol-la-mi-fa-mi).[37] This title derives from Thomas Ashwell's Mass 'God save kyng Herry' which survives incomplete in the East Anglian UJ partbook pair of c.1530, and which was copied into two lost sources:[38] a copy made at New College, Oxford, in 1518–19;[39] and a lost Triplex partbook whose orphaned index is preserved in Merton College Library.[40] Robert Fayrfax, the doyen of early Tudor composers, had probably set the trend for dynastic anthems with his *Lauda vivi alpha et O*, which commends the king within its concluding petitions to St Mary.[41] An anonymous fragmentary motet *Potencia patris* also contains a petition on behalf of Henry VIII (and against his enemies) and may well have been composed in 1513.[42] Ludford's *Salve regina pudica mater* is in a similar vein: the text adapts the well-known Marian antiphon, recalling Mary's 'groans and pains' at the foot of the cross and invoking her as protector and patron of the English: 'O kindly one, protect the king and the queen likewise with their children and subjects from the neighbours [presumably the French]; granting that they might rejoice in prosperity.'[43]

A more direct link between Ludford and the royal household can be found in a weekly cycle of his Lady Masses preserved in BL, Royal Appendix MSS 45–8. Sometimes confused for a four-partbook set, these visually uniform books were in fact copied for a three-part vocal ensemble singing in alternation with an organist (as indicated by the fact that the polyphonic verses in RA 45–7 set different verses from those copied into RA 48 as monophonic chant and squares).[44] Aside from its context, the set is of historic interest as the first witness to the printing of blank five-line staves for the purpose of copying polyphony (i.e. manuscript paper).[45] The books were copied by an experienced

---

[37] William Alen, *Gaude virgo mater Christi* and William Pashe, *Sancta Maria mater Dei* are in the Peterhouse partbooks; the theme was used twice by Richard Alwood, in his Mass *Praise him praiseworthy* and in an instrumental 'In nomine'. See N. Sandon, 'F G A B-flat A: Thoughts on a Tudor Motif', *Early Music*, 12 (1984), 58–63. Based on a numerological reading of Thomas Ashwell's eponymous Mass, Sandon has cautiously suggested the second half of 1513 for its composition (Sandon, 'F G A B-flat A', p. 62).
[38] Cambridge, Cambridge University Library, MS Dd.xiii.27 and St John's College, MS K.31 [James 234].
[39] Oxford, New College, Muniment 7476 (Bursars' account, 1518–19), under *Custus capelle*: 'Et solutum Nichole Hokar pro notacione missis vulgariter nuncupatur god save kynge Harry, xvj d.' Nicholas Hoker of Basingstoke, Hants. (d.1546), was a fellow of New College, gaining BCnL in 1522, and taking up a fellowship Winchester College from 1527 (A. B. Emden, *A Biographical Register of the University of Oxford, A.D. 1501 to 1540* (Oxford, 1974), p. 293). He composed or copied a set of Lady Masses at Winchester in 1529/30: Winchester College, Muniment 22188 (Bursar's Account, 1528/9), under *Custus capelle*.
[40] Oxford, Merton College, MS 62.f.8.
[41] An earlier royal anthem of this type is discussed in M. Williamson, 'Royal Image-Making and Textual Interplay in Gilbert Banaster's *O Maria et Elizabeth*', *Early Music History*, 19 (2000), 237–78.
[42] BL, Add. MS 34191, fols 34r–35r (possibly the same as *Altissimi potencia* mentioned above: Daisy Gibbs, 'England's Most Christian King: Henry VIII's 1513 Campaigns and a Lost Votive Antiphon by William Cornysh', *Early Music*, 46 (2018), pp. 131–48).
[43] 'O clemens/Regem simul et reginam/Cum natis et subditis/Tuaeris a vicinis/Dans gaude prospere' (translation adapted from Skinner, *Nicholas Ludford*, I, p. 95).
[44] Squares used as cantus firmi by Ludford include *Le Roy* (for the Sunday's Mass) which he also used in the fragmentary Mass (in BL, Add. MS 30520), and *Or me veult* (for Tuesday). This latter melody is found in the Mellon Chansonnier of c.1475 (USA-NHub 91, fols 69v–71r), an important source for Bedyngham's song *Myn hertis lust*; it was also used as cantus firmus in the earliest surviving keyboard Kyrie (in GB-Lbl Royal Appendix MS 56, a manuscript probably from London). On squares, see Hugh Baillie, 'Squares', *Acta Musicologica*, 32 (1960), 178–93.
[45] John Milsom, 'The Date of Ludford's Lady Masses: A Cautionary Note', *Music and Letters*, 66 (1985), 367–8; Iain Fenlon and John Milsom, '"Ruled Paper Imprinted": Music Paper and Patents in Sixteenth-Century England', *Journal of the American Musicological Society*, 37 (1984), 139–63.

and clear-headed musician. Musical notation is in square- and lozenge-headed notes with text underlay in an unfussy cursive, minimizing the number of pen lifts. There is very little paratext and no polychrome ornamentation, but the books are elegant and free of error. Every element is planned to the last detail: at the head of each side, the day of the week is given in regularly alternating roman and arabic numerals on verso and recto respectively. This alternation is repeated in the binding: RA 45 and 47 have Henry VIII's arms stamped onto the front board and Katherine of Aragon's on the rear, an order of precedence reversed in RA 46 and 48.[46]

The Lady Masses were in Westminster New Palace by 1542, when the Whitehall inventory was drawn up: the inventory number 99 can be found on the first folio of each volume.[47] Given the careful manner of the books' preparation, and given their presence in the royal collection six years before the dissolution of St Stephen's and the dispersal of the college's book collection, we can assume that this sole surviving source of Ludford's Masses was carefully copied for use in the royal household while Katherine was queen, even if Ludford had originally written them for use elsewhere (whether for St Stephen's, St Mary Undercroft, the Abbey's Lady Chapel, or St Margaret's church).[48] The diminutive size and oblong format of the books (190 × 110 mm) suggest their use in performance by a small ensemble in a relatively intimate space: a handful of boys singing from the two children's books, RA 46 and 47, perhaps two or three to a part, with their master reading from the adult singer's book RA 45, and the organist improvising *alternatim* versets from RA 48. Surviving pre-Reformation inventories suggest that small ensembles regularly performed polyphony at Lady Mass (and other votive Masses), including movements of both the Proper and Ordinary;[49] at Durham Cathedral, for instance, Jesus Mass was sung each Friday within a designated loft (containing its own organ) by the singing boys, the cantor, and an organist.[50] Combined with an organ blower, this chamber-style ensemble need have numbered no more than seven people at St Stephen's (perhaps fewer: six if the choristers' master also operated the organ bellows instead of the sexton, and four if the two children's parts were each taken by a single soloist). Given his dual role as organist-verger, Ludford almost certainly would have improvised organ versets at Lady Mass; a colleague directed the boys.[51]

---

[46] J. Basil Oldham, *English Blind-Stamped Bindings* (Cambridge, 1952): HE3 for Henry and HE4 for Katherine. Roy App 45: HE3/HE4, Roy App 46: HE4/HE3, Roy App 47: HE3/HE4, Roy App 48: HE4/HE3. Basil Oldham found pairings of HE3 and HE4 in at least 23 books from 1508 to 1533 (I am most grateful to Philippa Marks for sharing Basil Oldham's working notes at the BL).

[47] James P. Carley (ed.), *The Libraries of King Henry VIII*, Corpus of British Medieval Library Catalogues, 7 (London, 2000), p. 40: 'Bookes of priksong masses four: 98'. On the relationship between the putative and the actual inventory numbers, see Carley, *The Libraries*, pp. lxvi–lxxii.

[48] There is no biographical data to place Ludford in Westminster in the early 1510s. Until 1512, when the Palace was damaged by fire, St Mary Undercroft may have functioned as a chapel for the royal household (see John Harper's chapter in this volume).

[49] Ordinary: Kyrie, Gloria, Credo, Sanctus-Benedictus, and Agnus Dei. Proper: Introit, Gradual-Alleluia, Sequence, Offertory, and Communion. The Offertory was frequently played on the organ, as witnessed by numerous settings of *Felix namque* in manuscripts such as BL, Add. MS 29996. The conflation of the verger and organist roles prior to Bedyngham's appointment suggests that the organ played a structured role within worship at St Stephen's from the mid fifteenth century.

[50] Harrison, *Music in Medieval Britain*, p. 188.

[51] As David Skinner noted ('At the mynde', p. 396), the posts of organist and instructor were separate; in Nov. 1545 Thomas Wallis was appointed instructor (TNA, E 40/13431).

By chance another book has survived from the 1542 inventory of Westminster Palace, an edition of the Sarum Processional printed in Antwerp by Cristoffel Ruremund in 1528.[52] Among various manuscript addenda on the final verso and rear flyleaf is to be found a single mensural voice-part or 'square' for the refrain of the processional hymn *Salve festa dies*. Music of this kind can be found in numerous printed Processionals; it provided an easy-to-read aide-mémoire from which the walking singers could realize semi-scripted polyphony. Although less neatly copied than Roy App 45–8, and not directly associable with Ludford himself, the added *Salve festa dies* is its calligraphic kin. Sung on many calendar feasts, the hymn refrain invariably began with 'Salve festa dies toto venerabilis evo Qua […]' [Hail, feast day, hallowed in all time, On which […]]; in the Westminster copy a Tudor reader added 'sterilis Mariam protulit anna piam' [the sterile Anne bore holy Mary], a rare variant of this hymn refrain. The adaptation was for the feast of Mary's Nativity (8 September), but nods deferentially towards Anne, suggesting a date between 1533 and 1536.

Thomas Cranmer's archiepiscopal consecration in St Stephen's in 1533 and the religious reforms precipitated by it have left no discernible traces by way of musical repertories that can demonstrably be associated with St Stephen's.[53] Similarly, although Ludford remained in post until 1548, all of his surviving pieces appear to have been composed before the early 1530s, and the polyphonic culture of the college in its final years has left only faint traces in the surviving musical sources.[54]

After 1540: The Ceremonial Transformation of Westminster

The demise of St Stephen's in 1548 resolved a duplication created by the refoundation of Westminster Abbey. Until January 1540, a town of 2,400–3,000 inhabitants had been home to a Benedictine monastery, a secular college, a parish church, the king's household and, until 1529 the residence of the Archbishops of York, each with its own distinctive and complementary ceremonial traditions.[55] The Abbey's conversion from a Benedictine monastery to a diocesan cathedral in December 1540 created within a stone's throw of St Stephen's a secular college which comprehensively outshone it: from this point, references to 'the college' in administrative records can be taken to refer to the new collegiate foundation rather than the old one. By 1541 this new cathedral was served by a dean, twelve prebendaries, eleven minor canons, ordained gospel- and epistle-readers, masters of grammar and song, an usher, eleven vicars choral, and five choristers (soon to double in number), as well as a grammar school, almshouse, and domestic staff.[56] By Christmas 1540, this new community created new opportunities for students and musicians, as well as a demand for

---

[52] BL, C.35.f.10 (RSTC 16237), catalogue No. 681, corresponding with inventory No. 679 (Carley, *Libraries of Henry VIII*, p. 95).
[53] On the consecration, Biggs, 'College and Canons', pp. 101–2.
[54] David Skinner has suggested the obsequies of Westminster's Abbot John Islip in 1532 as the occasion for Ludford's Jesus anthem *Domine Jesu Christe*, which is found in the Peterhouse partbooks of c.1540 (Skinner, *Ludford, I*, p. xviii). The piece's syllabic incisiveness would suit a date of 1532 or later, but nothing in the text ties it firmly to that specific occasion. An anthem *Trium regum tuum* attributed in the same source to 'Catcott', and copied immediately after Ludford's *Salve regina mater misericordiae*, may have been composed by John Calcost, instructor of choristers at St Stephen's in 1535 (Skinner 'At the mynde', p. 396).
[55] Rosser, *Late Medieval Westminster*, p. 475.
[56] TNA, LR 2/111 (quarterly running accounts, 1540–2), fols 59, 68v.

new books: although much of the polyphonic repertoire of the old Lady Chapel choir could be transferred to the main quire, the secular Use of Salisbury displaced the old Benedictine Use, whose chant books were rendered obsolete.

Little thought seems to have been given to the interaction of the two neighbouring secular colleges during the Abbey's protracted refoundation in 1540–2.[57] None of the clergy and singers first nominated to posts in the new cathedral were drawn from St Stephen's. Priority was given instead to the redeployment of monks as prebendaries and minor canons, and to members of the Lady Chapel choir as lay vicars or choristers: so Roger Empson, an Abbey singer since 1522, continued in post until Christmas 1556 or later.[58] Where their careers can be traced, external appointees came from beyond Westminster, particularly from London parishes known to have actively cultivated polyphonic song.[59] The traffic also moved in the other direction: Lewis Mogge forsook a post at Westminster for St Paul's Cathedral, where he attended the organist John Redford's funeral in 1547.[60] None of the newly founded cathedral's nominees of 1540 came from St Stephen's – in other words, no steps were taken to mitigate the impact upon its current members of a dissolution which, before the chantries acts of 1545 and 1547, appears not to have been contemplated. In the mind of Henry VIII, at least, Westminster would become and remain a two-college town, however anomalous such institutional duplication might appear subsequently.[61]

The dissolution of St Stephen's in 1548 brought about the first, and only, transfusion of personnel to the cathedral.[62] Several junior clergy became minor canons in the new

---

[57] St Stephen's is correspondingly absent from recent studies of the Abbey after 1540: see, for instance, C. S. Knighton and Richard Mortimer (eds), *Westminster Abbey Reformed 1540–1640* (Aldershot, 2003).

[58] Roger Bowers, in Tim Tatton-Brown and Richard Mortimer (eds), *Westminster Abbey: The Lady Chapel of Henry VII* (Woodbridge, 2003), pp. 33–58; WAM 37709. The longest-serving ex-monastic employee, Christopher Bricket, was a chorister in 1540 when nominated to a scholarship (BL, Add. MS 40061; TNA, E 315/24, fol. 81), and was lay vicar 1549–97 (C. S. Knighton (ed.), *Acts of the Dean and Chapter of Westminster, 1543–1609, Part One: the First Collegiate Church, 1543–1556*, Westminster Abbey Record Series, 1 (Woodbridge, 1997), p. 103; Edward Pine, *The Westminster Abbey Singers* (London, 1953), p. 42; see also Stanford Lehmberg, 'The Musicians of Westminster Abbey, 1540–1640', in C. S. Knighton and Richard Mortimer (eds), *Westminster Abbey Reformed 1540–1640* (Aldershot, 2003), pp. 94–113, at pp. 99–102).

[59] From the church of St Mary-at-Hill came Thomas Yowell and William Foxe, nominated lay vicars in 1540 (BL, Add. MS 40061), and James Cancellar, whose subsequent career took him to the Chapel Royal (Andrew Ashbee and David Lasocki, *A Biographical Dictionary of English Court Musicians, 1485–1714* (2 vols, Aldershot, 1998), vol. 1, p. 228); Yowle had moved to Canterbury Cathedral by 1550 (Canterbury, Cathedral Archives CCc/DCc/MA40, fol. 21). Although nominated petty canon in 1540, Thomas Wharleton, a conduct at St Dunstan in the West, declined to move.

[60] BL, Add. MS 40061; TNA, LR 2/111, fol. 56v, and PROB 11/31/392. A Richard Mugge joined the new cathedral's choristers in Feb. 1541 and left (or died) in June 1542, simultaneously with Lewes' departure to St Paul's (TNA, LR 2/111, fols 57 and 75).

[61] From 1540, the Abbey was described as 'the Colledge' (e.g. TNA, LR 2/111, fol. 56). Elizabeth Biggs has suggested that the almshouse added to St Stephen's by John Chamber after 1542 may have compensated for eleemosynary provision lost at the Abbey's dissolution (Biggs, 'College and Canons', p. 111); but an almshouse was included in the successor foundation from the outset (TNA, LR 2/111, fol. 57).

[62] Clergy, singers, and choristers of St Stephens at dissolution are listed in C. J. Kitching (ed.), *London and Middlesex Chantry Certificate 1548*, London Record Society, 16 (London, 1980), p. 79: TNA, E 101/75/22, m. 1v (1548, vicars: Robert Skelton, Richard Matthew, James Rabone, John Mere, John Markaunt, John Pulford, William Langborne, John Rogers, Alexander Peryn; cantarists: John Fountayne, John Forster, Robert Skyres, and Hugh Shepey; ministers: William Pampyon and Thomas Wallys). Later pension lists: BL, Add. MS 8102 (1555), and TNA, E 164/31, fols 7v–8 (1555–6, vicars: John Varley, Robert Skelton, Richard Mathew, William Crose, James Rabone, John Meere, John Markaunt, John Pulforde, William Langeborne, John Rogers, and Alexander Peryn; cantarists: John Fountayn, John Forster, Robert Skyres and Hewe Shepye; clerks: Robert Lawney deceased, John Fuller deceased, William Pampion, and Thomas Walles; choristers: Thomas Clerk, Thomas Gilbert, William

cathedral: John Markaunt transferred almost immediately upon the dissolution,[63] as did William Langborne or Langborough;[64] John Rogers followed sometime later, and had become the new cathedral's epistle-reader by 1552;[65] Alexander Peryn also transferred sometime between the dissolution of St Stephen's and the burial of Edward VI in July 1553, and would later act as precentor after 1558 in Queen Elizabeth's refounded collegiate church.[66] The only lay singer known to have transferred from St Stephen's to the cathedral was William Pampyon. Appointed to a clerkship at St Stephen's in December 1540, just as the neighbouring monastery was being refounded, he would later serve Westminster Cathedral as lay vicar for a couple of years before the return of the monks in 1557.[67] By then he was a senior member of the local community, like Nicholas Ludford a churchwarden of St Margaret's parish and a pensioner of the conveniently located Exchequer; his service as lay vicar perhaps facilitated the grant to him of revenues from the plump London parish of St Bride's, Fleet Street.[68] Pampyon prospered, enjoying taxable wealth of £20 in 1555, twice that of his Long Woolstable neighbour and one-time colleague, Nicholas Ludford:[69] the revived pleasures of Latin liturgical song, rather than an urgent post-dissolution need to sing for his supper, caused him to join the cathedral choir under Mary Tudor.

By unfortunate happenstance Westminster Abbey's financial records, so detailed in the early 1540s, become inconveniently coy around the time St Stephen's was dissolved. Between 1545 and 1553 singers are seldom named, so we cannot discount the possibility that any of the six choristers of St Stephen's found a place at the cathedral, whether in the choir or grammar school. The last instructor of St Stephen's, Thomas Wallis, continued to receive a pension in 1555, as did Pampyon, Ludford, and four of the six choristers present at dissolution.[70] The other two St Stephen's song-men died at the time of the dissolution: John Fuller and Robert Lawney, brother of Thomas Lawney, wit and protégé of Archbishop Thomas Cranmer.[71] Superseded by the self-sufficiently ample cathedral foundation, and no longer required as a ceremonial pied-à-terre for the royal household, St Stephen's quickly faded from memory.[72]

Clerk, John Lane, Nicholas Roddes, and Richard Horpe; college officers include Nicholas Ludford with pension of £13 3s. 4d.

[63] Admitted 16 Nov. 1549, dismissed 22 Oct. 1552 for slander (Knighton, *Acts*, vol. 1, pp. 67 and 103–4).

[64] Admitted peticanon 20 Sept. 1548, and vacated by 8 April 1554, when superseded (Knighton, *Acts*, vol. 1, pp. 102 and 106).

[65] WAM 37387A; the Abbey's annual audits are sketchy and intermittent from 1549 to 1552.

[66] Andrew Ashbee (ed.), *Records of English Court Music, Volume VII (1485–1558)* (Aldershot, 1993), pp. 130–1.

[67] He was admitted on 5 Aug. 1555 (Knighton, *Acts*, vol. 1, p. 107); WAM 37709 and 37713–37714 (1555–6).

[68] TNA, E 40/13427 (confirmation of clerkship by John Chamber, Dean of St Stephen's, 5 Dec. 32 Henry VIII); WAM 33198E, wrapper (undated indenture between Pampyon and Westminster Cathedral); the lease was extended for twelve years at £40 p.a. by his widow Anne after his death in winter 1558 (Westminster Archives, Reg. Bracy, f. 1376; will 31 Oct. 1558; Walter H. Godfrey, 'History of St Bride's: The Advowson', in *Survey of London Monograph 15, St Bride's Church, Fleet Street* (London, 1944), p. 5); Pampyon also held an inn, the Rose and Axe in King Street (Skinner, 'At the mynde', p. 403).

[69] TNA, E 179/141/162, fol. 4.

[70] BL, Add. MS 8102, m. 6v (annuities: Ludford £12, Pampyon £7, Wallis £8 13s. 4d.) and m. 7 (pensions: Thomas Clerke, Thomas Gilberte, and Nicholas Roodes, choristers, and John Lane, minister, 53s. 4d. each).

[71] The Lawney brothers are first found in Boston in the mid-1520s (M. Williamson, 'Evangelicalism at Boston, Oxford and Windsor under Henry VIII: John Foxe's Narratives Recontextualized', in D. Loades (ed.), *John Foxe at Home and Abroad* (Aldershot, 2004), pp. 31–45, at p. 37).

[72] Diarmaid MacCulloch, 'The Great Transition: 1530–1603', in Cannadine, pp. 135–77, at pp. 152–3.

Aftermath

The total eclipse of St Stephen's is perhaps the more remarkable given the uncertain status of the new foundation, a diocesan cathedral from 1540, then a pro-cathedral following Westminster diocese's abolition in 1550, a Benedictine abbey once again from November 1556 and, finally, a collegiate church from 1559.[73] The Marian refoundation had a fleeting lifespan, and Queen Mary's death in 1558 forestalled any decision as to whether the old secular college of St Stephen would be revived along with the monastic community of St Peter. Once the monastery was restored, the Abbey choir reverted to its pre-1540 location and status as a modest-sized Lady Chapel ensemble:[74] in a strange inversion of the Marian norm, Westminster's choral foundations were probably more shrunken at Mary's death than they had been at Protestant Edward's five years earlier. Elizabeth's collegiate foundation has proved remarkably long-lived, but the future of Westminster Abbey might have seemed less certain in the 1550s.

For the three years between Mary's accession and the surrender of the secular chapter in September 1556, Hugh Weston championed the restored Catholic faith at Westminster. Numerous high-profile public events were performed in and around the Abbey, which also provided a sightseeing venue for the Muscovite ambassador in April 1557.[75] Other royal ceremonies took place in Whitehall Palace which could easily accommodate court worship and processions without the need for an adjunct collegiate foundation in the manner of St Stephen's.[76] King Street meanwhile afforded a ceremonial route from St Peter's through the complex of Whitehall Palace, through St Martin-in-the-Fields, and up the Strand to Temple Bar. This was the route taken in January 1555 when Dean Weston convened a grand processional Litany to pray for a safe delivery by Queen Mary, assumed to be pregnant.[77] Witnessing or participating in this dynastic spectacle may have prompted William Pampyon to join the choir of St Peter's a few months later.[78] Within a few years of its dissolution, St Stephen's had been entirely supplanted by the Abbey as a focus for dynastic ceremonial within Westminster. Dynastically, as well as doctrinally, it had become dispensable.

---

[73] C. S. Knighton, 'Westminster Abbey Restored', in E. Duffy and D. Loades (eds), *The Church of Mary Tudor* (Aldershot, 2006), pp. 77–123, at pp. 77–9.
[74] Stanford Lehmberg, *The Reformation of Cathedrals: Cathedrals in English Society, 1485–1603* (Princeton, 1988), pp. 130–1. On Mary's death the Abbey's Lady Chapel choir comprised just eight men and five boys.
[75] 12 Nov. 1554, king and queen attending Mass of the Holy Ghost before opening of Parliament; 1 Dec. 1555, reception of Cardinal Pole, with procession around church and cloister; Ascension day procession, 1557; 20 Jan. 1558, opening of Parliament (J. G. Nichols (ed.), *The Diary of Henry Machyn, Citizen and Merchant-Taylor of London, 1550–1563* (London, 1848), pp. 77, 98, 132, 137, 163).
[76] Such as the St George's Day procession on 23 April 1557 (*Machyn*, p. 137). The chapel of Whitehall Palace, built by Cardinal Wolsey, was shorter than St Stephen's (65 × 33 ft versus 90 × 30 ft; or 19.8 × 10.06 m versus 27.43 × 9.14 m), but better adapted to the needs of Tudor court ceremonial, with an Oxford-style ante-chapel housing royal closets (Simon Thurley, *Whitehall Palace: An Architectural History of the Royal Apartments, 1240–1698* (New Haven/London, 1999), pp. 30–1).
[77] On polyphonic music associated with this event, found in printed Processionals belonging to Westminster singers including Alexander Peryn, a transferee from St Stephen's, see M. Williamson, 'Queen Mary I, Tallis's *O sacrum convivium* and a Latin Litany', *Early Music*, 44 (2016), 251–70, and performances on *Queen Mary's Big Belly: Hope for an Heir in Catholic England*, Gallicantus/dir. Gabriel Crouch (Perivale, 2017).
[78] A few weeks later, Pampyon witnessed a violent assault on a priest in St Margaret's church on Easter Sunday, and the perpetrator's burning to death in the churchyard ten days later, on 24 April 1555; John Foxe mentions Pampyon as a witness (John Foxe, *Actes and Monuments* (London, 1570; RSTC 11223), pp. 1785–8). The Dean and Chapter paid the surgery costs of the victim, John Cheltham, a minor canon of St Peter's (WAM 37667, acquittance for £16 6s. 8d. for 'meate, drynke & surgerye').

Part II

St Stephen's and
the House of Commons

St Stephen's under the Tudors: From Royal Chapel to Commons Chamber

J. P. D. Cooper

Among the drawings of the Flemish artist Anthonis van den Wyngaerde held in the Ashmolean Museum in Oxford is a remarkable evocation of London's river frontage during the final years of Henry VIII's reign (fig. 1). A panorama of churches and bridges, houses and shops provides the backdrop for a celebration of English architectural splendour. Sketching swiftly in brown ink, Wyngaerde followed the course of the Thames from the Palace of Westminster and its magnificent new neighbour at Whitehall, past the Tower with its artillery and down to Greenwich Palace, where the king had been born.[1] To provide a sense of scale, the artist populated his studies with glimpses of everyday life: a lone wherryman plying the river at Queenhithe, horses grazing in a paddock in Southwark, or – grim reminder of the reality of Henry VIII's England – the severed heads of traitors displayed on poles at Aldgate. Dated to 1543–4 by Howard Colvin, Wyngaerde's panorama captures London at the moment that its topography began to be reshaped by the Reformation.[2] Of the many ecclesiastical buildings on the threshold of change, few were more beautiful or politically significant than St Stephen's Chapel at Westminster: royal place of worship, elite college of canons and crown servants, and origin of the modern House of Commons.

This chapter tracks the last years of St Stephen's as a functioning religious community, and its adaptation from 1548 to become the first permanent meeting-place of the elected house of Parliament. Early Tudor St Stephen's continued to enjoy royal patronage, its chapel a site of rich liturgy and its college broadly able to navigate the shifting currents of Henry VIII's Reformation.[3] When the religious tide finally turned, however, it swept all before it. The accession of the nine-year-old King Edward VI in 1547 unleashed a flood of evangelical reform and acquisitiveness for church assets that proved lethal to the chantries and colleges, institutions whose primary purpose was to pray for souls in purgatory. Dissolved and cleared of its altars and choir stalls, St Stephen's Chapel was converted into a debating chamber for the Commons and a lobby for clerks and petitioners: an arrangement that persisted, despite increasingly vocal arguments for a more capacious or convenient lower House, until the

---

[1] Oxford, Ashmolean Museum, Sutherland Collection WA.1950.206.1. I am grateful to the staff of the Print Room for time spent with this drawing.
[2] H. M. Colvin and Susan Foister (eds), *The Panorama of London circa 1544* (London, 1996), pp. 5–6.
[3] On the college and its personnel see the essay by Elizabeth Biggs in this volume.

Fig. 1. Anthonis van den Wyngaerde, *Panorama of London as seen from Southwark: Westminster*, 1543–4. Ink and chalk, on paper, 24.3 × 42.8 cm. Oxford, Ashmolean Museum, WA.1950.206.1.

devastating fire in the Palace of Westminster in 1834, and which continued to influence the design of replacement Commons chambers into the second half of the twentieth century.

The conversion of St Stephen's Chapel into the House of Commons took place within a wider realignment of ecclesiastical and political space at Westminster in response to the Tudor reformations of religion. The Commons had a long tradition of meeting in rooms borrowed from the Abbey, but the dissolution of its Benedictine community in 1540 prompted the demolition of the monks' refectory where MPs had formerly gathered; another temporary Commons chamber, the thirteenth-century Chapter House, was converted into a repository for the records of the Treasury of Receipt of the Exchequer.[4] The Reformation at Westminster thus denied the Commons their customary meeting-places within the Abbey complex, while offering an alternative – and permanent – home in the Palace of Westminster itself.

Precisely how that move into St Stephen's came about may never be known, though it is tempting to speculate that the royal administrator and politician Sir William Paget would have been involved. Paget's experience as an MP and privy councillor, in combination with his role as clerk of the parliaments and comptroller of the household, uniquely positioned him to advise the young king's uncle and governor the Duke of Somerset.[5] The role of John Chamber, last Dean of St Stephen's and senior physician to the late King Henry, may also be surmised.[6] However arrived at, the decision to repurpose the former royal chapel provided several hundred English and Welsh burgesses and knights of the shire with their first dedicated space within the Palace of Westminster. As an expanding intake of MPs took their places during the reigns of Mary and Elizabeth, so the architecture of St Stephen's came to inflect the political culture of the lower House: in practical ways, as cultures of debate and procedure were shaped by the size and space and layout of the former chapel, but also in terms of how the power of the Commons was conceptualized. Visual evidence reveals that by the mid seventeenth century, St Stephen's had become the symbol – as well as the location – of a more assertive and self-aware House of Commons.

Unplanned in advance and largely unremarked at the time, the Commons' move into St Stephen's was in the long run a profound influence on the development of the elected house of Parliament. The efforts of constitutional historians to trace the sixteenth-century ancestry of the modern British state have been challenged on grounds of the impermanence of the Tudor 'revolution in government', or the fluctuating relationship between Church and State long after the Elizabethan 'settlement' of religion, or indeed the whole notion that modern understandings of liberty and democracy have their roots in the early modern period. In the location of the House of Commons, however, it is possible to trace a line of descent between Reformation England and the present day: a sense of connection with the past that was perpetuated when the Commons was rebuilt after the 1834 Palace of Westminster fire and again following the Second World War, and which persists in the

---

[4] The refectory was demolished between 1542 and 1545: Alasdair Hawkyard, 'From Painted Chamber to St Stephen's Chapel: The Meeting Places of the House of Commons at Westminster until 1603', *PH*, 21:1 (2002), 62–84, at 76.
[5] For Paget's career in the 1540s see 'Paget, William (by 1505–1563)', in *Hist Parl 1509–1558*; Sybil M. Jack, 'Paget, William, first Baron Paget (1505/6–1563)', *ODNB* <http://www.oxforddnb.com> [accessed 11 Nov. 2023].
[6] His seniority among the royal physicians is recognized in Holbein's celebrated group portrait 'King Henry VIII and the Barber Surgeons' dating from 1541, in which Chamber appears immediately to the king's right.

arrestingly 'Tudor' decoration of the modern Palace of Westminster. For all these reasons – historical, political, cultural, and aesthetic – the story of St Stephen's Chapel and the House of Commons deserves to be better understood.

The Early Tudor Chapel

By the early sixteenth century, St Stephen's Chapel presided over a range of buildings belonging to the college, including a hall, a cloister with a belfry, houses for the vicars (on site) and canons (in Canon Row), and the Dean's residence. Collectively these comprised a religious complex at the centre of the Palace of Westminster, equivalent in number to the Benedictine community at the adjacent Abbey.[7] The exterior of the Chapel depicted in Wyngaerde's panorama, and in a pair of slightly earlier drawings (see Ayers, fig. 1, p. 14),[8] was little changed since its completion by Edward III: a soaring Perpendicular structure recalling the Sainte-Chapelle in Paris, commissioned 'to be the very latest word in Gothic magnificence, to be "sumptuous" to the last degree'.[9] The two-storey chapel was strikingly tall and slender, its proportion of breadth to height of a little more than 1:2 creating a dramatic effect similar to the chapel of King's College, Cambridge. Wyngaerde's drawing accentuates the graceful lines of St Stephen's, making Westminster Hall seem squat by comparison (the Chapel was fifteen feet higher) and inviting comparison with the early Tudor Gothic of Henry VII's Lady Chapel at the Abbey.[10] The embanked river frontage is labelled, in Flemish, 'Groen' for green, implying that the artist intended to produce a fully worked-up version of his sketches. Heraldic beasts decorate the landing-stage opposite New Palace Yard, proclaiming Westminster's status as royal *palatium* or seat of power: technically the only one of the king's houses to be called a 'palace'.[11]

According to the Elizabethan historian John Stow, 'a great part' of the privy palace was destroyed in a fire in the winter of 1512–13, 'since the which time, it hath not beene reedified: onely the great Hall, with the offices neare adioyning, are kept in good reparations'. As one of the buildings adjoining Westminster Hall, St Stephen's Chapel seems to have escaped the fire; the quality of its 'curious workemanship' was still apparent to Stow in 1598.[12] Positioned at the fulcrum of royal legislative and administrative authority exercised from Westminster, St Stephen's played a full part in the ceremonial splendour practised by the

---

[7] There were 24 monks at Westminster when Henry VIII dissolved the Abbey in 1540.
[8] The drawing of St Stephen's, perhaps by Lucas Cornelis de Kock, is split between London, Victoria & Albert Museum (acc. no. E 128–1924) and Paris, Musée du Louvre (INV 18702, verso). See Mark Collins, 'The Topography of the Old Palace of Westminster, 1510–1834', in BAA, *Westminster II*, pp. 205–56, at p. 207; Ann Saunders, 'Westminster Hall: A Sixteenth Century Drawing?', *The London Journal*, 12 (1986), 29–35.
[9] Maurice Hastings, *St Stephen's Chapel and its Place in the Development of Perpendicular Style in England* (Cambridge, 1955), p. 2. For a more recent interpretation, see the essay by Tim Ayers in this volume. A virtual reconstruction of the chapel in the 1360s, modelled by the AHRC 'St Stephen's Chapel, Westminster' project at the University of York, may be explored at <https://www.virtualststephens.org.uk/explore/section1> [accessed 13 Nov. 2023].
[10] St Stephen's Chapel stood an estimated 116 ft (35.35 m) to the parapet of the east gable. Information from Dr Anthony Masinton, calculated from the contemporary drawings by Anthonis van den Wyngaerde, another attributed tentatively to Lucas Cornelis de Kock (see Ayers, fig. 1, p. 14), surveys by the antiquaries John Carter and Frederick Mackenzie, and the Virtual St Stephen's digital modelling project at the University of York <https://www.virtualststephens.org.uk>.
[11] Simon Thurley, *The Royal Palaces of Tudor England* (New Haven/London, 1993), p. 1.
[12] John Stow, *A Survay of London* (London, 1598; STC 23341), pp. 389, 392.

early Tudor kings. As has often been observed, the circumstances of Henry VII's accession made the demonstration of his legitimacy an urgent political necessity. In the words of Kevin Sharpe, Henry's 'concern with public display was in direct relation to his dynastic insecurity'. Architecture, art, and liturgy were all employed to emphasize continuity in the line of kingship.[13] Royal chapels, including Edward IV's complex at St George's Windsor (continued by Henry VII and completed in 1528) and most famously the Henry VII Chapel of Westminster Abbey (1503–12), were particularly potent sites in the display of sacred royal power.[14] Capable of the highest standards of liturgy and music, and accessible to litigants and others with business at Westminster as well as the royal family and household, St Stephen's was a showcase for the beauty of holiness performed by the pre-Reformation crown.

As a secular college of canons, vicars, and choristers, St Stephen's most closely resembled Edward III's college of St George at Windsor founded on the same day in 1348; the key difference being that St George's was home to the Order of the Garter, enabling it – uniquely – to weather the Reformation. St Stephen's maintained a perpetual round of prayer for the royal dead, Edward III and Queen Philippa and their successors including both Henry VII and Henry VIII.[15] But it also functioned as the Chapel Royal when the king was in residence at Westminster, bearing comparison with the chapels newly built at Greenwich (structurally complete by c.1506 and fronting the river, its brick composition contrasting with the pale limestone of St Stephen's) and St James' (where the iconography of the chapel ceiling celebrated Henry VIII's brief marriage to Anne of Cleves). Other comparator buildings include Cardinal Wolsey's chapels at York Place (adapted with new choir stalls carved with royal beasts and roses) and at Hampton Court (provided with a timber vault and 'holyday closets' for the king and queen).[16] At St Stephen's the king's pew seems to have been towards the east end rather than being located in a closet above as in other royal chapels, perhaps because the structure was already double height; a factor which would have made the royal presence all the more evident when the king was required to worship in public.

Though sometimes neglected by historians of Tudor ceremonial and magnificence, music and liturgy were vital – and portable – resources for the projection of royal power. One of the few specialist studies, by Fiona Kisby, describes services in the Chapel Royal as 'the regular creation of a platform for the staging of majesty'.[17] Building on Kisby's work, Elizabeth Biggs has suggested that the singers of the Chapel Royal may have merged with the 'king's chaplains' or canons of St Stephen's when the sovereign came to Westminster, creating a combined choir of up to sixty voices. Several deans of the early Tudor Chapel Royal also held canonries at St Stephen's, illustrating the extent to which the two institutions overlapped.[18]

---

[13] Kevin Sharpe, *Selling the Tudor Monarchy: Authority and Image in Sixteenth-Century England* (New Haven/London, 2009), p. 66; Fiona Kisby, '"When the King Goeth a Procession": Chapel Ceremonies and Services, the Ritual Year, and Religious Reforms at the Early Tudor Court, 1485–1547', *Journal of British Studies*, 40:1 (2001), 44–75, at 64.
[14] Tim Tatton-Brown, 'The Constructional Sequence and Topography of the Chapel and College Buildings at St George's', in Colin Richmond and Eileen Scarff (eds), *St George's Chapel, Windsor, in the Late Middle Ages* (Windsor, 2001), pp. 3–38; *HKW*, vol. 3, pp. 210–22.
[15] See the essay by Elizabeth Biggs in this volume.
[16] *HKW*, vol. 4, pp. 97–9, 134–5, 241–2, 315; Julian M. C. Bowsher, 'The Chapel Royal at Greenwich Palace', *The Court Historian*, 11:2 (2006), 155–61.
[17] Kisby, '"When the King Goeth a Procession"', p. 65.
[18] Elizabeth Biggs, *St Stephen's College Westminster: A Royal Chapel and English Kingship 1348–1548* (Woodbridge, 2020), pp. 119–22.

The output of one early Tudor composer is known to have been closely associated with the college and chapel. Nicholas Ludford was verger and organist at St Stephen's from 1527, in effect the chief musician of the Chapel. His mass setting *Lapidaverunt Stephanum* was presumably composed for its patronal festival (26 December) for the benefit of the court assembled at Westminster (see Williamson, fig. 3, p. 179). The decorated covers of the partbooks containing Ludford's lady masses imply they were a presentation copy to Henry VIII and Queen Katherine; the settings may have been sung in the lower or Lady Chapel, now known as St Mary Undercroft.[19] Katherine's presence is similarly signalled by the pomegranate device among the carved bosses decorating the fan-vaulting of St Stephen's cloister.[20]

These surviving examples of musical and visual culture remind us that queens had a matching role to play within the public piety of the early Tudor monarchy. Queen Elizabeth (of York)'s privy purse expenses include offerings to the oratory of St Mary le Pew attached to the main chapel, demonstrating that St Stephen's was a conduit of female royal devotion as well as a celebration of male kingship.[21] The women of the royal family and court took centre stage in November 1487 when the queen, Lady Margaret Beaufort, and eighty ladies accompanied Henry VII to mass in St Stephen's the day after Elizabeth's coronation at Westminster Abbey: a ritual transition from public celebration to the private thanksgiving of the royal household. The newly crowned queen then 'kepte her Astate in the Parlyament Chamber', otherwise known as the Queen's Chamber (or House of Lords), thus reinforcing the spatial connections between crown and Parliament.[22]

Whether for a coronation, a royal entry to the city, or the opening of Parliament, the procession was a key moment in the ceremonial life of the early Tudor monarchy. When Henry VII landed at the King's Bridge (also known as Westminster Stairs) in June 1486 following his first great progress to York, during which he had faced down an attempted rebellion in the north, the 'procession of Sent Stevens Chapell' were waiting to welcome the king back to his Palace: part of a great pageant of barges and banners accompanied by the mayor of London, city officials, and the monks of the Abbey.[23] Kisby's research alerts us to the precise meaning of holy day processions to chapel services, as an opportunity for the king to be seen and petitioned, to demonstrate the hierarchy of favour among attendant nobles and courtiers, and to represent a ritual journey from private to public sphere: 'a crucial instant set in a devotional context that drew attention to the king's conventional and conspicuous piety'. The feast of Epiphany, for instance, required a procession and crown-wearing.[24] When

---

[19] David Skinner, 'Ludford, Nicholas (c.1490–1557)', *ODNB* [accessed 13 Nov. 2023]. In 1548 there were three pairs of organs inventoried in the upper chapel, and another old pair in the 'nether' or lower chapel: TNA, E 117/11/49, fol. 5. In 2015 the choir of Gonville and Caius College Cambridge, organist Magnus Williamson, and the St Stephen's Chapel project collaborated to bring a performance of Ludford's lady masses and organ accompaniment back to the location for which they were probably composed. A film of the performance in St Mary Undercroft, including the *Missa Lapidaverunt Stephanum*, may be accessed at <https://www.virtualststephens.org.uk/blog/sacred-music-and-st-stephen%E2%80%99s-listening-ludford> [accessed 13 Nov. 2023].
[20] *Royal Commission on Historical Monuments: London*, vol. 2: *West London* (London, 1925), pp. 123–4 and pls 179, 184.
[21] N. H. Nicolas, *Privy Purse Expenses of Elizabeth of York* (London, 1830), pp. 2, 4, 22–3, 78.
[22] John Leland, *Joannis Lelandi Antiquarii De Rebus Britannicis Collectanea*, ed. Thomas Hearne (6 vols, London, 1774), vol. 4, pp. 228–9.
[23] Leland, *Collectanea*, vol. 4, p. 202.
[24] Kisby, '"When the King Goeth a Procession"', pp. 53–7 and tables.

the king's presence at Westminster for parliamentary business or other ceremonial occasions coincided with a Sunday or one of forty-five holy days, St Stephen's would have been the focus of this procession. Since the 1340s an *alura* or covered passage had allowed access from the east end of the upper chapel to the Painted Chamber and the personal apartments of the king.[25] We see this route in action during the investiture of Arthur as Prince of Wales in 1489, when the three-year-old heir and his entourage were 'princely conveid' through St Stephen's Chapel towards his ceremonial re-entry to Westminster Hall on horseback and his keeping of estate in the Parliament Chamber.[26]

Processional routes must have been disrupted by the fire of 1512–13, which damaged the royal apartments in particular. But Westminster remained a prominent site of royal power, as the location of Parliament (of which the monarchy was, of course, a key component) and other displays of royal magnificence including jousts and tournaments. The Eltham ordinances of 1526 list the salaries of royal servants including 20s. to the 'boy bishop of St Nicholas' at St Stephen's Chapel, confirming that the Palace of Westminster remained in ceremonial use after the fire; the feast of St Nicholas, 6 December, was another royal procession day. The last known payment to a boy bishop came in 1531, which coincides with work to take down a tower 'at the king's place within his paleis' to provide materials for the rebuilding of York Place as the new Palace of Westminster at Whitehall.[27] The demolition of the privy palace was a significant stage in the lengthy evolution of Westminster from royal residence to centre of crown administration, accompanied by construction work on the Star Chamber and a new Court of Augmentations.[28] Within this shifting environment, however, St Stephen's continued to represent the personal authority of the king at Westminster.

As Henry VIII turned away from Rome, so the college and chapel became the means to proclaim the new relationship between church and state. On Passion Sunday 1533 Thomas Cranmer was consecrated Archbishop of Canterbury at St Stephen's, taking the still-necessary oath of allegiance to the papacy (hastily followed by a protestation of loyalty to the crown) and then processing into the Chapel for the formal liturgy of consecration. Diarmaid MacCulloch suggests that the royal chapel of St Stephen was the appropriate place for this 'symbolic transition from the papal obedience to a future national church'.[29] When a great banquet was held in Westminster Hall to celebrate the coronation of Anne Boleyn two months later, 'out of the Cloyster of S. Stephe[n]s, was made a litle Closet, in whych the kyng with diverse Ambassadors, stoode to behold' as the queen was served under her cloth of estate. A drawing of Anne under her canopy, with Cranmer by her side and a seating plan for the feast, includes a sketch of the king's closet in the top left-hand corner.[30] In 1534

---

[25] Elizabeth Biggs, 'The College and Canons of St Stephen's, Westminster, 1348–1548' (Ph.D. dissertation, University of York, 2016), pp. 75–6, 180–1, 236 (access diagram).
[26] Leland, *Collectanea*, vol. 4, pp. 252–3.
[27] *L & P Henry VIII 1524–6*, no. 1939; *HKW*, vol. 4, pp. 287–8, 304–5. A statute of 1536 renamed York Place as 'the King's Palace of Westminster' (generally known as Whitehall from *c.*1542), reflecting the migration of the royal presence and change of use of the old Palace since the fire of 1512/13. The old Palace was evidently still used for the Christmas festivities in 1549, when a fire in the kitchens and scullery destroyed quantities of plate on display: John Strype, *Ecclesiastical Memorials* (London, 1816), vol. 2, p. 316.
[28] *HKW*, vol. 4, pp. 288–9; W. C. Richardson, *History of the Court of Augmentations 1536–1554* (Baton Rouge, 1961), pp. 90–2.
[29] Diarmaid MacCulloch, *Thomas Cranmer: A Life* (New Haven/London, 1996), pp. 88–9.
[30] Edward Hall, *The Unyon of the Two Noble and Illustre Famelies of Lancastre and Yorke* (London, 1550; STC 12723a), 'Kyng Henry the viii', fol. ccxvii; BL, Harley MS 41, fol. 12.

Anne's influence helped to secure a canonry of St Stephen's for her almoner, the evangelical Cambridge preacher Nicholas Shaxton: another example of female royal influence in the college, albeit in a different theological direction from her predecessors. The following year Cranmer consecrated Shaxton Bishop of Salisbury in St Stephen's Chapel, one of several reformist canons appointed in the 1530s on route to bishoprics including John Skip (also almoner and chaplain to Queen Anne) and Thomas Goodrich.[31] St Stephen's College attempted to redefine its role in the 1540s, launching a campaign of weekly preaching and building an almshouse in St Stephen's Alley.[32] But in an atmosphere increasingly hostile to the doctrine of purgatory and impatient to secularize the chantries, its core activity was becoming indefensible.

The man responsible for commissioning the almshouse at St Stephen's, and for guiding the college through the turbulent years of Henry VIII's Reformation, was its last dean John Chamber. An influential if shadowy figure, Chamber had a long career taking in the royal court, senior church office in both England and Ireland, and the wardenship of Merton College in the University of Oxford. His appointment as Dean of St Stephen's in 1514 was probably related to his service to both Henry VII and his son as a personal physician. Some of Chamber's prescriptions survive, including a plaster devised 'to cease pain, and mollify the humours', especially ulcers on the legs – one of Henry VIII's particular torments.[33] Simultaneous service to the king's two bodies was not uncommon in the early sixteenth century. How Chamber may have petitioned or even advised the king in the process of treating him cannot be known, but it will have done St Stephen's no harm to have such an intimate royal servant as its dean.

John Stow gives us another tantalizing detail about Chamber: he was responsible for commissioning St Stephen's cloister. As it exists today, the cloister consists of two sides of a range matching the double height of the former chapel, with a small oratory or chantry chapel on each storey.[34] Put to a variety of post-Reformation uses including lodgings and offices for staff in the Exchequer of Receipt, St Stephen's cloister suffered significant damage during the Palace fire of 1834 and again in December 1940 during the Blitz on London.[35] Even in this reduced state, it has been described as 'one of the finest structures of its kind to survive in Britain'.[36] Given the loss during the Reformation of any coherent archive relating to St Stephen's College, our best evidence for the construction of the early-sixteenth-century cloister (on a site where Richard II's had stood) remains Stow's reference to the 11,000 marks spent on the 'cloyster of curious workemanship' built by Dr John Chamber.[37] Whether dated to the 1520s (as it conventionally has been) or to the previous decade, St Stephen's cloister is testament to the confidence of the college and its apparent security in royal favour.[38] With

---

[31] John Strype, *Memorials of the Most Reverend Father in God Thomas Cranmer* (3 vols in 4, Oxford, 1840), vol. 1, p. 53; Susan Wabuda, 'Shaxton, Nicholas (c.1485–1556)', *ODNB* [accessed 13 Nov. 2023].
[32] Biggs, *St Stephen's College Westminster*, pp. 185, 200–1.
[33] *L & P Henry VIII 1513–14*, no. 3499 (54); BL, Sloane MS 1047; Norman Moore rev. Sarah Bakewell, 'Chambre, John (1470–1549)', *ODNB* [accessed 13 Nov. 2023].
[34] For a recent reinterpretation of the oratories/'chapter house' see Biggs, 'College and Canons of St Stephen's', pp. 82–3.
[35] See the essay by Elizabeth Hallam Smith in this volume.
[36] John Goodall, 'St Stephen's Chapel, Westminster', in BAA, *Westminster II*, pp. 111–19, at p. 118.
[37] Stow, *Survay*, p. 392.
[38] The dating of the cloister is discussed by Biggs, *St Stephen's College Westminster*, pp. 172–9.

the death of Henry VIII, however, a rhetoric of reform which had been muted during the 1540s suddenly had the freedom to express itself. Rich in resources but lacking the defences of its sister foundation of St George's Windsor, St Stephen's had no option but to submit.

Conversion to the Commons

The deeper Reformation unleashed by Edward VI's accession was swift to secularize the majority of colleges and chantries that had evaded closure while Henry VIII still lived. The practice of praying for souls in purgatory had been openly ridiculed by English evangelicals since copies of Simon Fish's *Supplication for the Beggars* were scattered among the procession at the opening of the Reformation Parliament in 1529.[39] The 1545 Chantries Act empowered the crown to seize endowments providing for intercessory prayer, but was not systematically acted upon. Now Somerset and Cranmer declared purgatory to be an unscriptural fabrication and scheduled the chantries for confiscation.[40] A calendar rich in saints' days was stripped of its special liturgies and processions, interrupting centuries of ritual and rhythm within the king's houses. After four decades in royal service, John Chamber was not the man to resist this onslaught. Describing himself as 'late Deane of the Kinges free Chapell of Saynte Stephen the marter within the Kinges Palace of Westmynster' in his will of October 1548, Chamber contented himself with the affirmation that he would die 'in the true pure and intire faithe of the churche Catholicke of Christe' and the donation of his Canon Row and London houses to be sold for the relief of prisoners.[41]

Still functioning in September 1547, when instructions to Bishop Thirlby of Westminster refer to weekly sermons and occasional divinity lectures at St Stephen's, the college was swiftly dissolved under the provisions of the second Chantries Act passed in December of that year. An inventory of its treasures was drawn up, the mercer John Bowke brought in to supply an expert assessment of the vestments and altar hangings.[42] Everything was listed according to resale value: rich copes of needlework set with pearl and cloth of gold with raised red 'fygury'; altar frontals made of crimson velvet, and curtains of green and red sarsenet; albs and tunicles for deacons and boy choristers; textiles ornamented with stars and lions, birds and fleurs-de-lis. All the colours of the pre-Reformation church calendar were represented, from the purple of Advent to the white linen altar cloths used during Lent. Copes, hangings, and a hearse cloth in black velvet illustrate the work of the college in praying for the dead. Some of the vestments had been given by canons of the college, duly noted in the inventory: Henry VII's Latin secretary Pietro Carmeliano, the church lawyer Edward Higgons, Dean John Chamber.

The musical life of St Stephen's had been full to the end, to judge by the collection of antiphoners and grails, Psalters and 'iij gret pryke song bokes' which the commissioners

---

[39] Simon Fish, *A Supplicacyon for the Beggars* (Antwerp, 1529; STC 10883); J. S. W. Helt, 'Fish, Simon (d.1531)', *ODNB* [accessed 13 Nov. 2023].
[40] Peter Marshall, *Heretics and Believers: A History of the English Reformation* (New Haven/London, 2017), pp. 239–40, 294, 313–14; Alan Kreider, *English Chantries: The Road to Dissolution* (Cambridge, MA/London, 1979), chaps 7 and 8; Diarmaid MacCulloch, *Tudor Church Militant: Edward VI and the Protestant Reformation* (London, 1999), pp. 77, 81.
[41] Will of John Chamber, TNA, PROB 11/32.
[42] TNA, E 117/11/49.

reckoned to be worth a total of £5 10s. 4d. – a nominal sum, since they could no longer be used. Easier to monetize were the 'Plate and Juelles' which had enriched the liturgy of St Stephen's: two folios' worth of chalices and crosses, patens and candlesticks, from weighty images of St Stephen and Our Lady down to 'one litell box for Syngyng bred' and a silver-gilt spoon. The goods of the devotional cult of St Mary le Pew were separately listed, including hangings of purple velvet set with spangles of silver and gilt. Quantities of censers, ships (for incense), and a silver and gilt processional cross recall the movement of priests and choristers between the altars of the upper and lower chapels and through the cloister. A standing pyx 'to bere the Sacrement' was fashioned in silver and gilt set with precious stones and pearls; a second pyx was made of ivory. Two 'old Carpettes for the herse' depicted the founder's arms, in use perhaps since Edward III had endowed the college in 1348.

Signing the inventory document was John Chamber's poignant last duty as dean. Work to clear and convert the upper chapel had already begun, traceable in a series of payments 'in & upon the P[ar]lyament house at Westm[inster] some tyme Saynt Stephens Chappell' recorded by surveyor of the royal works Lawrence Bradshaw. Initial expenditure of £15 14s. in 1547/8 would have covered only basic preparations to make way for the new House of Commons: the removal of the altars and choir stalls, and (probably) the adaptation of the pulpitum to become the dividing line between the new debating chamber and the smaller lobby located in the ante-chapel.[43] If the Commons gathered in the former St Stephen's Chapel for the second session of Edward VI's parliament in the winter of 1548/9, then we may imagine the provision of a seat for the Speaker and benches for privy councillors with the majority required to stand. The alternative is that MPs met in the former dormitory of Westminster Abbey, cleared for reuse following the demolition of the refectory which had until recently doubled as the Commons chamber.[44] Either way, the location would have been emblematic of the Reformation.

A much more substantial sum was spent on the new Parliament House in advance of Edward's third parliamentary session in 1549/50: £344 16s. 10½d., readying the building for what would become its permanent occupation by the Commons in various iterations down to the Palace of Westminster fire of 1834. There is no breakdown of costs in Bradshaw's summary account, but the scale suggests a significant campaign of work to include the provision of four rows of tiered seating (as described by the Elizabethan MP John Hooker in 1572), the replacement of stained glass with clear, and the insertion of a ceiling to create an acoustic suited to the spoken word rather than the sung liturgy.[45] Separate payments totalling £39 19s. 6d. were made in 1552/3 'ov[er] the P[ar]lyament House at Westm[inster] for safe kepinge the Records there', including the wages of carpenters, bricklayers, and glaziers. Thus, the Commons acquired a dedicated record room with their new meeting-house, located above the ceiling of the chamber and accessible either by way of the staircase within the former pulpitum or via the spiral stairs in the eastern turrets: an archive of parliamentary business and procedure to supplement the individual memories of MPs. Since 1547 these

---

[43] TNA, E 351/3326. For a discussion of the pulpitum and the Commons chamber see J. P. D. Cooper, 'The Elizabethan House of Commons and St Stephen's Chapel Westminster', in *Space and Sound*, pp. 34–59, at pp. 46–7.
[44] Hawkyard, 'From Painted Chamber to St Stephen's Chapel', pp. 77–8.
[45] TNA, E 351/3326; V. F. Snow (ed.), *Parliament in Elizabethan England: John Hooker's Order and Usage* (New Haven/London, 1977), p. 163.

records included the Commons Journal, another element in the creation of a more stable political identity for the lower house within what Paul Seaward has described as 'the creation of a more routine and more systematic collection of information about, and record of, the transaction of bureaucratic and legal business'.[46]

From 1624 MPs and clerks of the parliaments could call on another site of memory in Cotton House, the home of the antiquary and politician Robert Cotton conveniently situated between the House of Commons and the Painted Chamber. Cotton's library preserved reams of material relevant to the self-identity of members including Parliament rolls and statutes, copies of Magna Carta and the fourteenth-century treatise *Modus Tenendi Parliamentum*, and other papers relating to the power, procedure, and antiquity of Parliament. For those with the inclination to think historically – and the early modern Commons had plenty of lawyers as well as antiquaries – Cotton House was a treasure trove of precedent. Charles I detected a threat to his prerogative, ordering in 1629 that the library be closed and catalogued to reveal any documents detrimental to royal authority. Cotton himself was granted access only in the company of the clerk of the council.[47] The Treasury of Receipt of the Exchequer, based close by in the north-east corner of Westminster Hall, was another rich archival resource which included the revered Domesday Book and the Red and Black Books of the Exchequer. More than a dedicated chamber for debate, the move into the Palace of Westminster provided the Commons with a physical corpus of records and memories that could give voice to the authority of the lower House: 'of great Use and Service for the Knowledge and Preservation of our Constitution both in Church and State', to quote John Strype's 1720 edition of Stow's *Survey*.[48]

The presence of a private dwelling within the precincts of a royal palace may look like an aberration, but in fact it was nothing unusual in early modern Westminster. The great (as distinct from privy) palace centred on the Hall had hosted shops and businesses for centuries, creating a forum in which many degrees of men and women could mingle.[49] The demolition of sections of the privy palace following the fire of 1512/13 enabled others to encroach on the spaces vacated by the king and his court. The magnificent cloister commissioned by John Chamber could be viewed in this context, as a private act of devotion under licence from the king. Legal and financial officers of the crown were the next to colonize the Palace, as the new courts channelling the profits of monastic dissolution were allocated premises adjacent to Westminster Hall. The more ancient Exchequer was also hungry for space, occupying the houses and cloister yielded up by the departing canons of St Stephen's and then getting a new chamber of its own in the 1560s.[50] The conversion of St Stephen's Chapel into the House of Commons should be seen within this longer-term context of the recycling of space at Westminster, a process in which fire and fashion (Henry VIII's

---

[46] TNA, E 351/3326; Paul Seaward, 'Institutional Memory and Contemporary History in the House of Commons, 1547–1640', in Paul Cavill and Alexandra Gajda (eds), *Writing the History of Parliament in Tudor and Early Stuart England* (Manchester, 2018), pp. 211–28, at p. 215.
[47] C. G. C. Tite, 'The Cotton Library in the 17th Century and its Manuscript Records of the English Parliament', *PH*, 14 (1995), 121–38; Stuart Handley, 'Cotton, Sir Robert Bruce (1571–1631)', *ODNB* [accessed 13 Nov. 2023].
[48] John Stow and John Strype, *A Survey of the Cities of London and Westminster* (2 vols, London, 1720), vol. 2, p. 55. Ownership of Cotton House passed from the Cotton family to the nation in 1707.
[49] J. Goodall, 'The Medieval Palace of Westminster', in Riding & Riding, pp. 49–67, at pp. 58–9.
[50] Collins, 'Topography of the Old Palace', pp. 214–16; Kirsty Wright, 'The Exchequer of Receipt in the Palace of Westminster, 1548–1662' (Ph.D. dissertation, University of York, 2023).

aspiration to create a Renaissance court at Whitehall) played their parts alongside the Reformation.

The repurposing of St Stephen's as part of this wider scramble for space, as distinct from a Tudor 'revolution in government' or any kind of constitutional grand plan, is illustrated by the fate of the former college site. On 22 July 1550 St Stephen's was granted to the Kentish landowner and soldier Sir Ralph Fane: as specified in the patent roll, 'the whole of the house and site of the late college or royal free chapel of St Stephen' to include its church, cloister, houses, and entrance porch, with the caveat that the upper chapel itself be reserved 'for the house of Parliament and for holding our Parliaments there'. Fane acquired the manor and park of Penshurst and other properties in the same transaction: belated recognition of his role in the 1547 English victory over the Scots at Pinkie, as claimed in the grant, but more plausibly part of John Dudley, Earl of Warwick's manoeuvres to detach clients of the now-disgraced Duke of Somerset to his own service.[51]

If this was indeed Warwick's strategy then it failed, since Fane was among the supporters of Somerset who had to be eliminated in October 1551 following an alleged conspiracy. The site of St Stephen's was regranted in April 1552 to Sir John Gates, a soldier not unlike Fane but closer in clientage to Dudley (who emerged from this latest round of politicking as Duke of Northumberland). Gates's acquisition of St Stephen's was justified on grounds of his service as captain of the guard.[52] When Gates in turn succumbed to the scaffold following Northumberland's attempt to place his daughter-in-law Jane on the throne, Queen Mary granted the former college site to a third soldier-courtier, Edward Hastings, who took the opposite side to Gates in summer 1553 and upheld Mary's right to rule. His religious conservatism makes it likely that this is the same Edward Hastings who witnessed the will of John Chamber, implying a prior connection to St Stephen's.[53] In common with both Fane and Gates, Hastings had the curious experience of sitting in the Commons while in possession of the rest of the former college site.[54] His death in 1572 returned St Stephen's to the crown, securing the future of the former college buildings as a home for the Auditor and Tellers of the Exchequer of Receipt.[55] The story of St Stephen's in these years demonstrates how the Palace of Westminster itself was evolving, from royal residence to epicentre of crown administration, Parliament, and the law: as contemporary theorists would have understood it, a transition from the body natural to the body politic.

When it has been considered at all, the post-Reformation history of St Stephen's has generally been thought about in isolation from other buildings. Comparisons with the Sainte-Chapelle in Paris, its closest surviving relative, debate the degree of imitation practised by the medieval architects of St Stephen's but neglect to carry the comparison into the modern era: the secularization of the Sainte-Chapelle as an archival repository following the French Revolution and its restoration by Duban, Lassus, and Viollet-le-Duc in the context of the

---

[51] TNA, C 66/834, m. 22; J. Andreas Löwe, 'Fane, Sir Ralph (b. before 1510, d.1552)', *ODNB* [accessed 13 Nov. 2023].
[52] TNA, C 66/846, m. 28; TNA, DL 10/404; TNA, DL 26/86; Narasingha P. Sil, 'Gates, Sir John (1504–1553)', *ODNB* [accessed 13 Nov. 2023].
[53] TNA, C 66/935, m. 35; TNA E 354/9; TNA, PROB 11/32; BL, Lansdowne MS 171, fol. 359; David Loades, 'Hastings, Edward, Baron Hastings of Loughborough (1512x15?–1572)', *ODNB* [accessed 13 Nov. 2023].
[54] *Hist Parl 1509–1558*, 'Vane (Fane), Sir Ralph (by 1510–52)', 'Gates, John (by 1504–53)', 'Hastings, Edward (by 1519–72)'.
[55] TNA, SC 6/ELIZI/1429, 1447; TNA, SC 6/JASI/644, 650.

Gothic Revival of the 1840s and 50s, a cycle of adaptation and renewal also recognizable at Westminster. Of course St Stephen's Chapel has a very particular significance, the place of worship for medieval kings and queens that ultimately became emblematic of the power of the people. But the processes that formed the House of Commons in St Stephen's were not unique; indeed they are quite familiar to historians and post-Reformation archaeologists who study buildings of this type.

Maurice Howard tells us that the recycling of monastic fabric was an everyday occurrence in later Tudor England, inviting imaginative architectural responses to the past. Perhaps half the buildings emptied by the dissolution may have been put to new use.[56] Inevitably houses for the gentry predominated, but numerous other solutions were found: town halls, workshops, schools, and hospitals were all housed in former monasteries and friaries. Holy Trinity Priory Aldgate became a city home for Thomas Audley and subsequently the Duke of Norfolk, its claustral buildings converted into a hall and tenements and mapped in c.1585 by John Symonds, who also surveyed St Stephen's cloister.[57] The London Charterhouse saw service as a storage facility for Henry VIII's tents and masquing costumes before its renovation as a house for the Chancellor of the Court of Augmentations; from 1613 it was converted into a hospital and school.[58] The Priory of St John of Jerusalem in Clerkenwell also hosted the king's tents and hunting gear, then was employed as a home for Princess Mary and a ready source of quality stone for building at Whitehall and Somerset House.[59] Set in context, the refurbishment of St Stephen's Chapel as the House of Commons fits a pattern of pragmatic solutions to practical problems: how to accommodate the needs of an expanding Tudor state and society, and what to do with prominent buildings made redundant by the Reformation. In terms of its political consequences, however, the decision to house the Commons in St Stephen's was in a league of its own.

Royal Chapel to Commons Chamber

According to the architectural historian Maurice Hastings, the Chapel of St Stephen 'practically disappeared' when it was converted – or 'relegated', as he puts it – to the use of the House of Commons. Although material and artistic evidence survived below the surface, to be rediscovered and reinterpreted by antiquaries before being obliterated by the renovations of James Wyatt and the fire of 1834, a lot was also destroyed during the long occupation of the Chapel by MPs.[60] The interior of St Stephen's by 1707, as reordered over the previous fifteen years by Surveyor of the King's Works Christopher Wren, bore little resemblance to the former chapel. The clerestory had been removed to allow for the lowering of the roof, the galleries extended (supported by eight iron columns with decorative capitals), and

---

[56] Maurice Howard, 'Recycling the Monastic Fabric: Beyond the Act of Dissolution', in David Gaimster and Roberta Gilchrist (eds), *The Archaeology of the Reformation 1480–1580* (Leeds, 2003), pp. 221–34, at p. 221.
[57] John Schofield and Richard Lea, *Holy Trinity Priory, Aldgate, City of London* (London, 2005), pp. 19–21.
[58] Bruno Barber and Christopher Thomas, *The London Charterhouse* (London, 2002), p. 73.
[59] Barney Sloane and Gordon Malcolm, *Excavations at the Priory of the Order of St John of Jerusalem, Clerkenwell, London* (London, 2004), p. 223.
[60] Hastings, *St Stephen's Chapel*, pp. 2, 28. For analysis of the pre-Reformation chapel and its rediscovery by antiquaries see Rosemary Hill, '"Proceeding like Guy Faux": The Antiquarian Investigation of St Stephen's Chapel Westminster', *Architectural History*, 59 (2016), 253–70.

the walls panelled in painted wood.[61] Such was the chamber depicted in Peter Tillemans' engaging study of *The House of Commons in Session* in Queen Anne's reign: a rationalized and classicized space, its fashionably dressed inhabitants posed in measured and leisurely discourse (fig. 2).[62]

Tillemans painted the House of Commons as it wanted to be seen, celebrating the Act of Union that had recently brought Scotland together with England and Wales to form the United Kingdom. Consider the chamber before its reordering by Wren, however, and a somewhat different picture emerges. Our understanding of the relationship between St Stephen's Chapel and the Commons in the century and a half following its conversion is hampered both by the scarcity of contemporary visual sources (the earliest engraving of the interior of the chamber dates from *c*.1624), and by questions relating to the interpretation of those images that have come down to us: whether intended to be realistic depictions of the lower House, or more representative in character. But when other evidence is brought to bear – financial records relating to the maintenance of the Commons, or the testimonies of MPs who knew the building – Hastings's divide between the chapel and the chamber becomes less absolute. Material traces of St Stephen's Chapel remained visible in the Commons chamber, the lobby, and the west entrance and stairway: for instance the rich display of heraldry referenced in a speech by MP and parliamentary diarist Hayward Townshend in 1601, or the statues of the twelve Apostles – headless, but stubbornly still in place on their image brackets forty years later.[63] Echoes of the former chapel could be heard as well as seen. Long after the dissolution of St Stephen's College, the soundscape at Westminster followed the rhythm of Edward III's clock tower located in New Palace Yard. Stow describes its great bell striking the hour, regulating the law-courts meeting in Westminster Hall; on a calm day it could be heard in the city of London. For coronations and other 'great triumphes' people would congregate at the foot of the tower, where the fountain was primed to spout wine.[64]

The architecture and decoration of St Stephen's Chapel reminded MPs that they met in residually royal space, even if its usage had changed. The pew once occupied by kings and queens disappeared with the rest of the choir stalls, probably in the initial clearance of the chapel during Edward VI's reign, but the royal presence remained in the form of the arms painted in a 'table' above the Speaker's chair as recorded in an Exchequer account for 1576; these may have replaced an earlier set.[65] Another instance of the queen's arms, carved in stone at the cost of 26*s*. 8*d*. in wages, is recorded in Exchequer payments for the roofing of the stair to the Commons lobby from the west, one of the access routes for MPs heading for the chamber; the work was carried out between 1567 and 1570.[66] The inclusion of the

---

[61] See the essay by Murray Tremellen in this volume. For a virtual reconstruction of the Commons chamber *c*.1707 modelled by the St Stephen's Chapel project, see <https://www.virtualststephens.org.uk/sites/virtualststephens.org.uk/files/panoramas/1707/tour.html> [accessed 13 Nov. 2023].
[62] John Goodall believes that 'the fabric of the chapel was largely intact beneath Wren's features': 'The Medieval Palace of Westminster', picture caption pp. 62–3.
[63] T. E. Hartley (ed.), *Proceedings in the Parliaments of Elizabeth I* (3 vols, Leicester, 1981–5), vol. 3, p. 470; Anon. artist, *Platform of this Lower House of the Present Parliament* (engraving, *c*.1641), BM, Prints & Drawings, 1885, 1114.124.1-3.
[64] Stow, *Survay*, pp. 392–3. The clock tower (a different structure from St Stephen's belfry mentioned above, also built by Edward III) was granted to the dean and canons of St Stephen's in 1443: *CPR 1441–46*, p. 113. The clock tower was finally demolished in 1692.
[65] TNA, E 351/3211, 20*s*. paid 'for armes to hang in the lower p[ar]liamente Howse'.
[66] TNA, E 351/3204.

Fig. 2. Peter Tillemans, *The House of Commons in Session*, 1709–14. Oil painting, 137.2 × 123.2 cm. WOA 2737.

Lesser or White Hall in the same account makes it impossible to be certain, but a plausible explanation is that the arms were displayed above the entrance to the former ante-chapel.

The ritual life of the Commons, its prayers before the start of business and the procession of the Speaker and Serjeant with his mace, was another means of ensuring that the authority of the crown was upheld in the daily life of Parliament.[67] Less easy to interpret are the wall paintings commissioned by Edward III, including St George presenting the king to the

---

[67] Parliamentary prayer, ceremony and the mace all discussed in greater detail in Cooper, 'Elizabethan House of Commons'.

Virgin and Child, recorded by antiquaries as still extant in the east end of the former chapel in the 1790s. Since Wren's time they had been hidden behind wainscot panelling, hence their preservation. But what was their history in the years following the Reformation? The paintings may have been concealed by the tiered seating constructed where the high altar had stood, or obscured by the tapestries that hung in the Commons as in the Lords. Workmen were paid in 1565/7 for 'whyting and plaistering bothe the houses' of Parliament, although modern pigment analysis shows no trace of whitewash on surviving sections of the paintings.[68] An alternative possibility is that part of Edward III's devotional sequence could still be seen, saved from destruction by its dynastic and national iconography and recalling a space that had been 'intently focused on the celebration of the royal family', as Emily Howe characterizes St Stephen's under the Plantagenets.[69] This is how the Elizabethan chamber appears in the virtual reconstructions modelled for the St Stephen's Chapel project: a speculative but informed response to Hayward Townshend's and other evidence, as a means of prompting further debate.[70]

A positive case has been made for the influence of the former chapel fabric on the layout of the early modern Commons. John Goodall sees a direct connection between the former choir stalls and the bench seating constructed for MPs, the one exactly reproducing the other: 'It is this confrontational arrangement of seats that has done so much to shape the style of debate at Westminster.'[71] Another account implies that the choir stalls themselves were initially reused.[72] A myth circulating at the modern Parliament, not helped by a Commons Information Office fact sheet, explains the custom of bowing to the Speaker as an acknowledgement of the altar in St Stephen's Chapel; in fact it was a conventional gesture of respect to the presence of the sovereign represented by the royal arms.[73]

As an explanation for the peculiarly British way of doing politics in the Commons, this continuity thesis between the chapel and the chamber has obvious appeal. The risk, however, is that it reads history backwards. Visual evidence for the early-seventeenth-century interior shows that the former choir stalls did not precisely mirror the seating provided for MPs, which was built in four (later five) tiers and carried around the east end of the former chapel to create an overall horseshoe shape. As pointed out by Alasdair Hawkyard, since the fourteenth century the Commons had regularly met in rectangular spaces – the Painted Chamber, the Abbey refectory – making the move into St Stephen's less of an innovation than it may appear. The exception was the octagonal chapter house of Westminster Abbey, but here too there may be similarities between the pre- and post-Reformation meeting-places of the Commons: when fitted out with tiered seating, the chapter house would have

---

[68] TNA, E 351/3203. For modern analyses of the wall paintings, see Helen Howard et al., 'The Wall Paintings at St Stephen's Chapel, Westminster Palace: Recent Imaging and Scientific Analysis of the Fragments in the British Museum', *British Art Studies* 16 (2020), <http://britishartstudies.ac.uk/issues/issue-index/issue-16/wall-painting-fragments-in-the-british-museum> [accessed 13 Nov. 2023]; and the essay by Jane Spooner in this volume.
[69] Emily Howe, 'Divine Kingship and Dynastic Display: The Altar Wall Murals of St Stephen's Chapel, Westminster', *Antiquaries Journal*, 81 (2001), 259–303, at 260.
[70] For the St Stephen's Chapel project virtual reconstruction of the Commons chamber in Elizabeth I's reign, see <https://www.virtualststephens.org.uk/explore/section3/elizabethan-commons-1559-1601> [accessed 13 Nov. 2023].
[71] Goodall, 'St Stephen's Chapel, Westminster', p. 118.
[72] Collins, 'Topography of the Old Palace', p. 215.
[73] 'Some Traditions and Customs of the House', <https://www.parliament.uk/documents/commons-information-office/g07.pdf> [accessed 13 Nov. 2023].

been 'strikingly like' the chamber described by John Hooker.[74] It is also worth noting that the Commons sat in St Stephen's for well over a century before the emergence of anything resembling an 'Age of Party', inviting questions about the immediate relationship between 'confrontational' politics and the architecture of the Commons chamber. The Tudor constitutional historian Geoffrey Elton was clear that the Elizabethan Commons 'did not include a group of opposition members anxious to raise issues displeasing to the Queen', denying the connections that his former tutor John Neale had made between the historical and modern-day House of Commons.[75]

This is not to play down the impact of St Stephen's on the Commons – the intention of this chapter, and much of the rest of this book, is precisely to explore the linked histories of the two spaces – but rather to focus attention on aspects of the former chapel that were the most significant in framing the political culture of Parliament. The size, as much as the shape, of St Stephen's was a defining feature of the new House of Commons. Of the spaces occupied by MPs since the later fourteenth century, the Chapel of St Stephen was by some way the most cramped. At 62 ft 5 in (19.04 m) in length, the debating chamber was half the size of the 'cavernous' monastic refectory which had served as the Commons' meeting-place before the Reformation. If Hawkyard is correct that the shape and fabric of the refectory were key determinants of the layout of the pre-Reformation Commons, for instance the location of the Speaker's chair, then the move into St Stephen's required fitting the same essential elements into a much more compact space.[76] Even with tiered seating and a general willingness to squash up, the newly converted Commons chamber would barely have been sufficient to seat all the elected Members at one time.[77] As the list of boroughs entitled to return Members to Parliament expanded during the later sixteenth century, so the problem became more acute. The number of MPs elected in England and Wales grew from 379 in Edward VI's reign, to 398 under Mary I, to 462 for the last of Elizabeth's parliaments.[78] The uncomfortable and unsanitary conditions may have diminished the appetite for lengthy sessions, or fuelled the absenteeism that continued to vex the authorities. A treatise prepared for Sir Christopher Hatton in 1572 contrasted the fresh intake of MPs who 'are commonly most adventurous and can be gladdest of long Parliaments to learn and see fashions', with the 'old continuers' who had learned to be more circumspect.[79] When the Commons was close to capacity, as it could be when a vote or division was called, the experience of debate would have been intimate and intense. Over time the crowdedness of the Commons became a political issue in itself: to radicals a symbol of the unreformed constitution, while to the Whig interpretation of history a defining virtue of its Britishness to be protected against clumsy innovation. Thanks to the design choices of Charles Barry in the 1840s and the

---

[74] Hawkyard, 'From Painted Chamber to St Stephen's Chapel', pp. 68, 84; Snow (ed.), *John Hooker's Order and Usage*, p. 163.
[75] Geoffrey Elton, *The Parliament of England 1559–1581* (Cambridge, 1986), p. 328.
[76] Chapel dimensions calculated for the St Stephen's project virtual reconstructions. On the refectory see Hawkyard, 'From Painted Chamber to St Stephen's Chapel', p. 74.
[77] Seating capacity for the chamber has been estimated at 334 MPs based on 50 cm of bench-space per member, a few dozen more if this allowance is reduced. By 1606 a gallery had been introduced to reduce overcrowding.
[78] Figures from *Hist Parl Online*: <https://www.historyofparliamentonline.org/volume/1509-1558/survey/appendix-iii-seats-available> and <https://www.historyofparliamentonline.org/research/constituencies/constituencies-1558-1603> [accessed 13 Nov. 2023].
[79] Elton, *Parliament of England 1559–1581*, p. 324.

determination of Winston Churchill to replace the chamber blitzed in 1941 with as near a restoration as possible, the crowded intimacy of St Stephen's continues to shape the House of Commons to this day.

Another distinctive feature of the modern Commons traceable to the deep past is the custom of voting by division. Again this predated the move into St Stephen's, but was then reshaped by the layout of the former chapel and ante-chapel. Division of the House was first recorded in the 1523 Blackfriars Parliament; whether an innovation or already familiar practice is not known.[80] The dimensions of St Stephen's Chapel made it impractical for the house to divide into two within the chamber, but a solution was at hand in the form of the liturgically redundant pulpitum (or whatever replaced it) and the ante-chapel or 'utter [outer] rowme' mentioned by Hooker, known by the seventeenth century as the lobby. Members voting in favour of a motion left the chamber to wait in the lobby, which had been cleared of clerks and messengers, servants and petitioners by the Serjeant. The number still sitting was taken by tellers appointed by the Speaker, before the voting Members were counted one-by-one on their return to the chamber.[81] The uncertainty of regaining a vacated seat was a practical disincentive to backing change in the law, as was perhaps the visible and personal nature of voting; a quaintly theatrical element of the process that the UK Parliament retains, at least for the present.

As for that lobby vacated in advance of a vote, the culture of petitioning Parliament was established long before the move to St Stephen's, and indeed was fundamental to the identity of the Commons. But the creation of a space where lobbyists could wait, adjacent to Westminster Hall where so many other forms of legal petitioning took place, undoubtedly funnelled the presentation of suits and pleas to the elected Members of Parliament. Chris Kyle and Jason Peacey have highlighted the Commons lobby as a political access point, whether to convey messages to Members, to post libels on the Commons door, or (by the 1640s) openly to protest.[82] Above the lobby stood the committee room where growing quantities of business were transacted, creating further opportunities to intercept Members on their way to work.[83]

The Chapel of St Stephen may have been smaller than the accommodation previously occupied by the Commons, but it was better located. Early modern England was intensely aware of the social gradation of space, and Parliament was no exception. The Lords had long been settled in the Queen's (or White) Chamber, known as the Parliament Chamber from the later Middle Ages, where they deliberated following the formal opening in the adjacent Painted Chamber. MPs were excluded from the procession to the opening of Parliament,

---

[80] Alasdair Hawkyard, *The House of Commons 1509–1558: Personnel, Procedure, Precedent and Change* (Chichester, 2016), pp. 5–6, 332–3.
[81] Snow (ed.), *John Hooker's Order and Usage*, p. 66. Evidence for the adaptation of the medieval pulpitum as the partition between the Commons chamber and the lobby is assessed in Cooper, 'Elizabethan House of Commons', pp. 46–7.
[82] Chris R. Kyle and Jason Peacey, '"Under cover of so much coming and going": Public Access to Parliament and the Political Process in Early Modern England', in Chris R. Kyle and Jason Peacey (eds), *Parliament at Work: Parliamentary Committees, Political Power and Public Access in Early Modern England* (Woodbridge, 2012), pp. 1–23, at pp. 4–5.
[83] Citing the evidence of the MPs and writers on Parliament William Lambarde and William Hakewill, the parliamentary historian David Dean notes that 'committees had become a regular and important feature of Parliamentary life' by 1610: D. M. Dean, 'Public Space, Private Affairs: Committees, Petitions and Lobbies in the Early Modern English Parliament', in Kyle and Peacey, *Parliament at Work*, pp. 169–78, at p. 172.

St Stephen's under the Tudors: From Royal Chapel to Commons Chamber 207

and were admitted to the sovereign's address on second-class terms. Formal conferences with the Lords emphasized their social inferiority, even in a Parliament where the political power of the lower House was challenging the dominance of the upper. From 1548, however, the Commons had to borrow space no longer. Their secure tenure of St Stephen's Chapel, reserved for their sole use and modified to fit the needs of an assembly growing in self-awareness, demands to be factored into what historians used to think of as the 'rise of Parliament' between the Reformation and the Civil War. The nature and timing of that rise have been debated many times, from multiple perspectives. What has until now been under-appreciated is the acquisition by the Commons of a permanent foothold within the ancient Palace of Westminster, with a dedicated record repository and committee room, and (from the 1620s) a research library of parliamentary privilege and precedent next door. Into the old debate about whether Tudor parliaments were 'institutions' or 'events', we can insert the creation of the House of Commons as a place.

How did members of the Commons react to their new home in St Stephen's? Architecture and politics seem to be intimately linked in the early modern period, yet explicit evidence for this can be hard to find. People rarely reflected in detail on their built surroundings, whether royal palaces or churches or urban environments, in the ways that historians and art historians might wish that they had done. The reign of Elizabeth witnessed a burgeoning culture of writing about Parliament, its antiquity and procedures and ceremonial, without it commenting in any detail on the architecture or decoration of the Palace of Westminster. A similar problem is faced by historians of royal magnificence and display, requiring anthropological 'thick description' and art-historical theorizing to compensate for the absence of contemporary first-hand testimony about the impact of representations of power.

Some conclusions may nonetheless be drawn. The dissolution of St Stephen's enabled the Commons to move from temporary to permanent housing, at the junction between the public and privy Palace of Westminster, with office and storage space to aid their deliberations and sustain their collective memory. Early modern MPs debated, objected, voted, and prayed together in close proximity, in a former chapel whose decoration and regalia proclaimed the sovereignty of the monarchy while at the same time legitimating loyal critique of crown policy. St Stephen's provided the seedbed in which the 'collective identity' and 'sense of shared experience' that Norman Jones and David Dean have claimed for Elizabethan MPs could take root.[84] Memory accumulated within and about the building, as 'old Parliament men' like William Fleetwood shared stories with each other and the younger generation of MPs.[85] The action of returning to the same meeting-place, from one parliament to another, created its own narrative about the permanence of the House of Commons and its equivalent status with the Lords. Member for Exeter John Hooker, the first writer on Parliament to comment in any detail on the layout of the Commons chamber, was firmly of the opinion that the 'nether' House (Hooker preferred this to 'Lower') was of 'like and equall authoritie' with the upper House; 'therefore the oppinion, censure and judgement

---

[84] D. M. Dean and Norman L. Jones, 'Representation, Ideology and Action in the Elizabethan Parliaments', in D. M. Dean and Norman L. Jones (eds), *The Parliaments of Elizabethan England* (Oxford, 1990), pp. 1–13, at p. 5.
[85] Cooper, 'Elizabethan House of Commons', p. 50; Seaward, 'Institutional Memory and Contemporary History', pp. 214–15.

of a mean Burgesse: is of as great avail: as is the best Lords'.[86] Hooker was among several MPs associated with the first Society of Antiquaries (active 1586–1607) including William Lambarde and William Hakewill, both of whom compiled notes relating to the power and procedure of Parliament.[87] Their work was continued in the 1620s by Sir Simonds D'Ewes, who looked to the Parliaments of Elizabeth's reign for contrasts and parallels with the politics of his own day. In the post-Reformation House of Commons a new sense of place, and a heightened awareness of history, went hand in hand.

Reflecting on this growing historical consciousness within the Parliaments of early modern England, Alexandra Gajda and Paul Cavill contend that 'While developing in many ways, Parliament still looked the same and proceeded similarly in 1485 and in 1642.'[88] As a means of taking us beyond exhausted debates about 'rise' and 'revolution' in parliamentary sovereignty, the point is well made. Parliament plainly took an increasingly active interest in its own history, citing precedent and claiming antiquity even when it was innovating. But in one crucial aspect, Parliament did not look the same by the civil war as it did in Henry VII's reign. At the midpoint in this Tudor–earlier Stuart parliamentary chronology, the Commons moved into the Palace of Westminster (technically *back* into the Palace if one takes the long view), refashioning a royal chapel into a space which remained their home until 1834 and went on to determine the layout of both the Houses of Commons that have so far succeeded it.

Reimagined as the Parliament House, St Stephen's became emblematic of the power of the Commons. The earliest known view of the Commons interior is an engraving from c.1624, preserved among the papers of Simonds D'Ewes.[89] A more detailed broadside of the Commons assembled at Westminster in early 1641 includes plans of parliamentary boroughs and a map of England and Wales to the side of the main image, conveying the sense that the Commons represented the nation even as Charles I was forced to summon the Short Parliament and put an end to his personal rule.[90] Three generations since it had been taken over by the elected house of Parliament, St Stephen's had come to stand for the legitimate political aspirations of the Commons. When decades of tension finally resolved into a civil war, the royal arms above the Speaker's chair enabled the Commons to sustain the fiction that they, rather than the king, represented the true authority of the crown.[91]

The extent to which the political landscape was transformed by the war is illustrated in two engravings by the émigré Bohemian artist Wenceslaus Hollar, a client of Thomas Howard, Earl of Arundel. Hollar's 1647 panorama of Westminster (see Introduction, fig. 1, p. 2) invites comparison with Wyngaerde's view across the river of a century earlier: the slender Gothic exterior of St Stephen's Chapel little altered architecturally, but appearing under its acquired name of 'Parliament House'.[92] The same image resurfaced in a more sectarian context two years later, when Hollar reworked William Marshall's frontispiece

---

[86] Snow (ed.), *John Hooker's Order and Usage*, p. 183.
[87] Christina DeCoursey, 'Society of Antiquaries (*act.* 1586–1607)', *ODNB* [accessed 13 Nov. 2023].
[88] Alexandra Gajda and Paul Cavill, 'Introduction', in Cavill and Gajda, *Writing the History of Parliament*, pp. 1–36, at p. 27.
[89] BL, Harley MS 158, fols 264–5.
[90] BM, Prints & Drawings, 1885, 1114.124.1-3.
[91] J. P. D. Cooper and James Jago, 'Picturing Parliament: The Great Seal of the Commonwealth and the House of Commons', *Antiquaries Journal*, 101 (2021), 369–89.
[92] Robert J. D. Harding, 'Hollar, Wenceslaus (1607–1677)', *ODNB* [accessed 13 Nov. 2023].

to the royalist text *Eikon Basilike* published within weeks of Charles I's execution.[93] The martyred king appears in prayer, his gaze fixed on a spiritual crown illuminated in radiant light while an earthly crown lies discarded at his feet. Behind Charles in the middle distance stands the Chapel of St Stephen, the perspective arranged in order to draw the viewer from the icon of the king towards the Commons that had authorized his execution. From sanctuary of early Tudor royal splendour to emblem of the regicide by 1649, St Stephen's Chapel was at once a location and a symbol of power in early modern England.

---

[93] Wenceslaus Hollar, frontispiece to *Eikon Basilike* (etching, ?1649), Metropolitan Museum of Art, New York, Drawings and Prints, 24.57.107, <https://www.metmuseum.org/art/collection/search/361501>.

The Wren Commons Chamber

Murray Tremellen

By the late seventeenth century, the ageing fabric of St Stephen's Chapel was causing concern among MPs. In 1678 Sir Christopher Wren, Surveyor-General of the King's Works, reported to the Commons that the roof was unsafe.[1] This prompted an extensive programme of repairs, but by 1691 MPs were again worried about the state of the clerestory. Wren was asked to prepare another report for the Commons; this time, he recommended that the clerestory be completely demolished and the roof lowered to suit.[2] The Commons accepted this advice, and decided that this would also be a good opportunity to refit the interior of the chamber. Inevitably the new fittings were designed by Wren's office, although there is only one known official drawing of the new scheme. This is a north-facing section drawn by Wren's assistant, Nicholas Hawksmoor (fig. 1).[3]

In 1691, the House of Commons was not in a position to make a bold architectural statement. The recent Glorious Revolution (1688–9) had, in some ways, strengthened the position of Parliament relative to the Monarch. Yet this resulted principally from the relatively low revenue settlement afforded to William and Mary, rather than from reforming legislation such as the Bill of Rights.[4] At any rate, the Commons needed the King's approval before repairs to the old chapel could be authorized.[5] At this stage, there was no question of replacing St Stephen's, or even of extending its shell; instead, MPs had to be content with relatively modest internal alterations. (Wren later made proposals for a new Parliament building as part of his 1698 scheme to rebuild Whitehall Palace, but Parliament refused to provide the necessary funds.)[6]

Although the scope of Wren's works was relatively modest, they were essentially modernizing in character. True, the Commons retained its traditional layout of opposing benches,

---

[1] *HKW*, vol. 5, p. 401.
[2] TNA, WORK 6/2, Office of Works: warrants and correspondence (1685–1702), fols 16d–18; *HKW*, vol. 5, pp. 401–2.
[3] Oxford, All Souls College, 344 (AS IV.91). For more information on this drawing see Anthony Geraghty, *The Architectural Drawings at All Souls College, Oxford: Wren and Hawksmoor* <https://library.asc.ox.ac.uk/wren/westminster_palace.html> [accessed 19 Aug. 2022].
[4] Julian Hoppit, *A Land of Liberty? England 1689–1727* (Oxford, 2000), p. 25; Henry Horwitz, *Parliament, Policy and Politics in the Reign of William III* (Manchester, 1977), pp. 85–8.
[5] *HKW*, vol. 5, p. 402.
[6] See A. Geraghty, 'Whitehall Palace Rebuilding Projects', <https://library.asc.ox.ac.uk/wren/whitehall_rebuilding.html#new_palace_1664> [accessed 19 Aug. 2022]. The All Souls collection also includes drawings of a Wren scheme for a new House of Lords, probably dating to 1706, but this project is not mentioned in official records.

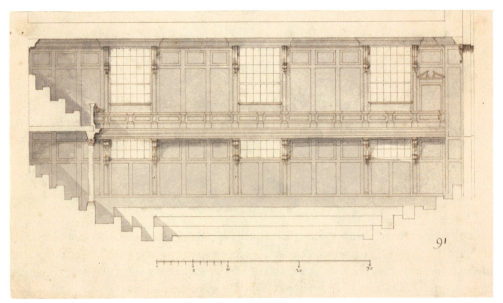

Fig. 1. Nicholas Hawksmoor, design for remodelling the House of Commons, section looking north, 1692. Ink and wash drawing, on paper, 27.2 × 46.8 cm. Oxford, All Souls College, 344 – AS IV.91.

but this was probably as much a consequence of the restricted space available as it was a reflection of conservatism among MPs. In its construction and decoration, Wren's new interior fully accorded with the most up-to-date architectural thinking; indeed, in some respects it was innovative and forward-looking. Work began on the project during the early months of 1692. On 11 March the Office of Works' carpenter, John Churchill, agreed to provide 'the new Roofe and other Carpenters Worke'.[7] Three days later, a mason was contracted to remove the stonework of the former clerestory, and the Serjeant Plumber was instructed to cover the new roof with lead.[8] On 5 May, Narcissus Luttrell MP noted in his diary that the Court of Requests was being fitted up to provide temporary accommodation for the Commons while the works continued.[9]

Despite the lowering of the roof, it appears that the internal height of the Commons chamber was not significantly altered. A flat ceiling had already been installed above the Commons by 1585, and as far as we know Wren did not change its height.[10] He did, however, replace its fabric. The old structure had been made of wooden laths faced with plaster of Paris, a method considered obsolete by the 1690s. Wren therefore replaced it with a more up-to-date construction covered with lime and animal hair.[11] It is not entirely clear why the

---

[7] TNA WORK 5/145, Office of Works: Accounts: Contracts (1668–1724), fol. 213.
[8] TNA, WORK 5/145, fols 213–15.
[9] Narcissus Luttrell, *A Brief Historical Relation of State Affairs from September 1678 to April 1714* (6 vols, Oxford, 1857), vol. 2, p. 607. The temporary fittings in the Painted Chamber are recorded in the Exchequer accounts (TNA, E 351/3304).
[10] The Exchequer accounts for 1584/5 (TNA, E351/3219, n. p.) mention 'Mendinge a p[art]icion and Celinge in the lower Howse'. See also J. P. D. Cooper, 'The Elizabethan House of Commons and St Stephen's Chapel Westminster', *PH*, 38:1 (Feb. 2019), 44.
[11] *HKW*, vol. 5, pp. 401, 403.

low ceiling was originally installed, but it may have been an attempt to improve the acoustics of the chamber. Whatever its advantages, it tended to make the chamber feel cramped and hot, especially when the House was full.[12] In 1701, ventilation holes were cut into it to try to improve the atmosphere, but with little success.[13]

By 1692, the basic seating layout of the Commons was well established: rows of benches for MPs down the north and south sides of the chamber, with the Speaker's chair at the east end.[14] However, it had long been recognized that the seating capacity of the House was totally inadequate. Even in the early years of the seventeenth century, the Commons could only offer enough seating for about half the total number of MPs; and membership continued to increase over the course of the century, from 493 MPs in 1629 to 512 in 1690.[15] Sometime between 1604 and 1624, an attempt had been made to alleviate this problem by adding a fifth row of benches to each side of the chamber. However, this necessitated situating the front row slightly below the principal floor level of the chamber, so that the lower legs of any Members sitting on it were tucked out of sight. This arrangement evidently proved unsatisfactory, as the fifth row was removed sometime after 1645.[16] Wren now adopted a different solution to this problem: he installed side galleries above the existing seating. There was already a gallery at the west end of the chamber (installed by 1621 at the latest), so Wren now extended this down the north and south sides of the room.[17] To provide access, he cut staircases through the corner turrets at the east end of the building; these connected to a new passageway which ran behind the Speaker's chair.[18] The side galleries were supported by wooden brackets, carved by renowned woodcarver Grinling Gibbons.[19] Meanwhile, the west end gallery was mounted on slender cast-iron columns. These were manufactured by Jean Tijou, a renowned French émigré metalworker who had previously produced decorative ironwork for Hampton Court Palace and St Paul's Cathedral.[20] It has previously been suggested that they may have been the world's first structural iron columns.[21] However, more recent research has revealed that two of Wren's City churches – St Bride's, and St Stephen's Coleman Street – also had cast-iron columns installed in about 1692.[22] Regardless of which

---

[12] For a comprehensive history of the ventilation problems in the Commons see Elizabeth Hallam Smith, 'Ventilating the Commons, Heating the Lords, 1701–1834', *PH*, 38:1 (Feb. 2019), 74–102.

[13] *HKW*, vol. 5, p. 404.

[14] The benches were almost certainly upholstered in 'Commons green', a colour choice which seems to have been well established by 1692 (G. Chowdharay-Best, 'The Colours of the Two Houses of Parliament at Westminster', *Notes and Queries*, 16:3 (March 1969), 89; *HKW*, vol. 5, p. 400). Sections of green upholstery are just visible in both the Tillemans and Hickel paintings.

[15] John P. Ferris and Andrew Thrush (eds), *The History of Parliament: The House of Commons 1604–1629* (Cambridge, 2021), p. 205. Membership data taken from *Hist Parl*: <https://www.historyofparliamentonline.org/volume/1604-1629/survey/ii-membership> and <https://www.historyofparliamentonline.org/volume/1690-1715/parliament/1690> [accessed 4 Sept. 2022].

[16] A. Hawkyard, 'Inigo Jones, the Surveyors of the Works and the "Parliament House"', *PH*, 32:1 (Feb. 2013), 18, 28–9.

[17] There is some disagreement among historians as to when the west gallery was first introduced as a permanent feature. Andrew Thrush argues for 1621, but Alasdair Hawkyard suggests it may have occurred earlier, c.1604. See Ferris and Thrush, *The History of Parliament*, p. 206 and Hawkyard, 'Inigo Jones', p. 18.

[18] *HKW*, vol. 5, p. 403. These external additions are not shown on Hawksmoor's drawing, but the passage behind the Speaker's chair is visible in Sandby's illustration (fig. 2), projecting from the east front of the chapel.

[19] *HKW*, vol. 5, p. 404.

[20] Raymond Lister, *Decorative Wrought Ironwork in Great Britain* (London, 1957), pp. 93–4.

[21] John Harris, 'History: Cast Iron Columns 1706', *Architectural Review*, 130 (July 1961), 60–1.

[22] My thanks to Dr Mark Kirby for this information. See also Andrew Saint, *Architect and Engineer: A Study in Sibling Rivalry* (New Haven, 2008), pp. 70–1.

came first, there is a certain irony that the secularization of St Stephen's reflected an emerging trend in church design. The Georgian Church of England faced a similar challenge to the House of Commons: namely, a need to maximize the capacity of their buildings while still ensuring that all congregants could hear the sermon. Consequently, side galleries with iron columns became a common feature of Georgian church design.[23]

Wren's interior was finished with new wainscot (i.e. oak) panelling.[24] The panels were designed in Wren's usual classically derived Baroque style, and they completely covered the walls so as to totally obscure any surviving medieval Gothic features. This stylistic change also extended to the fenestration: the large east window of the old chapel was replaced by three small, round-headed windows. These are clearly visible in Peter Tillemans' picture of the House of Commons in session, painted between 1709 and 1714 (see Cooper, fig. 2, p. 203). Wren disliked mixing classical and Gothic styles: in a well-known letter, he claimed that any attempt to do so would produce a 'disagreeable mixture'.[25] It was therefore important to maintain stylistic consistency within the new chamber. On the other hand, Wren did not necessarily see it as a problem if the interior and exterior of a building did not match. He wrote in his 'Tracts' that 'Variety' was 'commendable' in parts of a building which were 'not seen at once, and have no Respect to one another'.[26] All the same, it is striking that Wren made no effort to disguise his new round-headed windows on the east façade, as shown in a later illustration by Thomas Sandby (fig. 2). The new windows arguably presented a 'disagreeable mixture' when juxtaposed with the surviving lancet windows of the undercroft below it. The most likely explanation for this is that MPs were simply unwilling to spend money on major aesthetic changes to the exterior. Indeed, Sandby's drawing also shows that the new passageway behind the Speaker's chair was completely utilitarian in character.

Despite the thoroughgoing redecoration of the interior, the Chapel's medieval wall paintings remained undisturbed beneath Wren's new panelling. Indeed they had probably already been covered by cloth, tapestries, or panelling long before the 1690s.[27] There was apparently enough space – just – for a person to crawl between the panels and the wall. Antiquary John Carter did exactly this in the 1790s, in order to record the wall paintings for posterity.[28] Meanwhile, the new panels were given a much plainer decorative finish: surviving images suggest that they were either varnished, or painted plain brown. Similarly, the ceiling was plain white. Despite this restrained finish, painting of the chamber was entrusted to the King's Serjeant-Painter, Robert Streeter II.[29]

The Speaker's chair was the most prominent item of furniture in the chamber, but it was also an ephemeral one. Until at least 1834, it was customary to provide a new chair every time

---

[23] Christopher Webster, 'Late Georgian Churches: "Absolutely Wretched" or the Triumph of Rational Pragmatism?', *Architectural History*, 60 (2017), 170. See also Saint, *Architect and Engineer*, pp. 70–5.
[24] TNA, WORK 5/1, Office of Works: accounts, fols 216–17.
[25] Christopher Wren Jr, *Parentalia* (London, 1750), p. 302.
[26] Wren Jr, *Parentalia*, p. 352.
[27] The Great Seal of the Commonwealth appears to show the Commons hung with tapestries: Rosemary Hill, '"Proceeding Like Guy Faux": the Antiquarian Investigation of St Stephen's Chapel, Westminster, 1790–1837', *Architectural History*, 59 (2016), 253–79, at 261. However, Hawkyard, 'Inigo Jones', p. 19, argues that panelling had been installed by 1640, based on a print of that date in the British Museum (1885,1114.124).
[28] Hill, '"Proceeding Like Guy Faux"', p. 255.
[29] Edward Croft-Murray (ed.), *Decorative Painting in England, 1537–1837* (2 vols, London, 1962), vol. 1, pp. 226–8. Streeter's father, Robert I, had produced the elaborate ceiling painting for the Sheldonian Theatre.

Fig. 2. John Thomas Smith, *North East view of the House of Commons, from a Drawing by Thomas Sandby Esq. R.A., in the possession of Paul Sandby Esq. R.A., F.A.S.* From Smith, *Antiquities*, facing p. 145. WOA 7518.

a Speaker was elected or re-elected, and the incumbent kept the old chair as a perquisite. In retirement, Henry Addington kept two of his chairs beside his dining room fireplace.[30] Charles Manners Sutton accumulated no less than five chairs, but sold them off after his retirement in 1835.[31] Only one of these chairs is now known to survive: a chair used by Sir John Cust (Speaker 1761–70) is preserved at Belton House, Lincolnshire.[32] The Speaker's chair was set against an elaborate baldachin embellished with a full Corinthian order and surmounted by the royal arms. The famous Tillemans painting of the House of Commons (see Cooper, fig. 2, p. 203) suggests that the baldachin was painted to imitate white

---

[30] George Pellew, *The Life and Correspondence of Henry Addington, 1st Viscount Sidmouth* (3 vols, London, 1847), vol. 1, pp. 67–8.
[31] PA, ARC/VAR/189, *Catalogue of […] the Official Residence of the Speaker in New Palace Yard* (1835), pp. 42–3.
[32] Chair, 18th century, wood/textile, National Trust, Belton House (434879). For a complete list of surviving fragments and furniture from the old Palace, see Mark Collins, 'The Topography of the Old Palace of Westminster, 1510–1834', in BAA, *Westminster II*, pp. 244–50.

marble.³³ In 1707, the English royal arms above the chair were replaced by the new arms of the Union.³⁴ Immediately in front of the Speaker's chair was the clerks' table. Today there is a large eighteenth-century table, rescued from St Stephen's cloister in 1834 and recently in the Speaker's study, which was traditionally believed to be the table of the old House of Commons.³⁵ However, this identification has never been certain, not least because the surviving pictures of Wren's chamber always show the table covered by a green cloth. Wren's financial statement to the Treasury also mentions 'a new Clock with carved workes [sic] & ornaments'.³⁶ Karl Anton Hickel's 1793 painting of the chamber appears to show a clock inserted into the panelling of the gallery above the government front bench, but this is not visible in any other illustrations.³⁷

On 3 November 1692, Luttrell noted that the refurbishment of the Commons was complete and the temporary facilities in the Court of Requests were being dismantled.³⁸ This was not the end of the story, however, as several modifications were made to Wren's chamber over its lifetime. In 1707, following the Act of Union, the side galleries had to be extended in order to provide two rows of seats, sufficient to accommodate forty-five Scottish MPs.³⁹ To provide additional support, eight more iron columns had to be installed; this time they were fitted with wooden capitals carved by Gibbons.⁴⁰ Another change came in the 1790s, when Henry Holland was asked to make further improvements to the ventilation. He opened up the octagonal panel in the centre of the ceiling and installed a large ventilation shaft in the attic space above it. This was the famous 'ventilator' around which society ladies subsequently gathered to listen to proceedings in the Commons.⁴¹

The most radical changes came in 1800, when the Union with Ireland prompted a major programme of alterations to the Palace masterminded by Wren's successor James Wyatt. His first objective was to increase the capacity of both Houses in order to accommodate the Irish MPs and Peers. One hundred extra seats were needed in the Commons, and Wyatt decided that the only way to provide them was to carve niches within the thick medieval walls, into which additional benches could be inserted.⁴² To support these voids, yet another row of narrow columns had to be installed behind the galleries; these are just visible in an early 1820s illustration of the House (fig. 3).⁴³ When Wyatt removed Wren's

---

[33] A closer view of the Speaker's chair can be found in Thornhill and Hogarth's 1730 portrait of Speaker Arthur Onslow in the Commons (Sir J. Thornhill and W. Hogarth, *Speaker Arthur Onslow calling upon Sir Robert Walpole to Speak in the House of Commons*, 1730, oil on canvas, 991 × 9270 mm, National Trust, Clandon Park, Guildford (1441463)).
[34] *HKW*, vol. 5, p. 404; Croft-Murray, p. 228.
[35] Alexandra Wedgwood, *Guide to the Speaker's House* (London, 1994), pp. 9–10; PA, ARC/VAR/123, draft catalogue of an exhibition commemorating the 150th anniversary of the 1834 fire, pp. 11–12.
[36] TNA, WORK 6/2, fol. 31; *HKW*, vol. 5, p. 403. TNA, E 351/3304 mentions a payment of £20 to Thomas Herbert 'for a long pendulem [sic] clock' during the 1692/3 financial year, but this is listed under the heading of 'the Parliam[en]t House' rather than specifically the House of Commons.
[37] Anton Hickel, *The House of Commons*, 1793–4. Oil on canvas, 3226 mm × 4496 mm. National Portrait Gallery, London.
[38] Luttrell, *A Brief Historical Relation*, p. 607.
[39] TNA, WORK 6/14 Office of Works: memorials, fols 146–7; A. A. Hanham (ed.), 'England, Scotland and the Treaty of Union, 1706–08', *Hist Parl Online* <https://www.historyofparliamentonline.org/england-scotland-and-treaty-union-1706-08> [accessed 5 Aug. 2022].
[40] TNA, E 351/3312, Exchequer Pipe Office: declared accounts, n. p.; *HKW*, vol. 5, p. 403.
[41] Hallam Smith, 'Ventilating the Commons', pp. 76, 81–2.
[42] *HKW*, pp. 525–6.
[43] Harris, 'History: Cast Iron Columns 1706', p. 60.

Fig. 3. James Scott, James Stephanoff, and Augustus Charles Pugin, *View of the Interior of the House of Commons during the Session 1821–3*, 1836. Mezzotint, 42 × 54.6 cm. WOA 3102.

Fig. 4. Robert William Billings, *Exterior of St Stephen's Chapel, East End from Speaker's Garden*, 1834. Watercolour, 36.8 × 28 cm. WOA 1663.

panelling, the medieval paintings were briefly revealed; but they were broken up in the process of cutting back the walls.[44] This act of destruction proved hugely controversial, but it should not obscure the fact that Wyatt's wider vision for the Palace of Westminster was fundamentally historicist. He attempted to 'restore' the eastern façade of St Stephen's to a fourteenth-century appearance, adding new Gothic details in stucco. He even attempted to disguise Wren's round-headed windows by adding blind tracery around them to give the illusion of a large, pointed east window (fig. 4). In the following years Wyatt rebuilt the neighbouring Speaker's House in a complementary Gothic style (see Collins, fig. 3, p. 284); his intention was that, when viewed together, this ensemble would look like an old country mansion with an attached chapel.[45]

Wyatt's approach to the Houses of Parliament reflects a deep-rooted change in attitudes towards the Palace, and to architecture more broadly, over the course of the eighteenth century. For all its limitations, Wren's work was essentially contemporary, even forward-looking. Wyatt, by contrast, consciously attempted to evoke the architecture of an earlier period in British history. These two remodelling schemes, almost exactly a century apart, provide a vivid architectural demonstration of Britain's transition from the Age of Enlightenment to the Age of Romanticism.

---

[44] See the essay by Rosemary Hill in this volume.
[45] *The Times*, 28 March 1805, p. 3.

Architecture and Revolution at St Stephen's and Beyond

Paul Seaward

> We shape our buildings and afterwards our buildings shape us. Having dwelt and served for more than 40 years in the late Chamber, and having derived fiery great pleasure and advantage therefrom, I, naturally, would like to see it restored in all essentials to its old form, convenience and dignity.
>
> HC Deb 28 Oct 1943, vol. 393, col. 403

Oblongs and Hemicycles

Winston Churchill's remark, delivered during the 1943 debate on rebuilding the chamber of the Commons following its destruction by bombing, is probably the second most famous about the Westminster Parliament. There were two characteristics of the old chamber that Churchill specifically wanted to defend. The first was 'that its shape should be oblong and not semi-circular':

> Here is a very potent factor in our political life. The semi-circular assembly, which appeals to political theorists, enables every individual or every group to move round the centre, adopting various shades of pink according as the weather changes. I am a convinced supporter of the party system in preference to the group system. I have seen many earnest and ardent Parliaments destroyed by the group system. The party system is much favoured by the oblong form of Chamber. It is easy for an individual to move through those insensible gradations from Left to Right but the act of crossing the Floor is one which requires serious consideration. I am well informed on this matter, for I have accomplished that difficult process, not only once but twice. Logic is a poor guide compared with custom. Logic which has created in so many countries semi-circular assemblies which have buildings which give to every Member, not only a seat to sit in but often a desk to write at, with a lid to bang, has proved fatal to Parliamentary Government as we know it here in its home and in the land of its birth.

The second was its size:

> The essence of good House of Commons speaking is the conversational style, the facility for quick, informal interruptions and interchanges. Harangues from a rostrum would be a bad substitute for the conversational style in which so much of our business is done. But the conversational style requires a fairly small space, and there should be on great occasions a sense of crowd and urgency.[1]

The shape of the Commons chamber is a historical accident, the result of the pre-Reformation St Stephen's Chapel being adapted to serve as accommodation for a legislature. Churchill made it into an essential feature of the British constitution and the British parliamentary tradition. Following Churchill's line of thinking, many have associated the alternative design – the hemicycle so common in continental European parliaments – with proportional representation systems of voting and coalition governments, as opposed to the tradition in the United Kingdom and a good deal of the anglophone world of first-past-the-post elections and two large main parties. The Labour MP (and later Peer) Frank Judd, speaking in 1978, for example, suggested that 'the interests of democracy can be best protected by honest confrontation of ideas and priorities rather than by slithering uncertainties of semicircular Assemblies where truth and facts may become blurred in the consequential game of constantly changing alliances'.[2] And many supporters of the hemicycle have shared the same basic assumption – that much of the form and style of British politics can be traced to the shape of the chamber of the House of Commons.

Tony Banks, for example, complained in 1994 that 'the layout of the Chamber derives from the fact that, in 1547, Edward VI gifted his chapel to the Commons – and we are left with this ridiculous choir stall arrangement and no facilities'; the chamber, he continued,

> is confrontational. If we took 650 people from the telephone directory and stuck them in this place they would behave in exactly the same way as hon. Members behave at Prime Minister's Question Time. In many respects, the Chamber is like a football pitch with banks of supporters on each side looking down to the pitch, each group cheering on its own side even when it is playing rubbish.[3]

Contemporary discussions of the style of British politics return, time and again, to the fact that the shape of the chamber was determined by the shape of a medieval ecclesiastical building.[4] The two associated ideas – that hemicycles are for continental coalitions elected by proportional representation, not no-nonsense British first-past-the-post majoritarianism, and that the Westminster oblong gives rise to a peculiarly confrontational, 'Punch and Judy' style of politics – are deeply embedded in the way we think about the British Parliament. A moment's thought, however, suggests that while there may be elements of truth within them, they both, to say the least, lack subtlety. The United States seems to manage with a first-past-the-post system and chambers arranged in a semicircle; there are oblong, or near oblong chambers which work with coalition governments elected by proportional

---

[1] HC Deb 28 October 1943, vol. 393, cols 403–4.
[2] HC Deb 23 Feb. 1978, vol. 944, col. 1725.
[3] HC Deb 24 June 1994, vol. 245, col. 524.
[4] See the essay by Mark Collins in this volume.

representation;[5] and confrontations can occur in the best-regulated hemicycles (as even the *Daily Mail* commented about an eruption of fighting in the semicircular Ukrainian Parliament in 2012, 'say what you like about their adversarial style, but at least the great and good of British politics keep the fisticuffs for the Commons bar').[6] Nevertheless, deeply – and interestingly – embedded they are, for the argument has a long history. Ever since the 1730s, if not before, those considering the reconstruction of the Commons chamber have thought about alternative shapes; and ever since the French and American Revolutions resulted in the creation of chambers conceived very differently, the discussion about the shape of the Westminster chamber has been imbued with politics, just as much as with architecture.

The Premodern Deliberative Chamber

Most premodern deliberative chambers seem to have used square or rectangular rooms. The celebrated Roman architect and architectural theorist Vitruvius, in the little he said on the subject, seems to have regarded this as the only option for a Senate House, and the surviving Roman Senate House, the Curia Julia, is an oblong in shape. Its other meeting-places, the Curia Julia's predecessors and various temples, seem to have been of a similar shape.[7] Little is known about the organization of the meetings of medieval assemblies; the frequency with which religious buildings were used may have meant that an arrangement with seating round the four sides of a square room was the most practical, but it is difficult to be sure.[8] When reasonably reliable images of other assemblies do become available in the late sixteenth or early seventeenth century, they often do look like the seventeenth-century House of Commons: the Synod of Dort (fig. 1), an ecclesiastical body which met in Dordrecht in the Netherlands in 1619, remarkably so. The Commons, from when they first met as a separate body, mostly sat in a variety of square or rectangular rooms: the Painted Chamber in the Palace of Westminster; the refectory at the Abbey; and beyond Westminster, in various monastic refectories, and dormitories, before it became established at St Stephen's.[9] Other secular bodies in Europe met in similar square or rectangular spaces: the Estates General of France is pictured meeting at Blois in 1577 – a complex arrangement given that the three estates are all gathered together for the opening ceremony (fig. 2); the Dutch States General met in the Ridderzaal, the medieval great hall of the Binnenhof Palace complex in The Hague, arranged with opposing sets of benches, rather like a chapel (fig. 3).

But there were other models too. The polygonal chapter house is the obvious example: the Commons, as is well known, did sometimes meet in the Chapter House of Westminster

---

[5] The obvious example is New Zealand after it changed from a first-past-the-post system in 1996.
[6] 'That's One Way to Communicate: Fists Fly in Ukrainian Parliament in Clash over Language Law', *Daily Mail*, 25 May 2012.
[7] Vitruvius, *De Architectura*, 2.1; Richard J. A. Talbert, *The Senate of Imperial Rome* (Princeton, 1984), p. 124; Andrew Lintott, *The Constitution of the Roman Republic* (Oxford, 1999), pp. 72–3.
[8] See, for example, Agustin Bermudez, 'Ceremonial Spaces for Parliamentary Sessions in the Kingdom of Valencia (XII–XVII Centuries)', *Parliaments, Estates and Representation*, 32 (2012), 1–19.
[9] J. S. Roskell, *The History of Parliament: The House of Commons, 1386–1421* (4 vols, Stroud, 1991), vol. 1, p. 46. See also A. D. K. Hawkyard, 'From Painted Chamber to St Stephen's Chapel: The Meeting Places of the House of Commons at Westminster until 1603', *PH*, 21 (2002), 62–70, and *The House of Commons 1509–1558: Personnel, Procedure, Precedent and Change*, PH Texts and Studies, 12 (Chichester, 2016), pp. 189–99.

Fig. 1. After François Schillemans, *The Opening of the Synod of Dort*, 1619. Etching and engraving, 45.3 × 40.5 cm. Amsterdam, Rijksmuseum, RP-P-OB-77.278.

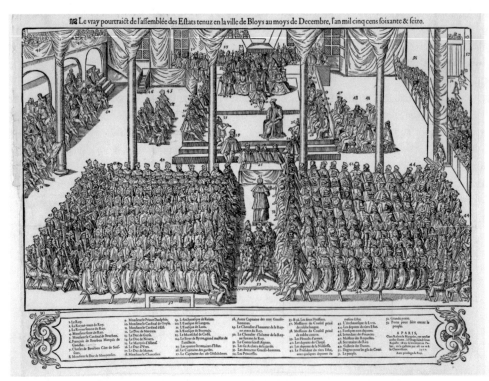

Fig. 2. Robert Le Mangnier (publisher), *Le vray pourtraict de L'assemblée des Estats tenuz en la ville de Bloys au moys de Decembre, l'an mil cinq cens soixante & seize*, 1577. Woodcut, 39.1 × 51.1 cm. New York, Metropolitan Museum of Art, acc. no. 1998.4681.

Fig. 3. Bartolomeus van Bassen/Antonie Palamedesz., *The Great Assembly of 1651*, c.1651. Oil on panel and metal, 52 × 66 cm. Amsterdam, Rijksmuseum, SK-C-1350.

Fig. 4. Claudio Duchetti (publisher), *The General Assembly of the Council of Trent, 1565*, 1565. Etching and engraving, 33.5 × 49.7 cm. New York, Metropolitan Museum of Art, 41.72 (3.70).

Abbey during the fourteenth century; the Anonimalle Chronicle's account of the meeting of the Good Parliament of 1376 in Westminster Abbey Chapter House describes individual Members addressing the assembly from a lectern in the middle of the floor.[10] A remarkable image of the Council of Trent in session (fig. 4) suggests that the hemicycle was not an eighteenth-century invention, and could be fitted into a square or rectangular architectural space, although the council is being harangued rather curiously from the side of the chamber, rather than from in front. It was not, therefore, always assumed that deliberative assemblies had to sit in a square or rectangular, or, indeed, any other, format.

Westminster and Dublin

The House of Commons chamber after the Wren alterations of 1692 occupied, according to William Kent, a space of 60 ft 8 in (18.49 m) by 32 ft 4 in (9.85 m). Kent thought it could hold reasonably comfortably three hundred in the body of the House, with an additional 120 spaces in the gallery (the membership of the House of Commons after the Union of 1707 was 558) (see Cooper, fig. 2, p. 203). It was cramped, uncomfortable, poor as an auditorium, and just about the only way to reach anywhere was by walking right across the floor of the House. It, or more generally the Palace complex in which it was situated, was commonly thought of as a national disgrace.[11] There was, in fact, a striking alternative model in the recent work carried out in Dublin to create a new home for the Irish Parliament. The architect chosen in 1727 was Edward Lovett Pearce, a man of Irish background who was related to, and possibly trained under, John Vanbrugh, and had worked for William Connolly, the then Speaker of the Irish House of Commons. Pearce was himself a Member of the Irish House, though his connection with Connolly was no doubt also helpful in securing for him the commission. His remarkable octagonal design for the chamber of the Commons owed very little to the Westminster example, and dealt with many of the issues with which subsequent architects would grapple (fig. 5). In the memorandum he provided to the Committee overseeing the project he explained its virtues: the Speaker, placed virtually equidistant from all seats, can see and hear easily what is going on; the gallery (unlike that in the Westminster chamber) did not overhang the chamber, interrupting sight-lines and creating problems for those sitting below it, but receded from it; an arcade gave access to a corridor running right around the chamber making it easy for a Member to move from one part to another, or reach his seat without crossing in front of the Speaker or the person addressing the House.[12]

At Westminster itself, schemes to rebuild the Cottonian Library after the disastrous fire of 1731 helped to trigger the consideration of plans about rebuilding the British legislature.[13] In designs of 1733 (his so-called 'Pantheon' design) Burlington's protégé William Kent envisaged a circular Commons chamber within a roughly square space at one end of an immense new

---

[10] In R. G. Davies and J. H. Denton, *The English Parliament in the Middle Ages* (1979), p. 124.
[11] *HKW*, vol. 5, pp. 416–25.
[12] Edward McParland, 'Edward Lovett Pearce and the Parliament House in Dublin', *The Burlington Magazine* 131:1031 (Feb. 1989), 100; Edward McParland, 'Building the Parliament House in Dublin', in Clyve Jones and Sean Kelsey (eds), *Housing Parliament: Dublin, Edinburgh and Westminster* (Edinburgh, 2002), pp. 130–40.
[13] Frank Salmon, 'Public Commissions', in Susan Weber (ed.), *William Kent: Designing Georgian Britain* (New Haven, 2013), pp. 315–63, at p. 329. See the *Report from the Committee appointed to view the Cottonian Library* (London, 1732), p. 10. The proposal to build a library or record repository in relation to a new building for Parliament perhaps linked later associations of libraries with parliaments.

Fig. 5. Peter Mazell, after Rowland Omer, *A Section of the House of Commons Dublin*, 1767. Engraving with etching. Dublin, National Library of Ireland, ET C466.

Palace, with a House of Lords at the other.[14] The discussions spawned further suggestions. In a pamphlet written in 1734, James Ralph, the probably American-born Grub-street writer and later historian, complained that 'nothing can be more unworthy of so august a body as the parliament of *Great Britain*, than the present place of their assembly: ... so detach'd in parcels, so incumber'd with wretched apartments, and so contemptible in the whole'.[15] He offered a remarkable proposal that both Houses should be

> under the same roof, built on the same line, exactly opposite to each other, the seats rang'd theatrically; the throne in the midst of one semi-circle, the Speaker's chair in the other; and that when the King made his speech, ways and means might be found to remove the partitions from between the two houses, and present the whole Parliament of Britain at one view, assembled in the most grand, solemn, and elegant manner.[16]

Ralph's hemicycle/circle idea was not taken up, and the 1733 scheme itself got nowhere. In 1739, though, a new impetus was given to the moves to rebuild. Kent produced several designs for remodelling the House of Commons, and the Treasury went so far as to initiate

---

[14] Salmon, 'Public Commissions', p. 335, fig. 13.23.
[15] James Ralph, *A Critical Review of the Publick Buildings ... in and about London and Westminster* (London, 1734), p. 57.
[16] Ralph, *Critical Review*, pp. 57–8.

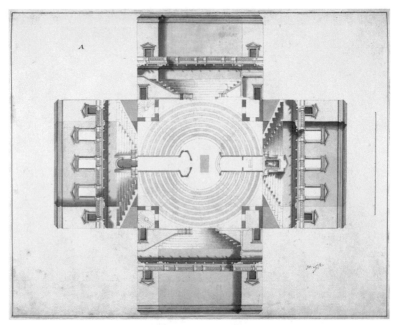

Fig. 6. William Kent, unexecuted design for the Houses of Parliament, Palace of Westminster, London: plan and laid out elevations for the House of Commons chamber (Design A), 1739. Pen and wash, 355 × 451 mm. London, RIBA Collections, VOS/150, fol. 17.

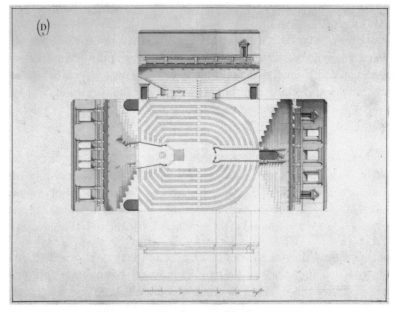

Fig. 7. Unexecuted designs for the Houses of Parliament, Palace of Westminster, London: plan and laid out elevations for the House of Commons chamber (Design D2), 1739. Pen and wash, 327 × 430 mm. London, RIBA Collections, VOS/150, fol. 20.

consultations with the Speaker, the legendary Arthur Onslow. The designs Kent showed him were: (A) circular (fig. 6); (B) elliptical; (C) two semicircles joined with a rectangle; and (D) one semicircle abutting a rectangle (fig. 7). All the drawings have galleries. 'D' offered the greatest accommodation: with 520 seats in the body of the chamber and 220 in the galleries it must have been intended to provide a significant amount of space for the public. Nothing came of the Kent proposals, though we do not know the reasons for their failure.[17] Several others, including James Adam and John Soane, toyed in a speculative fashion with designs from the late 1770s to the 1790s, but there was no political will behind it before the discussions of the early 1830s, to which we will return.[18]

France and the Revolution

Well before the 1830s other legislatures had come into existence, the development of which would not only become critical to the design of legislative chambers but was also interwoven with the history of their Westminster counterparts. The contribution of the philosopher and polymath Jeremy Bentham to the subject is a case in point. In 1788 the profound economic and political crisis in France had brought Louis XVI to agree, reluctantly, to a summons of the Estates General for the first time in 175 years. With deadlock over the format it should take (whether the three Estates of the Nobility, Clergy, and the Third Estate should meet separately, as was traditional, or as a single Assembly), there was intense interest in France in the details of legislative practice. In the winter and spring of 1788/9 Bentham, encouraged by contacts in France, produced a study from first principles of the procedure and operation of parliamentary assemblies that would eventually become published, in part, as *Political Tactics*, designed to inform the rules of procedure of the Estates General.[19]

Bentham's proposals for the best way of setting out a chamber were governed by three 'essential points', namely 'facility of hearing for the Members'; 'facility of seeing for the president'; and 'personal convenience for the individuals'. The dominance of 'the great popular assemblies, in the ancient republics', by 'two or three demagogues', was because only they could make themselves heard. Unless this were avoided, the 'first quality required would no longer be mental superiority, but a physical advantage, which, without being incompatible with talent, does not necessarily imply it'. The best option, Bentham thought, was

> a form nearly circular, seats rising amphitheatrically above each other – the seat of the President so placed that he may see all the assembly – a central place for the secretaries and papers – contiguous rooms for Committees – a gallery for auditors – a separate box for the reporters for the public papers.[20]

One influential French politician, the Abbé Sièyes, shared Bentham's view that a circular Assembly was the most practical, though in his case it was for different reasons: 'it is easy',

---

[17] See *HKW*, vol. 5, pp. 416–25; Salmon, 'Public Commissions'.
[18] See Sean Edward Sawyer, 'Soane at Westminster: Civic Architecture and National Identity, 1789–1834' (Ph.D. dissertation, Columbia University, 1999), pp. 71–115.
[19] Jeremy Bentham, *Political Tactics*, ed. Michael James, Cyprian Blamires, and Catherine Pease-Watkin (Oxford, 1999), pp. xvi–xxii.
[20] Bentham, *Political Tactics*, p. 45.

Fig. 8. Isidor Stanislas Helman, after Charles Monnet, *Ouverture des Etats Généraux à Versailles le 5 Mai 1789*, La Salle des Menus-Plaisirs arranged for the opening of the Estates, 1789. Etching, 34.9 × 45.4 cm. Amsterdam, Rijksmuseum, RP-P-OB-63.129.

he wrote, 'to set up the Assembly as a circle or an oval, so that there will not be anywhere that is the most prominent place, and that no province and no order can be seen as below another'.[21] However, when the Estates General met in the Hôtel des Menus-Plaisirs du Roi at Versailles in May 1789, it was in a large hall whose principal space was about 120 by 57 ft (c.37 × 17 m) adapted from a workshop building, and set out in a very traditional form. Created by those responsible for the ceremonies and spectacles in the court, the layout was poorly designed both for sight and sound (notoriously, the opening three-hour speech of the King's First Minister to the Assembly was just about inaudible), and also cramped for the full Assembly – around three hundred for each of the first two Estates, and six hundred for the Third, so 1,200 in total – but well-equipped with space for spectators: it was said to be able to accommodate two thousand (fig. 8). The room was rearranged in July, after the Third Estate, or 'Communes', had adopted the term *Assemblée Nationale*, and the resistance of the King and the other Estates of the Nobility and Clergy to meeting jointly with the Third Estate collapsed (fig. 9). Now the 'Salle Nationale' was transformed with seating arranged elliptically, and raked, with a corridor running behind the seats in front of the raised galleries

---

[21] *Instructions donnée par SAS Monseigneur le duc d'Orléans a ses Répresentans aux bailages, suivies de délibérations à prendre dans les assemblées* (1789), p. 35.

Fig. 9. Isidor Stanislas Helman, after Charles Monnet, *Assemblée Nationale: Abandon de tous les Privilèges*, La Salle des Menus-Plaisirs rearranged as the Assemblée Nationale, 1790. Etching, 35.8 × 46.4 cm. Amsterdam, Rijksmuseum, RP-P-OB-132.

(the 'tribunes') on all sides of the chamber. The 'tribune' for the President of the Assembly was placed in the middle of one of the long sides; another tribune on the other side for the person addressing the Assembly, with a 'bar' below it, for non-members (such as petitioners) who were addressing it.[22]

This was what the Assemblies looked like during the early debates of the Revolution, until a little after the invasion of Versailles by crowds of Parisians on 5 October. After the King was hauled off to the Tuileries Palace in Paris, semi-captive, the Assembly decided (against the advice of its architect) that it, too, should move to Paris. It settled on the Salle du Manège, or riding school, at the Tuileries, built originally for the education of Louis XV: partly because it was the largest space it could find, and partly because of the existence in nearby monastic buildings of spaces where the Bureaux of the Assemblies could be established (including several which would become notorious as the sites of the political clubs which operated as effective and very public caucuses). The arrangement of the Manège was broadly similar to that in the Menus-Plaisirs, but the Manège was much longer – 34 ft (10.36 m) longer than the Menus-Plaisirs – and very narrow, making the ellipsis of the previous chamber

---

[22] Armand Brette, *Histoire des Édifices où ont siégé les Assemblées Parlementaires de la Révolution Française I* (Paris, 1902), pp. 22, 25, 34.

difficult to achieve: the seating against the long walls was straight, rather than curved. It had a vault that was said to absorb sound, making it difficult to distinguish one speaker from another.[23] It was difficult to speak, difficult to see, and difficult to hear. There were calls for a more satisfactory arrangement including a more circular or elliptical form.[24] The problem became more apparent with the new constitution of September 1791, which replaced the National Assembly with the smaller Legislative Assembly, of 745 members instead of 1200. The Assembly appointed a Committee late that year to look at adaptation of the chamber, and agreed that the most satisfactory arrangement would be for the benches to be 'laid out as a semi-ellipse, placing the president at the centre of the ellipse', but they drew back from recommending it because of the disruption it would cause, at a time of intense crisis, shortly before Austria's declaration of war.[25]

A number of architects had already offered plans for a more satisfactory home for the Assembly.[26] One of the places that had been considered in the search for a new building in 1789 had been the School of Surgery, designed by Jacques Gondouin in the early 1770s, and echoing both the Roman Pantheon and the amphitheatres of antiquity. The search committee had dismissed it as being too small for their purposes, but it would have a big impact on those tasked with thinking about alternative designs.[27] This was particularly the case for the plans presented in February 1792 by the naval officer and substitute deputy, Armand Guy de Kersaint, and drawn up by Jacques-Guillaume Legrand and Jacques Molinos, to convert the then unfinished Madeleine Church into a massive Palais National with at its centre a chamber for the Assembly. This was much closer to a hemicycle – a sort of extended semicircle. Moreover, it had both the President's and the speaker's tribunes on the same side, speaking out towards all of the Deputies, and also out towards the public galleries.[28]

The storming of the Tuileries in August 1792 and the fall of the monarchy put an end to the Kersaint-Legrand-Molinos plan, as it offered the cheaper alternative of moving to the Tuileries Palace itself. It also resulted in the replacement of the Legislative Assembly with a new legislature, the National Convention, which would put the King on trial and execute him in January 1793. It was the Convention that made the move to the Tuileries in May 1793. The old Salle des Machines – a theatre dating back to the 1660s with a backstage area of about 126 ft (c.38.4 m) long by 55 ft (c.18.8 m) broad, out of all proportion to its auditorium, had until recently been the home of the Comédie Française.[29] An original scheme by Pierre Vignon, which would have tacked onto this rectangular building a hemicycle protruding from its side, was abandoned for a rather cheaper option drawn up by Pierre Gisors, in which the existing space was arranged with seating in a sort of stretched semicircle, with (as with the plan for the Madeleine) the President's tribune above, rather than facing, the

---

[23] Brette, *Histoire des Édifices*, pp. 165–6, 168.
[24] Brette, *Histoire des Édifices*, pp. 205–6.
[25] Brette, *Histoire des Édifices*, pp. 216–17.
[26] See especially Claudine de Vaulchier, 'La Recherche d'un Palais pour l'Assemblée Nationale', in Annie Jacques and Jean-Pierre Mouilleseaux (eds), *Les Architectes de la Liberté 1789–1799* (Paris, 1989), pp. 137–63.
[27] Brette, *Histoire des Édifices*, p. 95. See Jean-Philippe Heurtin, 'Architectures Morales de L'Assemblée Nationale', *Politix*, 7:26 (1994), 114–15, for the designs of Pierre Rousseau and Pierre Vignon.
[28] *Discours sur les Monuments Publics, Prononcé au Conseil du Département de Paris, le 15 Décembre 1791, par Armand-Guy Kersaint* (Paris, 1792), pp. 33–8, plates V, VII, VIII.
[29] For a description of the Salle des Machines in its theatre days, see Barbara Coeyman, 'Theatres for Opera and Ballet during the Reigns of Louis XIV and Louis XV', *Early Music*, 18:1 (1990), 23–7.

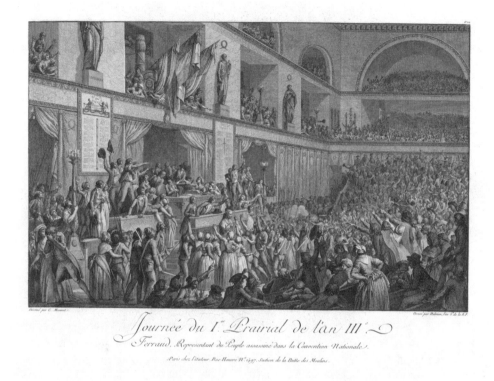

Fig. 10. Isidor Stanislas Helman, after Charles Monnet, *Journée du 1er Prairal de l'an III*, The Assassination of Féraud in the Convention at the Tuileries, 1797. Engraving, 36 × 47.2 cm. Amsterdam, Rijksmuseum, RP-P-OB-63.139.

speaker's.[30] In the stands on both short sides of the chamber, and in the window recesses on the long sides, were found space for 1400 spectators. It was a considerably better-appointed chamber than its predecessors, with an ambitious and portentous scheme of decoration asserting a link to ancient lawmakers, philosophers, and orators. But the acoustic problems remained, as did the stuffiness of the chamber. The Convention was housed in the Salle des Machines throughout the Terror, the coup that disposed of Robespierre in July 1794, and the reaction that followed leading to the crisis of May 1795 in which the Deputy, Féraud, was shot and decapitated (fig. 10).

A fourth legislature was introduced by the new reactionary constitution of August 1795, bringing in a British-style bicameral Parliament. A Lower House, the Conseil des Cinq-Cents, possessed the power to initiate legislation; and an Upper, the Conseil des Anciens, with 250 members, would accept or reject it. Two chambers were therefore required, and the Palais Bourbon, across the river, was commandeered to house the Cinq-Cents. Gisors, with the assistance of Etienne-Charles Leconte, added a hemicycle to the existing palace.

[30] See Patrick Brasart, *Paroles de la Révolution: Les Assemblées Parlementaires 1789–1794* (Minerve, [1989]), pp. 127–30, and also p. 251 for an analysis of the relative merits of the Vignon and Gisors plans, carried out for the Convention, which observed that the Gisors scheme would cost less, though it preferred it for several other reasons as well.

Fig. 11. Louis-Marie Normand, *Hémicycle de l'Assemblée Nationale*, as altered in 1827–32, 1837. Engraving, 48.8 × 63.1 cm. Paris, Musée Carnavalet.

The chamber was essentially in the same form as that of the Salle des Machines, with the speaker below the President, but it was now genuinely semicircular. The world's first legislative hemicycle was first used as such on 21 January 1798, only about 20 months before both parts of what was known as the Corps Legislatif were dissolved by Napoleon's coup of 18 Brumaire. There is no image of the chamber at work before the alterations carried out by Jules de Joly in 1827–32, though these left it broadly similar in its basic structure (fig. 11).[31]

The Salle des Machines and the Palais Bourbon crystallized a new type of chamber, in terms of their shape – the hemicycle – and also the arrangement in which the speaker addressed his colleagues, the other members of the Assembly, and a large body of the public sitting behind and above the Members. It made explicit the relationship between the Assembly and a theatre, rather than a church or chapel. The proceedings of the French National Assembly had already been famous for the eagerness with which its novice Members would produce speeches of theatrical rhetoric and ludicrous pretensions, as British observers were keen to point out, although the challenges of speaking in the cavernous Salle du Manège partly solved the problem, as few had the lung power to make themselves heard.[32] It seemed to confirm the tendency for politics in France apparently to assimilate themselves to models of theatricality, rather than conventions of deliberation; and it crowned a period in which the public had been already deeply engaged with the proceedings of the various legislatures, attending in droves, applauding and commenting loudly and volubly on the proceedings, and on occasion straying onto the floor, or even invading it in strength.[33] The interaction between the public and the Assembly horrified foreign, particularly British observers, and a good number of members of the Assembly as well.[34] The hemicycle arrangement seemed

---

[31] Jules de Joly, *Plans, Coupes, Élévations et Détails de la Restauration de la Chambre des Députés* (Paris, 1840).
[32] Timothy Tackett, *Becoming a Revolutionary: The Deputies of the French National Assembly and the Emergence of Revolutionary Culture* (Princeton, 1996), pp. 225–34.
[33] Paul Friedland, *Political Actors: Representative Bodies and Theatricality in the Age of the French Revolution* (Ithaca, NY, 2002), pp. 180–2. For Edmund Burke's reaction to the theatricality of French revolutionary politics, see Peter H. Melvin, 'Burke on Theatricality and Revolution', *Journal of the History of Ideas*, 36:3 (1975), 447–68.
[34] See the speeches of d'André in 1791 and the Comte de Sade in 1830, quoted in Heurtin, 'Architectures Morales', pp. 121, 123.

to affirm it: here was a legislative Assembly that was designed precisely like an ancient theatre, focusing all attention on a single speaker, rather than the more complex dialogue between speakers that might be symbolized by a circular, or a square chamber. Legislators were speaking directly to the people, rather than to each other.

The United States

At the same time as the French, the leaders of the United States of America were also seeking to construct a pair of new legislative chambers, in no less tortuous a fashion. There was no shortage of existing models, in the Colonial, then State, Assemblies, though most of these were designed for very small bodies. The Virginia House of Burgesses in Williamsburg destroyed by fire in 1747 (as now reconstructed), for example, might have been based on the House of Commons; but the Assembly Room of the Pennsylvania State House, otherwise known as Independence Hall, resembles a drawing room, though the present arrangement of its furniture is certainly semicircular. These were clearly inadequate for a new national legislature. The First US Congress met in New York in 1789–91, and among its first acts was to establish at Philadelphia the temporary capital for ten years while a permanent one was built on the Potomac River.[35]

Thomas Jefferson, the first Secretary of State, had himself been responsible for the new Virginian State Legislature built in 1786, a rectangular construction, based on the celebrated Roman Maison Carrée at Nîmes. He proposed that the new seat of national government be designed after 'one of the models of antiquity', which distanced it from the British Legislature.[36] A drawing by Jefferson, dated to 1792, shows that he hankered after a circular building, housing four *oval* rooms, one each for the Senate, House of Representatives, the Courts, and joint Conferences or Committees.[37] But a competition for the new Capitol, as it was called after the Virginian example, produced a series of designs with rectangular or almost square chambers. None of them was regarded with any enthusiasm. An unhappy compromise resulted in the only professional architect among the competitors, the Frenchman, Etienne-Sulpice Hallet, being asked to develop a scheme entered late by Dr William Thornton, a remarkable West Indian-born Quaker educated in England and Scotland. In the bad-tempered collaboration between them, over 1793–7, the plan that emerged incorporated a semicircular chamber for the Senate, an elliptical one for the House of Representatives, and a circular Conference Room. The seating in the latter two was arranged oddly in semi-concentric rings (fig. 12).

Dogged by money problems, Jefferson's obsession with the dome of the Halle aux Blés in Paris, and the sniping between the two architects which led to Hallet's dismissal in 1794, only the North (Senate) wing was ready by the deadline of 1800: the second session of the Sixth Congress convened there in November 1800. There is unfortunately no visual record of this first Senate chamber, the second purpose-built legislative chamber built on a semicircle

---

[35] William C. Allen, *Capitol: A Chronicle of Design, Construction and Politics* (Washington, DC, 2001), p. 6.
[36] Jefferson to Madison, Paris, 20 Sept. 1785, https://founders.archives.gov/documents/Madison/01-08-02-0191> [accessed 16 Nov. 2023]; Jefferson to Buchanan and Hay, Paris, 26 Jan. 1786, https://founders.archives.gov/documents/Jefferson/01-09-02-0194> [accessed 16 Nov. 2023].
[37] Allen, *Capitol*, pp. 10, 13 (Jefferson to L'Enfant, 10 April 1791).

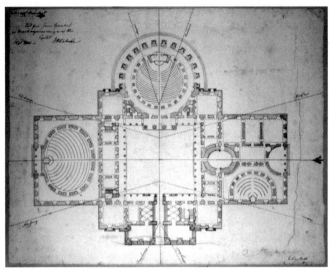

Fig. 12. Etienne-Sulpice Hallet, *Federal Capitol*, design, with the House of Representatives on the left, *c*.1793–5. Ink and watercolour drawing. Washington, DC, Library of Congress, Prints and Photographs Division, ADE – UNIT 2461, no. 6 (D size).

plan. It, too, possessed a gallery. The House of Representatives met in the rectangular room of the Library of Congress, apparently with a gallery provided, before being moved to a temporary elliptical chamber (known as 'the oven', presumably because of the heat, though it looked more like a casserole dish).

The hiring of Benjamin Latrobe as surveyor of public buildings in 1803 resulted in a drastic rethink of the design of both South and North wings. Latrobe's memorandum to Jefferson itemized numerous defects in the current scheme, which did not endear him to the prickly Dr Thornton with whom Latrobe eventually found himself in litigation.[38] Writing the same year to a Philadelphia Quaker who sought advice on 'the best form of a room for hearing and speaking', Latrobe remarked on the lack of real understanding among current architects of the subject. Even though he classified Quaker meeting houses, the halls of literary societies and legislative assemblies as rooms 'in which the place of the voice is unfixed and uncertain', he nevertheless thought Gondouin's semicircular École de Chirurgie in Paris 'one of the most beautiful rooms and perhaps the best lecture room in the world for speaking, hearing and seeing'. He referred to Kersaint's recommendation of a domed semicircle for the Convention, and the endorsement of the plan by French architects as 'the best adapted for the purposes of deliberation'.[39]

Latrobe proposed a redesign of the chamber of the House of Representatives along these lines, offering a domed room seating 360 members in a semicircle, based, Latrobe said, on 'the ancient theatre'.[40] But Jefferson rejected it, as too far a departure from the design that had been originally agreed in 1793. So Latrobe's 1804 plan, in which he had to accept Jefferson's pet idea of the colonnade running around the chamber, was two semicircles (60 ft or 18.29 m in diameter) joined by a rectangle with sides of 25 ft (7.62 m), giving an overall space of

---

[38] John C. Van Horne and Lee W. Formwalt (eds), *The Correspondence and Miscellaneous Papers of Benjamin Henry Latrobe, Volume I, 1784–1804* (New Haven, 1984), pp. 268–83.
[39] Allen, *Capitol*, p. 89. *Correspondence of Benjamin Henry Latrobe*, vol. 1, pp. 405, 406.
[40] Allen, *Capitol*, p. 52.

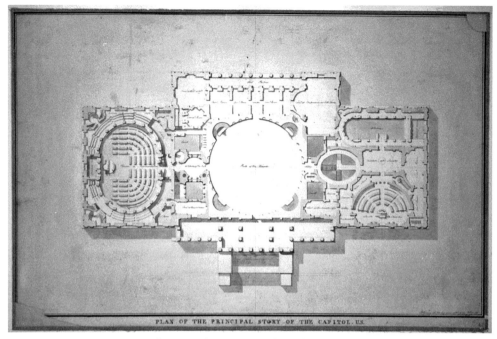

Fig. 13. Benjamin Henry Latrobe, *United States Capitol, Washington, DC*, 1804 design, with plan of principal story and chambers, c.1808–9. Drawing, 49.5 × 75.5 cm. Washington, DC, Library of Congress, Prints and Photographs Division, ADE – UNIT 2462, no. 3 (Cabinet B).

around 85 by 60 ft (25.9 × 18.28 m) (fig. 13). The room was finally available for occupation at the end of 1807. It attracted applause for its appearance ('the handsomest room in the world occupied by a deliberative body'), but was regarded acoustically as a disaster, 'admirably suited to every purpose which would be required except one ... that of debate'.[41]

Financial problems led to a virtual cessation of work on completing the Capitol before it and other public buildings were burnt down by the British army in 1814. Latrobe seized his opportunity (with Jefferson no longer president) to reconstruct the House chamber as a semicircle, but retaining the colonnade of the previous chamber (fig. 14). He argued that the existing semicircular Senate Chamber was 'the best room of debate in America', and referred to his own anatomical theatre at the University of Pennsylvania, the ancient Theatre of Bacchus in Athens, and the Palais Bourbon as other examples of semicircular rooms used successfully for lectures and debates.[42] Eventually approved by Madison over the objections of Thornton (who argued that the ellipse was better because it lacked 'those little breaks that destroy the unity, grandeur, and dignity of architecture', and contained no part of a circle that creates 'repercussion of sound'), the House of Representatives had moved into its new chamber by 1819.[43] Despite Latrobe's views, the chamber was soon found to be acoustically poor, like its predecessor: Samuel Morse's painting of it in 1825 shows the drapery used to attempt to overcome the problem (fig. 15).

[41] Allen, *Capitol*, p. 71.
[42] *The Correspondence of ... Latrobe*, vol. 1, p. iii.
[43] Allen, *Capitol*, p. 105.

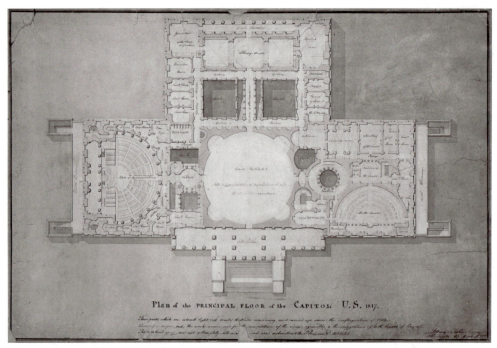

Fig. 14. Benjamin Henry Latrobe, *United States Capitol, Washington, DC*, 1817 design, with principal floor plan, vestibule, library and Senate chamber, House of Representatives, 1817. Ink, wash and watercolour drawing, 53.6 × 79.9 cm. Washington, DC, Library of Congress, Prints and Photographs Division, ADE – UNIT 2463, no. 2 (D size).

Fig. 15. Samuel Morse, *The House of Representatives*, 1822–3. Oil painting, 220.7 × 331.8 cm. Washington, DC, National Gallery of Art, 2014.79.27.

Redesigning Westminster

These examples of new, purpose-built legislatures served to emphasize the inadequacy of the accommodation for the House of Commons at Westminster, more acute still after the arrival of the hundred new Members following the Union with Ireland in 1800. The chamber's problems had long been acknowledged and frequently remarked upon.[44] But it was not until 1831 – in the middle of the debates on parliamentary reform – that an attempt to do anything about them (other than tinkering with the ventilation system) attracted serious political interest.

The original proposal for major alterations to the chamber did not come from political radicals, but the reaction to it suggested that an association with political radicalism was quickly perceived. The Select Committee appointed that year was the initiative of the Tory developer and urban improver Frederick Trench, whose schemes over the previous ten years included one for the embankment of the Thames, and a new royal palace to replace Buckingham House. Trench complained of insufficient seating room, poor audibility, with sound 'wafted directly across the House by the draught of air from the windows, and … lost in the lantern above', 'the constant interruption occasioned now by hon. Members rising and crossing each other, so as to escape through the north and south doors into the lobby, without passing through the House', and the inadequate seating for visitors.[45] He planned to promote a design by an associate, the architect Benjamin Wyatt, based on extending the chamber into the lobby, but it foundered on the opposition of the rest of the Committee.[46] Nevertheless the Committee concluded, against Trench's objections, that the only practical solution was to build a new chamber.[47]

In the debate on the Committee's report Trench sought again to promote his own scheme, only to be ridiculed by a colleague, John Wilson Croker, a minor office-holder and one of the leaders of the charge against the Reform Bill. Croker concluded his sarcastic speech with a rhetorical appeal to the associations of the existing chamber, and an attack on the alternative models:

> He did not blindly reverence the mere antiquity of the edifice; but he could not forget that it was the place in which the Cecils and the Bacons, the Wentworths and Hampdens, the Somers's and the St. Johns, the Walpoles and the Pulteneys, the Pitts, the Foxes, the Murrays, and the Burkes, had 'lived, and breathed, and had their being.' … The Irish House of Commons and the French Chambers, which were built according to all the rules of architecture and all the theory of acoustics, were the worst constructed buildings for hearing that was possible, while the English House of Commons, patched and pieced as it was, contained nearly all the advantages a Legislative Assembly could desire.[48]

---

[44] For a discussion of these, see Paul Seaward, 'A Sense of Crowd and Urgency? Atmosphere and Inconvenience in the Chamber of the Old House of Commons', in *Space and Sound*, pp. 103–18.
[45] Explained by Frederick Trench on 12 Aug. 1831 (though appointed earlier): HC Deb. 12 Aug. 1831, vol. 5, cols 1261–3.
[46] See the entry on Frederick William Trench (?1777–1859), in *Hist Parl 1820–32*, vol. 7, pp. 497–505.
[47] *Report from the Select Committee on House of Commons Buildings*, HC 308 (1831).
[48] HC Deb 11 October 1831 vol. 8, col. 558.

The argument was apparently irrelevant, since there was no proposal on the table as yet to create a new chamber. But it was clearly an attempt to pre-empt one, and was perhaps a recognition that there were radical voices now arguing for a new chamber on continental lines. Croker may have particularly disliked Trench's proposal that space for visitors in the gallery be increased. Some months later, in a second debate, Trench attempted to revive his own proposals, obliquely attacking the inveterate, and to many insufferable, radical Joseph Hume, who had been a member of the 1831 Committee, as wanting to erect a 'new and magnificent' House, and calling for a new Committee. Hume's close ally, the philosophic radical and Benthamite Henry Warburton, pointed out that magnificence had not been part of Hume's plan, but made clear that a simple extension to the already inconvenient oblong chamber was no solution. 'One of the theatres of London University' was a more desirable model, 'where every person was at the same distance from the President'. This time it was Sir Robert Peel who poured scorn on the idea as expensive and unnecessary, dismissing objections to the oblong shape of the room: 'with all the imperfections of the oblong, the real business of the country could always be transacted between the two sides'. Besides, he said, he was attached to the existing building, because of its powerful associations: 'it was with a feeling of pride that he sat in the same House where Chatham, and Pitt, and Fox, and Wyndham, had made their greatest and most splendid orations'.[49]

Trench was defeated in the post-reform 1832 general election, which returned a new and energetic cohort of reforming and radical Members, and offered some hope of a new impetus to the moves to replace, and indeed to reshape, the chamber. At the beginning of March 1833, the reforming polemicist William Cobbett, one of those newly elected the year before, chose to fill his *Weekly Political Register* with a piece on the arrangement and organization of the House of Commons, in which he drew explicit comparisons with the chambers of the US Congress and of State Legislatures (Cobbett had lived in exile in America in 1792–1800 and 1817–19): 'an Englishman would blush were he to see the House of Assembly of one of the states of America, not to mention that of the congress of the United States'. In the State House of Connecticut, in which the seating was placed in a horseshoe,

> The arrangement of the space is so contrived, that no member, and no person ever crosses the floor, or even steps his foot upon the floor while the Speaker is in his chair. … Every member comes to his seat from an opening in the outside part of the horseshoe. His seat is always the same seat, and he comes to it, and goes from it, without interrupting any other member … Every member has a little desk fixed before him, in his lodge, as it may be called, for the purpose of locking up his papers, or for the purpose of writing on.[50]

The galleries were spacious enough for people to come and go without causing any disturbance. At Westminster, he complained, the lack of space led to disorder and confusion that

> beggars all description. The business is retarded by it; the crowds about the Speaker's Chair, while the Private Bills are going on, the everlasting trampling backward and

---

[49] HC Deb 14 Feb. 1832, vol. 10, col. 336.
[50] *Weekly Political Register*, vol. 79, no. 9, Saturday 2 March 1833, pp. 524–5. I owe this reference to Leanne Marie Cotter.

forward on the floor; the interruption which men give to one another, in spite of their desire to avoid it; the calls of 'order, order,' incessantly recurring; all these absolutely distract men's minds, and they render it impossible for them to do that which it is their duty to do, and which they wish to do. The House necessarily thus becomes a place for doing little business, and that little not well.[51]

Cobbett may have published his article to support Hume, who only a few days later revived the subject in the House, and pushed for a new Select Committee. Warburton elaborated on his view that the oblong shape of the House was 'inconvenient and every way inferior to a semicircular form'.[52] The conservatives remained out in force. The Ultra Tory opponent of Catholic Emancipation and political reform Sir Robert Inglis thought that recalling 'the eloquence of some of the greatest and the wisest men who ever dignified a deliberative assembly' would prevent members 'from readily accommodating themselves to a House, the idea or notion of which would have been borrowed from the new – and he might add vulgar – legislative assemblies on the other side of the Atlantic'. Such a plan for 'a degraded council chamber', he fulminated, was 'unworthy of the Legislature of such a country as this'.[53] A moderate reformer, the young Catholic Philip Howard, also weighed in, vigorously rejecting the idea of 'pulling down that building hallowed by its recollections for the purpose of erecting in its stead a semicircular theatrical edifice like that proposed. For hearing, and the transaction of business, the House of Commons was preferable to the French Chamber of Deputies.'[54]

Despite their opposition, a Committee was appointed as Hume had proposed, and proceeded to take evidence from the most prominent practising architects in the country. One of the themes of the Committee's discussions was the shape of the chamber. There was no consensus. Sir John Soane was the only one to advance the benefits of a semicircle, arguing that Palladio's Teatro Olympico in Vicenza and 'all the ancient theatres, both Greek and Roman' were semicircular.[55] Sir Jeffry Wyatville's plan was a semicircle with its ends extended.[56] But others made the customary point that the House of Commons was not like a theatre. The Office of Works architect and designer of the British Museum, Robert Smirke, wanted a rectangle with an apsidal end.[57] Decimus Burton, Thomas Hopper, George Basevi, and John Deering all told the Committee that while a semicircular chamber was most suitable where the speaking was done from a single point, it would not work in a situation where Members spoke from their places.[58] Hopper, whose plan to take down the side walls of the chamber and extend it at both sides was closely associated with the Member and amateur architect Charles Hanbury Tracy, argued for a square: 'in a lecture room, where one person is to address an assembly, an amphitheatre or semicircular form is the best; but

[51] Ibid.
[52] HC Deb 7 March 1833, vol. 16, cols 374–5.
[53] Ibid., col. 376.
[54] Philip Henry Howard (1801–82), the son of Henry Howard, was an antiquary and a friend of Louis Philippe; he spent much time in his early years on the continent: *Hist Parl 1820–32*, vol. 5, pp. 733–5.
[55] *Report from the Select Committee on the House of Commons Buildings*, HC (1833), 269, Q. 144.
[56] Ibid., Q. 274. There is a copy of Wyatville's plans in the Library of the Royal Institute of British Architects, at SB73/WyJe[20](8).
[57] HC (1833), 269, Ibid., Q. 152.
[58] Ibid., Q. 386, 445.

where Members have to debate with each other, it seems to me that the quadrangular form is best'.[59] George Basevi concurred that 'If the members were to speak from a tribune, as in the Chamber of Deputies in Paris, there is no doubt the semicircular shape would be best; but speaking from all parts of the House, I fear the speaker would be but very imperfectly heard'.[60] Smirke commented, apparently favourably, on the provision of desks in the chamber of the House of Representatives, though as he said, the semicircle had a diameter of around 100 ft (*c.*30.5 m) and accommodated just 213 Members. He suggested that if a semicircular chamber with as generous provision for seating as was provided for members in Paris, it would need to be 100 by 60 ft (30.48 × 18.28 m), 'inconvenient' in size, though a gallery could reduce this.[61] John Wilson Croker, who had declined to offer himself for election in 1832, regarding the Reform Act as not only illegal but 'a *usurpation* leading to as complete a subversion of our ancient constitution as that of the Long Parliament', turned up rather improbably arguing for a scheme of his own. Still condemning the acoustic properties of the National Assembly and claiming that a simple semicircle 'would not be consistent with our Parliamentary habits', he now thought that the best plan was a sort of 'semi-circle with elongated sides', or an 'oblong room with semi-circular seats in the two angles opposite the Chair'.[62] Rigby Wason, who was a Member of the House, offered the most innovative scheme. His plan was 'designed upon the principle of the ancient Chapter-house, a form which our scientific ancestors uniformly adopted for deliberative assemblies, where it was necessary that each Member should deliver his sentiments from his place, sure of being heard equally well by all present'.[63]

The Committee, unsurprisingly, failed to come to any conclusion other than to reiterate the need for a new chamber, and to condemn the existing arrangement as injurious to the health of the Members. Hume was supported in a debate on the report by Warburton and by the independent Whig Thomas Henry Hastings Davies; but as before, Peel tore into it, 'the most imperfect and, with every respect for the Chairman, the most discreditable report he had seen'.[64] Hume's proposed resolution in favour of a new chamber was lost by a large majority.

Do Our Buildings Shape Us?

About 15 months after that debate, the fire that destroyed almost all of the Palace of Westminster, including the chamber, would open up the issue in a way that was impossible before. Conservatives immediately expressed anxiety that the radicals would now press for a considerably increased public gallery, and that it might be used to overawe the House.[65] In the arguments that ensued over the new building, Tories and Whigs argued over whether to

---

[59] Ibid., Q. 445. Hanbury Tracy would be Chairman of the Commission that judged the designs for the new Palace of Westminster after the fire: see *Mr Barry's War*, p. 43.
[60] Ibid., Q. 586.
[61] Ibid., Q. 151, 152, 191.
[62] Ibid., Q. 938.
[63] Ibid., Q. 1048.
[64] HC Deb 2 July 1833, vol. 19, cols 59–66.
[65] See Charles S. Parker, *Life and Letters of Sir James Graham, Second Baronet of Netherby, 1792–1871* (2 vols, London, 1907), vol. 1, p. 211, Graham to E. G. Stanley, 21 October 1834.

rebuild on the same site, or to move to somewhere more commodious.[66] While it was now unconstrained by the difficulties of adapting the old chamber, argument would continue over the relative merits of the hemicycle and the oblong, most notably as Members criticized the inadequacies of the temporary chamber, and the merits of the French, American, and by now also the Belgian examples.[67]

Britain was not, of course, to get a hemicycle, not in 1833, not after the fire, and not after the chamber was destroyed by bombing in 1941. As we have seen, the United Kingdom Parliament remained attached to its oblong legislative chambers, and for many Members, close acquaintance with the continental hemicycle tradition, through travel, and, over the last seventy years through participation in international assemblies such as the Parliamentary Assemblies of the Council of Europe and the Western European Union, and the European Parliament itself, served only to confirm their views.

Many of those views were presented as practical in nature. During the debates of the 1830s technical issues – the quality of sound principally, but also ventilation, heating, sight-lines, and access for Members – were naturally uppermost in consideration of the various schemes. These could be complex and (as experience of the chambers in both Paris and Washington showed) did not straightforwardly argue for the adoption of either structure: the discussion of the acoustic properties of hemicycles or oblongs, as well as of the various different building materials, was confused and contradictory. But the practical issues could themselves have political implications. The greatest technical stumbling block to the adoption of the hemicycle was the fact that the speaker was meant to address the assembly from a fixed point, the tribune, rather than (potentially) anywhere in the House. It meant that rather than turning to face the Chair, and turning his back on the public gallery, he would be talking directly to the spectators, sitting in large numbers behind and above the hemicycle. For the defenders of the oblong chamber, not only was this a rejection of the values of parliamentary debate – civilized discussion designed to persuade and convince – but it also implied an appeal beyond Parliament to the people at large, a complete abnegation of the point of representative government. With the experience of the French Revolution behind it, it seemed an obvious offence against the British conception of Parliament.

When we talk now about the confrontational aspects of the Westminster system, we link the oblong chamber with the intense drama of Prime Minister's Questions: the theatrical, gladiatorial, spectator-pleasing aspects of the weekly comedy of the chamber. It is notable, then, that in the nineteenth century, the hemicycle struck commentators as more inherently dramatic, at least for those watching: a chamber designed like a Greek or Roman amphitheatre, oriented towards the spectators. No doubt it is the development of Prime Minister's Questions that influences our current perceptions, as well as the calming down of the atmosphere on the floor of the US Congress. It is true that hemicycles lack the sense of

---

[66] *Mr Barry's War*, pp. 13–15.
[67] HC Deb 10 Aug. 1836, vol. 35, cols 1070–1. The speaker was the exotic reformer, traveller, and writer James Silk Buckingham. See also the discussion in *Report of the Committee of the House of Commons on Ventilation, Warming and Transmission of Sound, Abbreviated with notes, by W. S. Inman* (London, 1836), in which he drew on the work of George Saunders, *A Treatise on Theatres* (London, 1790). On this, Wyatt had drawn and expanded in his evidence to the 1833 Committee, and the views of Robert Mills, *Guide to the Capitol of the United States* (Washington, DC, 1834), p. 38, supporting Latrobe's decision to base the House of Representatives on a semicircle, and discussing the chamber of the French legislature.

dialogue that is seen as a great virtue of the Westminster chamber, and also the sense of intensity and drama, though there is a tendency to exaggerate this; many defenders of the Westminster oblong, moreover, will point out that PMQs is only a small slice of each week's *mise-en-scène*, and that much of the week is spent in debates that are no more dramatic or confrontational than any meeting.

But technical arguments can also be surrogates for deeper objections. British attitudes to the hemicycle have reflected not only views of its value as a debating chamber, but also differing attitudes towards the work that went on inside the chamber, and towards the idea and the processes of democratic and parliamentary government. Whatever the practical issues, British reactions to the hemicycle were profoundly influenced by an emotional attachment to the existing chamber, and by a powerful association of the hemicycle with radicalism and revolution. The espousal of the hemicycle by radicals such as Henry Warburton or William Cobbett was perhaps as much an indication of their broader political affiliations as of their commitment to a more practical and workable chamber; conversely, its dismissal by conservatives betrayed a visceral dislike of bodies so associated with the challenge to the old order.

In the end, technical issues are far less significant in governing our attitudes towards the architecture of legislative chambers than are our attitudes towards the political systems, structures, and values of which they are part. In time, a new science of amplification, and the development of mechanical systems for ventilation and heating would render the technical issues much less important in practice, though no less a preoccupation for those responsible for designing them. The divergent political attitudes towards different shapes of chambers live on. The shape and location of Parliament and its chambers *can* have a significant influence on the way any legislature operates – exactly how the interactions between politicians take place – and they have even more on the way we conceptualize and talk about our politics, such as our mental or actual maps of political gradations from left to right, terms reliant on where the different factions sat during the French Revolution. But these are generally topographical metaphors for deeper and sometimes very complex political realities, rather than facts created by the shape of a room. Churchill was verging on a subtle version of what one might call the topographical fallacy, or morphological determinism. He was undoubtedly onto *something*. But it was not so much that the shape of the chamber determines our political system, than that it becomes a symbol of that system, to be defended, as Croker so histrionically argued, as its first bastion. We shape our buildings, Churchill might more accurately have said, but once we have stopped complaining about them, we find that we have built them into our whole structure of thought.

Antiquaries, Architects, and St Stephen's Chapel, Westminster, 1790–1837

Rosemary Hill[1]

I have done my duty as an Englishman to save this palace. (John Carter)[2]

After its glorious medieval heyday the story of St Stephen's Chapel is one of adaptation, decline and, ultimately, destruction. In the last decades of its existence, however, it enjoyed a brief renaissance. Between 1790 and 1837 St Stephen's was studied, drawn, discussed, and interpreted as never before by a number of antiquaries and architects. Their findings were published as the late-Georgian Gothic Revival was gathering pace and they met with an enthusiastic reception among a readership saturated in Walter Scott's Romantic vision of the 'olden times'. Thus, by a sad irony, the Chapel was finally lost at a moment when it was better understood and more admired than at any time since the Middle Ages. How and why that should have been is one question which this chapter seeks to answer. The individual antiquarian studies of St Stephen's have been discussed in detail elsewhere; the intention here is to set the growing understanding of the Chapel in the context of Westminster Palace as a whole, and to chart the shifting relationship between antiquarianism and architecture on the cusp of the Victorian age.[3]

Almost everything that is now known about the physical appearance of the medieval Palace is due to the efforts of a handful of antiquaries of whom the most important were John Carter (1748–1817), William Capon (1757–1837), John Chessell Buckler (1793–1894), Charles Stothard (1786–1821), John Thomas Smith (1766–1833), and Edward Blore (1787–1879). They drew and measured the details of the building at a time when medieval architecture was regarded as of little value and 'Gothic' was a derogatory term, indicative of the crude art of an age that had not yet rediscovered the classical principles of design. When the original decoration in the Painted Chamber was uncovered, the wall paintings were dismissed by *The Literary Gazette* as being

---

[1] I am as ever grateful to Julian Pooley for his help and for access to the Nichols archives and to Maria Singer of the Yale Center for British Art for information on the Carter drawings in that collection.
[2] *GM*, 71 (1800), 837–40.
[3] See Rosemary Hill, '"Proceeding like Guy Faux": The Antiquarian Investigation of St Stephen's Chapel Westminster, 1790–1837', *Architectural History*, 59 (2016), 253–79.

of course, more interesting to the antiquary than to the artist; for in our early ages, Painting [...] was compelled to take a subordinate and mechanical place in the estimation of the times, until the revival of the Arts in Italy and the incomparable and unrivalled talents of the Italian painters fixed the attention of Europe upon the great capabilities of their art.[4]

Not only was medieval art despised, the taste for it was considered declassé, even subversive. Gentlemen took the Grand Tour and studied the antiquities of Greece and Rome. With the exception of a few coat-trailing mavericks of whom Horace Walpole was the most prominent, it was only the lower orders, those uneducated in the classics and too poor to travel, who had to make do with their native architecture. It is notable that the antiquaries who recorded Westminster Palace all belonged to the working or artisan classes. Carter was the son of a monumental mason, Capon worked as theatrical scene-painter, Buckler had been articled to a builder, Smith's father was a print-seller, Blore had been apprenticed to an engraver and Stothard, who had trained at the Royal Academy, was a professional artist. Theirs was a milieu with more connections in the world of the theatre and Grub Street than the universities. The most important forum for their debates was the *Gentleman's Magazine*, which after 1780 was largely under the editorship of the publisher and antiquary John Nichols (1745–1826). The reviews editor was Richard Gough (1735–1809), Director of the Society of Antiquaries. Beyond the pages of the *Gentleman's Magazine* admirers of Gothic were not only considered uncultivated, they were suspected of Catholic sympathies, at a time when Catholicism was still almost entirely suppressed. A significant number of Fellows of the Society of Antiquaries objected to funding Carter's engravings of the English cathedrals. Their reasons were both aesthetic and religious, he recalled:

> The chief of those adverse to the measure argued that the illustration of our Cathedrals was not of that importance so as to need any further notice by them, such objects having but <u>little</u> to recommend them (insinuations at the same time flying about the room that to encourage such subjects were to encourage the cause of Popery etc). Yet should the Society be desirous to expend money on the representations to be made of any foreign antiquities how they would with pleasure agree to any desired aid [...] They who thus conquered by such their opposition concluding an end was put to the said 'Popish Plott' [*sic*] of bringing into notice once more those 'Relics of Superstition' the cathedrals of this kingdom.[5]

Thus the handful of men who preserved the memory of St Stephen's and much of the rest of the medieval Palace should be seen as pioneers, working against the social and cultural grain, for the most part without patronage and with limited resources.

---

[4] *The Literary Gazette and Journal of the Belles Lettres*, 11 Sept. 1819, p. 587.
[5] John Carter, MS volume, 'Pursuits of Antiquaries', London, King's College London, Leathes Collection 7/5 [unfoliated].

The Suffering Majesty of the Place

Carter was one of the most energetic and combative of antiquaries and he seems to have been the first to start drawing at Westminster. He had admired medieval architecture from childhood, when

> as Windsor was the nearest market town it may be supposed I barely passed the week without beholding the stupendous walls, and romantic scenery of the castle [...] no wonder my purile [sic] mind imbibed those seeds of delight in witnessing and propensity to draw from our antiquities, which since that period marked the progress of my life.[6]

In 1780 he was at work in Westminster Hall, where alterations were taking place. As was often to be the case, building work was both the antiquary's friend and his enemy. It created opportunities to examine the exposed medieval fabric which, all too often, it went on to destroy. For most of the eighteenth century Westminster Hall had been lined with stalls: 'Book and printsellers, Mathematical Instrument Makers, Sempstresses, Haberdashers and other tradespeople' paid rent for their pitches to the Warden of the Fleet, who was Keeper of the Palace.[7] This somewhat shambolic bazaar was increasingly the subject of complaints and the stalls were eventually cleared away, thereby revealing the damage they had caused 'the disgraceful appearance of the inside of the walls and the very bad state of the paving'.[8]

Between 1780 and 1782 the walls were relined and a new floor laid. Carter took the opportunity to draw the interior and some of the sculpture, which he illustrated in his *Specimens of Ancient Sculpture and Painting*, which appeared in parts between 1780 and 1794. This was his first important publication and it boldly asserted the historical and aesthetic value of medieval art, but the notes on his drawings also record that the two statues on the north front of Westminster Hall were 'destroyed next day after this sketch was taken'.[9] In the rebuilding of the stairs at the northern end of the Hall the damaged effigy of a figure in armour was discovered in the rubble. Carter drew it but it was 'afterwards broken to pieces'.[10] Twenty years later, reviewing the latest alterations, he was still lamenting the impossibility of persuading the authorities to value the building. Writing in the *Gentleman's Magazine* he protested that:

> This wondrous hall [is] thrown into the power of those who, from being insensible of its grandeur, have left no means unused to render it as contemptible as possible; while we, who may be said almost to idolize it, are cut out from raising a hand to preserve it from insult, and can only deplore its unfortunate lot. Yet not wholly so, my friends; for in this survey some satisfaction may fall to our share by catching at the hope that we may have made one convert to venerate and to feel for the suffering majesty of the place. If so, our labour is not in vain.[11]

---

[6] Carter, MS volume, 'Occurrences in the life, and memorandums relating to the professional Persuits [sic] of J C F.A.S. Architect', London, King's College London, Leathes Collection 7/4.
[7] Brayley & Britton, p. 462.
[8] Quoted in *HKW*, vol. 5, p. 388.
[9] H. M. Colvin, 'Views of the Old Palace of Westminster', *Architectural History*, 9 (1966), 34.
[10] *GM*, 70 (1800), 215.
[11] *GM*, 70 (1800), 300.

Fig. 1. John Carter, *South View in the Entrance or Porch at the west end of St Stephen's chapel, Westminster*, c.1790. Pen and pencil sketch, on paper, 22 × 33 cm. New Haven, Yale Center for British Art, Paul Mellon Collection, B1977.14.22482.

It was not in vain, but it was still a most unequal struggle. In 1790 events took a turn for the better with the appointment of John Soane as Clerk of Works at St James', Whitehall and Westminster. Carter had known Soane for about ten years since Soane had been 'a drawing and measuring clerk at Mr Hollands, Half-moon Street' and knew that although he was a classicist he was respectful of historic buildings.[12] Though it has never been established, it seems likely that it was due to Soane's influence that Carter was able to get into St Stephen's Chapel that year and crawl behind Wren's wainscoting to draw the surviving structure and the wall paintings, as well as other parts of the fabric (fig. 1).[13] In 1793 Carter's friend Capon began work on a ground plan of the Palace, a project that would occupy him periodically for thirty years (fig. 2). Though a less prolific and vocal advocate of the Gothic than Carter, he was a better draughtsman and 'he had something of an archaeologist's ability to disentangle one period from another'.[14] He was also able to set out the results in a clear, intelligible form. His perspective view of the Prince's Chamber is one of the first examples of the use of different colours to distinguish the work of different dates. Capon's crowning

---

[12] Carter, 'Occurrences'.
[13] The details of Carter's activities at this date are described in Hill, '"Proceeding like Guy Faux"'.
[14] Colvin, 'Views of the Old Palace', p. 25.

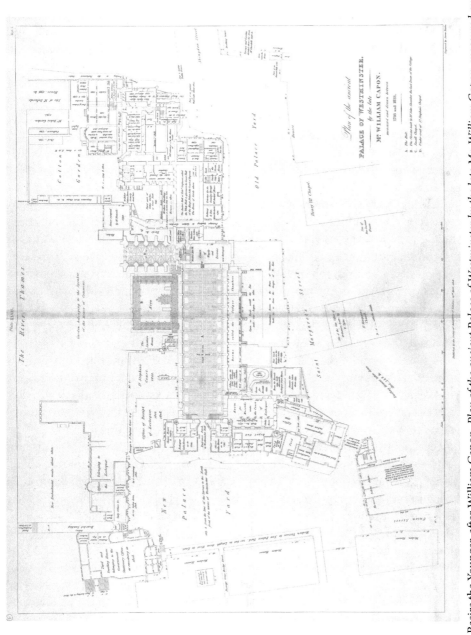

Fig. 2. James Basire the Younger, after William Capon, *Plan of the ancient Palace of Westminster by the late Mr. William Capon, measured and drawn between 1793 and 1823*, 1828. Engraving, 52.9 × 68.3 cm. New Haven, Yale Center for British Art, Paul Mellon Collection, B1977.14.22448.

achievement, however, was his great coloured ground plan, which remains 'of fundamental importance for the study of the Palace'.[15] He took numerous interior and exterior views and drew details as well as undertaking a particular study of the Painted Chamber.

After this relatively productive decade, the year 1800 marked the best and worst of times for the antiquaries at the Palace. Extensive works, including the creation of a new House of Lords, were undertaken by James Wyatt (1746–1813) who had used his influence with George III to snatch the commission from Soane, who had been virtually promised it. Wyatt and the antiquaries were by now in a state of open war. Carter had been attacking him regularly in the *Gentleman's Magazine* for his cavalier 'improvements' at Salisbury, Durham, and Lichfield Cathedrals and elsewhere. He had also been criticized in print by the Catholic bishop and antiquary John Milner and by Richard Gough. In 1797 Wyatt was proposed for membership of the Society of Antiquaries, the election supposedly a formality. Thanks to Gough and his allies, however, Wyatt was blackballed, an almost unprecedented insult that infuriated many people including the King. Now Wyatt took his revenge. In August 1800, while adapting the Commons for the accession of Irish MPs following the Union, he set about destroying the wall paintings. Carter tried in vain to be allowed to record them as they appeared in daylight for the first time in centuries. As he told Gough: 'I said here is a public building of the first consequence in the kingdom, losing some of the most exquisite beauties of ancient art therefore I thought it a laudable act in me to endeavour to preserve them by my pencil'. But it was to no avail. Wyatt had him barred. 'The reasons are obvious', Carter concluded: the authorities must 'dread the censure' of the public for 'destroying what they should have preserved with a religious zeal'.[16]

However, Wyatt was briefly taken ill and another antiquary John Thomas Smith took advantage of his absence to make drawings of the 'invaluable' paintings, 'many whole length figures and some in armour &c with inscriptions under them'.[17] Meanwhile Capon was at work in the Painted Chamber, which was to be fitted up as a conference room. It was so long since it had been whitewashed and hung with tapestry that, as Carter wrote in the *Gentleman's Magazine*: 'Upon what account this chamber has obtained the name of the Painted Chamber, we are at a loss to ascertain.'[18] Capon drew the tapestry, a cycle depicting the Siege of Troy (fig. 3). In describing it Carter argued not only for its beauty but for its value as an historic document. It was in this, the use of material artefacts, art, architecture, armour, costume, and other physical remains of the past as historical records, that the Georgian antiquaries made their greatest contribution to the development of historical method. Carter's discussion of the tapestries is exemplary. Aware that in medieval art mythical, biblical, or historic events appear as if set in the present, he read the tapestries as 'a striking representation of the manners and customs of the time in which it is supposed to have been executed […] for neither the buildings, dresses or other appearances, have the least tendency to illustrate Troy's ten years' siege'.[19] The hangings were also useful as architectural history for, as Carter reasoned, if the lower parts of the buildings depicted corresponded to the architecture

---

[15] Colvin, 'Views of the Old Palace', p. 25.
[16] Carter to Richard Gough, 15 Aug. 1800, Nichols Archive, Private Collection 1 PC1/96/26 NAD8839.
[17] Carter to Richard Gough, 15 Aug. 1800, Nichols Archive, Private Collection 1 PC1/96/26 NAD8839.
[18] John Carter, 'The Ancient Palace of the Kings at Westminster', *GM*, 70 (1800), 423.
[19] Carter, 'Ancient Palace', p. 424.

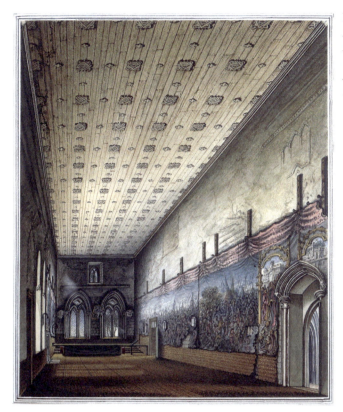

Fig. 3. William Capon, *Painted Chamber, 1799: Interior view looking east with Trojan War tapestries shown.* Watercolour, on paper, 23.5 × 19 cm. WOA 1648.

of the period still extant, then the depiction of the upper parts, which had so often been lost or replaced, could be taken as a reliable indication of the original appearance. He was distraught when the tapestry was taken down and dumped in a cellar. In about 1820 it was sold to Charles Yarnold of Great St Helen's for £10 and has since disappeared from view.[20]

As well as documenting the tapestry Capon was also exploring the basement of the Painted Chamber, discovering that

> at the east end is a fine piece of masonry, consisting of four broad ribs, and groinings between them, and three narrow windows, with round heads, inserted in a very thick wall; and at the distance of about twelve feet, four inches, is another wall, parallel to that, of the thickness of five feet, eight inches. This latter wall now goes up no higher than to the floor of the Painted Chamber; but it could never have been built of such a vast thickness, unless to carry a wall of superstructure.[21]

Capon hypothesized a structure taken down in the reign of Henry III to make space for 'a room of such vast length' as the Court of Requests.[22] He also glimpsed beneath the

---

[20] Brayley & Britton, p. 420n.
[21] Quoted in John Gage Rokewode, *An Account of the Painted Chamber in the Royal Palace at Westminster with designs by C. A. Stothard, and with a biographical note signed W T* (London, 1842), p. 7.
[22] Quoted in Gage Rokewode, *An Account of the Painted Chamber*, p. 7.

Fig. 4. Isaac Cruickshank, *View of the Houses of Lords and Commons from Old Palace Yard*, 1808. Watercolour, on paper, 26.7 × 39.4 cm. New Haven, Yale Center for British Art, Paul Mellon Collection, B1977.14.17696.

whitewash some traces of painting, but there was neither time nor opportunity to examine them as Wyatt's workmen went on with their job until 'every part' of the Palace bore 'the marks of hammer, brush, or trowel'.[23]

When Wyatt had finished Carter was far from alone in disparaging the resulting 'mixture of discordant particles' as a 'random shew [sic]', a '*monstrosity* of barefaced *improvement*'.[24] Writing in 1807 he noted that the new buildings had 'already become food for criticism' in the press.[25] Much of the medieval fabric had been lost, and what had been newly built was universally deplored. Taste had moved on. Sash windows in the cloister of St Stephen's, thin crockets, flimsy plasterboard and oil cloth were now seen as gross solecisms. In a parliamentary debate in 1808 a number of MPs, including Richard Brinsley Sheridan, called for Wyatt's new House of Lords, fitted within the sturdy walls of the Romanesque Lesser Hall, with its 'piazza or Gothic arcade embattled on the top', to be demolished (fig. 4). However, as Wyatt's work had not only been unsatisfactory but wildly over budget, costing in the end more than £200,000, the House decided that it 'preferred the eyesore of the present building to the expense of pulling it down'.[26] The change in polite taste and increasingly informed interest in the Gothic was reflected in the reception of Smith's *Antiquities of Westminster*,

[23] *GM*, 77 (1807), 134.
[24] *GM*, 77 (1807), 135.
[25] *GM*, 77 (1807), 214.
[26] Quoted in *HKW*, vol. 6, p. 519.

Fig. 5. John Thomas Smith, *Cotton Garden, Westminster*, 1800, showing masonry from St Stephen's Chapel, published 1804. Etching, 21 × 17.8 cm. WOA 630b.

published in 1807, which reproduced his own drawings of the lost wall paintings as well as a number of historic illustrations of the Palace (fig. 5). It was an expensive book and included several plates in the still novel form of lithography. The list of subscribers was headed by George III and it included twenty earls, five dukes, two duchesses on their own account, twelve Oxford colleges, and the Archbishop of Canterbury. Among the artists to subscribe were William Blake, John Flaxman, John Constable, and Benjamin West.

Carter was so incensed at the desecration of St Stephen's that he ended his description of Wyatt's work at Westminster with a threat. Did Wyatt not know, he asked rhetorically, 'that at the completion of antient religious buildings, a solemn service was performed, wherein a curse was pronounced against all those who might in aftertimes defile, dilapidate, or destroy such works?'[27] Six years later Wyatt was thrown from his carriage and killed instantly. Certainly he was not much mourned among the antiquaries. Carter himself died in 1817. While he still found much to deplore, he had at least lived to see the architecture of the Middle Ages more admired and better understood, not least due to his own efforts. He had, as he said, done his duty by the Palace. By the time of his death Carter's strictures on Wyatt's work had been vindicated. Soane reported that year that 'considerable repairs' were

[27] *GM*, 78 (1807), 800.

needed to the new House of Lords, and the next year the roof of the Painted Chamber was found to require immediate attention.[28] Once again the antiquaries sensed an opportunity.

Discoveries and Souvenirs

Charles Stothard was in East Anglia, drawing medieval monuments for the book he hoped to produce as an advance on Carter's *Specimens of Ancient Sculpture*, when he read in a newspaper that repairs to the Painted Chamber (fig. 6) had led to certain 'discoveries'.[29] He hurried back to London and got a commission from the Society of Antiquaries to draw these 'very early and interesting vestiges of art'.[30] His wife Eliza, later Eliza Bray, describes a scene that must have been familiar to all antiquaries:

> Enthusiastic and fearless in his pursuit, Charles took his stand upon the highest and most dangerous parts of the scaffold erected in the Painted Chamber for the repairs; and there, almost stunned by the incessant noise of the workmen, amidst dust and every possible annoyance, he actually commenced and finished these beautiful productions of his pencil.[31]

Edward Crocker, an antiquary of whom little seems now to be known, oversaw the uncovering of the wall paintings. He and Stothard, with others including J. C. Buckler and Capon, battled on amid the uproar. The resulting discoveries were duly relayed through the *Gentleman's Magazine* and the *Literary Gazette*, which in September had been so dismissive of the paintings as art. By December it was describing at considerable length these 'precious relics' of special interest to 'the artist' and emphasizing that its earlier contribution had been based on 'extraneous sources'.[32] The *Gazette* had seen the antiquaries at work 'clambering over scaffoldings, and catching glimpses of their subjects' through the workman's tools, and complained that 'the wall of a parish workhouse could not have been treated with greater disregard […] in the hurry to get the place ready for the meeting of Parliament'.[33]

Dust was not the only problem; there was also 'the indiscreet folly' of souvenir hunters who took fragments of painted stone which had been thrown out with the rubbish and were 'of no value individually'.[34] Visitors carried away 'several of the heads of the figures' from a sequence of months of the year which Stothard had found broken up and used to block earlier windows. He had hoped to reassemble them but now 'the whole was rendered incomplete'.[35] One of the ceiling pateras is now in the Soane Museum, for the Clerk of Works himself was not above 'salvage'.[36] Of the wall paintings Stothard reported that the subjects were arranged in six bands 'something similar to the Bayeux Tapestry', which he

---

[28] Quoted in *HKW*, vol. 6, p. 519.
[29] Mrs Charles Stothard, afterwards Mrs A. E. Bray, *Memoirs […] of the late Charles Alfred Stothard, FSA* (London, 1823), p. 304.
[30] Stothard, *Memoirs*, p. 304.
[31] Stothard, *Memoirs*, p. 305.
[32] *Literary Gazette*, 4 Dec. 1819, pp. 776–9; 11 Dec. 1819, pp. 794–5.
[33] *Literary Gazette*, 4 Dec. 1819, p. 776.
[34] Quoted in Gage Rokewode, *An Account of the Painted Chamber*, p. 2.
[35] Quoted in Gage Rokewode, *An Account of the Painted Chamber*, p. 2.
[36] There are several fragments from Westminster in Soane's Monk's Parlour at the Soane Museum.

Fig. 6. John Thomas Smith, *East End of Painted Chamber*, from Smith, *Antiquities*, facing p. 45.

had drawn for the Society of Antiquaries the year before.[37] In the Painted Chamber each band of subjects increased in breadth 'the further it is removed from the eye' until the top one was three times the width of the lowest.[38] Thus, as the *Literary Gazette* pointed out, 'we have the same skill evinced as in the noblest Grecian temples', the artists of the Middle Ages understood the effects of perspective and were not, after all, mere 'house painters'.[39] The revelation of a painting of the coronation of Edward the Confessor explained why this had sometimes been known as St Edward's Chamber (fig. 7). When the refitting work was complete the *Gazette* felt that 'a very laudable spirit' was shown in attempts to preserve something of the Chamber's original character.[40] The ceiling was still visible, as were some of the wall paintings, but regrettably the Tudor chimney-piece had been 'modernized' and, still worse, below the depiction of Edward's coronation a quatrefoil opening had been cut 'about a foot in diameter'. The effect, 'like a mortal wound to a living body' would 'remain for ever a monument of barbarism'.[41]

---

[37] Quoted in Gage Rokewode, *An Account of the Painted Chamber*, p. 2.
[38] Quoted in Gage Rokewode, *An Account of the Painted Chamber*, p. 2.
[39] *Literary Gazette*, 4 Dec. 1819, p. 778.
[40] *Literary Gazette*, 11 Dec. 1819, p. 795.
[41] *Literary Gazette*, 11 Dec. 1819, p. 795.

Fig. 7. James Basire the Younger, after Charles Alfred Stothard, *The Coronation of Edward the Confessor*, 1842. Hand-coloured engraving, 36.5 × 44.8 cm. New Haven, Yale Center for British Art, Paul Mellon Collection, B1977.14.22593.

Despite the difficulties, Stothard was pleased with what he had managed to record and was making speculations about the painters, wondering whether they were Italian or English, the date and the materials they had used. He was too busy with his monuments project in 1820, however, to publish anything and it was only early in 1821 that he got down to 'preparing the materials for an essay concerning the age of these curious paintings'.[42] But on 28 May, when he was tracing a stained-glass window in the church of Bere Ferrers in Devon, the step of his ladder broke. He fell and was killed instantly. The Society of Antiquaries had his drawings of the Painted Chamber, but it would be more than twenty years before they were published.

Antiquaries and Architects

In 1820, after a decade of Regency, George IV became King and immediately demanded alterations to the Palace of Westminster. Soane, once more in charge, was first faced with the unusual task of fitting up the House of Lords for the trial of Queen Caroline, from whom the King was anxious to obtain a divorce. It was another three years before major works began. The first necessary step in Soane's scheme was the demolition of the old House of Lords and the Prince's Chamber beyond it (fig. 8). While this was regretted by antiquaries and others, Soane was a man of conscience where historic fabric was concerned. He allowed Capon to make drawings as the work went on and he made records himself (fig. 9). On 3 October 1823 the building work started in earnest and at high speed to provide the new Royal Gallery and Scala Regia. By March 1824 Soane reported that 'The approach for His

---

[42] Stothard, *Memoirs*, p. 305.

Fig. 8. John Thomas Smith, *Views of the East side of the House of Lords; the East end of the Prince's Chamber; etc.*, published 1807. Etching, 15.2 × 24.1 cm. WOA 630a.

Fig. 9. John Soane, *House of Lords: perspective view of the old House of Lords, with elevations, plans and details of arches*. Pen and ink drawing, on paper, 61.5 × 75 cm. TNA, WORK 29/17.

Majesty to the House of Lords is completed and the Record Rooms, Committee Rooms, and Journal Rooms are in a progressive state of finishing.'[43]

Among those on site during the demolition was Edward Blore. He was one of the rising generation of antiquaries who included Buckler, Lewis Cottingham, who published *Plans etc of Westminster Hall* in 1822, Thomas Rickman, and Robert Billings, one of the able draughtsman trained by the indefatigable publisher and antiquary John Britton to illustrate his own books.[44] These men had much in common with their predecessors. They all belonged to the artisan classes and they pursued their interest in historic buildings through commissions from publishers and contributions to the *Gentleman's Magazine*. They had, however, the advantage of a larger public. Britton was a great popularizer. His multivolume surveys of the *Beauties of England and Wales*, the *Architectural Antiquities of England* and the *Cathedral Antiquities* catered for a wide readership among the middling classes who by now knew their Waverley novels, appreciated picturesque scenery and had had more than twenty years, while the Continent was largely closed by war, to become curious about their native architecture. There was no need by now to apologize for the Gothic, it was only necessary to illustrate and elucidate.

There was another significant difference between this generation and the last. Many of them practised as architects. In an age when formal architectural training was rare and, where it did exist, was heavily biased still towards the classical, it was a short step from drawing medieval buildings and studying their construction to recreating them. Carter had put up a few buildings, but it was hard to find patrons. As the Gothic Revival advanced, however, any antiquary who could produce convincing designs, based on historic precedent from the Middle Ages, and understand how to construct them, was in demand. Blore was consulted by Walter Scott about designs for Abbotsford and ended his career as architect to Buckingham Palace. His friend Thomas Rickman, whose analysis of the periods of Gothic gave us the terms still in use for Early English, Decorated, and Perpendicular, had an extensive church practice. The way in which architecture and antiquarianism fed into one another is clearly illustrated in the letter Rickman wrote to Blore when he heard about the discoveries in the Painted Chamber. He wanted detailed information, not only for interest but for direct application to his own designs:

> In the Literary Gazette for the last 2 weeks there has been given some account of the alterations going on in the painted Chamber Westminster, & from their description (tho not very clear) it should appear that the ceiling I understand them [sic] an <u>original flat one</u>, is if not in its original state, yet so far so as that the original <u>moulded work & forms</u> are left; now I believe thee well know how important in modern Gothic work is a flat ceiling, hitherto I cannot go back earlier than middle perpendicular for a flat ceiling, & that in wood, now if this ceiling is really original, it is at least early decorated, if not late Early English, and as some new accident or repair may destroy it entirely, I am very anxious to possess an account & sketch of it [...] I expect that by application to the Housekeeper of the House of Lords, there will be no difficulty to

---

[43] Quoted in *HKW*, vol. 6, pp. 521–3.
[44] Colvin in 'Views of the Old Palace' suggests that both John Buckler (1770–1851) and his son John Chessell (1793–1894) both worked at Westminster, but I can find no record of Buckler Senior's involvement.

get into the painted chamber, & make a sketch (any fees for which may be required I shall gladly repay).[45]

The next and worst accident to befall the Chamber and the whole Palace was the fire of October 1834. The young A. W. N. Pugin, who happened to be in London that day, watched the conflagration. He himself was in many ways typical of the late-Georgian antiquary-architect. His father Auguste Pugin (1767/8–1832) had been an architectural draughtsman working from time to time for Britton and producing measured details of Gothic buildings intended for copying by architects. From childhood Pugin had explored medieval buildings in a completely empirical way, but he had no other training. His much-quoted description of the fire comes from a letter to another antiquary-architect, his old friend Edward Willson of Lincoln. Willson, who had written the text for Pugin's father's books, had learned his craft by helping his own father with the restoration of the cathedral. He now had a modest practice as a church architect and restorer. This circle of antiquarian architects habitually despised and bemoaned the ignorance of professional architects, but Pugin spoke no more than the truth when he told Willson that 'a vast quantity of Soanes mixtures & Wyatts heresies have been effectually consigned to oblivion'.[46] It was indeed the latest additions to the Palace, the 'composition mullions & cement pinnacles', sash windows and brick walls that went 'flying & cracking' while much of the medieval stonework survived or, as Pugin put it, 'stood triumphantly amidst this scene of ruin'.[47]

Thus the antiquaries were not unduly dismayed by the fire. Like the building campaigns, it offered opportunities for enquiry and there seemed a reasonable chance that some at least of the ruins would be restored. Public opinion was increasingly on the side of the antiquaries and Cottingham seized the day. He made a model of St Stephen's as he believed it had once been and might be again. This 'exquisitely finished' piece of work was shown in March 1835 to the King and Queen. Their majesties, according to the press, inspected it 'with great attention'.[48] The King concluded 'emphatically' that 'so beautiful a building ought not to perish', adding 'It is my hope and my wish that it may be restored.'[49] In April William Etty (1787–1849), one of the most popular painters of the day and a close friend of Pugin, wrote a letter to the *York Chronicle* which was reprinted in the *Morning Post*. It was a rallying cry to his fellow artists who ought, of all people, to be 'the most deeply interested' in the preservation of historic buildings. 'Use your influence', he urged, 'with "the great ones of the earth" [...] instruct the ignorant and put to flight the barbarians'.[50] It was a plea for conservation in general, but it lit on Westminster as the most urgent case. There the Hall, the Abbey, and St Stephen's stood, Etty wrote, 'Three majestic sisters of this noble English race [...] the last remaining relics of the age of romance. In them is history in them is poetry'. Yet of the trio St Stephen's, the youngest, 'sits all desolate'.[51] The restoration of England's ruins, he concluded, should begin with the Chapel. It was stirring stuff, and the editor of the *Post*

---

[45] Thomas Rickman to Edward Blore, 20 Dec. 1819, BL, Add. MS 56296 [unfoliated].
[46] Pugin to Willson, 6 Nov. 1824, in Pugin, *Letters*, vol. 1, p. 42.
[47] Pugin to Willson, 6 Nov. 1824, in Pugin, *Letters*, vol. 1, p. 42.
[48] *Hampshire Advertiser*, 7 March 1835, p. 4.
[49] *Hampshire Advertiser*, 7 March 1835, p. 4.
[50] *Morning Post*, 9 April 1835, p. 3.
[51] *Morning Post*, 9 April 1835, p. 3.

added a note to the effect that 'even in these disjointed times there can be no difference of opinion' about the desirability of restoring the Chapel.[52]

Among the visitors to the site was the young George Gilbert Scott. He had known St Stephen's as the Commons, when it was fitted up like 'a rather sumptuous Methodist chapel' but now 'how changed was its aspect! It seemed as if the subject of an enchanter's spell, and converted suddenly from a mean conventicle into a Gothic ruin of unrivalled beauty, glowing with the scorched but quite intelligible remnants of its gorgeous decorative colouring.'[53] Britton and Billings meanwhile had been exploring the ruins from the day after the fire and the resulting publication, *The History of the Ancient Palace and later Houses of Parliament at Westminster*, was issued smartly in 1836 with extensive illustrations of the ruins of St Stephen's Chapel, the adjoining cloister, and the Painted Chamber. It was dedicated to the President of the newly founded Institute of British Architects (soon to be the Royal Institute) Earl de Grey. Architecture and antiquarianism were presented seamlessly as aspects of the same subject. In his preface Britton spoke for a large section of the public in denouncing the 'lamentable mismanagement' of public works in recent years.[54] Wyatt's work was by now anathema to most people. The scandal of Nash's financially questionable dealing over Buckingham Palace, and the perception of Soane as old-fashioned, combined in a general feeling that there should be a competition for the new building rather than the commission being simply given to Robert Smirke, the only one of the Office of Works architects still active, who had been called in to fit up temporary chambers for the Lords and Commons.

When the terms of the competition were published and it was announced that the style was to be Gothic or Elizabethan, many an antiquarian architect reached for his pencil. The tables were at last turned. Architects, the *Gentleman's Magazine* noted with some satisfaction, would now have to take notice of the medieval: 'a class of buildings which they have hitherto regarded with contempt or apathy'. Furthermore, since 'the architecture of their own country has formed no part of the study of our present race of architects', the antiquaries were in with a chance.[55] 'Professional men have not studied the subject while *amateurs* have devoted their time and abilities in making themselves acquainted with the merits and details of English architecture.'[56] Rickman, Cottingham, Buckler, and Blore all entered and Buckler was one of the four prize winners. Pugin, who did not enter on his own account, worked on two of the entries, Gillespie Graham's and Charles Barry's. His contribution as a draughtsman with an unrivalled repertoire of medieval details in sketchbooks filled on his travels in England, Scotland, Germany, and France, was critical, all the more so since the judging committee included no professional architects and so its members were not used to reading plans or section drawings. The attractiveness of the presentation mattered, indeed it mattered rather too much in the opinion of the *Gentleman's Magazine* which worried that 'the unpractised eye is too easily captivated by detail, to regard the proportions of the building on which it is so lavishly displayed'.[57]

---

[52] *Morning Post*, 9 April 1835, p. 3.
[53] George Gilbert Scott, *Personal and Professional Recollections*, ed. Gavin Stamp (1879; facsimile edn, Stamford, 1995), p. 76.
[54] Brayley & Britton, p. x.
[55] *GM*, NS, 5 (1836), 523.
[56] *GM*, NS, 5 (1836), 524.
[57] *GM*, NS, 5 (1836), 635.

When the designs were exhibited it was clear that Barry had taken full advantage of his young ghost's expertise; indeed the *Gentleman's Magazine* critic thought it seemed as if 'Mr Barry [...] considered nothing so attentively as the enrichment of his design'.[58] Casting his own more practised eye over the scheme, he concluded, as Pugin himself said years later, that the elaborate detail obscured the essentially classical conception, that it was 'a *Grecian* design overlaid with *Gothic* ornament'.[59] Reviewing the other entries when they were exhibited at the new National Gallery in the summer of 1836, the *Gentleman* was naturally in favour of preserving as much of the medieval fabric as possible and was pleased to note that 'The majority of the architects have considered it an object of primary importance to save from total destruction the chapel of St Stephen', while some hoped to save the Painted Chamber too.[60] Barry's design showed the Chapel 'proposed to be rebuilt and called St Stephen's Hall'.[61] 'Rebuilt' was an ambiguous term that might imply anything from restoration to demolition. The article shrewdly observed that whatever Barry did to St Stephen's would be largely concealed by his new porch and the rebuilding of the South end of Westminster Hall, which it deplored. The author went on to suggest that while Barry was preserving the remains of St Stephen's 'out of deference to the public voice' he actually considered them a nuisance, interfering 'with the harmony of his design'.[62] The course of later events suggests that this was indeed the case.

Barry and Pugin's drawings are long lost, but they were clearly open to interpretation on the question of St Stephen's. *The Athenaeum* magazine approved of the scheme and in its issue of 21 May 1836 reproduced a perspective and ground plan as well as 'the paper submitted by Mr Barry with his design'.[63] Barry wrote of his intentions that 'St Stephens Chapel, the Crypt and Cloisters, are proposed to be restored'.[64] The *Athenaeum* clearly understood this to mean a reinstatement of the lost chapel, going on to enthuse about the bold effect that would be gained from the lengthening of the Hall and the new South window which would throw 'a flood of light' on the visitor ascending the steps to the new St Stephen's lobby from whence 'the eye will range upwards, through the old Chapel of St Stephen's, with its light attached pillars and richly-groined roof'.[65] In fact nobody knew at this date whether the roof had been 'richly groined' or not. What the *Athenaeum* describes sounds very much like one of the richly detailed 'Ideal Schemes' that Pugin was in the habit of making for his own amusement and had inserted into this part of Barry's design.

True Principles

After the competition, Pugin helped Barry with the estimate drawings and then they went their separate ways. While Pugin's architectural career rapidly gathered pace, Barry began embanking the Thames and constructing the coffer dam. He had said that the Palace would

---

[58] GM, NS, 5 (1836), 635.
[59] GM, NS, 5 (1836), 634.
[60] GM, NS, 5 (1836), 523.
[61] GM, NS, 5 (1836), 527.
[62] GM, NS, 5 (1836), 634.
[63] The Athenaeum, 21 May 1836, p. 362.
[64] The Athenaeum, 21 May 1836, p. 362.
[65] The Athenaeum, 21 May 1836, p. 363.

be finished by 1841, but it was not until 1840 that the foundation stone was laid. By the time the building started to appear above ground the Victorian Gothic Revival was well under way. The choice of Gothic for a major public building marked a permanent change. From a novelty style, a niche taste or an antiquarian hobby, the medieval was now the national style of a great imperial power. There was a new and serious mood among the young generations. In November 1841, with the Palace barely started, the Cambridge Camden Society (CCS) published the first number of its monthly magazine *The Ecclesiologist*. The Society had been founded by a group of undergraduates for the study of church architecture, with a hefty high-church bias. Within three years the members included sixteen Bishops and thirty-one Peers, and it had become the most authoritative critical voice in the discussion of Gothic architecture. The half-century since Carter had crept behind the wainscot had seen a revolution. The *Ecclesiologist* paid him due tribute, for having 'stood almost alone at that tasteless period'.[66] Ever since 1836, the year of the Palace competition, the magazine noted 'the state of religious feeling' had developed and by 1842 'more correct principles' obtained, in theology and in architecture.[67] That year saw the long-delayed publication of Stothard's drawings of the Painted Chamber in a volume edited by John Gage. As Director of the Society of Antiquaries, Gage had made his own explorations since the fire with antiquarian friends including Blore, and brought his considerable scholarship to bear on Stothard and Capon's work which he combined with the other discoveries of the last forty years to make a remarkably complete account.

The Camdenians now turned their attention to the fate of St Stephen's. Access to the works at Westminster was strictly controlled and few people knew what exactly had happened to the Chapel. In May 1842 Barry exhibited a picture at the Royal Academy entitled 'New Houses of Parliament'.[68] This reawakened speculation as to 'the condition of this beautiful and deeply interesting monument of national and ecclesiastical architecture', it having been 'the belief [...] of many', according to the *Ecclesiologist*, that Barry's plan had been for a complete restoration.[69] The picture apparently still left room for doubt. Press reports and rumours abounded. Barry replied with a letter for publication stating that 'the dangerous state of the ruins' had required him 'to remove them entirely', but even this apparently unequivocal statement was qualified to the point where its exact import was unclear.[70] 'All such parts of the moulded and carved details [...] were carefully preserved', he wrote, and could be seen by the CCS whenever they chose. It was, however, an error to suppose he had ever meant to restore the Chapel: 'the only portions of the ancient Palace of Westminster which I proposed to retain and restore were the Crypt of the Chapel, the adjoining cloisters and Westminster Hall'.[71] That was, he said, the understanding on which his designs had been accepted. He went on to add that restoration had been impossible for two reasons. The first was that insufficient evidence survived for a 'perfect and faithful restoration', so that any attempt would be 'purely speculative, and consequently unsatisfactory'.[72] While

---

[66] *The Ecclesiologist*, 12–13 (Aug. 1842), p 187.
[67] *The Ecclesiologist*, 12–13 (Aug. 1842), p. 185.
[68] Ex. inf. Royal Academy archivists.
[69] *The Ecclesiologist*, 8 (May 1842), p. 117.
[70] *The Ecclesiologist*, 8 (May 1842), p. 118.
[71] *The Ecclesiologist*, 8 (May 1842), p. 118.
[72] *The Ecclesiologist*, 8 (May 1842), p. 118.

this argument might carry some weight with ecclesiologists, his second reason flatly contradicted it. Even if it were possible, Barry added, restoration would be 'impracticable' because it would not fit in with his plan, in which the new Hall on the site of the Chapel would form the public approach to the Houses. Thus Barry appeared to be saying that even if it was possible to restore St Stephen's from one point of view, from another it was impossible because, as the *Gentleman's Magazine* had observed, it was in his way.

A reply came in August from 'An Architectural Conservative' who pointed to the flaws in Barry's logic. He could have retained the Chapel by simply not deciding to turn it into a corridor, and even if knowledge of the original design was incomplete that did not mean nothing could be done: 'to sacrifice the majority which we know, merely because there are parts which we do *not* know, is absolutely absurd'.[73] The 'Conservative' suggested that a Committee of both Houses of Parliament be formed to consult 'with some of the most eminent ecclesiastical and architectural antiquaries' on the future of St Stephen's.[74] As for the cost of restoration, the *Ecclesiologist* considered that 'In a country which spends its thousands in importing mutilated remnants of pagan art, it seems monstrous to give up for ever the infinitely more valuable remains of the best age of Christian and native architecture, sculpture and painting.'[75]

In fact the debate was futile. St Stephen's was lost. Five years earlier, on 25 July 1837, Barry had requested that the ruins be 'immediately taken down'.[76] Demolition took place over the next few months. The Chapel had never been more famous or admired in its post-medieval history than it was in 1842 when it became one of England's great ghost buildings, and it was a ghost that haunted Barry.[77] The implementation of his design was, in many ways, a Pyrrhic victory. By the time the new Palace was up it already looked old-fashioned. The world of late-Georgian Classical architecture which had shaped Barry was passing. The coming age belonged to George Gilbert Scott and the ecclesiologists. Scott, naturally, was 'exceedingly irate at the projected destruction' of St Stephen's Chapel, 'the single blot upon the fair shield of Sir Charles Barry'.[78] Having begun his career designing workhouses, he had undergone a Damascene conversion in the early 1840s. Pugin's *True Principles of Pointed or Christian Architecture*, his articles in the *Dublin Review* and the publications of the CCS brought about in Scott an 'awakening' to the moral and social power of architecture. Using the campaign for St Stephen's as an opening, he wrote to Pugin whose works, he recalled, excited him 'almost to fury […] I suddenly found myself like a person awakened from a long feverish dream, which had rendered him unconscious of what was going on about him'.[79] To Scott's 'almost tremulous delight' Pugin invited him to call.[80]

Neither Scott nor Pugin left any surviving record of their 'tremendously jolly' conversation.[81] Pugin was then living in Chelsea. He was famous and frantically busy with dozens

---

[73] *The Ecclesiologist*, 12–13 (Aug. 1842), p. 184.
[74] *The Ecclesiologist*, 12–13 (Aug. 1842), p. 185.
[75] *The Ecclesiologist*, 12–13 (Aug. 1842), p. 185.
[76] PA, ARC/PRO/WORK11/26/6.
[77] For Barry's subsequent protective attitude to preserving the fabric of St Mary Undercroft, see Elizabeth Hallam Smith's essay in this volume.
[78] Scott, *Recollections*, pp. 76, 87.
[79] Scott, *Recollections*, p. 88.
[80] Scott, *Recollections*, p. 89.
[81] Scott, *Recollections*, p. 89.

of commissions, but he was in close touch with the CCS who, though they could not accept him as a member because he was a Catholic, were vocal in their admiration of his work; indeed he had designed the Society's seal. There can be no doubt that Pugin knew all about the row. It seems almost certain that he would have favoured the restoration of St Stephen's to something like what he had drawn in Barry's competition entry, but he also felt personal loyalty and gratitude to Barry. History must therefore leave him there, caught on the horns of a dilemma. Two years later, he reluctantly went back to work for Barry at Westminster. Pugin was now a hero to Scott's generation. His designs for the interior decoration and furnishing of the Palace were admired, and rumours went round that Barry was taking credit for his work. To some extent that was true. When the House of Lords was opened in 1847 Barry's office gave out a list of designers and contractors. Pugin, who was responsible for all the details of the interior, was not mentioned. It was the mean act of a decent man under immense pressure who perhaps could not forgive Pugin for representing the future, while Barry himself seemed increasingly to belong to the past. Even today, his reputation is less than he deserves. The Victorians did not forgive him for St Stephen's. To the end of his life Scott could not forget the one, indelible stain on Barry's character.

St Stephen's, Temporary Accommodation, and the New House of Commons

Rebekah Moore

On 16 October 1834 the medieval Palace of Westminster was destroyed by fire, beginning the process that led to the construction of the first purpose-built Parliament at Westminster. The fire happened at a critical juncture in British politics, for the period between 1828 and 1836 was a 'constitutional turning point', witnessing rapid political, social, and economic change.[1] Catholic emancipation was achieved in 1829, followed by the passing of the Reform Act in 1832, ushering in a period of transition and modernization in British public life.

Despite these profound and wide-ranging developments, parliamentary spaces continued to be strongly influenced by the past as much as the political realities of the present. Many historians have emphasized the sense of continuity between the old and the new, post-fire, Palace of Westminster. Roland Quinault, for instance, has argued that the new home of Parliament was 'designed and built as a royal Palace', which left little room for expressions of parliamentary sovereignty.[2] Its design was indeed palatial, and the importance of royalty was emphasized throughout its decoration and iconography, in spite of a perceptible decrease in royal authority after the Reform Act. Similarly, the decision to build the new Palace in the Gothic style also provided a visual link with the past rather than with modernity, prioritizing the history of the building, a distinct 'English national identity', and the ancient Protestant constitution over the reformed values of modern government.[3] The intention of the new Palace, through both its style and its design, was to emphasize continuity with history rather than to recognize the upheaval, and the important constitutional changes, of the more recent past.

However, while the new Palace was under construction, Parliament was housed in temporary accommodation which provided an unexpected opportunity for experimentation. Previous accounts of innovation within the temporary House of Commons have

---

[1] Angus Hawkins, *Victorian Political Culture: Habits of Hearts and Minds* (Oxford, 2015), pp. 65–99.
[2] Roland Quinault, 'Westminster and the Victorian Constitution', *Transactions of the Royal Historical Society*, 2 (1992), 80.
[3] Linda Colley, *Britons: Forging the Nation, 1707–1837* (London, 2003), p. 330. See also Mark Collins's essay in this volume; Gerald Newman, *The Rise of English Nationalism: A Cultural History, 1740–1830*, rev. edn (New York, 1997), pp. 231–6, and R. J. Smith, *The Gothic Bequest: Medieval Institutions in British Thought, 1688–1863* (Cambridge, 1987), pp. 171–95.

focused on the scientific and engineering aspects: warming and ventilation, acoustics and lighting.[4] Yet this sense of innovation was not confined to these technological areas. There were also spatial and procedural experiments within the chamber, denoting a modernization of the political and constitutional practices of Parliament. Kathryn Rix has investigated the evolution of the reporters' gallery and the division lobby as an expression of the desire of radical Members for increased public accountability.[5] This chapter further explores these spaces, analysing how they evolved within the temporary House of Commons, which replaced St Stephen's. This building was in its turn an important influence upon Charles Barry's new permanent chamber, which again reflected the changes and challenges within politics in the age of reform.

'The worst imaginable chamber of legislation'

Throughout its long and chequered history, the old Palace of Westminster had been a building shaped by the political pressures of the moment, and consequently one which demonstrated little architectural coherence. The Acts of Union of 1800–1 stimulated the biggest programme of improvements since Christopher Wren's remodelling. The consequence of these extensive alterations was that by 1834, both the Commons and Lords had been meeting 'in what amounted to a perpetual building site for well over thirty years'.[6] Despite attempts to make the exterior more aesthetically pleasing, the Palace remained a mix of medieval Gothic, castellated Georgian Gothic additions, and classical improvements.

The interior of the old Palace of Westminster also offered little coherence in its arrangement. It was divided over four roughly defined floors. The ground floor contained many of the cellars and storerooms for facilities, including the furnaces for heating, while some of the Lords committee rooms were located at the south-eastern end of the site.[7] Also at ground floor level was the former lower storey of St Stephen's Chapel (today the Chapel of St Mary Undercroft), part of which was used as the Speaker's dining room. The House of Commons and the House of Lords were both at Principal Floor level of the Palace (fig. 1). A mezzanine floor was located one level up from the floor of the Commons chamber, featuring galleries for Members, the strangers' gallery (for men), and rooms for journalists. The upper floor contained committee rooms and prison rooms, while the ventilator within the roof of the House of Commons was used unofficially as a space in which women could gather to watch debates.[8] The floor levels were not uniform, and to walk between the Lords and Commons Members were obliged to walk up fourteen steps and down seven.[9]

---

[4] M. H. Port, 'Problems of Building in the 1840s', in Port, *HoP*, pp. 97–121; Denis Smith, 'The Building Services', in Port, *HoP*, pp. 218–31; Henrik Schoenefeldt, 'The Temporary Houses of Parliament and David Boswell Reid's Architecture of Experimentation', *Architectural History*, 57 (2014), 173–213; Edward Gillin, *The Victorian Palace of Science: Scientific Knowledge and the Building of the Houses of Parliament* (Cambridge, 2017), pp. 149–53.
[5] Kathryn Rix, '"Whatever passed in Parliament ought to be communicated to the public": Reporting the Proceedings of the Reformed Commons, 1833–1850', *PH*, 33 (2014), 453–74.
[6] Philip Salmon, 'The House of Commons, 1801–1911', in Clyve Jones (ed.), *A Short History of Parliament: England, Great Britain, the United Kingdom, Ireland and Scotland* (Woodbridge, 2009), p. 250.
[7] Michael Port, *The Palace of Westminster Surveyed on the Eve of the Conflagration, 1834* (London, 2011), p. 5.
[8] Sarah Richardson, 'Parliament as Viewed through a Woman's Eyes: Gender and Space in the 19th-Century Commons', *Space and Sound*, pp. 119–34 at pp. 120–5.
[9] Port, *HoP*, p. 9.

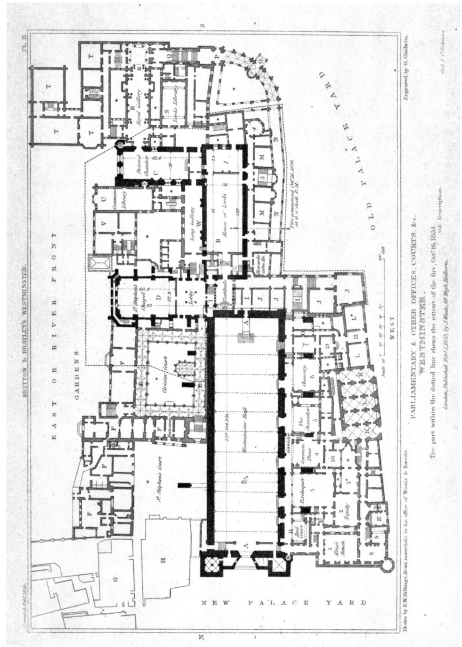

Fig. 1. Robert William Billings, *Parliamentary & Other Offices, Courts, &c, Westminster*, principal floor plan, showing the extent of the fire of 1834 (within dotted line), 1835. Engraving, 14.6 × 22.4 cm. PA, HC/LB/1/114/17.

The parliamentary reporter James Grant noted that 'there were so many passages and rooms in the old House of Commons that it was with great difficulty strangers could find their way to the gallery'. This could lead to some entertainment within the chamber. In 1833 a Scottish Highlander 'wearing highland costume' accidentally ended up in the side galleries, rather than in the strangers' gallery. 'Donald' knew no more 'of the rules or localities of the House than he did of the politics of Timbuctoo', and never suspected he was in breach of the rules. It was only the kind intervention of a Member, who advised him to make his way to the strangers' gallery, which prevented him from being taken into the custody of the Serjeant-at-Arms.[10] In another incident in 1834, a woman entered the side galleries of the chamber, rather than making her way to the ventilator from which women were by then watching and listening to debates. The Speaker, Charles Manners Sutton, was said to be 'quite delighted at the sight of a politician in petticoats'. The woman left after around a minute when she realized that she was in the wrong location.[11]

Despite extensive modifications, the Palace of Westminster was increasingly unsuited to the needs and expectations of politicians. The former St Stephen's Chapel was particularly ill-suited as the Commons chamber (see Tremellen, fig. 3, p. 217).[12] James Fenimore Cooper, the popular American author, visited St Stephen's prior to the conflagration and wrote to Thomas James de Lancey:

> I should think that the whole chapel internally might be about fifty-five feet long, by about forty-one or two wide. The floor I paced and made it about forty feet square [...] A good deal of even these straightened limits is lost, by a bad arrangement of the seats behind the Speaker's Chair, which is about a fourth of the way down the Chapel; the seats rising about each other like the transoms of a ship [...] The wood is all of oak, unpainted; the place is lighted by candles, in very common brass chandeliers, and the whole has a gloomy and inconvenient air.[13]

James Grant agreed with this assessment, stating that the House

> was dark, gloomy and badly ventilated [...] when an important debate occurred, but especially when that debate was preceded by a call of the House, the Members were really to be pitied; they were literally crammed together, and the heat of the house rendered it in some degree a second edition of the black hole of Calcutta.[14]

The *Mirror of Literature* concurred with Grant's appraisal of the chamber, stating that St Stephen's Chapel was the 'worst imaginable Chamber of legislation'.[15]

The appearance and inconvenience of the Chapel were all the more concerning given the expansion in Parliamentary business. The 1820s had seen a significant increase in

---

[10] The incident is recounted in James Grant, *Random Recollections of the House of Commons: From the Year 1830 to the Close of 1835, including Personal Sketches of the Leading Members of All Parties* (London, 1836), pp. 12–13.
[11] Grant, *Random Recollections*, pp. 13–14.
[12] Paul Seaward, 'A sense of Crowd and Urgency? Atmosphere and Inconvenience in the Chamber of the Old House of Commons', in *Space and Sound*, pp. 103–18.
[13] James Fenimore Cooper, *Gleanings in Europe: England. By an American* (2 vols, Philadelphia, 1837), vol. 1, pp. 65–6.
[14] Grant, *Random Recollections*, p. 2.
[15] *The Mirror of Literature, Amusement, and Instruction*, 24 (1834), 325.

the amount of legislation, leading to MPs spending more time in the chamber. In 1828 the House sat after midnight on 52 occasions, increasing to 62 in 1830. Between 1828 and 1830 the Commons devoted an average of 720 hours per session to debate.[16] The 1830 session was described by Huskisson as 'one of the longest and most arduous Sessions ever known'.[17] There was also additional public scrutiny of Parliament. The wide-ranging impact of Catholic emancipation and parliamentary reform, and the increased level of attention from the press, made it increasingly problematic for them to be dealt with behind closed doors at Westminster.[18] This was particularly evident during the passage of the Reform Bill, when political unions and other organizations sprang up across the country to support reform.[19]

This increased level of interest in the proceedings of Parliament prompted concern about the state of the chamber, and the difficulty of hearing speeches and debates in the Commons.[20] Frederick Trench, MP for the borough of Cambridge, who considered himself a great urban improver, asserted – inaccurately – in 1831 that 'the bad state of the atmosphere, and the exposure to unequal draughts of air had already caused the death of several hon. Members in the course of this arduous Session'.[21] During a debate on the House of Commons buildings in 1833, there were numerous criticisms of the chamber by Members. Henry Warburton, MP for Bridport and a radical reformer, complained about its 'deficiency of accommodation, the inconvenient shape and the bad arrangement'.[22] The Scottish MP Robert Cutlar Fergusson argued that

> the present building might be large enough for the discussion of Turnpike Bills, Road Bills and so on, but it was most certainly far from affording adequate accommodation for the reception of that collective body of Representatives of the Empire who duty imperatively called upon them to be present at the discussion on every important question.

Even the conservative Robert Inglis, who strongly opposed plans to alter the chamber, conceded that there was not sufficient accommodation for 'full Houses'.[23]

Across the political spectrum, Members were concerned that the restrictions imposed by St Stephen's were an obstacle to the transaction of business. But despite this, there was little support among Members for change. Select Committees were established in 1831 and 1833 to investigate measures to improve the spaces of the House of Commons. The first concluded that owing to the situation of other buildings in the Palace of Westminster, particularly the residence of the clerk of the Commons to the south-east, 'no such alterations or improvements could be made in the present House of Commons as would afford adequate

---

[16] Peter Jupp, *British Politics on the Eve of Reform: The Duke of Wellington's Administration, 1828–30* (Basingstoke, 1998), pp. 198–9.
[17] Quoted in Jupp, *British Politics on the Eve of Reform*, p. 198.
[18] Boyd Hilton, 'The Political Arts of Lord Liverpool', *Transactions of the Royal Historical Society*, 5th ser., 38 (1988), 168.
[19] See Nancy D. LoPatin, *Political Unions, Popular Politics and the Great Reform Act of 1832* (Basingstoke, 1999).
[20] HC Deb 11 Oct. 1831, vol. 8, cols 554–60.
[21] HC Deb 11 Oct. 1831, vol. 8, col. 555.
[22] HC Deb 7 March 1833, vol. 16, col. 374.
[23] HC Deb 7 March 1833, vol. 16, cols 375–7.

accommodation for Members'.[24] In 1833 Members returned to their discussion of the subject, briefly considering moving the legislature to another location.[25] Once again, a suitable way to increase parliamentary accommodation could not be agreed. The imputation from some members of the Committee, such as Joseph Hume, was that despite the Whig Government's attempts to eradicate abuses, parliamentary space was adding a physical barrier to their efforts. And some of these abuses would only be cured when the Commons moved to a chamber that was suitable for its needs and could accommodate all of its members.[26]

Although radical MPs were in favour of this change, the majority resisted any idea of leaving the traditional Westminster site. The Palace acted as a place of collective memory, in which Britain's long history of links between Parliament and royalty was embedded, representing continuity with the past, while also celebrating a Whig version of history emphasizing the progress of parliamentary institutions.[27] This was particularly important given the tumultuous political context. There was a palpable sense that the political world had changed: for those fearful of further disruption, emphasis on the longevity of British institutions was an important symbol of stability. This view was expressed by Philip Howard, who objected to any prospect of 'pulling down a building hallowed by its recollections'.[28] Even after the 1834 fire, there was a reluctance to move. Despite the inconvenience of constructing temporary accommodation on the same site occupied by the old Palace, Lord Melbourne was 'unwilling to be the Minister who should advise your Majesty, upon his responsibility, to remove the Houses of Parliament from their ancient and established place of assembly at Westminster'.[29]

Continuity and Innovation in the Temporary Chamber

Following the conflagration of 16 October 1834, temporary accommodation was constructed within the charred and damaged remains of the ancient Palace of Westminster. On 24 October the Treasury authorized attached architect Sir Robert Smirke to begin the creation of temporary housing for the Commons and Lords,[30] and a detailed plan was presented by Smirke to the Office of Woods and Forests soon afterwards.[31] Construction of the temporary chambers at Westminster proceeded so rapidly that the new parliamentary session was able to start there in February 1835. The House of Lords was displaced from its large and airy space in the Romanesque Lesser Hall so that the area could be occupied by the Commons in a new temporary building. The Peers were relocated to the much smaller Painted Chamber, located at right angles to and to the east of their previous accommodation, until they moved into their new House in 1847 (fig. 2).

---

[24] *Report from the Select Committee on the House of Commons Buildings; together with the minutes of evidence taken before them*, HC 308 (1831), p. 3. See the essay by Paul Seaward in this volume.
[25] *Report from the Select Committee on House of Commons Buildings*, HC 269 (1833), p. 33.
[26] HC Deb 7 March 1833, vol. 16, col. 371.
[27] Andrea Fredericksen, 'Parliament's *genius loci*: The Politics of Place after the 1834 Fire', in Riding & Riding, p. 99.
[28] HC Deb 7 March 1833, vol. 16, col. 378.
[29] Lord Melbourne to William IV, 1 Nov. 1834, in Lloyd C. Sanders (ed.), *Lord Melbourne's Papers* (London, 1889), p. 214.
[30] Treasury Chambers to His Majesty's Commissioners of Woods, 24 Oct. 1834, TNA, WORK 11/10/2, fol. 1.
[31] Sir Robert Smirke (n. d.), TNA, WORK 11/10/2, fol. 3.

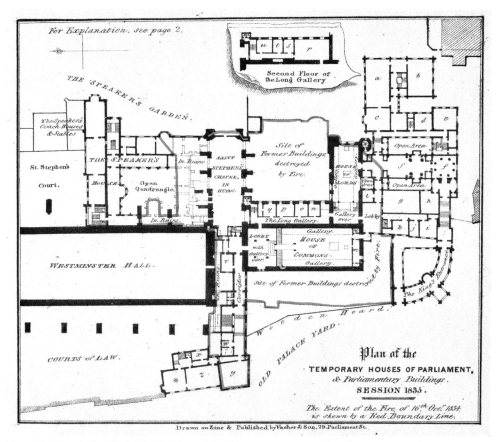

Fig. 2. Vacher & Son (publisher), *Plan of the Temporary Houses of Parliament, & Parliamentary Buildings. Session 1835*, 1835. Zincograph, 21 × 25.8 cm. PA, HC/LB/1/114/18.

The temporary House of Commons was both larger and more convenient than St Stephen's. The temporary building contrived by Smirke in the shell of the Lesser Hall provided comfortable seating for an increased number of MPs attending debates in the aftermath of reform (fig. 3). Following the first reformed election the old St Stephen's chamber was home to 658 MPs, yet could offer accommodation on the floor of the House of Commons only for 305 MPs with 82 more in the galleries. Although approximately the same width, the temporary Commons was seventeen feet (5.2 m) longer and could accommodate 450 Members.[32] It was this increased size that led *The Times* to conclude that the temporary House of Commons was 'altogether as superior to the old House, both for appearance and utility, as it is well possible to conceive'.[33]

The Reform Act had an important impact on politics within the Commons chamber. It was intended as an essentially conservative piece of legislation, framed by the Whig leadership as a means of 'reasserting the constitutional tradition protecting British liberties

[32] *Report from the Select Committee on State of Building of Houses of Parliament*, HC 448 (1844), p. 15; Salmon, 'The House of Commons, 1801–1911', p. 250. See also Mark Collins's essay in this volume.
[33] *The Times*, 4 Feb. 1835, p. 3.

Fig. 3. Robert William Billings, *The Temporary House of Commons as fitted up in 1835.* Pencil drawing, on paper, 27.9 × 19.8 cm. WOA 15.

which had been established by their ancestors in 1688/9, and which had later been eroded by Tory corruption and exclusiveness'.[34] Although many elements of continuity and conservatism can be discerned, at the same time the Reform Act initiated a process of transition in British politics.[35] There was 'the *sense*, on both sides of the House, that a venerable historic constitution was being irrevocably changed'.[36]

Incremental but significant change to the layout and functionality of the Commons chamber between 1832 and 1852 paralleled and reflected this constitutional and political

---

[34] Jonathan Parry, *The Rise and Fall of Liberal Government in Victorian Britain* (London/New Haven, 1993), p. 8.
[35] Emphasizing continuity, see Frank O'Gorman, *Voters, Patrons, and Parties: The Unreformed Electoral System of Hanoverian England, 1734–1832* (Oxford, 1989); James Vernon, *Politics and the People: A Study in English Political Culture, c.1815–1867* (Cambridge, 1993), pp. 99, 163. On transition, see John A. Phillips and Charles Wetherell, 'The Great Reform Act of 1832 and the Political Modernization of England', *American Historical Review*, 100:2 (1995), 411–36; Angus Hawkins, '"Parliamentary Government" and Victorian Political Parties, c.1830–c.1880', *English Historical Review*, 104 (1989), 638–69; Matthew Cragoe, 'The Great Reform Act and the Modernization of British Politics: The Impact of Conservative Associations, 1835–1841', *Journal of British Studies*, 47 (2008), 581–603.
[36] William Thomas, *The Quarrel of Macaulay and Croker: Politics and History in the Age of Reform* (Oxford, 2000), pp. 7–8 (my emphasis).

transition, and was made possible by the prevailing climate of scientific experimentation at Westminster. A key driver for these changes was MPs' concern with appearing accountable to the people, which prompted the creation of a reporters' gallery in the temporary Commons chamber. The House of Commons had historically been reluctant to engage with the press, and parliamentary reporting had had a short but tumultuous evolution before the conflagration of 1834. The verbatim reporting of debates was forbidden by a standing order of the House,[37] but following the American Revolution there was heightened interest in the proceedings of Parliament, and newspapers were increasingly inclined to push the boundaries of the standing order. In 1771 reporters from eight newspapers were called to the bar of the House to answer charges relating to the publication of debates. While minor punishments were handed out by the Commons, it was clear that the expense of enforcing the ban on parliamentary reporting was beyond the means of the state. After this episode, reports of debates appeared more frequently in the press in blatant defiance of the standing order.[38]

Further concessions were made in 1803. In anticipation of a speech by William Pitt, the House was filled to capacity, and there were no available seats for journalists; thus no accounts of the speech appeared in the press the next day. This provoked complaints from the press, who claimed that despite their best attempts 'reporters could neither by persuasion nor force obtain a seat'.[39] Following that incident, the Speaker arranged with the Serjeant-at-Arms to allow reporters into the strangers' gallery before the general public was admitted.[40] The same year saw William Cobbett begin producing his *Parliamentary Debates*, printed by Thomas Curson Hansard. In 1812 Hansard purchased the rights, the title changing to *Hansard's Parliamentary Debates* in 1829. Between 1828 and 1843 the rival *Mirror of Parliament* also published verbatim accounts of Parliamentary proceedings.[41]

Despite these minor concessions, there was no change to the standing order and technically parliamentary reporting still took place in breach of the rules. Its uncertain status was demonstrated by the lack of accommodation for journalists in St Stephen's. Reporters shared the strangers' gallery with members of the public, and were confined to the back row of the gallery. They had to contend with the noise and chatter of other strangers, as well as the poor acoustics within the chamber itself. While official figures suggested that the gallery could seat sixty-four, it could have one hundred and fifty people 'wedged into it' when an important debate was taking place.[42] The gallery was also located opposite the Speaker's chair, meaning that MPs spoke with their backs to reporters.

Although the addition of a gallery for reporters was a change that was 'long sought', the constraints of space in St Stephen's prevented its construction.[43] In 1830, reporters for

---

[37] Peter Jupp, *The Governing of Britain, 1688–1848: The Executive, Parliament and the People* (London, 2006), p. 206.
[38] The episode is recounted in more detail in Peter D. G. Thomas, 'The Beginning of Parliamentary Reporting in Newspapers, 1768–74', *English Historical Review*, 74 (1959), 623–36.
[39] Charles Gratton, *The Gallery: A Sketch on the History of Parliamentary Reporting and Reporters* (London, 1860), p. 76.
[40] Salmon, 'The House of Commons, 1801–1911', p. 259.
[41] Salmon, 'The House of Commons, 1801–1911', p. 259; David Lewis Jones, 'Hansard, Thomas Curson (1776–1833)', *ODNB*.
[42] HC 448 (1844), p. 15; Grant, *Random Recollections*, p. 9; Seaward, 'A Sense of Crowd and Urgency?', pp. 112–17.
[43] *The Times*, 9 Dec. 1834, p. 4.

The Times conceded that there was 'little, if any, further accommodation that could be extended to them, as the present House is constructed'.[44] But the additional space offered by the temporary House of Commons provided an opportunity to recognize the importance of Parliamentary reporting, as a designated press gallery was now included for the first time. This was an acknowledgement that the presence of the press was 'a vital element in the practical functioning of the relationship between Parliament and the people'.[45] The new reporters' gallery was situated opposite the public gallery and above the Speaker's chair, increasing the efficiency and ease with which reporters could hear debates:

> The gallery is immediately behind the Speaker's Chair, so that they will enjoy the advantage of hearing distinctly the various Members who address the House, who will now of necessity turn their faces towards them, instead of, as before, their backs.[46]

However, there were some initial problems due to the placement of the gallery. Walter Henry Watts, reporter for the *Morning Chronicle*, complained that when Members were seated in certain parts of the chamber, journalists in the gallery could neither see them nor hear their speeches.[47] To correct this, both the strangers' and reporters' galleries were lowered and the size of the Speaker's chair was reduced, so that there was increased visibility for reporters. The screen separating the galleries from the chamber was also removed.[48] The alterations to the gallery demonstrate the importance placed by Members upon the ability of reporters to see and hear what was happening below them, and to communicate this accurately to the public. At the same time, sound-absorbing carpets were fitted to enhance audibility. Most strikingly, a false ceiling was constructed with distinctive sloping panels (fig. 4).[49]

The arrangements for the press within the temporary House of Commons were recreated in the new chamber, with further minor improvements. As in the temporary chamber, the reporters' gallery was situated behind the Speaker's chair, but there was now a series of rooms behind the gallery for the use of parliamentary journalists. These included refreshment facilities and rooms where reports could be written up before being sent to the newspaper offices.[50] In addition there was a small social space, where reporters could rest or compare notes on the speeches made that evening. The addition of a telegraph machine in the Central Lobby also allowed them to communicate their summaries of debates to their newspapers with comparative ease.[51] The gallery was now a permanent fixture, so that 'at last, the reporters' gallery was erected on a firm and enduring basis. It was an acknowledgement that henceforth it was to be an abiding adjunct of Parliament.'[52] One of several innovations within the temporary Houses of Parliament, the gallery demonstrated an intention to engage

---

[44] *The Times*, 22 June 1830, p. 5.
[45] Rix, 'Whatever passed in Parliament', p. 453.
[46] *The Times*, 4 Feb. 1835, p. 3.
[47] *Report from the Select Committee on the Admission of Ladies to the Strangers' Gallery*, HC 437 (1835), p. 5.
[48] *The Times*, 22 Oct. 1836, p. 3.
[49] Henrik Schoenefeldt, *Rebuilding the Houses of Parliament: David Boswell Reid and Disruptive Environmentalism* (Abingdon, 2021), pp. 37–8.
[50] 'Plan of first floor of the House of Commons', TNA, WORK 29/103.
[51] Thomas Erskine May, *The Machinery of Parliamentary Legislation Reprinted from the Edinburgh Review of January 1854 with a letter from the author 23 March 1881* (London, 1881), p. 11.
[52] Michael Macdonagh, *The Reporters' Gallery* (London, 1913), p. 392.

Fig. 4. Anon., *T. Duncombe, Esq: Presenting the Petition*. Engraving, 17.8 × 12.7 cm. WOA 80.

with the newly expanded electorate, and recognition of the fact that 'all that passed within these walls ought to be communicated to the public'.[53]

By contrast, the facilities offered to women to view Commons debates were diminished in the temporary chamber, with a small space seating no more than 13 women being concealed behind the strangers' gallery. Despite strong initial resistance by many MPs in 1835–7, a far more substantial area was allocated as the ladies' gallery in the permanent House, although like its predecessors it was screened off to keep the ladies out of sight.[54]

Another innovation in the temporary House of Commons was the addition of a second division lobby. Before the 1834 fire, the lobby of the House of Commons – originally the ante-chapel of St Stephen's – had doubled as the sole division lobby. Described as a 'landing place' approached by a 'broad stone staircase, traversed by Strangers and Members alike', the

---

[53] HC Deb 22 May 1834, vol. 23, col. 1229 (William Tooke MP).
[54] Richardson, 'Parliament as Viewed through a Woman's Eyes', pp. 126–9. See also the chapter by Caroline Shenton and Melanie Unwin in this volume.

lobby gave access both to the Commons chamber and the staircase to the strangers' gallery. It was populated with members of the public, doorkeepers wearing seventeenth-century court dress, and refreshment stands at the entrance.[55] When a division was called before 1834, the Speaker decided whether the ayes or noes should move out into the lobby, with the perceived majority being told to remain in the chamber – a practice dating back to Tudor times.[56] Before a division could take place, the strangers' gallery had to be emptied and the lobby cleared of members of the public and officers. As a consequence divisions were lengthy, consuming a significant proportion of parliamentary time.[57]

Before the destruction of the old Palace of Westminster, division lists were not routinely published. Accounts of divisions often appeared in the national press on the following day, albeit only after important votes, or those that the press believed would be of interest to the newspaper-reading public. However, the arrangement was problematic. Although information about debates was relatively well circulated due to the presence of parliamentary reporters, accounts of the results of votes often contained numerous mistakes.[58] There were also issues relating to the casting of votes. When a division was called, Members were often reluctant to leave the Commons for fear of losing their precious seat within the chamber – a sentiment already familiar to Elizabethan MPs meeting in the recently converted St Stephen's Chapel.[59] Consequently Members would be more likely to cast a vote for the side that was remaining in the chamber, which led the *Spectator* to suggest that close divisions, such as one against establishing a ladies' gallery in 1835, had been decided by the number of MPs who were unwilling to leave their seats.[60]

In 1833, when the motion officially to publish the lists of divisions of the House was raised, there was little agreement on the proposal. While the practical advantages of accurate division lists were strongly emphasized, the motion provoked debate about the place of the electorate in politics and the limits of their influence within the chamber. Daniel Harvey, MP for Colchester, suggested that the publication of division lists was essential due to increased public participation in politics:

> Their proceedings were closely watched by the public, who, till the Reform Bill was passed, were estranged from the Parliament, which had no sympathy with them. Now a sympathy had been restored between them, and the people looked with confidence to their deliberations.[61]

Harvey stressed the responsibility of Members to the electorate, and suggested that the publication of division lists would demonstrate that MPs were acting in accordance with the wishes of voters. However, the motion was strongly opposed. Viscount Stormont,

---

[55] [Anon], 'A Crush in the Commons', *The Leisure Hour*, 15:753 (2 June 1866), 341.
[56] *Report from Select Committee on Means of Taking Divisions of House of Commons*, HC 147 (1834), p. 3. See also J. P. D. Cooper's essay in this volume.
[57] Ryan Vieira, *Time and Politics: Parliament and the Culture of Modernity in Britain and the British World* (Oxford, 2015), p. 31.
[58] HC Deb 10 March 1835, vol. 26, col. 834; Rix 'Whatever passed in public', p. 465.
[59] J. P. D. Cooper, 'The Elizabethan House of Commons and St Stephen's Chapel Westminster', in *Space and Sound*, pp. 34–59 at pp. 46–7.
[60] *The Spectator*, 27 Feb. 1836, p. 201.
[61] HC Deb 21 Feb. 1833, vol. 15, col. 1080.

member for Norwich, declared that to publish such a list would be an 'infringement on the constitutional privileges of the House, and would only encourage the people to watch their proceedings'.[62] Sir Robert Peel did not see the need for official publications, pointing out that the division lists for major debates were already in the public domain, and fearing that an MP could be voted out at the next election if the electorate disagreed with the stance of the Member. The motion for allowing the publication of debates was rejected by 49 to 142. However, the issue was revisited early in the next session and was sent to committee to discuss the practicalities of the publication of division lists.[63]

In 1834, before the Palace fire, a Select Committee of the House of Commons had advised that the addition of a second division lobby could reduce the time taken to complete divisions and provide a more efficient means of counting votes, thus recognizing that the arrangements at St Stephen's Chapel were a barrier to the accurate collection of division lists.[64] A second lobby would allow the House to be cleared upon division, and enable the tellers more easily (and importantly more accurately) to record Members as they entered one of the lobbies. But none was constructed, due to the lack of available space. Suitable accommodation could only be located at a considerable distance from the Commons, since the chamber was surrounded by buildings and corridors on three sides. As with the reporters' gallery, the division lobby was considered by members to be a desirable change in the aftermath of constitutional reform, but the spatial limitations of St Stephen's had prevented the Commons from innovating in response to the newly expanded electorate.

Following the fire, however, it did become possible, as there was ample space for the construction of a new lobby near to the temporary House of Commons. The issue of divisions was revisited in a Select Committee in 1835, when Sir Robert Smirke assured Members that the cost of an additional lobby capable of holding five hundred members and appropriate passageways would not exceed £1,500.[65] With the promise that the building could be completed quickly, construction of the second division lobby began between the parliamentary sessions and was completed by February 1836.[66] There was now a separate space for both the 'ayes' and the 'noes' when recording the result of a division.[67] For the first time, the chamber was entirely cleared during a vote. Two tellers from each side of the question were sent to count the Members in each lobby, whose numbers were then used to create accurate division lists. This compelled MPs to make an active decision about which lobby they would enter (and consequently whether they supported a measure) rather than passively remaining in their seats.[68]

This new and widespread availability of accurate information about Parliament constituted an 'information revolution'.[69] Politicians were increasingly aware of the need to court

---

[62] HC Deb 21 Feb. 1833, vol. 15, col. 1083.
[63] HC Deb 11 Feb. 1834, vol. 21, cols 239–45.
[64] HC 147 (1834), p. 3.
[65] *Report of the Select Committee appointed to take into consideration the best mode of publishing correct and authentic lists of the divisions of the House*, HC 66 (1835), p. 1.
[66] *Journals of the House of Commons*, vol. 91 (1836), p. 67.
[67] Thomas Erskine May, 'The Imperial Parliament', in *Knight's Store of Knowledge for All Readers being a collection of treatises in various departments of knowledge by several authors* (London, 1841), p. 107.
[68] Rix, 'Whatever passed in parliament', p. 471.
[69] Jupp, *The Governing of Britain*, p. 207.

popular opinion, and clerk of the House Thomas Erskine May asserted that the Commons was a 'representative body [that] is in close communication with the people and gives expression to public opinion'. The Lords, by contrast, was 'constitutionally independent of public opinion'.[70] The publication of division lists consequently cemented the relationship between the Commons and the people, meaning that 'public opinion could be effectively brought to bear as the most efficient safeguard of party discipline'.[71] Division lists allowed Parliament to respond more effectively to the will of the people, thanks to the innovative reassignment of space in the temporary chamber.

The fact that the right to publish debates was not guaranteed by the standing orders and privileges of the Commons meant that the principle of the publication of division lists was still debated. However, the inclusion of these new spaces in first the temporary chamber, and then (crucially) the new permanent Commons chamber at Westminster led to a sense that these concessions were immovable. The discussions over the reporters' gallery and the division lobby demonstrate that the layout of the building was being shaped by constitutional change rather than faithfully recreating St Stephen's Chapel and its many constraints.

The Response to Charles Barry's House of Commons

While Parliament was housed in temporary accommodation, the new Palace designed by Charles Barry was under construction.[72] After several years of delay the new Commons chamber was eventually opened in 1850 (see Collins, fig. 8, p. 293), so that it could be tried out by MPs. But members returned a far from favourable verdict, for after the test run both Barry's design and his management of the building project were heavily criticized. Colonel Charles Sibthorp complained that 'the New Palace at Westminster was not a House built for business'. Joseph Hume judged the Commons chamber 'utterly unfit for its purpose', while Montagu Bertie, Lord Norreys, crushingly declared that 'there had been universal acknowledgement that the New House was a failure'.[73]

Throughout the tests, the Conservative leader Robert Peel and Prime Minister Lord John Russell moved around the chamber, trying out the acoustics from different areas of the building. One of the places they visited was the reporters' gallery. Following complaints from MPs about their ability to hear each other and the Speaker, and concern that reporters would not be able to hear the debates below them, substantial changes were made to the Chamber.[74] The roof was lowered into the same shape as the temporary chamber, obscuring the tops of the windows and hiding Barry's Gothic tracery. As one Edwardian historian noted, 'it may be said, indeed, that they willingly spoiled the architectural beauty of their House so that the reporters might hear their debates'.[75] This is something of an exaggeration: the roof was pitched to improve the acoustics for the benefit of everyone within the

---

[70] Erskine May, *Machinery of Parliamentary Legislation*, p. 16.
[71] Joseph Redlich, *The Procedure of the House of Commons: A Study of its History and Present Form*, trans. A. Ernest Steinthal, preface by Sir Courtenay Ilbert (London, 1908), p. xvi.
[72] See Mark Collins's essay in this volume and *Mr Barry's War*, pp. 103, 194–9, 205–8, 213–14.
[73] HC Deb 2 August 1850, vol. 113, pp. 727–8, 737.
[74] The incident is recounted in Macdonagh, *Reporters' Gallery*, p. 394.
[75] Macdonagh, *Reporters' Gallery*, p. 395.

Fig. 5. Joseph L. Williams, *The New House of Commons, From the Bar*. Published in *The Illustrated London News*, 7 Feb. 1852, p. 121. WOA 6109.

chamber. However, the attention paid by Russell and Peel to what debates sounded like in the reporters' gallery indicates that they were concerned at least to some degree about how well the journalists would hear them. To Barry's chagrin, the ability to hear Commons proceedings, and the need for unhindered Parliamentary reporting, assumed far greater significance than his Gothic design.

The changes to the new House of Commons meant that its appearance was closer to the temporary House than to the former St Stephen's (fig. 5). A contemporary guidebook commented that, in contrast to the 'almost perfect' appearance of the House of Lords, the Commons was 'more plainly decorated' due to the 'overwhelming impression of dark wood' and the artificial roof which restricted light from entering into the chamber.[76] Many of the features of the new House were also directly copied from the temporary accommodation. The redesigned roof, ladies' gallery, reporters' gallery, and division lobbies were all features that had been initially tried and tested in the temporary House.

[76] [Anon.], *The New Palace of Westminster*, 7th edn (London, 1852), p. 42.

The Influence of the Temporary Chamber

The traditions of St Stephen's and the innovations of the temporary House of Commons were combined to influence the design and appearance of the Commons chamber in the new Palace of Westminster. The spaces of the temporary chamber, and subsequently of the new House, were themselves shaped by the changing political context. The new House of Commons as opened in 1852 bore a strong visual similarity to its temporary predecessor, emphasizing the continuity between the two. Indeed, Members later looked back to the temporary chamber, rather than to St Stephen's, with a degree of fondness. Alexander Beresford Hope, the Conservative politician and author, may have compared the temporary chamber to a 'hideous barn', but he also felt that it was 'larger and more convenient in some respects that the present one'.[77] The Great Reform Act of 1832 was passed two years before the conflagration which destroyed the Palace of Westminster, and its influence permeated the re-creation of the House of Commons in both its temporary and permanent forms. The innovations and experiments of the temporary chamber proved indispensable to the functioning of the elected house, recognizing and facilitating increased communication between Parliament and the people.

---

[77] HC Deb 9 April 1866, vol. 172, cols 925–6.

'Going to St Stephen's':
The Gothic Legacy of the Chapel in the Nineteenth and Twentieth Centuries

Mark Collins

This chapter tracks the location and design of the Commons chamber from the fire of 1834 to its most recent incarnation: Giles Gilbert Scott's 'neo-Gothic' House opened in 1950. It explores in some depth the rationale for the choice of Gothic Revival style for the Victorian Palace of Westminster, which was strongly supported by Members. The House of Lords chamber exemplifies this style at its most glittering and impractical, yet for the Commons the Gothic styling was, as the chamber took shape, relatively muted. Initially a reflection of the Commons' working ethos, this was compounded by the changes imposed by Members, many to improve their working conditions, which privileged practicality over aesthetics. After its destruction in 1941 by enemy action, the Commons chamber rose again once more clothed in a Gothic style mediated to reflect contemporary taste and underpinned by the finest engineering of the day. All of this was informed by the ghostly but powerful legacy of St Stephen's Chapel.

On the night of 16 October 1834, fire left about two-thirds of the old Palace of Westminster burnt out, St Stephen's Chapel sustaining fatal damage (fig. 1). Although its lower storey (now St Mary Undercroft) survived, the upper chapel formerly housing the Commons chamber was declared too costly and precarious to rescue.[1] Destruction on such a scale offered the possibility of a new and more convenient chamber at the heart of a far more functional Palace of Westminster. In March 1835 Prime Minister Sir Robert Peel set up a Select Committee to formulate requirements for a new Houses of Parliament, with the intention that these would then go out to a public design competition.[2] Along with its House of Lords equivalent, after considerable debate, the Committee resolved that the new Palace was to remain on its original site.[3]

---

[1] TNA, WORK 11/26/6, 25 July 1837; *HKW*, vol. 6, p. 601.
[2] 'Report from the Select Committee on Rebuilding Houses of Parliament; with the minutes of evidence, and an appendix', HC 262 (1835), pp. 3–4; *Mr Barry's War*, pp. 10–13.
[3] Andrea Fredericksen, 'Parliament's *genius loci*: The Politics of Place after the 1834 Fire', in Riding & Riding, pp. 99–111.

Fig. 1. Anon., *St Stephen's Chapel looking east after the fire of 1834*, c.1834. Pen and ink drawing, on paper, 29.2 × 26.7 cm. WOA 3639.

It was to be on a scale fit to represent the most powerful political and economic power in the world. Yet instead of taking the opportunity to mandate a progressive style, reflecting the changing mood of the times, the Committee opted for tradition. Contemporary architectural conventions for a public building would have favoured the classical style, which in the case of the Palace of Westminster would also have evoked cultural links with the early legislatures of ancient Greece and imperial Rome. Instead of this, however, the members stipulated that 'the style of the buildings should be either Gothic or Elizabethan'. The new Palace, and with it the Commons chamber, would thereby explicitly reference the very era when the Gothic chapel of St Stephen's was first converted for the use of the Commons.[4] Although many contemporaries were angered by this choice, few were surprised. In an age of 'associative architecture', the Committee had a number of reasons for making it.[5]

The first was derived from nationalism and a desire for architectural preservation which had initially manifested itself in literature during the eighteenth century. Yet right up to the 1790s, Gothic was still very much a minority interest, its medieval architectural jewels recorded passively and frequently swept aside in improvements; most notably by James

---

[4] HC 262 (1835), p. 4.
[5] Port, *HoP*, pp. 30–2.

Wyatt, whose influence was so great that he was tantamount to being the 'state architect'.[6] Paradoxically, he was at the same time also a key proponent of the Gothic Revival, as exemplified in his numerous commissions for houses in the style such as Lee Priory, Kent (c.1785–90) Fonthill Abbey, Wiltshire (1796–1812) and Ashridge Park, Hertfordshire (1808–13).

Wyatt became the pre-eminent exponent of what became known as 'gothick' architecture before it grew more archaeologically accurate as the revival progressed. He had a greater understanding of the style than did his predecessors, because of his knowledge of cathedrals and from his connection with medieval scholars such as James Bentham of Ely. But under the leadership of Richard Gough (1735–1809), the Society of Antiquaries, in a quest to promote authenticity over artifice, began an active campaign to record and publicize ancient buildings and campaign for their preservation, bringing them into conflict with Wyatt.[7] Nevertheless, it may be that Charles Barry was not above taking inspiration from the regular cross-formation plan and octagonal central hall at Fonthill for his own design of the new Houses of Parliament in the 1830s.

A leading light in this movement was the controversial antiquarian John Carter (1748–1817), who in the early 1790s painfully recorded the wall paintings hidden behind Wren's panelling in the former St Stephen's Chapel.[8] In 1800–1, following the Act of Union with Ireland, Wyatt destroyed many of these paintings while expanding the chamber to make space for the consequential extra hundred MPs. He barred Carter, one of his leading critics, from drawing them, prompting an onslaught from Carter in the *Gentleman's Magazine*. But the somewhat more emollient antiquarian draughtsman John Thomas Smith (1766–1833) was able to draw a substantial number, publishing them in 1807 in his important *Antiquities of Westminster*.[9] In their different ways both Smith and Carter were influential in bringing the increasingly degraded Gothic glories of St Stephen's Chapel to a wider audience, and in making the case for informed conservation of the medieval past.

The second reason was that by the late eighteenth century, and especially after the onset of war with France in 1793, the classical style began to be perceived by Carter and his supporters, such as Sir Henry Englefield and John Milner, as both foreign and 'heathen'. For a country looking for a settled identity against an underlying murmur of revolution and the upheavals of industrialization, the Gothic was seen to be a refuge, simultaneously English and Christian (albeit Catholic). Vitriol was reserved for the French, and here again Carter was influential in his determination to link the origins of Gothic architecture with England.[10] Carter emphasized that it was a national style belonging to the English first and foremost: 'The admiration that has been conjured up in support of (the Roman and Grecian) styles has necessarily turned the genius of Englishmen from their national architecture to toil in an inglorious and servile pursuit to imitate a foreign manner.'[11] Carter wanted his countrymen

---

[6] Rosemary Hill, '"Proceeding like Guy Faux": The Antiquarian Investigation of St Stephen's Chapel Westminster, 1790–1837', *Architectural History*, 59 (2016), 253–7; John Martin Robinson, *James Wyatt (1746–1813), Architect to George III* (New Haven/London, [2012]).
[7] Hill, '"Proceeding like Guy Faux"', pp. 256–9.
[8] Hill, '"Proceeding like Guy Faux"'; Topham; John Carter and James Basire, *Some Account of the Collegiate Chapel of St Stephen's Westminster* (London, 1795).
[9] Smith, *Antiquities*.
[10] John M. Frew, 'Gothic is English: John Carter and the Revival of the Gothic as England's National Style', *The Art Bulletin*, 64:2 (1982), 315–19.
[11] *GM*, 69 (1799), 92.

'to think well of their own national memorials, the works of art of ancient times, and not to hold up any foreign works as superior to our own; and in particular the name of *France* should never be introduced, but to raise ideas of terror and destruction'.[12]

Ever since 1789, there had been a growing reaction against the prevailing classical idiom so closely associated with French architecture and with continental revolution and republicanism. For the Commons chamber, the model of a neoclassical, semicircular form as exemplified by the debating chamber of the Palais Bourbon in Paris was set aside in favour of a reassuring vision of a traditional English system. A challenge to that vision had been posed by the *Historical Survey of the Ecclesiastical Antiquities of France* of 1809, in which George Whittington laid out evidence that the royal Abbey of St-Denis outside Paris represented the first example of Gothic architecture.[13]

Although awkward for English patriots, this finding could be countered by the fact that English Gothic had produced a particular style of its own, namely Perpendicular: the late Gothic style that had developed from the fifteenth century and appeared in its last, luxurious flourish just before the dissolution of the monasteries. In 1817, the architect Thomas Rickman (1776–1841) published his categorization of medieval architecture as 'Early English', 'Decorated English', and 'Perpendicular English', terms that are often still employed today.[14]

Thirdly, since the late eighteenth century, popular movements in British domestic architecture had also reacted against the prevailing classicism. The castellated and 'Jacobethan' styles had become popular for country houses, running in parallel with the classical *palazzo* manner, and were an attempt to evoke a noble ancestral lineage, either real or imaginary. Early examples of castellated mansions include Downton Castle in Herefordshire (Richard Payne Knight, *c.*1772–8), Taymouth Castle (Alexander Nasmyth and William Atkinson, 1800–34), and Eastnor Castle (Robert Smirke, 1808–11), each with symmetrical façades. Of the 'Jacobethan' style, Canford Manor (Edward Blore, 1825–36) was an early exemplar, while Costessey Park in Norfolk (John Chessell Buckler, 1826 onwards) was more Tudor. All such houses harked back stylistically to the notion of an 'old England' and an apparently settled social order which provided comfort at a time of rapid change. The style attracted royal patrons too. From 1801 to 1811 Wyatt created the Tudor-style castellated palace at Kew for George III (demolished in 1827). The ultimate royal seal of approval for the Tudor Gothic style came with the major recasting of Windsor Castle by James Wyatt's nephew Jeffry Wyatville (1766–1840), undertaken for George IV between 1823 and 1840.

Such was the influence of the style that by the 1820s, even among the Italianate villas of the middle classes in towns and cities a movement was under way towards the 'stucco Gothic' of gables, battlements, and pinnacles. At the same time, popular interest in the medieval period was kindled by the romantic novels of Walter Scott (1771–1832). The Waverley novels – in particular, *Ivanhoe* (1820) – had an early and profound influence on the revival of interest in the Middle Ages. Scott had meanwhile built a faux Scottish baronial ancestral home in the Borders: Abbotsford (by William Atkinson, with contributions from Edward Blore and others, 1812–18), which opened to the public in 1833 a few months after Scott had died. By this time,

---

[12] *GM*, 69 (1799), 190.
[13] George Downing Whittington, *An Historical Survey of the Ecclesiastical Antiquities of France* (London, 1809).
[14] George Millers, *A Description of Ely Cathedral* (London, 1807); Thomas Rickman, *An Attempt to Discriminate the Styles of Architecture from the Conquest to the Reformation* (London, [?1817]).

popular guides to Gothic buildings and Gothic pattern books were reaching wide audiences and helping to define popular taste.[15] The Labourer-in-Trust – a deputy clerk of works – at the Palace of Westminster, Adam Lee, produced one such illustrated, conjectural, reconstruction of St Stephen's Chapel in plans and elevations which was intended to popularize the medieval fabric. Lee also created large-scale paintings for exhibition to the public.[16]

Fourthly, the Gothic had a long connection with Westminster. The *genius loci* of the old site was strongly bound up with that great survivor of the fire, Westminster Hall. Unlike the rest of the old Palace its fabric was seen as special: it excited strong feelings of national pride and evoked a long parliamentary history known to date back to the Middle Ages. Its remarkable hammer beam roof and its statues of English kings were widely recognized as authentic embodiments of the Gothic era.[17] Within the Hall, in 1739 William Kent had created a screen housing the courts of King's Bench and Chancery in Strawberry Hill Gothic style, while by 1772 Edward Hussey Delaval had built a small and elegant riverside villa, near the Parliament Stairs in Gothic Revival style. In 1816 this became Black Rod's Official Residence.[18]

These were precursors to Wyatt's Gothic showy remodelling of parts of the Palace from 1796 to 1808. After starting to improve the interior of the Speaker's House, he introduced his own version of the Tudor style at the Palace in 1799, with his new front to the House of Lords overlooking Old Palace Yard (fig. 2). In 1802–8 he united St Stephen's Chapel and its cloister behind a Tudor Gothic façade cloaking the exterior of the now considerably remodelled Speaker's House. The east façade of the chapel was restored to Wyatt's style of Gothic, Wren's earlier classicizing work having been removed (fig. 3).[19] Wyatt wrote that he wanted 'the whole [Palace] to assume the appearance of a large Gothic edifice',[20] and drew up schemes for this, including a Gothic Royal Entrance, which remained unrealized. That was not least because many contemporaries, including MPs, derided his efforts, although others found them pleasingly picturesque.

Adjacent to the chapel was the cloister of St Stephen's College, rebuilt for Henry VIII between about 1515 and 1527. Its ground-storey fan-vaults and fine upper and lower chapels had survived the fire, albeit in a damaged state (see Biggs, fig. 1, p. 118). More significantly still, Henry VII's Chapel at Westminster Abbey, just opposite the Palace, was one of the most magnificent examples of the Perpendicular style, and the burial place of the founder of the Tudor dynasty. The chapel, dating from 1503–19, had been carefully repaired by Wyatt and the Abbey mason, Thomas Gayfere (1720–1812) and his son, true to the original detail, the work completed in 1823 (fig. 4). The strong local architectural links to the splendour of the

---

[15] William J. Rorabaugh, 'Politics and the Architectural Competition for the Houses of Parliament, 1834–1837', *Victorian Studies*, 17:2 (1973), 155–75, esp. 157.
[16] Hill, '"Proceeding like Guy Faux"', 269; Mireille Gallinou, 'Adam Lee's Drawings of St Stephen's Chapel, Westminster: Antiquarianism and Showmanship in Early Nineteenth-century London', *Transactions of the London and Middlesex Archaeological Society*, 34 (1983), 231–44.
[17] Frederickson, 'Parliament's *genius loci*'.
[18] For Delaval's house see TNA, CRES 2/588 and [Samuel Leigh], *Panorama of the Thames: A Riverside View of Georgian London*, [1829], ed. John R. Inglis and Jill Sanders (London, 2015), frontispiece. My thanks to Dr Elizabeth Hallam Smith for this information.
[19] For the date of the illustration (fig. 3), see Murray Tremellen, '"A Palace within a Palace": The Speaker's House at Westminster, 1794–1834' (Ph.D. dissertation, University of York, 2023), pp. 134–5, 138–9, 143–6 <https://etheses.whiterose.ac.uk/33678/>.
[20] *The Times*, 23 Oct. 1806, p. 3, col. 3.

Fig. 2. Robert Havell the Elder and Robert Havell the Younger, *View of the House of Lords and Commons from Old Palace Yard*, 1821. Colour aquatint, 20.3 × 30.5 cm. WOA 1085.

Fig. 3. After James Wyatt, *Speaker's House in about 1800* [sic], *c.*1807. Watercolour, 59.1 × 71.1 cm. WOA 2873.

Fig. 4. Anon., *Henry VII Chapel, Westminster Abbey*, date unknown. Wash drawing, 25.4 × 13.5 cm. WOA 3589.

Plantagenets and Tudors, as well as to the royal burial church, were to provide continuity with a noble past and inspiration for the new Palace. For this was above all a royal palace, its conception, layout, and elaborate decoration showcasing the role of the crown in Parliament.[21]

By the time of Wyatt's death in 1813 his Gothic work at Westminster was attracting almost universal opprobrium, and Soane, now Attached Architect, was able to introduce the classical with impressive effect, most notably in his Royal Entrance to the House of Lords. Completed in 1824, this played to King George IV's sense of ceremonial and pageantry (fig. 5).[22] For this royal patron, too, Soane, John Nash, and Robert Smirke created a series of great classical public buildings in London, ranging from the British Museum to Regent Street. Yet even in the 1820s Soane had been compelled by MPs to remodel the northern façade of his Law Courts, next to Westminster Hall, in Gothic style; and by the mid-1830s, the classical idiom, so strongly associated with the now late King George and with radical

---

[21] Roland Quinault, 'Westminster and the Victorian Constitution', *Transactions of the Royal Historical Society*, 2 (1992), 79–104.
[22] Sawyer, 'Delusions of National Grandeur', pp. 245–9.

Fig. 5. Office of John Soane, *Approved design for the Scala Regia [interior perspective]*, *February 1822*, 1822. Wash drawing, 45.1 × 33.6 cm. London, Sir John Soane's Museum, SM 71/2/72.

politics, was in turn increasingly gathering its own detractors. A defining moment was Nash's remodelling of Buckingham Palace, completed in 1834. Soane's work too was now regarded by many of the new taste-makers as heavy and outdated.[23]

The architectural bones of St Stephen's Chapel were placed on full view by the 1834 fire which stripped away Wren's panelling and ceiling which had so effectively hidden its medieval origins in the late seventeenth century. Widespread concerns about the practical limitations of the old House of Commons soon gave way to a romanticized sense of mourning for its loss, reflected in a host of newspaper accounts, popular prints and drawings, commemorative paintings by leading artists of the day, and numerous souvenirs created from its tangible remains. Publications such as those by John Britton and Frederick Mackenzie memorialized the chapel while maintaining the public's interest in

[23] Rorabaugh, 'Politics and the Architectural Competition', pp. 157–9; Sawyer, 'Delusions of National Grandeur', pp. 237–50.

Fig. 6. William Heath, *The Destruction of the Houses of Lords and Commons by Fire on the 16th of October 1834*, 1834. Hand-coloured lithograph, 37 × 46.9 cm. WOA 589.

it.[24] Moreover, the long association of the chapel with the Commons would be preserved in its name. Although after Wren's alterations little of the original fabric of the chapel had been visible from within the chamber, Members had long said that they were 'going to St Stephen's' when they were on their way there, a usage which transferred to its replacement and survived into the twentieth century.[25]

After watching the fire of 1834, the ardent Gothic Revival architect and designer, A. W. N. Pugin (1812–52), who was soon to be closely involved at Westminster, wrote: 'There is nothing much to regret, and a great deal to rejoice in. A vast quantity of Soane's mixtures and Wyatt's heresies have been effectually consigned to oblivion'[26] (fig. 6). It was to the older and more authentic Gothic survivals at Westminster that he and Charles Barry would now turn for inspiration in clothing their new Palace. Thus, a Tudor-style new Palace would reinforce the Gothic spirit of Westminster in a defining and dramatic contrast to the classical style of St Paul's Cathedral and the City of London to the east.

The choice of the Gothic or Elizabethan style was nevertheless a major departure for such a significant new building as the Palace of Westminster, and it came as a rude awakening

[24] John Britton, *The Architectural Antiquities of Great Britain represented and illustrated in a series of views, elevations, plans, sections, and details of various ancient English edifices* (London, 1826); Brayley & Britton; Mackenzie.
[25] For the continuing use of the name see Arnold Wright and Philip Smith, *Parliament Past and Present* (London, [1902]), e.g. pp. 252, 269, 522.
[26] Augustus W. N. Pugin, letter to E. J. Wilson, 6 Nov. 1834, in Pugin, *Letters*, vol. 1, p. 42.

to those architects who were so devoted to – and so well versed in – the formal language of classicism. The new Palace marked a turning point in the Gothic Revival and set it on a new course, away from the dreams of private country houses and villas and into the serious world of public architecture. But the choice of style was roundly criticized by some contemporaries as unsuitable for a modern Parliament 'in this enlightened age'. The historicism was viewed as antiquated in both ideas and decorative detail, reflecting the old politics before reform.[27]

Its style was to be Gothic but, in its dimensions, there was now the chance for the Commons chamber to break away from the straitjacket of St Stephen's Chapel. Thus the Committee's specifications of accommodation of June 1835 instructed:

> That the length of the New House [of Commons] ought not greatly to differ from the breadth; that sitting room be provided for from 420 to 460 members in the body of the House and adequate accommodation for all the rest in the galleries [...] Special provision for ventilation of all rooms.

This allowed for a larger and squarer chamber than at St Stephen's Chapel, with more space for visitors, and is likely to reflect the positive experience of the more commodious temporary chamber in the Lesser Hall.[28]

The government's public design competition for the new Palace drew applications from ninety-seven architects, but one, by Charles Barry (1795–1860), stood out for its skilful floor plan and elevations, and was praised for the 'superior merit of the internal arrangements'.[29] Barry was selected as the Architect for the new Palace on 31 January 1836, and the design was published on 29 February. He had already built up a strong reputation with several notable buildings, including the Royal Manchester Institution (now City Art Gallery, 1824) and the Travellers Club, Pall Mall, London (1829). Later he displayed a new and influential early-sixteenth-century Italian Renaissance style in the design for his Reform Club on Pall Mall (1837–41), which was equipped with state-of-the-art ventilation systems.

In common with other architects of his generation, Barry turned out buildings in both classical and Gothic styles depending on the requirements of the commission. Before winning the contract for the new Palace, he had designed churches and a school – King Edward's, Birmingham (1833–8) – in Tudor Gothic. Here Barry had employed the brilliant Pugin, whose passion and advocacy for the more accurate representation of medieval architecture was profoundly to influence the Gothic Revival. Barry's drawings for the new Palace were embellished by beautiful detailing from Pugin. A few months after the competition results were announced, Pugin published his *Contrasts* between modern buildings and their 'noble' medieval antecedents, and Gothic was now established in deliberate opposition to classical.[30]

---

[27] Charles Fowler, *The New Houses of Parliament, Remarks as to Site* (London, 1836), p. 1; Edward J. Gillin, *The Victorian Palace of Science: Scientific Knowledge and the Building of the Houses of Parliament* (Cambridge, 2017), pp. 35–8.
[28] HC 262 (1835), p. 4; *Mr Barry's War*, pp. 32–3.
[29] Report from Select Committee on Houses of Parliament; with the minutes of evidence, HC 245 (1836), p. 1; Port, *HoP*, pp. 32–49.
[30] Augustus Welby Northmore Pugin, *Contrasts: or, A parallel between the noble edifices of the fourteenth and fifteenth centuries and similar buildings of the present day. Shewing the present decay of taste. Accompanied by appropriate text* (London, 1836).

The Gothic Legacy of the Chapel in the Nineteenth and Twentieth Centuries 289

Fig. 7. Joseph Nash, *The House of Lords*, 1857. Print, 29 × 22.2 cm. WOA 6281.

Nevertheless, the extended and regular façades of the new Palace, and its ordered internal planning, owe more to the logical, clear, and uniform arrangements of classical architecture than to earlier Gothic models, deriving from the order and harmony of the eighteenth century. Barry's new Commons chamber was not to be a reincarnation of the fourteenth-century chapel of St Stephen. Instead it echoed the early-sixteenth-century Tudor Gothic of Henry VII's Chapel nearby, a Perpendicular style more compatible with the regular rhythm of classical symmetry as well as with the needs of an active legislature. Barry and Pugin discovered inspiring examples of this style in the Low Countries, especially in Flemish town halls, and incorporated them into their designs.[31]

The House of Lords chamber was to be 90 ft (27.43 m) long, 45 ft (13.72 m) wide, and 45 ft (13.72 m) high, thereby forming a double cube: considered the most perfect shape for a room of any significance, and also noted for its good acoustics (fig. 7). At 300 members, the capacity of the Lords chamber was not to disappoint the upper house.[32] Barry's original plan for the Commons chamber put it on a par with the Lords. At 83 ft (25.30 m) long, 46 ft (14.02 m) wide, and 50 ft (15.24 m) high, it was larger and squarer in plan than St Stephen's,

---

[31] Alfred Barry, *The Life and Works of Sir Charles Barry* (London, 1867), pp. 242–3.
[32] Port, *HoP*, p. 312.

in accordance with the *Specifications of Accommodation*, reflecting the more spacious temporary chamber. The government favoured accommodation which would house all 658 MPs, with between 420 and 460 in the body of the House, and the rest in the galleries.[33]

Judged too dangerous to be repaired, and potentially impeding his plans for a grand public entrance to his new Palace, the tottering ruins of the old St Stephen's Chapel were demolished by Barry in 1837. On their site he now established St Stephen's Hall, joining Westminster Hall and Central Hall, as a hall of patriots displaying marble statues of leading Parliamentarians who had once spoken there. This would in due course necessitate repairing and partly rebuilding the Chapel of St Mary Undercroft beneath it.[34]

Barry's proposed House of Commons was thus a key element in his plans. Yet even among the gargantuan challenges he faced in bringing his great new building to fruition, it would prove to be one of the most problematical. As his biographer and second son Alfred Barry (1826–1910), recounted:

> The House of Commons underwent many changes. The accommodation required by the original instructions, and the recommendation accompanying them, that every member should be brought as near to the Speaker as possible, necessitated enormous size and a nearly square form; but on consultation with the authorities of the House, it was found that they considered the accommodation, both for Members and for Strangers, as unnecessarily and inconveniently large, and that the preponderance of their opinion was in favour of the old oblong form. On their authority the width and available accommodation of the House were greatly reduced.[35]

When its foundations were laid in the spring of 1840, Barry's Commons chamber came in at 68 ft (20.73 m) by 45½ ft (13.87 m), considerably shorter in length than the Lords and little larger than its earlier St Stephen's home. A government side and opposition side were to be maintained, with crossbenches in the return stalls. Five rows of seats were to be set against the longer walls, the same number as there had been in St Stephen's in the seventeenth century, and able to hold 450 members from a total of 658. Reflecting the design of the temporary Commons chamber, Barry made provision for curved seats opposite to the Speaker's chair, instead of behind the Speaker as in St Stephen's.[36]

In 1842 the contract for constructing the new Commons chamber was awarded to Barry's lead contractors Grissell and Peto, and work at last began.[37] But when the Lords occupied their chamber in April 1847, the Commons was still far from complete; it did not reach its final form until 1852. Its birth was particularly painful. Over more than a decade its design underwent numerous modifications, reflecting the acute political complexities around the rebuilding project and its lack of a single controlling authority. The difficulties were compounded by economic pressures, in turn driving demands for cost savings to budgets for the new Palace.

---

[33] Port (ed.), *HoP*, p. 312.
[34] TNA, WORK 2/2, p. 296; A. Barry, *The Life and Works of Sir Charles Barry*, p. 240. See also the essays by Rosemary Hill, Elizabeth Hallam Smith and Caroline Shenton and Melanie Unwin in this volume.
[35] A. Barry, *The Life and Works of Sir Charles Barry*, pp. 248–9.
[36] TNA, WORK 29/81.
[37] TNA, WORK 11/7/3.

The most immediate cause of the delay was the appointment, on 24 January 1840, of Dr David Boswell Reid (1805–63) to devise a system for the warming and ventilation of both Houses.[38] This was a major and long-standing preoccupation of Members of both Houses. For the Commons, Reid – a physician and scientist who had specialized in the ventilation of coal mines – had recently installed a relatively successful system in the temporary chamber.[39] In September 1841 Robert Peel announced in the House a further £80–90,000 to fund substantial changes to the warming and ventilation arrangements for the chamber to bring them up to the standard to which MPs had become accustomed. The ventilation arrangements caused disputes between Reid and Barry so acrimonious that in 1845 work on much of the new Palace was halted. The Lords rescinded Reid's authority, enabling Barry to complete their chamber, but the Commons kept their faith in him, consequently requiring major modifications to Barry's design.[40]

Additional complications arose from a decision of November 1841, when Peel appointed the Royal Fine Art Commission with Prince Albert as its chairman. Its purpose was to oversee the paintings and portrait sculpture in the new Palace, but Barry was not a member.[41] Moreover the later stages of the chamber's construction coincided with an era of austerity and public and political hostility to the building of the new Palace. Even as the walls of the Commons finally began to rise, expenditure was diverted by the Treasury onto defence and Barry's vote was cut by £50,000 in 1847 and 1848.[42]

Nevertheless, in 1848 George Bankes MP (1788–1856) criticized Barry for wasteful expenditure: 'He recollected well that the Members before the days of Reform were satisfied with St Stephen's Chapel – now they must have a palace. Since the Reform Bill passed they must be accommodated like princes; but the people must pay for their accommodation [...] and the people would not be very well pleased.'[43] In an attempt to overcome such widespread concerns, a Royal Commission was appointed in that year to oversee the completion of the House and the rest of the Palace including fixtures and fittings – and to oversee all of Barry's expenditure on the project.[44] By then the wooden ceiling of the chamber had been partly fixed, the iron floor was on order, and the gas lighting was in design; and during 1849 the chamber was fitted out.[45] Seating plans had now been specified more exactly: 'There will be seats, 20 inches [0.5 m] wide, for 462 Members. Each Lobby will afford accommodation, in Divisions, for from 450 to 500 Members.'[46]

Had very much changed from St Stephen's? Barry wrapped seats for MPs at the south end opposite the Speaker's chair instead of behind it, providing better vision. There were now two voting lobbies instead of one (an innovation carried on from the temporary

---

[38] TNA, WORK 1/20; Gillin, *Victorian Palace of Science*, 161–83.
[39] The full story of Boswell Reid's work at the Palace is in Henrik Schoenefeldt, *Rebuilding the Houses of Parliament: David Boswell Reid and Disruptive Environmentalism* (Abingdon/New York, 2021).
[40] *Mr Barry's War*, p. 103; HC Deb 16 Sept 1841, vol. 59, col. 512. See also the chapter by Elizabeth Hallam Smith in this volume.
[41] Robert Bargery, *Decorating Parliament; Prince Albert and the first Royal Fine Art Commission 1841–1863* ([London], 2017), p. 32; Pugin, *Letters*, vol. 2, p. 209.
[42] TNA, WORK 11/9/7, 10 July 1847; *Mr Barry's War*, pp. 178–9.
[43] HC Deb 1848, vol. 196, cols 578–80.
[44] Port, *HoP*, pp. 142, 146.
[45] TNA, WORK 11/9/7, 6 July 1848, 18 May 1849.
[46] *New Houses of Parliament; A Return, showing how many Members the New House of Commons will accommodate, specifying the Space allowed for each*, HC 325 (1849), p. 1.

chamber),[47] and there was a little more legroom. The new chamber for the Commons, like the new Lords chamber, was provided with galleries all the way round to accommodate extra seating for Members, for the press, and for visitors to listen to debates. The Commons chamber in St Stephen's already had galleries on three sides, so this was not an innovation, but it was an improvement in terms of the numbers that could be accommodated. Yet when she visited the almost-complete chamber in March 1850, Queen Victoria commented that 'it certainly seems small'.[48]

In 1843 the Fine Art Commission had observed that the new chamber

> will have a flat ceiling. It is proposed to be finished in the same style as the House of Lords, but with less enrichment and less of colour and gold in its decorations. The nature of its design, and the extent of the fittings for the accommodation required, will not admit of the aid of either painting or sculpture.[49]

Barry, who held responsibility for the decorative arts for the new Palace, was therefore unencumbered by the Commission in his plans for decorating the Commons chamber. Wooden panelling, stained glass, and metalwork were included in the contract which he made with Pugin in June 1844 to execute these decorative details throughout the new Palace. Thus, respecting the chaste nature of the previous Commons chambers, there was to be none of the drama and dazzle which had been created for the Lords. Barry's new House of Commons was to be a businesslike space, lacking in any fine art. Stencil patterns on the ceiling panels, painted heraldry and stained glass were to be the sum total of the coloured decoration; the majority of the decorative detail was to be confined to elaborately carved, unstained oak and plain stone window tracery.

In its overall appearance, however, the room was remarkably similar to the Lords which had opened in 1847, with six clerestory windows on each side, a flat, ribbed and panelled ceiling and galleries all the way round (fig. 8). A raised Speaker's chair in the centre with a wooden canopy and a Clerks' table in front of it repeated the arrangements of the St Stephen's and temporary Commons chambers. Seating, arranged in five rows on each side and covered with dark green buttoned leather, was provided for the government on the right of the Speaker and for the opposition on the left. Independent MPs would use small seats opposite the Speaker at the south end, adjacent to the Bar of the House, with the Serjeant-at-Arms' chair next to them on the east side. The gallery over the Bar was to be used by the diplomatic corps and distinguished foreigners in the front seats, although these were often occupied by Peers, behind which there was a Speaker's gallery for his guests, and then behind that, a strangers' gallery for male visitors who had applied to an MP for a ticket.

On the wall above the north gallery, behind the Speaker's chair, and reflecting the new Lords chamber once again, three large, Tudor arches were situated, the upper half filled with blind stone tracery, rather than with frescos as in the Lords. Below this tracery, each arch contained three smaller round-headed open arches: an incongruous classical intrusion in the Gothic chamber, and an apparent echo of Wren's three east windows at

---

[47] The addition of the second lobby is discussed in Rebecca Moore's essay in this volume.
[48] Quoted in *Mr. Barry's War*, p. 195.
[49] *Second Report of the Commissioners on the Fine Arts; Architect's report as to internal decorations, addition to building, and local improvements*, HC 499 (1843). p. 10.

Fig. 8. Anon., *The New House of Commons, Westminster.* Published in *The Builder*, 5, Jan. 1850, facing p. 36.

St Stephen's. These nine arches concealed a long, narrow room with a particular purpose; set high above the chamber floor and the reporters' seating, a small and restricted ladies' gallery – the concept introduced in 1842 in the temporary chamber – was now a permanent feature.[50] Two voting lobbies, the west division lobby for 'Ayes' and the east division lobby for 'Noes', each with a barrier for tellers to allow only two MPs through at a time, were provided on either side of the chamber and lined with oak panelling. Above the lobbies were Members' writing rooms. Behind the Speaker's chair were two corridors, one which led to the Speaker's retiring room and his house, and a second leading to the official residences of the Clerk of the House and Serjeant-at-Arms. The spacious Commons House lobby stood to the south, 45 ft (13.72 m) square, with carved but unpainted stonework, stained glass displaying heraldry and an encaustic tile floor. Leading from the lobby were a post office and Doorkeepers' rooms.

On 10 May 1850, more than fifteen years since fire had destroyed St Stephen's, MPs departed from their temporary chamber in the former Lesser Hall for the first time for trials of their new one. Leaving it meant leaving behind also many improvements to the heating and ventilation systems and to the acoustics introduced there. In their testing of their new chamber, Members noticed the absence of them. They found their new accommodation draughty, its heating and ventilating system causing cold feet and hot heads. Poor acoustics

[50] See Caroline Shenton and Melanie Unwin's essay in this volume. There was another, smaller ladies' gallery to the west of this one set aside for the Speaker's women guests.

were diagnosed as a particular problem – MPs thought the new chamber too high, with the result that their voices disappeared into the empty space above their heads.

Worse still, although its dimensions and seating arrangements had been agreed at the behest of Committees, this was forgotten: now that it was complete, the new chamber, with space for 462 out of 658 MPs, was declared too small for comfort, as 91 of these seats were in galleries, which members disliked and wished to see modified.[51] Barry's cost overruns were also excoriated, even though, as was pointed out, they 'had been incurred in consequence of alterations and additions which had been suggested by various Committees and Members of Parliament'.[52] The levity with which many MPs approached the trials were reflected by *The Spectator*, which expressed astonishment that 'In the vast Parliamentary Palace at Westminster, room has not been provided for the House of Commons! [...] Decidedly, the Architect, or the Committee of Taste that controlled him, should be called upon to make atonement by providing camp-stools and speaking-trumpets.'[53]

The sympathy and esteem in which Barry was held by fellow-professionals was demonstrated by the Royal Institute of British Architects, which presented him with its Royal Gold Medal in June 1850, the President commending him for overcoming 'unprecedented political and bureaucratic obstacles'.[54] In the same month, however, a Select Committee was appointed by the Commons to oversee modifications to its chamber. One of its members, Sir Benjamin Hall soon put forward a plan 'to afford increased accommodation', which the Committee instructed Barry to follow in preference to his own proposals to elongate and reconfigure the House. These involved extending the lobbies to the north and widening and adjusting the galleries, enabling up to 488 Members to be seated. To improve the acoustics, Barry was instructed to replace the ceiling with

> one that shall rise from some point not higher than the transoms of the windows, and which, instead of being a flat surface, shall rise from the sides towards the centre in such form, and of such a pitch, as Mr Barry shall consider best calculated to make the voice of the Member speaking audible in every part of the House, and which in architectural effect and detail shall be justified by the best precedents of the architectural period to which the general arrangements and detail of the rest of the building are referable.[55]

MPs then went back to their temporary chamber in the Lesser Hall, after fewer than three months in their new one. A number of further trials took place over the summer and autumn of 1850,[56] but it was on the basis of Hall's recommendations that Barry – most reluctantly – modified the chamber. Most of this work was effected by March 1851, and the final works were completed in December.[57] When they inspected their new chamber in April following these alterations, MPs found that Barry had maintained the chamber's

---

[51] E.g. HC Deb 10 June 1850, vol. 111, cols 981–3 (Joseph Hume).
[52] HC Deb 24 May 1850, vol. 111, cols 333–7.
[53] *The Spectator*, 1 June 1850, p. 1.
[54] *Mr Barry's War*, p. 197.
[55] *First report from the Select Committee on New House of Commons*, HC 650 (1850), part I, p. 3; part II, pp. 4–5.
[56] *Sydney Morning Herald*, 5 Nov. 1850, p. 2.
[57] *The Builder*, 8 (1850), 370, 392; TNA, WORK 1/35, p. 394; TNA, WORK 11/9/7, 21 March 1851.

floor dimensions of 68 ft (20.73 m) by 45½ ft (13.87 m), now seating 346 MPs in this space. But by widening the side galleries to give a second row of seats Barry had created room for 437 altogether. Greater provision had also been made for officials, reporters, and visitors who had their own gallery, entrance, and stairs.[58] But to re-establish the notion that women should not be admitted into the chamber during debates, the ladies' gallery had been concealed behind a brass grille, soon seized upon as an infamous symbol of their exclusion.[59]

To improve the acoustics, a new, lower, false ceiling had been installed at a cost of £6,200, its sloping sides cutting the windows in half. The two lobbies were given oriels, costing a total of £8,600.[60] Despite many setbacks and delays, Barry had, however, managed to complete much of his decorative scheme, including the armorial shields and stained glass.[61] In common with the rest of the new Palace, royal symbols took precedence; they were featured in the heraldic shields, in the Tudor roses carved on the back of the Speaker's chair and in the arms above its canopy, and in the ceiling decoration with stencilled panels showing alternately the Tudor rose and portcullis.

The loyal motto, '*Domine salvam fac reginam nostram*' was carved over the door to the Commons House lobby. The badges and monograms of the sovereigns in succession and the arms of the three kingdoms had been emblazoned along the front of the gallery, and the coving under the galleries had been gilded with the intention of placing there the coats of arms of all former Speakers in chronological order. The latter scheme was never carried out, apparently because of fears that too much painted decoration would detract from the practical appearance of the House.[62] The stained glass depicted arms of some of the cities and boroughs which returned a Member, although a few years later these were found to be too dark and were changed for badges of the sovereigns. Moreover, the new ceiling had cut out so much light that the stained glass had to be illuminated externally by gas lighting.

'The general aspect of the House of Commons and its adjacent parts is quiet and grave', declared the official description. But it was not without 'exquisite' detail, a reference to the fine woodcarving.[63] Not all Members agreed. In a heated debate in the new chamber in April 1851 Barry's gilding and brightly painted shields were censured, and he was accused of installing 'wretched fantastic carving, so that it looked more like some monastery of the tenth or twelfth century, than a representative chamber of the nineteenth' (fig. 9).[64]

To meet Members' demands, the layout and facilities of the new chamber had thus come a long way from the original fourteenth-century style of St Stephen's, although, despite all the modifications, its Gothic Revival style and its layout still paid homage to those origins. The *New Statesman* judged it to be a 'magnificent and imposing apartment', and the Queen commented

---

[58] Andrew James Moyes, *Debating Chambers of the House of Commons* (London, 1950), p. 11.
[59] See Caroline Shenton and Melanie Unwin's essay in this volume.
[60] Port, *HoP*, p. 148, plate 91; *HKW*, vol. 6, p. 624.
[61] Port, *HoP*, p. 149; Pugin, *Letters*, vol. 4, p. 560.
[62] The Commons 'should be finished in the plainest style possible', according to Sir Denham Norreys MP: HC Deb 7 July 1851, vol. 118, col. 302.
[63] Charles Barry, *Illustrations of the New Palace of Westminster*, First Series (London, 1849), House of Commons chamber.
[64] HC Deb 14 April 1851, vol. 116, cols 190–200.

Fig. 9. E. Chavanne, after Read, *Interior of the House of Commons*, c.1852. Coloured engraving, 19.5 × 14 cm. WOA 1643.

that it was 'most beautiful'. Yet, so devastated was Barry by the effect of the changes imposed upon him that thereafter he refused to enter the chamber unless absolutely necessary.[65]

As the Commons chamber was now deemed complete, demolition of the temporary chambers was ordered in June 1851, at the end of the session; the work began in early September.[66] The Commission supervising the new Palace of Westminster was closed on 19 December 1851, and oversight of completing the huge project handed over to the newly constituted Office of Works.[67] Queen Victoria opened the whole of the new Palace on 3 February 1852, and Barry was knighted a few days later. Soon after this, in September 1852, at the age of 40, Pugin met an early death.

Barry's chamber as modified by the end of 1851 would remain substantially unaltered as the sitting place of the House of Commons until its destruction on the night of 10–11 May 1941 during the Blitz. Along with the division lobbies and much of the Commons lobby, the chamber was lost during the bombing. When both the chamber and the roof of Westminster Hall caught alight, it was decided to leave Barry's Gothic Revival pastiche Commons chamber to burn while every effort was made to save the fourteenth-century Gothic roof of the Hall.[68] The chamber had been 'christened' by the delivery of Disraeli's first Budget in

[65] *Mr Barry's War*, pp. 213–14.
[66] TNA, WORK 11/10/2, fol. 76, 26 June 1851.
[67] TNA, WORK 11/9/5, fol. 31.
[68] Hilary St George Saunders, *Westminster Hall* (London, 1951), pp. 13–17.

THE PRIME MINISTER INSPECTING THE RUINED HOUSE OF COMMONS.

AMIDST A HIDEOUS CONFUSION OF TWISTED GIRDERS, BLOCKS OF STONE AND CHARRED WOODWORK, MR. CHURCHILL SURVEYS THE MOTHER OF PARLIAMENTS, BOMBED DELIBERATELY ON MAY 10 BY GERMAN RAIDERS. ON THE RIGHT IS LORD REITH.

Fig. 10. Anon., *The Prime Minister [Winston Churchill] Inspecting the Ruined House of Commons*. From *The Illustrated London News*, 17 May 1941, p. 641.

April 1852, and Churchill's first rousing speeches as Prime Minister in the early part of the war had been its swansong (fig. 10).

In the late summer of 1940, a large, newly constructed building nearby, considered to be bomb-proof, had already been selected in case of aerial attack: the headquarters of the Church of England at Church House. The building was close to the Palace, but it was used only for a few of the most dangerous weeks of the war in 1940–1 and 1944. Following the loss of their own chamber, the Commons borrowed the Lords chamber for most of its sittings from 1941 to 1950. The Lords took over the Robing Room.[69]

However unwelcome its impact, the wartime bombing offered another opportunity for remodelling the House of Commons. Planning for a new chamber began before the end of the war. In his speech to the House in October 1943 launching the Select Committee on rebuilding the Commons, Winston Churchill (1874–1965) pushed for continuity of layout and style with the Victorian past, not change. 'We shape our buildings and afterwards our buildings shape us', he famously declared. He also proposed conditions for the new chamber:

---

[69] Jennifer Tanfield, *In Parliament 1939–50: The Effect of the War on the Palace of Westminster* (London, 1991); Miles Taylor, 'St Stephen's in War and Peace: Civil Defence and the Location of Parliament, 1938–51' in *Space and Sound*, pp. 135–48.

The first is that its shape should be oblong and not semi-circular. Here is a very potent factor in our political life. I am a convinced supporter of the party system in preference to the group system. I have seen many earnest and ardent Parliaments destroyed by the group system. The party system is much favoured by the oblong form of chamber.[70]

The Select Committee Report on the rebuilding, published in October 1944, reflected Churchill's views and was unanimous that 'the sense of intimacy and almost conversational form of debate encouraged by the dimensions of the Old chamber should be maintained'.[71] This sentiment was echoed by Labour Prime Minister Clement Attlee (1883–1967) after the war. Giles Gilbert Scott (1880–1960) was appointed to design and reconstruct the House: work began on 10 May 1945, exactly four years after the old one had been destroyed, and the new chamber was opened in October 1950. Although the galleries were widened to accommodate additional press and visitors, the floor of the chamber itself was precisely the same dimensions as its Victorian predecessor, and the ceiling had the same sloped profile as that forced upon Barry in the modifications of 1852. Yet in its secular, crisp neo-Gothic aesthetics and advanced mechanical and electrical services, it is very much a mid-twentieth-century creation[72] (fig. 11).

Derided by some contemporaries as a pastiche and greatly underestimated by many commentators ever since, Scott's Commons chamber, melding the traditional with the modern, and in its precise detailing drawing on the skills of the finest craftsmen of the day, has at last over recent decades come to be recognized as a remarkable achievement. Having inherited a complex and overlaid accretion of assumptions about the style and layout of the Commons chamber, Scott interpreted them perfectly to reflect the continuity of the British parliamentary tradition in the spirit of the post-war age.

In 1970 the Palace of Westminster was listed Grade I, imposing major limitations on the alterations that may now be given consent. Then in 1987 the Palace was encompassed in UNESCO's inscription of the Westminster World Heritage Site, further staying the hand of change. Crown Immunity was removed in 2006, allowing the Local Authority even greater powers to insist that the building be maintained in its current state. The building has also come to be perceived as an enduring representation of British democracy – and despite its many inconveniences in today's world is therefore apparently untouchable.

The 2015 scheme to refurbish the Palace of Westminster maintained the traditional form of the Commons chamber unaltered, ruling out the possibility of rethinking its configuration or that of the surrounding spaces.[73] A proposed temporary decant chamber once again replicated its essential layout and features, although by 2022 the future of this had become far less clear given changes to House of Commons procedures wrought by the coronavirus

---

[70] HC Deb 28 Oct 1943, vol. 393, col. 403.
[71] *Report from the Select Committee on House of Commons (Rebuilding) together with photographs, plans and sections, and the proceedings of the Committee*, HC 109 (1943–4), p. 4.
[72] Gavin Stamp, '"We Shape our Buildings and Afterwards Our Buildings Shape Us": Sir Giles Gilbert Scott and the Rebuilding of the House of Commons', in Riding & Riding, pp. 149–63. See also the essay by Paul Seaward in this volume.
[73] *House of Lords, House of Commons Joint Committee on the Palace of Westminster; Restoration and Renewal of the Palace of Westminster, First Report of Session 2016–17*, HL 41 and HC 659 (2016–17).

Fig. 11. House of Commons chamber (interior view looking towards the Speaker's Chair).

pandemic and a reappraisal of the Restoration and Renewal programme. As in the years between 1789 and 1834, the story continues to unfold. A constant, however, remains the formula for a Commons chamber set down in the sixteenth century. Although modified through each successive reincarnation, its fundamentals have remained unchanged into modern times. Without a change in the way that voters are represented, it seems likely that the inherited layout of St Stephen's Chapel will continue to influence political behaviour into the future.

St Mary Undercroft, 1548–1870:
'A dull sort of ecclesiastical lumber-room'?

Elizabeth Hallam Smith[1]

St Mary in the Vaults in 1548

An important and fragile survival from the old Palace of Westminster, the chapel of St Mary in the Vaults was completed by 1348 and originally formed the lower, ground-level storey of the now-lost royal chapel of St Stephen. After the demolition of the upper chapel in 1837 it became known as St Stephen's crypt. It retained this name until in 1972 it was officially redesignated as the chapel of St Mary Undercroft (fig. 1).[2] Within Parliament, it is still widely described as the crypt chapel, reflecting its subterranean ambience. Having suffered an equally damaging and even more complex cycle of abuse and repair than the adjoining St Stephen's cloister,[3] its story from 1548 to 1870 is the focus of this chapter.

Medieval St Mary in the Vaults was far from the uniform space suggested by the version bequeathed to us by its Victorian restorers (fig. 2).[4] Most notable were the differences in floor levels between its nave and chancel, separated by a stone screen, and the irregularities in the ribs in the chancel.[5] Reserved for royal baptisms and for memorializing the royal family through the daily offices for the dead, it had long been significant as a place of burial.[6]

On the eve of the Reformation, overshadowed perhaps by the much-venerated chapel of St Mary le Pew nearby, it was clearly not much used, although it still had a font in its nave. Its pre-Reformation inventory of about 1548 lists two organs and some copper candlesticks, consistent with a single altar, although there is no record of any services being held. Whereas above in St Stephen's Chapel the Royal Commissioners found a dazzling array of crosses,

---

[1] This chapter arose from a Leverhulme Trust-funded research project on St Stephen's cloister and undercroft, grant no. EM-2017-078, based at the University of York and the Houses of Parliament. My thanks to Professor Tim Ayers, Dr Elizabeth Biggs, Dr Mark Collins, Dr John Cooper, Simon Neal, Dr Caroline Shenton, Dr Murray Tremellen, and Dr Kirsty Wright for their invaluable advice.
[2] *Westminster Abbey and St Margaret Act* (1972 chapter 26), para. 18: 'the Chapel of St Mary Undercroft (commonly known as the Crypt Chapel of the Palace of Westminster)'.
[3] Elizabeth Hallam Smith, 'The "Gothic slum": MPs and St Stephen's Cloister, 1548–2017', *PH*, 41 (2022), 279–302.
[4] See the essay by Tim Ayers in this volume.
[5] John Carter, 'Ground Plan of the Undercroft of St Stephen's Chapel', SAL, Red Portfolio 236/E, publ. in Topham, plate II; Smith, *Antiquities*, p. 148 and facing p. 45.
[6] Elizabeth Biggs, *St Stephen's College, Westminster, a Royal Chapel and English Kingship, 1348–1548* (Woodbridge, 2020), pp. 133–4, 149.

Fig. 1. Chapel of St Mary Undercroft, interior view looking east.

statues, reliquaries, and costly ecclesiastical garb, St Mary in the Vaults below offered them far slimmer pickings: a few old vestments and the royal hearse.[7]

From Reformation to Restoration, 1548–1660

After the dissolution of St Stephen's College in 1548, St Stephen's Chapel was given to the House of Commons as its sitting place. 'A dull sort of ecclesiastical lumber-room' was how in 1864 *The Times* would characterize the fate of its undercroft thereafter.[8] Initially this seems right: like similar spaces in comparable decommissioned monastic buildings in London and beyond, it was probably used as a storeroom.[9] Directly to its north, most of the college's domestic buildings, centred around the elegant perpendicular St Stephen's cloister, became a highly desirable residence, passing to three royal courtiers in rapid succession. The crypt was clearly attached to this grand dwelling, as the grants made of that portion of the former college precinct excluded only the upper chapel, not its lower level.[10]

---

[7] Biggs, *St Stephen's College*, pp. 133–4, 149, 159; TNA, E 117/11/49. See also the essay by John Cooper in this volume.
[8] *The Times*, 11 Aug. 1864, p. 9.
[9] E.g. Bruno Barber and Christopher Thomas, *The London Charterhouse* (London, 2002), pp. 73–5.
[10] Biggs, *St Stephen's College*, p. 206.

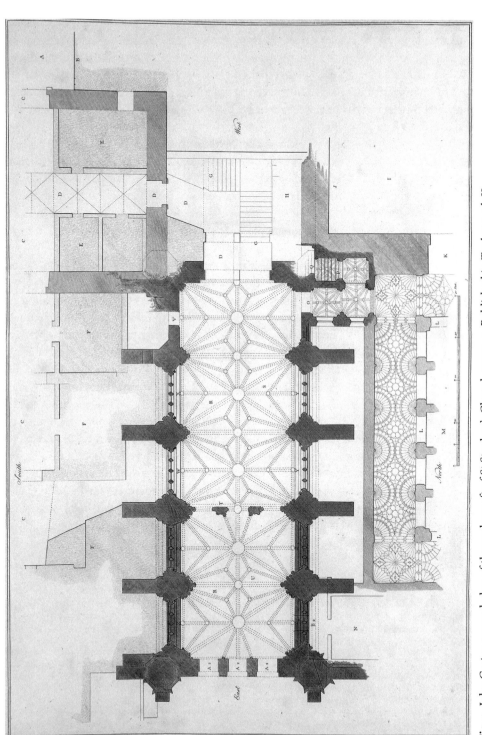

Fig. 2. John Carter, ground plan of the undercroft of St Stephen's Chapel, c.1791–2. Published in Topham, pl. II.

The final occupant, Edward, Lord Hastings, died without heirs in 1572, and the house at St Stephen's came back into royal hands, providing an opportunity for the crown to reassess its use in response to the growing needs of its administrators. The house was soon repaired and split into two apartments used as offices and dwellings, one going to Sir Walter Mildmay, Chancellor of the Exchequer, and the rest to his deputy, the Auditor of the Exchequer, Robert Petre. Mildmay's part next passed to one of the four Tellers of the Receipt, perhaps before 1586/7 when further repairs to it were made.[11]

But as is clear from a detailed plan of these apartments, made in 1593 to settle an accommodation dispute, the undercroft was not attached to either of these dwellings.[12] By 1583 it had, rather, been allocated to the City of Westminster Burgess Court. Overseen by the Dean of Westminster Abbey and managed by the vestry of St Margaret's parish church, the court had since 1559 met in Westminster Hall or in local taverns.[13] Exchequer building accounts for 1582/3 locate it clearly at St Stephen's, itemizing works for a new great door to the town courthouse here. For fitting it out, payments were also made for a 'bridge' with posts and rails and for boarding.[14]

The undercroft was evidently allocated to the Burgesses at the behest of the Lord Treasurer, Lord Burghley, who with the Dean of Westminster presided over a powerful web of patronage in this area.[15] A Burghley adherent, senior Burgess Court member Maurice Pickering, led the way in obtaining statutory regulation for the Court in 1585 and in embellishing the courthouse.[16] Pickering would also facilitate the first proud trappings of civic authority for Westminster's government: the grant of a coat of arms in 1601 and a magnificent silver-gilt cup he bequeathed in 1603.[17]

Thus set up in some splendour, for almost two centuries the Westminster Burgess Court would convene weekly in the undercroft, while the House of Commons met above it in St Stephen's Chapel. Space in the old Palace was, however, always at a premium, and from the mid seventeenth century there were increasing attempts to squeeze the Burgesses out. These began in 1650 when the House of Commons attempted to requisition 'the Court House in Westminster' in order to store its records – without success.[18] This episode debunks the colourful and persistent parliamentary legend that the undercroft was used to stable Oliver Cromwell's horses during the Interregnum.[19] Had that been needed, there was in fact a purpose-built and long-standing stables and coach-house nearby in St Stephen's Court, known later as Speaker's Court.[20]

---

[11] TNA, E 351/3221.
[12] Hatfield, Hatfield House, Cecil Papers 24/61 (112) and 24/62 (113).
[13] Julia Merritt, *The Social World of Early Modern Westminster: Abbey, Court and Community, 1525–1640* (Manchester, 2005), esp. pp. 225–56. See also William Manchée, *The Westminster City Fathers, 1585–1901* (London, 1924).
[14] TNA, E 351/3217.
[15] Julia Merritt, 'The Cecils and Westminster 1558–1612: The Development of an Urban Power Base', in Pauline Croft (ed.), *Patronage, Culture and Power: The Early Cecils* (New Haven/London, 2002), pp. 231–46.
[16] London, Westminster City Archives, E2413, fols 17–18.
[17] Merritt, *Social World*, pp. 91–2; Manchée, *Westminster City Fathers*, pp. 25–6.
[18] Julia Merritt, *Westminster 1640–60: A Royal City in a Time of Revolution* (Manchester, 2013), pp. 168, 176–7; *Journals of the House of Commons*, vol. 6 (1648–51), p. 350.
[19] See e.g. Roger Sands et al., *The Houses of Parliament: An Illustrated Guide to the Palace of Westminster* (London, 1977), p. 20.
[20] TNA, E 351/3271 (1637/8).

Those stables belonged to the Auditors of the Exchequer, who since 1610 had occupied almost all of the cloister residence.[21] Now formally attached to the office of Auditor, this was fashioned gradually into an impressive and prestigious town house, much coveted for its proximity to the centre of political power.[22] Having passed to influential affiliates of Cromwell during the Interregnum, at the Restoration in 1660 the house was returned to its previous royalist occupant, Auditor Sir Robert Pye.[23]

The Auditors and the Burgesses, 1660–1794

By the time that the crypt first appears on a plan, in 1711–16,[24] it had been divided into two parts along the line of its medieval stone screen. The Burgess Court still occupied the three western bays, but the two eastern bays – the former chancel – were by now attached to the Auditor's house. The division seemingly took place in 1661/2, when a substantial 'pallisado' or partition was built within the 'court house' to infill the screen.[25] This coincided with – and may be the consequence of – a major rearrangement of the adjoining parts of Westminster Hall and the cloister, in preparation for the coronation of Charles II.[26] Those works lost the Auditor some important circulation space in the cloister's south-west corner, which now became an access route to the House of Commons.[27] The allocation of the former chancel of the undercroft to the Auditor could have provided some compensation.

The Auditor's newly acquired space was soon deployed to create a storage cellar for beer and wine. It was underpinned in the 1660s and again between 1671 and 1674, when its drains, windows, and paving were renewed, a pump installed and new partitions and door-cases built.[28] The names used in the accounts which identify the storeroom with the two bays of the former chancel – the Auditor's 'great cellar', 'vault', and 'dark cellar' – suggest that all of the windows were covered up. By the time of the 1711–16 plan the cellar had been dubbed the 'grotto room'.

Meanwhile, next door, in the three bays still occupied by the Burgesses, substantial stonework, brickwork, paving, and plastering was required in 1661/2, including 'raising the wall of the little buttry in the Courte house'.[29] In 1691–2 Sir Christopher Wren undertook a major remodelling of the House of Commons above, removing the roof and clerestory and restyling the whole of the east end's exterior, but no further works in either part of the undercroft are recorded at that time.[30]

---

[21] TNA, E 351/3245.
[22] Hallam Smith, 'The "Gothic slum"', pp. 281–2.
[23] John C. Sainty, *Officers of the Exchequer* (London, 1983), p. 207.
[24] Oxford, All Souls, MS III, 14, published in Anthony Geraghty, *The Architectural Drawings of Sir Christopher Wren at All Souls College, Oxford* (Aldershot, 2007), pp. 13, 230, 233.
[25] TNA, WORK 5/3, fols 295–6. The 'pallisado' was 7 ft high and 23 ft long (2.13 × 7.01 m). Although the internal width of the undercroft was 27 ft 6 in (8.38 m), the stone screen jutted out into the body of the chapel. See TNA, WORK 29/20–27, published by Michael H. Port, *The Palace of Westminster Surveyed on the Eve of the Conflagration, 1834* (London, 2011), plan 2.
[26] Elizabeth Hallam Smith and John Crook, 'Westminster Hall's Lost Stuart Door-Passage Rediscovered', *Antiquaries Journal*, 102 (2022), 389–417, at 393–5, 401–2, 412–13.
[27] See e.g. Brayley & Britton, pls 16, 19.
[28] TNA, WORK 5/3, fols 274d, 287, 295–6; E 351/3285; WORK 5/25, fols 381d, 383; Smith, *Antiquities*, p. 264.
[29] TNA, E 351/3276; WORK 5/2, fols 222, 228d, 347, 349d; WORK 5/3, fol. 296.
[30] See the chapter by Murray Tremellen in this volume; *HKW*, vol. 5, pp. 402–5.

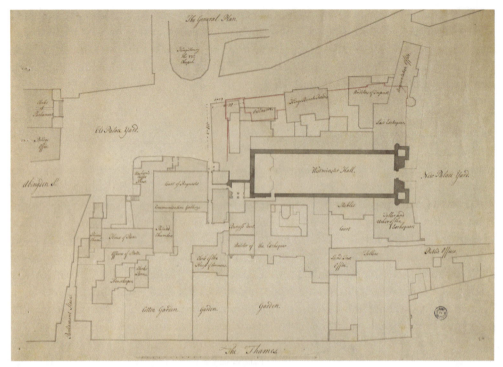

Fig. 3. Office of John Soane, *Survey of the Palace of Westminster, 1760–6* (part). Pen and wash drawing, 37 × 53.1 cm. London, Sir John Soane's Museum, SM 37/1/24.

Another round of repairs and decoration in the courthouse took place between 1706 and 1708, encompassing more new brickwork, paving, plastering, and the painting and gilding of the union arms.[31] The Court's own minutes for 1712 also note a spend of 9d. for repairing the windows. On 7 March 1709 the Burgesses were unable to meet because the throngs of spectators attending the trial of the high-church controversialist Doctor Henry Sacheverell in Westminster Hall blocked the courthouse's entrance.[32]

Thereafter, the problems from the court's neighbours increased. In February 1725, the Burgesses were caught up in a dispute about access to the recently remodelled vaults under the adjoining Lesser Hall (Court of Requests). In the fallout they lost their small annexe which included the base of the medieval south-western turret of the chapel – which it is tempting to connect with their aforementioned 'buttry' – to the storage of King's Bench records.[33] By about 1760 their space had been constricted yet further to improve the main access route to Old Palace Yard and the south end of the Palace (fig. 3).

Worse still, in 1736 two major floods engulfed parts of the old Palace of Westminster, bringing with them a most adverse impact on the courthouse from the House of Commons

---

[31] TNA, E 351/3312–13.
[32] Westminster City Archives, WCBG/WCB/3, fols 2, 208.
[33] TNA, T1/252, fols 256–9; John Crook and Roland B. Harris, 'Reconstructing the Lesser Hall: An Interim Report from the Medieval Palace of Westminster Research Project', *PH*, 21 (2002), 22–61, esp. 30–1; *HKW*, vol. 5, p. 397.

lavatory which directly adjoined its southern side.[34] The Burgesses petitioned the Commissioners of Works to inspect the courthouse and to authorize repairs, since 'from the great sinking of the floor that is the covering of the Bogghouse of the House of Commons and other visible decays your memorialists are extreamly apprehensive that they cannot assemble together in the said Court House without very great danger'.[35] In 1756 the problem still remained unsolved: a further petition to the Treasury reiterated the need for repairs and complained that the well-attended courthouse was far too small and incommodious. A promise from the Treasury of an alternative site came to naught.[36]

Auditor George Montagu, Earl of Halifax, was similarly afflicted by the two major inundations of 1736, which washed into his house and badly affected the health of his servants 'for want of the lower floors being raised and proper drains being made'. The Treasury granted funding for repairs, which included raising some of the floor levels, probably including his two eastern bays of the crypt.[37] Soon after that, in 1739, the next Auditor, the lacklustre Robert, Lord Walpole, son of Prime Minister Robert Walpole, arranged for further 'reparations and alterations' to the house.[38] It is likely that the first stages at least of his conversion of the grotto from a 'receptacle for coals, wood and lumber' into a 'handsomely-appointed domestic apartment' was carried out as part of this refurbishment.[39]

Like his predecessors, Walpole wanted to be seen as a man of power and taste by displaying his fine collections in his highly desirable residence.[40] In his conversion of the grotto room, he seems to have been inspired by the increasingly modish gothick style, installing against the partition wall a chimney piece designed by Batty Langley, whose showroom was located nearby at the Parliament Stairs.[41] Walpole himself or his successor the Duke of Newcastle also unblocked the three lancet windows at the undercroft's east end.[42]

Although neither taste-maker Horace Walpole, the Auditor's younger brother, nor antiquary John Carter, who later disparaged the fireplace, approved of Batty Langley's designs,[43] this new entertaining space was evidently a great success. In March 1756, royal confidante and artist Mary Granville, Mrs Delany, attending a magnificent soirée at the Auditor's house, was particularly impressed with this 'fine old Gothic room'. Speculating that it had once been part of a monastery, she contrasted the imagined ecclesiastical vestments

[34] *GM*, 6:110 (1736–1833), 747; for the lavatory see Alasdair Hawkyard, 'From Painted Chamber to St Stephen's Chapel: The Meeting-Places of the House of Commons until 1603', *PH*, 21 (2002), 62–94, esp. 82.
[35] Westminster City Archives, WCBG/WCB/10, fol. 288.
[36] TNA, T 1/364, no. 46, 24 Dec. 1756.
[37] *GM*, 6:110, 747; William Arthur Shaw (ed.), *Calendar of Treasury Books and Papers, 1729–1745, Preserved in the Public Record Office* (5 vols, London, 1897–1903), vol. 3, pp. 171, 221, 227; TNA, T 29/27, 383–4; T 56/19, 46; 51.
[38] Shaw, *Calendar of Treasury Books and Papers*, vol. 4, pp. 113; TNA, T 27/25, 511.
[39] Smith, *Antiquities*, p. 264.
[40] Wilmarth Sheldon Lewis (ed.), *The Yale Edition of Horace Walpole's Correspondence* (48 vols, New Haven, 1937–83), vol. 9, p. 109, vol. 17, pp. 299–300, vol. 18, p. 249.
[41] Christine McAleavy, 'Batty Langley's Early Years in London, 1729–35 […]', *Garden History*, 44:2 (2016), 191–208, esp. 204–5. For examples of his gothick chimney pieces see Batty Langley, *Gothic Architecture Improved by Rules and Proportions* (London, 1747), plates 42–4, 47.
[42] For visual evidence of the changes to the east end compare 'The House of Commons', an engraving by Charles Grignion after Samuel Wale, for *London and its Environs Described* (London, 1761), vol. 2, p. 165 with e.g. Paul Sandby, 'View of the south end of the old House of Commons', 1794, at BM, Prints and Drawings Collection, 1880,1113.1290.
[43] Horace Walpole, *Anecdotes of Painting in England* (1808; repr. London, 1871), p. 380; John Carter in *GM*, 77:2 (1807), 735.

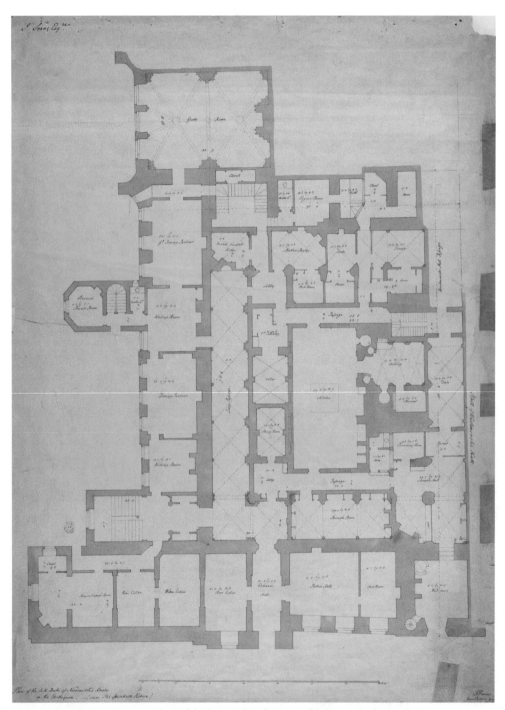

Fig. 4. John Thomas Groves, *Plan of the late Duke of Newcastle's House in the Exchequer, since the Speaker's House* [*ground floor*], 1794. Wash drawing, 84.3 × 61.6 cm. London, Sir John Soane's Museum, SM 37/1/28.

of the former occupants with the female partygoers' costumes: 'enormous hoops, gold and silver braid, exposed heads and shoulders, and the numberless adornments for the head!'[44]

The host of this grand party was fellow-attendee Horace Walpole's close friend, and the last Auditor to possess the house, namely Henry Fiennes Clinton, Earl of Lincoln, later Duke of Newcastle-under-Lyme.[45] When he died in 1794 – still in office and on the premises – his residence was surrendered to the crown once more under the terms of the 1783 Exchequer Act.[46] Soon after that the house was allocated to Henry Addington, Speaker of the House of Commons, probably at the behest of his patron Prime Minister William Pitt.[47] As the first official residence for the Speaker, this would serve to relieve some of the pressures on Commons accommodation – and also enhanced his role.[48] A plan of the ground floor of the house from 1794, drawn at the time of the transfer by J. T. Groves, Clerk of Works (fig. 4), shows the grotto room to the south of the house (top) with an engine room next to it in the space between the cloister and undercroft. The vaults at the east end are irregular, as in John Carter's plan (see above, fig. 2). The western part of the crypt is not shown.

Meanwhile in the 1780s the antiquaries had begun to record St Stephen's Chapel and its surroundings, providing posterity with invaluable evidence about these buildings in their damaged but unrestored state. Alongside that went a stalwart antiquarian defence of the old Palace's medieval heritage.[49] Writing in about 1790 in response to a parliamentary plan to renew the old Palace of Westminster, Francis Douce spoke up for the crypt's damaged remains: 'it is to be hoped that there will not be found wanting also a portion of national taste, to rescue from destruction the most beautiful specimen of Gothic architecture which this country has to boast of'.[50]

The antiquaries' work was taken up and popularized by influential travel writer Thomas Pennant. The undercroft was once, he said, 'a most beautiful building. The far greater part is preserved, but frittered into various divisions, occupied principally by the passage from Westminster Hall to Palace Yard. [...] In what is called the grotto room, are fine remains of the roof and columns of this sub-chapel.'[51] The decayed state of the Speaker's House and the aspirations of the new occupants would, however, soon bring further major changes to these fragile survivals of an already distant medieval past.

From Burgess Court to Boiler House, 1766–1834

By 1766 the Burgesses had left the western end of the undercroft for a brand-new Guildhall in King Street, provided by their powerful new benefactor Hugh Percy, Earl of Northumberland,

---

[44] Lady Llanover (ed.), *The Autobiography and Correspondence of Mary Granville, Mrs Delany* (6 vols, London, 1861–2), vol. 3, pp. 416–21; Lewis, *Walpole's Correspondence*, vol. 37, pp. 453–4.
[45] Sainty, *Officers of the Exchequer*, p. 209; Lewis, *Walpole's Correspondence*, vol. 9, p. 386; vol. 17, p. 210; vol. 30, p. 41.
[46] *Receipt of the Exchequer Act* (23 George III, chapter 82); Sainty, *Officers of the Exchequer*, pp. 203–4, 209.
[47] TNA, WORK 6/22, fol. 142, 20 June 1794.
[48] Philip Zeigler, *Addington: A Life of Henry Addington, Viscount Sidmouth* (London, 1965), p. 69; Orlo Williams, *Topography of the Old House of Commons* (London, 1953), pp. 7–8.
[49] Rosemary Hill, '"Proceeding like Guy Faux": The Antiquarian Investigation of St Stephen's Chapel, Westminster, 1790–1837', *Architectural History*, 59 (2016), 253–79, esp. 253.
[50] Printed in Carter, *Ancient Sculpture and Painting*, vol. 2, pp. 28–9.
[51] Thomas Pennant, *Some Account of London*, 2nd edn (London, 1791), pp. 88–90.

a major player in Westminster politics.[52] Grim memories of their courthouse in the undercroft – 'small, dark, close and inconvenient, [with its] stench so intolerable' – would, however, live on in popular guidebooks to London for several decades to come.[53]

Two significant relics of the Court also remained there, until 1801. The first, in plain sight, was a stained-glass window showing the City of Westminster coat of arms, situated on the south side of the chapel. The date of its creation is unknown. Sketched by John Carter in 1791,[54] and four years later described as the 'perfect window' and with its heraldry correctly identified, it was published by John Topham from further Carter drawings.[55] It was lost during the remodelling of this area in 1801. The second relic, a painted and gilt Tudor oak door with its hinges still intact, was discovered during those works. Seemingly a tangible link to the Court's origins, it had been entombed in the cross wall, presumably when the space was partitioned. Carefully recorded and published by antiquary John Thomas Smith,[56] it too was subsequently lost.

After the departure of the Burgesses, the three western bays of the undercroft were initially partitioned as offices for the Auditor's servants, while the passage from Westminster Hall through to Cotton Garden continued to traverse the most western bay.[57] All this changed in 1791, however, with the advent of a huge 'empyreal' stove, 6 ft (1.82 m) square and 14 ft (4.27 m) high, filled with earthen pipes and retorts and placed in the second bay from the west end. Its task was to purify the air in the House of Commons, to which it was attached by clay flues pierced through the undercroft's vaults. The hot air emerged through a floor grate 3 ft 6 in (1.06 m) in diameter into the chamber, within 2 ft (*c.*0.6 m) of the Clerks' table, often overheating the chamber and prompting several subsequent and largely ineffective experiments with air extractors in the roof space above.[58]

These changes elicited much criticism from John Carter, who in 1800 complained that this end of the undercroft accommodated not just a 'lamplighter's lumber hole' in the old staircase leading up to the House of Commons, but also the long-standing 'common thoroughfare' from Westminster Hall to Old Palace Yard. The second bay accommodated 'all the rubbish of a low mechanic and his necessary receptacles, with the Westminster pillory and 'till within these few years, the Westminster ducking stool', these scorned receptacles evidently including the stove. In the third bay was to be found the hapless mechanic's apartments.[59] The system was modified in 1800 and, with a short interruption in 1819–20, continued to operate for almost two decades.[60]

The year 1819 saw a short-lived but dramatic episode in the Commons' endless quest for an effective heating and ventilation system. A very large copper steam boiler, specified by

---

[52] *Special and Annual Report with Notes on Local Government in Westminster from Pre-Reformation times to the Present Day* (London, 1889), pp. 174–5, 201; Westminster City Archives WCBG/WCB/13, 23 Oct., 5 Nov. 1766.
[53] E.g. *The Antiquities of London* [...] *Chiefly from the Works of Thomas Pennant*, 2nd edn (London, 1818), p. 74.
[54] BL, Add. MS 29930, fol. 101.
[55] Topham, pls 5, 7.
[56] Smith, *Antiquities*, pp. 149, 253.
[57] John Carter, *Plan of the remains of the old Palace of Westminster*, 1788, Poughkeepsie, NY, Frances Lehman Loeb Art Center, Vassar College, 1864.2.2787; Carter, *Ancient Sculpture and Painting*, vol. 2, p. 27.
[58] Elizabeth Hallam Smith, 'Ventilating the Commons, Heating the Lords, 1701–1834', in *Space and Sound*, pp. 74–102, at pp. 80–2; *Kentish Gazette*, 6 May 1791, p. 3.
[59] John Carter in *GM*, 70:2, 722–5.
[60] TNA, WORK 6/23, fols 182–3, 216; Rudolph Ackermann, *Microcosm of London* (London, 1808–10), pp. 190–1.

French inventor Jean Frédérique, Marquis de Chabannes, made a brief appearance in the undercroft. It was a major element in the Marquis's elaborate, noisy, and erratic steam-driven heating arrangements introduced at the behest of Speaker Charles Manners Sutton. This invention was also dangerous: steam pumps were at this time a relatively new technology and were liable to unexpected explosions.[61] Moreover, one of the workmen overseeing the system attested years later that Adam Lee, Labourer-in-Trust, was perpetually urging that the fires in the boiler be kept safe lest the House should burn down.[62]

Worst of all from the viewpoint of the Members, the ventilating arrangements were wholly ineffective, temperatures in the Commons chamber rapidly rising to unbearable levels. After several fruitless attempts to ameliorate these problems, Chabannes' contraptions were hastily removed and much of the previous heating and ventilation system was reinstated by early in 1820, with further work in 1822.[63] Perhaps then, and certainly by 1828, the more traditional boiler required was now relocated outside the undercroft in the furnace room abutting the second bay from the west end of the undercroft. This also adjoined the Commons lavatory.[64] The space thus liberated was soon deployed as a wine cellar,[65] but in 1834 the undercroft's western end lay empty apart from a few discarded barrels.[66]

The Speaker's Dining Room, 1795–1834

Armed with a vote from the Commons of more than £2,500, in 1795 Henry Addington began a programme of piecemeal repairs to his house, at public expense. This was overseen by James Wyatt, Surveyor-General of the King's Works from 1796 and celebrity architect to King George III.[67] Addington saw lavish political hospitality as an important and congenial way to enhance the prestige of his office, and soon pressed the undercroft into service to that end. By mid-1795 he had furnished his 'great room under St Stephen's' with ostentatious red hangings and gilt chairs; and although the house already had two dining parlours in its east wing (see fig. 4, above), in February 1796 the crypt was repurposed and added to these as his State Dining Room.[68]

Here Addington hosted his splendid official (and male only) banquets, usually on a Saturday, starting at 5.30 p.m. and ending at 9.00 p.m. In his diary Charles Abbot MP, a future Speaker, described one which he attended in February 1796. Twenty parliamentary diners in full dress, including William Wilberforce, met 'in a vaulted room under the House of Commons, looking towards the river'. Here they were served numerous lavish courses on plates bearing the royal arms.[69] Prodigious quantities of alcohol were also consumed. As John Carter lamented of these events:

---

[61] Hallam Smith, 'Ventilating the Commons', pp. 86–9.
[62] *Report of the Lords of the Council respecting the destruction by fire of the two Houses of Parliament*, HC 1 (1835), pp. 58–9.
[63] Hallam Smith, 'Ventilating the Commons', pp. 89–90; *Morning Post*, 28 Nov. 1822, p. 3.
[64] PA, OOW/51, 1828.
[65] Hallam Smith, 'Ventilating the Commons', p. 99; Port, *Palace of Westminster Surveyed*, p. 36.
[66] WOA 1300A.
[67] John Martin Robinson, *James Wyatt, Architect to George III* (New Haven/London, 2012), pp. 271–4.
[68] Ex inf. Murray Tremellen, citing Exeter, Devon Heritage Centre, 152M/C1795/F/7, letter of 6 July 1795.
[69] *The Diary and Correspondence of Charles Abbot, Lord Colchester*, ed. Charles Abbot Baron Colchester (3 vols, London, 1861), vol. 1, pp. 34–5; Port, *HoP*, p. 198; Smith, *Antiquities*, pp. 149, 252.

> Surloins of beef and drinking glasses
> Are here the only sight that passes,
> Where erst in solemn pomp took post
> The silver chalice, wafer'd host.[70]

Addington's refurbishments were interrupted by his departure for his (short-lived) elevation to the role of Prime Minister. The tenure as Speaker of his reluctant successor, Sir John Mitford, lasted only a year, from 1801 to 1802. Before his promotion to Lord Chancellor of Ireland in February 1802 he was, however, said to have ensured that his apartments were further 'advanced in beauty and convenience'.[71] The grand official dinners continued, and Mitford commissioned an impressive new service of silver plate for these, its 160 pieces costing more than £2,700.[72]

Mitford was in turn succeeded as Speaker by the far more dynamic Charles Abbot: combative, proactive, and reforming. On taking up office Abbot, dissatisfied with the 'damp insecure state of the Speaker's House', decided that parts of it should be pulled down and rebuilt to remedy the problems.[73] It fell to James Wyatt as Surveyor-General to carry out the works, and with much direction from Abbot he transformed it into a spectacular Gothic mansion.[74]

By the time that Abbot and his family first occupied parts of the house, in July 1802, one major building project was, however, already completed and awaiting decoration and furnishing: the extension of the State Dining Room.[75] During Mitford's Speakership, or perhaps in Addington's last year, the decision had already been made to enlarge it by taking into it the central bay from the area formerly occupied by the Burgess Court. That work probably accounted for the vast bulk of the substantial £4,000 spent by Wyatt on the Speaker's House in 1801–2.[76] This followed on from his damaging alterations to the House of Commons between August 1800 and January 1801, the very public controversies around that perhaps distracting attention from the extent of the alterations taking place below.[77]

This project necessitated the demolition of the medieval stone screen including its later infill. John Carter criticized the consequential removal of the 'Batty Langley grotesque' fireplace from its previous location against the partition over to the south wall where it now blocked the windows. Other than that, perhaps unwilling to offend Abbot, he noted little to suggest that the walls had been 'havocked'.[78] But in fact, major changes had been wrought. As subsequent plans clearly demonstrate, the ribs of the second and third bays had to be rebuilt on structural grounds and now formed a symmetrical pattern (e.g. fig. 5).[79] Moreover, parts of the vaults were cut into by one foot to add extra height, presumably

---

[70] John Carter in *GM*, 70:2, 725.
[71] Smith, *Antiquities*, p. 264.
[72] Ex inf. Murray Tremellen, citing Gloucester, Gloucestershire Archives, D2002/3/1/9, tradesmen's estimates.
[73] *Diary and Correspondence of Charles Abbot*, vol. 1, p. 285.
[74] *HKW*, vol. 6, pp. 496–7; e.g. TNA, PRO/30/9/14, II #4.2.0, 24 June 1802.
[75] TNA, PRO/30/9/14, II #4.2.0, 26 July 1802.
[76] Ex inf. Murray Tremellen, citing TNA, PRO 30/9/14, Box 2, I. §.1. 2. c.
[77] *HKW*, vol. 6, pp. 525–6 and n. 1.
[78] Carter in *GM*, 77:2, 735; Brayley & Britton, pp. 455–6 and pl. 28.
[79] See also Adam Lee, 'Plan of the Palace of Westminster', 1807, London, Museum of London Prints and Drawings Collection, A 15453.

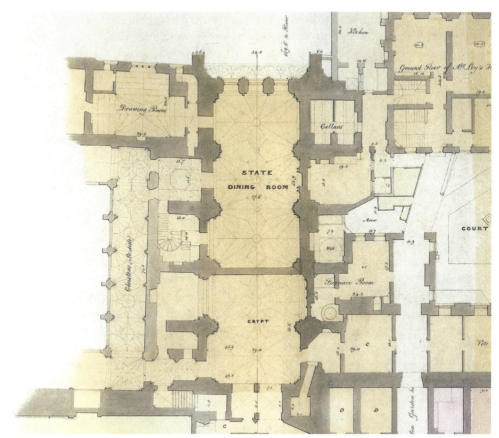

Fig. 5. Thomas Chawner and Henry Rhodes, *No. 2 Ground Storey Offices of the House of Commons together with the adjoining portions of the House of Lords and of other Public Buildings*, 1834. Pen and ink, 92 × 122.5 cm. TNA, WORK 29/22.

because the floor, which had been raised incrementally at least three times, was by now in places 4 ft 3 in (*c*.1.3 m) above its original level.[80]

In addition, the medieval Purbeck columns were concealed behind new Portland stone piers, and as was observed by Thomas Grissell, Charles Barry's lead contractor, in 1844, 'the beautiful and elegant architecture of the apartment [was] disfigured and obscured by unsightly and huge casings of composition and plaster' (see fig. 12 below).[81] The 'carvings', presumably the bosses, in the central bay were, however, said to have been carefully repainted and regilt to return them to their 'original' colours, and the spandrels of the vaults were covered with red broadcloth.[82]

The State Dining Room was intended for public use and therefore, unlike the Speaker's private apartments, was furnished at public expense.[83] Fitted up with Wyatt's finest

[80] Port, *Palace of Westminster Surveyed*, no. 7; Mackenzie, pp. 5, 23.
[81] Brayley & Britton, p. 449; Mackenzie, p. 23; Thomas Grissell, 'Observations on a Portion of the Crypt of St Stephen's Chapel Westminster', *Archaeologia*, 31 (1846), 323–5. See also *West Kent Guardian*, 15 March 1845, p. 2.
[82] Smith, *Antiquities*, p. 264; Carter in *GM*, 77:2, 735.
[83] TNA, PRO 30/9/31, fol. 54.

chandeliers, dramatic crimson hangings set in gilt mouldings, and mahogany and black lacquer furniture, it now became an elegant and perfectly staged setting for Abbot's lavish banquets and levées, over which he presided from his seat stationed directly beneath his chair in the House of Commons.[84] To access the space from the east cloister walk, Wyatt created a small saloon designed in homage to the octagon at Ely Cathedral.[85]

This was but one element in a major, costly, and protracted transformation of the house. Not completed until 1809, it provided Abbot with a striking and magnificent Gothic Revival mansion, a setting fit to entertain the highest in the land.[86] In 1815, for example, Abbot hosted 'a party of grandees [...] to luncheon in the House of Commons Dining Room. It was Queen Charlotte and the Duke and Duchess of Wellington after the battle of Waterloo [...] [on] the day when the Duke came to the House of Commons to receive Public Thanks.'[87]

Elected in 1817, the last Speaker to inhabit the cloister house was the gregarious and urbane Charles Manners Sutton. Ellen Home Purves, his 'châtelaine' from 1823 and from 1828 his wife, was famously hospitable, and some of the improvements made at the Speaker's House in the 1820s – most notably the remodelling of Wyatt's east range next to the State Dining Room – would certainly have enhanced Manners Sutton's entertaining space.[88] In 1823 the State Dining Room itself, used as before for official banquets, was redecorated and new Gothic ogee gilt mouldings ordered for the red curtains.[89]

Brayley and Britton later opined that this Speaker had 'manifested great anxiety to preserve all the fine and beautiful parts of the cloister and crypt [...] from further injury and defacement'.[90] But the removal of the ever-active kitchens from Cloister Court in 1824–7 was seemingly prompted by the nuisance from their smoking chimneys rather than by aesthetic considerations.[91]

Destruction and Change, 1834–44

Many decades of warnings about the hazards of fire at Westminster were realized when on 16–17 October 1834 much of the old Palace was consumed in an inferno. This left the House of Commons in St Stephen's Chapel as a standing but empty shell. Yet the undercroft below showed great resilience. The press reported that as the roof of St Stephen's Chapel crashed down upon it, like a volcanic eruption from the 'caverns of Etna', the crypt's 'noble groined roof withstood and flung off the flames and molten furnace of the conflagration', surviving intact.[92]

---

[84] TNA, LC 5/163, 268; LC 11/8, quarters ending 5 Jan., 5 April 1803; PA, OOW/3, fols 56–63; Smith, *Antiquities*, p. 264; Caroline Shenton, *The Day Parliament Burned Down* (Oxford, 2012), p. 159.
[85] Carter in *GM*, 77:2, 735.
[86] Hallam Smith, 'The "Gothic slum"', pp. 282–5.
[87] Mary Constance Hill, *Good Company in Old Westminster and the Temple* (London, 1925), pp. 7–8, quoting the memoirs of Anne Rickman.
[88] TNA, LC 11/38, fols 52d–53; *HKW*, vol. 6, pp. 533–4; David R. Fisher, 'Manners Sutton, Charles, 1780–1845', *Hist Parl*.
[89] TNA, LC 11/38, fols 23v, 32v.
[90] Brayley & Britton, p. 456.
[91] TNA, WORK 1/14, fol. 409; WORK 1/15, fol. 161; WORK 1/16, fol. 86; WORK 5/109; *HKW*, vol. 6, p. 534; Mari Takayanagi and Elizabeth Hallam Smith, *Necessary Women: The Untold Story of Parliament's Working Women* (Cheltenham, 2023), p. 32.
[92] *Sun* (London), 8 Nov. 1834, p. 4; *London Evening Standard*, 27 Nov. 1834, p. 4; *Sussex Advertiser*, 9 March 1835, p. 2.

Fig. 6. J. Mackenzie, *The Crypt*, 1834. Wash drawing, 42.3 × 53.2 cm. WOA 84.

A more considered view, this time in the official report of the damage to the old Palace, explained that 'the State Dining Room under the House of Commons is much damaged, but capable of restoration'.[93] Contemporary images of the ruins show fire damage to parts of the upper cloister nearest to the crypt, but here too the older stonework emerged relatively unscathed. Another building surviving the fire was the Commons lavatory, in its distinctive tower directly to the south of the undercroft.[94]

The shell of the large Romanesque Lesser Hall – used most recently as the House of Lords, and the place where the fire had first broken out – also remained standing, as did the smaller but similarly robust medieval Painted Chamber. With remarkable despatch, by February 1835 Attached Architect Sir Robert Smirke had fitted them up as temporary chambers for the Commons and the Lords respectively.[95]

The Manners Suttons reoccupied the undamaged parts of the Speaker's House in November 1834, remaining there – and inappropriately staging political soirées – for several months after his removal from office in February 1835.[96] It is unlikely that the State Dining Room was in any fit state to be used for these entertainments, but as the clear-up operations began, the undercroft's western bays were soon deployed as a builder's yard and a store for stone. The vaults here were in a sound state and even retained some paint (fig. 6).[97]

June 1835 saw the announcement of a competition to design a new Palace of Westminster, with Charles Barry emerging as the winner early the following year. His plan, which reflected the approach of the majority of the judging panel and of many of the other competitors, was to retain and incorporate in his new building the three most renowned structures from the old Palace to survive the fire: St Stephen's Chapel, St Stephen's cloister, and Westminster Hall. Those other parts of the old Palace that were still usable were to be deployed as temporary

---

[93] Brayley & Britton, pp. 412–13; *HKW*, vol. 6, p. 534.
[94] Depicted in London, Museum of London Prints and Drawings Collection, A 12137 (reproduced on the cover of this volume).
[95] PA, HC/LB/1/114/18.
[96] *London Evening Standard*, 14 Nov. 1834, p. 3; *Evening Chronicle*, 18 July 1835, p. 3; Takayanagi and Hallam Smith, *Necessary Women*, p. 38.
[97] See also WOA 5195.

accommodation until they were superseded and could be demolished. Thus, over the next quarter of a century, the vast new Palace of Westminster rose gradually around the ever-diminishing remains of its predecessor. At the heart of this complex and constantly changing building site the two Houses of Parliament would continue to operate in often unpleasant and dangerous conditions.

In 1835, Barry may have believed that the ruined House of Commons could and should be repaired. However, acting on the advice of a panel of architects and masons, in July 1837 he controversially took down the walls of the upper chapel on the grounds that they posed a safety risk.[98] The Office of Woods, now superintending, was taking no chances with the crypt, ordering it to be roofed over to protect the vaults.[99] Barry went further, erecting temporary buildings on top of it, which in January 1838 were appropriated as a smoking room, dining room, and kitchens for MPs. Bellamy's parliamentary catering operation, renowned for its meat pies and insubordinate serving staff, soon took up residence.[100] Despite the convenience afforded by their proximity to the temporary House of Commons, MPs soon criticized these facilities for their lack of comfort.[101] Down below, the former Speaker's dining room was meanwhile converted into two committee rooms for the Commons, as was now much of the rest of the former Speaker's House (fig. 7).[102]

Looming over the crypt were two vital services: the Commons lavatory in its tower, back in use, and next to that, an enormous 210 ft (64 m) tall industrial chimney, with a roaring coal fire at its base, to drive the heating and ventilation arrangements for the two temporary Houses (fig. 8).[103] This latter was a key element in the innovative and constantly evolving system installed by scientist and inventor Dr David Boswell Reid. After impressing their Select Committee in 1835, he was brought in by MPs to oversee the latest chapter in their never-ending quest for effective ventilation.[104]

Reid's first attempt at a temporary heating and ventilation scheme was up and running by November 1836, and, after numerous further iterations, would be needed right up until 1851, when MPs moved into their new House. In their spacious and airy temporary chamber, the Commons generally liked the results of Reid's experiments; the Lords, tightly packed into the Painted Chamber, which was connected up in 1839, were far less impressed.[105] Reid aspired to use the crypt to house steam engines to drive his system, but for now, Barry prevented this from happening. He also quashed on structural grounds Reid's plan to take over the whole of the undercroft as an air chamber.[106]

After Reid's appointment as Ventilator for the new Palace in 1840, he worked, increasingly uneasily, with Barry over the next four years to produce plans for a complex and costly

---

[98] TNA, WORK 1/22, 296; WORK 11/26/6; Alfred Barry, *The Life and Works of Sir Charles Barry, RA, FRS* (London, 1867), pp. 239–40; *HKW*, vol. 6, p. 601. See also Rosemary Hill's essay in this volume.
[99] TNA, WORK 1/22, 296, 26 July 1837.
[100] TNA, WORK 2/2, 186.
[101] TNA, WORK 1/23, 21, 229, 241; WORK 2/2, 186, 214; *Mr Barry's War*, p. 78.
[102] PA, HC/LB/1/114/19; TNA, WORK 2/2, 157.
[103] See also London, Museum of London Prints and Drawings Collection, 27/18.1.
[104] Henrik Schoenefeldt, 'The Temporary Houses of Parliament and David Boswell Reid's Architecture of Experimentation', *Architectural History*, 57 (2014), 175–215, at 190–7.
[105] Edward J. Gillin, *The Victorian Palace of Science: Scientific Knowledge and the Building of the Houses of Parliament* (Cambridge, 2017), pp. 161, 172.
[106] *Minutes of the Proceedings [...] Relative to the Warming and Ventilating of the New Palace of Westminster*, HL 35 (1846), pp. 297, 324, 346, 355, 360, 362.

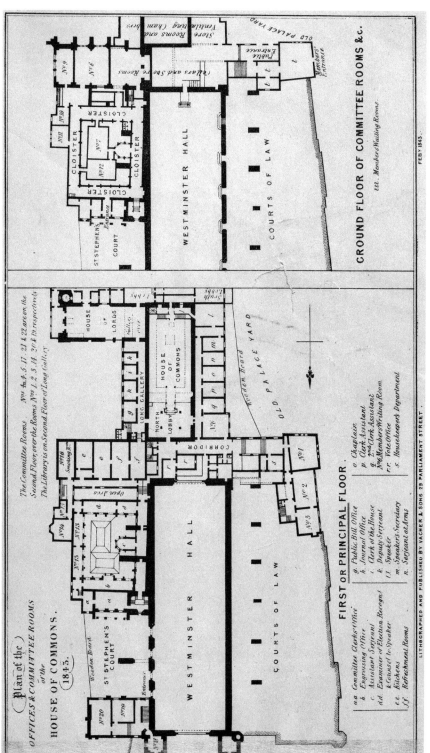

Fig. 7. Vacher & Sons (publisher), *Plan of the Offices and Committee Rooms of the House of Commons*, 1843. Lithograph, 14.3 × 24 cm. PA, HC/LB/1/114/19.

Fig. 8. George Moore, *St Stephen's Chapel, Palace of Westminster*, 1836–7. Watercolour, 36 × 26 cm. London Metropolitan Archives, Prints Collection, record no. 313151.

grand system.[107] This development was one reason why Barry rethought elements of his own original design. Although the Architect's intention remained to retain and restore the undercroft and to build St Stephen's Hall above it on the footprint of the lost upper chapel, the new buildings directly adjacent to it at each end were now considerably modified. The Central Hall (today Central Lobby) to its east was to be set within a substantially redesigned central ventilation tower, the epicentre of Reid's permanent system, separated from the crypt only by a narrow passageway.[108]

Directly to the west of the undercroft was now to be St Stephen's Porch, a new and imposing public entrance coming in from Old Palace Yard and leading through St Stephen's Hall to Central Hall (fig. 9).[109] Some of the main arteries for Reid's air-handling system were to flow through channels at different levels within this area.[110] These developments would leave the undercroft at the heart of a highly complex – and contested – part of the building site.

[107] *HKW*, vol. 6, pp. 604–5.
[108] Gillin, *Victorian Palace*, pp. 162–5; TNA, WORK 29/3053.
[109] *HKW*, vol. 6, pp. 598, 600.
[110] Henrik Schoenefeldt, *Rebuilding the Houses of Parliament: David Boswell Reid and Disruptive Environmentalism* (London, 2020), p. 107.

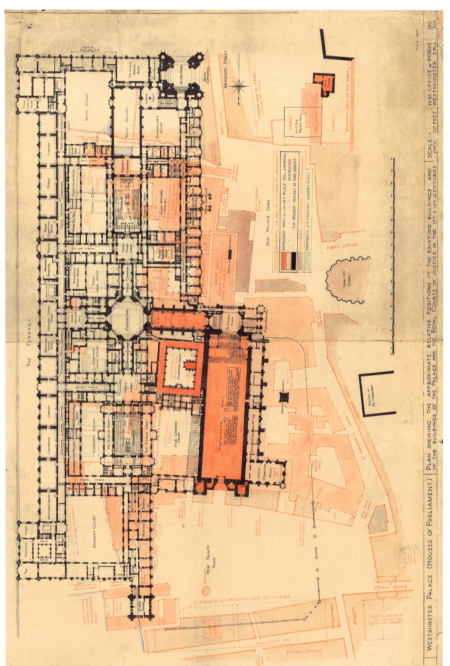

Fig. 9. G. H. Checkley, *Westminster Palace (Houses of Parliament): Plan Shewing [sic] the Approximate Relative Positions of the Existing Buildings and of the Buildings of the Palace and the Royal Courts of Justice in the 17th and 18th Centuries*. Swindon, Historic England Archive, Palace of Westminster Collection, PSA01/08/00003.

Frozen in Time, 1844–52

In 1844, Bellamy's rooms on top of the undercroft were pulled down so that work on St Stephen's Porch and Hall could begin.[111] Barry also started work on the crypt to prepare it for a new identity: a place of worship for the inhabitants of the new Palace of Westminster.[112] The floor level was taken down to the original medieval paving, several human skeletons being discovered in the layer just above.[113] On 15 March 1845, Prince Albert visited the 'crypt of St Stephen's, […] now in course of restoration […] The old plaster casings, which had so much disfigured this exquisite piece of architecture, have been entirely removed, and the building is now almost restored to its pristine beauty.'[114]

As was also the case with St Stephen's cloister,[115] Barry was very protective of the fabric of 'St Stephen's crypt', as it was now named in his plans. Perhaps this was in part a reaction to the controversies arising from the demolition of the upper Chapel in 1837.[116] Now, as one of his subordinates told an Inquiry in 1845, 'Mr. Barry always rigidly refused to allow the crypt to be touched'.[117] A plan that Barry drew up in April 1845 marked in black the extensive original fabric that was to be retained.[118] But soon afterwards, in June 1845, he also introduced new features: an octagonal lobby at its south-west corner, later used to house the baptistery, and a robing room or vestry at its north-east corner.[119] The more slender walls of St Stephen's Hall were to be constructed above the undercroft, supported by new buttresses which rested on and wrapped around the medieval fabric.[120] The Hall as built followed these plans, except that the mass and therefore the strength of its external buttresses was increased.

The cramped nature of the building site (fig. 10)[121] gave Barry little room for manoeuvre: it was hemmed in by Westminster Hall to its north, Central Hall to its east, and to its south, the temporary House of Commons with its protruding lavatory tower and Reid's ventilation chimney. But Reid also needed access to this area to run his heating and ventilation systems, both for the temporary chambers and for the new Palace. Because the reporting lines between Barry and Reid were unclear, Reid was able to liaise directly with the Office of Woods to promote his interests against those of Barry. The strong support that Reid commanded from MPs meant that at times his needs trumped Barry's, leading the Office of Woods to countermand the Architect's instructions on the Ventilator's behalf. The undercroft soon fell victim to such a conflict of interests.

In November 1845 Barry reported that 'the excavation of St Stephen's porch is in hand and a considerable advance is made with the masonry of the crypt and superstructure of St Stephen's Hall'.[122] In June 1846, however, the picture was very different: 'the works at the

---

[111] *Morning Post*, 5 Aug. 1844, p. 2; TNA, WORK 11/10/2, 27, 29, 31 July 1844.
[112] *Third Report from the Select Committee on Westminster Bridge and the New Palace*, HL 13 (1847), pp, 111–12.
[113] *Sussex Advertiser*, 30 April 1844, p. 4; Grissell, 'Observations', pp. 323–5. See also the essay by Caroline Shenton and Melanie Unwin in this volume.
[114] *West Kent Guardian*, 15 March 1845, p. 2.
[115] Hallam Smith, 'The "Gothic slum"', pp. 287–8.
[116] See the essay by Rosemary Hill in this volume.
[117] HL 35 (1846), p. 355.
[118] TNA, WORK 29/811–12, 802. See also WORK 29/771.
[119] TNA, WORK 29/778, and see WORK 29/779, 783.
[120] TNA, WORK 29/810, 16 May 1845, WORK 29/805 and 807, an earlier version made on 17 April 1845.
[121] See also plans at TNA, WORK 11/10/2, 24 Sept. 1845; WORK 11/6/4, 22 Sept. 1847.
[122] TNA, WORK 11/9/7, 1 Nov. 1845.

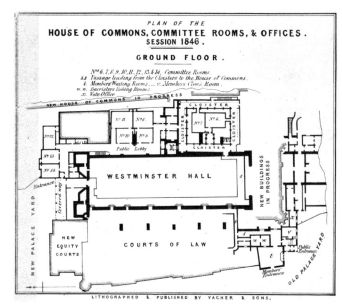

Fig. 10. Vacher & Sons (publisher), *Plan of the House of Commons, Committee Rooms & Offices, Session 1846, Ground Floor*, 1846. Lithograph, 14.3 × 24 cm. PA, HC/LB/1/114/21.

crypt of St Stephen's chapel and contiguous portions of the building [...] are at a stand, owing to difficulties in respect of warming and ventilation arrangements'.[123] This was because in May 1846 Reid, by appealing to the Office of Woods, had managed to bring Barry's work on St Stephen's Hall and crypt to a halt: his team needed to make a large cutting through the undercroft's east end, to create an air channel for Reid's permanent House of Lords ventilation system. Barry excoriated the results, not only for displaying a major 'want of taste' but also for endangering the stability of the buildings.[124]

The scale of the challenges and the poor state of the site at this moment are vividly illustrated by this lithograph (fig. 11),[125] produced by Reid in August 1846 to explain the acute difficulties he faced in sourcing fresh air for his temporary system. At the centre is the crypt, with, to its left, the south end of Westminster Hall. To its right are the north end of the temporary House of Commons (the Lesser Hall), with its lavatory tower and Reid's ventilation chimney. On top of the unexcavated undercroft, St Stephen's Hall is starting to rise, with the River Front of the new Palace beyond it. In the foreground are the foundations of St Stephen's Porch, flooded and dispersing 'most offensive emanations from drains, cesspools and ground saturated with noxious products'. Barry's response to Reid's complaint was dismissive – not least since many of Reid's problems had resulted from his own interventions, and on 18 July had been exacerbated by a dangerous fire in his ventilation chimney caused by the experimental burning of wood.[126]

---

[123] TNA, WORK 11/9/7, 30 June 1846.
[124] TNA, WORK 11/12, 4, 5, 18 May 1846; WORK 1/29, fols 262–3.
[125] TNA, WORK 11/12, fol. 204; and see Elizabeth Hallam Smith, 'St Stephen's in 1846: Ventilation Wars, "Offensive Emanations" and Lost Buildings', <https://www.virtualststephens.org.uk/blog>, blog posted 7 Jan. 2022 [accessed 20 Nov. 2023].
[126] TNA, WORK 11/12, 31 Aug., 5 Sept. 1846; WORK 1/30, 79, 91–2; *Morning Post*, 22 July 1846, 2.

Fig. 11. Office of Works, sketch to illustrate problems with the ventilation of the Temporary Houses, 1846. TNA, WORK 11/12, fol. 204.

By this time, in June 1846, following three major Inquiries, Barry had been awarded primacy over most of the new air-handling systems including that for the House of Lords. However, Reid retained responsibility not only for maintaining the temporary system but also for designing a separate system for the new House of Commons.[127] As a result, between September 1846 and February 1852, two complex and competing networks of air channels for fresh and vitiated air were constructed incrementally – and rancorously – throughout the new Palace.[128] In St Stephen's Porch and Hall, Reid's air channels were to occupy the roof of the new Hall and Barry's, a triple-aisled brick basement to be contrived within the foundations of the undercroft.[129]

At the same time, the flues for Barry's local system to ventilate St Stephen's Porch and Hall required two further air channels, which were to be concealed between the floor of St Stephen's Hall and the 'groins' of the crypt, and like their pre-fire predecessors were to debouch warm air through grilles in the floor of the Hall.[130] The design for these was completed in 1848 and they were probably built soon afterwards. Damage to the bosses and ribs at this time may well have prompted the comment in an 1849 guidebook that 'the crypt of St Stephen's has been mutilated more by abuse than by the fire'.[131] The carelessness of workmen using a raised gangway which had been built too close to the vaults was subsequently given as the reason.[132]

Other than that, the undercroft's fabric seemingly remained untouched until early in 1852, even though Barry continued to report steady progress with St Stephen's Hall and Porch, which rose around it and were structurally complete by that time.[133] The most likely explanation for the suspension of the works within the crypt is that, as was later reported, Reid was using it to house gas retorts and a gasometer.[134] For while the Lords moved into their grand new chamber in April 1847, the heating and ventilation system for the Commons temporary chamber and for the Painted Chamber, now repurposed as the access corridor to the new Peers' Lobby,[135] remained *in situ* for a further four years. Reid's system was a continuing block on progress and required space for its industrial machines. It could not be removed until MPs had occupied their own new House, which had to wait until April 1851.[136]

The order to demolish the Lesser Hall, which had served well as the temporary House of Commons, together with the Painted Chamber – and with them the Commons lavatory and Reid's huge ventilation chimney – came eventually in June 1851.[137] That allowed the final stages of the work at St Stephen's to commence, including the excavation of the undercroft's floor to strengthen the foundations and to allow the construction of the long-planned brick basement for the air channels.

---

[127] TNA, WORK 1/30, 217–18; Schoenefeldt, *Rebuilding the Houses*, pp. 123–6; *HKW*, vol. 6, pp. 603, 616.
[128] Schoenefeldt, *Rebuilding the Houses*, p. 172; *HKW*, vol. 6, pp. 619–23.
[129] TNA, WORK 11/13, 5 May (plans), 2 June 1848; WORK 29/2769, 2960, 3067.
[130] TNA, WORK 29/816, 833–4; WORK 11/13, 6 July 1848.
[131] Peter Cunningham, *A Handbook for London, Past and Present* (3 vols, London, 1849), vol. 1, p. 397.
[132] *Pall Mall Gazette*, 6 May 1865, p. 9.
[133] TNA, WORK 11/9/7, Christmas 1846, 30 June, 23 Dec. 1847; 7 April and 30 June 1848, 31 March 1849, 21 March 1851, 18 June 1852.
[134] *The Times*, 11 Aug. 1864, 9; *Illustrated Times*, 21 Jan. 1865, pp. 5–6.
[135] TNA, WORK 1/31, 103; WORK 29/3207.
[136] See the essay by Mark Collins in this volume.
[137] TNA, WORK 11/10/2, 26 June, 25 Aug. 1851; *Reynolds's Newspaper*, 14 Oct. 1851, p. 13.

Fig. 12. John Wykeham Archer, *Crypt of St Stephen's Westminster [east end], drawn 1852*, 1852. Watercolour, 22.7 × 32.8 cm. BM, mus. no. 1874,0314.191.

This important depiction of the three eastern bays of the crypt (fig. 12), evidently made just before the works began, corroborates contemporary comments that it had been 'sadly abused' but was 'still a beautiful building'. The remains of Wyatt's alterations are discernible, including in the foreground the ribs he had reconstructed in the central bay. So too are signs of its recent industrial uses. Its fine medieval bosses, although defaced, were said to have showed 'traces of the gilding and colour with which the whole of the interior was once embellished'.[138]

It was now that, after many years of obscurity, in January 1852 the undercroft suddenly and briefly became a place of interest and pilgrimage, when workmen removing a stone seat discovered human remains below the window at the north-east corner. After the find was announced to the press, the celebrated surgeon and antiquary Thomas Pettigrew soon identified the body as William Lyndwood (d.1446), Bishop of St David's and a significant benefactor of St Stephen's College.[139] The Society of Antiquaries enjoyed two site visits during January, the second hosted by Barry, where they recorded the remains and endorsed this attribution.[140] Many other images of the undercroft and of the burial were also made and

---

[138] *The New Palace of Westminster*, 7th edn (London, 1852), pp. 36–8.
[139] *The Times*, 28 Jan. 1852, p. 3; *Illustrated London News*, 28 Feb. 1852, p. 180; Biggs, *St Stephen's College*, pp. 133–4.
[140] 'Report of the Committee appointed by the Society of Antiquaries to investigate [...] the discovery of a body in St Stephen's Chapel, Westminster', *Archaeologia*, 34 (1852), 406–40. See also the chapter by Elizabeth Biggs in this volume.

Fig. 13. George Scharf, *View through the S. E. Window of the Crypt Beneath St Stephen's, Westminster*, 1852. Graphite, watercolour and ink, on paper, 33 × 27.6 cm. New Haven, Yale Center for British Art, Paul Mellon Collection, B1977.14.22534.

circulated (e.g. fig. 13),[141] providing posterity with final glimpses of the east end of the still unrestored crypt. The 'mummy' was handed over to the Dean of Westminster Abbey for reburial.[142]

Work on the undercroft's foundations and on the triple-aisled brick basement within them now proceeded apace and was finished in June 1852.[143] This did not involve the method which Barry had used for the rest of the new Palace, including St Stephen's Porch: namely excavating down to the deep layer of gravel beneath the site and building a concrete raft at that level to support the new fabric. By contrast for the crypt, as also with the cloister, Barry preserved the original foundations which rested on a layer of alluvium above the gravel and constructed his concrete raft here. At that time still supported on their original oak piles, the crypt's massive medieval foundations were incorporated into the new work to a height of 2.23 m.

In addition, Barry seemingly retained some supporting stonework from the Lesser Hall and Westminster Hall at the north-east and south-east corners of the crypt, which the medieval builders of St Stephen's chapel had incorporated into their own foundations. Barry's work was completed as specified, but the subsequent slow drying out of the site's

---

[141] See also e.g. London Metropolitan Archives Prints Collection, record no. 311129.
[142] TNA, WORK 1/38, pp. 780–1.
[143] TNA, WORK 29/2955; WORK 11/9/7, 18 June 1852; *HKW*, vol. 6, p. 625.

substrate was not foreseen. By the 1990s this had caused the oak piles to crumble away, and the resulting voids were infilled with concrete to prevent subsidence. But the medieval foundations of St Stephen's Chapel, built in Kentish ragstone, may still be viewed from Barry's lowest service passageway.[144]

The Undercroft Repaired, 1852–60

Although the engineering work on the crypt was completed in June 1852, its stonework would remain unrestored for several more years. The dismissal of Reid in October 1852 removed one major source of distraction, but Barry remained under considerable pressure to complete other more high-profile parts of the new Palace.[145] By 1855, however, he was starting to plan the undercroft's restoration, proposing to the Office of Works a budget of £7,200 for that, raised to £7,297 in the Estimates for November 1857. In 1855–7 Barry prepared a specification for the works and high quality and detailed drawings for the stonework, including the windows, screen, east end and vestry.[146]

The work began in March 1858 and by the end of September Barry, on returning to his duties after 'a long and serious illness', reported the completion of 'a considerable portion of the groined vaulting; a portion of the masonry of the walls, screens etc.; the paving of the floor, the steps from the exterior; access to the cloister; the glazing of the windows, and decorations'.[147] A press report from December said that 'workmen are busily engaged restoring its richly carved bosses and groined roof and replacing the polished columns of Purbeck marble which have been defaced and sadly misused in times bygone. [...] Every minute detail of the original structure is being carefully restored.'[148] Another, more critical, view was that the restoration was too severe: 'everything, to the minutest ornament, is to be replaced'.[149] In February 1859 the *Illustrated London News* printed an invaluable view of the work in progress (fig. 14), which shows the restoration of the ribs and central bosses.

Barry continued to report developments right up to what turned out to be his final return, on 31 March 1860.[150] He commissioned the flooring and masonry work from William Field, including Purbeck marble columns and encaustic tiles.[151] He also ordered from John Hardman the metalwork screen for the west end, modelled on the 1294 grille for Eleanor of Castile's tomb in Westminster Abbey, along with a set of stained-glass windows. These were to represent scenes from the life of St Stephen, who – rather than its original dedicatee, the Blessed Virgin Mary – was to become the focus of the undercroft's decorative scheme.[152] That tied the crypt to the lost chapel of St Stephen and to its later House of Commons heritage.

---

[144] Museum of London Archaeology Service, *St Stephen's Chapel, an Archaeological Watching Brief* (London, 1994), pp. 25–34; PA, PSA/16: Alan Baxter and Associates, *Palace of Westminster Structural Engineering Report* (1991), esp. vol. 2, pp. 23–6, 32–3, 39–40, 53–4 and related plans.
[145] Gillin, *Victorian Palace*, p. 181; *Mr Barry's War*, pp. 216–18, 220–1.
[146] TNA, WORK 11/9/6, 9 Jan, 21 March 1855; WORK 29/785–90; *Correspondence between the First Commissioner of Works and Sir C Barry in relation to expenditure on New Palace of Westminster*, HC 49 (1857–8), pp. 8, 11.
[147] TNA, WORK 11/9/6, 18 Feb., 31 March, 29 Sept. 1858.
[148] *Evening Mail*, 27 Dec. 1858, p. 7.
[149] *Falkirk Herald*, 27 Jan. 1859, p. 4.
[150] TNA, WORK 11/9/7, 31 March, 19 Nov. 1859, 31 March 1860.
[151] TNA, WORK 29/791.
[152] TNA, WORK 29/792, 1859–60; WORK 11/22/2, 15 Nov. 1861; WORK 11/159, 30 April 1865.

Fig. 14. *The Crypt under St Stephen's Chapel, Westminster, now in Course of Restoration.* From *The Illustrated London News*, 5 Feb. 1859, p. 129.

Less happily, as his son – and successor as Architect – Edward Barry explained in August 1860, in the course of the restoration his father had encountered major and unforeseen structural problems in the undercroft. He incurred substantial unbudgeted extra costs of £2,200 over and above his 1857 Estimates, for 'entire new stone work instead of repairs to old structure, in consequence of decayed state of the same. Temporary support of the floor of St Stephen's Hall and protection to public using the same.'[153] The extent of the remedial work needed clearly stemmed from the direct and indirect results of all the disruptions of the previous decade, although Edward Barry's public line was that it was the 1834 fire that had damaged the stonework.[154] Yet despite these significant challenges, the structural restoration was nearing completion when Charles Barry died on 12 May 1860.[155]

'Bedizening with Gold', 1860–70

On taking over his father's responsibilities at the Palace of Westminster, Edward Barry soon found himself under budgetary pressure over the many parts of the new Palace that remained uncompleted. For the undercroft, the tasks still outstanding were the final stages

---

[153] TNA, WORK 11/9/6, 15 Aug. 1860.
[154] *Morning Post*, 3 Feb. 1858, p. 2.
[155] TNA, WORK 11/159, 1 June 1869.

of restoring the bosses and the decayed portions of the walls, finishing the baptistery and vestry, laying the floor tiles, completing the windows and stained glass, painting, and doors – and work on the 'hot air flues and ventilating openings'. Edward Barry's estimate for all that was £3,476, but most, he averred, could if necessary be deferred apart from completing the doors and some paintwork.[156] In the event, following his assurance that while unbudgeted, his father's extra expenditure had been necessary, the Office of Works increased his funds so that he could proceed with the work.[157]

Once he had finished his father's work on the floor, stained glass, and Purbeck marble columns, Edward Barry now had the opportunity to design his own decorative scheme to embellish the walls. In July 1863, in putting this forward to the Office of Works, now supervising, he praised the chapel as 'one of the most interesting remains of the architecture of the 14th century [and] I propose that the decoration should bear reference to its former character'.[158] But Edward Barry's elaborate and exuberant adornment of the crypt in a High Victorian neo-Byzantine style, executed between 1863 and 1869, is far more redolent of Ruskin's *Stones of Venice* than of the building's English origins.

This watercolour, attributed to the Architect himself (fig. 15), vividly illustrates his decorative scheme for the crypt, which could be viewed by an admiring public from January 1865.[159] His dazzling design for gilding the vaults and embellishing them with painted vine scrolls was executed by J. G. Crace, who was also responsible for the dramatic *trompe l'oeil* masonry-effect murals on the north and south walls.[160] William Field fashioned the highly ornate inlaid alabaster and marble dado, altar rails, pulpit, font, and communion table. The elaborate reredos was created by Clayton and Bell, who also adorned the east wall with panel paintings of eight saints and a cross at the centre.[161] Finally, the baptistery was decorated to match the rest of the chapel.[162] The interior was lit by candlelight, with gas lamps shining inwards from the exterior through the stained-glass windows to enhance the effect.[163]

Edward Barry's restoration of St Mary Undercroft was signed off by the Office of Works in June 1869 at a relatively modest figure of £6,568. The decoration, coming in at £837, accounted for less than a third of the total. General construction costs were £3,499 and gas mains and fittings, £1,116.[164] However, the grand total for the rebuilding and restoration of the crypt was widely, and often critically, stated to have been in the region of £30,000.[165] This was almost double the restoration costs which had been officially itemized by Charles Barry and Edward Barry since 1858 (£16,065), but those figures excluded all the major structural costs which had long been subsumed into those for the Palace as a whole. Some idea as to

---

[156] TNA, WORK 11/9/7, 27 Aug. 1860.
[157] TNA, WORK 11/9/6, 24 Sept. 1860; WORK 2/23, 406–7, 410.
[158] TNA, WORK 11/9/7, 31 July 1863.
[159] *The Times*, 3 Jan. 1865, p. 4; *Sussex Advertiser*, 10 Jan. 1865, p. 3.
[160] TNA, WORK 11/159, 11 Aug. 1863; Megan Aldrich (ed.), *The Craces: Royal Decorators, 1769–1899* (Brighton, 1990), pp. 110–12; *Illustrated Times*, 21 Jan. 1865, p. 6.
[161] TNA, WORK 11/159, 11 Jan., 1 Mar. 1865, 3 Feb. 1866; Riding & Riding, pp. 133–4; *The Builder*, 9 July 1864, p. 514; *The Times*, 9 May 1865, p. 11.
[162] TNA, WORK 11/159, 8 Nov. 1866; WORK 11/21, 10 June, 15 June, 18 June 1869.
[163] TNA, WORK 11/20, 7 Dec. 1865.
[164] TNA, WORK 11/159, 1 June 1869, printed 7 July 1871; WORK 11/21, 10 June, 15 June, 18 June 1869.
[165] HC Deb 12 May 1865, vol. 179, cols 251–2; Port, *HoP*, p. 180.

Fig. 15. Edward M. Barry, *Houses of Parliament, St Stephen's Crypt, Restored about 1863*, 1863. Watercolour, 66 × 90.2 cm. WOA 1601.

their scale can be derived from an estimate of £22,000 agreed back in 1849, for structural repairs to the crypt and the adjacent cloister – likely to have been exceeded for both.[166] On that basis the widely quoted total spend of £30,000 on restoring St Mary Undercroft, which derived probably from Office of Works figures, may be about right.

Further finishing touches necessitated another £500 for the 'decoration of entrance iron gate and to baptistery and font cover', work that was not completed until well into 1870.[167] By that time Edward Barry's contract as Architect to the Palace of Westminster had been summarily terminated by Acton Ayrton MP, First Commissioner of Works.

Edward Barry regarded the undercroft's embellishment as his finest achievement at Westminster.[168] Many contemporaries agreed. The *Morning Post* declared it to be England's Sainte-Chapelle,[169] and in the House of Lords, the Bishop of Gloucester and Bristol extolled the way in which the chapel 'had been beautifully restored. He could not think this an improper expenditure on a place possessing so much historical interest.'[170] Barry's own depiction of the restored undercroft won plaudits at the Royal Academy in 1863, and when

---

[166] *Estimate of Sums Required for Completion of Building of New Houses of Parliament*, HC 404 (1849), p. 3; HC Deb 4 May 1865, vol. 178, cols 1468–9.
[167] TNA, WORK 11/159, 8 Feb. 1870; WORK 11/22/2, 11 July 1870.
[168] Port, *HoP*, pp. 178–90.
[169] *Morning Post*, 18 Jan. 1865, p. 6; 1 Feb. 1866, p. 5.
[170] HL Deb 24 June 1870, vol. 202, col. 857.

exhibited at the Paris Universal Exhibition in 1867 received an 'outspoken commendation' from none other than the leading architect of the French gothic revival, Eugène-Emmanuel Viollet-le-Duc, who had played his own part in the restoration of the Sainte-Chapelle.[171]

However, Edward Barry's reimagined crypt also elicited some criticism in the press. Some of this balanced admiration for the effects of the decorative scheme with regret for the way in which its medieval identity had been submerged by what was regarded as Barry's stylistic excesses.[172] Moreover, many MPs objected to the strong impression created of a high-church – or even a Roman Catholic – place of worship.[173] For by the time that the work was finished, the appearance of the chapel was very much at variance with the prevailing Low Church sentiments in the House of Commons.[174] In the chamber, Barry's nemesis, First Commissioner Acton Ayrton, thundered

> that £30,000 had been spent in bedizening with gold a part of the building which in former times was used as a coal cellar and lumber room, and which was subsequently used as a dining room for the Speaker […] The vault was not now used for any purpose and never could be, so that it remained a spectacle of the most absolute waste of public money.[175]

Ayrton was far more dismissive of the crypt's history and significance than most contemporaries. Even those who disdained it, quite mistakenly, as having been 'a dull sort of ecclesiastical lumber-room',[176] welcomed its rebirth as a religious space. But there was widespread concern that, although fitted out with seating in readiness to be used as the chapel for the Palace of Westminster, it had not as yet assumed that role.[177] The planned reinstatement of daily worship was strongly resisted by many MPs and officials, and in 1870 Prime Minister William Ewart Gladstone firmly if pedantically quashed it 'until multiplied indications lead us to believe that it would be in conformity with the general wish of the House'.[178]

In 1871, efforts by the Lord Great Chamberlain and the Bishop of Gloucester and Bristol to open the undercroft for regular Sunday services similarly foundered for lack of support in Parliament.[179] Over the next few decades the crypt chapel was therefore used only occasionally and in a low-key way, mostly for christenings. Not until 1907 was the first wedding celebrated there, followed in 1911 by the first Holy Communion service since the Reformation.[180] That same year, suffragette Emily Wilding Davison would conceal herself in a cupboard next to the west end of the crypt for two nights, so that she could be recorded in the census returns as resident in the Palace of Westminster.[181]

---

[171] G. W. Burnet and David G. Blisset, 'Barry, Edward Middleton', *ODNB*.
[172] *Illustrated Times*, 21 Jan. 1865, p. 6, 20 July 1867, p. 6.
[173] *Morning Post*, 13 July 1867, p. 3.
[174] Port, *HoP*, p. 180.
[175] HC Deb 27 June 1871, vol. 207, cols 648–86 at col. 656.
[176] *The Times*, 11 Aug. 1864, p. 9.
[177] TNA, WORK 11/159, plan of Nov. 1866; *Leeds Intelligencer*, 30 July 1864, p. 3; *Illustrated Times*, 5 Feb. 1870, p. 6; HC Deb 14 Feb. 1870, vol. 199, col. 236.
[178] HC Deb 14 Feb. 1870, vol. 199, col. 236.
[179] PA, LGC/5/6.
[180] *Daily Mirror*, 22 Nov. 1907, p. 1; Donald Gray, *Chaplain to Mr Speaker: The Religious Life of the House of Commons* (London, 1991), p. 92 n. 63.
[181] Takayanagi and Hallam Smith, *Necessary Women*, pp. 125–6, 131–4.

How much of the fabric of the chapel of St Mary in the Vaults, as completed in 1348, has survived? Contemporaries were divided on this issue, some declaring the restored stonework to be a lifeless modern pastiche,[182] others praising the way in which the original vaults, ribs, and bosses had been carefully kept.[183] In 1925, the view of the Royal Commission on the Historical Monuments of England was that 'with the exception of the vaulting and possibly some of the supporting shafts the whole of the face-work of the building is modern'.[184] Archaeological investigations in the 1990s established that the foundations and supporting walls of the undercroft are largely medieval, but that, while the crypt is fundamentally a pre-1834 structure, 'it has almost all been encased or refaced following the fire'.[185] Certainly, any original stonework still remaining on the surface of its interior after Charles Barry's structural repairs would be visually overwhelmed by the lavishness of Edward Barry's decorative scheme. It would also not be immediately apparent given the outstanding skills of the crypt's Victorian restorers in replicating medieval work.

Other comparative evidence hints at a rather more nuanced picture than is often supposed. The great care with which Charles Barry repaired the adjoining St Stephen's cloister, one of the other survivals from the old Palace, is well documented. In 1850-2 he instructed the masons restoring it to keep as much of the original stonework as possible, and to replicate only the missing parts. To that end he provided them with detailed colour-coded plans and drawings. Trial restoration work undertaken in the cloister in 2019-20 demonstrated that his instructions were observed to the letter. Consequently the external stonework of the two walks of the cloister which survived the Blitz is today a meticulous and sensitive patchwork of material from several different eras.[186]

For the undercroft, comparable detailed instructions from Charles Barry to his masons have not come to light; and here as in the cloister he created new features, for example the baptistery, and replaced the damaged stonework in the windows.[187] But as noted above, he was adamant that the old structure should be preserved, and as far as circumstances allowed, he remained extremely protective of its fabric over two decades. Depictions of the crypt in 1852 show that much of its original stonework, along with Wyatt's changes to the ribs, had survived its years of abuse since the 1834 fire, so there was plenty there to preserve.

Observationally, the central bosses seem very close to those drawn by John Carter *c.*1786 (see Binski, fig. 3, p. 127), and some of them at least may still be the originals. Even more convincing are the central parts of the doorway on the south side of the former nave, which now leads into the baptistery. This appears, apparently unchanging, in numerous depictions of the undercroft's west end.[188] Perhaps therefore, beneath its lavish decoration, the stonework of the undercroft's ribs and bosses is, like that of the cloister, a careful mix of old and new.

---

[182] *Pall Mall Gazette*, 6 May 1865, p. 9.
[183] *The Builder*, 9 July 1864, p. 514; *Morning Post*, 18 Jan. 1865, p. 6.
[184] Royal Commission on the Historical Monuments of England, *An Inventory of the Historical Monuments in London, West London* (London, 1925), p. 123.
[185] PA, PSA/16, 39-40.
[186] Hallam Smith, 'The "Gothic slum"', pp. 287-9.
[187] TNA, WORK 29/785.
[188] E.g. Ayers, fig. 3, on p. 18. See also Smith, *Antiquities*, pp. 148, 264.

The status of St Mary Undercroft today, as a marginalized ecclesiastical space at the heart of the Palace of Westminster, in many ways echoes its final and neglected years before the Reformation. But a fascinating story lies behind the apparent uniformity of its glittering Victorian interior surfaces, so 'terribly scraped and garnished'.[189] Moreover, Edward Barry's bedizening may have served to disguise more of its earlier fabric than has hitherto been recognized.

---

[189] William R. Lethaby, *Westminster Abbey and the King's Craftsmen* (London, 1906), p. 18.

From Valhalla to New Dawn: Commemoration and Gender in the Afterlife of St Stephen's

Caroline Shenton and Melanie Unwin

'It is my object, as an architect', Charles Barry (fig. 1) told a Committee of MPs considering the decoration of the new Houses of Parliament in 1841, 'to give the most striking effect to the building as a whole, and I think that the effect of architecture can in no way be so highly enhanced as by the arts of painting and sculpture'. Given the national role of the Palace of Westminster, the subjects most applicable would be those which referred to famous events in British history and should – in his view – 'most decidedly' not be allegorical. The purpose should be celebratory, and the walls should not all be decorated at the same time: each successive generation should have the opportunity of adding its own people and events to the scheme.[1] How Barry's vision for the interior design of the Palace – specifically St Stephen's Hall, the site previously occupied by the upper chapel of St Stephen and subsequently the House of Commons chamber – has been transformed by political protest, gender politics, and curatorial interpretation since then is the subject of this chapter.

Destruction and Restoration

Seven years before Barry's appearance at that Committee, both he and A. W. N. Pugin had watched the destruction by fire of the old Palace of Westminster. Pugin exclaimed,

> Oh it was a glorious sight to see [James Wyatt's] composition mullions & cement pinncles [*sic*] & battlements flying and cracking While his 2.6 turrets were smoking Like so many manufactoring [*sic*] chimnies till the heat shivered them into a thousand pieces – the old walls stood triumphantly amidst this scene of ruin while brick walls & frames sashes slate roofs &c fell faster than a pack of cards.

Shortly before eight in the evening the wind changed direction, veering westerly over the Thames and driving the flames from the Lords, where the fire had begun, onto the roof of

---

[1] *Report from the Select Committee on Fine Arts; together with the minutes of evidence, appendix and index*, HC 423 (1841 Session 1), p. 8.

Fig. 1. Henry W. Pickersgill, R.A., *Sir Charles Barry, R.A. 1795–1860*. Oil painting, 144.8 × 111.8 cm. WOA 2729.

St Stephen's, where the flames spread with the rapidity of wildfire. Pugin was astonished: 'From the time of the House of Commons first taking fire till the flames were rushing out of every apperture [sic] it could not be more than five or six minutes and the effect of the fire behind the tracery &c was truly curious and awfully grand.'[2]

Barry's experience of that chilly night was similar. Returning from a work trip to Brighton on the evening of 16 October 1834, his eldest son Alfred later described how,

> a red glare on the London side of the horizon showed that a great fire had begun […] and that all attempts to stop the conflagration were unavailing. No sooner had the coach reached the office, than he hurried to the spot, and remained there all night. All London was out, absorbed in the grandeur and terror of the sight. The destruction was so far complete, that preservation or restoration was out of the question; the erection of a new building was inevitable, on a scale and with an opportunity for the exercise of architectural genius, hitherto unexampled in England.[3]

---

[2] Caroline Shenton, *The Day Parliament Burned Down* (Oxford, 2012), pp. 94–5, 101.
[3] Alfred Barry, *The Life and Works of Sir Charles Barry, RA, FRS* (London, 1867), pp. 145–6.

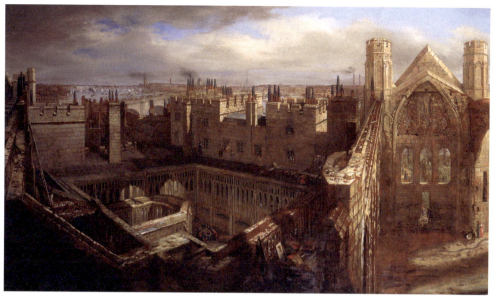

Fig. 2. George Scharf, *Panorama of the Ruins of the Old Palace of Westminster*, 1834. Oil painting, 80.5 × 140 cm. WOA 3793.

In December 1834, Pugin wryly complained to a friend that Robert Smirke (the government in-house architect who had obtained the commission to fit out the temporary chambers and was seeking to extend that into rebuilding the Palace as a whole) had not yet been killed by any of the falling ruins at St Stephen's – in an allusion to St Stephen Protomartyr's death by stoning.[4] However, as Rosemary Hill shows elsewhere in this volume, the demolition of the triumphant old walls of St Stephen's was by no means a foregone conclusion (fig. 2). In the final site plans issued for the architectural competition for the new Palace of Westminster on 25 August 1835, colour washes indicated which buildings in the complex were to be demolished (such as the Painted Chamber), which were definitely to remain (including Westminster Hall), and those which competitors could keep or destroy at their discretion. Among these last was St Stephen's Chapel.[5]

Barry fudged what he intended to do with the ruins of St Stephen's. Most competitors had tried to incorporate it into their proposals and Barry was no different, indicating that he might restore it as a grand space leading from the main entrance by Westminster Hall into the heart of his new Palace. But 'restoration' in the 1830s was a loose concept indeed. By the middle of 1837 Barry had consulted a panel of architects and had decided that the walls of the upper chapel would need to come down. In their place would go new ones, though with the same dimensions as the old. He told the Office of Woods his intentions at the end of July, and by the early autumn the upper chapel had disappeared forever.[6]

During the first half of 1838 Barry created temporary Dining Rooms for MPs in the flattened area over the lower crypt of St Stephen's, where the upper chapel had formerly

[4] Pugin, *Letters*, vol. 1, p. 44.
[5] *Mr Barry's War*, pp. 35–6.
[6] HKW, vol. 6, p. 601.

stood. By the following winter, the Members eating their suppers were complaining of the cold so Barry had to install swing doors to keep the draughts out, the Treasury having turned down his proposal for fireplaces.[7] A temporary Tea Room and Smoking Room were subsequently added.[8] Architecturally expedient though the removal of the upper chapel was to Barry's plans – ruthless even – it may not have been without a twinge of regret. There are today two watercolours of the ruins in the Parliamentary Art Collection which his youngest son, the civil engineer Sir John Wolfe-Barry (1836–1918), later donated to Parliament. One (WOA 257) shows a labourer resting in an ogival gothic doorway at the east end while smoking a pipe, in between salvage operations. The other (WOA 259) is a scene of the clearance, or shoring up, of the south-east wall, showing the ruined interior and east end. Intriguingly, they seem to be copies of two original watercolours also today in Parliament's Art Collection (WOA 6924 and WOA 6925 respectively) by George Belton Moore. Belton Moore (1805–75) was a landscape painter and pupil of A. C. Pugin, but also a drawing master at various London institutions, and a frequent exhibitor at the Royal Academy and elsewhere.[9] How these watercolours came into Wolfe-Barry's possession is not known. Both he and his elder brother Edward Middleton Barry (who completed the 'restoration' of the lower chapel, after his father's death) were too young to have made contemporaneous copies, though Wolfe-Barry might have done so in later life if he had somehow gained access to the originals. He may simply have picked them up on the open market. But it is an intriguing thought that he might have inherited them from his father, who was no mean architectural watercolourist himself, and who may have wished to have a record of his own of the great building which he razed flat in the summer of 1837.[10]

St Stephen's Hall and Valhalla

By the early 1840s, a new building was rising on exactly the same footprint as St Stephen's and the former Commons chamber, but slightly lower in height than the medieval chapel as it missed out the clerestory: St Stephen's Hall (fig. 3). This was in effect, a ceremonial corridor, intended by Barry to be a splendid route from his remodelled south end of Westminster Hall to the octagonal Central Hall (now Central Lobby), planned as the crossroads of the new Houses of Parliament. St Stephen's Hall, thought Barry, was one of several locations ideal for decoration, but was probably the only one which could be entirely filled with painting and some sculpture.[11]

Fresco had already been proposed for the interior of Barry's Reform Club in Pall Mall, but had not yet been executed and he thought it would be difficult to find British or Irish artists capable of handling it 'owing to the want of experience with reference to that kind of painting in this country'.[12] When questioned on this at the 1841 Committee hearing, Barry

---

[7] TNA, WORK 1/23, 74, 95, 229, 241.
[8] HC 423 (1841 Session 1), p. 10.
[9] L. H. Cust, 'Moore, George Belton (1805–1875)', rev. Emily M. Weeks, *ODNB*.
[10] Barry funded two years of his Grand Tour between 1817 and 1820 by creating a watercolour portfolio of the great buildings of France, Italy, Greece, and the Ottoman Empire as a travelling companion to a rich patron, David Baillie. See *Mr Barry's War*, pp. 22–4.
[11] HC 423 (1841 Session 1), p. 10.
[12] HC 423 (1841 Session 1), p. 4.

Fig. 3. St Stephen's Hall, Palace of Westminster (present day view). UK Parliament/Estates Archive.

stated that oil was also a possibility, but overall he 'should prefer having it upon the wall itself, as it would then become an integral part of the building', and there was a limit to the size of wall a canvas could cover. If time and encouragement were given to artists to undertake the development of unfamiliar techniques, 'I see no reason,' he said, 'why the efforts of our own artists should not equal those of any other country'. The walls of Westminster Hall could be experimented upon, he thought, to give the effect of tapestry, or several of the corridors off the Central Lobby he had designed. Did he think the Peasants' Revolt a good subject? enquired one member: clearly a trap. 'Any leading event in English history would be a good subject', responded Barry, mildly. Free-standing monumental sculpture could also be employed 'with very great effect', though not reliefs, which were a continental Gothic style; Barry was 'not quite sure that I altogether approve' of the effect of coloured statues of the kind which Pugin had introduced at Alton Towers.[13]

The report of the Committee led to the establishment of the Fine Arts Commission, to be chaired by Prince Albert, aided and abetted by Charles Eastlake as Secretary, a friend of Barry's from his Grand Tour days. Albert quickly became deeply engaged in the plans for artworks to decorate the new Palace, and in the cartoon competitions to decide on subjects and artists. As a result he was regularly briefed by Barry on progress with the building and on the spaces suitable for wall paintings. Some of this immersion in the history and architecture of the Palace, and particularly St Stephen's, must have influenced Victoria and Albert's decision in the spring of 1842 to hold a *Bal Costumé* at Buckingham Palace, to which (as Victoria recorded in her diary) 'we have settled to go as Edward IIIrd & Queen Philippa, & there is such trouble in getting the costumes correct'.[14] By early May Victoria

---

[13] HC 423 (1841 Session 1), pp. 4–9.
[14] *Queen Victoria's Journal* (Princess Beatrice's copies), 18 April 1842, <http://www.queenvictoriasjournals.org> [accessed 20 Aug. 2017].

declared herself most satisfied with her 'really very handsome' fancy-dress outfit.[15] On the morning of 12 May, she

> went with Albert to look at the arrangement of the rooms for our great 'Bal Costume' [...] [we] remained principally in the Throne Room, which is really quite beautiful, the alcove & throne, all hung with dark blue cloth with gold crown & Garter printed all over the hangings. We met Lord Liverpool there, really beautifully got up, in a tight white satin dress, his arms embroidered in gold, all over it, red hose & gold shoes, a long mantle, & a velvet cap [...] Many Ladies, with powered coiffures were very handsome, 2, in particular, Miss Bolland, & Mme Lionel de Rothschild. – The procession walking up, slowly, 2 by 2, hand in hand, & bowing at the foot of the Throne, had a very fine effect [...] Nothing could have gone better, than the whole did, &, it was a truly splendid spectacle.[16]

Albert, who had studied art history at Bonn University, was absolutely determined that the Palace should contain a monumental series of narrative wall paintings based on his knowledge of the German Nazarene movement.[17] Meanwhile Barry's fertile imagination continued to run riot over the remnants of the old Palace as well. His plans for Westminster Hall were startling, despite having ruled out the possibility – suggested by one MP – of transferring all the burial monuments in Westminster Abbey and St Paul's there:

> In the event of the law courts being removed, which is quite essential to the treatment of Westminster Hall as a whole, I should say that the Hall might be appropriated to the reception of statutes of eminent public men of past times, to be arranged on each side, and at a short distance from the walls, and that they should be placed with reference to the ribs of the roof: that is, a statue might be placed opposite to each rib, by which arrangement the wall would in effect be divided into sections or compartments, and so fitted for the reception of a distinct subject of painting. I merely mention this as an instance of the mode of applying the two arts with reference to architectural arrangement [...] Single statues I think would be most applicable in the situations which I have mentioned. With reference to further effect in Westminster Hall, if the proposed arrangements of painting and sculpture were adopted in connexion with a display of armorial bearings and ancient armour on the sides and above the windows, trophies and banners &c suspended from the roof, ornamental glass, and tessellated pavement and decorative painting, the whole would have a peculiarly striking appearance, and tend to awaken old and interesting associations connected with our national history.[18]

In the autumn of 1842 these thoughts inspired one of the rare holidays which Charles Barry took during his life, to the Kingdom of Bavaria. He enjoyed the mountains just as much as he had in the Alps on his Grand Tour twenty-five years before, and he toured Munich, Regensburg, Nuremberg, and Constanz, sketching as he went. But he also took the opportunity to visit the newly opened *Walhalla*, perched on a cliff above the Danube at

---

[15] *Queen Victoria's Journal* (Princess Beatrice's copies), 9 May 1842.
[16] *Queen Victoria's Journal* (Princess Beatrice's copies), 12 May 1842. There is a painting by Landseer of Victoria and Albert in their costumes in the Royal Collection (RCIN 404540).
[17] Stanley Weintraub, *Albert: Uncrowned King* (London, 1997), pp. 57, 60–1.
[18] HC 423 (1841 Session 1), p. 9.

Fig. 4. Pisan (engraver), *Interior of the Valhalla at Regensburg*, for *Magasin Pittoresque*, 12, Jan. 1844, p. 37.

Regensburg (fig. 4).[19] This neoclassical temple, built to honour the achievements of ethnic Germans since ancient times, contained a Hall full of statues and plaques commemorating rulers, politicians, men of letters, artists, and scientists – exactly the sort of thing Barry had envisaged for Westminster. He returned inspired by what he had seen.

By the start of 1845 the temporary restaurant and tearooms on the site which became St Stephen's Hall had been cleared. *The Times* reported that two survivors of the fire, the Speaker's dining room (the undercroft chapel of St Stephen's) and its gorgeous Tudor cloister, Barry intended to renovate to their 'original architectural elegance'.[20] On the afternoon of Friday 7 March, Prince Albert and the rest of the Fine Arts Commissioners came to inspect progress and the areas set aside for fine art. Included in their tour was the site of St Stephen's Hall, eagerly anticipated as 'one of the grandest edifices in London', to be lavishly decorated with artworks on historical themes.[21]

Then into the crypt of old St Stephen's they went, where the partition walls and plastering of the Speaker's dining room, with its neighbouring coal holes and lumber rooms, 'which had so much disfigured this exquisite piece of architecture', had been removed – and the medieval vaulted structure was revealed once more. There had been gruesome discoveries down there during the strip-out, as probing the foundations had allegedly revealed several

[19] London, RIBA Library, SKB 402/3.
[20] *The Times*, 4 Jan. 1845, p. 6.
[21] *The Times*, 11 March 1845, p. 6.

skeletons which had 'belonged to men of immense proportions and gigantic stature', their giant jaws containing perfect sets of teeth.[22] Certainly plenty of archaeological finds were made during the digging out of the foundations of the new Palace, and this sensational story of giants buried in the lower chapel of St Stephen's (its original function long forgotten) came partly true seven years later with the discovery of the tomb of William Lyndwood, Bishop of St David's (1442–6), in one of the walls.[23]

Happily, Barry's plans for Westminster Hall (including raising its roof) were not executed. Instead a *Valhalla* was created in St Stephen's Hall, which during his lifetime was lined with monumental sculptures of Walpole, Pitt the Younger, Fox, and other notable Parliamentarians – all, obviously, male. By 1853, the entrance and stairs from Westminster Hall into St Stephen's Hall were completed, as was the stairway from St Stephen's Porch to the outside world, offering in the form of a tall, elegant passage the ghostly image of the former chapel and debating chamber.[24]

When Barry died in 1860 some suggested that he be buried in St Mary Undercroft, the lower chapel of St Stephen's, much as Wren had been buried in his masterpiece of St Paul's. At the time, this 'matchless crypt' was undergoing a wholesale restoration, virtually in secret due to the fear of complaints about expenditure, under the supervision of Barry's son Edward. Though few visitors were aware of its existence, workmen were busily restoring the carved bosses and groined roof, and replacing the polished Purbeck marble columns defaced and 'sadly misused in centuries bygone'.[25] But in the end Charles Barry was buried in the nave of Westminster Abbey, somewhat against the wishes of Lady Barry and his children.

A statue of Charles Barry, carved by J. H. Foley, who had produced those of the Parliamentarians John Hampden and John Selden for St Stephen's Hall, was commissioned by his best friend John Lewis Wolfe, and had many subscribers. Placing it in St Stephen's Porch at the head of Westminster Hall was deemed to be inappropriate, so instead it was installed on the Grand Staircase, part of the public route from the Lower Waiting Hall to the Committee Corridor, where it remains today. Foley's statue shows Barry seated with his coat thrown open, vigorously sketching the design of the Victoria Tower on a drawing board balanced on his knee. All agreed it was an inspired rendering of the friend they had known, and of the part of the building he thought would be his memorial.[26] But it was also an addition of yet another worthy male to a scheme which offered no females (with the exception of queens: honorary men in all but dress), and only three named non-royal women in the wall painting cycles.[27]

Barry had intended that successive generations would add their own commemorations to the decorative scheme, thereby keeping the Palace relevant to the society which Parliament

---

[22] *The Times*, 11 March 1845, p. 6.
[23] J. Hunter, 'A Few Notices Respecting William Lynwode, Judge of the Arches, Keeper of the Privy Seal, and Bishop of St. David's', *Archaeologia*, 34 (1852), 403–5. For archaeological finds during construction see Shenton, *Mr Barry's War*, p. 92. See also Elizabeth Biggs's essay in this volume.
[24] *Biographical Dictionary of Civil Engineers in Great Britain and Ireland*, vol. 2, 1830–1900, ed. M. M. Chrimes et al. (London, 2008), pp. 531–2; *Illustrated London News*, 12 Feb. 1853, p. 127.
[25] *Illustrated London News*, 5 Feb. 1859, p. 125. See also Elizabeth Hallam Smith's essay in this volume.
[26] Barry, *Life*, pp. 350–1.
[27] Melanie Unwin, 'New Dawn: Celebrating Feminist Collective Action in the Landscape of the Heroic Male Parliamentarian', in Jenna C. Ashton (ed.), *Feminism and Museums: Intervention, Disruption and Change* (2 vols, Edinburgh/Boston, 2017), vol. 2, pp. 106–37 at p. 117.

Fig. 5. Charles H. Sims, *King John Assents to the Magna Carta, 1215*. Oil painting, 304.8 × 442 cm. WOA 2602.

represented. The Fine Arts Commission had a different plan: to fill all the walls and spaces of the Principal Floor with contemporary wall paintings and sculpture, thus presenting a finished and complete scheme by the end of the 1860s. It was only the combination of the death of Prince Albert, Chairman of the Commission, in 1861, massive budgetary overspend, and the impatience of Parliamentarians to be rid of the artists whose activity prevented them inhabiting the working rooms of the Palace, which eventually left any walls free of decoration.[28] Of the later schemes which eventually filled the four main incomplete spaces at Albert's death in 1861 – the Royal Gallery, Princes' Chamber, East Corridor, and St Stephen's Hall – only the Royal Gallery, with its display of royal portraits up to and including Elizabeth II, and St Stephen's Hall, had any intention of appealing to a contemporary audience or reflecting modern subjects as they were produced.[29] In St Stephen's the result was a mural cycle of British history – *The Building of Britain* (1927) – which, however, ended at 1707 (fig. 5). Again it was populated by a majority of men, with the honourable exceptions of Elizabeth I sending Raleigh off to find the New World and Queen Anne assenting to the Union of Scotland and England.

[28] Riding & Riding, p. 223.
[29] The Royal Gallery in the House of Lords was proposed as the site of a First World War memorial. Initially a huge wall painting was proposed, but ultimately an allegorical statue group was commissioned which was installed but soon moved to an external location. The empty wall compartments have since the mid twentieth century housed portraits of monarchs.

Women and Westminster

The absence of women in the Victorian and early-twentieth-century parliamentary *mise-en-scène* reflected the reality of the institution itself. However, despite not being able to be MPs until 1918, women have had an active presence in the Palace of Westminster as residents, workers, visitors, subjects, and politically engaged citizens for as long as it has been there.[30] During the eighteenth century, women had even briefly been able to sit in the public gallery alongside men, but were then banned in 1778 following a protest by Sophia Musters who had refused to clear the gallery on the Speaker's instruction.[31] Sometime after this expulsion women discovered the loft space of St Stephen's, which enclosed what remained of the upper parts of the old chapel as altered by Wren and housed the 'ventilator' constructed above a grille in the Commons' ceiling, designed to draw out the foul air from the chamber (fig. 6). At first they made their entrance by stealth, bribing doorkeepers to let them into the space. But by the Regency period matters were more formalized, with a ticketing system and refreshments, while the authorities turned a blind eye. Despite the unpleasant conditions, women – predominantly those related to Parliamentarians, but including visitors from further afield such as the Anglo-Irish writer Maria Edgeworth – regularly congregated there to listen to debates via the ventilator opening.[32] An account by Anne Rickman (b.1808) daughter of the Commons' Clerk Assistant explained, 'this upper storey was frequented by ladies who had itching ears for the Debates [...] They looked down thro' peep holes [...] which encircled the aperture over the chandelier of wax candles and could see fairly well by glasses to the right and left.' She went on to describe her own experience:

> We were very pleased when sometimes Papa came in to his late tea and said that a good Debate was coming on unexpectedly, no doubt the roof was pretty vacant [...] and we might go up there. So I have heard Cauning [sic], Lord Castlereagh, Peel, Joseph Hume, Lord Palmerston.[33]

Hidden in the attic, out of sight and out of mind, there is intriguing evidence that female spectators of debates may in fact have ended up being more privileged than ordinary males in the open public gallery below. When the House was cleared on the orders of the Speaker in order to discuss private business – 'I spy strangers!' – male spectators would leave, while the women, upstairs and hidden, remained. Furthermore, acoustic research on the pre-fire Commons chamber suggests that, far from being consigned to the worst seats in the House, women may in fact have had an advantage when it came to the audibility of debates.[34]

---

[30] The passing of the Parliament (Qualification of Women) Act (1918 chapter 47) allowed women to stand as MPs for the first time. For further information, see Mari Takayanagi and Elizabeth Hallam Smith, *Necessary Women: the Untold Story of Parliament's Working Women* (Cheltenham, 2023).
[31] Paul Seaward, 'Gallery' (History of Parliament Director's Blog, 2017) <https://historyofparliamentblog.wordpress.com/2017/05/21/304/> [accessed 21 Nov. 2023] and Amy Galvin, 'From suffragette to citizen: female experience of parliamentary spaces in long nineteenth-century Britain', Ph.D. dissertation, University of Warwick, 2020.
[32] Barbara Leah Harman, *The Feminine Political Novel in Victorian England* (Charlottesville/London, 1998), p. 154.
[33] Copy of unpublished typed manuscript of a letter from Anne Rickman to her nieces, undated, Private Collection. Anne and her sister Frances lived in their father's dwelling in the precincts of Parliament. John Rickman (1771–1840) was Clerk Assistant in the Commons, 1820–40.
[34] Catriona Cooper, 'The Sound of Debate in Georgian England: Auralising the House of Commons', in *Space and Sound*, pp. 60–73.

Fig. 6. Frances Rickman, *Sketch of Ventilator in Ladies Gallery Attic in St Stephen's*, 1834. Pencil, on paper, 17.8 × 22.9 cm. WOA 26.

Following the 1834 fire, women were allowed to watch the debates in a partitioned area of the public gallery in the temporary chamber constructed while the new Palace of Westminster was being built.[35] Though in 1835 the Commons then voted by 86 to 83 against ladies being admitted to the planned gallery in the new Palace, in 1836 a majority of 42 in favour was achieved.[36]

The ladies' gallery in the new Commons chamber was immediately unpopular with women, who wrote complaining of its poor view, being situated high above the Speaker's chair and reporters' gallery; its lack of ventilation; and most of all the ornamental metal grilles which were placed in front of the unglazed openings, not for any reason of safety but to prevent the women being seen from the chamber: the result of concerns that MPs would find their feminine presence distracting.[37] The gallery was soon nicknamed 'the Cage', and allusions to harems were regularly made.[38] The grilles remained in place until 1917 when, as the Representation of the People Bill began its legislative passage through

---

[35] *Mr Barry's War*, p. 63.
[36] *Mr Barry's War*, pp. 34, 63.
[37] Mari Takayanagi, 'GONE GRILLE: The removal of the Ladies' Gallery Grilles', at <https://ukvote100.org/2017/08/23/the-ladies-gallery-grilles/> [accessed 29 Aug. 2023].
[38] Ruth Bernard Yeazel, *Harems of the Mind: Passages of Western Art and Literature* (London/New Haven, 2000), pp. 54–5.

the Commons, it became evident that women's exclusion was almost over: the writing was on the wall.

It was from the ladies' gallery that the suffragist Millicent Garrett Fawcett observed the Commons at work in May 1867 when John Stuart Mill proposed an amendment to the Reform Bill, replacing the word 'man' with 'person'. The previous year, Garrett (she married in April 1867) had been actively involved in the creation of the 1866 petition to the Commons, which Mill had presented in the chamber. This first mass petition asking for the extension of the franchise to female voters, and signed by 1,521 women, marked the beginning of the formal women's suffrage campaign in the UK. Though an activist, Fawcett was too young at 19 to sign the petition, but the following year she joined the executive of the newly founded London National Society for Women's Suffrage. An intellectual, she wrote extensively on women's rights and was a leading figure in the suffrage movement, eventually becoming the President of the National Union of Women's Suffrage Societies, the largest constitutional organization, from 1907 to 1919.

St Stephen's and the Suffrage Campaign

As the long campaign for women's suffrage entered its militant phase, with the establishment of the Women's Social and Political Union (WSPU) in 1903 and the Women's Freedom League (WFL) 1907, 'the Cage' became the site of a number of important suffragette protests. Access was closely regulated and restricted, and opportunities were limited. However, it was through St Stephen's Hall that campaigners for votes for women, peaceful as well as disruptive, entered and left the building daily in the latter half of the nineteenth and early twentieth centuries. Initial suffragette disturbances took place predominantly in Central Lobby, but on 14 February 1907 women were banned from entering it following a number of protests and riots. This forced militant activity westwards, back towards Westminster Hall and St Stephen's Entrance, and in the process transformed St Stephen's Hall, Barry's 'ceremonial corridor' and narrative Valhalla of the male great and good, into a major symbolic space for female protest inside the Houses of Parliament.

At this time, St Stephen's was decorated with the Fine Arts Commission's statue scheme of twelve marble seventeenth- and eighteenth-century parliamentarians: 'men of eloquence and ability in the chamber'. Its intended wall paintings had not been commissioned, and only easel paintings hung in three of the eight empty wall compartments. It is not without irony that the women whose voices could not be heard in the chamber and whose cause was not, in their view, being satisfactorily addressed by politicians, were confined to the site of the former Commons' chamber to campaign for their rights – a chamber from which they had also been historically excluded. The statues of great parliamentary orators were now silent witnesses to (and on one occasion, participants in) a series of protests by the WSPU and WFL. Although only a total of seven incidents in St Stephen's Hall are recorded in police reports, they are highly significant at a time when many WSPU members and others were banned from the building or halted at the main entrance. The first was on 30 June 1908 when Miss Jessie Stephens entered the Hall and asked that her card be sent

Fig. 7. H. K. Porters, Boston, USA, Porter's 'Easy' Bolt Clippers No. 2, c.1908–9. Principal Doorkeeper's Office, House of Commons.

to an MP.[39] When her card was returned, she yelled 'Votes for Women!' and was ejected by the police.[40] This minor disturbance was built on dramatically the following year by two iconic protests.

In April 1909, five women were admitted accompanied by two men. On asking to see two MPs, the men were granted access to Central Lobby while the women, 'in accordance with regulations', remained in St Stephen's Hall. The women quickly sprang into action. Three of them – Margery Humes, Theresa Garnet, and Sylvia Russell – were wearing locked leather belts around their waists (hidden by their coats) with chains with which they shackled themselves to the statues of Robert Walpole, John Selden, and Viscount Falkland. Meanwhile Bertha Quinn chained a notice of a public meeting at the Albert Hall to the statue of Somers and began 'to blow on a whistle loudly'.[41] The fifth woman, Joan Geast, pulled open the door to Central Lobby, thereby attracting the attention of the men inside to the protest. Spectacular though the demonstration was, the police report boasts that, thanks to the aid of some newly purchased bolt clippers (fig. 7), 'it was only the work of about 7–8 minutes from the commencement to the end of the whole proceeding'. The report identifies the women as members of the WSPU. They were never charged, though the First Commissioner of Works was consulted regarding Margery Humes, whose chains had caused the only casualty of the incident: the spur on the boot of the Falkland statue had been broken off. It still bears the scar, a reminder of its part in this protest since the spur was never reattached.

It was perhaps the efficiency of the bolt clippers which inspired artist Marion Wallace Dunlop, a member of the Fabian Women's Group and the WSPU, to devise a rather very different form of protest the following month (fig. 8). When Dunlop entered St Stephen's Hall on 22 June with a gentleman, the same police officer, P.C. Boyce, happened to be on duty.

---

[39] Then as now, any member of the public can enter Parliament and ask for their MP, although MPs are not obliged to attend unless an appointment has been made.
[40] PA, HC/SA/SJ/10/12/4.
[41] PA, HC/SA/SJ/10/12/18. Mary Branson was shown a similar leather belt by curator Beverley Cook: Museum of London. Artist's Residency Diary, 9 May 2017 at <https://newdawnartwork.com/2016/08/11/friday-9th-may-2014/> [accessed 29 Aug. 2023].

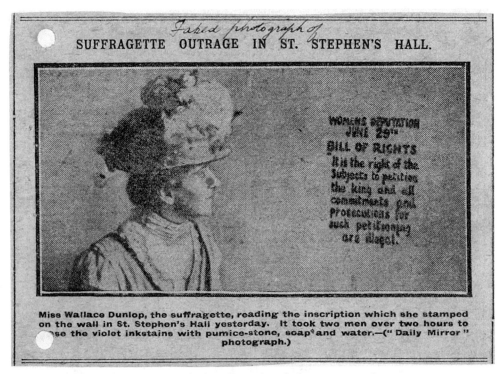

Fig. 8. *Suffragette Outrage in St. Stephen's Hall.* Unidentified press cutting, June 1905. PA, HC/SA/SJ/10/12/21.

The previous month's protest must have made him wary. Following the usual procedure, the man was directed to Central Lobby, and Dunlop was asked to take a seat on one of the benches which ran the length of the Hall, punctuated only by the statue plinths. After a while, Boyce spotted her acting suspiciously and ran over to find her, rubber ink pad in hand, trying to print text onto the stonework of the wall: 'his action prevented the reading becoming legible'.[42] Once again the First Commissioner decided to release the suspect rather than have her charged. This proved to be unwise, for only two days later Dunlop was back in the company of Victor Duval, a member of a family of suffrage campaigners and a year later founder of the Men's Political Union for Women's Enfranchisement. Duval went through to the Central Lobby as usual and returned shortly after, passing the police officer on duty. P.C. Parsons, watching Dunlop start to leave her seat, spotted text printed in violet ink on the wall: he 'accused the lady who had the pad in her hand of disfiguring the stonework, which she admitted'.[43] This time, no doubt in response to what seemed to be a potentially escalating series of protests, the First Commissioner instructed both participants (Duval had been picked up in Westminster Hall) to be charged. Dunlop had stamped on the wall an extract from the Bill of Rights together with the date of a WSPU deputation to Parliament:

[42] PA, HC/SA/SJ/10/12/19.
[43] PA, HC/SA/SJ/10/12/20.

> Women's Deputation June 29th
> BILL OF RIGHTS
> It is the right of the Subjects to petition the king and all commitments and prosecutions for such petitioning are illegal.

In a neat coincidence, the Fine Arts Commission had chosen over sixty years earlier to include a wall painting of William and Mary being read the Bill of Rights by the Clerk of the Parliaments (1689) as part of the decorative scheme on the north corridor leading from Central Lobby to the House of Commons.[44] The Monarchs' coronation was dependent on their acceptance of its terms and marked the point – in the eyes of Whig historians – when Parliament, and the House of Commons specifically, gained significant power and independence from the Monarch. The right to petition the crown enshrined in the Bill of Rights was adopted by the WSPU as evidence of their right to make their case in Parliament unfettered.[45] Wallace Dunlop's protest advertised the first WSPU deputation to petition the Prime Minister. Later in their campaign they made sustained efforts to communicate directly with the King; WSPU suffragette Emily Wilding Davison's disruption of the Epsom Derby in 1914, when she attempted to interfere with the King's horse and was killed, being the most extreme example.

Dunlop was subsequently found guilty and, having refused a fine, was sentenced to a month in prison. However much publicity Dunlop's protest and consequent trial gained for the WSPU, it was her next action which was to cause a seismic change to the course of the campaign. As Annie Kenney, a leading member of the WSPU recounted:

> Miss Wallace Dunlop went to prison, and defied the long sentences that were being given by adopting the hunger strike. 'Release or death' was her motto. When asked by the prison authorities what she would have for dinner, her reply was, 'My own determination'. From that day July 5th, 1909, the hunger-strike was the greatest weapon we possessed against the government.[46]

Dunlop had decided on her action alone, but in the process forged an extraordinary weapon of passive resistance which would famously be used by hundreds in the cause of women's suffrage, and had done so directly as a result of being prosecuted for protest on the site of the former home of the House of Commons.

After the 1909 insurgency, the police and parliamentary authorities became substantially better at stopping WSPU protesters at the gates, or allowing only prearranged and regulated access by named individuals. The notable exception was Emily Wilding Davison, who succeeded in gaining unauthorized access to the Palace and its precincts five times between April 1910 and June 1911. Although none of the police reports mention how she got into the building, given her high profile and the fact that she was formerly banned from the Palace in June 1910 following two of these incursions it is reasonable to assume her access was more clandestine than entering via St Stephen's Hall with its watchful police constables.

---

[44] Edward Matthew Ward, *The Lords and Commons presenting the Crown to William and Mary*, waterglass painting, 1867, WOA 2606.
[45] June Purvis, *Emmeline Pankhurst: A Biography* (London/New York, 2002), pp. 129–31.
[46] Annie Kenney, *Memories of a Militant* (London, 1924), p. 45.

However, it is worth noting that her second most notorious protest took place at the time of the 1911 census, when she managed to gain access to the building and secrete herself in a cupboard adjoining St Mary Undercroft, the former lower chapel of St Stephen's as restored by Barry. This was to ensure that she could claim her residence on census night as the House of Commons for the purpose of the national statistical record.[47]

Even regulated access could not prevent protest. On 20 January 1913 Speaker James Lowther announced his decision that, if a proposed amendment was made to include women's suffrage in the government's own Franchise and Registration Bill which addressed issues of male suffrage, the Bill would need to be reintroduced, wiping out months of talks, negotiations and hopes. The repercussions among the WSPU were significant. Emmeline Pankhurst had written to her members on 10 January 1913, ten days before the proposed debate and the very day Mr Speaker announced his ruling, saying that any defeat of the amendment would make militancy 'more of a moral duty and more of a political necessity than it has ever been before', and that to refrain from militant protest 'will itself be a crime'. She warned her members to prepare for action.[48]

It was in this atmosphere that the WSPU held a meeting that same evening. Sylvia Pankhurst attended and recounted later in her autobiography that: 'the burden of its speeches was "we told you so" [...] To me this was maddening [...] I fled the meeting; I could endure no more speeches. Hurrying home to Linden Gardens I groped in the darkness of the little courtyard, grasping for the largest stones.'[49]

Sylvia Pankhurst then went to the House of Commons. She was undoubtedly well known to the police, and had been at Parliament earlier in the day lobbying MPs in St Stephen's Hall in advance of the debate; she once again gained admittance to it. Pankhurst's account and the police report vary in detail, but the substance of what happened next is undisputed. Pankhurst threw one of her stones at an easel painting, newly installed in St Stephen's, which appropriately showed a past Speaker also in difficult circumstances: 'The House of Commons, 2 March 1629 (Holles and Valentine holding the Speaker in the Chair)'.[50] The police report continued: 'fortunately no damage was done and before she could throw another stone, which she also took from her pocket, she was seized [...] When asked she said, "The glass is hard [and] if I had known it would not break I would have broken something else".'[51]

Pankhurst was released uncharged later that evening. Following the Speaker's decision and the failure of the Bill, hers was the first protest in what in her own words was a period of 'destructive militancy on a hitherto unparalleled scale, petty injuries and annoyances continuing side by side with large-scale damage'.[52] Sylvia Pankhurst was banned from the Palace later that year.[53] Similarly excluded was Marguerite Sidley, who was nevertheless

---

[47] 'Emily Wilding Davison and Parliament', at <https://www.parliament.uk/about/living-heritage/transformingsociety/electionsvoting/womenvote/case-studies-women-parliament/ewd/> [accessed 29 Aug. 2023].
[48] TNA, CRIM 1/139/2.
[49] E. Sylvia Pankhurst, *The Suffragette Movement* (London, 1972), p. 432.
[50] Andrew Carrick Gow, *House of Commons Speaker Finch held by Holles and Valentine*, oil painting, 1912, WOA 2950.
[51] PA, HC/SA/SJ/10/12/40.
[52] Pankhurst, *The Suffragette Movement*, p. 434.
[53] PA, HC/SA/SJ/10/12/64.

discovered in St Stephen's Hall in February 1914 along with seven other WFL members and was removed by Sergeant Kearney.[54] The following month Sidley was arrested for speaking on the steps of a government building in Whitehall and spent four days in prison, her third period behind bars.[55] The last St Stephen's protest before the outbreak of war, when the WSPU ceased its active militancy, was on 11 June 1914. A Mrs McCombley and a Mrs Skiffington travelled from Belfast and were admitted to St Stephen's in order to send in cards to MPs. Receiving no responses, they remonstrated loudly with the constable at the door to Central Lobby, clearly irritated at having come so far to no avail. They were asked to leave, having caused a disturbance, which they duly did.[56]

These incidents show the variety of experiences of militant suffrage campaigners who attracted the attention of the police in St Stephen's Hall, from iconic protests to minor incidents. They reflect the frustration, ingenuity, and persistence of the women involved, as well as their lack of regard for what the penalty of their actions might be. Indeed, in the case of Wallace Dunlop, the penalty itself grew into the most iconic suffragette protest of all.

New Dawn

Over one hundred years later, St Stephen's Hall is now at the heart of Parliament's commemorative and curatorial activity relating to the history of the campaign for female suffrage in the UK. Self-guided tours and interpretation are available explaining the history of suffragette activity in this historic space. It also houses the 'Dearsley Windows', a series of four stained-glass windows illustrating the history of the franchise. The final window illustrates key moments in women's struggle for the franchise, including Wallace Dunlop's hunger strike, Wilding Davison's symbolic night in the crypt, and the infamous 'Cat and Mouse' Act. The most recent artwork to be added permanently to the decorative scheme of St Stephen's is *New Dawn* by artist Mary Branson, installed in 2016 on the 150th anniversary of the 1866 petition, commemorating and celebrating the women's suffrage movement in Parliament in all its manifestations (fig. 9).

The commissioning of *New Dawn* was the second stage of a process which had started with a residency for an artist to research how the suffrage campaign had been played out in Parliament. Mary Branson was selected after an open call for applicants. The first location Branson visited in the Palace was the Victoria Tower, Barry's masterpiece and the home of the original Act Room in the Parliamentary Archives.[57] Later the same day she went on a tour of the Principal Floor, commenting in her residency diary, 'I'm already searching for potential spaces that could be suitable for an artwork. Worryingly, for such an enormous place, there seems to be little room left!'[58]

New Dawn was underpinned by Branson's intensive research. In addition to studying the records in the Parliamentary Archives, the building itself and its role in the suffrage

[54] PA, HC/SA/SJ/10/12/52.
[55] Elizabeth Crawford, *The Women's Suffrage Movement. A Reference Guide 1866–1928* (London/New York, 2001), p. 637.
[56] PA, HC/SA/SJ/10/12/56.
[57] Artist's residency diary, 17 April 2014 <https://newdawnartwork.com/2016/07/28/thursday-17th-april-2014/> [accessed 29 Aug. 2023].
[58] Artist's residency diary, 17 April 2014.

campaign, the artist spoke to experts, historians, and academics inside and outside Parliament as well as MPs, Peers, and staff. In preparing a design for Parliament Branson had been asked to propose an innovative, dynamic, ambitious, and inspiring artwork which would engage building users and visitors and be of museum standard. The new commission would also seek to redress some of the imbalance inevitably found in the twenty-first-century Parliamentary Art Collection due to its legacy of male portraiture and patriarchal history painting. Her research swiftly identified St Stephen's Hall as a 'corridor of power' for women.[59] She proposed the wall compartment above the entrance to St Stephen's Hall – the blank space once occupied by the west end of St Stephen's Chapel – as the site for her work. This location was another of the casualties of the incomplete Fine Arts Commission wall painting schemes, overlooked by subsequent generations not least due to its darkness, a property which for Branson – an artist who works in light – only added to its suitability. On the question of the compatibility of ornamental glass with painting for the Palace of Westminster, Barry himself had been firm: 'it must be used with great care, so as not to produce improper lights'.[60]

Branson noted quite early in her research the sheer quantity of women involved in the suffrage campaign:

> One of the questions that goes around in my head as I see the many refusals by Asquith to see deputations of women is: How many petitions were put before the government before we got the vote? I ask [a Senior Archivist in Parliament]. She says no one knows, as the actual petitions are not kept, but there are records – and if I like I could find out.[61]

The volume of signed petitions presented to the Commons between 1866 and 1918 would have a dramatic impact on the scale of the design for *New Dawn*. As well as counting petitions, Branson also read the police reports to the Serjeant-at-Arms from 1906 documenting 'suffragette' disturbances which required police action within the Palace precincts.[62] The women involved came from a variety of backgrounds and areas of the country, and were of a broad range of ages. On reading the full police file of 67 reports, Branson remarked, 'Once again I made a mental note that I must find a way to represent all women.'[63] This is because the police files did not record the numbers of women who entered St Stephen's peacefully to lobby MPs and hand in petitions, such as the members of the NUWSS and the other constitutional suffrage organizations who continued to press for suffrage without disrupting the House.

Having identified the location and the need to reflect the large numbers of women involved, both peaceful and militant, Branson's visit to the Act Room provided the strongest visual reference. *New Dawn*'s coloured blown glass scrolls draw directly on the aesthetic

---

[59] See <https://www.youtube.com/watch?v=KGMvQVg1d2E&list=PLj3mInRJqIekWo8zm2keMIpv3ApeS3dBb&index=36> [accessed 29 Aug. 2023].
[60] HC 423 (1841 Session 1), p. 9.
[61] Artist's residency diary, 1–2 May 2014 <https://newdawnartwork.com/2016/08/06/thursday-1st-and-friday-2nd-may-2014/> [accessed 29 Aug. 2023].
[62] PA, HC/SA/SJ/10/12.
[63] Artist's residency diary, 1–2 May 2014.

of the rolled parchment Acts of Parliament, as well as alluding to the fact that women's lives were bound by those statutes despite their exclusion from the franchise. Indeed, some were specifically aimed at controlling women including the 1913 'Cat and Mouse' Act, introduced by the government in response to the suffragette hunger strikes and the consequent abhorrent force-feeding. But the enrolled Acts also symbolize the subsequent passage of laws which started to protect women's rights and promote equality.

New Dawn is not a static artwork. Its lighting slowly and constantly changes, reflecting the ebb and flow of the Thames tides. At high tide the artwork is fully lit; at low tide just one glass scroll is illuminated. The period between these two extremes has been designed by the artist to highlight the colours of particular suffrage organizations, reflecting the diversity of the suffrage campaigners: alongside the NUWSS (red, white, and green) and WSPU (purple, green, and white) are the colours of organizations such as the Jewish League for Women (purple and celestial blue), and the Men's League (black and gold). The metaphor of the 'tide of change' was a frequently occurring theme in suffrage literature and promotional materials, both in terms of campaigners wishing to achieve change and their satirization of the anti-suffrage movement as Canute-like characters opposing the inevitable.[64] The phrase itself, and its linkage to the river outside the building, allows the artwork to connect to the world outside Parliament, reminding viewers of continuing campaigns for equality.[65]

Despite Barry's stricture that artworks in the Palace should decidedly not be allegorical, *New Dawn* was not only metaphorical but abstract as well; it was in fact the first abstract art commissioned by Parliament for the Palace. The portcullis, official symbol of Parliament and originally used by Barry to identify his competition entry for the new Palace, was adopted by Sylvia Pankhurst for her Holloway Prison brooch awarded by the WSPU to all its members who were imprisoned for the cause.[66] Pankhurst surmounted the portcullis with an enamelled arrowhead in the WSPU's colours. Branson used a vast circular portcullis on which to mount her lit scrolls. Over three metres in diameter, the horizontal bars of the portcullis combined with the multitude of circular scrolls create numerous, repeating, 'Venus' symbols. This feminized Portcullis (both in terms of the Venus symbol and its overall circular shape) is described by Branson as having been raised up over the doorway to St Stephen's to give permanent access into Parliament for all women.

Unlike the pre-1834 chamber destroyed by fire, or Barry's chamber bombed out in 1941, St Stephen's Hall still exists with all its ghostly echoes of its past (see fig. 3). Barry's architecture, the Commission's statues and the subsequent 1920s wall painting scheme all contribute to what Branson recognized as 'a cold, masculine area. It was built by men and for men. I wanted the piece to insert a warm energy.'[67] Until *New Dawn* was installed, St Stephen's Hall's temporary conversion by the suffrage campaigners into a transgressive radicalized space was invisible save for the one small scar on the Falkland statue. Branson's

[64] See for instance 'The New Mrs Partington …', postcard by Ernestine Mills, *c.*1910, seen by Mary Branson at the Museum of London. London, Museum of London, 50.82/864.
[65] For further information about Mary Branson, *New Dawn*, sculpture, 2016, WOA 7538, see <https://heritagecollections.parliament.uk/exhibits/new-dawn/>; <https://marybranson.com/newdawn> and <https://www.youtube.com/results?search_query=art+in+parliament+new+dawn-> [all accessed 29 Aug 2023].
[66] For Barry and the portcullis, see *Mr Barry's War*, pp. 42–3.
[67] Mary Branson, quoted in *The Independent*, 11 June 2016 <http://www.independent.co.uk/arts-entertainment/art/suffragist-light-sculpture-marking-womens-right-to-vote-battle-sets-british-parliament-aglow-a7074526.html> [accessed 29 Aug. 2023].

New Dawn has recognized and made visible that campaign, as well as the historic presence of women in Parliament.

The House of Commons first tried to make women absent by banning them from the pre-fire chamber at St Stephen's, then tried to hide them behind grilles in Barry's ladies' gallery, and finally threw them out of Central Lobby and tried to police their access to St Stephen's Hall. Today women still struggle to find equality in all things inside Parliament, as they do outside. The installation of *New Dawn*, an explicitly feminist artwork, is one way in which Parliament has recognized the challenge – this time not to keep women out, but to recognize historic injustice, to celebrate women's achievements, and to encourage women to enter and participate as equals.

Fig. 9. Mary Branson, *New Dawn*, 2016. Sculpture. WOA S753.

Index

Page numbers in *italics* refer to figures.

Abbot, Charles, Speaker of House of Commons   311–12, 314
Abbotsford, Roxburghs.   282
Abraham, biblical patriarch   133
Act of Union (1707)   202, 216, 224, 237, 264, 281, 341
Adam, James, architect   227
Addington, Henry, Speaker of House of Commons, Prime Minister   215, 309, 311–12
Aiscough, William, Bishop of Salisbury   112
Albert, Prince, husband of Queen Victoria   291, 320, 337–9, 341
   Albert Memorial Chapel   55
Aleyn, John, canon of Windsor, composer   73–4
Ammonias, Andreas   121
Anne, Queen of England   202, 341
Anne of Cleves, wife of Henry VIII   193
Anonimalle Chronicle   224
Anthony, Lord Rivers   117
antiquaries, importance of (general)   5–6, 8–9, 16, 34, 137, 208, 243–62, 281
Arthur, Prince of Wales, son of Henry VIII   116, 195
Ashridge Park, Herts.   281
Ashwell, Thomas   178, 180
Assisi, Basilica of St Francis of Assisi, Lower Church   155
Athelard, John, painter and glazier   140
Athens   235
Atkinson, William, architect   282
Attlee, Clement, Prime Minister   298
Audley, Thomas   201
Avignon   104, 153, 154
Ayrton, Acton, MP, First Commissioner of Works   329–30

Bankes, George, MP   291
Banks, Tony, MP   220
Barbara, saint   70
Bardi of Florence, banking firm   102–3
Barking Abbey, Essex   33
Barowe, Thomas   114
Barry, Alfred   290, 334
Barry, Sir Charles, architect
   burial   340
   Houses of Parliament, rebuilding of   3–6, 8–9, 205, 258–62, 264, 276–7, *277*, 281, 287–96, *293*, 298, 315–16, 318, 320–1, 323–8, 331, 333, *334*, 335–40, 348–9, 351–2
   other buildings   288
Barry, Edward, architect   327–32, *329*, 336, 340
Basevi, George, architect   239–40
Beaufort, Lady Margaret   117, 194
Becket, Thomas, Archbishop of Canterbury, saint   42–3
Bedyngham, John, composer   8, 68, 173–8, *176*
Bel and the Dragon   134
Bellamy, John, caterer to House of Commons   316, 320
Belton Moore, George   336
Benet, William, canon of St Stephen's   121
Benn, Tony, MP   5
Bentham, Jeremy   227, 238, 281
Berkeley, Thomas II   90, *93*
Berkeley Castle, Gloucs.   50
Bertie, Montagu, Lord Norreys   276
Beverley, William   113
Bibles moralisées   157, 159, 161–5, *164*, *165*, 169
Biblia Pauperum   145
Bigod, Roger, Marshal of England   84
Bill of Rights   211, 346–7
Billings, Robert, antiquary   256, 258
Binchois (Gilles de Bins)   175

Birmingham, King Edward's School   288
Black Death   36, 38, 49, 52, 158
Blake, William   251
Blanche of Castile, wife of Louis VIII   161
Blois   221, 222
Blore, Edward, antiquary and architect   243–4, 256, 258, 282
Bohun, Humphrey de, Constable of England   84
Boleyn, Anne, wife of Henry VIII   119, 195–6
books, for chapels   3, 60, 63–4, 71–2, 194, 197
Bosworth, battle of (1485)   113
Bowke, John, mercer   197
Box, John, master mason   77
Boyce, Police Constable   345–6
Branson, Mary, sculptor   349–51, 353
Brayley, Edward Westlake   6, 139, 314
Bristol, St Augustine's Abbey, Som.   18, 24, 90, 93
Britton, John, antiquary   6, 139, 256–8, 286, 314
Bruges, Nicholas, painter   141
Brut Chronicle   115
Buckingham, John, canon of St Stephen's   53
Buckler, John Chessell, antiquary and architect   243–4, 256, 258, 282
Burghley, Lord (William Cecil)   304
Burton, Decimus, architect   239

Caen   15, 17
    stone   2, 88
Calais, siege of (1346–7)   36
Cambridge, University of   46–7
    King's College   13, 15, 68, 134, 192
Canford Manor, Dorset   282
Canterbury, Kent   178
    Castle   60
    Cathedral   24, 25, 43, 98, 171
    St Augustine's Abbey   24, 25, 92, 95
Capel, Sir Giles   117
Capon, William, antiquary   243–4, 246, 247, 248–9, 249, 254, 260
Carmeliano, Pietro, Latin secretary to Henry VII   121, 197
Caroline, wife of George IV   254
Carter, John, antiquary   6, 82, 92, 104, 126, 214, 243–6, 246, 248, 250–2, 256, 260, 281, 307, 309–10, 312, 331

Chamber, John, Dean of St Stephen's College   122
    cloister, commissioning of   119, 121, 196, 199
    and dissolution of college   3, 191, 197–8
    as Henry VIII's physician   1, 196
    will of   200
Chantries Act   109, 122, 183, 197
Charles, Duke of Orléans   176
Charles I, King of England   208–9
Charles IV, Holy Roman Emperor   34, 131
Charles IV, King of France   97
Charles V, Holy Roman Emperor   131
Charlotte, wife of George III   314
Cherde, Philip de, mason   77, 104
Chesterfield, Adam, canon of St Stephen's   70
Chesterfield, John, canon of St Stephen's   53
Chesterfield, Roger, canon of St Stephen's   112
Chichele, Henry, Archbishop of Canterbury   116
Christ, Jesus   136, 161–2, 166
    images of   28, 62, 134, 139–40
Churchill, John, Office of Works' carpenter   212
Churchill, Winston, Prime Minister   9, 206, 219–20, 297–8, 297
Civil War, English (1642–51)   207–8
Clarendon, Wilts.   58–9, 62
Clayton and Bell, glaziers   328
Clement VI, Pope   114
Clinton, Henry Fiennes, Earl of Lincoln, Duke of Newcastle-under-Lyme   309
Clipstone, Notts.   60–1
Cobbett, William, MP   238–9, 242, 271
Cobham, Eleanor, Duchess of Gloucester   115–16
Codex Balduineus   131
Cologne Cathedral   154
    choir   126, 129, 153
    inscriptions, painted   152, 153
    Three Kings (Magi), shrine   43, 50, 131, 132
Company of the Star   48
Connolly, William, Speaker of Irish House of Commons   224
Constable, John, artist   251
Cooper, James Fenimore, author   266
Corby, John de, canon of St Stephen's   73
Corfe Castle, Dorset   60
Costessey Park, Norf.   282
Coton, John de, painter   141

Cottingham, Lewis, antiquary   256–8
Cotton, Sir Robert, antiquary   199
Couper, Alice, painter   141
courts of law   13, 117, 119, 202, 285
   Augmentations   115, 119, 122, 195, 201
   Chancery   2, 49, 52–3, 112, 114, 283
   Common Pleas   2, 49, 52, 174
   King's Bench   2, 49, 52, 283, 306
   Requests   212, 216, 249, 306
Crace, John Gregory, artist   328
Cranmer, Thomas, Archbishop of Canterbury   182, 184, 195–7
Crécy, battle of (1346)   36, 106
Crocker, Edward, antiquary   252
Croker, John Wilson, MP   237–8, 240, 242
Cromwell, Oliver, Lord Protector   304–5
Crook, John   115
Crowland Chronicle   110
crusades   85
Cust, Sir John, Speaker of House of Commons   215

Daniel, biblical prophet   134
Dartford, Dominican nunnery, Kent   46
David II, King of Scotland   102
Davies, Thomas Henry Hastings, MP   240
Davison, Emily Wilding, suffragette   5, 330, 347–9
Day, Thomas, canon of St Stephen's   121
D'Ewes, Sir Simonds   208
Deering, John   239
Delaval, Edward Hussey, architect   283
Denny, Anthony   123
Devizes, Wilts.   60
Disraeli, Benjamin, Prime Minister   296
Ditton, John de, clerk of works   87
Dixon, John   142
Domesday Book   199
Dordrecht   221
Dort, Synod of (1619)   221, 222
Douce, Francis, antiquary   309
Dover Castle, Kent   59–60
Downton Castle, Herefords.   282
drawings, architectural   26, 68, 76, 78–9, 81, 142, 192, 211, 212, 225, 226, 227, 233, 258–9, 288, 326, 331
Du Fay, Guillaume   176
Duban, Félix, architect   200

Dublin
   Castle   60
   Parliament   248, 249
Dudley, John, Earl of Warwick, Duke of Northumberland   200
Dunlop, Marion Wallace, suffragette   345–7, 349
Durham Cathedral, Co. Durham   178, 181, 248
Duval, Victor, suffragist   346

Eastnor Castle, Herefords.   282
Edgeworth, Maria, author   342
Edington, William, Bishop of Winchester, Treasurer of England   31, 48, 52–3, 110, 112
Edmund of Canterbury, saint   62
Edmund the Martyr, King of East Anglia, saint   82, 131
Edmund of St Andrew, Augustinian canon, master carpenter   33, 77
Edward I, King of England   54, 63
   and castles, Welsh   38
   coronation   50
   finances   84–6
   foundations, royal   45–6, 49
   religiosity of   41–5, 53, 62
   St Stephen's Chapel, rebuilding of   2, 7–8, 15, 29, 55, 66, 75, 78, 80–6, 107, 125–6
   tomb, Westminster Abbey   50
Edward II, King of England   49
   coronation   50
   death   44, 50
   deposition   83, 98
   finances   7, 86–7, 97
   foundations, royal   46–7, 53
   religiosity of   41–5, 53
   St Stephen's Chapel, rebuilding of   7, 15, 30, 72, 83, 86–97, 107
   tomb, Gloucester   27, 43, 50
   and wife, Isabella, relationship with   84, 97
Edward III, King of England   72, 97, 192, 202, 337
   coronation   131
   death and funeral   44–5, 114–15
   finances   7, 101–6, 109
   foundations, royal   45–8, 53
   France, war with   102–6
   prayers for   193
   religiosity of   41–5, 49, 53, 111

royal apartments, building of   36
St George's Chapel and College, Windsor,
   foundation of   3, 48, 55–7, 193
St Stephen's Chapel, decoration of   125,
   128–9, *130*, 131, 134, 136, 137, 140, 153,
   161–3, 166–7, 169–70
St Stephen's Chapel, rebuilding of   7, 9,
   15–16, 36–8, 50–1, 53, 72, 98–107
St Stephen's College, foundation of   2–3, 9,
   52–3, 55–7, 66, 109–12, 114, 116, 198
Scotland, invasion of   102
tomb, Westminster Abbey   131, *133*
and wall paintings   3, 8, 36, *37*, *130*, 131, 134,
   203–4
Edward IV, King of England   3, 113, 116
Edward V, King of England   115
Edward VI, King of England   184, 205
   dissolution of St Stephen's   3–4, 122, 189,
      197–8, 202, 220
Edward the Black Prince   46, 111
Edward the Confessor, King of England, saint
   253, *254*
   arms of   82
   canonization   62
   chapel at Windsor   3, 44, 55–6, *57*, 58, 62–6
   cult of   61–2
   shrine at Westminster Abbey   43, 50
   statues of   30, 98, 128
Eglesfield, Robert, chaplain of Philippa of
   Hainault   46
Eikon Basilike   209
Eleanor of Castile, wife of Edward I   84, 326
   Eleanor Crosses   44
Eleanor of Provence, wife of Henry III   62, 161
Elizabeth I, Queen of England   184, 191, 205,
   207, 341
Elizabeth II, Queen of United Kingdom   3, 341
Elizabeth of York, wife of Edward IV   111, 194
Ely Cathedral   125, 281
   Lady Chapel   21, *21*, 24
   Octagon   28, *28*, 314
   Prior Crauden's Chapel   154
Empson, Roger, singer at Westminster Abbey
   183
Englefield, Sir Henry   281
Erasmus, Desiderius   121
Estates General, France   227–33, *228*, *229*, *231*,
   232
Esther, biblical figure   134, 160–1

Estney, John, Abbot of Westminster   177
Eton College, Berks.   69–70
Etty, William, artist   257
Eugenius IV, Pope   174
Eustace, saint   134, *135*, 139
Exchequer   1–3, 6, 13, 17, 31, 39, 49, 52–3, 85, 87,
   109, 112, 184, 191, 196, 199–200, 202, 304–5
Exeter Cathedral, Devon   29, 90, 92

fabric accounts   6–8, 16, 24, 36
Falkland, Viscount (Lucius Cary)   345, 351
Fane, Sir Ralph   200
Fawcett, Millicent Garrett, suffragette   344
Fayrfax, Robert, composer   180
Féraud, Jean-Bertrand   231
Fergusson, Robert Cutlar, MP   267
Field, William   326, 328
Fish, Simon, *Supplication for the Beggars*   197
Flaxman, John, sculptor   251
Fleetwood, William, MP   207
Flemyng, Giles, painter   141
Foley, J. H., sculptor   340
Fonthill Abbey, Wilts.   281
Forbes, Vivian   5
Fotheringhay College, Northants.   173
Fox, Charles James, MP   238, 340
Frédérique, Jean, Marquis de Chabannes   311
Fredi, Bartolo di, painter   157
Froissart, Jean   39
Fuller, John   184

Gage, John, antiquary   260
Gardiner, Stephen, Bishop of Winchester   121
Garnet, Theresa, suffragette   345
Gates, Sir John   200
Gaveston, Piers   46
Gayfere, Thomas, mason   283
Geast, Joan, suffragette   345
Geddington, Northants.   59–60
Geneville, Geoffrey de   82–4
Geoffrey Plantagenet, Count of Anjou   82
George, saint   44, 70, 203
   heraldry and images   128, 131, 136
   See also Windsor Castle, St George's Chapel
George III, King of Great Britain   248, 251,
   282, 311
George IV, King of Great Britain   254, 282, 285
Gibbons, Grinling, master woodcarver   213,
   216

Index

Gillingham, Dorset 58
Giotto (da Bondone), artist 155
Gisors, Pierre, architect 230–1
Gladstone, William Ewart, Prime Minister 330
Glorious Revolution 211
Gloucester, St Peter's Abbey (now Cathedral), Gloucs. 18, 27, *27*, 43, 50
Godmered, Janyn, painter 141
Gondouin, Jacques, architect 230, 234
Goodrich, Thomas, Bishop of Ely 196
Gough, Richard, antiquary 244, 248, 281
Graham, Gillespie, architect 258
Grant, James 266
Granville, Mary (Mrs Delany) 307
Greenwich 117, 189, 193
Gregory I the Great, Pope, *Morals on the Book of Job* 156
Grey, Lady Jane 200
Grissell, Thomas, contractor 313
Groves, John Thomas, Clerk of Works *308*, 309

Hague, The 221, *223*
Hall, Sir Benjamin 294
Hallet, Etienne-Sulpice, architect 233, *234*
Hampden, John, MP 340
Hampton Court Palace, Middx 213
Hansard, Thomas Curson, publisher 271
Hardman, John 326
Harvey, Daniel, MP 274
Hastings, Edward 200, 202, 304
Hatton, Sir Christopher 205
Havering, Essex 58–9
Hawksmoor, Nicholas, architect 211, *212*
Heath, Nicholas, Archbishop of York 121
Henry III, King of England 8, 49, 84, 249
    and chapel of St Edward the Confessor 3, 55–6, 62–5
    chapels of 3, 55–6, 58–66, 134, 157
    religiosity of 43
    St Stephen's Chapel, decoration of 125
    tomb, Westminster Abbey 29
Henry IV, King of England 42, 113
Henry V, King of England 43, 116
Henry VI, King of England 13, 69–70, 112–13, 115, 173–4
Henry VII, Holy Roman Emperor 131, *132*

Henry VII, King of England 113–14, 116, 194, 196–7, 208
    accession 193
    chapel in Westminster Abbey 2, 9, 192–3, 283, *285*, 289
    death 197
    prayers for 193
Henry VIII, King of England 1, 117, 119, 123, 180–1, 183, 189, 191, 194, 283
    death 197
    divorce 121
    prayers for 115, 122, 193
    and Reformation 121, 189, 195–7, 201
    and Trinity College, Cambridge 47
heraldry/coats of arms 82–4, 160, 202, 292–3, 306
    of City of Westminster 304, 310
    royal 33, 36, 119, *120*, 159, 181, 198, 202–4, 208, 215–16, 295, 311
    of St George 128
    of Speakers of the Commons 295
    of Wolsey, Thomas 119, *120*
Hereford, Herefords. 171
    castle 58, 60
Herland, William, master carpenter 33, 51, 77
Hickel, Karl Anton, artist 216
Higgons, Edward, Master of Trinity College, Arundel 178, 197
Hodsock, Notts. 60
Holland, Henry 216
Hollar, Wenceslaus, artist 2, 208
Hooker, John, MP 198, 205–8
Hope, Alexander Beresford, MP 278
Hopper, Thomas 239
Horspath, Oxon. 117
House of Commons 215, *217*, 250, 304–5, *313*
    acoustics 198, 213, 231, 237, 241–2, 264, 271–2, 276–7, 293–5, 342
    development of 191–2, 207–8, 263, 266–7
    divisions 206, 264, 273–7, 291, 293, 296
    Estates General, compared to 227–33, 241
    fire (1834). *See under* Westminster, Palace of
    heating 213, 241–2, 264, 293, 310–11, 316, 320, 323
    Irish Parliament, compared to 225–7, 241
    ladies' gallery 273–4, 277, 293, 295, 343–4, 352
    lavatory for 307, 311, 315–16, 320–1, 347
    lighting 4, 264, 291, 295

lobby   5, 8, 189, 198, 202, 206, 237, 264,
    272–6, 291, 293, 295–6, 318, 320, 323,
    336–7, 344–7, 349, 352
  number of MPs   205, 213, 216, 224, 237, 275
  panelling   4, 6, 204, 214, 216, *217*, 218, 281,
    286, 292–3
  rebuilding after 1834 fire   257–62, 263,
    276–8, 279–80, 286–96, *296*, 315–16, *317*,
    318, *321*, 333
  redesign, eighteenth-century plans for
    237–42
  reporters' gallery   264, 271–2, 275–7, 343
  in St Stephen's Chapel   3–6, 8, 33, 109, 123,
    189, 191–2, 197–209, *203*, 211–18, 219–21,
    224–7, 237–42, 263–4, 266–8, 274, 278
  seating   198, 204–6, 211–13, *217*, 237, 240,
    269, 291–2, 294–5
  shape, importance of   220–7, 292
  Speaker's chair   202, 205, 208, 213–16, 225,
    238, 266, 271–2, 290–3, 295, 343
  strangers' gallery   264, 266, 271–4, 292
  temporary accommodation after 1834 fire
    9, 263–4, 268–76, *269*, *270*, *273*, 278,
    293–4, 296, 316, 323, 335–6
  United States legislative chambers, compared
    to   233–6, 238, 241
  ventilation   4, 213, 216, 237, 241–2, 264–7,
    288, 291, 293, 310–11, 316, 318, 320–1, 322,
    323, 328, 342–3, *343*
  in Westminster Abbey   1, 4, 51, 191, 198, 204,
    221, 224
  windows   211, 214, 292, 295
  and women   5–6, 9, 216, 264, 266, 273–4,
    277, 293, 330, 342–52
  World War II
    destruction in   5, 9, 191, 196, 219, 279,
      296–7, *297*, 351
    rebuilding after   9, 192, 219–20, 279,
      297–8, 299
  Wren, Christopher, reordering by   4, 8,
    201–2, 204, 211–18, *212*, 224, 246, 264,
    281, 283, 286–7, 292, 305, 342
  See also Parliament
House of Lords   4, 194, 204, 206–7, 225, 248,
    250, *250*, 252, 254, 264, 276–7
  acoustics   289
  demolition and rebuilding, eighteenth
    century   254, *255*, 256, 283, *284*, 285

fire of 1834, accommodation after   268,
    276–7, 279, 289, 289–91, 315, 323
  in Painted Chamber   268, 316
  in Robing Room   297
  See also Parliament
Howard, Philip, MP   239, 268
Hugh of St Albans, master painter   129, 136,
    137, 140–1, 154–5
Hume, Joseph, MP   238–40, 268, 276
Humes, Margery, suffragette   345
Hurley, William, master carpenter   28, 33, 77,
    88, 107

indulgences   39, 117
Inglis, Sir Robert, MP   239, 267
Isabella of France, wife of Edward II   44, 84,
    97–8, 111, 154–5

Jean II, King of France   47, 161–2
Jefferson, Thomas, US President   233–5
Jeremiah, biblical prophet   134, 159
Joan, daughter of Edward III   169
Job, biblical patriarch   *158*, *164*, *165*, 166
  Book of   156–7
  in context   157–8
  in French royal art   134, 158–62
  See also under St Stephen's Chapel, chapel,
    upper, paintings
John, King of England   42
John the Baptist, saint   131
John of Eltham, Earl of Cornwall   50
John the Evangelist, saint   98, 104, 126, 128
Jonas, biblical figure   134
Joseph, biblical patriarch   134
Judas Maccabeus, biblical figure   136
Judd, Frank, MP   220
Judith, biblical figure   134, 159

Karlštejn, Bohemia, castle chapel of Christ's
    Passion   34, 125
Katherine, saint   62, 104, 126
Katherine of Aragon, wife of Prince Arthur and
    of Henry VIII   116, 119, *120*, 121, 181, 194
Kempton, Middx   58, 61, 66, 70
Kenilworth Castle, Warwicks.   59, 65
Kenney, Annie, suffragette   347
Kent, William, architect   224–5, *226*, 227, 283
Kersaint, Armand Guy de   230, 234
Kew, Surrey, castellated palace at   282

King's Cliffe, Northants.   58, 60
Kings Langley, Herts.   46
Kirton, William, verger of St Stephen's   176–7
Knight, Richard Payne, architect   282

Lancey, Thomas James de   266
Langborne (Langborough), William   184
Langley, Batty, designer   307, 312
Larke, Thomas, canon of St Stephen's   121
Lassus, Jean-Baptiste, architect   200
Latrobe, Benjamin, US surveyor of public buildings   234–5, *235*, *236*
Lawney, Robert   184
Lawney, Thomas   184
Lawrence, saint   104, 126, 128
Leconte, Etienne-Charles, architect   231
Lee, Adam, Labourer-in-Trust at Palace of Westminster   283, 311
Lee, Edward, Archbishop of York   121
Lee Priory, Kent   281
Legrand, Jacques-Guillaume, architect   230
Lichfield Cathedral, Staffs.   248
Lincoln, Edward Willson, antiquary and architect   257
Lincoln Cathedral, Lincs.   22, 29
London   52
 Black Death   36
 Blackfriars   70, 119
 Bridewell Palace   117, 121
 British Museum, paintings from St Stephen's Chapel   8, 137, *138*, *139*, 141–4, *143*, *144*, *145*, *146*, *147*, *148*, 148–9, *149*, *150*, *151*, 153, 162–70
 Buckingham Palace   256, 258, 286, 337
 Charterhouse   201
 Greyfriars   112
 Holborn, chapel of Bishops of Ely   22, 126, 127
 Holy Trinity Priory, Aldgate   201
 Hospital of St Anthony   174
 London Bridge   39
 panorama of   189, *190*
 Priory of St John of Jerusalem   201
 Reform Club   288
 St Bride's   212
 St Martin le Grand   52
 St Mary Graces, Cistercian abbey   46, 111
 St Paul's Cathedral   183, 287, 340
  altar, high   128
 metalwork   213
 monuments   338
 Old (before 1666)   22, 26, 27, 39, 116, 128
 St Stephen's Coleman Street   213
 Tower of   2, 33, 59–60, 82, 141, 176
 Travellers Club   288
Lorenzetti, Pietro, painter   155
Louis VIII, King of France   161
Louis IX, King of France, saint   3, 29, 44, 125, 159–61
Louis XV, King of France   229
Louis XVI, King of France   227, 229–30
Lowther, James, Speaker of House of Commons   348
Ludford, John, composer   177
Ludford, Nicholas, composer   8, 68, 73, 173, 176–8, *179*, 180–2, 184, 194
Ludgershall Castle, Wilts.   60
Luttrell, Narcissus, MP   212, 216
Lyndwood, William, Bishop of St David's   112, 324, 340
 Provinciale   113

Mackenzie, Frederick, antiquary   6, 77, 100, 103, 286
Madison, James, US president   235
Magi (Kings), Three   43, 50, 131, *132*
Magna Carta   199
Manchester, Royal Manchester Institution   288
March, William, Bishop of Bath and Wells, Treasurer of England   31
Margaret, saint   104, 126
Margaret of Anjou, wife of Henry VI   111
Margaret of France, wife of Edward I   84
Markaunt, John   184
Marlborough Castle, Wilts.   59
Marshall, William, artist   208
Martin, Walter, clerk at St Stephen's   176
Martini, Simone, painter   154
Mary, Virgin   43, 126, 128, 180
 iconography   62, 65, 70, 111–12, 116, 125, 129, 131, 136, 204, 326
 Mass of   56, 60–1, 65, 72
Mary I Tudor, Queen of England   184–5, 191, 200–1, 205
Mary II, Queen of Great Britain   211, 347
Matthew of Vendôme, *Tobias*   156

May, Sir Thomas Erskine, clerk of House of Commons   276
Maynard, William, painter   141
Mercurius, saint   135, 136
Mettingham, Matthew, organist   177
Mettingham, Walter   176
Michael of Canterbury, master mason   24, 26–7, 72, 78–9, 87, 92, 96
Milano, Giovanni da   155
Mildmay, Sir Walter, Chancellor of the Exchequer   123, 304
Mill, John Stuart, MP   344
Milner, John, Catholic Bishop of Midland District   248, 281
Mitford, Sir John, Speaker of House of Commons   312
Modus Tenendi Parliamentum   199
Mogge, Lewis   183
Molinos, Jacques, architect   230
Mons   175
Montagu, George, Earl of Halifax   307
More, Sir Thomas, saint   5
Morse, Samuel, artist   235, 236
Mortimer, Joan, wife of Roger   83
Mortimer, Roger, Earl of March   83, 97–8
Mouter, Robert, canon of St Stephen's   112
Mowbray, Anne, wife of Richard, Duke of York   116
music and polyphony   8, 33, 72–4
    Caius Choirbook   68, 73, 178
    composers   173–82, 194
    Lambeth Choirbook   178
    in London churches   172–3
    purpose of polyphony   171
    St Stephen's, choristers at   71–4, 193–4
    and Westminster Abbey, ceremonial transformation of   182–5
    Windsor, choristers at   71
Musters, Sophia   342

Napoleon Bonaparte   231
Nash, John, architect   258, 285–6
Nasmyth, Alexander, architect   282
Nebuchadnezzar, biblical king   134
Neville, Richard, Earl of Warwick   113
Neville's Cross, battle of (1346)   43
New York   233
Newcastle, Northumb.   102
Nicholas, saint   62

Nichols, John, publisher and antiquary   244
Nightingale, Benedict, painter   141, 154
Nîmes   233
Nottingham Castle, Notts.   59–61

Onslow, Arthur, Speaker of House of Commons   227
Order of the Garter   3, 44, 48–9, 67, 109, 136, 193
Oxford, University of   46–7, 68, 178, 251
    Christ Church (Cardinal College)   119
    Magdalen College   68
    Merton College   196
    New College   112
Oxford Castle, Oxon.   59–61

Padua   125
Paget, Sir William   191
Pampyon, William   184–5
Pankhurst, Emmeline, suffragette   348
    Sylvia, suffragette   348, 351
Paris   154, 240, 282
    Halle aux Blés   233
    Tuileries Palace   229–30, 231
    See also Estates General, France; Sainte-Chapelle
Parliament   4, 30, 39, 49, 51–2, 102–3, 119, 195, 265
    Good   224
    Merciless   113
    Short   208
    See also House of Commons; House of Lords
Paulinus of Nola   134
Pearce, Edward Lovett, architect   224
Peel, Sir Robert, Prime Minister   238, 240, 275–7, 279, 291
Pennant, Thomas, travel writer   309
Penshurst, Kent   200
Perceval, Spencer, Prime Minister   6
Percy, Hugh, Earl of Northumberland   309
Peruzzi of Florence, banking firm   103
Peryn, Alexander   184
Petre, Robert, Auditor of the Exchequer   304
Pettigrew, Thomas, antiquary and surgeon   324
Philadelphia, Pennsylvania State House (Independence Hall)   233
Philip, Duke of Edinburgh   3
Philip VI, King of France   102–3
Philip the Good, Duke of Burgundy   175

Philippa of Hainault, wife of Edward III   46, 111, 337
  coronation   30
  prayers for   193
  and wall paintings   3, 36, *37*, *130*, 131, 134, 140, 163, 168
Pickering, Maurice   304
Pinkie, battle of (1547)   200
Pisan, Christine de   175
Pitt, William, the Elder, Earl of Chatham, Prime Minister   238
Pitt, William, the Younger, Prime Minister   238, 271, 309, 340
Poitiers, battle of (1356)   36, 161
Pole, William de la, Earl of Suffolk   175
polyphony. See music and polyphony
Pucelle, Jean, painter   153
Pugin, A. W. N., architect   261–2, 296, 336
  and Alton Towers   337
  and Palace of Westminster   4–5, 8–9, 257–9, 287–9, 292, 333–5
Pugin, Auguste, architect   257
Purves, Ellen Home, wife of Charles Manners Sutton   314
Pye, Sir Robert, Auditor of the Exchequer   305

Quinn, Bertha, suffragette   345

Raleigh, Sir Walter   341
Ralph, James, author   225
Ramsey, William, master mason   26–7, 36, 72, 102–7
Redford, John, organist   183
Reform Acts   237, 240, 263, 267–9, 278, 344
Regensburg, *Walhalla*   338–40, *339*
Reid, David Boswell   291, 316, 318, 320–1, 323, 326
Reigate, Surrey, stone   17
relics   244
  at Cologne   131, *132*
  Croes Nawdd   44–5
  Crown of Thorns   29, 160
  of Edward the Confessor   43
  Holy Rood of Scotland   43
  of St George   44
  at St George's Chapel, Windsor   44, 71, 114
  at St Stephen's Chapel   3, 30, 111, 128, 159
  at Sainte-Chapelle   3, 29–30, 159–60
  of True Cross   43–5

religiosity, royal   8, 41–5, 53
Reynolds, Walter, Archbishop of Canterbury   42
Rhuddlan Castle, Denbighs.   58, 60
Riccardi of Lucca, banking firm   85
Richard, Duke of York   116
Richard II, King of England   38, 51–2, 196
  deposition of   113
  religiosity of   43
  and Wilton Diptych   131
Richard III, King of England   113–15
Richard of Reading, sculptor   30
Richmond, Surrey   70, 117
Richmond, USA, Virginia State Legislature   233
Rickman, Anne   342
Rickman, Thomas, antiquary and architect   256, 258, 282
Ridderzaal, Binnenhof Palace, The Hague   221
Riga, Peter, *Aurora*   156
Robert the Bruce, King of Scotland   83, 97
Robespierre, Maximilien   231
Rochester, Kent   58–60
Rockingham, Northants.   60
Rogers, John   184
Rome, Sancta Sanctorum   125
Rothwell, William, canon of St Stephen's   53
Ruskin, John   328
Russell, Lord John, Prime Minister   276–7
Russell, Sylvia, suffragette   345

Sacheverell, Henry   306
Saint-Denis Abbey   282
Saint-Sardos, War of (1324–5)   97
St Stephen's Chapel
  buildings, range of   3, 38, 192, 199–200, 302, 304–7, *308*
  buttresses   21–2, 81–2, 84, 88, 320
  carpenters   24, 28–9, 33, 51, 77, 88, 107, 212
  and ceremonials, royal   194–5
  chapel, lower (St Mary in the Vaults; St Mary Undercroft)   17, *18*, 24, 36, 66, 68, 109, 111, 113, 116–17, 176, 181, 194, 198, 264, 279, 302, *302*, 315, *318*, 348
  in 1548   301–2
  altar   111, 301
  as Auditor's house   304, 307, *308*, 309
  as boiler house   310–11

bosses   17, 104, 126, *127*, 313, 323–4, 326, 328, 331
  as Burgess Court   304–7, 309–10, 312
  burials in   70
  dedication   126
  design and style of   75, 77–8, 80, *81*, 84, 104–7
  font   36, 59, 66, 70, 117, 301, 328, 329
  ground plans   *19*, *89*, *303*
  layout   17–18, 66, 70–1
  and Reformation   9, 301–5
  restoration after 1834 fire   4–5, 16, 320–32, *324*, *325*, *327*, *329*, 336, 339–40
  screen   17, 153, 301, 305, 312, 326
  sculpted images   126, *127*, 128
  as Speaker's dining room   9, 311–16, 339
  stained glass   310, 326
  tracery   18, *81*
  vault   17, 18, *18*, 19, 22, 104–6, 107, 126, *127*, 128, 309, 310, 312, 313, 315, 316, 323, 326, 328, 331, 339
  vestry   88, 90, 113, 326, 328
  windows   18, 27, 80, *81*, 88, *325*, 328, 331
chapel, upper   2, 17, *20*, 36–9, 49–51, 84, 88, 90, 100–1, 126, 193, 195, 283, 316, 320
  altars   3, *32*, 33, 36, 68, 70, 125, 128–31, 134, 155, 189, 198, 204
  arcading   21, 34, 90, *91*, 92, *94*, 107, 129
  bosses   107, 128
  clerestory   2, 4, 22, 26, 33, 98, 100, 107, 133, 201, 211–12, 305
  dedication   13, 15
  design and style of   2, 21–2, 24, 27–8, 75, 77–8, 81, 88, 90, *91*, 92, *94*, 95–6, 103, 107
  furnishings   31–6
  gables   100, 103
  ground plan   *140*
  heraldry, shields   33, 82–4, *82*, *83*, 136
  layout   21–2, 33, 67–70
  lectern   68, 69, 70
  martyrdom theme   136, 139–40
  material   141
  niches   21, 98, 125–6, 128
  paintings   3, 6–8, 34–6, *37*, 38, 111, 128–9, *129*, *130*, 131–4, *135*, 136–7, 139–40
    audience for   155
    and *Bibles moralisées*   157, 159, 161–5, *163*, *164*, *165*, *166*, *167*, 169

  BM fragments   8, 137, *138*, *139*, 141–5, *143*, *144*, 145, 146, *147*, *148*, 148–9, *149*, *150*, *151*, 153, 162–70
    in context   157–8
    iconography   137–70
    influences on   153–5, 170
    inscriptions   148–9, 153, 162, 170
    of Job   134, 136, 137, *138*, 140, 143–5, *146*, *147*, *148*, 149, *149*, *150*, *151*, 153, 155, 162–6, *163*
    panelling, hidden behind   204, 214, 218, 246–8, 251, 260, 281
    styles   136, 153–5
    of Tobit   134, 136, 137, 140, 142, 143, *143*, *144*, *145*, 149, 155, 156, 158, 159, 166–70, *167*, *168*
  pulpitum   2, 33, 67, *67*, 69–70, 128, 198, 206
  of royal family   3, 8, 36, *37*, *130*, 131, 134, 140, 163, 168, 203–4
  sculpted images   30, 33, *35*, 98, 125–6, 128–9, 133, 137, 159, 202
  stained glass   3, 8, 33, 125, 133–4, 137, 198
  stalls   31, *32*, 33, 67, *67*, 68–9, 72, 121, 122, 128, 189, 198, 202, 204
  tabernacles   95, 97, 103, 104, 107, 126, 129, 141
  tracery   22, 88, 95, 96, 98, 107, 218
  vault   22, 28, 33, 88, 96, 104, 126, 128
  vestibule (porch, galilee)   22, 23, 26, 38, 39, 65, *105*, *106*, 107
  vestry   24, 68, 88, 90, *91*, 113
  virtual visualization of   *7*, *67*
  windows   2, 21–2, 33, 34, 84, 88, 98, *100*, *101*, 103, 125, 128, 133, 142
collegiate chapel, change to   31, 66–71, *67*
demolition   3, 4–5, 9, 77, 261, 279, 290, 301, 316, 320, 335
dissolution   3, 8, 16, 74, 109, 122, 182–4, 189, 197, 202, 302
financing   1, 3, 84–6, 101–4, 109
fire (1834). *See under* Westminster, Palace of
first reference to   1–2
furnishings   3, 8, 31–4, *32*, *34*, *35*, 36, 59, 67–8, 71–4, 96, 197–8, 301–2
glaziers   38
jurisdiction   114
king's court, use by   115–16, 123
layout, original chapel   65–6

liturgical pattern and space   8, 66–74, 110–11, 116–17, 123
location of   13, 15, 22, 24
masons   22, 24, 26–7, 29–30, 36, 72, 77–80, 87, 92, 96, 98, 101, 102–7
painters, impressment of   140–1
pilgrimage and visitors to   2, 39, 111, 116–17, 123, 324
prayers for royalty   110–11, 115, 189, 193, 197
rebuilding (1292–1348)   7, 9, 15–16, 17–18, 21–2, 24, 26–31, 36–8, 50–1, 53, 72, 80–108
relics   3, 30, 111, 128, 159
Sainte-Chapelle, compared to   3, 29, 31, 34, 66, 125–6, 128, 136, 158–61, 192, 200, 329
statues   39, 70, 88, 98, 116
stone, type of   2, 17, 33, 80–1, 87–8, 95, 313, 326, 328, 340
turrets   13, 17, 22, 198, 213, 306, 333
Virtual St Stephen's project   7
Windsor, St George's Chapel, compared to   3, 31, 48, 50, 55, 56–7, 70–4, 110–11, 115, 174, 193
See also House of Commons, in St Stephen's Chapel; music and polyphony; St Stephen's College
St Stephen's College   2–3, 8
almshouse   196
canonries, as emoluments for clerks   53, 121
canons, housing of   3, 38, 112, 115, 192
cloister   8, 9, 23, 38, 115, *118*, 119, *120*, 121, 194, 199, 250, 283, 314–15, 331
dissolution of   3, 8, 16, 74, 109, 122, 182–4, 189, 197, 202, 302
endowments   109
foundation of   1, 2–3, 9, 31, 37, 41, 47–8, 52–3, 55–7, 66, 107, 109–12, 114, 115, 116, 125, 128, 155, 198
furnishings   31–4, *32*, *34*, *35*, 36, 71–4
links to wider Church   112–13
liturgy and prayers   36, 66–74, 110–11, 116–17, 123, 189, 197
location, importance of   112, 115, 123
Palace of Westminster, as part of   38–9
and Reformation   121–3, 182–5, 189, 195–7
statutes   71, 110, 114
See also music and polyphony
Sainte-Chapelle, Paris
college of   47

medallions, painted   126, *126*, 128, 133, 159, 161
relics   3, 29–30, 159–60
restoration of   200
St Stephen's Chapel, compared to   3, 29, 31, 34, 66, 125–6, 128, 136, 158–61, 192, 200, 329
stained glass   125, *126*, 133–4, 158–61
statues   126, *126*
Salisbury Cathedral, Wilts.   58, 73, 248
Sampson, Richard, Dean of the Chapel Royal   112
San Gimignano, Collegiata of   157, *158*
Sandby, Thomas, artist   214, *215*
Sarum Use   110, 171–2, 182, 183
Scott, Sir George Gilbert, architect   258, 261–2
Scott, Sir Giles Gilbert, architect   9, 279–80, 299
Scott, Sir Walter, author   243, 256, 282
Scrope, Richard, Archbishop of York   42
Selake, Sir John   117
Selden, John, MP   340, 345
Sennacherib, biblical figure   136
Seymour, Edward, Duke of Somerset   197, 200
Shaxton, Nicholas, Bishop of Salisbury   196
Sheppard, John, composer   177
Sherborne Castle, Dorset   60
Sheridan, Richard Brinsley, MP   250
Shrewsbury, Salop.   49
   St Mary's church   131
Sibthorp, Colonel Charles, MP   276
Sidley, Marguerite, suffragette   348–9
Sièyes, Abbé   227–8
Skip, John, Bishop of Hereford   196
Slake, Nicholas, Dean of Wells and of St Stephen's   113
Sleaford, William, Dean of St Stephen's   114
Sluys, battle of (1340)   103
Smirke, Sir Richard, architect   37, 129, *129*, *130*
Smirke, Sir Robert, architect   239–40, 258, 268–9, 275, 282, 285, 315, 335
Smith, John Thomas, antiquary   6, 92, 137, 139, 142, *142*, 243–4, 248, 250–1, *251*, 253, 255, 281, 310
Soane, Sir John, architect   227, 239, 246, 248, 251, 254, 255, 257, 285–7, *286*, 306
Solomon, biblical king   133
Stapeldon, Walter, Treasurer of England   31

Stephen, saint   125–6, 128–9, 133
    martyrdom   5, 134, 136, 335
    relics   43
    statues of   70
Stephens, Jessie, suffragette   344–5
Stormont, Viscount   274–5
Stothard, Charles, antiquary   243–4, 252, *254*, 260
Stothard (Bray), Eliza   252
Stow, John, antiquary   119, 192, 196, 199
Stratford, John, Archbishop of Canterbury   42
Strathbogie, David II de   82–3
Strathbogie, John de   82
Streeter, Robert II, King's Serjeant-Painter   214
Strype, John   199
Sturgeon, Nicholas, composer   173
styles, architectural   77–9
    and chronology   78–9
    Decorated   16, 24, 77, 256, 282
    Early English   256, 282
    French Rayonnant   21, 133
    Gothic   2, 9, 192, 208, 214, 244, 250, 256–7, 264, 280–3, 309, 336
    Gothic Revival   5, 8–9, 201, 218, 243–4, 246, 250, 256–60, 263–4, 276–7, 279–99, 307, 312, 314, 330, 337
    Jacobethan   282
    neoclassical   282, 339
    Perpendicular   2, 16, 27, 77, 192, 256, 281–3, 289
    proto-Perpendicular   78
    Romanesque   22
suffragettes/votes for women   5–6, 9, 330, 344–9
    New Dawn sculpture   349–53, *353*
Susanna, biblical figure   134, 139
Sutton, Charles Manners, Speaker of House of Commons   215, 266, 311, 314–15
Sylvester, Pope   *152*
Symonds, John   201

Tassyn, Lowen, painter   141
Taverner, John, composer   178
Taymouth Castle, Perth and Kinross   282
Thirlby, Thomas, Bishop of Westminster, and of Norwich, and of Ely   121–2, 197
Thomas of Canterbury, master mason   26–7, 87, 96, 98, 107

Thomas of Witney, master mason   29
Thornton, William, architect   233–5
Tiddeswell, William, canon of St Stephen's   73
Tijou, Jean, metalworker   213
Tillemans, Peter, artist   4, 202, *203*, 214–15
Tobit, biblical figure   134, 136, 137, *139*, 140–3, *143*, *144*, *145*, 149, 155, 166–70, *167*, *168*
    Book of   156–7
    in context   157–8
    in French royal art   158–62
    See also under St Stephen's Chapel, chapel, upper, paintings
Topham, John   310
touch, royal   45, 51
Tournai, siege of (1340)   103
Townshend, Hayward, MP   202, 204
Tracy, Charles Hanbury, MP   239
Trench, Frederick, MP   237–8, 267
Trent, Council of (1565)   223, 224
Tyrell, James   114

Underdown, William de, carpenter   88
Urswick, Christopher, Dean of York and of Windsor   114, 173

Vale Royal, Cheshire, Cistercian abbey   45
Vanbrugh, Sir John, architect   224
Versailles   228–9
vestments   43, 60–2, 302, 307
    in St Edward the Confessor's Chapel   63–4
    in St Stephen's   3, 70–1, 73, 197
Vicenza   239
Victoria, Queen of Great Britain   292, 295–6, 337–8
Vignon, Pierre, architect   230
Viollet-le-Duc, Eugène-Emmanuel, French architect   200
Viterbo   154
Vitruvius, Roman architect   221
Voragine, Jacobus de, *Golden Legend*   156, 166

Walby, Robert, sacristan at St Stephen's   176
Wallis, Thomas   184
Walpole, Horace, MP   244, 309
Walpole, Lord Robert   307
Walpole, Robert, Prime Minister   307, 340, 345
Walsingham, Thomas   104
Walter of Milemete   44

Walter of Weston, clerk of works   36
Warburton, Henry, MP   238, 242, 267
Washington, DC, federal Capitol buildings   233–5, *234*, *235*, *236*, 238
Wason, Rigby, MP   240
Waterloo, battle of (1815)   314
Watts, Walter Henry, reporter   272
Wellesley, Arthur, Duke of Wellington, Prime Minister   314
   Catherine, Duchess of Wellington   314
Wells Cathedral   24, 29, 113
   chapter house   31
   Lady Chapel   90, 92, *93*
West, Benjamin, painter   251
Westminster   2, 208
   as royal capital   8, 41, 49–54, 55
   St James' Chapel   193
   St James' Park   117
   Whitehall   70, 110, 117, 185, 189, 195, 199, 201, 211, 349
   See also House of Commons; House of Lords; St Stephen's Chapel; St Stephen's College; Westminster Abbey; Westminster Hall; Westminster, Palace of
Westminster, Palace of   1, 29–30, 86, 109–10, 112, 172, 181–2, 189, 200, 202, 207–8, 264
   alura (gallery, covered walkway) to Painted Chamber   24, 30, 39, 68, 88, 90, 92, 98, 107, 128, 195
   apartments, royal   26, 30, 36, 50, 57, 195
   clock tower   202
   fire (1512–13)   192, 195, 199, 268
   fire (1834)   3–4, 6–9, 16, 34, 77, 86, 113, 117, 191, 196, 198, 201, 240, 257–61, 263, *265*, *266*, 268, 275, 278, 279, *280*, 286, *287*, 293, 314–16, 318, 333–5, *335*, 343
   flooding of   306–7
   Lesser Hall   15, 22, 65, 107, 250, 268, 269, 288, 293, 294, 306, 315, 321, 323, 325
   New Dawn painting   349–53, *350*
   Painted Chamber (great chamber)   2, 15, 24, 29, 30, 49–51, 62, 65–6, 68, 88, 98, 128, 134, 136, 153, 157, 162, 195, 204, 206, 221, 243–4, 248–9, *249*, 252–4, *253*, 256–60, 315–16, *319*, 323, 335
   plan of   12, *173*, *247*, *248*, 265
   privy palace   2, 15, 17, 24, 30, 51, 68, 192, 195, 199, 207

royal administration at   13, 52–4, 117, 119. *See also* courts of law; Exchequer
St John's Chapel   30, 56, 61
St Lawrence, oratory   30, 56, 128
St Mary le Pew, chapel   30, 39, 68, 88, 109, 111, 116–17, 121, 128, 194, 198, 301
St Stephen's Hall   3–5, 9, 259, 290, 318, 320, 323, 333, 336–41, *337*, 347–9
Soane survey of   306
Speaker's House   118, 218, 283, *284*, *308*, 309, 312–16
Star Chamber   52, 119, 195, 199
as World Heritage Site   298
See also House of Commons; House of Lords; St Stephen's Chapel; St Stephen's College; Westminster Hall
Westminster Abbey   29–30, 68, 98, 110, 112, 174, 192, 194, 304, 340
   conversion to diocesan cathedral   182–5
   coronations   1, 50
   Edward the Confessor's Chapel, and shrine   3, 43, 55–6, 62–5
   Henry VII's Chapel   2, 9, 192–3, 283, *285*, 289
   House of Commons, meeting at   1, 4, 51, 191, 198, 204, 221, 224
   income of   3
   and indulgences   117
   music   171–2, 177, 181–5, 193
   privileges   114, 116
   rebuilding of   58
   retable   159
   rose window   22
   stone, type of   2, 17
   and Stone of Scone   50
   tombs, royal   29, 50, 54, 131, *133*, 326, 338
   visitors to   39
Westminster Hall   2, 9, 27–8, 38–9, 116–17, 119, 192, 195, 199, 206, 245, 259–60, 283, 290, 296, 304, 309–10, 320, 325, 335, 337–8, 340
   and St Stephen's Porch   318, 320, 323, 325, 340
Whittington, George   282
Wilberforce, William, MP   311
William I, the Conqueror, King of England, Duke of Normandy   15
William III, King of Great Britain   211, 347
William of Edington, Treasurer of England   37
William the painter   63
William of Patrington, sculptor   129

William of Walsyngham, painter   141
William of Windsor, son of Edward III   48
Williamsburg, Virginia House of Burgesses   233
Wilton Diptych   131
Winchelsey, Robert, Archbishop of Canterbury   42
Winchester, Hants.   56, 58–9, 61–2, 66, 70, 157
Windsor Castle, Berks.   38, 56, *57*, 60, 62, 66, 69, 157, 169, 282
  Albert Memorial Chapel   55
  apartments, royal   57, 70–1
  Edward the Confessor, chapel of   3, 44, 55–6, *57*, 58, 62–6
  music at   71–4, 174–5
  Round Table   103–6
  St George's Chapel and College   3, 31, 44, 47–8, 55, 62, 67, 70–1, 73–4, 109–11, 115–16, 174–5, 193, 197
Wolfe, John Lewis   340
Wolfe-Barry, Sir John, engineer   336
Wolsey, Thomas, Cardinal   5, 70, 117, 119, *120*, 193
Woodrove, John, prior of Kings Langley and Dartford   46

Woodstock, Oxon.   58
World War, Second   5, 9, 191, 196
Wren, Sir Christopher, architect   98, 213
  burial   340
  Commons chamber, reordering of   4, 8, 201–2, 204, 211–18, *212*, 224, 246, 264, 281, 283, 286–7, 292, 305, 342
Wyatt, Benjamin, architect   237
Wyatt, James, architect
  commissions for houses   280
  House of Commons, remodelling of   4, 6, 8–9, 201, 216, 218, 248, 250–1, 257–8, 280–1, 283, 285, 311, 324, 331
  House of Lords, rebuilding of   248, 250, 252
  Speaker's House   283, *284*, 312–14
Wyatville, Sir Jeffry, architect   239, 282
Wykeham, William, Bishop of Winchester, Chancellor of England   112
Wyngaerde, Anthonis van den   189, *190*, 192, 208

Yarnold, Charles   249
Yevele, Henry, master mason   51
York   49, 52, 60, 171–2, 194
  Minster   28

Printed in the United States
by Baker & Taylor Publisher Services